ETHICAL CHALLENGES

INVITATION TO INSIGHTS

SKILL BUILDERS

Looking Out/Looking In

Interpersonal Communication

First Canadian Edition

Looking Out/Looking In

Interpersonal Communication

First Canadian Edition

Ronald B. Adler
Santa Barbara City College

Neil Towne
Grossmont College

Judith A. Rolls
University College of Cape Breton

Harcourt College Publishers

Fort Worth   Philadelphia   San Diego   New York   Orlando   Austin   San Antonio
Toronto   Montreal   London   Sydney   Tokyo

Publisher	Earl McPeek
Acquisitions Editor	Steve Dalphin
Market Strategist	Laura Brennan
Developmental Editor	Martina van de Velde
Project Editor	Laura J. Hanna
Art Director	David A. Day
Production Manager	Lois West

Cover credit: Donald Martin, *Spring*, Private Collection/Donald C. Martin/SuperStock.

ISBN: 0-15-506436-3

Library of Congress Catalog Card Number: 00-106152

Printed in the United States of America

2 3 4 5 6 7 8 9   048   9 8 7 6 5 4 3 2 1

Harcourt College Publishers

Preface

Over its quarter-century lifetime, *Looking Out/Looking In* has changed in many ways, as has the academic study of interpersonal communication. When we look back at the earliest editions, we realize how much the field has evolved. We have worked hard to ensure that this edition reflects the increasingly sophisticated understanding that scholars have gained of the communication process.

WHAT'S FAMILIAR

Despite many changes, this edition of *Looking Out/Looking In* retains the qualities that have distinguished it from the beginning: a personal focus that helps students apply scholarly findings to their own lives, a writing style that strives to be readable without compromising academic integrity, and an inviting design that uses the work of other writers and artists to present material in a compelling way.

As in the past, *Looking Out/Looking In* refuses to take sides in the theory versus skills debate that seems to rage endlessly in some quarters of our discipline. Instead, this book uses contemporary scholarship to suggest ways that readers can become more effective communicators. While *Looking Out/ Looking In* does introduce readers to new skills, the book emphasizes that effective communication doesn't come from learning and using a collection of techniques on others. Instead, it shows readers that competence is a matter of expanding one's repertoire of skills and then learning to choose the approach that is most appropriate and effective in a given situation.

This edition retains an integrated approach to the influences of gender and culture on communication. Discussions of these topics are integrated into every chapter rather than being segregated in their own sections, and these topics are treated in an evenhanded way that reflects research findings that communication between men and women and among people from various backgrounds is shaped by similarities as well as differences. As in the past, a series of "Looking at Diversity" profiles provides first-person accounts of how cultural, co-cultural, and physical factors influence interaction.

Long-time users will also recognize the repeated emphasis that communication is not a panacea that guarantees "happily ever after" outcomes. In fact, the book makes it clear that competent communication does not always mean striving for deep, meaningful relationships. As in the past, *Looking Out/Looking In* suggests that even less personal or adversarial interactions usually have the best outcomes when they are handled in a constructive, respectful way.

Finally, this edition retains the basic structure that has served users well. The number of chapters has remained steady to make sure the book fits comfortably within the length of most academic terms. The order and basic approach of chapters are fundamentally similar to the previous edition, with a few exceptions noted below. As in the past, Chapters 2–10 can be covered in whatever order works best for an individual syllabus.

WHAT'S NEW

Most visibly, this edition of *Looking Out/ Looking In* is illustrated with images created by artists from a wide range of eras and cultures. We think this visually appealing and thought-provoking approach will help readers see how many themes in the book have a universality that reaches across time and culture background.

At the request of many users, this edition has an expanded treatment of ethical issues related to interpersonal communication. A series of extended "Ethical Challenges" present the views of a wide range of thinkers from various eras and backgrounds. Readers learn how the precepts of Aristotle, Lao Tsu, Martin Buber, Sissela Bok, Immanuel Kant, Carl Rogers, and others raise questions that thoughtful communicators must answer as they decide how to treat one another. Along with these "Ethical Challenges," the implicit theme in *Looking Out/Looking In* is that both pragmatic and ethical considerations dictate that the best way to treat others is with respect and concern for meeting their needs, as well as taking care of one's self.

Besides an overall updating of research, this edition contains some subtle but useful changes. Key Terms boldfaced in the text and defined in the Glossary have been edited to emphasize most important terminology and avoid confusing readers with less critical (and often more confusing) jargon. Marginal readings have been updated to reflect the interests of today's readers. For instance, as part of an increased focus on computer-mediated relationships, Chapter 1 contains a newspaper account of an online romance. New song lyrics (from artists including Sarah MacLachlan, Sheryl Crow, Alanis Morissette, Shania Twain, Our Lady Peace, and The Tragically Hip) help give this edition a contemporary focus.

Changes within individual chapters update the book without forcing a wholesale revision of course outlines. For example, in Chapter 1 the old sequence of linear-interactive-transactional models which confused many students has been replaced with a two-step discussion of models. The

transactional nature of communication is presented with less jargon and more clarity. New characteristics of transactional communication have been introduced. For example, the text now clarifies the fact that not all communication is aimed at mutual understanding. The relational nature of communication competence is highlighted, emphasizing that effective communication arises out of co-ordinated interaction and reminding readers that communication is something we do *with* others, not *to* them. This theme is continued in Chapter 2, where identity management is described as a mutual process and not a one-way affair.

Chapter 3 now introduces shared narratives as an additional influence on perceptions of relationships and individual behaviour, and it contains an expanded discussion of the nature of empathy and its roots. It also contains new information on how culture influences emotional expression.

Chapter 4 offers new material on emotional contagion, explaining the effect that one communicator's feelings have on the moods of another. In addition, the "Guidelines for Emotional Expression" have been revised. Parts of Chapter 5 dealing with gender and communication have been rewritten to emphasize that differences between male and female language use are characteristic, but not representative, of how all men or women speak. The discussion of listening in Chapter 7 contains new research-based advice on when and how to offer social support and how to choose a helping response style, as well as more-detailed advice on approaches to paraphrasing.

Chapter 8, now titled "Communication and Relational Dynamics," introduces readers to relational dialectics (moved and expanded from its former location in Chapter 1). There is still a discussion of the inherent tension between intimacy and distance, but other relational themes are also considered. In addition, the discussion of reasons for forming and maintaining relationships has been expanded. Chapter 10 clarifies the influence of gender on conflict styles, explaining other factors which are at least as powerful in influencing how individuals manage conflict.

In summary, these changes keep *Looking Out/Looking In* current without forcing users to revise their time-tested approaches to organizing the course.

TEACHING AND LEARNING RESOURCES

Looking Out/Looking In is accompanied by an extensive array of materials that help make the book more useful.

- The *Activities Manual and Study Guide,* developed by Mary Wiemann and Judith A. Rolls, includes a revised set of individual and group student activities that can be used both in and outside of class. The *Guide* also contains materials to help students improve their academic success: Expanded chapter outlines help students relate the textbook to class lectures; new crossword puzzles review key terms; and self-tests allow students to check their understanding of each chapter before they take graded exams.

- **ExamMaster,** a computerized test-generating program, makes the task of constructing and printing examinations quicker and easier than ever before. The program contains more than 1,200 class-tested questions and allows instructors to add their own.

- Two **videotapes,** *Understanding Interpersonal Misunderstandings* and *Interpersonal Communication in Action* (prepared by Sharon Ratliffe and David Hudson), show how principles from the textbook operate in everyday life.

- A comprehensive *Instructor's Manual* offers a wide variety of instructional strategies, course plans, and exercises that are useful for both first-time and experienced instructors.

- An extensive set of **PowerPoint slides** and **colour overhead transparencies** help instructors present concepts from the textbook in class lectures.

- A **World Wide Web site** contains a wealth of communication-related information, with links to resources that will help students and instructors explore many topics introduced in this book.

ACKNOWLEDGEMENTS

Any project with the scope of *Looking Out/ Looking In* is a team effort. We gratefully thank the following colleagues whose suggestions helped us decide what to keep and what to change in this edition: Ray Archee, University of Western Sydney; Betsy Bach, University of Montana; Marian Boyer, Kalamazoo Valley Community College; Mary Brignall, Northeast Wisconsin Technical College; Bonnie Casey, North Seattle Community College; Lyall Crawford, Weber State University; Carol Davis, Oakton Community College; Layne Dearden, Ricks College; Maureen Dingham, Durham College; Jackie Ganschow, Del Mar College; Charlotte Hammett, Jefferson Community College; Todd Harrison, Iowa Western Community College; Sherry Holmen, Albuquerque Community College; Diana Hutchinson, Scottsdale Community College; Jayne Landon, Bakersfield College; Shelley Lane, Collin County Community College; Jo Ann Lawlor, West Valley College; Michael Leigh, Orange Coast College; Tricia Light, Tarrant

County Junior College; Debra Mazloff, University of Saint Thomas; Steve McCornack, Michigan State University; Rebecca Mikesell, University of Scranton; Judy Motion, University of Waikato; Mary Jo Popovich, Monroe Community College; Eileen Berlin Ray, Cleveland State University; George Ray, Cleveland State University; Susan Richardson, Prince Georges Community College; Paul Rousseau, Saint Clair College; Glen Stamp, Ball State University; Tara Stuart, Keen State College; Pam Tobin, Camosun College; Theresa Turner, Shasta College; Lee Wertzler, Mount Royal College; Jerry Winsor, Central Missouri State University; Charles Wise, El Paso Community College; Stephen Wood, University of Rhode Island.

We continue to appreciate the comments of reviewers from earlier editions, whose comments have continued to be helpful over the years: Roberta Duncan, University of Wyoming; Char Berquist, Bellevue Community College; Robert Johnson, Pensacola Junior College; Miriam Zimmerman, University of San Francisco; Jeanne Elmhorst, Albuquerque Technical-Vocational Institute; Nan Peck, Northern Virginia Community College; Lynn Phelps, Ohio University; Deborah Pearce, Xavier University; Peter Bridge, Champlain College; Paul Aschenbrenner, Hartnell College; Diane M. Hill, University of Rhode Island; Joanne G. Clayton, Davenport College; Sherry J. Holmen, Albuquerque Technical-Vocational Institute; Stephen L. Coffman, Eastern Montana College; Joyce Taylor, City College of San Francisco; David H. W. Smith, Monroe Community College; Dick Stine, Johnson County Community College; Colan T. Hanson, North Dakota State University; David E. Axon, Johnson Community College; Ruth F. Eisenberg, Pace University; Vernon Gantt, Murray State University; M. Nicholas Gilroy, Bronx Community College; Virginia Katz, University of Minnesota at Duluth; Nancy Lampen, Monroe Community College; Jim Mammarella, San Antonio College; Gerard F. McDade, Community College of Philadelphia; Patsy Meisel, Mankato State University; Ramona Parrish, Virginia Western Community College; Wesley L. Robertson, Jefferson College; and Katherine M. Stannard, Framingham State College.

In addition, our special thanks go to Russ Proctor, Lawrence Rosenfeld, Jeanne Elmhorst, and Mary Wiemann, all of whom have been an ongoing source of good ideas and support over the years. We are grateful to Em Griffin, Jim Chesher, and Joe White for their help in developing the "Ethical Challenges" in this edition. The art program in this edition owes much of its success to the suggestions of Diane Handloser and Pamela Zwehl-Burke, as well as Skip Cole and Bret Rothstein. Lili Weiner worked hard to suggest art ideas and secure permission to use each of the images in this edition. Thanks go to many people for suggestions about contemporary song lyrics that illustrate themes in *Looking Out/Looking In:* Adams Stephens, Tracy Miller, Glenn Gallo, Elaine Manke, Tom and Claire Brantley, Marie Kent Stewart, Allen Kozlowski, and John Wiemann IV.

We want to express our appreciation to the professionals at Harcourt, whose hard work helped develop and deliver the book you are now reading: Steve Dalphin, Martina van de Velde, Steve Drummond, Laura Hanna, David Day, and Lois West. We feel lucky to work with such a fine group of people.

Finally, we want to express our deepest gratitude to our families, who have helped to keep our theoretical treatment of communication grounded in reality, and who have given us the support to make this book possible. They are the best reminders that "books aren't everything."

R.B.A.
N.O.T.

TO THE STUDENT

"So what?"

In our opinion, that's the fundamental question to ask when reading a college textbook. We are convinced that every well-constructed academic course and every textbook can and should have relevance to the lives of the people studying it.

We think you will find that *Looking Out/Looking In* answers the "So what?" question quite completely. Every page contains information to help you understand how communication operates in your own relationships, and every chapter offers tools to help you communicate more successfully. The information in these pages is based on sound scholarship, which we have tried to make come alive by showing how it applies to the world in which you live.

We have worked hard to make *Looking Out/Looking In* a "good read," and users over the past 25 years have told us that these efforts have been successful. A quick look shows that the book is filled with an array of words and images created by others: poetry, literary selections, interviews, cartoons, song lyrics, epigrams, newspaper clippings, photographs, and artwork. In every case, these pieces illustrate principles from the text. Rather than provide captions to explain the significance of these selections, we invite you to make your own connection to the communication principles in the text. If some words or images generate discussion between you, your classmates, and your professor, so much the better.

We believe strongly in the saying "It's not what you know that counts, it's what you use." We think the best measure of success for a course in interpersonal communication isn't the grade you earn; it's how much of the information you can apply in your life. Long after your transcript is forgotten and your class notes have disappeared, we hope you'll find yourself using the insights and skills you have learned here. If that happens, this book has done its job.

Preface to the Canadian Edition

When I was invited to join the Adler-Towne team, I was excited at the prospect of adding a Canadian viewpoint to *Looking Out/Looking In.* I had taught from an earlier edition of this textbook a number of years ago, and I knew that students responded favourably to it. However, they often asked why I couldn't find a Canadian textbook–one that more accurately reflected their cultural point of view. The answer to this question is straightforward: Most of the research in interpersonal communication comes from the United States out of the "speech" communication discipline, one that is not as developed here in Canada. As a result, fewer Canadian professors specialize in this area, which in turn results in reduced numbers of individuals who are interested in writing interpersonal communication textbooks. In fact, in 1997, to encourage research in this area, the *Canadian Journal of Communication* devoted a special volume (Volume 22, Number 1) to interpersonal communication topics.

However, interpersonal communication is widely taught across Canada, and student demand for Canadian textbooks continues to grow. This is one of the reasons I agreed to adapt *Looking Out/Looking In.* The second reason is the text itself. Ron Adler and Neil Towne have created a strong, well-researched textbook that incorporates the latest interpersonal communication research findings. The text contains skill-building exercises and clear examples, as well as strategically placed artwork that creates an aesthetically pleasing look. I also believe in the authors' outlook and approach to interpersonal communication.

So why is an American textbook that has been adapted for the Canadian market a better choice for Canadian students? First, students learn more when the subject matter is framed within their own cultural values and experiences. Therefore, I have included quotations, artwork, and diversity boxes that contain material created by Canadians about issues that are relevant to them. For example, there is an article about an adult's response to her school years enrolled in French Immersion, as well as an excerpt depicting a Native woman's experience in a residential school during the 1950s. I have also included Canadian poetry, quotations, and song lyrics that emphasize the interpersonal theories and concepts being explained. Wherever possible, I have included Canadian examples, statistics, names, nuances, and perspectives to give this textbook an overall Canadian cultural flavour that is substantially different from its American counterpart. Further, I have tried to be aware of gender, class, race, ethnicity, and sexual orientation issues so that this textbook will be of interest to all Canadian readers. I believe that this Canadian edition of *Looking Out/Looking In* will better serve our Canadian students.

ACKNOWLEDGEMENTS

I gratefully acknowledge the people at Harcourt who have made this project possible. Thanks to Heather McWhinney, Martina van de Velde, Larry Gillevet, Joan Smith, Laura Hanna, and Steve Dalphin. Thanks also to Lee Wertzler of Mount Royal College, who reviewed early chapters and provided useful suggestions for the Canadian edition. I also thank the members of the Department of Communication at the University College of Cape Breton for their continued support, and my students, who keep me centred. Finally, I express my gratitude to my family members, John, Jo-Anne, and Caleigh, who always know when I need to be working and when I need to stop.

Judith A. Rolls

Introduction

Since this is a book about interpersonal communication, it seems appropriate for us to introduce ourselves to you, the reader. The "we" you'll be reading throughout this book isn't just an editorial device: It refers to us—Ron Adler, Neil Towne, and Judy Rolls.

Ron lives in Santa Barbara, California, with his wife, Sherri, and their twelve-year-old son, Daniel. Their oldest daughter, Robin (who had just been born when the first edition of this book was published), now works in the publishing industry. Rebecca, their other daughter, just graduated from college.

Ron spends most of his professional time teaching and writing about communication. In addition to helping create *Looking Out/Looking In,* he has contributed to six other books about topics including business communication, public speaking, small group communication, assertiveness, and social skills. Besides writing and teaching, Ron helps professional and business people improve their communication on the job.

RON ADLER

Ron still loves to travel. Since the last edition of *Looking Out/Looking In* was published, he and his family lived and taught in Cambridge, England. Running, cycling, and hiking keep him physically and emotionally healthy. Ron cherishes his family and friends. His biggest challenge remains balancing the demands of his career with the other important parts of his life. His only regret is that there aren't more hours in the day.

Finally, after four decades of teaching, Neil has retired. He and his wife, Bobbi, now live on the shore of beautiful Clear Lake in Northern California. For them, retirement is not a lean-back and do-nothing time. Instead, they explain

NEIL TOWNE

that they have been "overworked and underpaid" as they go about making their new house a home and settling into a new community. Neil and Bobbi don't complain and agree that their efforts are truly a labor of love.

Neil stays active in the communication field through his continuing involvement in *Looking Out/Looking In,* and by directing workshops, teaching short classes in Couple Communication with Bobbi, and working with their church community in the area of conflict resolution.

Now, add their growing family—their greatest love—and you have an inkling of why the Townes often experience retirement as exhaustion. Currently the family includes their five adult children along with their spouses, and eight grandkids. Sharing in the lives of their family members now involves traveling, which is another joy in Neil's and Bobbi's lives.

JUDY ROLLS

Along with work and family, Neil enjoys reading, water skiing, wind surfing, singing in the choir, learning about the flora and fauna around their new home, volunteering as a docent at the nearby state park, making new friends, walking, and looking for any new adventure that may be just around the corner.

Judy is new to the team and brings in the Canadian dimension. She lives on beautiful Cape Breton Island in Nova Scotia with her husband, John MacLean, and cat, Sparkey. She's been teaching communication at the University College of Cape Breton for some twenty years. She truly loves her work, and always has great students. She is also an active researcher and her work is published in both Canadian and American scholarly journals. Further, Judy works as a communication consultant/trainer and has designed and facilitated workshops for over 100 organizations.

With all her work related activites, she seems to have little spare time. When she does, she heads for her cottage on the Bras d'Or Lake. She and her husband built the one-and-a-half story house with manual hand tools because electricity wasn't available in the area at the time. They also carried materials down a steep path because there was no road either! Judy also enjoys travelling, reading, making and listening to music (she used to sing in pubs as an undergraduate), and having good laughs with her family and friends.

Brief Contents

Contents

PART ONE: LOOKING IN 1

PART TWO: LOOKING OUT 167

PART THREE: LOOKING AT RELATIONSHIPS 317

Part One

Looking In

Chapter 1

A First Look at Interpersonal Relationships

I n a study of isolation, subjects were paid to remain alone in a locked room. Of the five subjects, one lasted for eight days. Three held out for two days, one commenting, "Never again." The fifth subject lasted only two hours.[1]

The need for contact and companionship is just as strong outside the laboratory, as individuals who have led solitary lives by choice or necessity have discovered. W. Carl Jackson, an adventurer who sailed across the Atlantic Ocean alone in 51 days, summarized the feelings common to most loners:

> I found the loneliness of the second month almost excruciating. I always thought of myself as self-sufficient, but I found life without people had no meaning. I had a definite need for somebody to talk to, someone real, alive, and breathing.[2]

WHY WE COMMUNICATE

It's true that all of us need solitude, often more than we get. On the other hand, each of us has a point beyond which we do not *want* to be alone. Beyond this point solitude changes from a pleasurable to a painful condition. In other words, we all need relationships. We all need to communicate. In fact, communication allows us to fulfil our physical, identity, and social needs and to attain practical goals.

Physical Needs

Communication is so important that its presence or absence affects physical health. In extreme cases communication can even become a matter of life or death. Frederick II, emperor of Germany from 1196 to 1250, may inadvertently have been the first person to prove the point systematically. A medieval historian described one of his significant, if inhuman, experiments:

> He bade foster mothers and nurses to suckle the children, to bathe and wash them, but in no way to prattle with them, for he wanted to learn whether they would speak the Hebrew language, which was the oldest, or Greek, or Latin, or Arabic, or perhaps the language of their parents, of whom they had been born. But he laboured in vain because all the children died. For they could not live without the petting and joyful faces and loving words of their foster mothers.[3]

Today's medical researchers have identified a wide range of health threats that can result from a lack of close relationships. For instance:

* A lack of social relationships jeopardizes coronary health to a degree that rivals risk factors including cigarette smoking, high blood pressure, blood lipids, obesity, and lack of physical activity.[4]

Maternal dislike is more crippling than clubs.

June Caldwell

- Socially isolated people are four times more susceptible to the common cold than those who have active social networks.[5]

- Social isolates are two to three times more likely to die prematurely than are those with strong social ties. The type of relationship doesn't seem to matter: Marriage, friendship, religious, and community ties all seem to increase longevity.[6]

- Divorced men (before age 70) die from heart disease, cancer, and strokes at double the rate of married men. Three times as many die from hypertension; five times as many commit suicide; seven times as many die from cirrhosis of the liver; and ten times as many die from tuberculosis.[7]

- The rate of all types of cancer is as much as five times higher for divorced men and women, compared with their married counterparts.[8]

- The likelihood of death increases when a close relative dies. In one Welsh village, citizens who had lost a close relative died within one year at a rate more than five times greater than those who had not suffered from a relative's death.[9]

Research like this demonstrates the importance of satisfying personal relationships. Not everyone needs the same amount of contact, and the quality of communication is almost certainly as important as the quantity. The important point is that personal communication is essential for our well-being.

Identity Needs

Communication does more than enable us to survive. It is the way—indeed, the *only* way—we learn who we are. As Chapter 2 explains, our sense of identity comes from the way we interact with other people. Are we smart or stupid, attractive or ugly, skillful or inept? The answers to these questions don't come from looking in the mirror. We decide who we are based on how others react to us.

Deprived of communication with others, we would have no sense of ourselves. In his book *Bridges, Not Walls,* John Stewart dramatically illustrates this fact by citing the case of the famous "Wild Boy of Aveyron," who spent his early childhood without any apparent human contact. The boy was discovered in January 1800 digging for vegetables in a French village garden. He showed no behaviours one would expect in a social human. The boy could not speak but uttered only weird cries. More significant than this absence of social skills was his lack of any identity as a human being. As author Roger Shattuck put it, "The boy had no human sense of being in the world. He had no sense of himself as a person related to other persons."[10] Only with the influence of a loving "mother" did the boy begin to behave—and, we can imagine, think of himself—as a human.

The Wild Boy of Aveyron

http://www.staff.uiuc.edu/ ~linneman/diss/jeanmarc.html

Like the boy of Aveyron, each of us enters the world with little or no sense of identity. We gain an idea of who we are from the way others define us. As Chapter 2 explains, the messages we receive in early childhood are the strongest, but the influence of others continues throughout life.

Some scholars have argued that we are most attracted to people who confirm our identity.[11] This confirmation can come in different forms, depending on the self-image of the communicator. People with relatively high self-esteem seek out others who confirm their value and as much as possible avoid those who treat them poorly. Conversely, people who regard themselves as unworthy may look for relationships in which others treat them badly. This principle offers one explanation for why some people maintain damaging or unsuccessful relationships. If you view yourself as a loser, you may associate with others who will confirm that self-perception. Of course, relationships can change a communicator's identity as well as confirm it. Supportive relationships can transform feelings of inadequacy into self-respect, and damaging ones can lower self-esteem.

Athena Hampton ©96

Social Needs

Besides helping define who we are, communication provides a vital link with others. In fact, some social scientists have argued that communication is the principal way relationships are created.[12] Researchers and theorists have identified a whole range of social needs we satisfy by communicating: *pleasure* (e.g., "because it's fun," "to have a good time"); *affection* (e.g., "to help others," "to let others know I care"); *inclusion* (e.g., "because I need someone to talk to or be with," "because it makes me less lonely"); *escape* (e.g., "to put off doing something I should be doing"); *relaxation* (e.g., "because it allows me to unwind"); and *control* ("because I want someone to do something for me," "to get something I don't have").[13]

As you look at this list of social motives for communicating, imagine how empty your life would be if these needs weren't satisfied. Then notice that it would be impossible to meet them without communicating with others. Because relationships with others are so vital, some theorists have gone as far as to argue that communication is the primary goal of human existence. Anthropologist Walter Goldschmidt terms the drive for meeting social needs the "human career."[14]

Practical Goals

Besides satisfying social needs and shaping our identity, communication is the most widely used approach to satisfying what communication scholars call **instrumental goals:** getting others to behave in ways we want. Some instrumental needs are quite basic: Communication is the tool that lets you tell the hairstylist to take just a little off the sides, makes it possible to negotiate household duties, and enables you to convince the plumber that the broken pipe needs attention *now!*

Other instrumental goals are more important. Career success is the prime example. As Table 1–1 shows, communication skills—the ability to speak and listen effectively—are the top factors in helping college graduates find jobs in an increasingly competitive workplace.[15] Good communication on the job is just as important. For example, in 1992 the Conference Board of Canada identified a set of characteristics required for present and future employees. Called the "Employability Skills Profile," it noted that to be successful in a high-quality Canadian workforce, employees must have the "(1) ability to communicate, think, and continue to learn throughout life; (2) ability to demonstrate positive attitudes and behaviours, responsibility, and adaptability; and (3) ability to work with others."[16] Good personal skills aren't just a social nicety: They can mean the difference between success and failure on the job.

> "If it weren't for the people, the goddamned people," said Finnerty, "always getting tangled up in the machinery. If it weren't for them, earth would be an engineer's paradise."
>
> Kurt Vonnegut, Jr., *Player Piano*

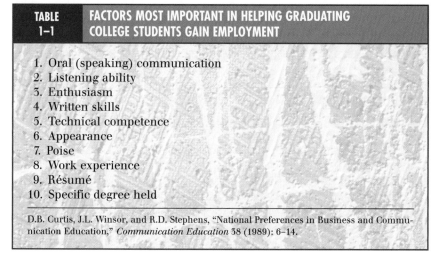

TABLE 1–1	FACTORS MOST IMPORTANT IN HELPING GRADUATING COLLEGE STUDENTS GAIN EMPLOYMENT

1. Oral (speaking) communication
2. Listening ability
3. Enthusiasm
4. Written skills
5. Technical competence
6. Appearance
7. Poise
8. Work experience
9. Résumé
10. Specific degree held

D.B. Curtis, J.L. Winsor, and R.D. Stephens, "National Preferences in Business and Communication Education," *Communication Education* 38 (1989): 6–14.

Psychologist Abraham Maslow suggested that human needs such as the preceding fall into five hierarchical categories, each of which must be satisfied before we concern ourselves with the following ones.[17] As you read on, think about the ways in which communication is often necessary to satisfy each need. The most basic of these needs are *physical:* sufficient air, water, food, and rest, and the ability to reproduce as a species. The second of Maslow's needs involves *safety:* protection from threats to our well-being. Beyond physical and safety concerns are the *social needs* we have mentioned already. Even beyond these, Maslow suggests that each of us has *self-esteem* needs: the desire to believe that we are worthwhile, valuable people. The final category of needs described by Maslow involves *self-actualization:* the desire to develop our potential to the maximum, to become the best person we can be.

THE PROCESS OF COMMUNICATION

We have been talking about communication as though the actions described by this word were perfectly clear. Before going further we need to explain systematically what happens when people exchange messages with one another. Doing so will introduce you to a common working vocabulary and, at the same time, preview some of the topics that are covered in later chapters.

A Linear View

As recently as 50 years ago, researchers viewed communication as something one person "does" to another.[18] In this **linear communication model,** communication is like giving an injection: A **sender encodes** ideas and feelings into some sort of **message** and then conveys them by means of a **channel** (speech, writing, and so on) into a **receiver,** who **decodes** the message (see Figure 1–1).

This perspective does provide some useful information. For instance, it highlights how different channels can affect the way a receiver responds to a message. Should you say "I love you" in person?

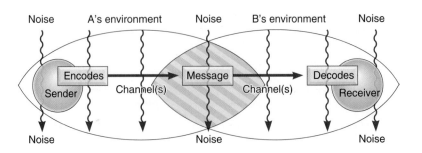

FIGURE 1–1

Linear Communication Model

Over the phone? By renting space on a billboard? By sending flowers and a card? With a singing telegram? Each channel has its differences.

Computer-mediated communication (CMC) offers a good example of how channels affect the way in which people interact. At first, some theorists predicted that CMC would be less personal than face-to-face communication. With no nonverbal cues, it seemed that CMC couldn't match the rich interaction that happens in person, or even over the phone. While some people become inhibited when engaged in CMC, recent studies show that CMC can be at least as deep and complex as personal contact.[19] The news story on this page offers an extreme example of this fact and supports the suggestion of Steve Jobs, the co-founder of Apple Computer, that personal computers be renamed "*inter*-personal computers."[20] Sociolinguist Deborah Tannen describes how the computer-mediated channel of electronic mail (e-mail) transformed the quality of two relationships:

> E-mail deepened my friendship with Ralph. Though his office was next to mine, we rarely had extended conversations because he is shy. Face to face he mumbled so, I could barely tell he was speaking. But when we both got on e-mail, I started receiving long, self-revealing messages; we poured our hearts out to each other. A friend discovered that e-mail opened up that kind of communication with her father. He would never talk much on the phone (as her mother would), but they have become close since they both got on line.[21]

The linear model also introduces the concept of **noise**—a term used by social scientists to describe any forces that interfere with effective communication. Noise can occur at every stage of the communication process. Three types of noise can disrupt communication—external, physiological, and psychological. *External noise*

Computer-Mediated Communication *magazine*

http://www.december.com/cmc/ mag/current/toc.html

Communication Transcript

Online Affair Leads to Divorce

One e-mail message said: "I love you dearly. XXOOXX."

It was one of many sent to Diane Goydan by a computer-paramour calling himself "The Weasel," but it was her husband who saved them.

John Goydan filed for divorce on Jan. 23 after accusing his wife of carrying on a "virtual" affair with a married man who was identified in court papers only as Ray.

Mrs. Goydan's relationship with The Weasel apparently never was consummated, but her husband claimed the pair planned a real tryst this weekend at a bed-and-breakfast inn.

In a Nov. 23 message, The Weasel wrote: "I gotta tell you that I am one happy guy now and so much at peace again

anticipating us. I love you dearly. XXOOXX."

Goydan learned about the cyberspace relationship by reading his wife's electronic mail exchanges—some sexually explicit—with the man she met on an online service, according to court papers.

(also called "physical noise") includes those factors outside the receiver that make it difficult to hear, as well as many other kinds of distractions. For instance, too much cigarette smoke in a crowded room might make it hard for you to pay attention to another person, and sitting in the rear of an auditorium might make a speaker's remarks unclear. External noise can disrupt communication almost anywhere in our model—in the sender, channel, message, or receiver. *Physiological noise* involves biological factors in the receiver or sender that interfere with accurate reception: illness, fatigue, and so on. *Psychological noise* refers to forces within a communicator that interfere with the ability to express or understand a message accurately. For instance, fishers might exaggerate the size and number of the fish they catch in order to convince themselves and others of their talents. In the same way, a student might become so upset upon learning that she failed a test that she would be unable (perhaps *unwilling* is a better word) to understand clearly where she went wrong. Psychological noise is such an important communication problem that we have devoted much of Chapter 9 to investigating its most common form, defensiveness.

A linear model also shows that communicators often occupy different **environments**—fields of experience that help them understand others' behaviour. In communication terminology, *environment* refers not only to a physical location but also to the personal experiences and cultural background that participants bring to a conversation.

Consider just some of the factors that might contribute to different environments:

A might belong to one ethnic group and B to another;

A might be rich and B poor;

A might be rushed and B have nowhere to go;

A might have lived a long, eventful life and B might be young and inexperienced;

A might be passionately concerned with the subject and B indifferent to it.

Environments aren't always obvious. For example, one study revealed that college students who have been enrolled in debate classes become more argumentative and verbally aggressive than those who have not been exposed to this environment.[22]

Notice how the model in Figure 1–1 shows that the environments of A and B overlap. This area represents the background that the communicators must have in common. As the shared environment becomes smaller, communication becomes more difficult. Consider a few examples in which different perspectives can make understanding difficult:

Bosses who have trouble understanding the perspective of their employees will be less effective managers, and workers who do not appreciate the challenges of being a boss are more likely to be unco-operative (and probably less suitable for advancement).

Parents who have trouble recalling their youth are likely to clash with their children, who have never known and may not appreciate the responsibility that comes with parenting.

Members of a dominant culture who have never experienced how it feels to be "different" may not appreciate the concerns of people from nondominant co-cultures, whose own perspectives make it hard to understand the cultural blindness of the majority.

Differing environments make understanding others challenging, but certainly not impossible. Hard work and many of the skills described in this book provide ways to bridge the gap that separates all of us to a greater or lesser degree. For now, recognizing the challenge that comes from dissimilar environments is a good start. You can't solve a problem until you recognize that it exists.

A Transactional View

Despite its simplicity, the linear view of communication isn't completely accurate. One of its greatest weaknesses is the suggestion that communication flows in one direction, from sender to receiver. Although some types of messages (printed and broadcast messages, for example) do flow in a one-way, linear manner, most types of communication—especially the interpersonal variety—are two-way exchanges.

Consider, for instance, the significance of a friend's yawn as you describe your romantic problems. Or imagine the blush you may see as you tell one of your raunchier jokes to a new acquaintance. Nonverbal behaviours like these show that most face-to-face communication is a two-way affair. The discernible response of a receiver to a sender's message is called **feedback.** Not all feedback is nonverbal, of course. Sometimes it is oral, as when you ask an instructor questions about an upcoming test or volunteer your opinion of a friend's new haircut. In other cases it is written, as when you answer the questions on a midterm exam or respond to a letter from a friend. Figure 1–2 makes the importance of feedback clear. It shows that most communication is, indeed, a two-way affair.

Another weakness of the traditional linear model is the questionable assumption that all communication involves encoding. We

It's not surprising that communication between human beings is so difficult, considering that so much of what each of us feels most deeply can't help but seem the merest trivia to almost everyone else.

Alden Nowlan,
Various Persons Named

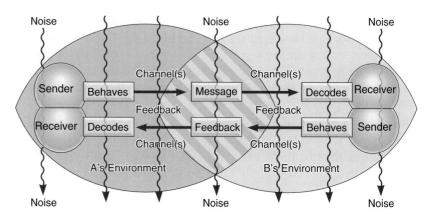

FIGURE 1–2

Transactional Communication
Model

certainly do choose symbols to convey most verbal messages. But what about the many nonverbal cues that occur whether or not people speak: facial expressions, gestures, postures, vocal tones, and so on? Cues like these clearly do offer information about others, although they are often unconscious and thus don't involve encoding. For this reason, the transactional model replaces the term *encoding* with the broader label **behaviour,** because it describes both deliberate and unintentional actions that can be observed and interpreted.[23]

Perhaps the most fundamental limitation of the linear model is the implicit but flawed assumption that the goal of all communication is to create shared understanding between communicators. In fact, there are many types of communication in which understanding isn't necessary. Consider, for example,

- The social rituals we enact every day: "How's it going?" you ask. "Great," the other person replies. The primary goal in exchanges like these is mutual acknowledgement: There's obviously no serious attempt to exchange information.

- Many attempts to influence others. A quick analysis of most television commercials shows that they are aimed at persuading viewers to buy products, not to understand the content of the ad.

- The multitude of times when we definitely do *not* want others to understand us clearly. When you decline an unwanted invitation by saying "I can't make it," you probably want to create the impression that the decision is really beyond your control. (If your goal was to be perfectly clear, you might say, "I don't want to get together. In fact, I'd rather do almost anything than accept your invitation.") As Chapter 5 explains in detail, we often equivocate precisely because we want to obscure our true thoughts and feelings.

As you study the information in *Looking Out/Looking In,* you will begin to realize that communicating to satisfy our social, physical, practical, and identity needs doesn't always require mutual understanding between communicators.

A **transactional communication model** represents communication accurately in other respects. It reveals that we usually encode, send, receive, and decode messages simultaneously, and not in a back-and-forth manner suggested by the linear model. Consider, for example, what might occur when you and a housemate negotiate how to handle household chores. As soon as you begin to hear (receive) the words sent by your partner, "I want to talk about cleaning the kitchen . . . ," you grimace and clench your jaw (sending a nonverbal message of your own while receiving the verbal one). This reaction leads your partner to interrupt him or herself, defensively sending a new message: "Now wait a minute. . . ." Because communicators send and receive messages simultaneously, the transactional model pictured in Figure 1–2 combines these functions into the single role of "communicator."[24]

A transactional view of communication recognizes that it's difficult to isolate a single discrete "act" of communication from the events that precede and follow it.[25] Consider the example in the preceding paragraph: Your partner's comment about cleaning the kitchen (and the way it was presented) probably grew from exchanges you had in the past. Likewise, the way you'll act toward each other in the future depends on the outcome of this conversation. As communication researcher Steve Duck put it, "Relationships are best conceived . . . as unfinished business."[26]

Now we can summarize the definition of communication we have been developing. **Communication** is a continuous, transactional process involving participants who occupy different but overlapping environments and create relationships through the exchange of messages, many of which are affected by external, physiological, and psychological noise.

INVITATION TO INSIGHT

A MODEL MUDDLE

You can gain appreciation for the transactional communication model by using Figure 1–2 to analyze a communication challenge you recently experienced. Which elements described in the model help explain the problem? What steps might you and the other person or people involved have taken to overcome these difficulties?

COMMUNICATION PRINCIPLES AND MISCONCEPTIONS

Before we look at the qualities that distinguish interpersonal communication, it's important to define what communication is and what it isn't, and to discuss what it can and can't accomplish.

Sometimes she thought the trouble was, she and Leon were too well acquainted. The most innocent remark could call up such a string of associations, so many past slights and insults never quite settled or forgotten, merely smoothed over. They could no longer have a single uncomplicated feeling about one another.

Anne Tyler,
Morgan's Passing

Communication Principles

It's possible to draw several important conclusions about communication from what you have already learned in this chapter.

WE COMMUNICATE *WITH* OTHERS   Unlike the one-way communication of the mass media, personal interaction isn't something we do *to* others; rather, it is an activity we do *with* them. In this sense, person-to-person communication is rather like dancing—at least the kind of dancing we do with partners. Like dancing, communication depends on the involvement of a partner. And like good dancing, successful communication doesn't depend only on the person who takes the lead. A great dancer who forgets to consider and adapt to the skill level of his or her partner can make both people look bad. In communication and dancing, even two talented partners don't guarantee success. When two skilled dancers perform without coordinating their movements, the results feel bad to the dancers and look foolish to an audience. Finally, relational communication—like dancing—is a unique creation that arises out of the way in which the partners interact. The way you dance probably varies from one partner to another. Likewise, the way you communicate almost certainly varies with different partners.

A fascinating study on relational satisfaction illustrates how satisfying communication depends on co-ordination between partners.[27] Researchers Brent Burleson and Wendy Sampter hypothesized that people with sophisticated communication skills (such as managing conflict well, giving ego-support to others, and providing comfort to relational partners) would be better at maintaining friendships than less-skilled communicators. To their surprise, the results did not support this guess. In fact, friendships were most satisfying when partners possessed matching skill levels. Apparently, relational satisfaction arises in part when our style matches those of the others with whom we interact.

The transactional nature of communicators shows up dramatically in relationships between parents and their children. We normally think of "good parenting" as a skill that some people possess and others lack. We judge the ability of a mother and father in terms of how well their children turn out. In fact, research suggests that the quality of interaction between parents and children is a two-way affair—that children influence parents just as much as the reverse.[28] For example, children who engage in what social scientists call "problematic behaviour" evoke more high-control responses from their parents than do co-operative children. By contrast, youngsters with mild temperaments are less likely to provoke coercive reactions from their parents than more aggressive children. Parents with low self-esteem tend to send more messages that weaken the self-esteem of their children, who in turn are likely to act in ways that make the parents feel even worse about themselves. Thus, a mutually reinforcing cycle arises in which parents and children shape one another's feelings and behaviour. In cases like this it's at least difficult and probably impossible to identify who is the "sender" and who is the "receiver" of messages. It's more accurate to acknowledge that parents and children—just like husbands and wives, bosses and employees, teachers and students, or any other people in relationships—act in ways that mutually influence one another.

COMMUNICATION CAN BE INTENTIONAL OR UNINTENTIONAL

Some communication is clearly deliberate: You probably plan your words carefully before asking the boss for a raise or offering constructive criticism. Some scholars argue that only intentional messages like these qualify as communication. Others suggest that even unintentional behaviour is communicative. Suppose, for instance, that a friend overhears you muttering complaints to yourself. Even though you didn't intend for her to hear your remarks, they certainly did carry a message. In addition to these slips of the tongue, we unintentionally send many nonverbal messages. You might not be aware of your sour expression, impatient shifting, or sigh of boredom, but others view them nonetheless. Scholars have debated without reaching consensus about whether unintentional behaviour should be considered communication, and it's unlikely that they will ever settle this issue.[29]

In *Looking Out/Looking In* we will look at the communicative value of both intentional and unintentional behaviour. This book takes the position that whatever you do—whether you speak or remain silent, confront or avoid, act emotional or keep a poker face—you provide information to others about your thoughts and feelings. In this sense we are like transmitters that can't be shut off.

Of course, the people who decode your message may not interpret it accurately. They might take your kidding seriously or underestimate your feelings, for example. The message that you intend to convey may not even resemble the one others infer from your actions. Thus, when we talk about "a communication breakdown" or "miscommunication," we rarely mean that communication has ended. Instead, we mean that it is inaccurate or unsatisfying.[30]

This explains why the best way to boost understanding is to discuss your intentions and your interpretations of the other person's behaviour until you have negotiated a shared meaning. The perception-checking skills described in Chapter 3, the tips on clear language in Chapter 5, and the listening skills introduced in Chapter 7 will give you tools to boost the odds that the meanings of messages you send and receive are understandable to both you and others.

> *A word is not a bird: Once on the wing, it can never be caught again.*
>
> Russian proverb

COMMUNICATION IS IRREVERSIBLE   We sometimes wish that we could back up in time, erasing words or acts and replacing them with better alternatives. Unfortunately, such reversal is impossible. There are certainly occasions when further explanation can clear up another's confusion or when an apology can mollify another's hurt feelings: "I've been thinking about what I said last week, and I'm sorry. . . ." In other cases, though, no amount of explanation can erase the impression you have created. Despite the warnings judges issue in jury trials, it's impossible to "unreceive" a message. Words said and deeds done are irretrievable.

COMMUNICATION IS UNREPEATABLE   Because communication is an ongoing process, it is impossible to repeat the same event. The initial friendly smile that worked so well when meeting a stranger last week might not succeed with the person you encounter tomorrow. It might feel stale and artificial to you the second time around, or it might be wrong for the new person or occasion. Even with the same person, it's impossible to re-create an event. Why? Because neither of you *is* the same person. You've both lived longer. The behaviour isn't original. Your feelings about one another may have changed. You need not constantly invent new ways to act around familiar people, but you should realize that the "same" words and behaviour are different each time they are spoken or performed. Chapter 8 will alert you to the stages through which a relationship progresses.

Communication Misconceptions

It's just as important to know what communication is *not* as to understand what it is.[31] Avoiding the following misconceptions can save you a great deal of personal trouble.

MEANINGS ARE NOT IN WORDS The biggest mistake we can make is to assume that *saying* something is the same thing as *communicating* it. To use the terminology of our communication model, there's no guarantee that a receiver will decode a message in a way that matches the sender's intention. (If you doubt this proposition, list all the times you've been misunderstood in the past month.) Chapter 3 outlines the many reasons why people can interpret a statement differently from the way you intended it, and Chapter 5 describes the most common types of verbal misunderstandings and suggests ways to minimize them. Chapter 7 introduces listening skills that help ensure that the way you receive messages matches the ideas a speaker is trying to convey.

MORE COMMUNICATION IS NOT ALWAYS BETTER Whereas not communicating enough can cause problems, there are also situations when *too much* talking is a mistake. Sometimes excessive communication is simply unproductive, as when two people "talk a problem to death," going over the same ground again and again without making progress. There are other times when talking too much actually aggravates a problem. We've all had the experience of "talking ourselves into a hole"—making a bad situation worse by pursuing it too far. As one communication book puts it, "More and more negative communication merely leads to more and more negative results."[32]

There are even times when *no* communication is the best course. Salespersons attest that it's often best to stop talking and let the customer think about the product. Or, two people who are hurt and angry are better served by spending time cooling off and thinking about what to say and how to say it, rather than lashing out and saying things they don't mean and may later regret. Chapter 4 will help you decide when and how to share feelings.

NO SINGLE PERSON OR EVENT CAUSES ANOTHER'S REACTION Although communicative skill can often make the difference between satisfying and unpleasant outcomes, it's a mistake to suggest that any single thing we say or do causes an outcome. Many factors play a role in how others will react to your communication in a single situation. Suppose, for example, that you lose your temper and say something to a friend that you regret as soon as the words escape your lips. Your friend's reaction will depend on a whole host of events besides your unjustified remark: her frame of mind at the moment (uptight or mellow), elements of her personality (judgemental or forgiving), your relational history (supportive or hostile), and her knowledge of any factors in your life that might have contributed to your unfair remark. Because communication is a transactional, ongoing, collaborative process, it's usually a mistake to think that any event occurs in a vacuum.

COMMUNICATION WILL NOT SOLVE ALL PROBLEMS Sometimes even the best-planned, best-timed communication won't solve a problem. Imagine, for example, that you ask an instructor to explain why you received a poor grade on a project you believe deserved top marks. The professor clearly outlines the reasons why you received the low grade and sticks to that position after listening thoughtfully to your protests. Has communication solved the problem? Hardly.

Sometimes clear communication is even the *cause* of problems. Suppose, for example, that a friend asks you for an honest opinion of the $200 outfit he has just bought. Your clear and sincere answer, "I think it makes you look fat," might do more harm than good. Deciding when and how to self-disclose isn't always easy. See Chapter 8 for suggestions.

COMMUNICATION IS NOT A NATURAL ABILITY   Many people assume that communication is an aptitude that is developed without the need for training—rather like breathing. Although almost everyone does manage to function passably without much formal communication training, most people operate at a level of effectiveness far below their potential. In this sense, communication is rather like playing a sport—a skill that can be developed by training and practice.

THE NATURE OF INTERPERSONAL COMMUNICATION

Now that you have a better understanding of the overall process of human communication, it's time to look at what makes some types uniquely interpersonal.

Two Views of Interpersonal Communication

Scholars have characterized **interpersonal communication** in a number of ways.[33] The most obvious definition focusses on the number of people involved. A **quantitative** definition of interpersonal communication includes any interaction between two people, usually face to face. Social scientists call two persons interacting a **dyad,** and they often use the adjective "dyadic" to describe this type of communication. So, in a quantitative sense, the terms *dyadic communication* and *interpersonal communication* can be used interchangeably. Using a quantitative definition, a salesclerk and customer or a police officer ticketing a speeding driver would be examples of interpersonal acts, whereas a teacher and class or a performer and audience would not.

Dyadic communication *is* different from the kind of interaction that occurs in larger groups. For example, two-person exchanges are the earliest form of interaction we experience, and throughout life they are the most common type of communication. Unlike threesomes and other groups, dyads are complete and cannot be subdivided. If one person withdraws from the other, the relationship is finished. This indivisibility means that, unlike groups, the partners in a dyad can't form coalitions to get their needs met: They must work matters out with one another.

Despite the unique qualities of dyads, you might object to the quantitative definition of interpersonal communication. For example, consider a routine transaction between a sales clerk and customer, or the rushed exchange when you ask a stranger on the street for directions. Communication of this sort hardly seems interpersonal . . . or personal in any sense of the word. In fact, after transactions like this we commonly remark, "I might as well have been talking to a machine."

The impersonal nature of some two-person exchanges has led some scholars to argue that quality is what denotes **interpersonal communication.**[34] Using a **qualitative** definition, interpersonal communication occurs when people treat one another as unique individuals, regardless of the context in which the interaction occurs or the number of people involved.

Several features distinguish qualitatively interpersonal communication from less-personal exchanges.[35] The first is *uniqueness*. Communication in impersonal exchanges is determined by social *rules* (laugh politely at others' jokes, don't dominate a conversation, and so on) and by social *roles* (the customer is always right, treat authority figures with deference, say "fine" when others ask how you're doing). Qualitatively interpersonal relationships are characterized by the development of unique rules and roles. For example, in one relationship you might exchange good-natured insults, while in another you are careful never to offend your partner. Likewise, you might handle conflicts with one friend or family member by expressing disagreements as soon as they arise, whereas the unwritten rule in another relationship is to withhold resentments until they build up and then clear the air periodically.

Even within a single relationship, communication can vary from ritualistic to unique. Sometimes your relationship with friends, family, neighbours, or co-workers might fit the standard cultural pattern; but, on occasion, you might behave in quite different ways that reflect your feelings at the moment.

A second characteristic of qualitatively interpersonal relationships is *irreplaceability*. Because interpersonal relationships are unique, they can't be replaced. This explains why we feel so very sad when a close friend or relative dies. No matter how many other relationships fill our lives, none of them will ever be quite like the one that just ended.

Interdependence is a third characteristic of qualitatively interpersonal relationships. At the most basic level the fate of the communication partners is connected. For example, you might be able to brush off the anger, affection, excitement, or depression of someone you're not involved with personally, but in an interpersonal relationship the

Having just heard that his dear friend of 25 years had died of a heart attack, stockbroker Bernard Pechter was crying as he drove down Market St. at 6:15 a.m. on his way to work. A policewoman in a patrol car flashed her red lights and motioned him to pull over. She then ordered him out of the car, saying, "You look so sad I figured you need a hug." She held him for a few moments and drove off, leaving Bernard dumbfounded and also openmouthed. But definitely feeling better.

Herb Caen,
San Francisco *Chronicle*

other's life affects you. Sometimes interdependence is a pleasure, and at other times it is a burden. In either case, it is a fact of life in qualitatively interpersonal relationships. Interdependence goes beyond the level of joined fates. In interpersonal relationships, our very identity depends on the nature of our interaction with others. As psychologist Kenneth Gergen puts it: "One cannot be 'attractive' without others who are attracted, a 'leader' without others willing to follow, or a 'loving person' without others to affirm with appreciation.[36] As Chapter 2 explains, our identity is shaped by interaction with many people, not just those with whom we have interpersonal relationships. But the "significant others" with whom we communicate in a qualitatively interpersonal manner have a profound influence on how we view ourselves.

A fourth yardstick of interpersonal relationships is often (though not always) the amount of *disclosure* of personal information. In

impersonal relationships we don't reveal much about ourselves, but in interpersonal ones we feel more comfortable sharing our thoughts and feelings. This doesn't mean that all interpersonal relationships are warm and caring, or that all self-disclosure is positive. It's possible to reveal negative, personal information: "I'm really mad at you . . ."

In **impersonal communication** we seek pay-offs that have little to do with the people involved. You listen to professors in class or talk to potential buyers of your used car in order to reach goals that have little to do with developing personal relationships. By contrast, you spend time in qualitatively interpersonal relationships with friends, lovers, and others because of *intrinsic rewards* that come from your communication. It doesn't matter *what* you talk about: Developing the relationship is what's important.

Qualitatively interpersonal communication is relatively scarce. We chat pleasantly with shopkeepers or fellow passengers on the bus or plane; we discuss the weather or current events with most class-mates and neighbours; we deal with co-workers and teachers in a polite way, but considering the number of people with whom we communicate, personal relationships are by far in the minority.

The rarity of personal relationships isn't necessarily unfortunate. Most of us don't have the time or energy to create personal relationships with everyone we encounter. In fact, the scarcity of qualitatively interpersonal communication contributes to its value. Like precious jewels and one-of-a-kind artwork, interpersonal relationships are special because of their scarcity.

Personal and Impersonal Communication: A Matter of Balance

Now that you understand the differences between qualitatively interpersonal and impersonal communication, we need to ask some important questions. Is interpersonal communication better than the impersonal variety? Is more interpersonal communication the goal?

Most relationships aren't *either* interpersonal *or* impersonal. Rather, they fall somewhere on a continuum between these two ex-tremes. Consider your own communication and you'll find that there is often a personal element in even the most impersonal situations. You might appreciate the unique sense of humour of a check-out clerk or connect on a personal level with the person cutting your hair. And even the most tyrannical, demanding, by-the-book boss might show an occasional flash of humanity.

Just as there's a personal element in many impersonal settings, there is also an impersonal side to our relationships with the people we care most about. There are occasions when we don't want to be personal: when we're distracted, tired, or busy, or just not interested. In fact, interpersonal communication is rather like rich food–it's fine in moderation, but too much can make you uncomfortable.

To know all your neighbors on the global level does not mean that you will automatically love them all; it does not, in and of itself, introduce a reign of peace and brotherhood. But to be potentially in touch with everybody at least makes fighting more uncomfortable. It becomes easier to argue instead.

Isaac Asimov,
"The Fourth Revolution"

INVITATION TO INSIGHT

HOW PERSONAL ARE YOUR RELATIONSHIPS?

Use the characteristics of qualitatively interpersonal communication described on pages 19–21 to think about your own relationships. Make a list of several people who are "close" to you–family members, people you live with, friends, co-workers, and so on.

   How would you rate these relationships on each of the following scales? After completing the exercise, ask yourself the important question: How satisfied are you with the answers you have found?

Uniqueness

1	2	3	4	5
Standardized, habitual				Unique

Replaceability

1	2	3	4	5
Replaceable			Irreplaceable	

Dependence

1	2	3	4	5
Independent			Interdependent	

Disclosure

1	2	3	4	5
Low disclosure			High disclosure	

The personal–impersonal mixture of communicating in a relationship can change over time. The communication between new lovers who only talk about their feelings may change as their relationship develops, so that several years later their communication has become more routine and ritualized, and the percentage of time they spend on personal, relational issues drops as conversation about less-intimate topics increases. Chapter 8 discusses how communication changes as relationships pass through various stages, as well as describes the role of self-disclosure in keeping those relationships strong. As you read this information, you will see even more clearly that, while interpersonal communication can make life worth living, it isn't possible or desirable all the time.

It's clear that there is a place in our lives for both impersonal and interpersonal communication. Each type has its uses. The real challenge, then, is to find the right balance between the two types.

COMMUNICATING ABOUT RELATIONSHIPS

By now you understand the characteristics that distinguish interpersonal relationships. But what kinds of messages do we exchange as we define our relationships?

Content and Relational Messages

Virtually every verbal statement has a **content** dimension, containing the subject being discussed. The content of such statements as "It's your turn to do the dishes" or "I'm busy Saturday night" is obvious.

Content messages aren't the only thing being exchanged when two people communicate. In addition, almost every message—both verbal and nonverbal—also has a second, **relational** dimension, which makes statements about how the parties feel toward one another.[37] These relational messages deal with one or more social needs, most commonly control, affection, or respect. Consider the two examples we just mentioned:

- Imagine two ways of saying "It's your turn to do the dishes": one that is demanding and another that is matter-of-fact. Notice how the different vocal nonverbal messages make statements about how the sender views control in this part of the relationship. The demanding tone says, in effect, "I have a right to tell you what to do around the house," whereas the matter-of-fact one suggests, "I'm just reminding you of something you might have overlooked."

- You can easily visualize two ways to deliver the statement "I'm busy Saturday night": one with little affection and the other with much liking.

Notice that in each of these examples the relational dimension of the message was never discussed. In fact, most of the time we aren't conscious of the many relational messages that bombard us every day. Sometimes we are unaware of relational messages because they match our belief about the amount of respect, control, and affection that is appropriate. For example, you probably won't be offended if your boss tells you to do a certain job because you agree that supervisors have the right to direct employees. In other cases, however, conflicts arise over relational messages even though content is not disputed. If your boss delivers the order in a condescending, sarcastic, or abusive tone of voice, you probably will be offended. Your complaint wouldn't be with the order itself but with the way it was delivered. "I may work for this company," you might think, "but I'm not a slave or an idiot. I deserve to be treated like a human being."

How are relational messages communicated? As the boss–employee example suggests, they are usually expressed nonverbally. To test this fact for yourself, imagine how you could act while saying "Can you help me for a minute?" in a way that communicates each of the following relationships:

superiority	friendliness	sexual desire
helplessness	aloofness	irritation

Although nonverbal behaviours are a good source of relational messages, they are also ambiguous. The sharp tone you take as a personal insult might be due to fatigue, and the interruption you assume is an

attempt to ignore your ideas might be a sign of pressure that has nothing to do with you. Before you jump to conclusions about relational clues, it's a good idea to check them out verbally. Chapter 3 will introduce you to the skill of perception checking—a useful tool for verifying your hunches about nonverbal behaviour.

Metacommunication

Not all relational messages are nonverbal. Social scientists use the term **metacommunication** to describe messages people exchange about their relationship. In other words, metacommunication is communication about communication. Whenever we discuss our relationship with others, we are metacommunicating: "I wish we could stop arguing so much" or "I appreciate how honest you've been with me." Verbal metacommunication is an essential ingredient in successful relationships. Sooner or later there are times when it becomes necessary to talk about what is going on between you and the other person. The ability to focus on the kinds of issues described in this chapter can be the tool for keeping the relationship on track.

An Outline of Human Language Functions

http://pubpages.unh.edu/~jel/
Lfunctions.html

Ethical Challenge

Martin Buber's "I and Thou"

Martin Buber is arguably the most influential advocate of qualitatively interpersonal communication as defined on pages 19–21 of this chapter. His book *Ich und Du* has been a worldwide classic, selling millions of copies since its publication in 1922.

In English, the book's title has sometimes been translated as "I and Thou," wording that both obscures and explains its central theme. The religious connotations of "Thou" have led some readers to think Buber was writing from a theological point of view. In fact, "Thou" reflects a distinction in German between two forms of address: the formal "sie" and the personal "du." Other languages make the same differentiation. In Spanish, for example, the terms are "usted" and "tu," and in French "vous" and "tu." Because "thou" connotes formality, the definitive English translation of Buber's work refers to its key concept as "I-You," the best English representation of the kind of intimate relationship that Buber was describing.

Buber states that "I-It" and "I-You" represent two ways in which humans can relate to one another. "I-It" relationships are stable, predictable, detached. In an "I-It" mode we deal with people because they can do things for us: pump gas, laugh at our jokes, buy products we are selling, provide information or amusement. "I-It" is also the approach of science, which attempts to understand what makes people tick in order to explain, predict, and control their behaviour. Buber would have regarded advertisers as operating in an "I-It" mode, crafting messages that lead people to buy their products or services. "I-It" relationships exist in personal relationships as well as between strangers: On an everyday basis parents and children, bosses and employees, service providers and customers . . . even lovers deal with one another

as objects ("I wish she would leave me alone"; "Can you pick me up after work?" "How can I get him/her to love me?").

In profound contrast to "I-It" relationships, Buber described an "I-You" way of interacting. "I-You" relationships are utterly unique. Because no two teachers or students, parents or children, husbands or wives, bosses or employees are alike, we encounter each person as an individual, and not as a member of some category. An "I-You" posture goes further: Not only are people different from one another; they, themselves, change from moment to moment. An "I-You" relationship arises out of how we are *now*, not how we might have been yesterday . . . or even a moment ago. In an "I-You" relationship, persuasion and control are out of the question: We certainly may explain our point of view, but ultimately respect the fact that others are free to act.

Buber acknowledges that it is impossible to create and sustain pure "I-You" relationships. But without this qualitatively interpersonal level of contact, our lives are impoverished. To paraphrase Buber, without "I-It" we cannot exist; but if we live only with "I-It," we are not fully human.

Think of your most important relationships. To what degree can they be described as "I-You" or "I-It"? How satisfied are you with this level of relating? What obligation do you have to treat others in an I-Thou manner? Based on your answers to these questions, how might you change your style of communication?

An English translation of Martin Buber's *I and Thou* was published in 1970 by Scribner's. For useful descriptions of its central themes, see John Stewart, "Interpersonal Communication: Contact between Persons," in J. Stewart, ed., *Bridges, Not Walls*, 6th ed. (New York: McGraw-Hill, 1995); and H.J. Paton's chapter "Martin Buber" in *The Modern Predicament* (London: Allen & Unwin, 1955).

Metacommunication is an important method for solving conflicts in a constructive manner. It provides a way to shift discussion from the content level to relational questions, where the problem often lies. For example, consider the conversation between Macon and Muriel in the Communication Transcript on page 27. Imagine how

The Martin Buber Home Page

http://www.buber.de/en/ index.html

QUALITY TIME   Gail Machlis

Quality Time © 1994 Gail Machlis. Reprinted with permission of Universal Press Syndicate.
All rights reserved.

the discussion might have been more productive if they had focussed
on the relational issue of Macon's commitment to Muriel and her
son. By sticking to the content level–the boy's math skill–Macon
avoided the kind of metacommunication that is often necessary to
keep relationships healthy.

Metacommunication isn't just a tool for handling problems. It is
also a way to reinforce the satisfying aspects of a relationship: "I really appreciate it when you compliment me about my work in front
of the boss." Comments like this serve two functions: First, they let
others know that you value their behaviour; second, they boost the
odds that others will continue the behaviour in the future.

Despite the benefits of metacommunication, bringing relational issues out in the open does have its risks. Discussing problems can be
interpreted in two ways. On one hand, the other person might see it
in a positive light–"Our relationship is working because we can still
talk things out." On the other hand, your desire to focus on the relationship might look like a bad omen–"Our relationship isn't working
if we have to keep talking it over."[38] Furthermore, metacommunication does involve a certain degree of analysis ("It seems like you're

Communication Transcript

Content and Relational Messages

Both content and relational communication are important. But when each person in a conversation focusses on a different level, problems are likely to arise. In this excerpt from Anne Tyler's novel The Accidental Tourist, Muriel tries to turn Macon's content-related remark about her son into a discussion about the future of their relationship. Until Macon and Muriel agree about whether they will focus on content or relational issues, they are likely to remain at an uncomfortable impasse.

"I don't think Alexander's getting a proper education," he said to her one evening.

"Oh, he's okay."

"I asked him to figure what change they'd give back when we bought the milk today, and he didn't have the faintest idea. He didn't even know he'd have to subtract."

"Well, he's only in second grade," Muriel said.

"I think he ought to switch to a private school."

"Private schools cost money."

"So? I'll pay."

She stopped flipping the bacon and looked over at him. "What are you saying?" she asked.

"Pardon?"

"What are you saying, Macon? Are you saying you're committed?"

Macon cleared his throat. He said, "Committed."

"Alexander's got ten more years of school ahead of him. Are you saying you'll be around for all ten years?"

"Um . . ?"

"I can't just put him in a school and take him out again with every passing whim of yours."

He was silent.

"Just tell me this much," she said. "Do you picture us getting married sometime? I mean when your divorce comes through?"

He said, "Oh, well, marriage, Muriel . . ?"

"You don't, do you. You don't know what you want. One minute you like me and the next you don't. One minute you're ashamed to be seen with me and the next you think I'm the best thing that ever happened to you."

He stared at her. He had never guessed that she read him so clearly.

"You think you can just drift along like this, day by day, no plans," she said. "Maybe tomorrow you'll be here, maybe you won't. Maybe you'll just go on back to Sarah. Oh yes! I saw you at Rose's wedding. Don't think I didn't see how you and Sarah looked at each other."

Macon said, "All I'm saying is—"

"All I'm saying," Muriel told him, "is take care what you promise my son. Don't go making him promises you don't intend to keep."

"But I just want him to learn to subtract!" he said.

———————

Anne Tyler,
The Accidental Tourist

angry with me"), and some people resent being analyzed. These cautions don't mean verbal metacommunication is a bad idea. They do suggest, though, that it's a tool that needs to be used carefully.

Types of Relational Messages

While the number and variety of content messages are almost infinite, the range of content messages fits into one of three categories: affinity, respect, and control.

"You say, 'off with her head,' but what I'm hearing is, 'I feel neglected.'"

Drawing by Mike Ewers. Reprinted by permission.

AFFINITY **Affinity** refers to the degree to which people like or appreciate one another.[59] Not all affinity messages are positive: A glare or an angry word shows the level of liking just as clearly as a smile or profession of love. The range of affinity messages shows that interpersonal relationships aren't always friendly. Friends who disagree or lovers who argue are still communication partners. As long as these relationships possess all the characteristics that distinguish them as interpersonal—uniqueness, irreplaceability, interdependence, and so on—we can say they are interpersonal. In this sense, liking and disliking (both signs that we care about the other person) are much more closely related to one another than either is to indifference.

RESPECT At first glance **respect** might seem identical to affinity, but the two attitudes are different.[40] It's possible to like others without respecting them. For instance, you might like—or even probably love—your 2-year-old cousin without respecting her. In the same way, you might have a great deal of affection for some friends, yet not respect the way they behave. The reverse is also true: It's possible to respect people we don't like. You might hold an acquaintance in high esteem for being hard working, honest, talented, or clever—yet not particularly enjoy that person's company.

Sometimes being respected is more important than being liked. Think about occasions in school when you were offended because an instructor or fellow student didn't seem to take your comments or questions seriously. The same principle holds on the job, where having your opinions count often means more than being popular. Even in more-personal relationships, conflicts often focus on the issue of respect. Being taken seriously is a vital ingredient of self-esteem.

CONTROL   A final way to look at relationships involves the question of **control**—the degree to which the parties in a relationship have the power to influence one another.

Types of Control   Communication researchers have commonly identified the balance of relational control in two ways. *Decision control* revolves around who has the power to determine what will happen in the relationship. What will we do Saturday night? Shall we use our savings to fix up the house or to take a vacation? How much time should we spend together and how much should we spend apart? As these examples suggest, some decisions are small, whereas others are major. It's important to realize that even the smallest decisions reveal something about the balance of power in the relationship.

A very different way to see how partners influence one another is to examine conversational control. Some common indicators of conversational control include who talks the most, who interrupts whom, and who changes the topic most often.[41] The person who exercises the greatest amount of conversational control doesn't always make decisions. A roommate who chatters constantly might not persuade you to accept his beliefs. Nonetheless, the ability to determine who talks about what does constitute one type of influence.

Distribution of Control   Control can be distributed in three ways within a relationship.[42] As you read each of these ways, decide which pattern describes each of your relationships.

A **complementary relationship** exists when the distribution of power is unequal. One partner says, "Let's go dancing tonight," and the other says, "Fine." The boss asks several employees to work late, and they all agree. You know your friend has been feeling low lately, and so you're willing to listen to her problems—even though you have other things to do. In complementary situations like these, one party exercises control, and the other is willing to go along. This structure explains why the controller is often labelled in communication jargon as "one up," whereas the party who is being controlled is termed "one down." As long as both parties are comfortable with their roles, a complementary relationship can be stable. On the other hand, relational problems are guaranteed if both parties struggle to occupy one-up positions. There are even situations in which both partners seek a one-down position. At first the idea of two partners striving to give up control may seem odd, but it is really quite common. Consider, for example, a couple discussing what to do during their evening out. "I don't care," one says, "whatever you want." The other replies, "I don't care either. Anything is fine with me." It's easy to imagine how the struggle to avoid responsibility could go on for some time—and how it could characterize some relationships.

Whereas power is unequal in complementary relationships, in a **symmetrical relationship** the partners seek the same degree of control. Although symmetry sounds like the best approach, it isn't always practical or necessary. On trivial issues (what to eat for dinner, whether to buy green or yellow tennis balls) equal decision making often isn't worth the effort. On major issues (whether to move to a new city, how many children to have) it may not be possible. Despite these difficulties, the shared power of a symmetrical relationship is a goal in many relationships, especially for "modern" couples who object to the unequal, complementary power structure of traditional marriages.

Unlike the lopsidedness of complementary relationships and the total equality of symmetrical ones, **parallel relationships** handle power in a much more fluid way. Partners shift between one-up controlling positions and one-down roles, so that each person leads in some areas and shares power equally in many situations. Kyle may handle the decisions about car repairs and menu planning, as well as taking the spotlight at parties with their friends. Ashley manages the finances and makes most of the decisions about child care, as well as controlling the conversation when she and Kyle are alone.

INVITATION TO INSIGHT

MEASURING YOUR RELATIONSHIPS

What kinds of relational messages do you communicate? What do they say about your relationship with others? You can find out by following these steps:

1. Choose an important interpersonal relationship.

2. Place your initials on each of the following scales to represent the kinds of relational messages you communicate to the other person. Be prepared to offer specific examples of situations that illustrate this type of relational communication.

3. Place your partner's initials on each scale representing your perception of his or her relational messages, and be prepared to offer examples to back up your choices.

4. Invite your partner to complete steps 2 and 3 using a different-colour ink to distinguish his or her responses from yours.

5. Now compare your answers with your partner's, and answer the following questions:
   a. Are your responses similar or different? If they differ, whose perception is more accurate?
   b. Are you satisfied with the relationship as it is described here? If not, what can you do to improve it?

Low		High
	AFFINITY	
Low		High
	RESPECT	
Complementary	Parallel	Symmetrical
	CONTROL	

When a decision is very important to one partner, the other willingly gives in, knowing that the favour will be returned later. When issues are important to both partners, they try to share power equally. But when an impasse occurs, each will make concessions in a way that keeps the overall balance of power equal. The same sort of parallel arrangement characterizes many working relationships, even among superiors and subordinates. The boss may assert authority in many cases while deferring to employees in others when their judgement or experience justifies that approach. And much of the time, both boss and employees will work together to develop a solution that makes sense to everyone.

COMMUNICATION COMPETENCE: WHAT MAKES AN EFFECTIVE COMMUNICATOR?

It's easy to recognize good communicators, and even easier to spot poor ones. But what are the characteristics that distinguish effective communicators from their less-successful counterparts? Answering this question has been one of the leading challenges for communication scholars.[43] Although all the answers aren't yet in, research has identified a great deal of important and useful information about communication competence.

Communication Competence Defined

Defining **communication competence** isn't as easy as it might seem. Although scholars are still struggling to agree on a precise definition, most would agree that effective communication involves achieving one's goals in a manner that, ideally, maintains or enhances the relationship in which it occurs.[44] This definition may seem vague on one hand and wordy on the other, but a closer look shows that it suggests several important characteristics of communication competence.

THERE IS NO "IDEAL" WAY TO COMMUNICATE   Your own experience shows that a variety of communication styles can be effective. Some very successful communicators are serious, while others use humour; some are gregarious, while others are more quiet; and some are more straightforward, while others hint diplomatically. Just as there are many kinds of beautiful music or art, there are many kinds of competent communication. It certainly is possible to learn new, effective ways of communicating from observing models, but it would be a mistake to try to copy others in a way that doesn't reflect your own style or values.

Cultural differences also illustrate the principle that there is no single model of competence. What qualifies as competent behaviour in one culture might be completely inept, or even offensive, in another.[45] On an obvious level, customs like belching after a meal or appearing nude in public that might be appropriate in some parts of the world would be considered outrageous in others. But there are more subtle differences in competent communication. For example, qualities like self-disclosure and speaking clearly that are valued in North America are likely to be considered overly aggressive and insensitive in many Asian cultures, where subtlety and indirectness are considered important. Even within a single society, members of various co-cultures may have different notions of appropriate behaviour. For instance, students from the Mi'kmaq nation have said in class that to avoid eye contact when speaking with their elders demonstrates respect. However, when this same behaviour is directed toward non-Aboriginal authority figures such as university professors, deans, judges, and so forth, it may be perceived as insolence rather than the courtesy and deference they mean to convey.

COMPETENCE IS SITUATIONAL   Even within a culture or relationship, the specific communication that is competent in one setting might be a colossal blunder in another. The joking insults you routinely trade with a friend might offend a sensitive family member, and last Saturday night's romantic approach would probably be out of place at work on Monday morning.

Because competent behaviour varies so much from one situation and person to another, it's a mistake to think that communication competence is a trait that a person either possesses or lacks. It's more accurate to talk about *degrees* or *areas* of competence.[46] You and the people you know are probably quite competent in some areas and less so in others. You might deal quite skillfully with peers, for example, while feeling clumsy interacting with people much older or younger, wealthier or poorer, more or less attractive than yourself. In fact, your competence with one person may vary from situation to situation. This means that it's an overgeneralization to say in a moment of distress, "I'm a terrible communicator!" when it's more accurate to say, "I didn't handle this particular situation very well."

COMPETENCE IS RELATIONAL   Because communication is transactional, something we do *with* others rather than *to* them, behaviour that is appropriate in one relationship isn't necessarily effective in others. For example, researchers have uncovered a variety of ways people deal with jealousy in their relationships.[47] The approaches included keeping closer tabs on the partner, acting indifferent, decreasing affection, talking the matter over, and acting angry. The researchers found that no one type of behaviour was effective or ineffective in every relationship. They concluded that approaches that work with some people would be harmful to others. Findings like these demonstrate that competence arises out of developing ways of interacting that work for you and for the other people involved.[48]

The number of forms that successful relationships can take is illustrated by research showing that there are three basic types of marriages: traditionals (who emphasize interdependence and harmony), independents (who value the relationship but emphasize individual differences between the partners), and separates (who view the marriage primarily as a matter of convenience).[49] In addition, the two partners in a marriage may have different orientations, such as separate/traditional or traditional/independent. While not all these types are equally successful, this typology shows that there is more than one way to have a successful marriage. For instance, the traditional arrangement that works so well for one couple might not suit another, whose independent lifestyle works just fine for them.

Characteristics of Competent Communicators

Despite the fact that competent communication varies from one situation to another, scholars have identified several common denominators that characterize effective communication in most contexts.

A WIDE RANGE OF BEHAVIOURS Effective communicators are able to choose their actions from a wide range of behaviours. To understand the importance of having a large communication repertoire, imagine that someone you know repeatedly tells jokes–perhaps racist or sexist ones–that you find offensive. You could respond to these jokes in a number of ways:

> You could decide to say nothing, figuring that the risks of bringing the subject up would be greater than the benefits.

> You could ask a third party to say something to the joke teller about the offensiveness of the stories.

> You could hint at your discomfort, hoping that your friend would get the point.

You could joke about your friend's insensitivity, counting on humour to soften the blow of your criticism.

You could express your discomfort in a straightforward way, asking your companion to stop telling the offensive stories, at least around you.

You could even demand that the other person stop.

With this choice of responses at your disposal (and you can probably think of others as well), you could pick the one that had the best chance of success. But if you were able to use only one or two of these responses when raising a delicate issue—always keeping quiet or always hinting, for example—your chances of success would be much smaller. Indeed, many poor communicators are easy to spot by their limited range of responses. Some are chronic jokers. Others are always belligerent. Still others are quiet in almost every situation. Like a piano player who knows only one tune or a chef who can prepare only a few dishes, these people are forced to rely on a small range of responses, whether or not they are successful.

ABILITY TO CHOOSE THE MOST APPROPRIATE BEHAVIOUR   Simply possessing a large array of communication skills is no guarantee of success. It's also necessary to know which of these behaviours will work best in a particular situation. Choosing the best way to send a message is rather like selecting a gift: What is appropriate for one person won't suit another. This ability to choose the best approach is essential, because a response that works well in one setting would flop miserably in another.

Although it's impossible to say precisely how to act in every situation, there are at least three factors to consider when you are deciding which response to choose. The first is the communication *context*. The time and place will almost always influence how you act. For example, the sombre, low-key communication style one finds at a funeral would be out of place at a graduation party.

Your goal will also shape the approach you take. Inviting a new neighbour over for a cup of coffee or dinner could be just the right approach if you want to encourage a friendship; but if you want to maintain your privacy it might be wiser to be polite but distant. Likewise, your goal will determine your approach in situations in which you want to help another person. As you will learn in Chapter 7, there are times when offering advice is just what is needed. But when you want to help others develop the ability to solve problems on their own, it's better to withhold your own ideas and function as a sounding board so they can consider alternatives and choose their solutions.

Finally, your *knowledge of the other person* should also shape the approach you take. If you're dealing with someone who is very sensitive or insecure, your response might be supportive and cautious. With an old and trusted friend you might be blunt. The social niche of the other party can also influence how you communicate. For instance, you would probably act differently toward an 80-year-old person than you would toward a teenager. You would probably behave differently toward the president of your institution than you would toward a classmate, even in identical circumstances.

SKILL AT PERFORMING BEHAVIOURS Once you have chosen the most appropriate way to communicate, it's still necessary to perform the required skills effectively. There is a big difference between knowing *about* a skill and being able to put it into practice. Simply being aware of alternatives isn't much help, unless you can skillfully put these alternatives to work.

Just reading about communication skills in the following chapters won't guarantee that you can start using them flawlessly. Like any other skill–playing a musical instrument or learning a sport, for example–the road to competence in communication is not a short one. As you learn and practise the communication skills in the following pages, you can expect to pass through several stages, shown in Figure 1–3.[50]

Beginning Awareness The first step in learning any new skill is a beginning awareness. This is the point at which you first learn that there is a new and better way of behaving. If you play tennis, for example, awareness might grow when you learn about a new way of serving that can improve your power and accuracy. In the area of communication, *Looking Out/Looking In* should bring this sort of awareness to you.

Awkwardness Just as you were clumsy when you first tried to ride a bicycle or drive a car, your initial attempts at communicating in new ways may also be awkward. This doesn't mean that there's anything wrong with these methods, but rather that you need more experience with them. After all, if it's reasonable to expect difficulty learning other skills, you ought to expect the same fumbling with the concepts in this book. As Ringo Starr put it when talking about music, "If you want to play the blues, you gotta pay your dues. . . . It don't come easy."

Consciously Skilled If you are willing to keep working at overcoming the awkwardness of your initial attempts, you will arrive at the third learning stage, which is one of skillfulness. At this point you'll be able to handle yourself well, although you will still need to think

You have to be willing to look bad in order to get good.

Jack Canfield

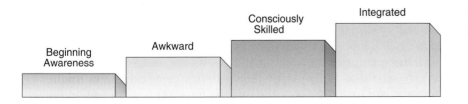

FIGURE 1–3

Stages in Learning Communication Skills

about what you're doing. As in learning a new language, this is the time when you're able to speak grammatically and use the correct words, even though you still need to think hard to express yourself well. As an interpersonal communicator, you can expect the stage of skillfulness to be marked by a great deal of thinking and planning and also by good results.

Integration Finally, after a period of time in the skillful phase, you'll find yourself at the final level of integration. This occurs when you're able to perform well without thinking about it. The behaviour becomes automatic, a part of you. Integrated speakers of a foreign language converse without translating mentally from their native tongue. Integrated cyclists ride skillfully and comfortably, almost as if the bike were an extension of each cyclist's own body. And integrated communicators express themselves in skillful ways, not as a self-conscious act but because that is who they have become.

It's important to keep these stages in mind as you try out the ideas in this book. Prepare yourself for the inevitable awkwardness, knowing that if you're willing to keep practising the new skills you will become more and more comfortable and successful with them. Realize that the effort is worth it, for once you have learned new methods of communicating you'll be rewarded with far more satisfying relationships.

COGNITIVE COMPLEXITY People have the best chance of developing an effective message when they understand the other person's point of view. And because others aren't always good at expressing their thoughts and feelings clearly, the ability to imagine how an issue might look from the other's point of view is an important skill. In fact, understanding the other person is so important that researchers have labelled *empathy* the most important aspect of communication competence.[51] Because empathy is such an important element of communicative competence, much of Chapter 3 is devoted to this topic.

Social scientists use the term **cognitive complexity** to describe the ability to construct a variety of different frameworks for viewing an issue. Researchers have found that cognitive complexity increases the chances of satisfying communication among married couples,[52] helping others who are feeling distressed,[53] and achieving career advancement,[54] to name a few contexts.

To understand how cognitive complexity can increase competence, consider an example. Imagine that a longtime friend seems to be angry with you. One possible explanation is that your friend is offended by something you've done. Another possibility is that something has happened in another part of your friend's life that is upsetting. Or perhaps nothing at all is wrong and you're just being overly sensitive. Considering the issue from several angles might prevent you from overreacting or misunderstanding the situation, increasing the odds of finding a way to resolve the problem constructively. The sections of Chapter 3 on empathy and perception checking, listening in Chapter 7, and preventing defensiveness in Chapter 9 provide specific tools for developing your cognitive complexity.

SELF-MONITORING   Whereas increased cognitive complexity helps you understand others better, self-monitoring is one way to understand yourself. Psychologists use the term **self-monitoring** to describe the process of paying close attention to one's behaviour and using these observations to shape the way one behaves. Self-monitors are able to separate a part of their consciousness and observe their behaviour from a detached viewpoint, making observations like

"I'm making a fool out of myself."

"I'd better speak up now."

"This approach is working well. I'll keep it up."

Although too much self-monitoring can be problematic (see Chapter 2), people who are aware of their behaviour and the impression it makes are more skillful communicators than people who are low self-monitors.[55] For example, they are more accurate in judging others' emotional states, better at remembering information about others, less shy, and more assertive. Whereas low self-monitors may blunder through life, succeeding or failing without understanding why, high self-monitors have the detachment to ask themselves the question "How am I doing?" and to change their behaviour if the answer isn't positive.

Calvin and Hobbes   by Bill Watterson

Looking at Diversity

Communication Competence and Context

In this profile **Maroushka Kanywani,** a Ugandan student living in Ethiopia and studying communication at the University College of Cape Breton, Nova Scotia, describes modifications in her communication style as she tries to meet the communication norms of both the African and Canadian cultures. This account demonstrates some of the elements of communication competence introduced in Chapter 1: a wide repertoire of behaviours, the ability to choose the best behaviour for a given situation, and skill at performing that behaviour.

Having lived in Canada for almost 2 years now, I realize that my communication style has changed a great deal. While I was aware it would alter, the differences really hit me when I went home for the summer in 1998. I had to use a different "tool box" at home in order to fit in with my family and friends.

The first change I made regarded my "Canadian" accent; I toned it down for fear of being made fun of. You see, once you leave Ethiopia and go to the United Kingdom, United States, or Canada, your accent is expected to change. The irony in the situation is that while your friends and family expect your speaking style to have changed, they are also the very same people who point out how "different" you are now. At the end of the day, you just don't measure up!

As far as my language style is concerned, it is more forward than it used to be. Not that I am a rude person, but I have learned to follow things up more than I did at home. In other words, I am more assertive than I was before. This assertiveness took some people (at home) by surprise because what we would normally define as assertive in Canada is seen as outright rudeness at home, particularly when aimed at elders. Assertiveness is equated with a lack of respect. I really had to watch that I didn't offend anyone. However, my relationship with my mother is very different. I can use

the assertive style with her without reprimand. Even if my opinions differ from hers, she always listens wholeheartedly to them. She has brought me up to be an independent person, although some of my relatives are not quite struck on the idea.

Another aspect of communication that took me a while to get used to upon returning to Ethiopia was the perception of time. Since living in Canada, I have come to realize that "time is money." At home, generally speaking, that is not the case. Punctuality is not a big thing; time tends to be more flexible than it is in Canada. If you're invited for lunch, for example, it is not wise to expect that the meal will be served between 12 and 1 P.M. I have been to many lunches where we started eating between 3 and 3:30 P.M.! In the past, I wouldn't have minded this. But on my last visit I found myself getting impatient when events, visits, or dates didn't occur when they were scheduled.

In terms of adapting my communication to meet Canadian expectations, I am far more aware of personal space here. Coming from a collective culture to an individualistic one, I find it is very easy to cross that invisible line and invade someone's personal space. It is something that I am very much aware of now; I always remind myself not to get too close to my Canadian friends. What sometimes happens is that the distance that I strive to maintain with my Cana-

dian friends spills over into relationships with other African students at the university. Then I'm accused of being too standoffish! It gets a bit frustrating sometimes because I am not always quick enough to alter my approach. The invisible line changes much too fast for my liking. I think it all lies in the fact that when you belong to a society that is traditionally collective, you get used to having a lot of people around you, regardless of whether or not there is enough space to contain these people.

My communication style has also changed quite a bit in terms of self-disclosure. I reveal a lot more about myself to my Canadian same-sex friends. I think this is because, as an international student with no family close by, I am forced to share my thoughts and feelings with my friends. However, in platonic opposite-sex friendships, I hardly disclose anything, which was not the case when I was home. I could say anything to the Ugandan guys. I do not feel as secure with Canadian men.

In sum, I find that the more often I go home, the more flexible I am with my communication tools and the easier it is for me to fit in with my friends and family. But once a lengthy period of time elapses, I find that consciously or otherwise, I begin to lose that flexibility and eventually stick to the tools that I use most often, rather than swapping them to meet the demands of the situation. This may not be so good.

SKILL BUILDER

CHECK YOUR COMPETENCE

Other people are often the best judges of your communication competence. They can also offer useful information about how to improve your communication skill. Find out for yourself by following these steps:

1. Choose a person with whom you have an important relationship.

2. In co-operation with this person, identify several contexts in which you communicate. For example, you might choose different situations, such as "handling conflicts," "lending support to friends," or "expressing feelings."

3. For each situation, have your friend rate your competence by answering the following questions:

   a. Do you have a wide repertoire of response styles in this situation, or do you always respond in the same way?
   b. Are you able to choose the most effective way of behaving for the situation at hand?
   c. Are you skillful at performing behaviours? (Note that knowing how you *want* to behave isn't the same as being *able* to perform.)
   d. Do you communicate in a way that leaves others satisfied?

4. After reviewing your partner's answers, identify the situations in which your communication is most competent.

5. Choose a situation in which you would like to communicate more competently, and, with the help of your partner,

   a. Determine whether your repertoire of behaviours needs to be expanded.
   b. Identify the ways in which you need to communicate more skillfully.
   c. Develop ways to monitor your behaviour in the key situation to get feedback on your effectiveness.

COMMITMENT   One feature that distinguishes effective communication—at least in qualitatively interpersonal relationships—is commitment. In other words, people who seem to care about the relationship communicate better than those who don't.[56] This concern shows up in several ways. The first is *commitment to the other person*. Concern for the other person is revealed in a variety of ways: a desire to spend time with him or her instead of rushing, willingness to listen carefully instead of doing all the talking, the use of language that makes sense to the other person, and openness to change after hearing the other person's ideas.

Effective communicators also care about *the message*. They appear sincere, seem to know what they are talking about, and demonstrate through words and deeds that their ideas matter. Phony communication turns people off. So do wishy-washy positions and uninformed, ignorant statements.

How do you measure up as a competent communicator? Competence isn't a trait that people either possess or lack. Rather, it's a state that we achieve more or less frequently. A realistic goal, then, is not to become perfect but to boost the percentage of time when you communicate in ways outlined in this section.

SUMMARY

Communication is essential on many levels. Besides satisfying practical needs, effective communication can enhance physical health and emotional well-being. As children, we learn about our identity through the messages sent by others, and as adults our self-concept is shaped and refined through social interaction. Communication also satisfies social needs: involvement with others, control over the environment, and giving and receiving affection.

The process of communication is not a linear one that people "do" to one another. Rather, communication is a transactional process in which participants create a relationship by simultaneously sending and receiving messages, many of which are distorted by various types of noise.

Interpersonal communication can be defined contextually by the number of people involved, or qualitatively by the nature of interaction between them. In a qualitative sense, interpersonal relationships are unique, irreplaceable, interdependent, and intrinsically rewarding. Qualitatively interpersonal communication is relatively infrequent, even in the strongest relationships. Both personal and impersonal communication are useful, and most relationships have both personal and impersonal elements.

Communication occurs on two levels: content and relational. Relational communication can be both verbal and nonverbal. Metacommunication consists of messages that refer to the relationship between the communicators. Relational messages usually refer to one of three dimensions of a relationship: affinity, respect, and control.

All communication, whether personal or impersonal, content or relational, follows the same basic principles. Messages can be intentional or unintentional. It is impossible not to communicate. Communication is irreversible and unrepeatable. Some common misconceptions should be avoided when thinking about communication: Meanings are not in words, but in people. More communication does not always make matters better. Communication will not solve all problems. Finally, communication—at least effective communication—is not a natural ability.

Communication competence is the ability to get what you are seeking from others in a manner that maintains the relationship on terms that are acceptable to all parties. Competence doesn't mean behaving the same way in all settings and with all people; rather, competence varies from one situation to another. The most competent communicators have a wide repertoire of behaviours, and they are able to choose the best behaviour for a given situation and perform it skillfully. They are able to take others' points of view and analyze a situation in a variety of ways. They also monitor their own behaviour and are committed to communicating successfully.

KEY TERMS

affinity
behaviour
channel
cognitive complexity
communication
communication competence
complementary relationship
content message
control (conversational and
    decision)
decode
dyad

encode
environments
feedback
impersonal communication
    (contextual and qualitative)
instrumental goals
interpersonal communication
    (quantitative and qualita-
    tive)
linear communication model
message
metacommunication

noise (external, physiological,
    psychological)
parallel relationship
receiver
relational message
respect
self-monitoring
sender
symmetrical relationship
transactional communication
    model

Communication and the Self

Who are you? Take a moment now to answer this question. List as many ways as you can to identify yourself. You'll need this list as you read the rest of this chapter, so be sure to complete it now. Try to include all the characteristics that describe you:

   your moods or feelings (e.g., happy, sad)

   your appearance (e.g., good-looking, unattractive)

   your social traits (e.g., friendly, shy)

   talents you possess or lack (e.g., musical, tone-deaf)

   your intellectual capacity (e.g., smart, stupid)

   your strong beliefs (e.g., religious, environmentalist)

   your social roles (e.g., parent, spouse)

   your physical condition (e.g., healthy, weak)

Now take a look at what you've written. How did you define yourself? As a student? A woman or man? By your age? By your geographical location? Your talents? Your physical stature? Your occupation? Your political affiliation? You'll probably see that the words you've chosen represent a profile of what you view as your most important characteristics. In other words, if you were required to describe the "real you," this list ought to be a good summary.

COMMUNICATION AND THE SELF-CONCEPT

Communication Theory: Identity and Gender Resources

http://www.theory.org.uk/ theory-r.htm

What you've done in developing this list is to give a partial description of your **self-concept:** the relatively stable set of perceptions you hold of yourself. If a special mirror existed that not only reflected your physical features but also allowed you to view other aspects of yourself—emotional states, talents, likes, dislikes, values, roles, and so on—the reflection you'd see would be your self-concept.

You probably recognize that the self-concept list you recorded earlier is only a partial one. To make the description complete, you'd have to keep adding items until your list ran into hundreds of words.

Take a moment now to demonstrate the many parts of your self-concept by simply responding to the question "Who am I?" over and over again. Add these responses to the list you started earlier.

Of course, not every item on your self-concept list is equally important. For example, the most significant part of one person's self-concept might consist of social roles, and for another it might be physical appearance, health, friendships, accomplishments, or skills.

You can discover how much you value each part of your self-concept by rank-ordering the items on the list you've compiled. Try it now: Place *1* next to the most fundamental thing about you, *2* next to the second most important term, and continue in this manner until you've completed your list.

This self-concept you've just described is extremely important. To see just how fundamental it is, try the following exercise.

INVITATION TO INSIGHT

TAKE AWAY

1. Look over the list of words you've just used to describe yourself. If you haven't already done so, pick the 10 items that describe the most fundamental aspects of who you are. Be sure you've organized these items so that the most fundamental one is in first place and the one that is least central to your identity is number 10, arranging the words or phrases in between in their proper order.

2. Now find a comfortable spot where you can think without being interrupted. You can complete this exercise in a group with the leader giving instructions, or you can do it alone by reading the directions yourself when necessary.

3. Close your eyes and get a mental picture of yourself. Besides visualizing your appearance, you should also include in your image your less-observable features: your disposition, your hopes, your concerns . . . of course, including all the items you described in step 1.

4. Keep this picture in mind, but now imagine what would happen if the 10th item on your list disappeared from your makeup. How would you be different? Does the idea of giving up that item leave you feeling better or worse? How hard was it to let go of that item?

5. Now, without taking back the item you just abandoned, give up the ninth item on your list, and see what difference this makes to you. After pausing to experience your thoughts and feelings, give up each succeeding item on your list one by one.

6. After you've abandoned the number-one feature of who you are, take a few minutes to regather the parts of yourself that you abandoned, and then read on.

For most people this exercise dramatically illustrates just how fundamental the concept of self is. Even when the item being abandoned is an unpleasant one, it's often hard to give it up. And when asked to let go of their most central feelings or thoughts, most people balk. "I wouldn't be *me* without that," they insist. Of course, this proves our point: The concept of self is perhaps our most fundamental possession. Knowing who we are is essential, for without a self-concept it would be impossible to relate to the world.

The self-concept isn't just an individual matter. Entire communities collectively develop an image of themselves. Communication scholar Donal Carbaugh describes how North Americans interact in

In order to get at any truth about myself, I must have contact with another person. The other is indispensable to my own existence, as well as to my knowledge about myself.

Jean-Paul Sartre

ways that collectively craft their identities in settings as varied as hockey games, the workplace, weddings, and public policy disputes.[1] You can probably understand this phenomenon by reviewing the self-concept list you just created. Several items probably refer to your identity as a member of various groups: ethnic, religious, family, social, and so on.

How the Self-Concept Develops

Most researchers agree that we are not born with a self-concept.[2] An infant lying in a crib has no notion of self, no notion—even if the ability to speak were miraculously made available—of how to answer the question "Who am I?" Consider what it would be like to have no idea of your characteristic moods, physical appearance, social traits, talents, intellectual capacity, beliefs, or important roles. If you can imagine this experience—*blankness*—you can begin to understand how the world might appear to someone with no sense of self. Of course, you have to take it one step further and *not know* you do not have any notion of self.

Soon after birth the infant begins to differentiate among the stimuli in the environment: familiar and unfamiliar faces, the sounds that mean food, the noises that frighten, the cat that jumps in the crib, the sister who tickles—each becomes a separate part of the world. Recognition of distinctions in the environment probably precedes recognition of the self.

During the first year of life the child begins to recognize "self" as distinct from surroundings. If you've ever watched children at this age you've probably marvelled at how they can stare with great fascination at a foot, a hand, and other body parts that float into view, almost as if they were strange objects belonging to someone else. Then the connection is made, almost as if the child were realizing "The hand is *me*," "The foot is *me*." These first revelations form the child's earliest concept of self. At this early stage, the self-concept is almost exclusively physical, involving the child's basic realization of existing and of possessing certain body parts over which some control is exerted. This limited self-concept barely resembles the more fully developed self-concepts older children hold.

Although children may behave more or less sociably, they don't automatically view themselves in a way that reflects their actual communication behaviour. In fact, the opposite is closer to the truth: The self-concept is extremely subjective, being almost totally a product of interaction with others.[3] You can begin to get a sense of how your self-concept has developed by trying the following exercise. Be sure to complete it before reading on.

To live in prison is to live without mirrors . . . To live without mirrors is to live without the self.

Margaret Atwood

INVITATION TO INSIGHT

"EGO BOOSTERS" AND "EGO BUSTERS"

1. Either by yourself or with a partner, recall someone you know or once knew who was an "ego booster"–who helped enhance your self-esteem by acting in a way that made you feel accepted, competent, worthwhile, important, appreciated, or loved. This person needn't have played a crucial role in your life as long as the role was positive. Often your self-concept is shaped by many tiny nudges as well as by a few giant events. A family member with whom you've spent most of your life can be an "ego booster," but so can the stranger on the street who spontaneously smiles and strikes up a friendly conversation.

2. Now recall an "ego buster" from your life–someone who acted in a large or small way to reduce your self-esteem. As with ego booster, ego buster messages aren't always intentional. The acquaintance who forgets your name after you've been introduced or the friend who yawns while you're describing an important problem can diminish your feelings of self-worth.

3. Now that you've thought about how others shape your self-concept, recall a time when you were an ego booster to someone else– when you deliberately or unintentionally boosted another's self-esteem. Don't merely settle for an instance in which you were nice: Look for a time when your actions left another person feeling valued, loved, needed, and so on. You may have to ask the help of others to answer this question.

4. Finally, recall a recent instance in which you were an ego buster for someone else. What did you do to diminish another's self-esteem? Were you aware of the effect of your behaviour at the time? Your answer might show that some events we intend as boosters have the effect of busters. For example, you might joke with a friend in what you mean as a friendly gesture, only to discover that your remarks are received as criticism.

After completing the exercise (you *did* complete it, didn't you?), you should begin to see that your self-concept is shaped by those around you. This process of shaping occurs in two ways: reflected appraisal and social comparison.

REFLECTED APPRAISAL: THE LOOKING-GLASS SELF   As early as 1912, sociologist Charles Cooley used the image of a mirror to identify the process of **reflected appraisal:** the fact that each of us develops a self-concept that matches the way we believe others see us.[4] In other words, we are likely to feel less valuable, lovable, and capable to the degree that others have communicated ego-busting signals; and we will probably feel good about ourselves to the extent that others seem to feel good about us. The validity of the principle of reflected appraisal will become clear when you realize that the self-concept you described in the list at the beginning of this chapter is a product of the positive and negative messages you have received throughout your life.

To illustrate this point further, let's start at the beginning. Newborn children aren't born with any sense of identity: They learn to judge themselves only through the way others treat them. At first the evaluations aren't linguistic. Nonetheless, even the earliest days of life are full of messages that constitute the first boosters and busters that start to shape the child's self-concept. The amount of time parents allow their baby to cry before attending to its needs nonverbally communicates over a period of time how important that child is to them. Their method of handling the child also speaks volumes: Do they affectionately play with it, or do they treat it like so much baggage, changing diapers, feeding, and bathing it in a brusque, businesslike manner? Does the tone of voice with which they speak express love and enjoyment or disappointment and irritation?

Of course, many of these messages are not intentional ones. It is rare when a parent will deliberately try to tell a child it's not lovable; but whether they're intentional or not doesn't matter–nonverbal statements play a big role in shaping a youngster's feelings of being "OK" or "not OK."

As the child learns to speak and understand language, verbal messages also contribute to a developing self-concept. Every day a child is bombarded with scores of messages about himself or herself. Some of these are positive: "You're so cute!" "I love you." "What a big girl." Other messages are more discouraging: "What's the matter with you? Can't you do anything right?" "You're a bad boy." "Leave me alone. You're driving me crazy!"

Evaluations like these are the mirror by which we know ourselves; and, because children are trusting souls who have no other way of viewing themselves, they accept at face value both the positive and negative evaluations of the apparently all-knowing and all-powerful adults around them.

These same principles in the formation of the self-concept continue in later life, especially when messages come from what sociologists term **significant others**–people whose opinions we especially value. (See the story "Cipher in the Snow" on page 52.) A look at the ego boosters and ego busters you described in the previous exercise as well as others you can remember will show that the evaluations of a few especially important people can have long-range

ZiGGY®

i've GOT A ReALLy iMPORTANT PATIENT
COMiNG iN ANy MiNUTe NOW...
CAN We WORK ON yOUR SeLF-esTeeM
SOMe OTHeR TiMe ?...

2-10   © 1986 Universal Press Syndicate

effects. A teacher from long ago, a special friend or relative, or perhaps a barely known acquaintance whom you respected all can leave an imprint on how you view yourself. To see the importance of significant others, ask yourself how you arrived at your opinion of yourself as a student . . . as a person attractive to others . . . as a competent worker . . . and you'll see that these self-evaluations were probably influenced by the way others regarded you.

Although messages from others have a powerful impact on shaping our identity, it is an exaggeration to suggest that feedback is *always* responsible for modifying the self-concept.[5] There are cases in which a person's actual abilities play a larger role in shaping both self-evaluations and the perceptions of others. For example, if you are an outstanding student or a computer whiz, your accomplishments will probably boost your self-esteem, even if others don't give you much praise.

The influence of significant others becomes less powerful as we grow older. After about the age of 30, most people don't radically change their self-concept, at least without a conscious effort, such as psychotherapy.[6] By contrast, the self-concept of younger people is still flexible. For example, in a 5-year American study of girls between the ages of 6 and 18, Carol Gilligan reported that although they started out feeling good about themselves, they experienced a clear decline in their confidence and self-esteem.[7] Reginald Bibby and Donald Poterski, who have studied teen trends across Canada, noted in 1985 that 35 percent of Canadian adolescent girls reported feeling inferior, as compared with 23 percent of the male participants.[8] In a 1992 survey they found that 33 percent of males versus 18 percent of females agreed that the statement, "I have a lot of confidence," described them very well.[9]

SOCIAL COMPARISON   So far we have looked at the ways others' messages shape our self-concept. In addition to incorporating these messages, each of us forms our self-image by the process of **social comparison:** evaluating ourselves in terms of how we compare with others.

Two types of social comparison need highlighting. In the first, we decide whether we are *superior* or *inferior* by comparing ourselves with others. Are we attractive or ugly? A success or failure? Intelligent or stupid? How we feel about ourselves depends on those against whom we measure ourselves.[10]

You might feel just ordinary or inferior in terms of talent, friendships, or attractiveness if you compare yourself with an inappropriate reference group. In one study, young women's perceptions of their bodies changed for the worse after watching just 30 minutes of televised images of the "ideal" female form.[11] You may never be as beautiful as a Hollywood star, as agile as a professional athlete, or as wealthy as a millionaire. When you consider the matter logically, these facts don't mean you're worthless. Nonetheless, many people judge themselves against unreasonable standards and suffer

If children live with criticism,
They learn to condemn.
If children live with hostility,
They learn to fight.
If children live with ridicule,
They learn to be shy.
If children live with shame,
They learn to feel guilty.
If children live with
encouragement,
They learn confidence.
If children live with tolerance,
They learn to be patient.
If children live with acceptance,
They learn to love.
If children live with approval,
They learn to like themselves.
If children live with honesty,
They learn truthfulness.
If children live with security,
They learn to have faith in
themselves and others.
If children live with friendliness,
They learn the world is a nice
place in which to live.

Dorothy Law Nolte,
"Children Learn What They Live"

accordingly.[12] You'll read more about how to avoid placing perfectionistic demands on yourself in Chapter 4. This principle is especially powerful when we compare ourselves with images in the media. Furthermore, these distorted self-images can lead to serious behavioural disorders, such as depression, anorexia nervosa, bulimia, and other eating disorders.

In addition to feelings of superiority and inferiority, social comparison also provides a way to decide if we are the *same as* or *different from* others. A child who is interested in ballet and who lives in a setting where such preferences are regarded as weird will start to accept this label if there is no support from others. Likewise, adults who want to improve the quality of their relationships but are surrounded by friends and family who don't recognize or acknowledge the importance of these matters may think of themselves as oddballs. Thus, it's easy to recognize that the **reference groups** against which we compare ourselves play an important role in shaping our view of ourselves.

Some people have so much respect for their superiors they have none left for themselves.

Peter McArthur

You might argue that not every part of one's self-concept is shaped by others, insisting there are certain objective facts that are recognizable by self-observation. After all, nobody needs to tell a person that he is taller than others, speaks with an accent, has acne, and so on. These facts are obvious. Though it's true that some features of the self are immediately apparent, the *significance* we attach to them—the rank we assign them in the hierarchy of our list and the interpretation we give them—depends greatly on the opinions of others. After all, many of your features are readily observable, yet you don't find them important at all because nobody has regarded them as significant.

Recently, we heard a woman in her 80s describing her youth. "When I was a girl," she declared, "we didn't worry about weight. Some people were skinny and others were plump, and we pretty much accepted the bodies God gave us." In those days it was unlikely that weight would have found its way onto the self-concept list you constructed because it wasn't considered significant. Compare this attitude with what you find today: It's seldom that you pick up a popular magazine or visit a bookstore without reading about the latest diet fads, and television ads are filled with scenes of slender, happy people. As a result you'll rarely find a person who doesn't complain about the need to "lose a few pounds." Obviously, the reason for such concern has more to do with the attention paid to slimness these days than with any increase in the number of people in the population who are overweight. Furthermore, the interpretation of such characteristics as weight depends on the way people important to us regard them. We generally see fat as undesirable because others tell us it is. In a culture where obesity is the ideal (and there are such cultures), a person who regards herself as extremely heavy would be a beauty. In the same way, the fact that one is single or married, solitary or sociable, aggressive or passive takes on meaning depending on the interpretation society attaches to those traits. Thus, the importance of a given characteristic in your self-concept has as much to do with the significance you and others attach to it as with the existence of the characteristic.

By now you might be thinking, "It's not my fault that I've always been shy or unconfident. Because I developed a picture of myself as a result of the way others have treated me, I can't help being what I am." Though it's true that to a great extent you are a product of your environment, to believe you are forever doomed to a poor self-concept would be a big mistake. Having held a poor self-image in the past is no reason for continuing to do so in the future. You *can* change your attitudes and behaviours, as you'll soon read. So don't despair, and most of all don't use the fact that others have shaped your self-concept as an excuse for self-pity or for acting helpless. Now that you know the effect overly negative evaluations have had on you in the past, you'll be in a better position to revise your perception of yourself more favourably in the future.

Cipher in the Snow

It started with tragedy on a biting cold February morning. I was driving behind the Milford Corners bus as I did most snowy mornings on my way to school. It veered and stopped short at the hotel, which it had no business doing, and I was annoyed as I had to come to an unexpected stop. A boy lurched out of the bus, reeled, stumbled, and collapsed on the snowbank at the curb. The bus driver and I reached him at the same moment. His thin, hollow face was white even against the snow.

"He's dead," the driver whispered.

It didn't register for a minute. I glanced quickly at the scared young faces staring down at us from the school bus. "A doctor! Quick! I'll phone from the hotel. . . ."

"No use, I tell you he's dead." The driver looked down at the boy's still form. "He never even said he felt bad," he muttered. "Just tapped me on the shoulder and said, real quiet, 'I'm sorry. I have to get off at the hotel.' That's all. Polite and apologizing like."

At school, the giggling, shuffling morning noise quieted as the news went down the halls. I passed a huddle of girls. "Who was it? Who dropped dead on the way to school?" I heard one of them half-whisper.

"Don't know his name; some kid from Milford Corners" was the reply.

It was like that in the faculty room and the principal's office. "I'd appreciate your going out to tell the parents," the principal told me. "They haven't a phone and, anyway, somebody from school should go there in person. I'll cover your classes."

"Why me?" I asked. "Wouldn't it be better if you did it?"

"I didn't know the boy," the principal admitted levelly. "And, in last year's sophomore personalities column I note that you were listed as his favourite teacher."

I drove through the snow and cold down the bad canyon road to the Evans place and thought about the boy, Cliff Evans. His favourite teacher! I thought. He hasn't spoken two words to me in two years! I could see him in my mind's eye all right, sitting back there in the last seat in my afternoon literature class. He came in the room by himself and left by himself. "Cliff Evans," I muttered to myself, "a boy who never talked." I thought a minute. "A boy who never smiled. I never saw him smile once."

The big farm kitchen was clean and warm. I blurted out my news somehow. Mrs. Evans reached blindly toward a chair. "He never said anything about bein' ailing."

His stepfather snorted. "He ain't said nothin' about anything since I moved in here."

Mrs. Evans pushed a pan to the back of the stove and began to un-tie her apron. "Now hold on," her husband snapped. "I got to have breakfast before I go to town. Nothin' we can do now anyway. If Cliff hadn't been so dumb, he'd have told us he didn't feel good."

After school I sat in the office and stared blankly at the records spread out before me. I was to close the file and write the obitu-ary for the school paper. The al-most bare sheets mocked the effort. Cliff Evans, white, never legally adopted by stepfather, five young half-brothers and sisters. These meagre strands of informa-tion and the list of D grades were all the records had to offer.

Cliff Evans had silently come in the school door in the mornings and gone out the school door in the evenings, and that was all. He had never belonged to a club. He had never played on a team. He had never held an office. As far as I could tell he had never done one happy, noisy kid thing. He had never been anybody at all.

How do you go about making a boy into a zero? The grade-school records showed me. The first- and second-grade teachers' annotations read "sweet, shy child," "timid but eager." Then the third grade note had opened the attack. Some teacher had written in a good, firm hand, "Cliff won't talk. Unco-operative. Slow learner." The other academic sheep had followed with "dull"; "slow-witted"; "low I.Q." They became correct. The boy's I.Q. score in the ninth grade was listed as 83. But his I.Q. in the third grade had been 106. The score didn't go under 100 until the seventh grade. Even shy, timid, sweet children have resilience. It takes time to break them.

I stomped to the typewriter and wrote a savage report pointing out what education had done to Cliff Evans. I slapped a copy on the principal's desk and another in the sad, dog-eared file. I banged the typewriter and slammed the file and crashed the door shut, but I didn't feel much better. A little boy kept walking after me, a little boy with a peaked, pale face; a skinny body in faded jeans; and big eyes that had looked and searched for a long time and then had become veiled.

I could guess how many times he'd been chosen last to play sides in a game, how many whispered child conversations had excluded him, how many times he hadn't been asked. I could see and hear the faces and voices that said over and over, "You're a nothing, Cliff Evans."

A child is a believing creature. Cliff undoubtedly believed them. Suddenly it seemed clear to me: When finally there was nothing left at all for Cliff Evans, he collapsed on a snowbank and went away. The doctor might list "heart fail-ure" as the cause of death, but that wouldn't change my mind.

We couldn't find 10 students in the school who had known Cliff well enough to attend the funeral as his friends. So the student body officers and a committee from the junior class went as a group to the church, being politely sad. I at-tended the services with them, and sat through it with a lump of cold lead in my chest and a big re-solve growing through me.

I've never forgotten Cliff Evans nor that resolve. He has been my challenge year after year, class af-ter class. I look for veiled eyes or bodies scrouged into a seat in an alien world. "Look, kids," I say silently, "I may not do anything else for you this year, but not one of you is going to come out of here a nobody. I'll work or fight to the bitter end doing battle with society and the school board, but I won't have one of you coming out of here feeling like a zero."

Most of the time—not always, but most of the time—I've suc-ceeded.

Jean Mizer

I am not what I think I am. I am not what you think I am. I am what I think you think I am.

Aaron Bleiberg and Harry Leubling

Characteristics of the Self-Concept

Now that you have a better idea of how your self-concept has developed, we can take a closer look at some of its characteristics.

THE SELF-CONCEPT IS SUBJECTIVE Although we may believe that our self-concept is accurate, in truth it may well be distorted. Some people view themselves more favourably than objective facts would suggest. For example, researchers have found that there is no relationship between the way post-secondary students rate their ability as interpersonal communicators, public speakers, or listeners and their true effectiveness. In all cases, the self-reported communication skill is higher than actual performance.

Not all distortion of the self-concept is so positive. Many people view themselves much more harshly than the objective facts warrant. We have all experienced a temporary case of the "uglies," convinced that we look much worse than others assure us we really appear. Research confirms what common sense suggests: that people are more critical of themselves when they are experiencing these negative moods than when they are feeling more positive.[13] Although we all suffer occasional bouts of self-doubt that affect our communication, some people suffer from long-term or even permanent states of excessive self-doubt and criticism.[14] It's easy to understand how this chronic condition can influence the way they approach and respond to others.

"Oh, thank you, I only wish I felt as good as I look."

Drawing by Schoenbaum, copyright © 1990 *The New Yorker Magazine*, Inc.

Distorted self-evaluations like these can occur for several reasons. One source is *obsolete information.* The effects of past failures in school or social relations can linger long after they have occurred, even though such events don't predict failure in the future. Likewise, your past successes don't guarantee future success. Perhaps your jokes used to be well received or your work was superior, but now the facts have changed.

Distorted feedback can also create a self-image that is worse or better than the facts warrant. Overly critical parents are one of the most common causes of a negative self-image. In other cases the re-marks of cruel friends, uncaring teachers, excessively demanding employers, or even memorable strangers can have a lasting effect. Other distorted messages are unrealistically positive. Bosses may think of themselves as excellent managers because their assistants shower them with false praise in order to keep their jobs or gain promotions. Likewise, a child's inflated ego may be based on the praise of doting parents.

Once communicators fasten onto a self-concept—whether it is pos-itive or negative—the tendency is to seek out people who confirm it. Recent studies show that both college students and married couples with high self-esteem seek out partners who view them favourably, while those with negative self-concepts are more inclined to interact with people who view them unfavourably.[15] The tendency to look for people who confirm our self-concept has been called *self-verification.*

Along with obsolete information and distorted feedback, another cause for a strongly negative self-concept is the emphasis on *perfec-tion,* which is common in our society. From the time most of us learn to understand language we are exposed to models who appear to be perfect. Children's stories and advertisements imply that the way to be a hero, the way to be liked and admired, is to show no flaws. Unfortu-nately, many parents perpetuate the myth of perfection by refusing to admit that they are ever mistaken or unfair. Children, of course, accept this perfectionist façade for a long time, not being in any position to dispute the wisdom of such powerful beings. And from the behaviour of the adults around them comes a clear message: "A well-adjusted, successful person has no faults." Thus, children learn that, in order to gain acceptance, it's necessary to pretend to "have it all together," even though they know this isn't the case. Given this naive belief that every-one else is perfect and the knowledge that one isn't, it's easy to see how one's self-concept would suffer.

Don't misunderstand: It's not wrong to aim at perfection as an *ideal.* We're suggesting only that achieving this state is usually not possible, and to expect that you should do so is a sure ticket to an in-accurate and unnecessarily low self-concept.

A final reason people often sell themselves short is also connected to *social expectations.* Canadians, for the most part, are modest peo-ple. We often consider those who honestly appreciate their strengths to be "braggarts" or "egotists," confusing them with the people who boast about accomplishments they do not possess.[16] This convention

Most forward looking people have their heads turned sideways.

Harold Innis

TABLE 2–1	DIFFERENCES BETWEEN COMMUNICATORS WITH HIGH AND LOW SELF-ESTEEM

PERSONS WITH HIGH SELF-ESTEEM

1. Are likely to think well of others.
2. Expect to be accepted by others.
3. Evaluate their own performance more favourably than people with low self-esteem.
4. Perform well when being watched: not afraid of others' reactions.
5. Work harder for people who demand high standards of performance.
6. Are inclined to feel comfortable with others they view as superior in some way.
7. Are able to defend themselves against negative comments of others.

PERSONS WITH LOW SELF-ESTEEM

1. Are likely to disapprove of others.
2. Expect to be rejected by others.
3. Evaluate their own performance less favourably than people with high self-esteem.
4. Perform poorly when being watched: sensitive to possible negative reaction.
5. Work harder for undemanding, less-critical people.
6. Feel threatened by people they view as superior in some way.
7. Have difficulty defending themselves against others' negative comments; more easily influenced.

Summarized by Don E. Hamachek, *Encounters with the Self,* 2nd ed. (New York: Holt, Rinehart and Winston, 1982), pp. 3–5.

leads most of us to talk freely about our shortcomings while downplaying our accomplishments. It's all right to proclaim that you're miserable if you have failed to do well on a project; but it's considered boastful to express your pride at a job well done. It's fine to remark that you feel unattractive, but egocentric to say that you think you look good.

After a while we begin to believe the types of statements we repeatedly make. The disparaging remarks are viewed as modesty and become part of our self-concept, and the strengths and accomplishments go unmentioned and are thus forgotten. And in the end we see ourselves as much worse than we are.

Self-esteem may be based on inaccurate thinking, but it still has a powerful effect on the way we relate to others. Table 2–1 summarizes some important differences between communicators with high and low self-esteem. Differences like these make sense when you realize that people who dislike themselves are likely to believe that others won't like them either. Realistically or not, they imagine that others are constantly viewing them critically, and they accept these imagined or real criticisms as more proof that they are indeed unlikable people. To use the well-known terminology of psychiatrist Eric Berne, they adopt an "I'm not OK–you're OK" orientation to life. Sometimes this low self-esteem is manifested in hostility toward others, because the communicator takes the approach that the only way to look good is to put others down.

One way to avoid falling into the trap of becoming overly critical is to recognize your strengths. The following exercise will give you a chance to suspend the ordinary rules of modesty and appreciate yourself publicly.

Self-love, My liege, is not so vile a sin as self-neglecting.

Shakespeare,
King Henry V

INVITATION TO INSIGHT

RECOGNIZING YOUR STRENGTHS

1. This exercise can be done either alone or with a group. If you are with others, sit in a circle so that everyone can see one another.

2. Each person should share three personal strengths or accomplishments. These needn't feature areas in which you are an expert, and they don't have to be concerned with momentous feats. On the contrary, it's perfectly acceptable to talk about some part of yourself that leaves you feeling pleased or proud. For instance, you might say that instead of procrastinating you completed a school assignment before the last minute, that you spoke up to a friend even though you were afraid of disapproval, that you bake a fantastic chocolate cake, or that you frequently drive hitchhikers to their destinations although it's out of your way.

3. If you're at a loss for items, ask yourself
    a. What are some ways in which you've grown in the past year? How are you more skillful, wise, or a better person than you previously were?
    b. Why do certain friends or family members care about you? What features do you possess that make them appreciate you?

4. After you've finished, consider the experience. Did you have a hard time thinking of things to share? Would it have been easier to list the things that are *wrong* with you? If so, is this because you are truly a wretched person or because you are in the habit of stressing your defects and ignoring your strengths? Consider the impact of such a habit on your self-concept, and ask yourself whether it wouldn't be wiser to strike a better balance distinguishing between your strengths and shortcomings.

THE SELF-CONCEPT RESISTS CHANGE   Despite the fact that we all change, there is a tendency to cling to an existing self-concept, even when evidence shows that it is obsolete. This tendency to seek and attend to information that conforms to an existing self-concept has been labelled **cognitive conservatism.**

It's understandable why we're reluctant to revise a previously favourable self-concept. Consider, for example, how some professional athletes doggedly insist that they can be of value to the team when they are clearly past their prime. It must be tremendously difficult to give up the life of excitement, recognition, and financial rewards that come with such a talent. Faced with such a tremendous loss, the athlete might well try to play one more season, insisting that the old skills are still there. In the same way, a student who did well in earlier years but now has failed to study might be unwilling to admit that the label "good scholar" no longer applies; and a previously industrious worker, pointing to past commendations in a personnel file and insisting that she is a top-notch employee, might resent a supervisor's mentioning increased absences and low productivity. (Remember that the people in these and other examples aren't *lying* when they insist that they're doing well in spite of the facts to the contrary; they honestly believe that the old truths still hold precisely because their self-concepts have been so resistant to change.)

Curiously, the tendency to cling to an outmoded self-perception also holds when the new image would be more favourable than the old one. We recall a former student whom almost anyone would have regarded as beautiful, with physical features attractive enough to appear in any glamour magazine. In spite of her appearance, in a class exercise this woman characterized herself as "ordinary" and "unattractive." When questioned by her classmates, she described how as a child her teeth were extremely crooked and how she had worn braces for several years in her teens to correct this problem. During this time she was often kidded by her friends, who never let her forget her "metal mouth," as she put it. Even though the braces had been off for two years, our student reported that she still saw herself as ugly and brushed aside our compliments by insisting that we were saying these things just to be nice—she knew how she *really* looked.

Examples like this show one problem that occurs when we resist changing an inaccurate self-concept. Our student denied herself a much happier life by clinging to an obsolete picture of herself. In the same way, some communicators insist that they are less talented or worthy of friendship than others would suggest, thus creating their own miserable world when it needn't exist. Some people resist change because they aren't willing to go through the disorientation that comes from redefining themselves, correctly anticipating that it *is* an effort to think of oneself in a new way. Whatever their reasons, it's sad to see people in such an unnecessary state.

A second problem arising from the persistence of an inaccurate self-concept is self-delusion and lack of growth. If you hold an unrealistically favourable picture of yourself, you won't see the real need for change that may exist. Instead of learning new talents, working to change a relationship, or improving your physical condition, you'll stay with the familiar and comfortable delusion that everything is all right. As time goes by, this delusion becomes more and more difficult to maintain, leading to a third type of problem: defensiveness.

To understand this problem, you need to remember that communicators who are presented with information that contradicts their self-perception have two choices: They can either accept the new data and change their perception accordingly, or they can keep their original viewpoint and in some way refute the new information. Because most communicators are reluctant to downgrade a positive image of themselves, their tendency is to opt for refutation, either by discounting the information and rationalizing it away or by counterattacking the person who transmitted it. The problem of defensiveness is so great that we will examine it in Chapter 9.

Culture and the Self-Concept

The challenges and opportunities that come from diversity are becoming more apparent in an increasingly multicultural society. But the power of culture is far more basic and powerful than most people realize. Although we seldom recognize the fact, our whole notion of the self is shaped by the culture in which we have been reared.[17]

The most obvious feature of a culture is the language members use. This is particularly evident in Canada, an officially bilingual country. However, in an attempt to maintain the distinct Québécois culture, the controversial Bill 101 makes French the official language in the province of Quebec. The French clearly recognize that to lose your language is to lose your sense of self. If you live in an environment where everyone speaks the same tongue, then language will seem to have little impact. But when your primary language is not the majority one, or when it is not prestigious, the sense of being a member of what social scientists call the "outgroup" is strong. At this point the speaker of a nondominant tongue can react in one of two ways: either to feel pressured to assimilate by speaking the "better" language, or to refuse to accommodate to the majority language and maintain loyalty to the ethnic tongue.[18] In either case, the impact of language on the self-concept is powerful. On one hand the feeling is likely to be "I'm not as good as speakers of the native language," and on the other the belief is "there's something unique and worth preserving in my language." This experience is exemplified by Canada's First Nations people who, during the 1950s and 1960s, were forced to speak English in residential schools. This resulted in the loss of their language and related cultural norms. It is only in recent years, with band-controlled schools adopting a bicultural/bilingual pedagogy, that Canada's Native peoples are reclaiming their cultural self.

Cultures affect the self-concept in more subtle ways too. Most Western cultures are highly individualistic, whereas traditional other cultures—most Asian ones, for example—are much more collective. When asked to identify themselves, Canadians, Americans, Australians, and Europeans would probably respond by giving their first name, surname, street, town, and country. Many Asians do it the other way around.[19] If you ask Hindus for their identity, they will

Cross-Cultural Awareness for the APEC Region

http://strategis.ic.gc.ca/SSG/mi0550Ze.html

In Japan, in fact, everything had been made level and uniform—even humanity. By one official count, 90 percent of the population regarded themselves as middle-class; in schools, it was not the outcasts who beat up the conformists, but vice versa. Every Japanese individual seemed to have the same goal as every other—to become like every other Japanese individual. The word for "different," I was told, was the same as the word for "wrong." And again and again in Japan, in contexts varying from the baseball stadium to the watercolor canvas, I heard the same unswerving, even maxim: "The nail that sticks out must be hammered down."

Pico Iyer,
Video Night in Katmandu

Canada is the only country I know of in which, throughout my lifetime, to be pro-Canadian has been interpreted in terms of a negative attitude towards other countries.

Norman Ward, in J.H. Bedekop (ed.),
The Star-Spangled Beaver

*Intercultural Conflict
Competence: Eastern & Western
Lenses*

http://www.cic.sfu.ca/forum/
STingToomeyJuly131999.html

give you their caste and village as well as their name. The Sanskrit formula for identifying one's self begins with lineage and goes on to state family and house, and ends with one's personal name.[20]

These conventions for naming aren't just cultural curiosities: They reflect a very different way of viewing one's self. In collective cultures a person gains identity by belonging to a group. This means that the degree of interdependence among members of the society and its subgroups is much higher. Feelings of pride and self-worth are likely to be shaped not only by what the individual does, but also by behaviour of other members of the community. This linkage to others explains the traditional Asian denial of self-importance–a strong contrast to the self-promotion that is common in individualistic Western cultures.[21] In Chinese written language, for example, the pronoun "I" looks very similar to the word for "selfish."[22] Table 2–2 summarizes some differences between individualistic cultures and more collective ones, and Table 2–3 shows where several countries fall on the individualism–collectivism spectrum.

This sort of cultural difference isn't just a matter of interest to anthropologists. It shows up in the level of comfort or anxiety people feel when communicating. In collective societies, there is a higher degree of communication apprehension. For example, as a group, residents of China, Korea, and Japan exhibit a significantly higher degree of anxiety about speaking out than do members of individualistic cultures, such as Canada.[23] It's important to realize that different levels of communication apprehension don't mean that shyness is a "problem" in some cultures. In fact, just the opposite is true: In these societies reticence is valued. When the goal is to *avoid* being the nail that sticks out, it's logical to feel nervous when you make yourself appear different by calling attention to yourself. A self-concept that includes "assertive" might make a Westerner feel proud, but in much of Asia it would more likely be cause for shame.

The difference between individualism and collectivism shows up in everyday interaction. Communication researcher Stella Ting-Toomey has developed a theory that explains cultural differences in important norms, such as honesty and directness.[24] She suggests that in individualistic Western cultures where there

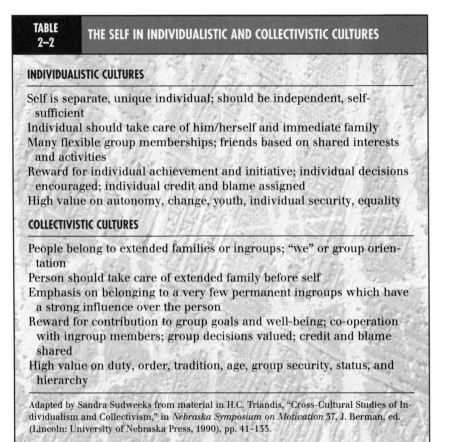

TABLE 2–2	THE SELF IN INDIVIDUALISTIC AND COLLECTIVISTIC CULTURES

INDIVIDUALISTIC CULTURES

Self is separate, unique individual; should be independent, self-sufficient

Individual should take care of him/herself and immediate family

Many flexible group memberships; friends based on shared interests and activities

Reward for individual achievement and initiative; individual decisions encouraged; individual credit and blame assigned

High value on autonomy, change, youth, individual security, equality

COLLECTIVISTIC CULTURES

People belong to extended families or ingroups; "we" or group orientation

Person should take care of extended family before self

Emphasis on belonging to a very few permanent ingroups which have a strong influence over the person

Reward for contribution to group goals and well-being; co-operation with ingroup members; group decisions valued; credit and blame shared

High value on duty, order, tradition, age, group security, status, and hierarchy

Adapted by Sandra Sudweeks from material in H.C. Triandis, "Cross-Cultural Studies of Individualism and Collectivism," in *Nebraska Symposium on Motivation* 37, J. Berman, ed. (Lincoln: University of Nebraska Press, 1990), pp. 41–133.

is a strong "I" orientation, the norm of speaking directly is honoured; whereas in collectivistic cultures, where the main desire is to build connections between the self and others, indirect approaches that maintain harmony are considered more desirable. "I gotta be me" could be the motto of a Westerner, but "If I hurt you, I hurt myself" is closer to the Asian way of thinking.

The Self-Fulfilling Prophecy and Communication

The self-concept is such a powerful force on the personality that it not only determines how you see yourself in the present but also can actually influence your future behaviour and that of others. Such occurrences come about through a phenomenon called the self-fulfilling prophecy.

A **self-fulfilling prophecy** occurs when a person's expectations of an event make the outcome more likely to occur than would

TABLE 2–3	INDIVIDUALISM INDEX OF SEVERAL COUNTRIES		
U.S.A.	91	India	48
Australia	90	Japan	46
Great Britain	89	Argentina	46
Canada	80	Iran	41
Netherlands	80	Brazil	38
New Zealand	79	Turkey	37
Italy	76	Greece	35
Belgium	75	Philippines	32
Denmark	74	Mexico	30
Sweden	71	Portugal	27
France	71	Hong Kong	25
Ireland	70	Chile	23
Norway	69	Singapore	20
Switzerland	68	Thailand	20
Germany	67	Taiwan	17
South Africa	65	Peru	16
Finland	63	Pakistan	14
Austria	55	Colombia	13
Israel	54	Venezuela	12
Spain	51	Mean of 39 countries	51

Adapted from Geert Hofstede, *Culture's Consequences* (Newbury Park, CA: Sage, 1984), p. 158.

otherwise have been true. Self-fulfilling prophecies occur all the time, although you might never have given them that label. For example, think of some instances you may have known:

You expected to become nervous and botch a job interview and later did so.

You anticipated having a good (or terrible) time at a social affair and found your expectations being met.

A teacher or boss explained a new task to you, saying that you probably wouldn't do well at first. You did not do well.

A friend described someone you were about to meet, saying that you wouldn't like the person. The prediction turned out to be correct—you didn't like the new acquaintance.

In each of these cases there is a good chance that the event occurred because it was predicted to occur. You needn't have botched the interview, the party might have been boring only because you helped make it so, you might have done better on the job if your boss hadn't spoken up, and you might have liked the new acquaintance if your friend hadn't given you preconceptions. In other words, what helped make each event occur was the expectation of it.

TYPES OF SELF-FULFILLING PROPHECIES There are two types of self-fulfilling prophecies. *Self-imposed prophecies* occur when your own expectations influence your behaviour. In sports you've probably "psyched" yourself into playing either better or worse than usual, so that the only explanation for your unusual performance was your attitude. Similarly, you've probably faced an audience at one time or another with a fearful attitude and forgotten your remarks, not because you were unprepared, but because you said to yourself, "I know I'll blow it." Research has demonstrated the power of self-imposed prophecies. In one study, communicators who believed they were incompetent proved less likely than others to pursue rewarding relationships and more likely to sabotage their existing relationships than did people who were less critical of themselves.[25] On the other hand, students who perceived themselves as capable achieved more academically.[26] In another study, subjects who were sensitive to social rejection tended to expect rejection, perceive it where it might not have existed, and overreact to their exaggerated perceptions in ways that jeopardized the quality of their relationships.[27] Research also suggests that communicators who feel anxious about giving speeches seem to create self-fulfilling prophecies about doing poorly that cause them to perform less effectively.[28] The self-fulfilling prophecy also operates on the job. For example, salespeople who perceive themselves as being effective communicators are more successful than those who view themselves as less effective, despite the fact that there was no difference in the approach that members of each group used with customers. In

Somehow the people who do as they please seem to get along just about as well as those who are always trying to please others.

Bob Edwards, publisher,
The Eye Opener

cathy®

by Cathy Guisewite

CATHY © 1994   Cathy Guisewite. Reprinted with permission of UNIVERSAL PRESS SYNDICATE. All rights reserved.

other words, the apparent reason some salespeople are successful is because they expect to succeed.

Self-imposed prophecies operate in a multitude of ways that affect everyday communication. You've had the experience of waking up in a cross mood and saying to yourself, "This will be a 'bad day.'" Once you made such a decision, you may have acted in ways that made it come true. If you approached a class expecting to be bored, you most probably did lose interest, owing partly to a lack of attention on your part. If you avoided the company of others because you expected they had nothing to offer, your suspicions would have been confirmed—nothing exciting or new did happen to you. On the other hand, if you approached the same day with the idea that it could be a good one, this expectation probably would have been met also. Smile at people, and they'll probably smile back. Enter a class determined to learn something, and you probably will—even if it's how not to instruct students! Approach many people with the idea that some of them will be good to know, and you'll most likely make some new friends. In these cases and ones like them, your attitude has a great deal to do with how you see yourself and how others will see you.

A second category of self-fulfilling prophecies is imposed by one person on another, so that the expectations of one person govern

There is a joke which goes right to the heart of this matter. It is about a man whose tire goes flat on a dark and lonely country road. When he discovers that he doesn't have a jack, he recalls seeing a farm house about a mile back. And so he starts to walk there in the hopes of borrowing one. While he is walking, he talks to himself about his situation: "Wow, I'm really stranded here. The guy will probably want a few dollars to lend me his jack. Why should he do it for nothing? Everyone wants to make a few bucks. A few bucks! If I don't get the jack, I'll never get out of here. He'll realize that, and probably want fifteen dollars, maybe twenty-five dollars. Twenty-five dollars? This guy's really got me by the old cashews. He'll ask fifty dollars, for sure—maybe a hundred."

Well, he goes on in this way until he reaches the farm house. He knocks at the door. An elderly farmer answers and with a cheerful smile asks, "Is there something I can do for you, young man?" "Do for me? Do for me?" says the man, "I'll tell you what you can do, you can take your goddamn jack and shove it!"

. . . If, as in this case, you predict that you will not be lent a jack in a spirit of gracious cooperation, you prepare yourself for the confrontation in such a way that you guarantee the jack will not be lent in a spirit of gracious cooperation. Your prediction is transformed into a fact, which then becomes the reality.

Neil Postman,
Crazy Talk, Stupid Talk

another's actions. The classic example was demonstrated by Robert Rosenthal and Lenore Jacobson in a study they described in their book *Pygmalion in the Classroom*.[29] The experimenters told teachers that 20 percent of the children in a certain elementary school showed unusual potential for intellectual growth. The names of these 20 percent were drawn by means of a table of random numbers, which is to say that the names were drawn out of a hat. Eight months later these unusual or "magic" children showed significantly greater gains in IQ than did the remaining children, who had not been singled out for the teachers' attention. The change in the teachers' expectations regarding the intellectual performance of these allegedly "special" children had led to an actual change in the intellectual performance of these randomly selected children. In other words, the children did better, not because they were any more intelligent than their classmates, but because they learned that their teachers–significant others–believed they could.

To put this phenomenon in context with the self-concept, we can say that when a teacher communicates to a child the message "I think you're bright," the child accepts that evaluation and changes her self-concept to include it. Unfortunately, we can assume that the same principle holds for students whose teachers send the message "I think you're stupid."

This type of self-fulfilling prophecy has been shown to be a powerful force for shaping the self-concept and thus the behaviour of people in a wide range of settings outside the schools.[30] In medicine, patients who unknowingly use placebos–substances such as injections of sterile water or doses of sugar pills that have no curative value–often respond just as favourably to treatment as those who actually received a drug. The patients believe they have taken a substance that will help them feel better, and this belief actually brings about a "cure." In psychotherapy Rosenthal and Jacobson describe several studies suggesting that patients who believe they will benefit from treatment do so regardless of the type of treatment they receive. In the same vein, when a doctor believes a patient will improve, the patient may do so precisely because of this expectation, whereas another person for whom the physician has little hope often fails to recover. Apparently the patient's self-concept as sick or well–as shaped by the doctor–plays an important role in determining the actual state of health.

Notice that it isn't just the observer's *belief* that creates a self-fulfilling prophecy for the person who is the target of the expectations. The observer must *communicate that belief* in order for the prediction to have any effect. If parents have faith in their children but the kids aren't aware of that confidence, they won't be affected by their parents' expectations. If a boss has concerns about an employee's ability to do a job but keeps those worries to herself, the subordinate won't be influenced. In this sense, the self-fulfilling prophecies imposed by one person on another are as much a communication phenomenon as a psychological one.

The difference between a lady and a flower girl is not how she behaves, but how she's treated. I shall always be a flower girl to Professor Higgins, because he always treats me as a flower girl, and always will; but I know I can be a lady to you, because you always treat me as a lady, and always will.

G.B. Shaw,
Pygmalion

There is an old joke about a man who was asked if he could play a violin and answered, "I don't know. I've never tried." This is psychologically a very wise reply. Those who have never tried to play a violin really do not know whether they can or not. Those who say too early in life and too firmly, "No, I'm not at all musical," shut themselves off prematurely from whole areas of life that might have proved rewarding. In each of us there are unknown possibilities, undiscovered potentialities–and one big advantage of having an open self-concept rather than a rigid one is that we shall continue to expose ourselves to new experiences and therefore we shall continue to discover more and more about ourselves as we grow older.

S.I. Hayakawa

INFLUENCE OF SELF-FULFILLING PROPHECIES   The influence of self-fulfilling prophecies on communication can be strong, acting either to improve or harm relationships. If, for instance, you assume that another person is unlikable, then you'll probably act in ways that communicate your feelings. In such a case, the other person's behaviour will probably match your expectations: We usually don't go out of our way to be nice to people who aren't nice to us. If, on the other hand, you treat the other person as likable, the results are likely to be more positive.

In business, the power of the self-fulfilling prophecy is also evident. More and more Canadian companies are reorganizing management to give employees input into decision making, goal setting, hiring practices, how much they earn, and so forth. Essentially entrusted with the success or failure of the operation, employees internalize this and become motivated to make the company a thriving enterprise. In other words, if upper management believes in employees, they, too, come to believe in themselves.

The self-fulfilling prophecy operates in families as well. If parents tell a child long enough that he can't do anything right, his self-concept will soon incorporate this idea, and he will fail at many or most of the tasks he attempts. On the other hand, if a child is told he is a capable or lovable or kind person, there is a much greater chance of his behaving accordingly.

The self-fulfilling prophecy is an important force in interpersonal communication, but it doesn't explain or affect all behaviour. There are certainly times when the expectation of an event's outcome won't bring it about. Your hope of drawing an ace in a card game won't in any way affect the chance of that card turning up in an already shuffled deck, and your belief that good weather is coming won't stop the rain from falling. In the same way, believing you'll do well in a job interview when you're clearly not qualified for the position is unrealistic. Similarly, there will probably be people you don't like and occasions you won't enjoy, no matter what your attitude. To connect the self-fulfilling prophecy with the "power of positive thinking" is an oversimplification.

In other cases, your expectations will be borne out because you're a good predictor and not because of the self-fulfilling prophecy. For example, some children are not equipped to do well in school; in such cases it would be wrong to say that the child's performance was shaped by a parent or teacher, even though the behaviour did match that which was expected. In the same way, some workers excel and others fail, some patients recover and others don't, in agreement with or contrary to our predictions, but not because of them.

Keeping these qualifications in mind, you will find it important to recognize the tremendous influence that self-fulfilling prophecies play in our lives. To a great extent we are what we believe we are. In this sense we and those around us constantly create our self-concepts and thus ourselves.

Changing Your Self-Concept

After reading this far, you know more clearly just what the self-concept is, how it is formed, and how it affects communication. But we still haven't focussed directly on perhaps the most important question of all: How can you change the parts of your self-concept with which you aren't happy? There's certainly no quick method for becoming the person you'd like to be: Personal growth and self-improvement are a lifetime process. But we can offer several suggestions that will help you move closer to your goals.

HAVE REALISTIC EXPECTATIONS It's extremely important to realize that some of your dissatisfaction might come from expecting too much of yourself. If you demand that you handle every act of communication perfectly, you're bound to be disappointed. Nobody is able to handle every conflict productively, to be totally relaxed and skillful in conversations, always to ask perceptive questions, or to be 100 percent helpful when others have problems. Expecting yourself to reach such unrealistic goals is to doom yourself to unhappiness at the start.

Sometimes it's easy to be hard on yourself because everyone around you seems to be handling themselves so much better than you. It's important to realize that much of what seems like confidence and skill in others is a front to hide uncertainty. They may be suffering from the same self-imposed demands of perfection that you place on yourself.

Self-Esteem Questionnaire

http://www.positive-way.com/ self-est1.htm

© Gahan Wilson

Even in cases where others definitely seem more competent than you, it's important to judge yourself in terms of your own growth and not against the behaviour of others. Rather than feel miserable because you're not as talented as an expert, realize that you probably are a better, wiser, or more skillful person than you used to be and that this is a legitimate source of satisfaction. Perfection is fine as an ideal, but you're being unfair to yourself if you expect actually to reach it.

HAVE A REALISTIC PERCEPTION OF YOURSELF   One source of a poor self-concept is an inaccurate self-perception. As you've already read, such unrealistic pictures sometimes come from being overly harsh on yourself, believing that you're worse than the facts indicate. By showing the self-concept list you developed on pages 44–45 to others who know you, it will be possible to see whether you have been selling yourself short. Of course, it would be foolish to deny that you could be a better person than you are, but it's also important to recognize your strengths. A periodic session of recognizing your strengths, such as you tried earlier in this chapter, is often a good way to put your strengths and shortcomings into perspective.

An unrealistically poor self-concept can also arise from the inaccurate feedback of others. Perhaps you are in an environment where

The Keirsey Temperament Sorter and Character Sorter

http://Keirsey.com/frame.html

you receive an excessive number of prickly messages, many of which are undeserved, and a minimum of positive messages. We've known many homemakers, for example, who have returned to college or university after many years spent in homemaking, where they received virtually no recognition for their intellectual strengths. Most are thrilled to find that they are much brighter and more competent intellectually than they suspected. In the same way, workers with overly critical supervisors, children with cruel "friends," and students with unsupportive teachers all are prone to low self-concepts owing to excessively negative feedback.

If you fall into this category, it's important to put the unrealistic evaluations you receive into perspective and then to seek out more supportive people who will acknowledge your assets as well as point out your shortcomings. Doing so is often a quick and sure boost.

HAVE THE WILL TO CHANGE   Often we say we want to change, but we aren't willing to do the necessary work. In such cases it's clear that the responsibility for growing rests squarely on your shoulders, as the following exercise shows.

SKILL BUILDER

RE-EVALUATING YOUR "CAN'TS"

1. Choose a partner and for 5 minutes or so take turns making and listing statements that begin with "I can't. . . ." Try to focus your statements on your relationships with family, friends, co-workers, students, and even strangers: anyone with whom you have a hard time communicating. Sample statements:

    "I can't be myself with strangers I'd like to get to know at parties."

    "I can't tell a friend how much I care about her."

    "I can't bring myself to ask my supervisor for the raise I think I deserve."

    "I can't ask questions in class."

2. Notice your feelings as you make each statement: self-pity, regret, concern, frustration, and so on, and reveal these to your partner.

3. Now repeat aloud each statement you've just made, except this time change each "can't" to a "won't." After each sentence, tell your partner whatever thoughts you have about what you've just said.

4. After you've finished, decide whether "can't" or "won't" is more appropriate for each item, and explain your choice to your partner.

5. Are there any instances of the self-fulfilling prophecy in your list—times when your decision that you "couldn't" do something was the only force keeping you from doing it?

"There is more to you than mere money-lust, Duddy, but I'm afraid for you. You're two people, that's why. The scheming little bastard I saw so easily and the fine, intelligent boy underneath that your grandfather, bless him, saw. But you're coming of age soon and you'll have to choose. A boy can be two, three, four potential people, but a man is only one."

Mordecai Richler,
The Apprenticeship of Duddy Kravitz

As this exercise demonstrates, we often maintain an unrealistic self-concept by claiming that we "can't" be the person we'd like to be when in fact we're simply not willing to do what's required. You *can* change in many ways, if only you are willing to make the effort.

You might, for instance, decide that you'd like to become a better conversationalist. Seeking the advice of your instructor or some other communication adviser, you receive two pieces of advice. First, you're instructed to spend the next three weeks observing people who handle themselves well in conversations and to record exactly what they do that makes them so skillful. Second, your adviser suggests that you read several books on the subject of conversational skills. You begin these tasks with the best intentions, but after a few days the task of recording conversations becomes a burden–it would be so much easier just to listen to others talk. And your diligent reading program becomes bogged down as the press of other work fills up your time. In other words, you find you just "can't" fit the self-improvement plan into your busy schedule.

Let's be realistic. Becoming a better communicator is probably one of many goals in your life. It's possible that other needs are more pressing, which is completely reasonable. However, you should realize that changing your self-concept often requires a good deal of commitment, and without that effort your good intentions alone probably won't get you much closer to this goal. In communication, as in most other aspects of life, "there's no such thing as a free lunch."

HAVE THE SKILL TO CHANGE   Often trying isn't enough. In some instances you would change if you knew how to do so. To see if this is the case for you, go back to your list of "can'ts" and "won'ts," and see if any items there are more appropriately "don't know how." If so, then the way to change is to learn how. You can do so in two ways.

First, you can seek advice–from books such as this one or from other printed sources. You can also get advice from instructors, counsellors, and other experts, as well as friends. Of course, not all the advice you receive will be useful, but if you read widely and talk to enough people, you have a good chance of learning the things you want to know.

A second method of learning how to change is to observe models– people who handle themselves in the ways you would like to master. It's often been said that people learn more from models than in any other way, and by taking advantage of this principle you will find that the world is full of teachers who can show you how to communicate more successfully. Become a careful observer. Watch what people you admire do and say, not so that you can copy them, but so that you can adapt their behaviour to fit your own personal style.

At this point, you might be overwhelmed at the difficulty of changing the way you think about yourself and the way you act. Remember, we never said that this process would be an easy one (although it sometimes is). But even when change is difficult, you know that it's possible if you are serious. You don't need to be perfect, but you can improve your self-concept if you choose.

PRESENTING THE SELF: COMMUNICATION AS IDENTITY MANAGEMENT

So far we have described how communication shapes the way communicators view themselves. In the remainder of this chapter we will turn the tables and focus on the topic of **identity management**–the communication strategies people use to influence how others view them. In the following pages you will see that many of our messages aim at creating a desired identity.

Public and Private Selves

To understand how identity management operates, we have to discuss the notion of self in more detail. So far we have referred to the "self" as if each of us had only one **identity.** In truth, each of us possesses several selves, some private and others public. Often these selves are quite different.

The **perceived self** is a reflection of the self-concept. Your perceived self is the person you believe yourself to be in moments of honest self-examination. We can call the perceived self "private" because you are unlikely to reveal all of it to another person. You can verify the private nature of the perceived self by reviewing the self-concept list you developed while reading pages 44–45. You'll probably find some elements of yourself there that you would not disclose to many people, and some that you would not share with anyone. You might, for example, be reluctant to share some feelings about your appearance ("I think I'm rather unattractive"), your intelligence ("I'm not as smart as I wish I were"), your goals ("The most important thing to me is becoming rich"), or your motives ("I care more about myself than about others").

In contrast to the perceived self, the **presenting self** is a public image–the way we want others to view us. In most cases the presenting self we seek to create is a socially approved image: diligent student, loving partner, conscientious worker, loyal friend, and so on. Social norms often create a gap between the perceived and presenting selves. For instance, Table 2–4 shows that the self-concepts of one group of male and female college students were quite similar, but their public selves differed in several respects from both their private selves and from the public selves of the other sex.[31]

You can recognize the difference between public and private behaviour by recalling a time when you observed a driver, alone in his or her car, behaving in ways that would never be acceptable in public. All of us engage in backstage ways of acting that we would never do in public. Just recall how you behave in front of the bathroom mirror when the door is locked, and you will appreciate the difference between public and private behaviour. If you knew someone were watching, would you behave differently?

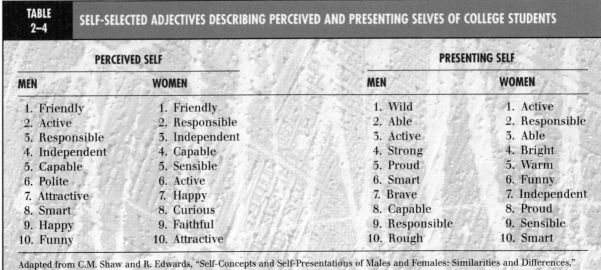

TABLE 2–4	SELF-SELECTED ADJECTIVES DESCRIBING PERCEIVED AND PRESENTING SELVES OF COLLEGE STUDENTS			
	PERCEIVED SELF		**PRESENTING SELF**	
MEN	**WOMEN**	**MEN**	**WOMEN**
1. Friendly	1. Friendly	1. Wild	1. Active
2. Active	2. Responsible	2. Able	2. Responsible
3. Responsible	3. Independent	3. Active	3. Able
4. Independent	4. Capable	4. Strong	4. Bright
5. Capable	5. Sensible	5. Proud	5. Warm
6. Polite	6. Active	6. Smart	6. Funny
7. Attractive	7. Happy	7. Brave	7. Independent
8. Smart	8. Curious	8. Capable	8. Proud
9. Happy	9. Faithful	9. Responsible	9. Sensible
10. Funny	10. Attractive	10. Rough	10. Smart

Adapted from C.M. Shaw and R. Edwards, "Self-Concepts and Self-Presentations of Males and Females: Similarities and Differences," *Communication Reports* 10 (1997): 55–62.

"Hah! This is the Old King Cole nobody ever sees."

Drawing by Dana Fradon; © 1983 *The New Yorker Magazine*, Inc.

Characteristics of Identity Management

Now that you have a sense of what identity management is, we can look at some characteristics of this process.

WE STRIVE TO CONSTRUCT MULTIPLE IDENTITIES   It is an oversimplification to suggest that each of us uses identity management strategies to create just one identity. In the course of even a single day, most people perform a variety of roles: "respectful student," "joking friend," "friendly neighbour," and "helpful worker," to suggest just a few.

The ability to construct multiple identities is one element of communication competence. For example, the style of speaking or even the language itself can reflect a choice about how to construct one's identity. We have a female colleague who plays hockey on the faculty/staff team that faces off against a student group on Friday afternoons. It is hard to imagine this petite, popular, scholarly biology professor on the ice. When asked how she manages her communication style, she responded that in the classroom, while she is dogmatic and authoritarian, she is also lively and enthusiastic. When delivering scientific papers, she eliminates any enthusiasm and minimizes the human element so as to appear serious and informative. But, on the ice, that's her time for fun. Changes in her communication style have less to do with verbal alterations and more to do with thought processes. To show that she means business, for example, she engages in light sticking and checking to be accepted as an equal.

We strive to construct different identities even with the same person. As you grew up you almost certainly changed characters as you interacted with your parents. In one context you acted as responsible adult ("You can trust me with the car!") and at another time you were the helpless child ("I can't find my socks!"). At some times–perhaps on birthdays or holidays–you were a dedicated family member, and at other times you may have played the role of rebel. Likewise, in romantic relationships we switch among many ways of behaving, depending on the context: friend, lover, business partner, scolding critic, apologetic child, and so on.

INVITATION TO INSIGHT

YOUR MANY IDENTITIES

You can get a sense of the many roles you try to create by keeping a record of the situations in which you communicate over a 1- or 2-day period. For each situation, identify a dramatic title to represent the image you try to create. A few examples might be "party animal," "helpful housekeeper," "wise older sibling," and "sophisticated film critic."

IDENTITY MANAGEMENT IS COLLABORATIVE Sociologist Erving Goffman used a dramatistic metaphor to describe identity management.[32] He suggested that each of us is a kind of playwright who creates roles that reflect how we want others to see us. But unlike most forms of acting, our "audience" is made up of other actors who are also trying to create their own characters. Identity-related communication can be viewed as a kind of process theatre in which we collaborate with other actors to improvise scenes in which our characters mesh.

You can appreciate the collaborative nature of identity management by thinking about how you might handle a gripe with a friend or family member who has failed to pass along a phone message that arrived while you were away from home. Suppose that you decide to raise the issue tactfully in an effort to avoid seeming like a nag (desired role for yourself: "nice person"), and also to save the other person from the embarrassment of being confronted (hoping to avoid suggesting that the other person's role is "screw-up"). If your tactful bid is accepted, the dialogue might sound like this:

You:	". . . By the way, Jenny told me she called yesterday. If you wrote a note, I guess I missed seeing it."
Other:	"Oh . . . sorry. I meant to write a note, but as soon as I hung up the doorbell rang, and then I had to run off to class."
You (in friendly tone of voice):	"That's OK. I sure would appreciate from now on if you'd leave me a note."
Other:	"No problem."

In this upbeat conversation, both you and the other person accepted one another's bids for identity. As a result, the conversation ran smoothly. Imagine, though, how differently the outcome would be if the other person didn't accept your role as "nice person":

You:	". . . By the way, Jenny told me she called yesterday. If you wrote a note, I guess I missed seeing it."
Other (defensively):	"OK, so I forgot. It's not that big a deal. You're not perfect yourself, you know!"

Your first bid as "nice, face-saving person" was rejected. At this point you have the choice of persisting in trying to play the original role: "Hey, I'm not mad at you, and I know I'm not perfect!" Or, you might switch to the new role of "unjustly accused person," responding with aggravation, "I never said I was perfect. But we're not talking about me here. . . . "

As this example illustrates, *collaboration* doesn't mean the same thing as agreement.[33] The small issue of the phone message might mushroom into a fight in which you and the other person both adopt the role of combatants. The point here is that virtually all conversations provide an arena in which communicators construct their identities in response to the behaviour of others. As you read in Chapter 1, communication isn't made up of discrete events that can be separated from one another. Instead, what happens at one moment is influenced by what each party brings to the interaction and by what happened in their relationship up to that point.

IDENTITY MANAGEMENT CAN BE DELIBERATE OR UNCONSCIOUS   At this point you might object to the notion of strategic identity management, claiming that most of your communication is spontaneous and not a deliberate attempt to present yourself in a certain way. You might acknowledge that some of your communication involves a conscious attempt to manage impressions.

There's no doubt that sometimes we are highly aware of managing impressions. Most job interviews and first dates are clear examples of deliberate identity management. But in other cases we unconsciously act in ways that are really small public performances.[34] For example, experimental subjects expressed facial disgust in reaction to eating sandwiches laced with a supersaturated saltwater solution only when there was another person present: When they were alone, they made no faces on eating the same snack.[35] Another study showed that communicators engage in facial mimicry (such as smiling or looking sympathetic in response to another's message) in face-to-face settings only when their expressions can be seen by the other person. When they are speaking over the phone and their reactions cannot be seen, they do not make the expressions.[36] Studies like these suggest that most of our behaviour is aimed at sending messages to others–in other words, identity management.

The experimental subjects described in the preceding paragraph didn't consciously think, "Somebody is watching me eat this salty sandwich so I'll make a face" or "Since I'm in a face-to-face conversation, I'll show I'm sympathetic by mimicking the facial expressions of my conversational partner." Decisions like these are often instantaneous and outside of our conscious awareness. In the same way, many of our choices about how to act in the array of daily interactions aren't highly considered strategic decisions. Rather, they rely on "scripts" that we have developed over time. You probably have a variety of roles for managing your identity from which to choose in familiar situations, such as dealing with strangers, treating customers at work, interacting with family members, and so on. When you find yourself in familiar situations like these, you probably slip into these roles quite often. Only when those roles don't seem quite right do you deliberately construct an approach that reflects how you want the scene to play out.

Despite the pervasiveness of identity management, it seems like an exaggeration to suggest that *all* behaviour is aimed at making impressions. Young children certainly aren't strategic communicators. A baby spontaneously laughs when pleased and cries when sad or uncomfortable without any notion of creating an impression in others. Likewise, there are times when we, as adults, act spontaneously. Despite these exceptions, most people consciously or unconsciously communicate in ways that help construct desired identities for themselves and others.

Some people are much more aware of their identity management behaviour than others. These high self-monitors have the ability to pay attention to their own behaviour and others' reactions, adjusting their communication to create the desired impression. By contrast, low self-monitors express what they are thinking and feeling without much attention to the impression their behaviour creates.[37] You can get an idea of whether you are a high or a low self-monitor by answering the following questions.

INVITATION TO INSIGHT

SELF-MONITORING INVENTORY

These statements concern personal reactions to a number of different situations. No two statements are exactly alike, so consider each statement carefully before answering. If a statement is true, or mostly true, as applied to you, circle the T. If a statement is false, or not usually true, as applied to you, circle the F.

1.	I find it hard to imitate the behaviour of other people.	T	F
2.	I guess I put on a show to impress or entertain people.	T	F
3.	I would probably make a good actor.	T	F
4.	I sometimes appear to others to be experiencing deeper emotions than I actually am.	T	F
5.	In a group of people I am rarely the centre of attention.	T	F
6.	In different situations and with different people, I often act like very different persons.	T	F
7.	I can argue only for ideas I already believe.	T	F
8.	In order to get along and be liked, I tend to be what people expect me to be rather than anything else.	T	F
9.	I may deceive people by being friendly when I really dislike them.	T	F
10.	I'm not always the person I appear to be.	T	F

SCORING: Give yourself 1 point for each of questions 1, 5, and 7 that you answered F. Give yourself 1 point for each of the remaining questions that you answered T. Add up your points. If you are a good judge of yourself and scored 7 or above, you are probably a high self-monitoring individual; 3 or below, you are probably a low self-monitoring individual.

Source: Mark Snyder, "The Many Me's of the Self-Monitor," *Psychology Today,* March 1983, p. 34. Reprinted with permission.

What is the ideal score for this self-quiz? There are certainly advantages to being a high self-monitor.[38] People who pay attention to themselves are generally good actors who can create the identity they want, acting interested when bored or friendly when they really feel quite the opposite. This allows them to handle social situations smoothly, often putting others at ease. They are also good "people-readers" who can adjust their behaviour to get the desired reaction from others. Along with these advantages, there are some potential drawbacks to being an extremely high self-monitor. Their analytical nature may prevent them from experiencing events completely, because a portion of their attention will always be viewing the situation from a detached position. High self-monitors' ability to act means that it is difficult to tell how they are really feeling. In fact, because high self-monitors change roles often, they may have a hard time knowing *themselves* how they really feel.

People who score low on the self-monitoring scale live life quite differently from their more self-conscious counterparts. They have a more simple, focussed idea of who they are and who they want to be. Low self-monitors are likely to have a more narrow repertoire of behaviours, so that they can be expected to act in more or less the same way regardless of the situation. This means that low self-monitors are easy to read. "What you see is what you get" might be their motto. While this lack of flexibility may make their social interaction less smooth in many situations, low self-monitors can be counted on to be straightforward communicators.

By now it should be clear that neither extremely high nor low self-monitoring is the ideal. There are some situations when paying attention to yourself and adapting your behaviour can be useful, and other times when reacting without considering the effect on others is a better approach. This need for a range of behaviours demonstrates again the notion of communicative competence outlined in Chapter 1: Flexibility is the key to successful relationships.

Why Manage Identities?

Why bother trying to shape others' opinions? Sometimes we create and maintain a front to follow social rules. As children we learn to act polite, even when bored. Likewise, part of growing up consists of developing a set of manners for various occasions: meeting strangers, attending school, going to a religious gathering, and so on. Young children who haven't learned all the do's and don'ts of polite society often embarrass their parents by behaving inappropriately ("Mommy, why is that man so fat?"); but, by the time they enter school, behaviour that might have been excusable or even amusing just isn't acceptable. Good manners are often aimed at making others more comfortable. For example, able-bodied people often mask their discomfort upon encountering someone who is disabled by acting nonchalant or stressing similarities between themselves and the disabled person.[39]

**"I do not want to be perfect.
I want to appear to be perfect."**

Social rules govern our behaviour in a variety of settings. It would be impossible to keep a job, for example, without meeting certain expectations. Salespeople are obliged to treat customers with courtesy. Employees need to appear reasonably respectful when talking to the boss. Some forms of clothing would be considered outrageous at work. By agreeing to take on a job, you are signing an unwritten contract that you will present a certain face at work, whether or not that face reflects the way you might be feeling at a particular moment.

Even when social roles don't dictate the proper way to behave, we often manage our own and one another's identities for a second reason: to accomplish personal goals. You might, for example, dress up for a visit to traffic court in hope that your front (responsible citizen) will convince the judge to treat you sympathetically. You might chat sociably with neighbours whom you don't find especially interesting so you can exchange favours or solve problems as they come up.

Sometimes identity management aims at achieving one or more of the relational goals we discussed in Chapter 1: affiliation, control, or respect. For instance, you might act more friendly and lively than you feel upon meeting a new person, so that you will appear likable. You could sigh and roll your eyes when arguing politics with a classmate to gain an advantage in an argument. You might smile and preen to show the attractive stranger at a party that you would like to get better acquainted. In situations like these you aren't being deceptive as much as putting "your best foot forward."

All these examples show that it is difficult—even impossible—*not* to manage identities. After all, you have to send some sort of message.

If you don't act friendly when meeting a stranger, you have to act
aloof, indifferent, hostile, or in some other manner. If you don't act
businesslike, you have to behave in an alternative way: weird, casual,
or whatever. Likewise, you have to play some role in constructing
others' identities. In conversations, you have to act either interested
or unattentive. If you don't act friendly with acquaintances, you have
to act in some other manner. These examples show that the question
usually isn't *whether* to manage identities; it's *how* you will do so.

How Do We Manage Identities?

Communicators manage their identities and those of others in three
ways: manner, appearance, and setting.[40] *Manner* consists of a communicator's words and nonverbal actions. Physicians, for example,
display a wide variety of manners as they conduct physical examinations. Some are friendly and conversational, while others adopt a
brusque and impersonal approach. Still others are polite but businesslike. Much of a communicator's manner comes from what he or
she says. A doctor who remembers details about your interests and
hobbies is quite different from one who sticks to clinical questions.
One who explains a medical procedure creates a different impression than another who reveals little to the patient. Along with the
content of speech, nonverbal behaviours play a big role in creating
impressions. A doctor who greets you with a friendly smile and a
handshake comes across quite differently from one who gives
nothing more than a curt nod. Manner varies widely in other professional and personal settings—professors, salespeople, hairstylists, and

Among connoisseurs, probably the most famous makeover in Canadian political history was that done by—and to—David Peterson before the 1985 Ontario provincial election. With the help of media guru Hershell Ezrin, Peterson metamorphosed from a frumpy, dumpy, bland, and bespectacled bore into a lean, mean, silver-haired, vote-getting machine who won two suc-

cessive elections. The tools of transformation included contact lenses, a diet, a well-publicized jogging regimen, and the public unleashing of Peterson's sharp wit. But consider the result when similar efforts were applied to former Ontario Progressive Conservative Leader Larry Grossman before the 1987 election. To match Peterson's newly hip image, Grossman was advised to doff his glasses in favour of contacts. He did, and liked it—but focus groups were unnerved by the change. As a result, Grossman ran the election campaign wearing non-prescription plain-glass spectacles—with contacts underneath. He lost. Similarly, Reform Leader Preston Manning several years ago had eye surgery, ditched his glasses, changed his hairstyle, swapped his off-the-rack clothes for Hugo Boss designer lines, and took lessons to rid his voice of its squeak. The efforts attracted no small ridicule, and few new votes.

The moral is that it's often not as much fun being an éminence grise (or "greasy eminence") as it's cracked up to be. In the political netherworld peopled by hacks (journalists) and flacks (political press secretaries), whatever a flack may do will never be quite enough to please nitpicky hacks. For one, it's considered a given that in public appearances, political leaders should always stick to the same one or two points. But when Liberal Leader Dalton McGuinty did that in an Ontario provincial leaders' debate—repeatedly referring to health and education issues as election priorities—he was criticized by the media for appearing inflexible. So much for the importance of staying "on message."

These days, the stakes for so-called spin doctors are higher than ever, both for their clients and themselves. Sometime Bill Clinton adviser James Carville has become a millionaire by appearing on ads, making speeches, and selling his Cajun-accented electioneering advice all over—most recently in Israel. White House spokesman Joe Lockhart talks with the press far more often than does Clinton. Prime Minister Jean Chrétien's communications director, Peter Donolo, seldom appears on television. But like Lockhart, Donolo represents the most regular contact that reporters have with the nation's leader, and thus is the unofficial keeper of his boss's image.

Chrétien chose well: Bill Fox, a former reporter and press secretary to Brian Mulroney, calls Donolo "the best spin doctor I've ever seen in Canada." Still baby-faced in his late 30s and perpetually upbeat, he orchestrated the strategy in the early 1990s that went head on against criticism that Chrétien was out of date as a politician. In the 1993 campaign, Chrétien donned denim shirts, was shown water-skiing and helping brewery workers hoist heavy cases of beer, and joked pointedly that politics is "the only profession in which people say you have too *much* experience." Now, Chrétien's problem is that Donolo, after eight years at his side, is leaving at the end of June for an unspecified new job. He won't be easily replaced.

Much as hacks belittle them, a good flack carries a remarkable skill set. Along with marketing ability, a flack must be a deft speechwriter, have a television producer's eye for the best camera angle at public appearances, have a print reporter's eye for a good anecdote, be conversant with major policy issues, and be able to deliver a sound bite interesting enough to get on the news, but not so compelling as to overshadow anything the boss says. Flacks should presume their boss will not understand what they do, but will take for granted it be done well. In Ottawa, bilingualism is often essential. Good flacks function as a bridge between two hostile groups—politicians and the people who cover them. Perhaps that's why prime ministers occasionally hire diplomats for the job. And perhaps that's why journalists now seldom cross the floor to become flacks: relations between the two sides are too polarized.

Anthony Wilson-Smith

so on—and the impressions they create differ accordingly. The same principle holds in personal relationships. Your manner plays a major role in shaping how others view you. Chapters 5 and 6 will describe in detail how your words and nonverbal behaviours create impressions. Since you *have* to speak and act, the question isn't whether your manner sends a message; rather, it's whether these messages will be intentional.

Along with manner, a second dimension of identity management is *appearance*–the personal items people use to shape an image. Sometimes appearance is part of creating a professional image. A physician's white lab coat and a police officer's uniform both set the wearer apart as someone special. A tailored suit or a rumpled outfit create very different impressions in the business world. Off the job, clothing is just as important. We choose clothing that sends a message about ourselves, sometimes trendy and sometimes traditional. Some people dress in ways that accent their sexuality, while others hide it. Clothing can say, "I'm an athlete," "I'm wealthy," or "I'm an environmentalist." Along with dress, other aspects of appearance play a strong role in

Looking at Diversity

Managing Sexual Identity

Ron Keough is a freelance journalist, playwright, and inventor living in a small, working-class city in eastern Canada. He is also gay and has been out since his teens. In this profile, Ron shows why heterosexual friends and acquaintances also seek the comforts offered by the sexual orientation closet.

I looked up the street. There was Joe, the young man who was by yesterday for the job interview, walking toward me. I really don't know if I'll hire him, but he seems like he'd fill the job very nicely. If he asks, I'll tell him I haven't made up my mind yet. Those must be some of the soccer players he chums around with.

I acknowledged his presence as we stepped by each other. He didn't return any gesture. He quickly darted across the street, beckoning for his buddies to follow. I really thought Joe was cool. Different. His demeanour in the interview was open, and I detected a worldly awareness in him. And that's rare in the students I interviewed over the years. But I guess he's not so different from Bob, John, or Chuck.

Sometimes I'd tell people. Other times I won't. Staying in a small town and incrementally disclosing my gayness since I was a young man has pretty well shut the closet door behind me. Although my first inclination is not to tell people I'm gay, I find it's best to reveal my sexual orientation upon first meeting. This came about because heterosexual guys with whom I'd eventually become friends informed me that they had actually been harassed by their friends if I said hello on the street, at a bar, or in a movie line-up. It

appears that to know and speak to me implies that they too must be gay. I have had friends ask me not to acknowledge them in public places. And when working at the university, I could always tell when new acquaintances found out. They'd decline a movie invitation, for instance, or make excuses or beg off a prearranged engagement for a drink or some other benign social interaction. Other acquaintances would often apologize when the group they were part of would hurl gay-unfriendly expletives my way. Their regret seemed sincere, but blossoming platonic relationships ironically were relegated to what I call a communication closet.

Even longtime friends, who publicly and openly showed their concern over intolerant and suggestive homophobic displays directed toward me, often visited the closet I left behind. Many times, well-intentioned friends, particularly when gathered together at a restaurant or party, would clearly set out to avow their openness by leaning across the table and saying, for all to hear, "Ronnie, I read something you would find really interesting." Invariably, that said piece from a popular news magazine or somewhat esoteric pop psychology

journal would deal with gayness—anything from the discovery of the "gay" gene to the outing of an underachieving celebrity on the *Hollywood Squares* circuit. But when it was time to take a stand, they just weren't there. One particular friend, who was almost oppressive with her overt openness, eventually was driven back into her communication closet when she felt obligated to ask a heterosexual male friend to stand as her newborn son's guardian. Her mother forbade her to ask me. After the event, she continued to shower me with insightful articles and armchair acceptance. The chair, however, was very close to the closet.

Being openly gay in a small town is what I chose. You don't know the consequences until the time passes and events remind you that the community perceives you as weak and just a little too strange. Having developed a public persona with radio journalism and a moderate acceptance as a current affairs–type playwright, I have had to weather a multitude of obscene phone calls, threatening correspondence, and crass cackles coming from hidden faces in the crowd. Unfortunately, so, too, have my heterosexual male friends.

identity management. Are you suntanned or pale? What is your hairstyle? Do you make an effort to look friendly and confident?

A final way to manage identities is through the choice of *setting*–physical items we use to influence how others view us. In modern Western society the automobile is a major part of identity management. This explains why many people lust after cars that are far more expensive and powerful than they really need. A sporty convertible or fancy imported sedan doesn't just get drivers from one place to another: It also makes statements about the kind of people they are. The physical setting we choose and the way we arrange it are another important way to manage identities. What colours do you choose for the place you live? What artwork? What music do you play? Of course, we choose a setting that we enjoy; but in many cases we create an environment that will present the desired front to others. If you doubt this fact, just recall the last time you straightened up the house before important guests arrived. Backstage you might be comfortable with a messy place, but your public front–at least to some people–is quite different.

Most of the preceding examples involve face-to-face interaction, but identity management is just as pervasive and important in other types of communication. Consider the care you probably take when drafting a résumé for a potential employer, a thank-you letter in response to a gift, or a love note to a sweetheart. Besides giving careful thought to the wording of your message, you probably make strategic decisions about its appearance. Will you use plain white paper or something more distinctive? Will you type out your words or write them in longhand? People think carefully about considerations like these because they instinctively know that the *way* a message is presented can say as much as the words it contains.

At first glance, the new technology of computer-mediated communication (CMC) seems to limit the potential for identity management. E-mail messages, for example, appear to lack the "richness" of other channels. They don't convey the tone of your voice, postures, gestures, or facial expressions. This absence of nonverbal cues isn't always a disadvantage. A telecommuter working at home can close a big deal via computer while chomping on an apple, muttering about the client, or even belching–none of which are recommended in face-to-face interaction!

In other words, communicating via computer can actually *enhance* the ability to manage one's identity strategically.[41] Authors of electronic messages can edit their messages until they create just the desired impression. E-mailers can choose the desired level of clarity or ambiguity, seriousness or humour, logic or emotion. Unlike face-to-face communication, electronic correspondence allows a sender to say difficult things without forcing the receiver to respond immediately, and it permits the receiver to ignore a message rather than give an unpleasant response. Options like these show that CMC can serve as a tool for identity management at least as well as face-to-face communication.

*Before flying to London
I must visit
Some downtown Fredericton
   hardware store
and invest
in a couple of modest but
   distinguishable nylon
Canadian flags to sew upon my
   baggage
and shoulders*

*Without them
Europeans will feel
that I have to be
American*

*And that
just isn't close
enough*

Joseph Sherman,
"The Colours"

*Identity Management in
Cyberspace*

*http://www.rider.edu/sites/suler/
psycyber/identitymanage.html*

"On the Internet, nobody knows you're a dog."

Drawing by P. Steiner; ©1993 *The New Yorker Magazine*, Inc.

Identity Management and Honesty

After reading this far, you might think that identity management sounds like an academic label for manipulation or phoniness. If the perceived self is the "real" you, it might seem that any behaviour that contradicts it would be dishonest.

There certainly are situations in which identity management is dishonest. A manipulative date who pretends to be affectionate in order to gain sexual favours is clearly unethical and deceitful. So are job applicants who lie about academic records to get hired, or salespeople who pretend to be dedicated to customer service when their real goal is to make a quick buck. But managing impressions doesn't necessarily make you a liar. In fact, it is almost impossible to imagine how we could communicate effectively without making decisions about which front to present in one situation or another. It would be ludicrous for you to act the same way with strangers as you do with close friends, and nobody would show the same face to a 2-year-old as they would to an adult.

Each of us has a repertoire of faces—a cast of characters—and part of being a competent communicator is choosing the best role for the situation. Consider a few examples:

* You offer to teach a friend a new skill: playing the guitar, operating a computer program, or sharpening up a tennis backhand. Your friend is making slow progress with the skill, and you find yourself growing impatient.

* At a party you meet someone whom you find very attractive, and you are pretty sure that the feeling is mutual. On one hand you feel an obligation to spend most of your time with the person whom you came with, but the opportunity here is very appealing.

* At work you face a belligerent customer. You don't believe that anyone has the right to treat you this way.

* A friend or family member makes a joke about your appearance that hurts your feelings. You aren't sure whether to make an issue of the remark or pretend that it doesn't bother you.

In each of these situations—and in countless others every day—you have a choice about how to act. It is an oversimplification to say that there is only one honest way to behave in each circumstance and that every other response would be insincere and dishonest. Instead, identity management involves deciding which face—which part of yourself—to reveal. For example, when teaching a new skill, you choose to display the "patient" instead of the "impatient" side of yourself. In the same way, at work you have the option of acting hostile or nondefensive in difficult situations. With strangers, friends, or family, you can choose whether to disclose your feelings. Which face to show to others is an important decision, but in any case you are sharing a real part of yourself. You may not be revealing *everything*—but as you will learn in Chapter 8, complete self-disclosure is rarely appropriate.

SUMMARY

The self-concept is a relatively stable set of perceptions individuals hold about themselves. It begins to develop soon after birth, being shaped by both verbal and nonverbal messages from significant others and from reflected appraisal based on comparison with reference groups. The self-concept is subjective and can vary in important ways from the way a person is perceived by others. Although the self may evolve over time, the self-concept resists change.

A self-fulfilling prophecy occurs when a person's expectations of an event influence the outcome. One type of prophecy consists of predictions by others, while another category is self-imposed. Self-fulfilling prophecies can be both positive and negative.

It is possible to change one's self-concept in ways that lead to more effective communication. It is necessary to have realistic expectations about how much change is possible and to begin with a realistic assessment of oneself. Willingness to exert the effort to change is important, and in some cases change requires new information or skills.

Identity management consists of strategic communication designed to influence others' perceptions of an individual. Identity management aims at presenting one or more faces to others, which may be different from private, spontaneous behaviour that occurs outside of others' presence. Some communicators are high self-monitors who are highly conscious of their own behaviour, while others are less aware of how their words and actions affect others.

Identity management occurs for two reasons. In many cases it is based on following social rules and conventions. At other times it aims at achieving a variety of content and relational goals. In either case, communicators engage in creating an identity by managing their manner, appearance, and the settings in which they interact with others. Although identity management might seem manipulative, it can be an authentic form of communication. Because each person has a variety of faces that he or she can reveal, choosing which one to present need not be dishonest.

KEY TERMS

cognitive conservatism
identity
identity management
perceived self

presenting self
reference groups
reflected appraisal
self-concept

self-fulfilling prophecy
significant other
social comparison

Perception: What You See Is What You Get

I've always admired those reporters who can descend on an area, talk to key people, ask key questions, take samplings of opinions, and then set down an orderly report very much like a road map. I envy this technique and at the same time do not trust it as a mirror of reality. I feel that there are too many realities. What I set down here is true until someone else passes that way and rearranges the world in his own style. In literary criticism the critic has no choice but to make over the victim of his attention into something the size and shape of himself. . . .

So much there is to see, but our morning eyes describe a different world than do our afternoon eyes, and surely our wearied evening eyes can only report a weary evening world.

John Steinbeck,
Travels with Charley

Study M.C. Escher's drawing "Relativity" on the opposite page. It pictures a strange universe in which the inhabitants of each world exist at right angles, using the same staircase but oblivious to one another's existence. Each has his or her own conception of up and down, right and left. If these characters were introduced to the residents of other worlds, they would find them odd, defying the rule of gravity.

This surreal vision provides a useful metaphor for challenges we encounter every day. Each of us experiences a different reality, and failing to understand other people's point of view can lead to problems on both practical and relational levels. But perceptual differences can enhance as well as interfere with relationships. By seeing the world through others' eyes you can gain insights that are different—and often more valuable—than those arising out of your own experiences.

This chapter will help you deal with the challenge of communicating in the face of perceptual differences. We will begin by looking at some of the reasons the world appears different to each of us. In our survey we'll explore several areas: how our psychological makeup, personal needs, interests, and biases shape our perceptions; the physiological factors that influence our view of the world; the social roles that affect our image of events; and finally the role culture plays in creating our ideas of what behaviour is proper. In doing so, we'll cover many of the types of physiological and psychological noise that were described in the communication model in Chapter 1. After examining the perceptual factors that can drive us apart, we will look at two useful skills for bridging the perceptual gap.

THE PERCEPTION PROCESS

We need to begin our discussion of perception by examining the gap between "what is" and what we know. At one time or another you've probably seen photos of sights invisible to the unaided eye: perhaps an infrared photo of a familiar area or the vastly enlarged image of a minute object taken by an electron microscope. You've also noticed how certain animals are able to hear sounds and smell odours that are not apparent to humans. Experiences like these remind us that there is much more going on in the world than we are able to experience with our limited senses, that our idea of reality is in fact only a partial one.

Even within the realm of our senses we're aware of only a small part of what is going on around us. For instance, most people who live in large cities find that the noises of traffic, people, and construction soon fade out of their awareness. Others can take a walk through the forest without distinguishing one bird's call from another or noticing the differences among various types of vegetation.

On a personal level, we've all had the experience of failing to notice something unusual about a friend—perhaps a new hairstyle or a sad expression—until it's called to our attention.

Sometimes our failure to recognize some events while noticing others comes from not paying attention to important information. But in other cases it's simply impossible to be aware of everything, no matter how attentive we might be: There is just too much going on.

William James said that "to the infant the world is just a big blooming, buzzing confusion." One reason for this is the fact that

When schemes are laid in advance, it is surprising how often the circumstances fit in with them.

Sir William Osler

infants are not yet able to sort out the myriad impressions with which we're all bombarded. As we grow, we learn to manage all this data, and as we do so, we begin to make sense out of the world.

Because this ability to organize our perceptions in a useful way is such a critical factor in our ability to function, we need to begin our study of perception by taking a closer look at this process. We can do so by examining the three steps by which we attach meaning to our experiences: selection, organization, and interpretation.

Selection

Because we're exposed to more input than we can possibly manage, the first step in perception is the **selection** of which data we will attend to. There are several factors that cause us to notice some messages and ignore others.

Stimuli that are *intense* often attract our attention. Something that is louder, larger, or brighter stands out. This explains why–other things being equal–we're more likely to remember extremely tall or short people and why someone who laughs or talks loudly at a party attracts more attention (not always favourable) than do quiet guests.

Repetitious stimuli, repetitious stimuli, repetitious stimuli, repetitious stimuli, repetitious stimuli, repetitious stimuli also attract attention.[1] Just as a quiet but steadily dripping faucet can come to dominate our awareness, people to whom we're frequently exposed become noticeable.

Attention is also frequently related to contrast or change in stimulation. Put differently, unchanging people or things become less noticeable. This principle gives an explanation (excuse?) for why we take wonderful people for granted when we interact with them frequently. It's only when they stop being so wonderful or go away that we appreciate them.

cathy®   **by Cathy Guisewite**

Motives also determine what information we select from our environment. If you're late for an appointment, you'll notice whatever clocks may be around you; and if you're hungry, you'll become aware of any restaurants or billboards advertising food in your path. Motives also determine how we perceive people. For example, someone looking for a romantic adventure will be especially aware of attractive potential partners, whereas the same person in an emergency situation might be oblivious to anyone but police or medical personnel.

Intensity isn't just a matter of physical properties or cues: We also pay more attention to people or behaviours once we have become attuned to them. If you are annoyed with a friend who talks too much or a boss who seems critical, you are likely to tune in to behaviours that feed your aggravation. If you find red-haired people, tall people, Asians, or people with nice smiles attractive, you're likely to spot them more than others who don't fit these attributes.

Selection isn't just a matter of attending to some stimuli: It also involves ignoring other cues. If, for example, you decide that someone is a terrific person, you may overlook some serious flaws. If you are focussed on examples of unfair male bosses, you might not recognize unfair female supervisors.

Organization

Along with selecting information from the environment, we must arrange it in some meaningful way. You can see how the principle of **organization** works by looking at Figure 3–1. You can view the picture either as one of a vase or as one of two twins, depending on whether you focus on the light or the dark areas. In instances such as this we make sense of stimuli by noticing some data that stand out as a *figure* against a less-striking *ground*. The "vase–face" drawing is interesting because it allows us to choose between two sets of figure–ground relationships.

This principle of figure–ground organization operates in nonvisual ways, too. Recall, for instance, how certain speech can suddenly stand out from a babble of voices. Sometimes the words are noticeable because they include your name, whereas at other times they might be spoken by a familiar voice.

In examples like the ones just mentioned, the process of organization is relatively simple. But there are other cases in which messages are ambiguous, having more than one possible way of being organized. You can see a visual example of such an ambiguous stimulus in Figure 3–2. How many ways can you view the boxes? One? Two? Three? Keep looking. If you're stumped, Figure 3–3 will help.

Just as you were inclined to view these boxes in one way, each of us uses a particular organizing scheme to make sense of the information about others. We do this by using **perceptual schemata**–cognitive frameworks that allow us to organize the raw data we have selected. Five types of schemata help us classify ourselves and others.

FIGURE 3–1

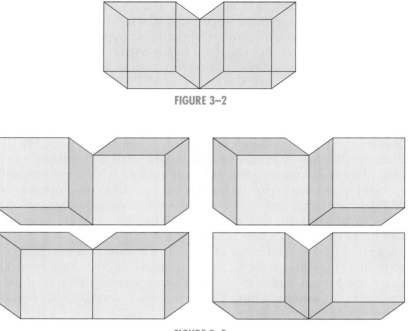

FIGURE 3–2

FIGURE 3–3

Physical constructs classify people according to their appearance: male or female, beautiful or ugly, fat or thin, young or old, and so on. **Role constructs** use social position: student, lawyer, wife, and so on. **Interaction constructs** focus on social behaviour: Friendly, helpful, aloof, and sarcastic are examples. The fourth organizing schema uses **psychological constructs:** curious, nervous, insecure, and so on. Finally, **membership constructs** help us identify others according to the group in which they belong: union rep, Liberal, and so on.

These schemata affect communication in two ways. First, they allow us to form impressions of others. Imagine that you've just met a new person at a party. Without these constructs, you would have no way to answer the question "What's this person like?" Once you have used various perceptual constructs to classify others, these classifications become a useful way to predict future behaviour. If you've classified a professor, for example, as "friendly," you'll handle questions or problems one way; if your analysis is "mean," your behaviour will probably be quite different. Note that there's an element of selection in the constructs we use: Choosing some constructs means that you ignore others. If you categorize people by their age or style of clothing, for example, you are likely to ignore other characteristics, such as their friendliness or intelligence.

The constructs we use strongly affect the way we relate to others. Young children usually don't classify people according to their skin colour until they become socialized. Then they learn that one common organizing principle in today's society is ethnicity, and their perceptions of others change. What constructs do you use to classify the people you encounter in your life? Consider how your relationship might change if you used different schemata.

INVITATION TO INSIGHT

YOUR PERCEPTUAL SCHEMATA

1. Identify the constructs described in the preceding section that you would use to categorize people in each of the following contexts. Describe both the *general type of construct* (e.g., "physical," "membership") and the *specific category* within each type (e.g., "attractive," "roughly the same age as me").
    a. Spending time with new acquaintances at a party
    b. Socializing with fellow workers on the job
    c. Choosing teammates for an important class project
    d. Offering help to a stranded motorist

2. Consider how valid the constructs you use are in making decisions about the type of communication in which you engage.
    a. Explain which of your constructs are valid.
    b. Explain which constructs are not valid, and suggest better alternatives.
    c. Describe how your relationships might change if you used different constructs.

Once we have selected an organizing schema to classify people, we use that schema to make generalizations about members of the groups who fit the categories we use. For example, if you were especially aware of gender, you might be alert to the differences between the way men and women behave or the way they are treated. If religion played an important part in your life, you might think of members of your faith differently from others. If ethnicity were an important issue for you, you would probably tune in to the differences between members of various ethnic groups. There's nothing wrong with generalizations as long as they are accurate. In fact, it would be impossible to get through life without them.

But when generalizations lose touch with reality, they lead to **stereotyping**–exaggerated generalizations associated with a categorizing system.[2] Stereotypes may be based on a kernel of truth, but they go beyond the facts at hand and make claims that usually have no valid basis.

You can begin to get a sense of your tendency to make generalizations and stereotype by completing the following sentences:

1. Women are_____
2. Men are_____

Farcus
by David Waisglass
Gordon Coulthart

"Kid, there are two types
of people in this world . . .
those who generalize, and
those who don't."

3. Inuit are_____

4. Wrestlers are_____

5. Whites are_____

6. Older people are_____

It's likely that you were able to complete each sentence without much hesitation. Does this mean you were stereotyping? You can answer this question by deciding whether your generalizations fit the three characteristics of stereotypes:

- You often categorize people on the basis of an easily recognized characteristic. For example, the first thing you notice about a person is his or her skin colour.

- You ascribe a set of characteristics to most or all members of this category. For example, you assume that all older people are doddering or all men are insensitive to women's concerns.

- You apply the set of characteristics to any member of the group. For example, when you meet an older person, you expect him or her to be senile.[3]

Stereotypes don't always lead to communication problems. If the person with whom you are interacting happens to fit the pattern in your mind, there may be no difficulties. But if your mental image does not happen to match the characteristics of the other person, problems can arise.

The process of organizing goes beyond our generalized perceptions of people. We also can organize our interactions with others in different ways; and these differing organizational schemata can have a powerful effect on our relationships with them. Communication theorists have used the term **punctuation** to describe the determination of causes and effects in a series of interactions.[4] You can begin to understand how the punctuation operates by visualizing a running quarrel between a husband and wife. The husband accuses the wife of being too critical, while she complains that he is withdrawing from her. Notice that the order in which each partner punctuates this cycle affects how the dispute looks. The husband begins by blaming the wife: "I withdraw because you're so critical." The wife organizes the situation differently, starting with the husband: "I criticize because you withdraw." Once the cycle gets rolling, it is impossible to say which accusation is accurate. The answer depends on how the sentence is punctuated. Figure 3–4 illustrates how this process operates.

Anyone who has seen two children argue about "who started it" can understand that haggling over causes and effects isn't likely to solve a conflict. In fact, the kind of finger-pointing that goes along with assigning blame will probably make matters worse. Rather than argue about whose punctuation of an event is correct, it's far more productive to recognize that a dispute can look different to each party, and then move on to the more important question of "What can we do to make things better?"

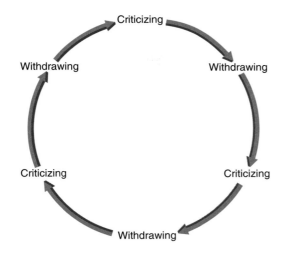

FIGURE 3—4
The same event can be punctuated in more than one way.

SKILL BUILDER

PUNCTUATION PRACTICE

You can appreciate how different punctuation patterns can influence attitudes and behaviour by following these directions.

1. Use the format pictured in Figure 3–4 to diagram the following situations:
   a. A father and daughter are growing more and more distant. The daughter withdraws because she interprets her father's coolness as rejection. The father views his daughter's aloofness as a rebuff and withdraws further.
   b. The relationship between two friends is becoming strained. One jokes to lighten up the tension, and the other becomes more tense.
   c. A dating couple is on the verge of breaking up. One partner frequently asks the other to show more affection. The other withdraws physical contact.

2. Identify two punctuating schemata for each of the situations described in step 1. Consider how the differing schemata would affect the way the two people in that situation respond to one another.

3. Now identify a difficult communication issue in your own life. Punctuate it in two ways: your own and the way it might be viewed by the other person. Discuss how seeing the issue from the other person's point of view might change the way you communicate as you discuss the issue.

Social Perception: How We See Others

http://www.as.ua.edu/psychology/social/socperc.htm

Interpretation

Once we have selected and organized our perceptions, we interpret them in a way that makes some sort of sense. **Interpretation** plays a role in virtually every interpersonal act. Is the person who smiles at you across a crowded room interested in romance or simply being polite? Is a friend's kidding a sign of affection or irritation? Should you take an invitation to "drop by any time" literally or not?

Several factors cause us to interpret an event in one way or another:

Relational satisfaction. The behaviour that seems positive when you are happy with a partner might seem completely different when the relationship isn't satisfying. For example, couples in unsatisfying relationships are more likely than satisfied partners to blame one another when things go wrong.[5] They are also more likely to believe that their partners are selfish and have negative intentions. Unhappy spouses are more likely than happy ones to make negative interpretations of their mate's behaviour. To see how this principle operates, recall the husband–wife quarrel we discussed earlier. Suppose the wife suggests that they get away for a weekend vacation. If the marriage has been troubled, the husband might interpret his wife's idea as more criticism ("You never pay attention to me"), and the fight will continue. If the relationship is solid, he is more likely to view the suggestion as a bid for a romantic getaway. It wasn't the event that shaped the reaction, but rather the way the husband interpreted the event.

Degree of involvement with the other person. We sometimes view people with whom we have or seek a relationship more favourably than those whom we observe from a detached perspective.[6] One recent study revealed how this principle operates in everyday life. A group of male subjects was asked to critique presentations by women who allegedly owned restaurants. Half of these presentations were designed to be competent and half incompetent. The men who were told they would be having a casual date with the female speakers judged their presentations–whether competent or not–more highly than did those who didn't expect any involvement with the speakers.[7]

Past experience. What meaning have similar events held? If, for example, you've been gouged by landlords in the past, you might be skeptical about an apartment manager's assurances that careful housekeeping will assure the refund of your cleaning deposit.

Assumptions about human behaviour. "People generally do as little work as possible to get by." "In spite of their mistakes, people are doing the best they can." Beliefs like these will shape the way we interpret another's actions.

Expectations. Anticipation shapes interpretations. If you imagine that your boss is unhappy with your work, you'll probably feel threatened by a request to "see me in my office first thing Monday morning." On the other hand, if you imagine that your work will be rewarded, your weekend will probably be pleasant.

Knowledge. If you know that a friend has just been jilted by a lover or laid off from a job, you'll interpret any aloof behaviour differently than you would if you were unaware of what had happened. If you know that an instructor speaks sarcastically to all students, you won't be as likely to take such remarks personally.

Self-concept. When you're feeling insecure, the world is a very different place from the world you experience when you're confident. For example, the recipient's self-concept has proved to be the single greatest factor in determining whether people who are on the receiving end of being teased interpret the teaser's motives as being friendly or hostile, and whether they respond with comfort or defensiveness.[8] The same goes for happiness and sadness or any other opposing emotions. The way we feel about ourselves strongly influences how we interpret others' behaviour.

Although we have talked about selection, organization, and interpretation separately, the three phases of perception can occur in differing sequences. For example, a parent's or baby-sitter's past interpretations (such as "Jason is a troublemaker") can influence future selections (his behaviour becomes especially noticeable) and the organization of events (when there's a fight, the assumption is that Jason started it). As with all communication, perception is an ongoing process in which it is hard to pin down beginnings and endings.

INFLUENCES ON PERCEPTION

Now that we've explored the psychological processes by which we perceive, it's time to look at some of the influences that cause us to select, organize, and interpret information.

Physiological Influences

The first set of influences we need to examine involves our physical makeup. Within the wide range of human similarities, each of us perceives the world in a unique way because of physiological factors. In other words, although the same events exist "out there," each of us receives a different image because of our perceptual hardware. Consider the long list of factors that shape our views of the world:

THE SENSES   The differences in how each of us sees, hears, tastes, touches, and smells stimuli can affect interpersonal relationships. Consider the following everyday situations:

"Turn down that radio! It's going to make me go deaf."
"It's not too loud. If I turn it down, it will be impossible to hear it."

"It's freezing in here."
"Are you kidding? We'll suffocate if you turn up the heat!"

"Why don't you pass that truck? The highway is clear for a mile."
"I can't see that far, and I'm not going to get us killed."

Sometimes very young children can look at the old, and a look passes between them, conspiratorial, sly, and knowing. It's because neither are human to the middling ones.

Margaret Laurence,
The Stone Angel

These disputes aren't over just matters of opinion. The sensory data we receive are different. Differences in vision and hearing are the easiest to recognize, but other gaps exist as well. There is evidence that identical foods taste differently to various individuals.[9] Odours that please some people repel others. Likewise, temperature variations that leave some of us uncomfortable are inconsequential to others. Remembering these differences won't eliminate them, but it will make it easier to remember that the other person's preferences aren't crazy, just different.

AGE Older people often view the world differently from younger ones because they have a greater scope and number of experiences. There are also developmental differences that shape perceptions. Swiss psychologist Jean Piaget described a series of stages that children pass through on their way to adulthood.[10] According to Piaget, younger children are incapable of performing mental feats that are natural to the rest of us. Until they approach the age of 7, for example, they aren't able to take another person's point of view. This fact helps explain why children often seem egocentric, selfish, and uncooperative. A parent's exasperated plea, "Can't you see I'm too tired to play?" just won't make sense to a 4-year-old full of energy, who imagines that everyone else must feel the same.

HEALTH Recall the last time you came down with a cold, flu, or some other ailment. Do you remember how different you felt? You probably had much less energy. It's likely that you felt less sociable, and that your thinking was slower than usual. These kinds of changes have a strong impact on how you relate to others. It's good to realize that someone else may be behaving differently because of illness. In the same way, it's important to let others know when you feel ill, so they can give you the understanding you need.

FATIGUE   Just as being ill can affect your relationships, so can being overly tired. Again it's important to recognize the fact that you or someone else may behave differently when fatigued. Trying to deal with important issues at such a time can get you into trouble.

HUNGER   People often get grumpy when they haven't eaten and sleepy after stuffing themselves. A number of physiological changes occur as we eat and become hungry again. Trying to conduct important business at the wrong time in this cycle can lead to problems.

BIOLOGICAL CYCLES   Are you a "morning person" or a "night person"? Most of us can answer this question pretty easily, and there's a good physiological reason behind our answer. Each of us is in a daily cycle in which all sorts of changes constantly occur, including body temperature, sexual drive, alertness, tolerance to stress, and mood.[11] Most of these changes are due to hormonal cycles. For instance, adrenal hormones, which affect feelings of stress, are secreted at higher rates during some hours. In the same manner, the male and female sex hormones enter our systems at variable rates. We often aren't conscious of these changes, but they surely influence the way we relate to one another. Once we're aware that our own cycles and those of others govern our feelings and behaviour, it becomes possible to manage our lives so that we deal with important issues at the most effective times.

For some women, the menstrual cycle plays an important role in shaping feelings and thus affects communication. Women aren't the only ones whose communication is affected by periodic changes in mood. Men too go through recognizable mood cycles, even though they aren't marked by obvious physical changes. Although they may not be aware of it, many men seem to go through biologically

---

INVITATION TO INSIGHT

NEW BODY, NEW PERSPECTIVE

You can get a clearer idea of how physiology influences perception by trying the following exercise.

1. Choose one of the following situations:
    An evening in a singles' bar
    A volleyball game
    A doctor's physical examination

2. How would the event you chose seem different if
    Your eyesight were much worse (or better)?
    You had a hearing loss?
    You were 8 inches taller (or shorter)?
    You were coming down with a serious cold?
    You were a member of the opposite sex?
    You were 10 years older (or younger)?

Trying on Old Age

How would you like to travel through time? That is, how would you like a glimpse into your golden years? That's the opportunity students are getting in psychologist Randall Wright's class on aging and human development.

Wright asked students to put together a costume that would make them look like senior citizens to casual observers. To create the illusion of age, Wright suggested wearing earplugs to reduce hearing, wrapping joints with elastic bandages to create stiffness, and using or discarding glasses to impair eyesight.

The students put in 5 hours of role-playing as older versions of themselves. They also submitted descriptions and ratings of the exercise as well as photographs of how they looked before and after donning their costumes.

Most of the students gained valuable insights during their sojourn in old age. Even such mundane activities as walking across the street took on new meanings, as one student observed: "With our legs wrapped, we walked considerably slower than most people. Inevitably, cars had to wait for us . . . not only do you feel a bother to other people, you worry about your life."

One student described how it felt to be ignored, while another was accosted by a group of boys in a passing car who screamed insults and demanded money.

Not all the experiences were frightening, however. One student was asked when he had last eaten

and was offered $10 as he pretended to rummage in a garbage can for food. Another male student said that "the highlight of my experiment came when a little old lady on the opposite bench winked at me."

Being old for a few hours was an eye-opening exercise, the students overwhelmingly agreed.

"Most felt that the simulation increased their knowledge and understanding of the elderly," says Wright. "In this case, living the lesson was better than learning it from a textbook."

Holly Hall

regulated periods of good spirits followed by equally predictable times of depression.[12] The average length of this cycle is about 5 weeks, although in some cases it's as short as 16 days or as long as 2 months. However long it may be, this cycle of ups and downs is quite regular.

Although neither men nor women can change these emotional cycles, simply learning to expect them can be a big help in improving communication. When you understand that a bad mood is predictable from physiological causes, you can plan for it. You'll know that every few weeks your patience will be shorter, so you'll be less likely to blame your mood swings on innocent bystanders. The people around you can also learn to expect your periodic lows. If they can attribute them to biology, maybe they will show you some understanding.

Oh, aren't the wrinkles coming in nicely!

Cultural Differences

So far you have seen how physical factors can make the world a different place for each of us. But there's another kind of perceptual gap that often blocks communication—the gap between people from different backgrounds. Every culture has its own worldview, its own way of looking at the world. Remembering these differing cultural perspectives can be a good way of learning more about both ourselves and others. But at times it's easy to forget that people everywhere don't see things the way we do. It is also important to note that many cross-cultural problems arise out of poor translation from one language to another:

- Chevrolet was baffled when its Nova model did not sell well in Latin American countries. Officials from General Motors finally realized the problem: In Spanish, *no va* means "does not go."

- One airline lost customers when it promoted the "rendezvous lounges" on its planes flying Brazilian routes. In Portuguese, *rendezvous* is a place to have sex.

- McDonald's Corporation was chagrined to learn that in French-Canadian slang, "big macs" are large breasts.[13]

Nonverbal behaviours, too, differ from one part of the world to another. In many cultures, the "OK" sign, made by touching the thumb and forefinger, is an obscene gesture representing the female

Judgement of Facial Expressions: Do Individuals of Different Cultures Provoke Different Reactions?

http://www.er.uqam.ca/nobel/ r24700/english/isre98.html

As only a sort of They!

We eat pork and beef
With cow-horn-handled knives.
They who gobble Their rice off a leaf
Are horrified out of Their lives;
While They who live up a tree,
Feast on grubs and clay,
(Isn't it scandalous?) look upon We
As a simply disgusting They!

We eat kitcheny food.
We have doors that latch.
They drink milk and blood
Under an open thatch.
We have doctors to fee.
They have wizards to pay.
And (impudent heathen!) They
look upon We
As a quite impossible They!

All good people agree,
And all good people say,
All nice people, like us, are We
And everyone else is They:
But if you cross over the sea,
Instead of over the way,
You may end by (think of it!)
looking on We
As only a sort of They!

Rudyard Kipling,
"We and They"

Father, Mother, and Me,
Sister and Auntie say
All the people like us are We,
And everyone else is They.
And They live over the sea
While we live over the way,
But—would you believe it?—
They look upon We

---

genitalia. To a woman, it is a proposition for sex, and to a man it suggests he is gay.[14] It's easy to imagine the problems that could result in an unsuspecting person's innocent gesture.

The range of cultural differences is wide. In Middle Eastern countries, personal odours play an important role in interpersonal relationships. Arabs consistently breathe on people when they talk. As anthropologist Edward Hall explains:

To smell one's friend is not only nice, but desirable, for to deny him your breath is to act ashamed. [North] Americans, on the other hand, trained as they are not to breathe in people's faces, automatically communicate shame in trying to be polite. Who would expect that when our highest diplomats are putting on their best manners they are also communicating shame? Yet this is what occurs constantly, because diplomacy is not only "eyeball to eyeball" but breath to breath.[15]

Even beliefs about the very value of talk differ from one culture to another.[16] Western cultures view talk as desirable and use it for social purposes as well as task performance. Silence has a negative value in these cultures. It is likely to be interpreted as lack of interest, unwillingness to communicate, hostility, anxiety, shyness, or a sign of interpersonal incompatibility. We are uncomfortable with silence, and find it embarrassing and awkward.

On the other hand, Asian cultures perceive talk quite differently. For thousands of years, Asian cultures have discouraged the expression of thoughts and feelings. Silence is valued, as Taoist sayings indicate: "In much talk there is great weariness," or "One who speaks does not know; one who knows does not speak." Unlike Westerners who are uncomfortable with silence, Japanese and Chinese believe that remaining quiet is the proper state when there is nothing to be said. To Asians a talkative person is often considered a show-off or an insincere individual.

It's easy to see how these different views of speech and silence can lead to communication problems when people from different cultures meet. Both the talkative Westerner and the silent Asian are behaving in ways they believe are proper; yet each views the other with disapproval and mistrust. Only when they recognize the different standards of behaviour can they adapt to one another, or at least understand and respect their differences.

It isn't necessary to travel overseas to encounter differing cultural perspectives. Within this country there are many subcultures, and the members of each one have backgrounds that cause them to see things in unique ways. For example, so as not to offend her newfound French companions, a Toronto student attending university in Montreal had to get used to greeting her friends with a kiss on each cheek. Upon returning to Toronto, she met her mother's Ukrainian friend, who would kiss her three times when they encountered one another. She had just become accustomed to this ritual when she moved to Vancouver, where no one kissed. She was surprised when she found herself having to hold back from displaying her newly acquired welcoming ritual. But not everyone is so aware of, or adapts so readily to, co-cultural differences. Take the notion of time, for instance. Aboriginal time is experiential in nature; that is, there is no particular time, only what is occurring at the moment. On the other hand, white Canadians (perceived as immigrants by Aboriginal peoples) think of time as event driven, or moving in a linear fashion. As a result of these perceptual differences, Aboriginal students who arrive late for class may be pigeonholed by white professors as apathetic, undependable, or irresponsible when in fact some other momentary matter may have consumed their attention. One Native student told us that if he was leaving for the university and his son wanted him to just hang out for a while, it would be more important to do that than to get to a scheduled class. As you can see, failure to recognize such perceptual differences can lead to unfortunate and unnecessary misunderstandings.

Along with ethnicity, geography influences perceptions. It is estimated that 60 percent of Canadians define themselves according to the region in which they live.[17] The distinct climates, histories, economics, and people found in each region influence how we think about ourselves and others. You can imagine, for instance, how a variety of events might be viewed very differently by individuals from the Prairies, downtown Toronto, or the North.

THE INVESTIGATION

Looking at Diversity

Ancestry vs. Environment: A Japanese-Canadian Perspective

David Suzuki

My genes can be traced in a direct line to Japan. I am a pure-blooded member of the Japanese race. And whenever I go there, I am always astonished to see the power of that biological connection. In subways in Tokyo, I catch familiar glimpses of the eyes, hairline, or smile of my Japanese relatives. Yet when those same people open their mouths to communicate, the vast cultural gulf that separates them from me becomes obvious: English is my language, Shakespeare is my literature, British history is what I learned, and Beethoven is my music.

For those who believe that in people, just as in animals, genes are the primary determinant of behaviour, a look at second- and third-generation immigrants to Canada gives powerful evidence to the contrary. The overriding influence is environmental. We make a great mistake by associating the inheritance of physical characteristics with far more complex traits of human personality and behaviour.

Each time I visit Japan, I am reminded of how Canadian I am and how little the racial connection matters. I first visited Japan in 1968 to attend the International Congress of Genetics in Tokyo. For the first time in my life, I was surrounded by people who all looked like me. While sitting in a train and looking at the reflections in the window, I found that it was hard to pick out my own image in the crowd. I had grown up in a Caucasian society in which I was a minority member. My whole sense of self had developed with that perspective of looking different. All my life I had wanted large eyes and brown hair so I could be like everyone else. Yet on that train, where I did fit in, I didn't like it.

On this first visit to Japan I had asked my grandparents to contact relatives and let them know I was coming. I was the first in the Suzuki clan in Canada to visit them. The closest relative on my father's side was my grandmother's younger brother, and we arranged to meet in a seaside resort near his home. He came to my hotel room with two of his daughters. None of them spoke any English, while my Japanese was so primitive as to be useless. In typical Japanese fashion, they showered me with gifts, the most important being a package of what looked like wood carved in the shape of bananas! I had no idea what it was. (Later I learned the package contained dried tuna fish from which slivers are shaved off to flavour soup. This is considered a highly prized gift.) We sat in stiff silence and embarrassment, each of us struggling to dredge up a common word or two to break the quiet. It was excruciating! My great-uncle later wrote my grandmother to tell her how painful it had been to sit with her grandson and yet be unable to communicate a word.

To people in Japan, all non-Japanese—black, white or yellow—are *gaijin* or foreigners. While *gaijin* is not derogatory, I find that its use is harsh because I sense doors clanging shut on me when I'm called one. The Japanese do have a hell of a time with me because I look like them and can say in perfect Japanese, "I'm a foreigner and I can't speak Japanese." Their reactions are usually complete incomprehension followed by a sputtering, "What do you mean? You're speaking Japanese." And finally a pejorative, "Oh, a *gaijin*!"

From John Borovilos, ed., *Breaking Through: A Canadian Literary Mosaic* (Scarborough, Ontario: Prentice-Hall, 1990), pp. 181–182.

Social Roles

So far you have seen how cultural and physiological variations can block communication. Along with these differences, another set of perceptual factors can lead to communication breakdowns. From

Online Discussion Forum on Interpersonal Relations

http://www.green-river.com/disc1PRS99_frm.htm

The primary area in which there remain dramatic differences between the values of men and women is in the orientation toward violence. Men are significantly more likely than women to believe that violence is an unavoidable fact of everyday life, and an acceptable way of resolving disputes; men are also much more likely than women to be entertained by violent sports, movies, or television. Women, on the other hand, are much less likely to accept violence as normative, and much more likely to worry about being violently attacked or victimized.

Michael Adams,
Sex in the Snow

almost the time we're born, each of us is indirectly taught a whole set of roles that we'll be expected to play. In one sense this collection of prescribed parts is necessary because it enables a society to function smoothly and provides the security that comes from knowing what's expected of you. But in another way, having roles defined in advance can lead to wide gaps in understanding. When roles become unquestioned and rigid, people tend to see the world from their own viewpoint, having no experiences that show them how other people view it. Naturally, communication suffers in such a situation.

GENDER ROLES In every society gender is one of the most important factors in determining how people perceive one another. Children learn the importance of sex-typed behaviour by watching other people and being exposed to media as well as by reinforcement.[18] Once members of a society learn customary sex roles, they tend to regard violations of those roles as unusual—or even undesirable.

Some theorists have suggested that stereotypical masculine and feminine behaviours are not opposite poles of a single continuum, but rather two separate sets of behaviour.[19] With this view, an individual can act in a masculine manner or a feminine manner, or exhibit both types of characteristics. The male-female dichotomy, then, is replaced with four psychological sex types, including masculine, feminine, **androgynous** (combining masculine and feminine traits), and undifferentiated (neither masculine nor feminine). Combining the four psychological sex types with the traditional physiological sex types produces the eight categories listed in Table 3–1.

Each of these eight psychological sex types perceives interpersonal relationships differently. For example, masculine males probably see their interpersonal relationships as opportunities for competitive interaction, as opportunities to win something. Feminine females probably see their interpersonal relationships as opportunities to be nurturing, to express their feelings and emotions. Androgynous males and females, on the other hand, probably differ little in their perceptions of their interpersonal relationships.

TABLE 3–1	PSYCHOLOGICAL SEX TYPES	
	MALE	**FEMALE**
Masculine	Masculine males	Masculine females
Feminine	Feminine males	Feminine females
Androgynous	Androgynous males	Androgynous females
Undifferentiated	Undifferentiated males	Undifferentiated females

Androgynous individuals probably see their relationships as opportunities to behave in a variety of ways, depending on the nature of the relationships themselves, the context in which a particular relationship takes place, and the myriad other variables affecting what might constitute appropriate behaviour. These variables are usually ignored by the sex-typed masculine males and feminine females, who have a smaller repertoire of behaviour.

OCCUPATIONAL ROLES   The kind of work we do often influences our view of the world. Imagine five people taking a walk through the park. One, a botanist, is fascinated by the variety of trees and plants. The zoologist is looking for interesting animals. The third, a meteorologist, keeps an eye on the sky, noticing changes in the weather. The fourth companion, a psychologist, is totally unaware of nature, instead concentrating on the interaction among the people in the park. The fifth person, being a pickpocket, quickly takes advantage of the others' absorption to make some money. There are two lessons in this little story. The first, of course, is to watch your wallet carefully. The second is that our occupational roles shape our perceptions.

Even within the same occupational setting, the different roles that participants have can affect their perceptions. Consider a typical college or university classroom, for example: The experiences of the instructor and students often are quite dissimilar. Having dedicated a large part of their lives to their work, most professors see their subject matter–whether French literature, physics, or speech communication– as vitally important. Students who are taking the course to satisfy a degree requirement may view the subject quite differently: maybe as one of many obstacles that stand between them and graduation, maybe as a chance to meet new people. Another difference centres on the amount of knowledge possessed by the parties. To an instructor who has taught the course many times, the material probably seems extremely simple; but to students encountering it for the first time, it may seem strange and confusing. Toward the end of a term the instructor might be pressing onward hurriedly to cover all the material in the course, whereas the students are fatigued from their studies and ready to move

OPERATION EMPATHY: PREPARATION FOR THE CHANGING POLICE ROLE

We are all aware that it is extremely difficult to immerse the average police officer into situations that will reveal the feelings of the down-and-outer, the social outcast, the have-nots, and show us their perspective of normal law-enforcement procedures. Obviously the officer, in his or her police role, would not fit into such a context. But suppose he or she was a person with a great deal of courage, willing for the sake of experimentation to become a bum, a skid row habitant.

A group of police officers who were willing to become skid row habitants were carefully selected and conditioned for the role they were about to play. Each was given three dollars with which to purchase a complete outfit of pawn shop clothing. Among other props were such items as a shopping bag filled with collected junk, and a wine bottle camouflaged with a brown paper sack.

Conditioned and ready, our officers, assigned in pairs, moved into an urban skid row district. They soon discovered that when they tried to leave the area, walking a few blocks into the legitimate retail sections, they were told, "Go back where you belong!" Our officers knew in reality they were not "bums," but they found that other citizens quickly categorized them and treated them accordingly.

During the skid row experiment, our officers ate in soup kitchens and shelters like the other outcasts and derelicts. They roamed the streets and the alleys, and discovered many levelling experiences. Some were anticipated, others were not. Perhaps the most meaningful experience of the skid row exercise occurred to Tom Courtney, a young juvenile officer with five years' police service.

It was dusk, and Tom and his partner were sauntering back to a prearranged gathering place. Feeling a little sporty, the pair decided to "polish off" the bottle of wine. They paused in a convenient parking lot, and Tom tipped the bottle up. As if from nowhere, two uniformed police officers materialized before the surprised pair. Tom and his partner were spread-eagled against a building and searched.

Forgetting the admonishment not to reveal identities and purpose unless absolutely necessary, Tom panicked and identified himself.

Later, Tom found it difficult to explain why he was so quick in his revelation. "You wouldn't understand," he told me; then blurted he thought he "might get shot."

I found it difficult to receive this as a rational explanation, especially since Tom stated that the officers, while firm, were courteous at all times. With some additional prodding, Tom admitted that as he was being searched, he suddenly thought of every negative thing he had ever heard about the police. He even perceived a mental flash of a newspaper headline: "Police Officer Erroneously Shot While on Field Experiment."

"I know better now," Tom continued, "but when you feel that way about yourself, you believe—you believe."

I attempted to rationalize with Tom his reason for fear. I asked if he was certain that the officers were courteous. He replied in the affirmative, but added, "They didn't smile, or tell me what they were going to do next." Tom had discovered a new emotional reaction within his own personal makeup, and it left a telling impression.

Today, Tom Courtney is still telling our department personnel, "For God's sake, smile when you can. And above all, tell the man or woman you're shaking down what you are going to do. Take the personal threat out of the encounter, if you can."

Equally important as Tom's experience, I believe, is the lesson we learned about personal judgements. Our men in the "Operation Empathy" experiment found they were adjudged by the so-called normal population as "being like" all the other inmates of skid row, simply because their appearance was representative.

Perhaps we would all do well to heed the lesson, for now, more than at any other time in our history, police officers and the RCMP must guard against the natural tendency to lump people into categories simply because they look alike.

R. Fred Ferguson

more slowly. We don't need to spell out the interpersonal strains and stresses that come from such differing perceptions.

Perhaps the most dramatic illustration of how occupational roles shape perception occurred in 1971.[20] A psychologist named Philip Zimbardo recruited a group of middle-class, well-educated young men. He randomly chose 11 to serve as "guards" in a mock prison set up in the basement of Stanford's psychology building. He issued the guards uniforms, handcuffs, whistles, and billy clubs. The remaining 10 subjects became "prisoners" and were placed in rooms with metal bars, bucket toilets, and cots.

Zimbardo let the guards establish their own rules for the experiment. The rules were tough: No talking during meals, rest periods, and after lights out. Head counts at 2:30 A.M. Troublemakers received short rations.

Faced with these conditions, the prisoners began to resist. Some barricaded their doors with beds. Others went on hunger strikes. Several ripped off their identifying number tags. The guards reacted to the rebellion by clamping down hard on protesters. Some turned sadistic, physically and verbally abusing the prisoners. They threw prisoners into solitary confinement. Others forced prisoners to call each other names and clean out toilets with their bare hands.

Within a short time the experiment had become reality for both prisoners and guards. Several inmates had stomach cramps and lapsed into uncontrollable weeping. Others suffered from headaches, and one broke out in a head-to-toe rash after his request for early "parole" was denied by the guards.

INVITATION TO INSIGHT

ROLE REVERSAL

Walk a mile in another person's shoes. Find a group that is foreign to you, and try to become a member of it for a while.

If you're down on the police, see if your local department has a ride-along program where you can spend several hours on patrol with one or two officers.

If you think the present state of education is a mess, become a teacher yourself. Maybe an instructor will give you the chance to plan one or more classes.

If you're adventuresome, follow the example of the police officers in the article on pages 108–109 and become a homeless person for a day. See how you're treated.

If you're right-winged, try getting involved in a radical organization; if you're more of a leftie, check out the conservatives.

Whatever group you join, try to become part of it as best you can. Don't just observe. Get into the philosophy of your new role and see how it feels. You may find that all those weird people aren't so strange after all.

The experiment was scheduled to go on for 2 weeks, but after 6 days Zimbardo realized that what had started as a simulation had become too intense. "I knew by then that they were thinking like prisoners and not like people," he said. "If we were able to demonstrate that pathological behaviour could be produced in so short a time, think of what damage is being done in 'real' prisons. . . . "

This dramatic exercise in which 21 well-educated, middle-class citizens turned almost overnight into sadistic bullies and demoralized victims tells us that *how* we think is a function of our roles in society. It seems that *what* we are is determined largely by society's designation of *who* we are. Fortunately, many officials in the field of law enforcement are aware of the perceptual blindness that can come with one's job. These professionals have developed programs that help to overcome the problem, as illustrated on pp. 108–109.

Self-Concept

Another factor that influences how we think of ourselves and interact with others is the self-concept. Extensive research shows that a person with high self-esteem is more likely to think well of others, whereas someone with low self-esteem is likely to have a poor opinion of others.[21] Your own experience may bear this out: Persons with low self-esteem are often cynical and quick to ascribe the worst possible motives to others, whereas those who feel good about themselves are disposed to think favourably about the people they encounter. As one writer put it, "What we find 'out there' is what we put there with our unconscious projections. When we think we are looking out a window, it may be, more often than we realize, that we are really gazing into a looking glass."[22]

Besides distorting the facts about others, our self-concepts also lead us to have distorted views of ourselves. We already hinted at this fact when we explained in Chapter 2 that the self-concept is not objective. "It wasn't my fault," you might be tempted to say, knowing deep inside that you were responsible. "I look horrible," you might think as you look into the mirror, despite the fact that everyone around you sincerely insists you look terrific.

Shared Narratives

Our interaction with other individuals and groups creates a shared perception of the world. Communication scholars have come to call this kind of shared perspective a **narrative.**[23] This term reflects the notion that humans make sense of the world by spinning a kind of story to explain events and behaviour. Shared narratives help groups of communicators make sense of themselves and others.[24]

Narratives evolve without any conscious strategy by the participants. One study of sense-making on the job illustrates how the process operates.[25] Researchers located employees who had participated in office discussions about "differential treatment"—cases where a fellow worker had received "differential treatment" from management about matters such as time off, pay, or work assignments. The researchers then analyzed the conversations employees held with fellow workers about the differential treatment. The analysis revealed that these conversations were the place in which workers created and reinforced the meaning of the employee's behaviour and management's response. For example, consider the way workers made sense of Jane Doe's habit of taking late lunches. As Jane's co-workers discuss her behaviours, they might decide that her late lunches aren't fair—or they might agree that late lunches aren't a big deal. Either way, discussion of office events *defines* those events. Once defined, co-workers tend to seek reinforcement for their perceptions by keeping a mental scorecard rating their fellow employees and management. ("Did you notice that Bob came in late again today?" "Did you notice that the boss chose Jane to go on that trip to New York?") Although most of us like to think we make judgements about others on our own, this research suggests that sense-making is an *interactive* process. In other words, reality in the workplace and elsewhere isn't "out there": We create it with others through communication.

Research on long-term happy marriages summarized by Judy Pearson demonstrates that shared narratives don't have to be accurate to be powerful.[26] Couples who report being happily married after 50 or more years seem to collude in a relational narrative that doesn't jibe with the facts. They agree that they rarely have conflict, although objective analysis reveals that they have had their share of disagreements and challenges. Without overtly agreeing to do so, they choose to blame outside forces or unusual circumstances for problems, instead of attributing responsibility to one another. They offer the most charitable interpretations of one another's behaviour, believing that their spouse acts with good intentions when things don't go well. They seem willing to forgive, or even forget transgressions.

Interestingly enough, divorce rates in Canada have been decreasing since the late 1980s. One might assume that Canadian couples are particularly adept at creating positive shared narratives. However, there has also been a 17.8 percent drop in the number of marriages between 1989 and 1996; thus the pool of potential divorces is reduced.[27] Further, twosomes are seeking separation rather than divorce, and a greater number of couples are opting to live together rather than to marry. In 1997, according to Statistics Canada, the highest divorce rates were in the Yukon, Alberta, and British Columbia, while the lowest were in the Northwest Territories, Newfoundland, and Prince Edward Island.[28]

THE ACCURACY—AND INACCURACY—OF PERCEPTION

By now it's obvious that many factors distort the way we interpret the world. Social scientists use the term **attribution** to describe the process of attaching meaning to behaviour. We attribute meaning both to our own actions and to the actions of others, but we often use different yardsticks. Research has uncovered several perceptual errors that lead to inaccurate attributions.[29]

We Often Judge Ourselves More Charitably Than Others

In an attempt to convince ourselves and others that the positive face we show to the world is true, we tend to judge ourselves in the most generous terms possible. Social scientists have labelled this tendency the **self-serving bias.**[30] When others suffer, we often blame the problem on their personal qualities. On the other hand, when we're the victims, we find explanations outside ourselves. Consider a few examples:

- When *they* botch a job, we might think they weren't listening well or trying hard enough; when *we* make the mistake, the problem was unclear directions or not enough time.

- When *he* lashes out angrily, we say he's being moody or too sensitive; when *we* blow off steam, it's because of the pressure we've been under.

- When *she* gets caught speeding, we say she should have been more careful; when *we* get the ticket, we deny we were driving too fast or say, "Everybody does it."

"The truth is, Cauldwell, we never see ourselves as others see us."

The Saturday Evening Post

I have heard students say things like, "It was John's fault, his speech was so confusing nobody could have understood it." Then, two minutes later, the same student remarked, "It wasn't my fault, what I said could not have been clearer. John must be stupid." Poor John! He was blamed when he was the sender and when he was the receiver. John's problem was that he was the other person, and that's who is always at fault.

Stephen W. King

The egocentric tendency to rate ourselves more favourably than others see us has been demonstrated experimentally.[31] In one study, a random sample of men were asked to rank themselves on their ability to get along with others.[32] Defying mathematical laws, all subjects—every last one—put themselves in the top half of the population. Sixty percent rated themselves in the top 10 percent of the population, and an amazing 25 percent believed they were in the top 1 percent. In the same study, 70 percent of the men ranked their leadership in the top quarter of the population, whereas only 2 percent thought they were below average. Sixty percent said they were in the top quarter in athletic abilities, whereas only 6 percent viewed themselves as below average.

Distortions like these usually revolve around the desire to maintain a presenting self-concept that has been threatened. The desire to maintain face is often strong. If you want to present yourself as a good student or musician, for example, an instructor who gives you a poor grade or a critic who doesn't appreciate your music *must* be wrong, and you'll find evidence to show it. If you want to think of yourself as a good worker or parent, you'll find explanations for the problems in your job or family that shift the responsibility away from you. Of course, the same principle works for people with excessively negative self-images: They'll go out of the way to explain any information that's favourable to them in terms that show they really are incompetent or undesirable. The list of defence mechanisms in Chapter 9 shows how inventive people can be when a threatened presenting image is at stake.

We Are Influenced by What Is Most Obvious

The error of being influenced by what is most obvious is understandable. As you read at the beginning of this chapter, we select stimuli from our environment that are noticeable: intense, repetitious, unusual, or otherwise attention grabbing. The problem is that the most obvious factor is not necessarily the only cause—or the most significant one for an event. For example,

- When two children (or adults, for that matter) fight, it may be a mistake to blame the one who lashes out first. Perhaps the other one was at least equally responsible, teasing or refusing to co-operate.

- You might complain about an acquaintance whose malicious gossiping or arguing has become a bother, forgetting that by putting up with such behaviour in the past you have been at least partially responsible.

- You might blame an unhappy working situation on the boss, overlooking other factors beyond her control, such as a change in the economy, the policy of higher management, or demands of customers or other workers.

We Cling to First Impressions

Labelling people according to our first impressions is an inevitable part of the perception process. These labels are a way of making interpretations. "She seems cheerful." "He seems sincere." "They sound awfully conceited."

If they're accurate, impressions like these can be useful ways of deciding how to respond best to people in the future. Problems arise, however, when the labels we attach are inaccurate; once we form an opinion of someone, we tend to hang on to it and then make any conflicting information fit our image.

Suppose, for instance, you mention the name of your new neighbour to a friend. "Oh, I know him," your friend replies. "He seems nice at first, but it's all an act." Perhaps this appraisal is off base. The neighbour may have changed since your friend knew him, or perhaps your friend's judgement is simply unfair. Whether the judgement is accurate or not, once you accept your friend's evaluation, it will probably influence the way you respond to the neighbour. You'll look for examples of the insincerity you've heard about . . . and you'll probably find them. Even if the neighbour were a saint, you would be likely to interpret his behaviour in ways that fit your expectations. "Sure, he *seems* nice," you might think, "but it's probably just a front." Of course, this sort of suspicion can create a self-fulfilling prophecy, transforming a genuinely nice person into someone who truly becomes an undesirable neighbour.

Given the almost unavoidable tendency to form first impressions, the best advice we can give is to keep an open mind and to be willing to change your opinion as events prove it mistaken.

We Tend to Assume Others Are Similar to Us

In Chapter 2 you read one example of this principle: that people with low self-esteem imagine others view them unfavourably, whereas people who like themselves imagine that others like them, too. The frequently mistaken assumption that others' views are similar to our own applies in a wide range of situations:

- You've heard a slightly raunchy joke that you think is pretty funny. You might assume that it won't offend a somewhat strait-laced friend. It does.

- You've been bothered by an instructor's tendency to get off the subject during lectures. If you were a professor, you'd want to know if anything you were doing was creating problems for your students, so you decide that your instructor will probably be grateful for some constructive criticism. Unfortunately, you're wrong.

- You lost your temper with a friend a week ago and said some things you regret. In fact, if someone said those things to you,

you'd consider the relationship was finished. Imagining that your friend feels the same way, you avoid making contact. In fact, your friend feels that she was partly responsible and has avoided you because she thinks you're the one who wants to end things.

Examples like these show that others don't always think or feel the way we do and that assuming similarities exist can lead to problems. How can you find out the other person's real position? Sometimes by asking directly, sometimes by checking with others, and sometimes by making an educated guess after you've thought the matter out. All these alternatives are better than simply assuming everyone would react as you do.

PERCEPTION CHECKING TO PREVENT MISUNDERSTANDINGS

Serious problems can arise when people treat interpretations as if they were matters of fact. Like most people, you probably resent others jumping to conclusions about the reasons for your behaviour.

"Why are you mad at me?" (Who said you were?)

"What's the matter with you?" (Who said anything was the matter?)

"Come on now. Tell the truth." (Who said you were lying?)

As you'll learn in Chapter 9, even if your interpretation is correct, a dogmatic, mind-reading statement is likely to generate defensiveness. The skill of **perception checking** provides a better way to handle your interpretations.

Elements of Perception Checking

A complete perception check has three parts:

* A description of the behaviour you noticed
* At least two possible interpretations of that behaviour
* A request for clarification about how to interpret the behaviour

Perception checks for the preceding three examples would look like this:

"When you rushed out of the room and the door slammed" *(behaviour),* "I wasn't sure whether you were mad at me" *(first interpretation)* "or just in a hurry" *(second interpretation).* "How did you feel?" *(request for clarification)*

"You haven't laughed much in the last couple of days" *(behaviour).* "It makes me wonder whether something's bothering you" *(first interpretation)* "or whether you're just feeling quiet" *(second interpretation).* "What's up?" *(request for clarification)*

"You said you really liked the job I did" *(behaviour)*. "On the other hand, there was something about your voice that made me think you may not like it" *(first interpretation)*. "Maybe it's just my imagination, though" *(second interpretation)*. "How do you really feel?" *(request for clarification)*

Perception checking is a tool for helping you understand others accurately instead of assuming that your first interpretation is correct. Because its goal is mutual understanding, perception checking is a co-operative approach to communication. Besides leading to perceptions, it minimizes defensiveness by preserving the other person's face. Instead of saying, in effect, "I know what you're thinking. . . ," a perception check takes the more respectful approach that states or implies, "I know I'm not qualified to judge you without some help."

Perception-Checking Considerations

Like every communication skill outlined in *Looking Out/Looking In,* perception checking isn't a mechanical formula that will work in every situation. As you develop the ability to check your perceptions fully, consider the following factors in deciding when and how to use this approach.

COMPLETENESS   Sometimes a perception check won't need all the parts listed earlier to be effective:

"You haven't dropped by lately. Is anything the matter?" *(single interpretation combined with request for clarification)*

"I can't tell whether you're kidding me about being cheap or if you're serious" *(behaviour combined with interpretations)*. "Are you mad at me?"

"Are you sure you don't mind driving? I can use a ride if it's no trouble, but I don't want to take you out of your way" *(no need to describe behaviour)*.

Sometimes even the most skimpy perception check—a simple question like "What's up?"—will do the job. You might also rely on other people to help you make sense of confusing behaviour: "Rachelle has been awfully quiet lately. Do you know what's going on?" A complete perception check is most necessary when the risk of sounding judgemental is highest.

NONVERBAL CONGRUENCY   A perception check can succeed only if your nonverbal behaviour reflects the open-mindedness of your words. An accusing tone of voice or a hostile glare will contradict the sincerely worded request for clarification, suggesting that you have already made up your mind about the other person's intentions.

CULTURAL RULES   The straightforward approach of perception checking has the best chance of working in what Chapter 5 identifies as

Apart from abstract propositions of comparison (such as two and two make four), propositions which tell us nothing by themselves about concrete reality, we find no proposition ever regarded by any one as evidently certain that has not either been called a falsehood, or at least had its truth sincerely questioned by someone else.

William James,
The Will to Believe

low-context cultures: ones in which members use language as clearly and logically as possible. The dominant cultures of North America and Western Europe fit into this category, and members of these groups are most likely to appreciate the kind of straight talking that perception checking embodies. On the other hand, members of *high-context cultures* (more common in Latin America and Asia) value social harmony over clarity. Low-context communicators are more likely to regard candid approaches like perception checking as potentially embarrassing, preferring instead less-direct ways of understanding one another. Thus, a "let's get this straight" perception check that might work well with a EuroCanadian manager who was raised to value clarity could be a serious mistake with a Mexican or Asian boss who has spent most of his or her life in a high-context culture.

Empathy in Communication

*http://wwwselfgrowth.com/
articles/winnett2.html*

EMPATHY AND COMMUNICATION

Perception checking is a valuable tool for clarifying ambiguous messages. But ambiguity isn't the only cause of perceptual problems. Sometimes we understand *what* people mean without understanding *why* they believe as they do. At times like this we are short on the vital ability to empathize.

Empathy Defined

Empathy is the ability to re-create another person's perspective; to experience the world from the other's point of view. It may be impossible to experience another person's perspective completely, but with enough effort we can certainly gain a better idea of how the world appears to her or him. As we'll use the term here, **empathy** involves three dimensions.[33] On one level, empathy involves *perspective taking*—an attempt to take on the viewpoint of another person. This understanding requires a suspension of judgement, so that for the moment you set aside your own opinions and try to understand the other person. Besides cognitive understanding, empathy also has an *emotional* dimension that helps us get closer to experiencing others' feelings: to gain a sense of their fear, joy, sadness, and so on. A third ingredient of empathy is a genuine *concern* for the welfare of the other person. When we empathize we go beyond just thinking and feeling as others do and genuinely care about their well-being.

The ability to empathize seems to exist in a rudimentary form in even the youngest children.[34] Research has verified what many parents know from experience: Virtually from birth, infants become visibly upset when they hear another baby crying, and children who are a few months old cry when they observe another child in tears. Young children have trouble distinguishing others'

SKILL BUILDER

PERCEPTION-CHECKING PRACTICE

Practise your perception-checking ability by developing three-part verifications for the following situations:

1. You made what you thought was an excellent suggestion to an instructor. The professor looked uninterested but said she would check on the matter right away. Three weeks have passed, and nothing has changed.

2. A neighbour and good friend has not responded to your "Good morning" for 3 days in a row. This person is usually friendly.

3. You haven't received the usual weekly phone call from the folks back home in over a month. The last time you spoke, you had an argument about where to spend the holidays.

4. An old friend with whom you have shared the problems of your love life for years has recently changed when around you: The formerly casual hugs and kisses have become longer and stronger, and the occasions where you "accidentally" brush up against one another have become more frequent.

Now he felt all that his mother had been thinking of as they walked along the street together a little while ago. He watched his mother, and he never spoke, but at that moment his youth seemed to be over; he knew all the years of her life by the way her hand trembled as she raised the cup to her lips. It seemed to him that this was the first time he had ever looked upon his mother.

Morley Callaghan,
All the Years of Her Life

distress from their own. If, for example, one child hurts its finger, another baby might put its own finger into its mouth as if she were feeling pain. Researchers report cases in which children who see their parents in tears wipe their own eyes, even though they are not crying.

Although infants and toddlers may have a basic capacity to empathize, studies with twins suggest that the degree to which we are born with the ability to sense how others are feeling seems to vary according to genetic factors.[35] Although some people may have an inborn edge, environmental experiences are the key to developing the ability to understand others. Specifically, the way in which parents communicate with their children seems to affect their ability to understand others' emotional states.[36] When parents point out to children the distress that others feel from their misbehaviour ("Look how sad Jessica is because you took her toy. Wouldn't you be sad if someone took away your toys?"), those children gain a greater appreciation that their acts have emotional consequences than when parents simply label behaviour as inappropriate ("That was a mean thing to do!").

It is easy to confuse empathy with **sympathy,** but the concepts are different in two important ways. First, sympathy means you feel compassion *for* another person's predicament, whereas empathy means you have a personal sense of what that predicament is like. Consider the difference between sympathizing with a pregnant teen or a homeless person and empathizing with them–imagining what it would be like to be in their position. When you sympathize, it is the

Empathy and Analogy

http://cogsci.uwaterloo.ca/ Articles/Pages/Empathy.html

Sibling Rivalry: A New Perspective

Empathizing with another person can be extremely difficult, especially when the other occupies a very different position. Authors Adele Faber and Elaine Mazlish help mothers find a way to understand how the arrival of a new brother or sister might seem to a preschool child.

Imagine that your spouse puts an arm around you and says, "Honey, I love you so much, and you're so wonderful that I've decided to have another wife just like you."

When the new wife finally arrives, you see that she's very young and kind of cute. When the three of you are out together, people say hello to you politely, but exclaim ecstatically over the newcomer. "Isn't she adorable! Hello, sweetheart . . . You are precious!" Then they turn to you and ask, "How do you like the new wife?"

The new wife needs clothing. Your husband goes into your closet, takes some of your sweaters and pants and gives them to her. When you protest, he points out that since you've put on a little weight, your clothes are too tight on you, and they'll fit her perfectly.

The new wife is maturing rapidly. Every day she seems smarter and more competent. One afternoon as you're struggling to figure out the directions on the new computer . . . she bursts into the room and says, "Oooh, can I use it? I know how."

When you tell her she can't use it, she runs crying to your husband. Moments later she returns with him. Her face is tear-stained, and he has his arm around her. He says to you, "What would be the harm in letting her have a turn? Why can't you share?"

One day you find your husband and the new wife lying on the bed together. He's tickling her, and she's giggling. Suddenly the phone rings, and he answers it. Afterwards he tells you that something important has come up, and he must leave immediately. He asks you to stay home with the new wife and make sure she's all right.

Adele Faber and Elaine Mazlish,
Siblings without Rivalry

120

Ethical Challenge

Empathy and the Golden Rule

Virtually everyone is familiar with the Golden Rule, which most of us learned in the form "Do unto others as you would have them do unto you." By obliging us to treat others as well as we would treat ourselves, this maxim seems to offer the foundation for a civil society in which everyone would behave with consideration.

Some ethicists have pointed out that the Golden Rule doesn't work well in situations where others don't want to be treated the same way you would. You may like to play heavy metal rock and roll at 3 A.M., but appeals to the Golden Rule probably won't placate your neighbours who don't share your musical tastes or late-night hours. Likewise, just because you enjoy teasing banter, you aren't entitled to joke with others who might find this type of humour offensive or hurtful. You may be infatuated with a potential lover who doesn't want to reciprocate your affections, but following the Golden Rule might lead to a restraining order against you.

The Golden Rule presents special problems in cases of intercultural contacts, where norms for what is desirable vary dramatically. For example, most speakers from low-context cultures where English is the first language value honesty and explicit communication, but this level of candour would be offensive in high-context cultures of Asia or the Middle East. A naive communicator following the Golden Rule might justify social blunders by claiming "I was just communicating the way I'd like to be treated." This sort of ethnocentrism is a recipe for unsuccessful communication, and perhaps very unpleasant consequences.

In response to the challenge of differing wants, Milton Bennett proposed a "Platinum Rule": "Do unto others as they themselves would have done unto them." Unlike the Golden Rule, this approach requires us to understand how others think and what they want before we can determine how to act ethically. Put differently, the Platinum Rule implies that empathy is a prerequisite for moral sensitivity.

Despite its initial appeal, the Platinum Rule poses its own problems. There are certainly cases where doing for others what they want might compromise our own needs, or even our ethical principles. It is easy to imagine cases in which the Platinum Rule would oblige us to cheat, steal, or lie on others' behalf.

Even if *acting* on the Platinum Rule is problematic, the benefit of *thinking* about it seems clear. An essential requirement for benign behaviour is the ability to empathize, helping us recognize that what others want may be different than what we would want under the same circumstances.

Describe how applying the Golden Rule and the Platinum Rule would affect one of your important interpersonal relationships. What communication is necessary before you could put each rule into practice? Which rule seems to be preferable?

For a discussion of the Golden and Platinum rules, see M. Bennett, "Overcoming the Golden Rule: Sympathy and Empathy," in *Communication Yearbook 3,* D. Nimmo, ed. (New Brunswick, NJ: Transaction Books, 1979), pp. 407–422; and J.A. Jaksa and M.S. Pritchard, *Communication Ethics: Methods of Analysis,* 2nd ed. (Belmont, CA: Wadsworth, 1994), pp. 101–105.

other's confusion, joy, or pain. When you empathize, the experience becomes your own, at least for the moment.

Empathy is different from sympathy in a second way. We sympathize only when we accept the reasons for another's pain as valid, whereas it's possible to empathize without feeling sympathy. You can empathize with a difficult relative, a rude stranger, or even a criminal without feeling much sympathy for them. Empathizing allows you to understand another person's motives without requiring you to agree with them. After empathizing you will almost certainly understand them better, but sympathy won't always follow.

It was six men of Indostan
    To learning much inclined,
Who went to see the elephant
    Though all of them were blind
That each by observation
    Might satisfy his mind.

The first approached the elephant
    And, happening to fall
Against the broad and sturdy side,
    At once began to bawl:
"Why, bless me! But the elephant
    Is very much like a wall!"

The second, feeling of the tusk,
    Cried: "Ho! What have we here
So very round and smooth and sharp?
    To me, 'tis very clear,
This wonder of an elephant
    Is very like a spear!"

The third approached the animal,
    And, happening to take
The squirming trunk within his hands
    Thus boldly up he spake:
"I see," quoth he, "the elephant
    Is very like a snake!"

The fourth reached out his eager hand
    And felt about the knee:
"What most this wondrous beast is like
    Is very plain," quoth he:
"'Tis clear enough the elephant
    Is very like a tree!"

The fifth who chanced to touch the ear
    Said: "E'en the blindest man

Can tell what this resembles most—
    Deny the fact who can:
This marvel of an elephant
    Is very like a fan!"

The sixth no sooner had begun
    About the beast to grope
Than, seizing on the swinging tail
    That fell within his scope,
"I see," quoth he, "the elephant
    Is very like a rope!"

And so these men of Indostan
    Disputed loud and long,
Each in his own opinion
    Exceeding stiff and strong;
Though each was partly in the right,
    And all were in the wrong.

John G. Saxe

Neither sympathy nor empathy is identical to the "I know how you feel" type of response that some people offer when faced with another's expression of emotion. Hearing someone else's account—of falling in love or losing a job, for example—might remind you of a similar experience, but it is highly unlikely that your experience matched hers. Furthermore, an "I know how you feel" response can be interpreted as a conversational "take away" in which you disregard the other person's story and begin telling yours. Chapter 7 offers more warnings about the perils of this type of apparent support.

No consistent evidence suggests the ability to empathize is better for one sex or the other.[37] Some people, however, seem to have a hereditary capacity for greater empathizing than do others.[38] Studies of identical and fraternal twins indicate that identical female twins are more similar to one another in their ability to empathize than are fraternal twins. Interestingly, there seems to be no difference between males. Although empathy may have a biological basis, the role of environment can still play an important role. For example, parents who are sensitive to their children's feelings tend to have children who also reach out to others.[39]

Total empathy is impossible to achieve. Completely understanding another person's point of view is simply too difficult a task for humans with different backgrounds and limited communication skills. Nonetheless, it is possible to get a strong sense of what the world looks like through another person's eyes.[40] The following method will help you become more empathic.

The "Pillow Method": A Tool for Building Empathy

Perception checking is a relatively quick, easy tool for clarifying potential misunderstandings. But some issues are too complex and serious to be handled with this approach. Writer Paul Reps describes a tool for boosting empathy when it seems impossible to find merit in another's position.[41]

Developed by a group of Japanese schoolchildren, the **pillow method** gets its name from the fact that a problem has four sides and a middle, just like a pillow (see Figure 3–5). As the examples on pages 123–127 show, viewing the issue from each of these perspectives almost always leads to valuable insights.

POSITION 1: I'M RIGHT, YOU'RE WRONG   This is the perspective we usually take when viewing an issue. We immediately see the virtues in our position and find fault with anyone who happens to disagree with us. Detailing this position takes little effort and provides little new information.

POSITION 2: YOU'RE RIGHT, I'M WRONG   At this point you switch perspectives and build the strongest possible arguments to explain how another person can view the issue differently from you. Besides

There are three sides to every argument. Yours. The other guy's. And the right side.

Mordecai Richler,
Son of a Smaller Hero

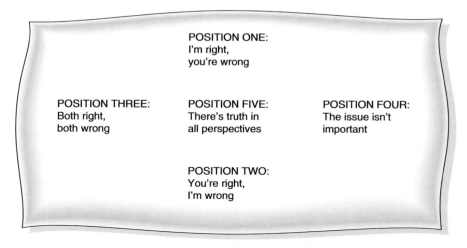

FIGURE 3–5
The Pillow Method

identifying the strengths in the other's position, this is the time to
play the devil's advocate and find flaws in yours.

Finding fault with your viewpoint and trying to support the other's
position require discipline and a certain amount of courage, even
though this is only an exercise and you will soon be able to retreat to
position 1 if you choose. But most people learn that switching perspectives shows that there is some merit to the other person's side of
the controversy.

There are some issues where it seems impossible to call the other
position "right." Criminal behaviour, deceit, and disloyalty often
seem beyond justification. At times like these it is possible to arrive
at position 2 by realizing that the other person's behaviour is understandable. For example, without approving you may be able to understand how someone would resort to violence, tell lies, or cheat.
Whatever the particulars, the goal of position 2 is to find some way of
comprehending how anyone could behave in a way that you originally found impossible to defend.

POSITION 3: BOTH RIGHT, BOTH WRONG   From this position you acknowledge the strengths and weaknesses of each person's arguments. If
you have done a good job with position 2, it should be clear that
there is some merit in both points of view and that each side has its
flaws. Taking a more evenhanded look at the issue can lead you to
be less critical and more understanding of another's point of view.

Position 3 can also help you find the commonalities between your
position and the other's. Perhaps you've both been right to care so
much about the issue, but both wrong in failing to recognize the
other person's concerns. Perhaps there are underlying values that you
both share and similar mistakes that you've both made. In any case,
the perspective of position 3 should help you see that the issue isn't as
much a matter of complete right and wrong as it first appeared to be.

POSITION 4: THE ISSUE ISN'T AS IMPORTANT AS IT SEEMS   This perspective will help you realize that the controversy isn't as critical as you thought. Although it is hard to think of some issues as unimportant, a little thought will show that most concerns aren't as vital as we make them out to be. The impact of even the most traumatic events—the

Communication Transcript

The Pillow Method in Action

Background

Who would have thought planning a wedding would be such a nightmare? My fiancé and I are struggling to decide whether we should have a large, festive wedding or a small, intimate one. I'm in favour of having a big, expensive ceremony and party. He wants a smaller, more affordable one.

Position 1: I'm right and he is wrong.

I have a big family, and I would feel guilty not inviting everyone. Also, we have lots of friends who would really miss not being present to celebrate our special day. If we invite one friend or relative, I say we have to invite them all to avoid hurting anybody's feelings. Otherwise, where do you draw the line? As far as money goes, I say that you get married only once, and this is no time to scrimp. My parents are willing to help pay the expenses because they want our entire family to be there at the wedding.

Position 2: He's right and I'm wrong.

My fiancé is right to say that we really don't have the funds to spend on a fancy

wedding. Every dollar we spend on a lavish event will be one less dollar we have to buy a house, which we hope to do soon. My boyfriend is right to say that a big wedding could postpone our house purchase for a year or two—maybe even longer, if real estate prices go up before we can buy. He's also right to say that no matter how many people we invite, someone is always going to be left out. It's just a case of where we draw the line. Finally, he's right to say that planning a big wedding will be a very stressful process.

Position 3: Both of us are right and both are wrong.

Both of us are right and both are wrong. I'm right to want to include our extended families and friends on this joyous day, and I'm right to say that a special wedding would be a lifetime memory. He's right that doing so could still leave some hurt feelings and that it will postpone our house purchase. He also has a good point when he says that planning a big event could drive us crazy and distract us from the real importance of joining our lives.

Position 4: The issue isn't important.

After thinking about it, I've realized that *getting* married is different from *being* married. The decision about what kind of ceremony to have is important, but ultimately it won't affect the kind of marriage we have. How we behave *after* we're married will be much more important. And we are going to face a lot of decisions together—about children and jobs, for example—that will have much bigger consequences than this ceremony.

Conclusion

Before using the pillow method to think through all sides of this issue, I was focussed on getting my way. This attitude was creating some feelings between my fiancé and I that were not what we should be having as we faced this most important event. I've realized that if one or the other of us "wins" but the result is injured feelings, it won't be much of a victory. I don't know what kind of ceremony we will finally decide to have, but I'm determined to keep my focus on the really important goal of keeping our relationship positive and respectful.

The test of a first-rate intelligence is the ability to hold two opposed ideas in mind at the same time and still retain the ability to function.

F. Scott Fitzgerald

death of a loved one or the breakup of a relationship, for example–usually fades over time. The effects may not disappear, but we learn to accept them and get on with life. The importance of a dispute can also fade when you realize you've let it overshadow other equally important parts of your relationship. It's easy to become so wrapped up over a dispute about one subject that you forget about the other ways in which you are close to the person.

CONCLUSION: THERE IS TRUTH IN ALL FOUR PERSPECTIVES After completing the first four positions, a final step is to recognize that each of them has some merit. Although logic might suggest that it's im-

---

SKILL BUILDER

PILLOW TALK

Try using the pillow method in your life. It isn't easy, but once you begin to understand it, the pay-off in increased understanding is great.

1. Choose a person or viewpoint with whom or which you strongly disagree. If you've chosen a person, it's best to have him or her there with you; but if that's not possible, you can do it alone.

2. What disagreement should you choose? No doubt there are many in your life:

   parent–child

   teacher–student

   employer–employee

   brother–sister

   friend–friend

   Reformer–NDPer

3. For each problem you choose, really place yourself in each position on the pillow as you encounter it:
   a. Your position is correct, and your opponent's is wrong.
   b. Your opponent's position is correct, and yours is wrong.
   c. Both your positions are correct, and both are wrong.
   d. It isn't important which side is right or wrong.
   e. Finally, affirm the fact that there is truth in all four positions.

4. The more important the problem is to you, the harder it will be to accept positions 2 through 5 as valid. But the exercise will work only if you can suspend your present position and imagine how it would feel to hold the other ones.

5. How can you tell if you've been successful with the pillow method? The answer is simple: If after going over all the steps you can understand–not necessarily accept but just understand–the other person's position, you've done it. After you've reached this understanding, do you notice any change in how you feel about the other person?

possible for a position to be both right and wrong, both important and unimportant, your own experience will show that there is some truth in each of the positions you have explored. This fifth position is very different from the "I'm right and you're wrong" attitude that most people bring to an issue. Once you have looked at an issue from these five perspectives, it is almost certain that you will gain new insights. These insights may not cause you to change your mind, or even solve the problem at hand. Nonetheless, the new understanding can increase your tolerance for the other person's position and thus improve the communication climate.

SUMMARY

There is more to the world "out there" than any person is capable of understanding. We make sense of our environment by the three-step process of selecting certain stimuli from the environment, organizing them into meaningful patterns, and interpreting them in a manner that is shaped by past experience, assumptions about human behaviour, expectations, knowledge, and personal moods.

A number of factors affect the way we select, organize, and interpret information. Physiological influences, such as the five senses, age, and health, play an important role. Cultural background also shapes the way we view the world, as do social roles and self-concept. Finally, communicators often construct shared narratives that create a common set of perceptions about themselves and others. In addition to these factors, we commonly make a number of perceptual errors when attributing meaning to others' behaviour.

Perception checking can be a useful tool for verifying interpretations of others' behaviour instead of assuming that the first hunch is correct. A complete perception check includes a description of the other's behaviour, at least two plausible interpretations of its meaning, and a request for clarification about what the behaviour does signify.

Empathy is the ability to experience another person's point of view. Empathy differs from sympathy because it more closely matches the other's experience and because it does not necessarily require agreement or pity. One means for boosting empathy is the pillow method, which involves viewing an issue from five different perspectives.

KEY TERMS

androgynous
attribution
empathy
interaction constructs
interpretation
membership constructs
narrative

organization
perception checking
perceptual schemata
physical constructs
pillow method
psychological constructs

punctuation
role constructs
selection
self-serving bias
stereotyping
sympathy

Emotions: Thinking, Feeling, and Acting

Ideas often last but a day;
feelings, dreams almost forever.

Gabrielle Roy, novelist

t's impossible to talk about communication without acknowledging the importance of emotions. Think about it: Feeling confident can make the difference between success and failure in everything from giving a speech to asking for a date, whereas insecurity can ruin your chances. Being angry or defensive can spoil your time with others, whereas feeling and acting calm will help prevent or solve problems. The way you share or withhold your feelings of affection can affect the future of your relationships. On and on the list of feelings goes: appreciation, loneliness, joy, insecurity, curiosity, irritation. The point is clear: Communication shapes our feelings, and feelings influence our communication.

The role of emotions in human affairs is apparent to social scientists and lay people alike. When psychologist Robert Sternberg asked people to describe an "intelligent person," one of the skills listed was the ability to understand and get along with others.[1] This ability to get along was characterized by psychologist Daniel Goleman as one aspect of "emotional intelligence."[2] Goleman makes the claim that intellectual ability is not the only way to measure one's talents and that success in the world depends in great part on the ability to understand and manage one's own emotions and be sensitive to others' feelings.

Because emotions are so important, we'll spend this chapter answering the following questions: Just what are feelings, and how can we recognize them? How are feelings caused, and how can we control them, increasing the constructive ones and decreasing ones that are less productive? When and how can we best share our feelings with others?

WHAT ARE EMOTIONS?

Suppose an extraterrestrial visitor asked you to explain emotions. How would you answer? You might start by saying that emotions are things that we feel. But this doesn't say much, for in turn you would probably describe feelings as synonymous with emotions. Social scientists generally agree that there are several components to the phenomena we label as feelings.

Physiological Changes

When a person has strong emotions, many bodily changes occur. For example, the physical components of fear include an increased heartbeat, a rise in blood pressure, an increase in adrenaline secretions, an elevated blood sugar level, a slowing of digestion, and a dilation of pupils. Some of these changes are recognizable to the person having them. These sensations are termed *proprioceptive stimuli,* meaning that they are activated by the movement of internal tissues. Proprioceptive messages can offer a significant clue to your emotions once you become aware of them. A churning stomach or tense jaw can be a signal that something is wrong. You can get a sense of your own proprioceptive messages by trying the following exercise.

INVITATION TO INSIGHT

HOW DOES IT FEEL?

Here's a way to learn more about yourself from your body. You can do this exercise with a group or individually outside the classroom. If you do it alone, read all the steps ahead of time so that you can work through the whole experience without interrupting yourself. However, the exercise will have more impact if you do it for the first time in a group because in this way your facilitator can read the instructions for you. Also, in a group your feelings can be shared and compared. The ellipses (. . .) in the instructions indicate points where you should pause for a moment and examine what you're feeling.

1. Wherever you are, find yourself a comfortable position, either lying or sitting. You'll need to find a quiet place with no distractions. You'll find that the exercise works better if you dim the lights.

2. Close your eyes. The visual sense is so dominant that it's easy to neglect your other senses.

3. Now that your eyes are closed and you're comfortable, take a trip through your body and visit its various parts. As you focus on each part, don't try to change what you find . . . just notice how you are, how you feel.

4. Now let's begin. Start with your feet. How do they feel? Are they comfortable, or do they hurt? Are your toes cold? Do your shoes fit well, or are they too tight?

Now move your attention to your legs. . . . Is there any tension in them, or are they relaxed? . . . Can you feel each muscle? . . . Are your legs crossed? Is there pressure where one presses against the other? . . . Are they comfortable?

Now pay attention to your hips and pelvis . . . the area where your legs and backbone join. Do you feel comfortable here, or are you not as relaxed as you'd like to be? If you're seated, direct your attention to your buttocks. . . . Can you feel your body's weight pressing against the surface you're sitting on?

Now move on to the trunk of your body. How does your abdomen feel? . . . What are the sensations you can detect there? . . . Is anything moving? . . . Focus on your breathing . . . .Do you breathe off the top of your lungs, or are you taking deep, relaxed breaths? . . . Does the air move in and out through your nose or your mouth? Is your chest tight, or is it comfortable?

Checking your breathing has probably led you to your throat and neck. Is your throat comfortable, or do you feel a lump there you need to keep swallowing? . . . How about your neck? . . . Can you feel it holding your head in its present position? . . . Perhaps moving your head

continued

INVITATION TO INSIGHT—Continued

slowly from side to side will help you feel these muscles doing their work. . . . Is there tension in your neck or shoulders?

Now let's move to your face. . . . What expression are you wearing? . . . Are the muscles of your face tense or relaxed? Which ones? Your mouth . . . brow . . . jaw . . . temples? Take a few moments and see. . . .

Finally, go inside your head and see what's happening there. . . . Is it quiet and dark, or are things happening there? . . . What are they? Does it feel good inside your head, or is there some pressure or aching? . . .

You've made a trip from bottom to top. Try feeling your whole body now. . . . See what new awareness of it you've gained. . . . Are there any special parts of your body that attract your attention now? . . . What are they telling you?

Now there's another very important part of your body to focus on. It's the part of you where you *feel* when you're happy or sad or afraid. Take a moment and find that spot. . . . See how you are now in there. . . . See what happens when you ask yourself, "How am I now? How do I feel?" . . . See what happens in that place when you think of a personal problem that's been bothering you lately. . . . Be sure it's something that's important to your life now. . . . Now see if you can get the feel of this problem there in the place where you feel things. . . . Let yourself feel all of it. . . . If the feeling changes as you focus on it, that's OK. Just stay with the feeling wherever it goes and see how it is. . . . If what you feel now makes a difference to you, see what that difference is. . . . Now, take a few minutes to use it in whatever way you like, and then slowly open your eyes.

5. Now think about the following questions. If you're with a group, you may want to discuss them there.
    a. Did you find out things about your body that you hadn't noticed before? Did you discover some tensions that you'd been carrying around? How long do you think you've been this way? Did recognizing them make any difference to you?
    b. Could you find the part of yourself where you usually feel things? Where was it? Or are there different spots for different feelings? Did focussing on your problem make some kind of difference to you?

Nonverbal Reactions

Not all physical changes that accompany emotions are internal. Feelings are often apparent by observable changes. Some of these changes involve a person's appearance: blushing, sweating, and so on. Other changes involve behaviour: a distinctive facial expression, posture, or gesture; or modification in vocal tone, rate, and so on.

Although it's reasonably easy to tell when someone is feeling a strong emotion, it's more difficult to be certain exactly what that emotion might be. A slumped posture could signify sadness or fatigue. Likewise, trembling hands might indicate excitement or fear.

As you'll learn in Chapter 6, nonverbal behaviour is usually ambiguous; and it's dangerous to assume that it can be "read" with much accuracy.

Although we usually think of nonverbal behaviour as the reaction to an emotional state, there may be times when the reverse is true—when nonverbal behaviour actually causes emotions. Research by Paul Ekman uncovered instances when experimental subjects were able to create various emotional states by altering their facial expressions.[5] When volunteers were coached to move their facial muscles in ways that appeared afraid, angry, disgusted, amused, sad, surprised, and contemptuous, the subjects' bodies responded as if they were having these feelings. Interestingly, the link between smiling and happiness was not as strong because, Ekman speculates, smiles can reflect so many different emotions: happiness, anger, sadness, humour, and so on.

Cognitive Interpretations

Although there may be cases in which there is a direct connection between physical behaviour and emotional states, in most situations

"What the hell was that? Something just swept over me—
like contentment or something."

Drawing by Weber © 1981 *The New Yorker Magazine, Inc.*

the mind plays an important role in determining how we feel. On page 130 you read that physiological components of fear include a racing heart, perspiration, muscle tension, and elevated blood pressure. Interestingly enough, these symptoms are similar to the physical changes that accompany excitement, joy, and other emotions. In other words, if we were to measure the physical condition of someone having a strong emotion, we would have a hard time knowing whether that person was trembling with fear or quivering with excitement. The recognition that the bodily components of most emotions are similar led some psychologists to conclude that the experience of fright, joy, or anger comes primarily from the *label* we give to the same physical symptoms at a given time.[4] Psychologist Philip Zimbardo offers a good example of this principle:

> I notice I'm perspiring while lecturing. From that I infer I am nervous. If it occurs often, I might even label myself a "nervous person." Once I have the label, the next question I must answer is "Why am I nervous?" Then I start to search for an appropriate explanation. I might notice some students leaving the room, or being inattentive. I am nervous because I'm not giving a good lecture. That makes me nervous. How do I know it's not good? Because I'm boring my audience. I am nervous because I am a boring lecturer and I want to be a good lecturer. I feel inadequate. Maybe I should open a delicatessen instead. Just then a student says, "It's hot in here, I'm perspiring and it makes it tough to concentrate on your lecture." Instantly, I'm no longer "nervous" or "boring."[5]

In his book *Shyness,* Zimbardo discusses the consequences of making inaccurate or exaggerated attributions. In a survey of more than 5,000 subjects, over 80 percent described themselves as having been shy at some time in their lives, whereas more than 40 percent considered themselves presently shy. Most significantly, those who labelled themselves "not shy" behaved in virtually the *same way* as their shy counterparts. They would blush, perspire, and feel their hearts pounding in certain social situations. The biggest difference between the two groups seemed to be the label with which they described themselves.[6] This is a significant difference. Someone who notices the symptoms we've described and thinks, "I'm such a shy person!" will most likely feel more uncomfortable and communicate less effectively than another person with the same symptoms who thinks, "Well, I'm a bit shaky (or excited) here, but that's to be expected."

We'll take a closer look at ways to reduce unpleasant emotions through cognitive processes later in this chapter.

The Shyness Page

http://www.shyness.com

TYPES OF EMOTIONS

So far our discussion has implied that although emotions may differ in tone, they are similar in most other ways. In truth, emotions vary in many respects.

Primary and Mixed Emotions

Emotions are rather like colours: Some are simple, whereas others are blends. Robert Plutchik's "emotion wheel" (see Figure 4–1) illustrates the difference.[7] For example, jealousy can be viewed as a combination of several different emotions: distress, anger, disgust, contempt, fear, and even shame.[8] Likewise, loneliness can include feelings of anger toward self and others, estrangement, and depression.[9] Plutchik has identified eight **primary emotions,** which are inside the perimeter of the wheel. He suggests that these primary feelings can combine to form other, **mixed emotions,** some of which are listed outside the circle.

Whether or not you agree with the specific emotions Plutchik identifies as primary and secondary, the wheel suggests that many feelings need to be described in more than a single term. To understand why, consider the following examples. For each one, ask yourself two questions: How would I feel? What feelings might I express?

> An out-of-town friend has promised to arrive at your house at six o'clock. When he hasn't arrived by nine, you are convinced that a terrible accident has occurred. Just as you pick up the phone to call the police and local hospitals, your friend breezes in the door with an offhand remark about getting a late start.

> You and your companion have a fight just before leaving for a party. Deep inside, you know you were mostly to blame, even though you aren't willing to admit it. When you arrive at the party, your companion leaves you to flirt with several other attractive guests.

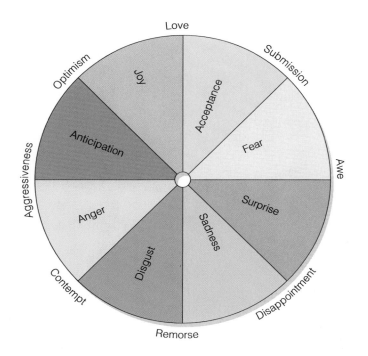

FIGURE 4–1

The Emotion Wheel: Primary and Mixed Emotions

In situations like these you would probably feel mixed emotions. Consider the case of the overdue friend. Your first reaction to his arrival would probably be relief–"Thank goodness, he's safe!" But you would also be likely to feel anger–"Why didn't he phone to tell me he'd be late?" The second example would probably leave you with an even greater number of mixed emotions: guilt at contributing to the fight, hurt and perhaps embarrassment at your friend's flirtations, and anger at this sort of vengefulness.

Despite the commonness of mixed emotions, we often communicate only one feeling . . . usually the most negative one. In both the preceding examples you might show only your anger, leaving the other person with little idea of the full range of your feelings. Consider the different reaction you would get by showing *all* your emotions in these cases, and others.

Intense and Mild Emotions

Another way emotions are like colours is in their intensity. Figure 4–2 illustrates this point clearly.[10] Each vertical slice represents the range of a primary emotion from its mildest to its most intense state.

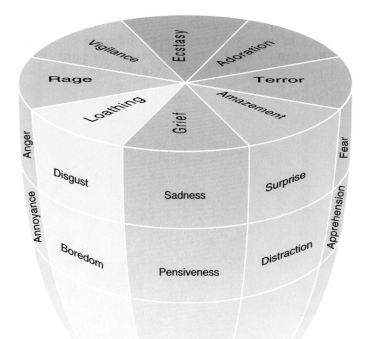

FIGURE 4–2

Intensity of Emotions

This model shows the importance not only of choosing the right emotional family when expressing yourself but also of describing the strength of the feeling. Some people fail to communicate clearly because they understate their emotions, failing to let others know how strongly they feel. To say you're "annoyed" when a friend breaks an important promise, for example, would probably be an understatement. In other cases, people chronically overstate the strength of their feelings. To them, everything is "wonderful" or "terrible." The problem with this sort of exaggeration is that when a truly intense emotion comes along, they have no words left to describe it adequately. If chocolate chip cookies from the local bakery are "fantastic," how does it feel to fall in love?

INFLUENCES ON EMOTIONAL EXPRESSION

Most people rarely express their emotions verbally. People are generally comfortable making statements of fact and often delight in expressing their opinion, but they rarely disclose how they feel. Why is it that people fail to express their feelings? Let's take a look at several reasons.

INVITATION TO INSIGHT

RECOGNIZING YOUR EMOTIONS

Keep a 3-day record of your feelings. You can do this by spending a few minutes each evening recalling what emotions you felt during the day, what other people were involved, and the circumstances in which the emotion occurred.

At the end of the 3-day period you can understand the role emotions play in your communication by answering the following questions:

1. How did you recognize the emotions you felt: through proprioceptive stimuli, nonverbal behaviours, or cognitive processes?

2. Did you have any difficulty deciding which emotion you were feeling?

3. What emotions do you feel most often? Are they primary or mixed? Mild or intense?

4. In what circumstances do you or don't you express your feelings? What factors influence your decision to show or not show your feelings? The type of emotion? The person or persons involved? The situation (time, place)? The subject that the emotion involves (money, sex, and so on)?

5. What are the consequences of the type of communicating you just described in step 4? Are you satisfied with these consequences? If not, what can you do to become more satisfied?

Culture

Over 100 years of research has confirmed the fact that certain basic emotions are experienced by people around the world.[11] No matter where a person is born and regardless of his or her background, the ability to feel happiness, sadness, surprise, anger, disgust, and fear seems to be universal. People from all cultures also express these emotions in the same way, at least in their facial expressions. A smile or scowl, for example, is understood everywhere.

Of course, this doesn't mean that the same events generate an emotion in all cultures. The notion of eating snails might bring a smile of delight to some residents of Québec, though it would cause many Canadians to grimace in disgust.

Differences also exist in the degree to which people in various cultures display their feelings. For example, social scientists have found support for the notion that people from warmer climates are more emotionally expressive than those who live in cooler places.[12] Over 2,900 respondents representing 26 nationalities reported that people from the southern part of their countries were more emotionally expressive than northerners.

One of the most significant factors that influences emotional expression is the position of a culture on the individualism–collectivism spectrum. Members of collectivistic cultures (such as Japan and India) prize harmony among members of their "ingroup" and discourage expression of any negative emotions that might upset relationships among people who belong to it. By contrast, members of highly individualistic cultures like Canada and the United States feel comfortable revealing their feelings to people with whom they are close.[13] Individualists and collectivists also handle emotional expression with members of outgroups differently: Whereas collectivists are quite frank about expressing negative emotions toward outsiders, individualists are more likely to hide such emotions as dislike.[14] It's easy to see how differences in display rules can lead to communication problems. For example, individualistic North Americans might view collectivistic Asians as less than candid, whereas a person raised in Asia could easily regard North Americans as overly demonstrative.

Cultural background influences the way we interpret others' emotions as well as the way we express our own. In one experiment, an ethnically varied group of students—Caucasian, Black, Asian, and Hispanic—identified the type, intensity, and appropriateness of emotional expression in 56 photos representing eight social situations (e.g., alone, with a friend, in public, with someone of higher status).[15] Results indicated that ethnicity led to considerable

Looking at Diversity

Out of the Depths

During the 1930s, 1940s, 1950s, and into the 1960s, Native children across Canada attended Indian Residential Schools. To this day, their emotional responses to the experience affect many aspects of their lives. In the reading below, "Out of the Depths," from the book of the same title, author Isabelle Knockwood provides some insight into life in a residential school.

Every one of the students who attended the Indian Residential School in Shubenacadie during the nearly 40 years it was open has their own story to tell. Some say, "Thank God for the Residential School" and that they learned valuable skills such as how to speak English, how to keep themselves and their homes clean, and how to sew and cook, and especially how to pray. Some of these people deny there were any beatings, while others say that the beatings were deserved and justified. Among this group were children who were "good" themselves or else had bigger sisters and brothers to look after them. Others were priests' and nuns' pets and favourites who were used as spies. Some looked on the school as a refuge from homes where they were abused, frequently by parents who had themselves attended the school and learned physical punishment as a method of child-rearing.

On the other hand many former students say that the Residential School was a terrible childhood experience and tell shocking stories of what happened to them there. Yet they all seem to make an effort to understand what motivated the priests and nuns who ran the school. "I've tried to understand why the priests and nuns acted the way they did toward us and I can't justify any of the beatings no matter how much

I try," a former student, who is now a grandmother, told me.

Nearly everyone had many difficulties when they left the school finding an identity and a place in the world. Some went home to the reserves after being discharged from the school only to find out that they didn't fit in, and when they tried to point out the social ills at home were told, "You don't belong here. Go back to where you came from." Even those of us who had parents who welcomed us home were suspended in limbo because we could no longer speak Mi'kmaw.

Despite school years where religion was practised as brutal compulsion, some former students still persist in endless churchgoing and expect God to come and solve everything. Others have become addicted to gambling in the false hope of becoming rich. Many others are staying home, collecting welfare instead of earning wages, because there are no jobs on the reserves. We have too many who are living in perpetual bliss under the influence of drugs and alcohol, thus becoming numb to the real problems and their practical solutions. However, others have claimed as adults the education they were denied as children. One person who has started on this path told me her reason for this: "The same treatment I suffered at the Resi will never again be inflicted on Native people."

These people include counsellors like Nora Bernard, who have examined their lives and traced patterns which developed in childhood. Nora realized that her alcoholism began with drinking altar wine while she was a teenager at the school serving as an altar girl. She is now a counsellor for the Native Alcohol and Drug Addiction Center. She says, "I had to experience all this in order to do the work that I have chosen."

Several former students have told me that one of the school's most devastating effects on their lives is that it instilled a fear of touching or of being physically close to other people. When Georgina Denny went to live at Eskasoni after spending her entire childhood at the school, she says that she was "fascinated" by the way people would show physical affection, "Everybody else seemed like they were so loving—holding and touching—I couldn't even have anyone sit next to me close." Another woman I talked to traced back her fear of touching to an incident at the school and the lessons instilled there:

> When I crawled in my sister's bed during a thunderstorm to keep warm, the Sister came along checking the beds and found me and my sister. I was cuddled up next to my sister and she said that we weren't allowed to sleep together because it's not clean to sleep with

someone. They taught us to stay away and not be touching. It's a natural thing to touch someone you love, be it your sister, brother, mother, father. It was pure innocence, real love. And they pushed that away from us and told us that it was dirty . . . Today I have a hard time. I don't want anybody to touch me unless I'm really close to them. I even have a hard time shaking hands. I want to be close to my family, but they're like me, afraid to hug me. The closest thing they ever tell me is, "See you tomorrow."

Her mother had also been a student at the school and she has no recollection of ever being hugged as a child. She speculates that her mother's refusal to touch her children was taught at the school, but she herself has deliberately changed the way she treats her own child. "I broke that cycle of not touching. I hug my daughter and tell her all the time that I love her."

Those who ran the school tried to rob us of our collective identity by punishing us for speaking our language, calling us "savages" and "heathens." They also tried to take away our individual identities. Often the nuns would arbitrarily change a child's name. Margaret Knockwood remembers, "Sister wrote 'Marjorie' on the board and told me, 'Your name is not Margaret. It's Marjorie.' So I was known as Marjorie at school." Another girl named Margaret was also renamed by the nuns. We had all been forced to call Margaret Julian "Peggy O'Neill." She had been so constantly punished at school that I somehow assume that she must have died. But 30 years later I met her. "Oh, Peggy, I thought they had killed you." She replied, "No, almost. But I'm Margaret Julian, remember? It's Johnson now." She had taken back her real name and identity and built another life

on it as a married woman.

Strangely enough, some of the students who were most seriously abused have been able to transform their lives and bring themselves "out of the depths." Wallis LeBillois ran away in 1939 and was hounded down by a police dog. He grew up to become a political activist, spending some of his time helping the National Indian Brotherhood, now the Assembly of First Nations (AFN), develop its policy on Native education, and eventually become elder-in-residence for the AFN.

Others have claimed their own identity and the meaning of their lives through the rediscovery of Native spiritual traditions. Despite the efforts of those who ran the school to instill hatred and contempt for Native traditions and culture, many of us have returned to a traditional path as the source of our strength. One man I interviewed joked that he now describes himself as "a born-again savage." Some of us have come to realize that we were abused not only physically but spiritually. For us, the Native Way with its Sacred Circle and respect for all living things is a means of healing that abuse.

The Talking Stick has come full circle. When Sister Mary Leonard told us that the Catholic Church believed in the saying, "Give me a child before the age of seven, and I will show you the adult," she was speaking a larger truth than she knew. Many years will have to pass before the damage inflicted by the residential school can be healed. I am still dealing with the mentally, emotionally, and spiritually damaged child of 5. It makes me angry that the people who almost destroyed me got away with it because they grew old and died before I could confront them. My

anger led to frustration because there is nothing I could do to even things up. I cannot confront those who lied to me about myself and about my people and withheld knowledge from me which could have allowed me to live up to my fullest potential. It made no real difference that government officials and some representatives of the Catholic Church apologized to Native people for the schools. Those individuals who directly caused our suffering never admitted their wrongdoing and were never called to account for their actions.

My path has taken many twists and turns which eventually led to the writing of this book. Long before I began writing it, Sulian Herney, my mentor at Mi'kmaw Lodge, had counselled me by saying, "Isabelle the adult has to go back into that school and find Isabelle the child, and take her by the hand and get her out of there." I have done that, and I find myself in a safer place where people are willing to listen, which is the first step of the healing process.

There is one story which I have not fully told till now. Two days before the derelict school burned down, when I went there with my daughter and granddaughter, they went ahead of me up the steps and stopped suddenly. They had heard a voice from behind the half-open door whisper, "Come in, you're welcome." My mother, Deodis, had always talked out loud to ghosts or spirits when she felt their presence. "Who's there?" I called out. "Is that you, Father Mackey? Is that you, Sister Superior? Show yourself." There was no answer, but I shouted back. "You got me when I was a child. But I'm here now and you can't have my children and my grandchildren."

I pass the Talking Stick to you.

differences in the way subjects gauged others' emotional states. For example, Blacks perceived the emotions in the photos as more intense than the Caucasian, Asian, and Hispanic respondents; Asians perceived them the least intense. Also, Blacks reported a greater frequency of anger expressions than the other groups. Ethnicity also shaped ideas about appropriate rules for expressing one's own emotions. For example, Caucasians perceived the display of the several emotions as more appropriate than did the other groups; Asians perceived their display as least appropriate. These findings remind us that, in a multicultural society, one element of communicative competence is the ability to understand our own cultural filters when judging others' behaviours.

Gender

Even within our culture, the ways in which men and women express their emotions vary in some significant areas.[16] Research on emotional expression suggests that there is at least some truth in the cultural stereotype of the unexpressive male and the more demonstrative female. As a group, women are more likely than men to express feelings of vulnerability, including fear, sadness, loneliness, and embarrassment. Men rarely express these sentiments, especially to their male friends, although they may open up to the person they love. On the other hand, men are less bashful about revealing their strengths and positive emotions. As Chapter 8 explains, neither stereotypical male nor female notions of emotional expressiveness are superior. Because the styles can be quite different, the challenge communicators face is how to co-ordinate their own style with others whose notions of appropriate emotional expressiveness are different.

Differences between the sexes also exist in the sensitivity to others' emotions. Psychologist Robert Rosenthal and his colleagues developed the Profile of Nonverbal Sensitivity (PONS) test to measure the ability to recognize emotions that are expressed in the facial expressions, movements, and vocal cues of others. Women consistently score slightly higher on this test than men.[17]

Of course, these gender differences are statistical averages, and many men and women don't fit these profiles. Furthermore, gender isn't the *only* variable that affects emotional sensitivity. Another factor is whether the other person is of the same or opposite sex: People generally are better at recognizing emotions of members of the same sex. Familiarity with the other person also leads to greater sensitivity. For example, dating and married couples are significantly better at recognizing each other's emotional cues than are strangers. A third factor is the difference in power between the two parties. People who are less powerful learn—probably from necessity—to read the more powerful person's signals. One experiment revealed that "women's intuition" should be relabelled "subordinate's intuition." In opposite-sex twosomes, the person with less control—regardless of sex—was better at interpreting the leader's nonverbal signals than vice versa.[18]

Experiencing Emotion: Facial Feedback

http://fccjvm.fccj.cc.fl.us/~jwisner/face.html

The Emotional Quotient Factor

http://www.seorf.ohiou.edu/~qf313/Brain/EmotionalQ/eq.htm

Social Conventions

Count the number of genuine emotional expressions you hear over a two- or three-day period and you'll discover that emotional expressions are rare. People are generally comfortable making statements of fact and often delight in expressing their opinions, but they rarely disclose how they feel.

Not surprisingly, the emotions that people *do* share directly are usually positive. Communicators are reluctant to send messages that embarrass or threaten the "face" of others.[19] We therefore strive to suppress these unpleasant emotions in almost every context, including child raising, the workplace, and personal relationships. One study of married couples revealed that the partners shared complimentary feelings ("I love you") or face-saving ones ("I'm sorry I yelled at you"). They also willingly disclosed both positive and negative feelings about absent third parties ("I like Jonathan," "I'm uncomfortable around Sarah"). On the other hand, the husbands and wives rarely verbalized face-threatening feelings ("I'm disappointed in you") or hostility ("I'm mad at you").[20]

Surprisingly, social rules even discourage too much expression of positive feelings.[21] While a hug and kiss for Mother is all right, a young man is more likely to shake hands with Dad. Affection toward friends becomes less and less frequent as we grow older, so

"I've been thinking—it might be good for Andrew if he could see you cry once in a while."

that even a simple statement such as "I like you" is seldom heard between adults. Just because we don't express our feelings toward others verbally doesn't mean we don't communicate them at all. As Chapter 6 explains in detail, a tremendous amount of the information carried via nonverbal communication involves relational messages, including our feelings of affinity (or lack of it) toward others.

Social Roles

Expression of emotions is also shaped by the requirements of many social roles. Salespeople are taught always to smile at customers, no matter how obnoxious they may be. Teachers and managers are expected to behave rationally and keep their emotions under control. Students are rewarded for asking "acceptable" questions and otherwise being submissive creatures.

Emotional Contagion

Cultural rules and social roles aren't the only factors that affect our feelings. Our emotions are also affected by the feelings of those around us through **emotional contagion:** the process by which emotions are transferred from one person to another.

Most of us recognize the degree to which emotions are "infectious." You can almost certainly recall instances in which being around a calm person leaves you feeling more at peace, or when your previously sunny mood was spoiled by contact with a grouch. Researchers have demonstrated that this process occurs quickly, and with very little apparent communication.[22] In one study, two volunteers completed a survey that identified their moods. Then they sat quietly, facing each other for a 2-minute period, ostensibly waiting for the researcher to return to the room. At the end of that time, they completed another emotion-identification survey. Time after time, the brief exposure resulted in the less-expressive partner's moods coming to resemble the feelings of the more-expressive one. If an expressive communicator can shape another person's feelings with so little input in such a short time, it's easy to understand how emotions can be even more "infectious" with more-prolonged contact. As one commentator observed, "We catch feelings from one another as though they were some kind of social virus."[23]

Fear of Self-Disclosure

In a society that discourages the expression of feelings, revealing your emotions can seem risky.[24] For a parent, boss, or teacher whose life has been built on the image of confidence and certainty, it may be frightening to say, "I'm sorry. I was wrong." A person who has made a life's work out of not relying on others has a hard time saying, "I'm lonesome. I want your friendship."

THE UNEXPRESSED

The unexpressed,
    the unarticulated
are frightening,
    when as fragments
they burn
    beneath the skin,
with no way at all
    to be scratched out,
plucked out,
    or brought to reason.

Events
    bricked up inside
cry out in despair:
    "We've been forgotten.
We'll be eliminated
    from history:
Let us out!
    Let us out!
Suffering rises up
    like a lump in the throat:
We are like stifled sobs.
    We long so for our liberation:
express us!
    express us!"

Yevgeny Yevtushenko

Moreover, someone who musters up the courage to share feelings such as these still risks unpleasant consequences. Others might misunderstand: An expression of affection might be construed as a romantic invitation, and a confession of uncertainty might appear to be a sign of weakness. Another risk is that emotional honesty might make others feel uncomfortable. Finally, there's always a chance that emotional honesty could be used against you, either out of cruelty or thoughtlessness. Chapter 8 discusses alternatives to complete disclosure and suggests circumstances when it can be both wise and ethical to keep your feelings to yourself.

GUIDELINES FOR EXPRESSING EMOTIONS

Emotions are a fact of life. Nonetheless, communicating them effectively isn't a simple matter. It's obvious that showing every feeling of boredom, fear, anger, or frustration would get you in trouble. Even the indiscriminate sharing of positive feelings—love, affection, and so on—isn't always wise. On the other hand, withholding emotions can be personally frustrating and can keep relationships from growing and prospering.

The following suggestions can help you decide when and how to express your emotions. Combined with the guidelines for self-disclosure in Chapter 8, they can improve the effectiveness of your emotional expression.

Recognize Your Feelings

Answering the question "How do you feel?" isn't always easy. As you've already read, there are a number of ways in which feelings become recognizable. Physiological changes can be a clear sign of your emotional state. Monitoring nonverbal behaviours is another excellent way to keep in touch with your feelings. You can also recognize your emotions by monitoring your thoughts, as well as the

EMOTIONAL ROLLER COASTER

Leo Cullum © 1998 from The Cartoon Bank. All Rights Reserved.

verbal messages you send to others. It's not far from the verbal statement "I hate this!" to the realization that you're angry (or bored, nervous, or embarrassed).

Think About How to Describe Feelings

Most people suffer from impoverished emotional vocabularies. Ask them how they're feeling and the response will almost always include the same terms: *good* or *bad, terrible* or *great,* and so on. Take a moment now and indicate how you are feeling. Write down as many descriptors as you can. After you've done your best, look at Table 4–1 and see which ones you've missed.

Many communicators think they are expressing feelings when, in fact, their statements are really emotional counterfeit. For example, it sounds emotionally revealing to say, "I feel like going to a show" or "I feel we've been seeing too much of each other." But, in fact, neither of these statements has any emotional content. In the first sentence

TABLE 4–1	SOME FEELINGS				
afraid	concerned	exhausted	hurried	nervous	sexy
aggravated	confident	fearful	hurt	numb	shaky
amazed	confused	fed up	hysterical	optimistic	shocked
ambivalent	content	fidgety	impatient	paranoid	shy
angry	crazy	flattered	impressed	passionate	sorry
annoyed	defeated	foolish	inhibited	peaceful	strong
anxious	defensive	forlorn	insecure	pessimistic	subdued
apathetic	delighted	free	interested	playful	surprised
ashamed	depressed	friendly	intimidated	pleased	suspicious
bashful	detached	frustrated	irritable	possessive	tender
bewildered	devastated	furious	jealous	pressured	tense
bitchy	disappointed	glad	joyful	protective	terrified
bitter	disgusted	glum	lazy	puzzled	tired
bored	disturbed	grateful	lonely	refreshed	trapped
brave	ecstatic	happy	loving	regretful	ugly
calm	edgy	harassed	lukewarm	relieved	uneasy
cantankerous	elated	helpless	mad	resentful	vulnerable
carefree	embarrassed	high	mean	restless	warm
cheerful	empty	hopeful	miserable	ridiculous	weak
cocky	enthusiastic	horrible	mixed up	romantic	wonderful
cold	envious	hostile	mortified	sad	worried
comfortable	excited	humiliated	neglected	sentimental	

the word *feel* really stands for an intention: "I *want* to go to a show." In the second sentence the "feeling" is really a thought: "I *think* we've been seeing too much of each other." You can recognize the absence of emotion in each case by adding a genuine word of feeling to it. For instance, "I'm *bored* and I want to go to a show" or "I think we've been seeing too much of each other and I feel *confined*."

Relying on a small vocabulary of feelings is as limiting as using only a few terms to describe colours. To say that the ocean in all its moods, the sky as it varies from day to day, and the colour of your true love's eyes are all "blue" tells only a fraction of the story. Likewise, it's overly broad to use a term like *good* or *great* to describe how you feel in situations as different as earning a high grade, finishing a marathon, or hearing the words "I love you" from a special person.

There are several ways to express a feeling verbally:

- Through *single words:* "I'm angry" (or "excited," "depressed," "curious," and so on).

- By describing *what's happening to you:* "My stomach is tied in knots," "I'm on top of the world."

- By describing *what you'd like to do:* "I want to run away," "I'd like to give you a hug," "I feel like giving up."

Sometimes communicators inaccurately minimize the strength of their feelings–"I'm a *little* unhappy" or "I'm *pretty* excited" or "I'm *sort* of confused." Of course, not all emotions are strong ones. We do feel degrees of sadness and joy, for example, but some people have a tendency to discount almost every feeling. Do you?

In other cases, communicators express feelings in a coded manner. This happens most often when the sender is uncomfortable about revealing the feeling in question. Some codes are verbal ones, as when the sender hints more or less subtly at the message. For example, an indirect way to say "I'm lonesome" might be "I guess there isn't much happening this weekend, so if you're not busy, why don't you drop by?" Such a message is so indirect that your real feeling may not be recognized. For this reason, people who send coded messages stand less of a chance of having their emotions understood– and their needs met.

If you do decide to express your feelings, you can be most clear by making sure that both you and your partner understand that your feeling is centred on a specific set of circumstances rather than being indicative of the whole relationship. Instead of saying, "I resent you," say, "I resent you when you don't keep your promises." Rather than "I'm bored with you," say "I'm bored when you talk about your money."

Share Multiple Feelings

Many times the feeling you express isn't the only one you're experiencing. For example, you might often express your anger but overlook the confusion, disappointment, frustration, sadness, or embarrassment that preceded it. In the following examples, notice how sharing multiple feelings increases the accuracy—and the value—of the message:

- "I'm mad at you for not showing up. *I'm also disappointed because I was looking forward to seeing you.*"

- "I get mad when you flirt at parties. *I care about you a lot, and I'd hate to think you don't feel the same way about me.*"

- "I get really angry when you tease me in front of our friends. *It's embarrassing to have you point out my flaws, even though I know you don't mean any harm.*"

SKILL BUILDER

FEELINGS AND PHRASES

You can try this exercise alone or with a group.

1. Choose a situation from Column A and a receiver from Column B.

2. Develop an approach for communicating your feelings for this combination.

3 Now create approaches for the same situation with other receivers from Column B. How are the statements different?

4. Repeat the process with various combinations, using other situations from Column A.

Column A: Situation	*Column B: Receivers*
a. You have been stood up for a date or appointment.	**a.** An instructor
b. The other person pokes fun at your schoolwork.	**b.** A family member (you decide which one)
c. The other person compliments you on your appearance, then says, "I hope I haven't embarrassed you."	**c.** A classmate you don't know well
d. The other person gives you a hug and says, "It's good to see you."	**d.** Your best friend

---

Recognize the Difference Between Feeling, Talking, and Acting

Just because you feel a certain way doesn't mean you must always talk about it, and talking about a feeling doesn't require you to act on it. This distinction is important because it can liberate you from the fear that acknowledging and/or expressing a feeling will commit you

Ethical Challenge

ARISTOTLE'S GOLDEN MEAN

Almost two and a half millennia ago, the philosopher Aristotle addressed issues that are just as important today as they were in classical Greece. In his *Nicomachean Ethics*, Aristotle explores the question of "moral virtue": What constitutes good behaviour, and what ways of acting enable us to function effectively in the world? One important part of his examination addresses the management and expression of emotion: what he defines as "passions and actions."

According to Aristotle, an important dimension of virtuous behaviour is moderation, which he defines as "an intermediate between excess and deficit . . . equidistant from the extremes . . . neither too much nor too little." Aristotle introduces the concept of virtue through moderation with a mathematical analogy: If ten is many and two is few, six is the intermediate. Applying this line of reasoning to emotional expression would reveal that, for example, the preferred form of expressing affection would fall equally between the extremes of being completely unexpressive and passionately effusive.

Aristotle points out that a formulaic approach to calculating the "Golden Mean" doesn't work in human affairs by illustrating the flaws in his earlier mathematical analogy: "If ten pounds are too much for a particular person to eat and two too little, it does not follow that the trainer will order six pounds, for this also is perhaps too much for the person who is to take it." In other words, Aristotle recognizes that people have different personalities; and he acknowledges that it isn't realistic or desirable for a passionate person to strive for the same type of behaviour as someone with a low-key temperament. After all, a world in which everyone felt and acted identically would be boring.

Instead of a "one type fits all" approach to emotional expression, Aristotle urges communicators to moderate their own style, to be "intermediate not in the object, but relative to us." Following Aristotle's injunction, a person with a hot temper would strive to cool down, while a person who rarely expresses his or her feelings ought to aim at becoming more expressive. The result would still be two people with different styles, but each of whom behaved better than before seeking the Golden Mean.

According to Aristotle, moderation also means that emotions should be suited to the occasion: We should feel (and express) them "at the right times, with reference to the right objects, towards the right people, with the right motive, and in the right way." We can imagine times when even a restrained person could reasonably act with anger, and times when a normally voluble person would appropriately behave with restraint. Even then, too much emotion (rage, for example) or too little falls outside the range of virtue. In Aristotle's words, when it comes to "passions and actions . . . excess is a form of failure and so is deficit."

Aristotle acknowledges that living a life of moderation is a challenge: "It is no easy task to find the middle. . . . Anyone can get angry: That is easy . . . but to do this to the right person, to the right extent, at the right time, with the right motive, and in the right way: That is not for everyone, nor is it easy." He warns us to especially guard against those extreme emotions that come most naturally. "We must drag ourselves away to the contrary extreme; for we shall get into the intermediate state by drawing well away from error."

How would your emotional communication be different if you strived for moderation? Answer this question by identifying the parts of your emotional expression that are most extreme, either in their intensity or their absence. How might your relationships change if you act more moderately? Are there any situations in your life when more extreme forms of emotional expression are both moral and effective?

To read Aristotle's full discussion of the Golden Mean, see Book Two of his *Nicomachean Ethics*, translated by H. Rachman and published by the Harvard University Press in 1934.

---

to some disastrous course of action. If, for instance, you recognize that you are upset with a friend, it becomes possible to explore exactly why you feel so furious. Sharing your feeling ("Sometimes I get so mad at you that I could punch you in the nose") might open the

Aristotle's Nicomachean Ethics

http://www.constitution.org/ari/ ethic_00.htm

door to resolving whatever is bothering you. Pretending that nothing is the matter, on the other hand, is unlikely to diminish your resentful feelings, which can then go on to contaminate the relationship.

Accept Responsibility for Your Feelings

It's important to make sure that your language reflects the fact that you're responsible for your feelings. Instead of "You're making me angry," say, "I'm getting angry." Instead of "You hurt my feelings," say, "I feel hurt when you do that." As you'll soon read, people don't make us like or dislike them, and believing that they do denies the responsibility each of us has for our own emotions. Chapter 5 introduces "I" language, which offers a responsible way to express your own feelings.

Consider When and Where to Express Your Feelings

Moderation is the wisdom which never quite exhausts its reservoirs of power; which never permits depletion, and is, therefore, never exhausted.

Bliss Carman,
The Kinship of Nature

Often the first flash of a strong feeling is not the best time to speak out. If you're awakened by the racket caused by a noisy neighbour, storming over to complain might result in your saying things you'll regret later. In such a case, it's probably wiser to wait until you have thought out carefully how you might express your feelings in a way that would be most likely to be heard.

Even after you've waited for the initial feeling to subside, it's still important to choose the time that's best suited to the message. Being rushed or tired or disturbed by some other matter is probably a good reason for postponing the expression of your feeling. Often dealing with your emotions can take a great amount of time and effort, and fatigue or distraction will make it difficult to follow through on the matter you've started. In the same manner, you ought to be sure that the recipient of your message is ready to hear you out before you begin.

MANAGING DIFFICULT EMOTIONS

Although feeling and expressing many emotions add to the quality of interpersonal relationships, not all feelings are beneficial. For instance, rage, depression, terror, and jealousy do little to help you feel better or improve your relationships. The following pages will give you tools to minimize these unproductive emotions.

Facilitative and Debilitative Emotions

We need to make a distinction between **facilitative emotions,** which contribute to effective functioning, and **debilitative emotions,** which keep us from feeling and relating effectively.

One difference between the two types is their *intensity*. For instance, a certain amount of anger or irritation can be constructive because it often provides the stimulus that leads you to improve the unsatisfying conditions. Rage, on the other hand, will usually make matters worse. The same holds true for fear. A little bit of nervousness before an important athletic contest or job interview might give you the boost that will improve your performance. (Mellow athletes or employees usually don't do well.) But total terror is something else. Even a little suspicion can make people more effective communicators. One study revealed that couples who doubted that their relational partners were telling the truth were better at detecting deception than were trusting mates.[25] Of course, an extreme case of paranoia would have the opposite and debilitative effect, reducing the ability to interpret the partner's behaviour accurately.

A second characteristic that distinguishes debilitative feelings from facilitative ones is their extended *duration*. Feeling depressed for a while after the breakup of a relationship or the loss of a job is natural. But spending the rest of your life grieving over your loss would accomplish nothing. In the same way, staying angry at someone for a wrong inflicted long ago can be just as punishing to you as to the wrongdoer.

Many debilitative emotions involve communication. Here are a few examples, offered by readers of *Looking Out/Looking In:*

> When I first came to college, I had to leave my boyfriend. I was living with three girls, and for most of the first semester I was so lonesome and unhappy that I was a pretty terrible roommate.

> I got so frustrated with my overly critical boss over several months that I lost my temper and quit one day. I told him what a horrible manager he was and walked off the job right then and there. Now I'm afraid to list him as a reference, and I'm afraid my temper tantrum will make it harder for me to get a new job.

> I've had ongoing problems with my family, and sometimes I get so upset that I can't concentrate on my work or school, or even sleep well at night.

In the following pages you will learn a method for dealing with debilitative feelings like these in a way that can improve your effectiveness as a communicator. This approach is based on the idea that one way to minimize debilitative feelings is to change unproductive thinking.

Thoughts Cause Feelings

For most people, emotions seem to have a life of their own. You wish you could feel calm when approaching strangers, yet your voice quivers. You try to appear confident when asking for a raise, yet your eye twitches nervously.

At times like these it's common to say that strangers or your boss *makes* you feel nervous just as you would say that a bee sting causes you to feel pain. The apparent similarities between physical and emotional discomfort become clear if you look at them in the following way:

Event		*Feeling*
Bee sting	→	physical pain
Meeting strangers	→	nervous feelings

When looking at your emotions in this way, you seem to have little control over how you feel. However, this apparent similarity between physical pain and emotional discomfort (or pleasure) isn't as great as it seems to be. Cognitive psychologists argue that it is not *events* such as meeting strangers or being jilted by a lover that cause people to feel bad, but rather the *beliefs they hold* about these events.

There is nothing good or bad but thinking makes it so.

Shakespeare, *Hamlet*

Albert Ellis, who developed the cognitive approach called *rational-emotive therapy,* tells a story that makes this point clear. Imagine yourself walking by a friend's house and seeing your friend stick his head out of a window and call you a string of vile names. (You supply the friend and the names.) Under these circumstances it's likely that you would feel hurt and upset. Now imagine that instead of walking by the house you were passing a mental institution when the same friend, who was obviously a patient there, shouted the same offensive names at you. In this case, your feelings would probably be quite different—most likely sadness and pity. You can see that in this story the activating event of being called names was the same in both cases, yet the emotional consequences were very different. The reason for your different feelings has to do with your thinking in each case. In the first instance, you would most likely think that your friend was very angry with you; further, you might imagine that you must have done something terrible to deserve such a response. In the second case, you would probably assume that your friend had some psychological difficulty, and most likely you would feel sympathetic.

From this example you can begin to see that it's the *interpretations* people make of an event, during the process of self-talk, that determine their feelings.[26]* Thus, the model for emotions looks like this:

Event	Thought	Feeling
Being called names→	"I've done some-→ thing wrong."	hurt, upset
Being called names→	"My friend must→ be sick."	concern, sympathy

The same principle applies in more common situations. For example, the words "I love you" can be interpreted in a variety of ways. They could be taken at face value as a genuine expression of deep affection. They might also be decoded in a variety of other ways; for example, as an attempt at manipulation, a sincere but mistaken declaration uttered in a moment of passion, or an attempt to make the recipient feel better. One study revealed that women are more likely than men to regard expressions of love as genuine statements, instead of attributing them to some other cause.[27] It's easy to imagine how different interpretations of a statement like "I love you" can lead to different emotional reactions:

---

* Two other sources of emotions do not involve self-talk. The first involves a conditioned response, in which a stimulus that was originally paired with an emotion-arousing event triggers the same emotion in future instances. You might, for instance, feel a wave of sadness when you catch a whiff of the perfume a former lover wore at the time of your breakup. The other cause of emotions that does not involve self-talk occurs when a person has learned that a certain feeling (or more correctly, behaviours that reflect that feeling) results in a desirable response from others. For example, some people cry or mope because doing so gets them a sympathetic response.

The Albert Ellis Institute

http://www.rebt.org/

The mind is its own place, and in itself can make a Heav'n of Hell, a Hell of Heav'n.

John Milton,
Paradise Lost

Event	Thought	Feeling
Hearing "I love you"→	"This is a genuine→ statement."	delight (perhaps)
Hearing "I love you"→	"S/he's saying→ this just to manipulate me."	anger

INVITATION TO INSIGHT

TALKING TO YOURSELF

You can become better at understanding how your thoughts shape your feelings by completing the following steps.

1. Take a few minutes to listen to the inner voice you use when thinking. Close your eyes now and listen to it. . . . Did you hear the voice? Perhaps it was saying, "What voice? I don't have any voice. . . ." Try again, and pay attention to what the voice is saying.

2. Now think about the following situations, and imagine how you would react in each. How would you interpret them with your inner voice? What feelings would follow from each interpretation?
   a. While sitting on a bus, in class, or on the street, you notice an attractive person sneaking glances at you.
   b. During a lecture your professor asks the class, "What do you think about this?" and looks toward you.
   c. You are telling friends about your vacation, and one yawns.
   d. You run into a friend on the street and ask how things are going. "Fine," she replies and rushes off.

3. Now recall three recent times when you felt a strong emotion. For each one, recall the activating event and then the interpretation that led to your emotional reaction.

Irrational Thinking and Debilitative Emotions

Focussing on the self-talk that we use to think is the key to understanding debilitative feelings. Many debilitative feelings come from accepting a number of irrational thoughts—we'll call them *fallacies* here—which lead to illogical conclusions and in turn to debilitating feelings. We usually aren't aware of these thoughts, which makes them especially powerful.[28]

1. The Fallacy of Perfection People who accept the **fallacy of perfection** believe that a worthwhile communicator should be able to handle every situation with complete confidence and skill.

   Once you accept the belief that it's desirable and possible to be a perfect communicator, the next step is to assume that people won't appreciate you if you are imperfect. Admitting your mistakes, saying, "I don't know," or sharing feelings of uncertainty

The juggler comes closest to our hearts when he misses the ball.

Richard J. Needham,
A Friend in Needham

seem like social defects when viewed in this manner. Given the desire to be valued and appreciated, it's tempting to try to *appear* perfect, but the costs of such deception are high. If others ever find you out, they'll see you as a phony. Even when your act isn't uncovered, such a performance uses a great deal of psychological energy and thus makes the rewards of approval less enjoyable.

Subscribing to the myth of perfection not only can keep others from liking you, but also can act as a force to diminish your own self-esteem. How can you like yourself when you don't measure up to the way you ought to be? How liberated you become when you can comfortably accept the idea that you are not perfect! That,

Like everyone else, you sometimes have a hard time expressing yourself.

Like everyone else, you make mistakes from time to time, and there is no reason to hide this.

You are honestly doing the best you can to realize your potential, to become the best person you can be.

2. **The Fallacy of Approval** The mistaken belief known as the **fallacy of approval** is based on the idea that it is not just desirable but *vital* to get the approval of virtually every person. People who accept this belief go to incredible lengths to seek acceptance from others even when they have to sacrifice their own principles and happiness to do so. Accepting this irrational myth can lead to some ludicrous situations:

Feeling nervous because people you really don't like seem to disapprove of you.

Feeling apologetic when others are at fault.

Feeling embarrassed after behaving unnaturally to gain another's approval.

In addition to the obvious discomfort that arises from denying your own principles and needs, the myth of approval is irrational because it implies that others will respect and like you more if you go out of your way to please them. Often this simply isn't true. How is it possible to respect people who have compromised important values just to gain acceptance? How is it possible to think highly of people who repeatedly deny their own needs as a means of buying approval? Though others may find it tempting to use these individuals to suit their ends or amusing to be around them, they hardly deserve genuine affection and respect.

Striving for universal acceptance is irrational because it's simply not possible. Sooner or later a conflict of expectations is bound to occur; one person will approve if you behave only in a certain way, but another will accept only the opposite course of action. What are you to do then?

Don't misunderstand: Abandoning the fallacy of approval doesn't mean living a life of selfishness. It's still important to consider the needs of others, and to meet them whenever possible. It's

that I would be good even if I did nothing
that I would be good even if I got the thumbs down
that I would be good if I got and stayed sick
that I would be good even if I gained ten pounds
that I would be fine even if I went bankrupt
that I would be good if I lost my hair and my youth
that I would be great if I was no longer queen
that I would be grand if I was not all knowing
that I would be loved even when I numb myself
that I would be good even when I am overwhelmed
that I would be loved even when I was fuming
that I would be good even if I was clingy
that I would be good even if I lost sanity
that I would be good
whether with or without you

Alanis Morissette

also pleasant—we might say even necessary—to strive for the respect of those people you value. The point here is that when you must abandon your own needs and principles in order to seek these goals, the price is too high.

3. **The Fallacy of Shoulds** One source of unhappiness is the **fallacy of shoulds,** the inability to distinguish between what *is* and what *should be.* You can see the difference by imagining a person who is full of complaints about the world:

"There should be no rain on weekends."

"People ought to live forever."

"Money should grow on trees."

"We should all be able to fly."

Beliefs like these are obviously foolish. However pleasant wishing may be, insisting that the unchangeable should be changed won't affect reality one bit. And yet many people torture themselves by engaging in this sort of irrational thinking when they confuse *is* with *ought.* They say and think things like this:

"My friend should be more understanding."

"She shouldn't be so inconsiderate."

"They ought to be more friendly."

"You should work harder."

The message in each of these cases is that you would *prefer* people to behave differently. Wishing that things were better is perfectly legitimate, and trying to change them is, of course, a good idea; but it's unreasonable to *insist* that the world operate just as you want it to or to feel cheated when things aren't ideal.

Imposing the fallacy of shoulds on yourself can also lead to unnecessary misery. Psychologist Aaron Beck points out some unrealistic self-imposed shoulds:[29]

"I should be able to find a quick solution to every problem."

"I should never feel hurt; I should always be happy and serene."

"I should always demonstrate the utmost generosity, considerateness, dignity, courage, unselfishness."

Becoming obsessed with shoulds like these has three troublesome consequences. First, it leads to unnecessary unhappiness, for people who are constantly dreaming about the ideal are seldom satisfied with what they have or who they are. A second drawback is that merely complaining without acting can keep you from doing anything to change unsatisfying conditions. A third problem with shoulds that you impose on others is that this sort of complaining can build a defensive climate with others, who will resent being nagged. It's much more effective to tell people about what you'd like than to preach: Say, "I wish you'd be more punctual" instead of "You should be on time." We'll discuss ways of avoiding defensive climates in Chapter 9.

4. **The Fallacy of Overgeneralization** The **fallacy of overgeneralization** comprises two types. The first occurs when we base a belief on a *limited amount of evidence*. For instance, how many times have you found yourself saying something like:

"I'm so stupid! I can't even understand how to do my income tax."

"Some friend I am! I forgot my best friend's birthday."

In cases like these, we focus on a limited type of shortcoming as if it represented everything about us. We forget that along with our difficulties we also have solved tough problems and that though we're sometimes forgetful, at other times we're caring and thoughtful.

A second related category of overgeneralization occurs when we *exaggerate* shortcomings:

"You *never* listen to me."

"You're *always* late."

"I can't think of *anything*."

On closer examination, absolute statements like these are almost always false and usually lead to discouragement or anger. You'll feel far better when you replace overgeneralizations with more-accurate messages to yourself and others:

"You often don't listen to me."

"You've been late three times this week."

"I haven't had any ideas I like today."

Many overgeneralizations are based on abuse of the verb *to be.* For example, unqualified thoughts such as "He *is* an idiot [all the time?]" and "I *am* a failure [in everything?]" will make you see yourself and others in an unrealistically negative way, thus contributing to debilitative feelings.

5. **The Fallacy of Causation** The **fallacy of causation** is based on the irrational belief that emotions are caused by others rather than by one's own self-talk.

This fallacy causes trouble in two ways. The first plagues people who become overly cautious about communicating because they don't want to "cause" any pain or inconvenience for others. This attitude occurs in such cases as:

Visiting friends or family out of a sense of obligation rather than a genuine desire to see them;

Keeping quiet when another person's behaviour is bothering you;

Pretending to be attentive to a speaker when you are already late for an appointment or feeling ill;

Praising and reassuring others who ask for your opinion when your honest response would be negative.

There's certainly no excuse for going out of your way to say things that will result in pain for others, and there will be times when you choose to inconvenience yourself to make life easier for those you care about. It's essential to realize, however, that it's an overstatement to say that you are the one who causes others' feelings. It's more accurate to say that they *respond* to your behaviour with feelings of their own. For example, consider how strange it sounds to suggest that you make others fall in love with you. Such a statement simply doesn't make sense. It would be closer to the truth to say that you act in one way or another, and some people might fall in love with you as a result of these actions, whereas others wouldn't. In the same way, it's incorrect to say that you *make* others angry or upset—or happy, for that matter. It's better to say that others create their own responses to your behaviour.

Restricting your communication because of the fallacy of causation can result in three types of damaging consequences. First, as a result of your caution you often will fail to have your own needs met. There's little likelihood that others will change their behaviour unless they know that it's affecting you in a negative way. A second consequence is that you're likely to begin resenting the person whose behaviour you find bothersome. Obviously, this reaction is illogical because you have never made your feelings known, but logic doesn't change the fact that burying your problem usually leads to a buildup of hostility.

Even when withholding feelings is based on the best intentions, it often damages relationships in a third way—once others find out

it's important to write down your **self-talk** when first learning to use this method. Putting your thoughts on paper will help you see whether they actually make any sense.

Monitoring your self-talk might be difficult at first. This is a new skill, and any new activity seems awkward. If you persevere, however, you'll find you will be able to identify the thoughts that lead to your debilitative feelings. Once you get in the habit of recognizing this internal monologue, you'll be able to identify your thoughts quickly and easily.

4. *Dispute your irrational beliefs.* Disputing your irrational beliefs is the key to success in the rational-emotive approach. Use the list of irrational fallacies on pages 154–160 to discover which of your internal statements are based on mistaken thinking.

You can do this most effectively by following three steps. First, decide whether each belief you've recorded is rational or irrational. Next, explain why the belief does or doesn't make sense. Finally, if the belief is irrational, you should write down an

---

SKILL BUILDER

RATIONAL THINKING

1. Return to the diary of irrational thoughts you recorded on page 160. Dispute the self-talk in each case, and write a more rational interpretation of the event.

2. Now try out your ability to think rationally on the spot. You can do this by acting out the scenes listed in step 4. You'll need three players for each one: a subject, the subject's "little voice"–his or her thoughts–and a second party.

3. Play out each scene by having the subject and second party interact while the "little voice" stands just behind the subject and says what the subject is probably thinking. For example, in a scene where the subject is asking an instructor to reconsider a low grade, the voice might say, "I hope I haven't made things worse by bringing this up. Maybe he'll lower the grade after rereading the test. I'm such an idiot! Why didn't I keep quiet?"

4. Whenever the voice expresses an irrational thought, the observers who are watching the skit should call out "Foul." At this point the action should stop while the group discusses the irrational thought and suggests a more rational line of self-talk. The players should then replay the scene with the voice speaking in a more rational way.

   Here are some scenes. Of course, you can invent others as well.
   a. A couple is just beginning their first date.
   b. A potential employee has just begun a job interview.
   c. A teacher or boss is criticizing the subject for showing up late.
   d. A student and an instructor run across each other in the market.

alternative way of thinking that is more sensible and that can leave you feeling better when faced with the same activating event in the future.

The approach of replacing self-defeating self-talk with more-constructive thinking provides an especially effective tool for improving self-confidence and relational communication.[32] Nonetheless, this method triggers objections for some readers.

"This rational-emotive approach sounds like nothing more than trying to talk yourself out of feeling bad." This accusation is totally correct. After all, since we talk ourselves *into* feeling bad, what's wrong with talking ourselves *out* of bad feelings, especially when they are based on irrational thoughts? Rationalizing may be an excuse and a self-deception, but there's nothing wrong with being rational.

"The kind of disputing we just read sounds phony and unnatural. I don't talk to myself in sentences and paragraphs." There's no need to dispute your irrational beliefs in any special literary style. You can be just as colloquial as you want. The important thing is to understand what thoughts led you into your debilitative feeling so you can clearly dispute them. When the technique is new to you, it's a good idea to write or talk out your thoughts in order to make them clear. After you've had some practice, you'll be able to do these steps in a quicker, less-formal way.

"This approach is too cold and impersonal. It seems to aim at turning people into cold-blooded, calculating, emotionless machines." This is simply not true. A rational thinker can still dream, hope, and love: There's nothing necessarily irrational about feelings like these. Basically rational people even indulge in a bit of irrational thinking once in a while. But they usually know what they're doing. Like healthy eaters who occasionally treat themselves to a snack of junk food, rational thinkers occasionally indulge themselves in irrational thoughts, knowing that they'll return to their healthy lifestyle soon with no real damage done.

"This technique promises too much. There's no chance I could rid myself of all unpleasant feelings, however nice that might be." We can answer this by assuring you that rational-emotive thinking probably won't totally solve your emotional problems. What it can do is reduce their number, intensity, and duration. This method is not the answer to all your problems, but it can make a significant difference—which is not a bad accomplishment.

SUMMARY

Emotions have several dimensions. They are signalled by internal physiological changes, manifested by nonverbal reactions, and defined in most cases by cognitive interpretations. Some emotions are primary, while others are combinations of two or more emotions. Some are intense, while others are relatively mild.

There are several reasons why people do not verbalize many of the emotions they feel. Social rules discourage the expression of some feelings, particularly negative ones. Many social roles do not allow expression of certain feelings. Finally, fear of the consequences of disclosing some emotions leads people to withhold expression of them.

Because total expression of feelings is not appropriate for adults, several guidelines help define when and how to share emotions effectively. Self-awareness, clear language, and expression of mixed feelings are important. Willingness to accept responsibility for feelings instead of blaming them on others leads to better reactions. Choosing the proper time and place to share feelings is also important.

Although some emotions are facilitative, others are debilitative and inhibit effective functioning. Many of these debilitative emotions are caused by various types of irrational thinking. It is often possible to communicate more confidently and effectively by recognizing troublesome emotions, identifying the activating event and self-talk that triggered them, and replacing any irrational thoughts with a more logical analysis of the situation.

KEY TERMS

debilitative emotions
emotional contagion
facilitative emotions
fallacy of approval
fallacy of catastrophic
    expectations

fallacy of causation
fallacy of helplessness
fallacy of overgeneralization
fallacy of perfection
fallacy of shoulds
mixed emotions

primary emotions
self-talk

Part Two

Looking Out

Language: Barrier and Bridge

And the whole earth was of one language and one speech. And it came to pass, as they journeyed from the East, that they found a plain in the land of Shinar; and they dwelt there.

And they said to one another, go to, let us make brick, and burn them thoroughly. And they had brick for stone, and slime had they for mortar.

And they said, go to, let us build us a city and a tower, whose top may reach unto Heaven; and let us make us a name, lest we be scattered abroad upon the face of the whole earth.

And the Lord came down to see the city and the tower, which the children of men builded.

And the Lord said, behold, the people is one, and they have all one language; and this they began to do: and now nothing will be restrained from them, which they have imagined to do.

Go to, let us go down, and there confound their language, that they may not understand one another's speech.

So the Lord scattered them abroad from thence upon the face of all the earth; and they left off to build the city.

Therefore is the name of it called Babel; because the Lord did there confound the language of all the earth; and from thence did the Lord scatter them abroad upon the face of all the earth.

Genesis 11:1–9

Just like in Babel, sometimes it seems as if none of us speaks the same language. Yet despite its frustrations and challenges, there is no question that language is a marvellous tool. It is the gift that allows us to communicate in a way that no other animals appear to match. Without language we would be more ignorant, ineffectual, and isolated.

In this chapter we will explore the nature of language and look at how best to take advantage of its strengths and how to minimize its limitations. After an overview of how language operates, we will focus on how to overcome the common barriers that occur when people encounter one another. We will then move beyond the challenges of simply understanding one another and explore how the language we use affects the climate of interpersonal relationships. Finally, we will broaden our focus even more to look at how linguistic practices shape the attitudes of entire cultures.

THE NATURE OF LANGUAGE

We will begin our survey by looking at some features that characterize all languages. These features explain why language can be so useful, yet so troublesome.

Language Is Symbolic

Words are arbitrary symbols that don't have any meaning in themselves. The word *five*, for example, is a kind of code that represents the number of fingers on your hand only because we agree that it does. As communication theorists have pointed out, there is nothing particularly five-like in the number "five." *Cinq* for French speakers, *fünf* for German speakers, and the coded symbol 00110101 for computer programmers represent the same concept.

Even sign language, as "spoken" by most deaf people, is symbolic in nature and not the pantomime it might seem. Because this form of communication is symbolic and not literal, there are hundreds of different sign languages spoken around the world that have evolved independently whenever significant numbers of deaf people are in contact.[1] These distinct languages include American Sign Language, British Sign Language, French Sign Language, Danish Sign

TYPOGRAPHY FOR THE WORD "MUSIC"

"I don't know what you mean by 'glory,'" Alice said.

Humpty Dumpty smiled contemptuously. "Of course you don't—till I tell you. I meant 'there's a nice knock-down argument for you!'"

"But 'glory' doesn't mean 'a nice knock-down argument,'" Alice objected.

"When I use a word," Humpty Dumpty said, in a rather scornful tone, "it means just what I choose it to mean—neither more nor less."

"The question is," said Alice, "whether you can make words mean so many different things."

"The question is," said Humpty Dumpty, "which is to be master—that's all."

Lewis Carroll,
Through the Looking Glass

Language, Chinese Sign Language . . . even Australian Aboriginal and Mayan Sign Languages.

Despite the fact that symbols are arbitrary, people often act as if they had some meaning in themselves. To illustrate the mistaken belief that words are inherently connected to the things they label, S.I. Hayakawa describes the little boy who was reported to have said, "Pigs are called pigs because they are such dirty animals."[2]

Language Is Subjective

Show a dozen people the same symbol and ask them what it means, and you're likely to get 12 different answers. For example, what associations do you have for a cross? Giving blood at a local Red Cross blood drive? The gentleness and wisdom of Jesus Christ? The necklace your friend always wears? How about the plus sign? A graveyard that you pass each day?

Like symbols such as a cross, words can be interpreted in many different ways. And, of course, this is the basis for many misunderstandings. It's possible to have an argument about feminism without ever realizing that you and the other person are using the word to represent entirely different ideas. The same goes for *socialism, alternative medicine, equality, independence,* and thousands of other symbols. Words don't have meaning; people do—and often in widely different ways.

Despite the potential for linguistic problems, the situation isn't hopeless. We do, after all, communicate with one another reasonably well most of the time. And with enough effort, we can clear up most of the misunderstandings that do occur. One key to more accurate use of language is to avoid assuming that others interpret words the same way we do. In truth, the chances for successful communication increase when we *negotiate* the meaning of a statement. By working to clarify the way language is used, we move closer to a shared understanding.

The need to negotiate meanings highlights both the shortcomings and strengths of language. On one hand, it is an imprecise tool for communicating. In any interchange we are likely to be misunderstood, and the odds are great that our understanding of others is flawed. On the other hand, the same language that works so imperfectly allows us to discover and clarify problems of understanding when they occur.

Language Is Rule-Governed

The only reason symbol-laden languages work at all is that people agree on how to use them. The linguistic agreements that make communication possible can be codified in rules. Languages contain several types of rules. **Phonological rules** govern how sounds are combined to form words. For instance, the words *champagne, double,* and *occasion* have the same meaning in French and English but are pronounced differently.

Whereas phonological rules determine how spoken language sounds, **syntactic rules** govern the way symbols can be arranged.

For example, in English, syntactic rules require every word to contain at least one vowel and prohibit sentences such as "Have you the cookies brought?" which would be a perfectly acceptable arrangement in German.

Although most of us aren't able to describe the syntactic rules that govern our language, it's easy to recognize their existence by noticing how odd a statement that violates them appears. Sometimes, however, apparently ungrammatical speech is simply following a different set of syntactic rules. For example, the way in which English is spoken by some members of the Black community (recently termed "Ebonics" by some) treats forms of the verb *to be* differently than does standard English.[3] An expression like "I be angry" that would be ungrammatical in standard English is perfectly correct in Ebonics, where it would be equivalent to the standard expression "I've been angry for a while." Ebonics might loosely be referred to as pidgin, a speech variety that blends two languages into a simplified syntactic structure. Typically, pidgins are marginalized languages. For example, in southeast New Brunswick, many francophones use a language variation called *chiac*, a combination of French and English. *Chiac* speakers, however, "experience disparaging remarks concerning their vernacular, and many experience significant hardships in learning 'standard' French in school."[4] Co-operative education placement officers note that students speaking *chiac* also have difficulty securing employment in companies and government offices where standard English or French is the norm.

Sign languages spoken by the deaf demonstrate the importance of syntactic rules. True sign languages have their own syntax and grammar, which have a completely different character from any spoken or written language. It is not possible to transliterate a spoken tongue into Sign word by word or phrase by phrase, as we often can do when switching between two spoken languages—their structures are just too different. Most uninformed people believe that sign language is unspoken English or French, but in truth it is nothing of the sort.

Calvin and Hobbes

by Bill Watterson

It's a Girl Thing for Women

AFTER YEARS OF BEING SPURNED AS A SEXIST PUT-DOWN, THE WORD IS BEING EMBRACED AS A HIP STATEMENT OF POWER AND VITALITY

When law professor and commentator Susan Estrich sent off her female research assistants after a long day of work, she cheerfully banished them with "Get out of here, girls."

When Richard Riordan's press secretary, Noelia Rodriguez, told a TV station official that she was finally taking a week's vacation, the woman executive exclaimed, "You go, girl!"

And in *Spin* magazine's special November issue on women in pop and rock music, the editors didn't mince words: On the cover they proclaimed it "The Girl Issue."

There was a time when Estrich wouldn't have dreamed of referring to any female adult as anything but a woman. Rodriguez has never used "girl" in her job and would be stunned if the word ever passed the Los Angeles mayor's lips. And virtually all of the musicians featured in the *Spin* issue are highly paid adult (or at least post-teenage) women.

So what's with all the girls?

With a significant degree of female equity and parity established in the workplace and other institutions, there has been a gradual social warming among women to the once-ostracized "girl"—a curiously defiant celebration of a word formerly fraught with oppression.

"We've taken back the word and are using it the way we want—girl power, girl talk," said Jane Pratt, the 34-year-old editor of her eponymous new magazine, *Jane*. "It's about girls supporting each other and revelling in what's fun about being a girl. . . . Girl power means something different from feminism."

This is not the old-school, coffee-making, office-slaving, husband's-credit-card-borrowing girl—although the word incorporates a dollop of old-fashioned girlishness. "Girl" has been reborn in the image of a modern woman: It borrows the youthful vigour and spontaneity of female adolescence and discards the meekness of the old-fashioned office girl. "I think women use it in a jocular, almost swaggering way," said Susan Faludi, author of the critically acclaimed *Backlash,* which examined society's resentment of feminism.

"It always implied somebody weak and feeble and ineffectual," said Barnard College professor Donna Gaines, who teaches about the sociology of youth and has written about the changing usage of "girl." "It's been appropriated as something very vital and strong."

Gaines says that use of the word has evolved among women in the same way that members of other groups sometimes convert an offensive term to an affectionate, even proud expression—the way, for example, that some gays use "queer."

Sometime around the rise of feminism and *Ms.* magazine a quarter of a century ago, "girl" was banned from the vocabulary of smart-thinking men and women when describing any female over 15.

It went the way of stewardesses and poetesses. There were no more office girls fetching coffee, no more college girls getting degrees or career girls working up the job ladder; no more girl Fridays, script girls, or hatcheck girls.

So why are "girls" back?

"Often after a social movement has been established for a while—like feminism—you can play around with certain terms," said Lynn Chancer, an assistant professor of sociology at Columbia University who studies feminism.

Now "girl" crops up throughout pop culture. "Girls rule" emblazons T-shirts. A college women's crew scrawls, "You row, girl" on the side of the team van. The clothing store X-Girl, in Los Feliz, is a spin-off for women of the hip-hop store X-Large.

As murky as the new "girl" may be, it comes with some rules.

One is that the conversation should be casual. Neither men—nor women—should be saying, 'I'll have my girl call your girl.' And no woman wants to use it in a serious office setting—or around impressionable minds.

"We have this 'Take Your Daughter to Work Day,'" said Robin Kramer, Riordan's chief of staff, "and the young women range in age from 7 to 17. Listening to both informal conversations and speeches, even those little ones are referred to as young women."

A second rule is that it's generally a woman's prerogative to use the word. Men treading into "girl" territory enter at their own risk.

Sometimes a gentle reminder is all it takes to separate the women from the girls.

Ms. magazine editor Barbara Findlen recalls a recent conversation with a man in which he referred to someone as "the girl who owns that business." "I said, 'God, a girl owns her own company! How old is she?' He laughed. He got it."

Carla Hall

TABLE 5–1	PRAGMATIC RULES GOVERN THE USE AND MEANING OF A STATEMENT	

Notice how the same message ("You look very pretty today") takes on different meaning depending on which of a variety of rules are used to formulate and interpret it.

	BOSS'S PERSPECTIVE	EMPLOYEE'S PERSPECTIVE
Content Actual words and behaviour	"You look very pretty today."	
Speech act The intent of a statement	Compliment an employee	Unknown
Relational contract The perceived relationship between communicators	Boss who treats employees like family members	Subordinate employee, dependent on boss's approval for advancement
Episode Situation in which the interaction occurs	Casual conversation	Possible come-on by boss?
Life script Self-concept of each communicator	Friendly guy	Woman determined to succeed on own merits
Cultural archetype Cultural norms that shape member's perceptions and actions	Middle-class Canadian	Middle-class Canadian

Adapted from W.B. Pearce and V. Cronen, *Communication, Action, and Meaning* (New York: Praeger, 1980).

Semantic rules also govern our use of the language. But where syntax deals with structure, semantics governs meaning. Semantic rules reflect the ways in which speakers of a language respond to a particular symbol. Semantic rules are what make it possible for us to agree that "bikes" are for riding and "books" are for reading, and they help us know whom we will and won't encounter when we use rooms marked "men" or "women." Without semantic rules, communication would be impossible, for each of us would use symbols in unique ways, unintelligible to one another.

Semantic rules help us understand the meaning of individual words, but they often don't explain how language operates in everyday life. Consider the statement "let's get together tomorrow." The semantic meaning of the words in this sentence is clear enough, yet the statement could be taken in several ways. We learn to make

INVITATION TO INSIGHT

YOUR LINGUISTIC RULES

To what extent do linguistic rules affect your understanding of and relationships with others? Explore this question by following these steps:

1. Recall a time when you encountered someone whose speech violated the system of phonological and/or syntactic rules that you are used to. What was your impression of this person? To what degree was this impression influenced by her or his failure to follow familiar linguistic rules? Consider whether this impression was or was not valid.

2. Recall at least one misunderstanding that arose when you and another person followed different semantic rules. Use hindsight to consider whether this misunderstanding (and others like it) could be avoided. If semantic misunderstandings can be minimized, explain what approaches might be useful.

3. Use the discussion of co-ordinated management of meaning theory in the preceding pages to identify at least two pragmatic rules that govern the use of language in one of your relationships. Share these rules with other students. Do they use language in the same way as you and your relational partner?

"Well, at any rate it's a great comfort," she said as she stepped under the trees, "after being so hot, to get into the–into the–into what?" she went on, rather surprised at not being able to think of the word. "I mean to get under the–under the–under this, you know!" putting her hand on the trunk of the tree. "What does it call itself, I wonder? I do believe it's got no name–why to be sure it hasn't!"

Lewis Carroll,
Through the Looking Glass

sense of speech acts like this through **pragmatic rules,** which help us decide what interpretation of a message is appropriate in a given context. The best way to appreciate how regulative rules work is to think of communication as a kind of co-operative game. Like all games, success depends on all the players understanding and following the same set of rules. The statement "let's get together tomorrow" illustrates this point. These words are likely to mean one thing when uttered by your boss and another entirely when spoken by your lover; one thing when uttered at the office and something quite different when whispered at a party. As long as everyone involved uses the same set of pragmatic rules to make sense of statements like this, understanding occurs. Problems arise, though, when communicators use different pragmatic rules to interpret a statement.

Pragmatic rules can be quite complex. Consider the use of humour: One study identified 24 different functions humour can serve in conversations.[5] These include showing the speaker's sense of humour, entertaining others, decreasing another person's aggressive behaviour, easing the disclosure of difficult information, expressing feelings, protecting the speaker's ego from attack, avoiding self-disclosure, and expressing aggression. It's easy to imagine how a joke aimed at serving one of these functions–reducing boredom, for example–might be interpreted by the recipient as an attack.

Co-ordinated management of meaning (CMM) theory describes some types of pragmatic rules that operate in everyday conversations. It suggests that we use rules at several levels to create our own messages and interpret others' statements.[6] Table 5–1 uses a CMM

Coordinated Management of Meaning Theory

http://oak.cats.ohiou.edu/ ~cz175996/CMM.htm

framework to illustrate how a sexual harassment claim might arise when two communicators use different rules to make sense of a statement. In situations like this, it's important to make sure that the other person's use of language matches yours before jumping to conclusions about the meaning of his or her statements. The skill of perception checking described in Chapter 3 can be a useful tool at times like this.

THE IMPACT OF LANGUAGE

So far, we have focussed on language only as a medium for helping communicators understand one another. But along with this important function, the words we use can shape our perceptions of the world around us and reflect the attitudes we hold toward one another.

On the broadest level, the language that communicators use can affect the way they view one another and the world around them. This chapter describes how language can shape an entire culture's worldview and how problems can arise when speakers of different languages encounter one another. But even among communicators who speak the same language, the labels we use to describe people, things, events, and ideas can affect our perceptions in a variety of ways.

Naming and Identity

"What's in a name?" Juliet asked rhetorically. If Romeo had been a social scientist, he would have answered, "A great deal." Research has demonstrated that names are more than just a simple means of identification: They shape the way others think of us, the way we view ourselves, and the way we act.

Different names have different connotations. In one study, psychologists asked college students to rate over a thousand names according to their likability, how active or passive they seemed, and their masculinity or femininity. In spite of the large number of subjects, the responses were quite similar.[7] Michael, John, and Wendy were likable and active and were rated as possessing the masculine or feminine traits of their sex. Percival, Isadore, and Alfreda were less likable, and their sexual identity was less clear. Other research also suggests that names have strong connotative meanings. More-common names are generally viewed as being more active, stronger, and better than unusual ones.[8] The impact of names does affect first impressions, but the effect doesn't seem so powerful once communicators become more familiar with one another.[9]

By the middle of childhood, we are able to start controlling the names by which we want to be called. The labels we choose for ourselves and encourage others to use say a great deal about who we

People often ask me whether Canadian English is getting more Americanized—if it's going to be swallowed up by American English. Working on the dictionary, we found that, in spite of living next to this behemoth for over 200 years, we've managed to maintain our own linguistic identity and continue to invent new Canadianisms every year. "Toonie" was a good example a few years ago, and just this year we've noted a new form of floor hockey called "schlockey." At the University of Guelph, they've just developed a new kind of genetically engineered pig that they've called the "Enviropig." Who knows, maybe "enviropig" will become as much a part of our common vocabulary as "canola" and "triticale" are now.

Katherine Barber, editor in chief,
The Canadian Oxford Dictionary

think we are and how we want others to view us. For many people, changes in age lead to changes in names. The diminutive that seemed to fit as a child doesn't fit as well in adolescence or adulthood. Thus, Vinnie may become Vince, and Danny may insist on being called Dan or Daniel. It still may be fine for close friends to use diminutives, but not others. The shift to more-formal, adult names may not be as pronounced for some women: It's not uncommon to meet an adult Betsy or Susie. But when being taken seriously is the goal in a world where women are all too often treated with less respect than they deserve, having a serious name can be an asset.

Many women in Western society, aware of the power of names to influence identity, are aware that choosing how to identify themselves after marriage can be a significant decision. They may follow the tradition of taking their husband's last name, hyphenate their own name and their husband's, or keep their birth name. A fascinating study by Karen Foss and Belle Edson revealed that a woman's choice is likely to reveal a great deal about herself and her relationship with her husband.[10] Surveys revealed that women who took their husband's name placed the most importance on relationships, with social expectations of how they should behave rated second and issues of self coming last. On the other hand, women who kept their birth names put their personal concerns ahead of relationships and social expectations. Women with hyphenated names fell somewhere between the other groups, valuing self and relationships equally. To date, Statistics Canada does not collect data on the number of Canadian women who change, retain, or hyphenate their names at marriage.

Female forms of address influence others' perceptions as well as shape the self-concept and behaviour of the women who choose them. Research conducted in the late 1980s showed that women who choose the title "Ms." give the impression of being more achievement oriented, socially assertive, and dynamic—but less interpersonally warm than counterparts who prefer more traditional forms of "Miss" or "Mrs."[11]

The power of naming extends beyond individuals. The terms used to label social groups can shape the way members of those groups regard themselves, and the way others view them. As the reading on the "S word" illustrates, some terms may seem familiar and thus innocuous; but their impact on both the namers and those being labelled can have subtle but profound effects.

Affiliation, Attraction, and Interest

Besides shaping an individual's identity, speech can be a way of building and demonstrating solidarity with others. Research has demonstrated that communicators are attracted to others whose style of speaking is similar to theirs.[12] Likewise, communicators who want to show affiliation with one another adapt their speech in a variety of ways, including their choice of vocabulary, rate of talking, number and placement of pauses, and level of politeness.[13] Adolescents who all adopt the same vocabulary of slang words and

The Etymology of First Names

http://www.pacificcoast.net/ ~muck/etym.html

I also have to thank my wife, Mrs. Hank Snow.

Hank Snow, born in Nova Scotia, accepting a country-and-western music award on television in the fall of 1979

Challenging the "S Word"

On the Leech Lake Reservation at the Cass Lake–Benz public school, students gather for Indian Culture class. A group of 11th-graders sits in a circle talking about their feelings about the word "squaw."

Ojibwae student Terry Johnson grew up on the Leech Lake Reservation. "I was always taught to respect things, respect the land, respect my people, respect the elders. And one thing I was taught was the word, the S–Q word was very offensive. And I was never to use it."

Terry is one of about 20 students who are active on the Name Change Committee, a group that formed 2 years ago to get rid of names it deemed derogatory to Native peoples. Students wrote to Crayola Crayon Company asking it to rename the crayon colour "Indian Red." Last year the Name Change Committee was successful working with neighbouring high school students to change the name of their sports teams from the "Indians" to the "Patriots." The Name Change Committee project started in the classroom of Indian Culture teacher Muriel Charwood-Litzau, who grew up in Squaw Lake. "I've always been ashamed of that name. It's not a good name. When you're called that, it's a put-down. It is a derogatory, demeaning word."

Two years ago Charwood-Litzau's daughter and another high school student traced the word *squaw* for a class project. They found an article in a Native American newspaper that said the word is a French corruption of Iroquois slang for *vagina*. Based on that one article, they wrote letters to their MLAs saying the use of the word *squaw* in name places was unacceptable and embarrassing. The lawmakers responded by passing a mandate to ban the word from lakes, creeks, and geographic features. Squaw Point near the high school is now known as Oak Point. And Squaw Pond is Scout Camp Pond.

Linguists and those who study Native languages disagree about the word's origins. One linguist at the Smithsonian Institution in Washington, Ives Goddard, says the word originated in an extinct Indian language known as Massachusett. Goddard says it simply meant "younger woman." Despite this innocent origin, it's generally considered to be demeaning or offensive, most standard dictionaries of English point out.

One of the high school students who started the Name Change Project, Dawn Litzau, says that when people have called her squaw, it's clearly been meant as an insult. "It's not just about a dictionary. It's not just about a word. It's about people's feelings."

Christina Koening, Robert Siegel, and Noah Adams

speech mannerisms illustrate the principle of linguistic solidarity. The same process works among members of other groups, ranging from street gangs to military personnel. Communication researchers call the process of adapting one's speech style to match that of others with whom the communicator wants to identify **convergence.**

When two or more people feel equally positive about one another, their linguistic convergence will be mutual. But when communicators want or need approval they often adapt their speech to accommodate the other person's style, trying to say the "right thing" or speak in a way that will help them fit in. We see this process when immigrants who want to gain the rewards of material success in a new culture strive to master the host language. Likewise, employees who seek advancement tend to speak more like their superiors, supervisors adopt the speech style of managers, and managers converge toward their bosses.

The principle of speech accommodation works in reverse, too. Communicators who want to set themselves apart from others adopt the strategy of **divergence,** speaking in a way that emphasizes their differences from others. For example, members of an ethnic group, even though fluent in the dominant language, might use their own dialect as a way of showing solidarity with one another—a sort of "us against them" strategy. Divergence also operates in other settings. A physician or a lawyer, for example, who wants to establish credibility with her or his client, might speak formally and use professional jargon to create a sense of distance. The implicit message here is, "I'm different (and more knowledgeable) than you."

Along with convergence and divergence, an individual's choice of words can reflect his or her liking and interest. Social customs discourage us from expressing like or dislike in an overt way. Only a social misfit would say "I don't like you" in most situations. Likewise, shy or cautious admirers might not admit their attraction to a potential partner. Even when people are reluctant to speak candidly, the language they use can suggest their degree of interest and attraction toward a person, an object, or an idea. Morton Weiner and Albert Mehrabian outline several linguistic clues that can reveal these attitudes.[14]

- *Demonstrative pronoun choice:*
  "These people want our help" indicates greater affinity than "Those people want our help."

- *Sequential placement:*
  "Jack and Jill are my friends" may suggest a different level of liking than "Jill and Jack are my friends."

- *Negation:*
  For the question, "What do you think of it?," the response "It's not bad" is less positive than "It's good."

- *Duration:*
  The length of time spent discussing a person or subject also can be a strong indicator of attraction to the subject or the person with whom the speaker is talking.

Power

Communication researchers have identified a number of language patterns that add to or detract from a speaker's power to influence others. Notice the difference between these two statements:

> "Excuse me, sir. I hate to say this, but I . . . uh . . . I guess I won't be able to turn in the assignment on time. I had a personal emergency and . . . well . . . it was just impossible to finish it by today. I'll have it on your desk on Monday, OK?"

> "I won't be able to turn in the assignment on time. I had a personal emergency, and it was impossible to finish it by today. I'll have it on your desk Monday."

Whether or not the professor finds the excuse acceptable, it's clear that the second one sounds more confident, whereas the tone of the first is apologetic and uncertain. Table 5–2 identifies several **powerless speech mannerisms** illustrated in the statements you just

"I love you" [is] a statement that can be expressed in so many varied ways. It may be a stage song, repeated daily without any meaning, or a barely audible murmur, full of surrender. Sometimes it means: I desire you or I want you sexually. It may mean: I hope you love me or I hope that I will be able to love you. Often it means: It may be that a love relationship can develop between us or even I hate you. Often it is a wish for emotional exchange: I want your admiration in exchange for mine or I give my love in exchange for some passion or I want to feel cozy and at home with you or I admire some of your qualities. A declaration of love is mostly a request: I desire you or I want you to gratify me, or I want your protection or I want to be intimate with you or I want to exploit your loveliness.

Sometimes it is the need for security and tenderness, for parental treatment. It may mean: My self-love goes out to you. But it may also express submissiveness: Please take me as I am, or I feel guilty about you, I want, through you, to correct the mistakes I have made in human relations. It may be self-sacrifice and a masochistic wish for dependency. However, it may also be a full affirmation of the other, taking the responsibility for mutual exchange of feelings. It may be a weak feeling of friendliness, it may be the scarcely even whispered expression of ecstasy. "I love you"—wish, desire, submission, conquest; it is never the word itself that tells the real meaning here.

J.A.M. Meerloo,
Conversation and Communication

TABLE 5–2	EXAMPLES OF POWERLESS LANGUAGE	
Hedges	"I'm *kind of* disappointed . . ."	
	"I *think* we should . . ."	
	"I *guess* I'd like to . . ."	
Hesitations	"*Uh*, can I have a minute of your time?"	
	"*Well*, we could try this idea . . ."	
	"I wish you would–*er*–try to be on time."	
Intensifiers	"*So* that's how I feel . . ."	
	"I'm not *very* hungry."	
Polite forms	"Excuse me, sir . . ."	
Tag questions	"It's about time we got started, *isn't it?*"	
	"*Don't you think* we should give it another try?"	
Disclaimers	"*I probably shouldn't say this but . . .*"	
	"*I'm not really sure but . . .*"	

read. A number of studies have shown that speakers whose talk is free of these mannerisms are rated as more competent, dynamic, and attractive than speakers who sound powerless.[15] One study revealed that even a single type of powerless speech mannerism can make a person appear less authoritative or socially attractive.[16]

Powerful speech that gets the desired results in mainstream North American and European culture doesn't succeed everywhere with everyone.[17] In Japan, saving face for others is an important goal, so communicators there tend to speak in ambiguous terms and use hedge words and qualifiers. In most Japanese sentences the verb comes at the end of the sentence so the "action" part of the statement can be postponed. Traditional Mexican culture, with its strong emphasis on co-operation, also uses hedging to smooth over interpersonal relationships. By not taking a firm stand with their speech language, Mexicans believe they will not make others feel ill at ease. The Korean culture represents yet another group of people who prefer "indirect" (for example, "perhaps," "could be") over "direct" speech.

Even in cultures that value assertiveness, language that is *too* powerful may intimidate or annoy others. Consider these two different approaches to handle a common situation:

"Excuse me. My baby is having a little trouble getting to sleep. Would you mind turning down the music just a little?"

"My baby can't sleep because your music is too loud. Please turn it down."

The more-polite, if less-powerful, approach would probably produce better results than the stronger statement. How can this fact be reconciled with the research on powerful language? The answer lies in the tension between the potentially opposing goals of getting immediate results and developing positive relationships. If you come across as too powerful, you may get what you're seeking in the short term but alienate the other person in ways that will make your relationship more difficult in the long term. Furthermore, a statement that is *too* powerful can convey relational messages of disrespect and superiority—just as likely to antagonize others as to gain their compliance.

In some situations polite, less apparently powerful forms of speech can even enhance a speaker's effectiveness.[18] For example, an administrator might say to an assistant, "Would you mind retyping this letter?" In truth, both know this is an order and not a request, but the questioning form is more considerate and leaves the assistant feeling better about the request.[19] The importance of achieving both content and relational goals helps explain why a mixture of powerful and polite speech is usually most effective.[20]

THE USES (AND ABUSES) OF LANGUAGE

By now it's apparent that language can shape the way we perceive and understand the world. Next we will look at some specific types of usage and explore both the value and potential problems they generate.

8-29 © 1986 Jim Unger

"Four blocks north. If it's not there, eight blocks south."

Precision and Vagueness

Most people assume that the goal of language is to make our ideas clear to one another. When clarity *is* the goal, we need language skills to make our ideas understandable to others. Sometimes, however, we want to be less than perfectly clear. The following pages will point out some cases where ambiguity and vagueness serve useful purposes as well as cases where perfect understanding is the goal.

EQUIVOCATION   **Equivocal language** consists of words that have more than one commonly accepted definition. Some equivocal misunderstandings are amusing, as the following newspaper headlines illustrate:

> Family Catches Fire Just in Time
>
> Man Stuck on Toilet; Stool Suspected
>
> 20-Year Friendship Ends at the Altar
>
> Trees Can Break Wind

Some equivocal misunderstandings are trivial. We recall dining at a Mexican restaurant and ordering a "tostada with beans." Instead of being served a beef tostada with beans on the side, we were surprised to see the waiter bring us a plate containing a tostada *filled* with beans. As with most equivocal misunderstandings, hindsight showed that the phrase "tostada with beans" has two equally correct meanings.

Other equivocal misunderstandings can be more serious. A nurse gave one of her patients a scare when she told him that he "wouldn't be needing" his robe, books, and shaving materials anymore. The patient became quiet and moody. When the nurse inquired about the odd behaviour, she discovered that the poor man had interpreted her statement to mean he was going to die soon. Instead, the nurse meant he would be going home shortly.

It's difficult to catch every equivocal statement and clarify it while speaking. For this reason, the responsibility for interpreting statements accurately rests in large part with the receiver. Feedback of one sort or another–for example, the kind of perception checking introduced in Chapter 3 and the paraphrasing described in Chapter 7– can help clear up misunderstandings.

Despite its obvious problems, equivocal language has its uses. As Chapter 8 describes in detail, there are times when using language that is open to several interpretations can be useful. It helps people get along by avoiding the kind of honesty and clarity that can embarrass both the speaker and listener. For example, if a friend proudly shows you a newly completed painting and asks your opinion about it, you might respond equivocally by saying, "Gee, it's really unusual. I've never seen anything like it" instead of giving a less ambiguous but more hurtful response such as "A 3-year-old could have done this!"

The animals have no need for speech, why talk when you are a word. I lean against a tree, I am a tree leaning.

Margaret Atwood,
Surfacing

ABSTRACTION High-level abstractions are convenient ways of generalizing about similarities between several objects, people, ideas, or events. Figure 5–1 is an **abstraction ladder** that shows how to describe the same phenomenon at various levels of abstraction.

We use higher-level abstractions all the time. For instance, rather than saying, "Thanks for washing the dishes," "Thanks for vacuuming the rug," "Thanks for making the bed," it's easier to say, "Thanks for cleaning up." In such everyday situations, abstractions are a useful kind of verbal shorthand.

As with equivocal language, the vagueness of abstractions allows us to avoid confrontations by deliberately being unclear.[21] Suppose, for example, your boss is enthusiastic about a new approach to doing business that you think is a terrible idea. Telling the truth might seem too risky; but lying—saying, "I think it's a great idea"—wouldn't feel right either. In situations like this an abstract answer can hint at your true belief without a direct confrontation: "I don't know . . . It's sure unusual . . . It *might* work." The same sort of abstract language can help you avoid embarrassing friends who ask for your opinion with questions like "What do you think of my new haircut?" An abstract response like "It's really different!" may be easier for you to deliver—and for your friend to receive—than the clear, brutal truth: "It makes your face look so fat!" Chapter 8 will have more to say about abstract equivocations as an alternative to complete self-disclosure on the one hand and lies on the other.

FIGURE 5–1

Abstraction Ladder A boss gives feedback to an employee about career advancement at various levels of specificity.

Although vagueness does have its uses, highly abstract language can cause four types of problems. The first is stereotyping. Imagine someone who has had one bad experience and, as a result, blames an entire group: "Marriage counsellors are worthless," "Mounties are rude," or "Men are no good." Overly abstract expressions like these can cause people to *think* in generalities, ignoring uniqueness. As you learned in Chapter 2, expecting people to act a certain way can become a self-fulfilling prophecy. If you expect the worst of people, you have a good chance of getting it.

Besides narrowing your own options, excessively abstract language can confuse others. Telling the hairstylist "not too short" or "more casual" might produce the look you want, or it might lead to an unpleasant surprise. The following conversation illustrates the kind of frustration and confusion that can arise from overly abstract descriptions.

A: We never do anything that's fun anymore.

B: What do you mean?

A: We used to do lots of unusual things, but now it's the same old stuff, over and over.

B: But last week we went on that camping trip, and tomorrow we're going to that party where we'll meet all sorts of new people. Those are new things.

A: That's not what I mean. I'm talking about *really* unusual stuff.

B: *(Becoming confused and a little impatient)* Like what? Taking hard drugs or going over Niagara Falls in a barrel?

A: Don't be stupid. All I'm saying is that we're in a rut. We should be living more-exciting lives.

B: Well, I don't know what you want.

Overly abstract language also leads to confusing directions. Have you had the following experience?

Professor:	I hope you'll do a thorough job on this paper.
Student:	When you say "thorough," how long should it be?
Professor:	Long enough to cover the topic thoroughly.
Student:	How many sources should I look at when I'm researching it?
Professor:	You should use several–enough to show me that you've really explored the subject.
Student:	And what style should I use to write it?
Professor:	It doesn't matter, as long as it's scholarly but not too formal.
Student:	Arrgh!!!

Even appreciation can suffer from being expressed in overly abstract terms. Psychologists have established that behaviours that are reinforced will recur with increased frequency. Your statements of appreciation will encourage others to keep acting in ways you like; but if they don't know just what it is that you appreciate, the chances of their repeating that behaviour are lessened. There's a big difference between "I appreciate your being so nice" and "I appreciate the way you spent time talking to me when I was upset."

Overly abstract language can leave you unclear even about your own thoughts. At one time or another we've all felt dissatisfied with ourselves and others. Often these dissatisfactions show up as thoughts such as "I've got to get better organized" or "She's been acting strangely lately." Sometimes abstract statements such as these are shorthand for specific behaviours that we can identify easily; but in other cases we'd have a hard time explaining what we'd have to do to get organized or what the strange behaviour is. Without clear ideas of these concepts, it's hard to begin changing matters. Instead, we tend to go around in mental circles, feeling vaguely dissatisfied without knowing exactly what is wrong or how to improve it.

Overly abstract language can lead to problems of a more serious nature. For instance, accusations of sexual assault can be reduced when males and females both hold to the notion that "no" means "no." To ensure that both partners who engage in sex do so willingly, a low-level abstraction code was developed at Antioch College in Ohio. The code minimizes the chances of anyone claiming confusion about a partner's willingness. For example, the code states

> To knowingly take advantage of someone who is under the influence of alcohol, drugs, and/or prescribed medication is not acceptable behaviour in the Antioch community.

> If sexual contact and/or conduct is not mutually and simultaneously initiated, then the person who initiates sexual contact/conduct is responsible for getting verbal consent of the other individual(s) involved.

> If one person wants to initiate moving to a higher level of sexual intimacy . . . that person is responsible for getting verbal consent of the other person(s) involved before moving to that level.

If someone has initially consented but then stops consenting during a sexual interaction, she/he should communicate withdrawal verbally and/or through physical resistance. The other individual(s) must stop immediately.[22]

Some critics have ridiculed rules like these as being unrealistically legalistic and chillingly inappropriate for romantic relationships. Whatever its weaknesses, the Antioch code illustrates how low-level abstractions can reduce the chance of a serious misunderstanding.

Research shows that low-level descriptions can help improve the quality of relationships, even when conflicts arise. One study found that well-adjusted couples had just as many conflicts as poorly adjusted couples, but the way well-adjusted pairs handled their problems was significantly different. Instead of blaming one another by using evaluative language, the well-adjusted couples expressed their complaints in behavioural terms.[23]

It's hard to overestimate the value of specific, behavioural language because speaking in this way vastly increases the chance not only of thinking clearly about what's on your mind but also of others understanding you. A behavioural description should include three elements: the participants, the circumstances, and the behaviour itself.

Who Is Involved?   At first the answer to this question might seem simple. If you're thinking about a personal problem or goal, you might reply, "I am"; if you're expressing appreciation, complaining, or making a request of another person, he or she would be the one who is involved. Although the question of involvement may be easy, it often calls for more detail. Ask yourself whether the problem or goal you're thinking about involves an entire category of people (women, salespeople, strangers), a subclass of the group (attractive women, rude salespeople, strangers you'd like to meet), or a specific person (Jen Doe, the salesclerk at a particular store, a new person in your

Ethical Challenge

Defining Rape

In 1983, Canadian Criminal Code legislation changed the legal definition of rape, reflecting the reorientation of rape as assault. Instead of being defined as penetration of the penis in the vagina, rape became sexual assault measured by the severity of violence and trauma suffered by the victim. Two sections in the code were designed to combat juridical bias deriving from the myth that women are responsible for being raped, particularly if they are not virgins. These provisions prevented women's sexual history and reputation from being presented as part of the court proceedings in a rape trial. In 1991, one

of these sections, dubbed the "rape-shield" provision, was quashed by the Supreme Court, which contended that the rape-shield provision might jeopardize alleged rapists' rights to a fair trial.

In your opinion, how do the change in language and change regarding which information is admissible in court impact on both the victim's and the alleged rapist's right to a fair trial?

From B.D. Warme, E. Malus, and K.L.P. Lundy, *Sociology: A Window on the World*, 3rd ed. (Scarborough, ON: Nelson, 1994), p. 165.

Now, if you want to please the great mass of mankind you must talk platitudes: when you can't do that, the next best thing is to talk nonsense.

J.J. Procter,
The Philosopher in the Clearing

neighbourhood). If you're talking to another person, consider whether your appreciation, complaint, or request is directed solely at him or her or whether it also involves others.

In What Circumstances Does the Behaviour Occur?   You can identify the circumstances by answering several questions. In what places does the behaviour occur? Does it occur at any particular times? When you are discussing particular subjects? Is there anything special about you when it occurs: Are you tired, embarrassed, busy? Is there any common trait shared by the other person or people involved? Are they friendly or hostile, straightforward or manipulative, nervous or confident? In other words, if the behaviour you're describing doesn't occur all the time (and few behaviours do), you need to pin down what circumstances set this situation apart from other ones.

What Behaviours Are Involved?   Although such terms as *more co-operative* and *helpful* might sound as if they're concrete descriptions of behaviour, they are usually too vague to explain clearly what's on your mind. Behaviours must be *observable,* ideally both to you and to others. For instance, moving down the abstraction ladder from the relatively vague term *helpful,* you might arrive at "does the dishes every other day," "volunteers to help me type my papers," or "fixes dinner once or twice a week without being asked." Terms like these are easier for both you and others to understand than are more-vague abstractions.

There is one exception to the rule that behaviours should be observable, and that involves the internal processes of thoughts and emotions. For instance, in describing what happens to you when a friend has kept you waiting for a long time, you might say, "My stomach felt as if it were in knots—I was really worried. I kept thinking that you were in an accident or something, and I was so upset." What you're doing when offering such a description is to make unobservable events clear.

You can better understand the value of behavioural descriptions by looking at the examples in Table 5–3. Notice how much more clearly they explain the speaker's thought than do the more-vague terms.

EUPHEMISM   **Euphemisms** (from the Greek word meaning "to use words of good omen") are pleasant terms substituted for blunt ones. Euphemisms soften the impact of information that might be unpleasant. Unfortunately, this pulling of linguistic punches often obscures the accuracy of a message.

There are certainly cases where tactless honesty can be brutal: "What do I think of your new perm? You could take them to small claims court!" or "How do I feel about the relationship? I can hardly wait for the semester to end and you'll go home." At the same time, being too indirect can leave others wondering where you stand: "What an original hairdo," or "We could grow closer than we are

TABLE 5–3	ABSTRACT VS. BEHAVIOURAL DESCRIPTIONS				
	ABSTRACT DESCRIPTION	**BEHAVIOURAL DESCRIPTION**			**REMARKS**
		WHO IS INVOLVED	**IN WHAT CIRCUMSTANCES**	**SPECIFIC BEHAVIOURS**	
Problem	I talk too much.	People I find intimidating	When I want them to like me	I talk (mostly about myself) instead of giving them a chance to speak or asking about their lives.	Behavioural description more clearly identifies behaviours to change.
Goal	I want to be more con-structive.	My roommate	When we talk about household duties	Instead of finding fault with her ideas, sug-gest alterna-tives that might work.	Behavioural description clearly outlines how to act; abstract description doesn't.
Appreciation	"You've really been helpful lately."	(Deliver to fel-low worker)	"When I've had to take time off work because of personal problems . . ."	". . . you took my shifts without com-plaining."	Give both abstract and behavioural descriptions for best results.
Request	"Clean up your act!"	(Deliver to target person)	"When we're around my family . . ."	". . . please don't tell jokes that involve sex."	Behavioural description specifies desired behaviour.

now." When choosing how to broach difficult subjects, the challenge is to be as kind as possible without sacrificing either your integrity or the clarity of your message. (The guidelines for self-disclosure outlined in Chapter 8 will help you.)

RELATIVE LANGUAGE   **Relative words** gain their meaning by comparison. For example, do you attend a large or small school? This depends on what you compare it with. Alongside a campus such as the University of British Columbia with over 30 000 students, your school may look small; but compared with a smaller institution, it may seem quite large. Relative words, such as "fast" and "slow," "smart" and "stupid," "short" and "long," are clearly defined only through comparison.

Some relative terms are so common that we mistakenly assume that they have a clear meaning. In one study, graduate students were asked to assign numerical values to such terms as "doubtful," "toss-up," "likely," "probable," "good chance," and "unlikely."[24] There was a tremendous variation in the meaning of most of these terms. For example, the responses for "possible" ranged from 0 to 99 percent. "Good chance" meant between 35 and 90 percent, while "unlikely" fell between 0 and 40 percent.

Using relative terms without explaining them can lead to communication problems. Have you ever responded to someone's question about the weather by saying it was warm, only to find out the person thought it was cold? Have you ever gone to a restaurant that advertised give-away prices, only to find that it was twice as expensive as you expected? Have classes you heard were "easy" turned out to be hard? The problem in each case resulted from failing to link the relative word to a more measurable term.

SKILL BUILDER

DOWN-TO-EARTH LANGUAGE

You can appreciate the value of non-abstract language by translating the following into behavioural terms:

a. An abstract goal for improving your interpersonal communication (for example, "be more assertive" or "stop being so sarcastic")

b. A complaint you have about another person (for instance, that he or she is "selfish" or "insensitive")

c. A request for someone to change (as "I wish you'd be more punctual" or "Try to be more positive")

d. An appreciation you could share with another person (such as "Thanks for being so helpful" or "I appreciate your patience")

In each case, describe the person or people involved, the circumstances in which the behaviour occurs, and the precise behaviours involved. What difference will using behavioural descriptions such as the ones you have created here be likely to make?

STATIC EVALUATION "Jamie is a nervous guy." "Caleigh is short-tempered." "You can always count on Yali." Statements that contain or imply the word "is" lead to the mistaken assumption that people are consistent and unchanging—clearly an incorrect belief. Instead of labelling Jamie as permanently and totally nervous, it would probably be more accurate to outline the situations in which he behaves nervously. The same goes for Caleigh, Yali, and the rest of us: We are more changeable than the way static, everyday language describes us.

Describing John as "boring" (you can substitute "friendly," "immature," or many other adjectives) is less correct than saying, "The John I encountered yesterday seemed to me to be. . . ." The second type of statement describes the way someone behaved at one point; the first categorizes him as if he had always been that way.

Subscripting is one linguistic device of dating to reduce **static evaluation.** Adding a subscript whenever appropriate will show the transitory nature of many objects and behaviours. For example, a teacher might write as an evaluation of a student: "Susan$_{\text{MAY 12}}$ had difficulty co-operating with her classmates." Although the actual device of subscripting is awkward in writing and impractical in conversation, the idea it represents can still be used. Instead of saying, "I'm shy," a more accurate statement might be "I haven't approached any new people since I moved here." The first statement implies that your shyness is an unchangeable trait, rather like your height, while the second one suggests that you are capable of changing.

The Language of Responsibility

Besides providing a way to make the content of a message clear or obscure, language reflects the speaker's willingness to take responsibility for her or his beliefs and feelings. This acceptance or rejection of responsibility says a great deal about the speaker and can shape the tone of a relationship. To see how, read on.

"IT" STATEMENTS   Notice the difference between the sentences of each set:

> "It bothers me when you're late."
> "I'm worried when you're late."

> "It's nice to see you."
> "I'm glad to see you."

> "It's a boring class."
> "I'm bored in the class."

As their name implies, **"it" statements** replace the personal pronoun "I" with the less immediate word "it." By contrast, **"I" language** clearly identifies the speaker as the source of a message. Communicators who use "it" statements avoid responsibility for ownership of a message, instead attributing it to some unidentified source. This habit isn't just imprecise; more important, it is an unconscious way to avoid taking a position. You can begin to appreciate the increased directness of "I" language by trying to use it instead of the less direct and more evasive "it" statements in your own conversations.

"BUT" STATEMENTS   Statements that take the form "X-but-Y" can be confusing. A closer look at the **"but" statement** explains why. In each sentence, the word "but" cancels the thought that precedes it:

the nature of the word being that when it's been said it will always be said—a recording exists in the main deep of sound.

Al Purdy, "Method for Calling Up Ghosts" (from Tom Marshall, *Multiple Exposures, Promised Lands*)

"You're really a great person, but I think we ought to stop seeing each other."

"You've done good work for us, but we're going to have to let you go."

"This paper has some good ideas, but I'm giving it a D grade because it's late."

These "buts" often are a strategy for wrapping the speaker's real but unpleasant message between more-palatable ideas in a "psychological sandwich." This approach can be a face-saving strategy worth using at times. When the goal is to be absolutely clear, however, the most responsible approach can be to deliver the central idea without the distractions that can come with "but" statements.

QUESTIONS Some questions are sincere requests for information. At other times, though, questions are a linguistic way to avoid making a declaration. "What are we having for dinner?" may hide the statement "I want to eat out" or "I want to get a pizza."

"How many textbooks are assigned in that class?" may hide the statement "I'm afraid to get into a class with too much reading."

"Are you doing anything tonight?" can be a less risky way of saying "I want to go out with you tonight."

"Do you love me?" safely replaces the statement "I love you," which may be too embarrassing, too intimate, or too threatening to say directly.

Sometimes being indirect can be a tactful way to approach a topic that would be difficult to address head on. When used unnecessarily, though, it can be a way to avoid speaking for yourself. See Chapter 8 for more details about the value and risks of using questions.

"I" AND "YOU" LANGUAGE We've already seen that "I" language is a way of accepting responsibility for a message. **"You" language** is quite different. It expresses a judgement of the other person. Notice how each of the following statements implies that the subject of the complaint is doing something wrong:

"You left this place a mess!"

"You didn't keep your promise!"

"You're really crude sometimes!"

Despite its name, "you" language doesn't have to contain the pronoun "you," which is often implied rather than stated outright:

"That was a stupid joke!" ["Your jokes are stupid."]

"Don't be so critical!" ["You're too negative."]

"Mind your own business!" ["You're too nosy."]

Whether the judgement is stated outright or implied, it's easy to see why "you" language can arouse defensiveness. A "you" statement implies that the speaker is qualified to judge the target—not an idea

Conversational Terrorism: How NOT to Talk

http://www.vandruff.com/ art_converse.html

that most listeners are willing to accept, even when the evaluation is correct.

Fortunately, "I" language provides a more accurate and less provocative way to express a complaint.[25] "I" language shows that the speaker takes responsibility for the gripe by describing his or her reaction to the other's behaviour without making any judgements about its worth.

A complete "I" statement has three parts: It describes

1. the other person's behaviour,
2. your feelings, and
3. the consequences the other's behaviour has for you.

These three elements can appear in any order. A few examples of "I" statements illustrate how they sound in everyday conversation:

> "I get embarrassed [Feeling] when you talk about my bad grades in front of our friends [Behaviour]. I'm afraid they'll think I'm stupid [Consequence]."

> "When you didn't pick me up on time this morning [Behaviour] I was late for class, and I wound up getting chewed out by the professor [Consequences]. That's why I got so mad [Feeling]."

> "I haven't been very affectionate [Consequence] because you've hardly spent any time with me in the past few weeks [Behaviour]. I'm confused [Feeling] about how you feel about me."

When the chances of being misunderstood or getting a defensive reaction are high, it's a good idea to include all three elements in your "I" message. In some cases, however, only one or two of them will get the job done:

"I went to a lot of trouble to get those tickets, and now it's too late to go. Of course, I'm mad!" [The behaviour is obvious.]

"I'm worried because you haven't called me up." ["Worried" is both a feeling and a consequence.]

Even the best "I" statement won't work unless it's delivered in the right way. If your words are non-judgemental but your tone of voice, facial expression, and posture all send "you" messages, a defensive response is likely to follow. The best way to make sure your actions match your words is to remind yourself before speaking that your goal is to explain how the other's behaviour affects you—not to act like a judge and jury.

Advantages of "I" Language   Using "I" language reduces defensiveness and increases honesty and information for both you and the recipients.

1. *Defense Reduction* Others are more likely to accept your message when it's delivered in "I" language than when you make judge-mental "you" statements. Even accurate "you" statements ("you're late," "you broke your promise") are hard to take. By contrast, "I" statements aren't a direct attack on the recipient. Because they de-scribe how the speaker feels, they are easier to accept without jus-tification. This doesn't mean using "I" language will *eliminate* defensiveness, but it will almost certainly *reduce* it.
2. *Honesty* Even though they are kinder than "you" comments, "I" statements are just as honest. They let you speak your mind and share what bothers you. They aren't artificially "nice" or watered down to avoid displeasing the other person. In fact, because "I" statements are easier on the recipient, you are more likely to use them when you might be reluctant to blurt out an accusing "you" message.
3. *Completeness* "I" statements deliver more information than "you" messages. Instead of making the other person guess about what's bothering you, they describe the other person's behaviour. "I" statements also describe how the other's behaviour affects you and how you are feeling—much more information than most "you" messages.

Problems with "I" Language   Some readers have reservations about us-ing "I" language, despite its theoretical appeal. Three common objections are addressed below.

1. *"I get too angry to use 'I' language."* It's true that when you're an-gry the most likely reaction is to lash out with a judgemental "you" message. But it's probably smarter to keep quiet until you've thought about the consequences of what you might say than to blurt out something you'll regret later. It's also important to note that there's plenty of room for expressing anger with "I" language. It's just that you own the feeling as yours ("You bet I'm mad at you!") instead of distorting it into an attack ("That was a stupid thing to do!").

2. *"Even with 'I' language, the other person gets defensive."* Like every communication tool described in this book, "I" language won't always work. You may be so upset or irritated that your judgemental feelings contradict your words. Even if you deliver a perfectly worded "I" statement with total sincerity, the other person might be so defensive or unco-operative that nothing you say will make matters better. But using "I" language will almost certainly *improve* your chances for success, with little risk that this approach will make matters worse.

SKILL BUILDER

PRACTISING "I" LANGUAGE

You can develop your skill at delivering "I" messages by following these steps:

1. Visualize situations in your life when you might have sent each of the following messages:

   You're not telling me the truth!
   You think only of yourself!
   Don't be so touchy!
   Quit fooling around!
   You don't understand a word I'm saying!

2. Write alternatives to each statement using "I" language.

3. Think of three "you" statements you might make to people in your life. Transform each of these statements into "I" language and rehearse them with a classmate.

---

3. *"'I' language sounds artificial."* "That's not the way I talk," you might object. Much of the awkwardness that comes with first using "I" language is due to its novelty. This is a normal feeling. As you become more used to making "I" statements, they will sound more and more natural—and become more effective.

One of the best ways to overcome your initial awkwardness is to practise making "I" statements in a safe way: by trying them out in a class, writing them in letters, and delivering them to receptive people on relatively minor issues. After your skill and confidence have grown, you will be ready to tackle really challenging situations in a way that sounds natural and sincere.

"WE" LANGUAGE   Despite its obvious advantages, even the best-constructed and delivered "I" messages won't always succeed. As author Thomas Gordon points out, "Nobody welcomes hearing that his behaviour is causing someone a problem, no matter how the message is phrased."[26] For this reason, Gordon points out that "I" statements can leave the recipient feeling "hurt, sorry, surprised, embarrassed, defensive, argumentative, or even tearful." Furthermore, "I" language in large doses can start to sound egotistical. Research shows that self-absorbed people, also known as "conversational narcissists," can be identified by their constant use of first-person-singular pronouns.[27] For this reason, "I" language works best in moderation.

One way to avoid overuse of "I" statements is to consider the pronoun "we." **"We" statements** imply that the issue is the concern and responsibility of both the speaker and receiver of a message. Consider a few examples:

> "We need to figure out a budget that doesn't bankrupt us."

> "I think we have a problem. We can't seem to talk about money without fighting."

> "We aren't doing a very good job of keeping the place clean, are we?"

It's easy to see how "we" language can help build a constructive climate. Besides being immediate, it suggests a kind of "we're in this together" orientation that reflects the transactional nature of communication. People who use first-person-plural pronouns signal their closeness, commonality, and cohesiveness with others.[28] Chapters 9 and 10 offer detailed advice on the importance and value of achieving a "we" orientation.

On the other hand, "we" statements aren't always appropriate. Sometimes using this pronoun sounds presumptuous, because it suggests you are speaking for the other person as well as yourself. It's easy to imagine someone responding to your statement "We have a problem . . ." by saying, "Maybe *you* have a problem, but don't tell me *I* do!"

Given the pros and cons of both "I" and "we" language, what advice can we give about the most effective pronouns to use in interpersonal communication? Researchers have found that "I"/"We" combinations (for example, "I think that we . . ." or "I would like to see us . . .") have a good chance of being received favourably.[29] Because too much of any pronoun comes across as inappropriate, combining pronouns is generally a good idea. If your "I" language reflects your position without being overly self-absorbed, your "you" language shows concern for others without judging them, and your "we" language includes others without speaking for them, you will probably come as close as possible to the ideal use of pronouns. Table 5–4 summarizes the advantages and disadvantages of each type of speech and offers suggestions for approaches that have a good chance of success.

Disruptive Language

Not all linguistic problems come from misunderstandings. Sometimes people understand one another perfectly and still wind up in a conflict. Of course, not all disagreements can, or should, be avoided.

Communication Transcript

"I" and "You" Language on the Job

For some time, Rebecca has been frustrated by her fellow worker Tom's frequent absences from the job. She hasn't spoken up because she likes Tom and also because she doesn't want to sound like a complainer. Lately, though, Tom's absences have become longer and more frequent. Today he extended his half-hour lunch an extra 45 minutes. When he returned to the office, Rebecca confronted him with her gripe using "you" language.

Rebecca   Where have you been? You were due back at 12:30, and it's almost 1:30 now.

Tom   *(Surprised by Rebecca's angry tone, which she has never used before with him)* I had a few errands to run. What's the problem?

Rebecca   We all have errands to run, Tom. But it's not fair for you to do yours on company time.

Tom   *(Feeling defensive after hearing Rebecca's accusation)* I don't see why you have to worry about how I do my job. Beth *(their boss)* hasn't complained, so why should you worry?

Rebecca   Beth hasn't complained because all of us have been covering for you. You should appreciate what a tight spot we're in, making excuses every time you come in late or leave early. *(Again, Rebecca uses "you" language to tell Tom how he should think and act.)*

Tom   *(Now too defensive to consider Rebecca's concerns)* Hey, I thought we all covered for one another here. What about the time last year when I worked late for a week so you could go to your cousin's wedding in Montreal?

Rebecca   That's different! Nobody was lying then. When you take off, I have to make up stories about where you are. You're putting me in a very difficult spot, Tom, and it's not fair. You can't count on me to keep covering for you.

Tom   *(Feeling guilty, but too angry from Rebecca's judgements and threat to acknowledge his mistakes)* Fine. I'll never ask you for a favour again. Sorry to put you out.

Rebecca may have succeeded in reducing Tom's lateness, but her choice of "you" language left him feeling defensive and angry. The climate in the office is likely to be more strained— hardly the outcome Rebecca was seeking. Notice how she could have handled the same issue using "I" language to describe her problem instead of blaming Tom.

Rebecca   Tom, I need to talk to you about a problem. *(Notice how Rebecca identifies the problem as hers, instead of attacking Tom.)*

Tom   What's up?

Rebecca   You know how you come in late to work sometimes or take long lunch hours?

Tom   *(Sensing trouble ahead and sounding wary)* Yeah?

Rebecca   Well, I need to tell you that it's putting me in a tight spot. *(Rebecca describes the problem in behavioural terms, and then goes on to express her feeling.)* When Beth asks where you are, I don't want to say you're not here because that might get you in trouble. So sometimes I make excuses or even lie. But Beth is suspicious of my excuses, and I'm worried about that.

Tom   *(Feeling defensive because he knows he's guilty, but also sympathetic to Rebecca's position)* I don't want you to get in trouble. It's just that I've got to take care of a lot of personal business.

Rebecca   I know, Tom. I just want you to understand that it's getting impossible for me to cover for you.

Tom   Yeah, OK. Thanks for helping out.

Notice how "I" language made it possible for Rebecca to confront Tom honestly, but without blaming or attacking him personally. Even if Tom doesn't change, Rebecca has gotten the problem off her chest in a way that didn't sound ugly or annoying.

TABLE 5–4	PRONOUN USE AND ITS EFFECTS		
	ADVANTAGES	**DISADVANTAGES**	**TIPS**
"I" language	Takes responsibility for personal thoughts, feelings, and wants. Less defence-provoking than "you" language.	Can be perceived as egotistical, narcissistic, and self-absorbed.	Use "I" messages when other person doesn't perceive a problem. Combine "I" with "we" language.
"We" language	Signals inclusion, immediacy, cohesiveness, and commitment.	Can speak improperly for others.	Combine with "I" language. Use in group settings to enhance unity. Avoid when expressing personal thoughts, feelings, and wants.
"You" language		Can sound evaluative and judgemental.	Use "I" language during confrontations.

But eliminating three linguistic habits from your communication repertoire can minimize the kind of clashes that don't need to happen, allowing you to save your energy for the unavoidable and important struggles.

FACT–OPINION CONFUSION   Factual statements are claims that can be verified as true or false. By contrast, opinion statements are based on the speaker's beliefs. Unlike matters of fact, they can never be proved or disproved. Consider a few examples of the difference between factual and opinion statements:

Fact	*Opinion*
It rains more in Vancouver than Kamloops.	The climate in Kamloops is better than Vancouver.
Kareem Abdul-Jabbar is the all-time leading scorer in the National Basketball Association.	Kareem is the greatest basketball player in the history of the game.
Big companies profit from selling sports clothes	I get ripped off every time I buy a new pair of sneakers.

When factual and opinion statements are set side by side like this, the difference between them is clear. In everyday conversation, however, we often present our opinions as if they were facts, and in doing so we invite an unnecessary argument. For example:

- "That was a dumb thing to say!"
- "Spending that much on _____ is a waste of money!"
- "You can't get a fair shake in this country unless you're a white male."

Notice how much less antagonistic each statement would be if it were prefaced by a qualifier such as "In my opinion . . ." or "It seems to me. . . ."

FACT–INFERENCE CONFUSION   Labelling your opinions can go a long way toward relational harmony, but developing this habit won't solve all linguistic problems. Difficulties also arise when we confuse factual statements with inferential statements—conclusions arrived at from an interpretation of evidence.

Arguments often result when we label our inferences as facts:

A: Why are you mad at me?
B: I'm not mad at you. Why have you been so insecure lately?
A: I'm not insecure. It's just that you've been so critical.
B: What do you mean, "critical"? I haven't been critical. . . .

Instead of trying to read the other person's mind, a far better course is to identify the observable behaviours (facts) that have caught your attention and to describe the interpretations (inferences) that you have drawn from them. After describing this train of thought, ask the other person to comment on the accuracy of your interpretation.

"When you didn't return my phone call [fact], I got the idea that you're mad at me [inference]. Are you?" [question]

"You've been asking me lately whether I still love you [fact], and that makes me think you're feeling insecure [inference]. Is that right?" [question]

> *Conversation has more vitality, more fun and more drama than writing. What I say is being used as a probe and it's not a package. I'm probing around without making special pronouncements. Most people say things as the result of thinking, but I use it to probe.*
>
> Marshall McLuhan,
> quoted in *Weekend Magazine*

EMOTIVE LANGUAGE **Emotive language** seems to describe something but really announces the speaker's attitude toward it. If you approve of a friend's roundabout approach to a difficult subject, you might call her "tactful"; if you don't like it, you might accuse her of "beating around the bush." Whether the approach is good or bad is more a matter of opinion than of fact, although this difference is obscured by emotive language.

You can appreciate how emotive words are really editorial statements when you consider these examples:

If you approve, say	*If you disapprove, say*
thrifty	cheap
traditional	old-fashioned
extrovert	loudmouth
cautious	cowardly
progressive	radical
information	propaganda
eccentric	crazy

Using emotive labels can have ugly consequences. Although experimental subjects who heard a derogatory label used against a member of a minority group expressed annoyance at this sort of slur, the negative emotional terms still had an impact.[30] Not only did the unwitting subjects rate the minority individual's competence lower when that person performed poorly, but also they found fault with others who associated socially with that minority person—even members of the subject's own ethnic group.

The best way to avoid arguments involving emotive words is to describe the person, thing, or idea you are discussing in neutral terms, and to label your opinions as such. Instead of saying "I wish you'd quit making those sexist remarks," say "I really don't like it when you call us 'girls' instead of 'women.'" Not only are non-emotive statements more accurate, but also they have a much better chance of being well received by others.

GENDER AND LANGUAGE

So far we have discussed language as if it were identical for both sexes. In many cases, however, there are significant differences between the ways men and women speak. As you read on, keep in mind that it is a mistake to think that *all* women use language in ways that are different from *all* men. What extensive research has uncovered is the fact that, in contemporary culture, there are some *characteristically* male and female ways of speaking. By the time you finish this section, you will see that gender is just one of many factors that shape the way we use language.

Content

Although a great deal of variation appears within each gender, on the average men and women discuss a surprisingly different range of topics. The first research on conversational topics was conducted over 70 years ago. Despite the changes in male and female roles since then, the results of several studies are remarkably similar.[51] In these surveys, women and men ranging in age from 17 to 80 described the range of topics each discussed with friends of the same sex. Certain subjects were common to both men and women: Work, movies, and television proved to be frequent topics for both groups. Both women and men reserved discussions of sex and sexuality for members of the same sex. The differences between men and women were more striking than the similarities. Female friends spent much more time discussing personal and domestic subjects, relationship problems, family, health and reproductive matters, weight, food and clothing, men, and other women. Men, on the other hand, were more likely to discuss music, current events, sports, business, and other men. Both men and women were equally likely to discuss personal

---

INVITATION TO INSIGHT

CONJUGATING "IRREGULAR VERBS"

According to S.I. Hayakawa, the game of conjugating "irregular verbs" originated with Bertrand Russell. The technique is simple: Just take an action or personality trait, and show how it can be viewed either favourably or unfavourably, according to the label it's given. For example:

> I'm casual.
> You're a little careless.
> He's a slob.

Or try this one:

> I'm thrifty.
> You're money conscious.
> She's a tightwad.

1. Try a few conjugations yourself, using the following statements:

   a. I'm tactful.
   b. I'm conservative.
   c. I'm quiet.
   d. I'm relaxed.
   e. My child is high-spirited.
   f. I have high self-esteem.

2. Now recall at least two situations in which you used emotive language as if it were a description of fact and not an opinion. A good way to recall these situations is to think of a recent disagreement and imagine how the other people involved might have described it differently than you.

appearance, sex, and dating in same-sex conversations. Regarding gossip, women were more likely to talk about close friends and family, while men gossiped about sports figures and media personalities. The gossip of neither sex was more derogatory than that of the other.

These differences can lead to frustration when women and men try to converse with one another. Researchers report that both men and women describe topics discussed by the opposite sex as "trivial." "I want to talk about important things," a woman might say, "like how we're getting along. All he wants to do is talk about the news or what we'll do this weekend."

Reasons for Communicating

Men and women, at least in the dominant cultures of Canada and the United States, often use language in different ways for different purposes. As a group, women are more inclined than men to use conversation to establish and maintain relationships with others. In fact, communication researcher Julia Wood flatly states that "for women, talk *is* the essence of relationships."[32] When a group of women was surveyed to find out what kinds of satisfaction they gained from talking with their friends, the most common theme mentioned was a feeling of empathy—"To know you're not alone," as some put it.[33] Whereas men commonly described same-sex conversations as something they *liked*, females characterized their woman-to-woman talks as a kind of contact they *needed*. The characteristically female orientation for relational communication is supported by studies of married couples showing that wives spend proportionately more time than husbands communicating in ways that help maintain their relationship.[34]

Because they use conversation to pursue social needs, women typically use statements showing support for the other person, offer demonstrations of equality, and make efforts to keep the conversation going. With these goals, it's not surprising that traditionally female speech often contains statements of sympathy and empathy: "I've felt just like that myself," "The same thing happened to me!" Women are also inclined to ask lots of questions that invite the other person to share information: "How did you feel about that?" "What did you do next?" The importance of nurturing a relationship also explains why female speech is often somewhat deferential and tentative. Saying, "This is just my opinion . . ." is less likely to put off a conversational partner than a more definite "Here's what I think. . . ."

The greater frequency of female conversations reflects their importance. Nearly 50 percent of the women surveyed said they called friends at least once a week just to talk, whereas less than half as many men did so. In fact, 40 percent of the men surveyed reported that they never called another man just to chat.

Men's speech is often driven by quite different goals than women's speech. Men are more likely to use language to accomplish the job at hand than to nourish relationships. This explains why men are less likely than women to disclose their vulnerabilities, which could be perceived as a sign of weakness. When someone is sharing a problem, instead of empathizing men are prone to offer advice: "That's nothing to worry about . . ." "Here's what you need to do. . . ." Besides taking care of business, men are more likely than women to use conversations to exert control, preserve their independence, and enhance their status. This explains why men are more prone to dominate conversations and one-up their partners. Men interrupt their conversational partners to assert their own experiences or point of view. (Women interrupt, too, but they usually do so to offer support: quite a different goal.) Just because male talk is competitive doesn't mean it's not enjoyable. Men often regard talk as a kind of game: When researchers asked men what they liked best about their all-male talk, the most frequent answer was its ease.[35] Another common theme was appreciation of the practical value of conversation: new ways to solve problems. Men also mentioned enjoying the humour and rapid pace that characterized their all-male conversations.

Differences like these begin early in childhood. Sociolinguist Deborah Tannen summarizes a variety of studies showing that boys use talk to assert control over one another, while girls' conversations are aimed at maintaining harmony.[36] Transcripts of conversations between preschoolers aged 2 to 5 showed that girls are far more co-operative than boys.[37] They preceded their proposals for action by saying "let's," as in "Let's go find some" or "Let's turn back." By contrast, boys gave orders like "Lie down" or "Gimme your arm."

Conversational Style

Women behave differently in conversations than do men.[38] For example, although both men and women use expletives, men swear more than women.[39] Women ask more questions in mixed-sex conversations than do men—nearly three times as many, according to one study. Other research has revealed that in mixed-sex conversations, men interrupt women far more than the other way around. Some theorists have argued that differences like these result in women's speech that is less powerful and more emotional than men's. Research has supported these theories—at least in some cases. Even when clues about the speaker's sex were edited out, raters found clear differences between transcripts of male and female speech. In one study women's talk was judged more aesthetic, while men were seen as more dynamic, aggressive, and strong. In another, male job applicants were rated more fluent, active, confident, and effective than females, all because of language style.

Other studies have revealed that men and women behave differently in certain conversational settings. For example, in mixed-sex dyads men talk longer than women, while in same-sex situations women speak for a longer time. In larger groups, men talk more, while in smaller settings women do more of the speaking. In same-sex conversations there are other differences between men and

Consider the marriage of a man who has had most of his conversations with other men, to a woman who has had most of hers with other women. . . . He is used to fast-paced conversations that typically stay on the surface with respect to emotions, that often enable him to get practical tips or offer them to others, and that are usually pragmatic or fun. She is used to conversations that, while practical and fun, too, are also a major source of emotional support, self-understanding, and the understanding of others. Becoming intimate with a man, the woman may finally start expressing her concerns to him as she might to a close friend. But she may find, to her dismay, that his responses are all wrong. Instead of making her feel better, he makes her feel worse. The problem is that he tends to be direct and practical, whereas what she wants more than anything else is an empathetic listener. Used to years of such responses from close friends, a woman is likely to be surprised and angered by her husband's immediate "Here's what ya do. . . ."

Mark Sherman and Adelaide Haas

women: Females use more questions, justifiers, intensive adverbs, personal pronouns, and adverbials. Men use more directives, interruptions, and filler words to begin sentences.[40]

Given these differences, a pessimist might wonder how men and women manage to communicate with one another at all. One reason cross-sex conversations do run smoothly so often is because women accommodate to the topics men raise. Both men and women often regard topics introduced by women as tentative, whereas topics that men bring up are more likely to be pursued. Thus, women seem to characteristically grease the wheels of conversation by doing more work than men in maintaining conversations. A complementary difference between men and women also promotes cross-sex conversations: Men are more likely to talk about themselves with women than with other men; and since women are willing to adapt to this topic, conversations are likely to run smoothly, if one-sidedly.

An accommodating style isn't necessarily a disadvantage for women. One study revealed that females who spoke tentatively were actually more influential with men than those who used more-powerful speech.[41] On the other hand, this tentative style was less effective in persuading women. (Language use had no effect on men's persuasiveness.) This research suggests that women who are willing and able to be flexible in their approach can persuade both other women and men . . . as long as they are not dealing with a mixed-sex audience.

Nongender Variables

Despite the differences in the way men and women speak, the link between gender and language use isn't as clear-cut as it might seem.[42] A large number of studies have found no significant difference between male and female speech in areas such as use of profanity, use of qualifiers such as "I guess" or "This is just my opinion," tag questions, and vocal fluency. Some on-the-job research shows that male and female supervisors in similar positions behave the same way and are equally effective. Other studies, however, have found differences between the styles of men and women. Female managers were rated as providing more information, putting more emphasis on happy interpersonal relationships, as well as being more encouraging, receptive to new ideas, concerned, and attentive. Male managers were rated as being more dominant, direct, and quick to challenge. The researchers concluded that "male and female managers [exerted] leadership in their own distinct fashions." They also argued that females may be superior managers because their verbal communication promotes more job satisfaction.

A growing body of research explains some of the apparent contradictions between the similarities and differences between male and female speech. Research has revealed other factors that influence language use as much as or more than gender does.[43] For example, social philosophy plays a role. Feminist wives talk longer than their partners, while nonfeminist wives speak less than their husbands. Orientation toward problem solving also plays a role in conversational style. The co-operative or competitive orientation of speakers has more influence on how they interact than does their gender.

The speaker's occupation also influences speaking style. For example, male day-care teachers' speech to their students resembles the language of female teachers more closely than it resembles the language of fathers at home. Overall, doctors interrupt their patients more often than the reverse, although male patients do interrupt female physicians more often than their male counterparts. A close study of trial transcripts showed that the speaker's experience on the witness stand and occupation had more to do with language use than did gender. If women generally use "powerless" language, this fact probably reflects their historical role in society at large.

To the degree that women use powerless language, there may be two explanations. One involves their historical role: Powerless speech may reflect the relative lack of power held by women. If this explanation is valid, the male–female differences in powerful and powerless speech are likely to diminish. A second, equally compelling explanation for the women-use-more-powerless-language finding comes from scholars, including Julia Wood[44] and Deborah Tannen,[45] who point out that what powerless speech sacrifices in potency it gains by building rapport between speaker and receiver. Because women have historically been more concerned with building harmonious relationships, it follows that typically feminine speech will sound less powerful.

Another powerful force that influences the way individual women and men speak is their **sex role.** Recall the various sex types described in Chapter 3 (pages 106–107): masculine, feminine, and androgynous. Remember that these sex types don't necessarily line up neatly with gender. There are "masculine" females, "feminine" males, and androgynous communicators who combine traditionally masculine and feminine characteristics. These sex roles can influence a communicator's style more than his or her biological sex. For example, one study revealed that masculine sex-type subjects used significantly more-dominant language than did either feminine or androgynous group members.[46] Feminine members expressed slightly more submissive behaviours and more equivalence behaviours than those of the androgynous group members, and their submissiveness and equivalence were much greater than those of the masculine subjects.

By now it should be clear that there are differences between the way men and women speak but that these differences are determined by a wide variety of factors that have little or nothing to do with biological sex. As men and women grow to have equal opportunities and more similar social experiences, we can expect that there will be fewer differences in the ways they speak.

Drawing by Leo Cullum; © *1996 The New Yorker Magazine, Inc.*

LANGUAGE AND CULTURE

Anyone who has tried to translate ideas from one language to another knows that conveying the same meaning isn't always easy.[47] Sometimes the results of a bungled translation can be amusing. For example, an American firm unknowingly introduced its product, Pet milk, to French-speaking markets without realizing that the word *pet* in French means "to break wind."[48] Likewise, the English-speaking representative of a soft drink manufacturer naively drew laughs from Mexican customers when she offered free samples of Fresca soda pop. In Mexican slang the word *fresca* means "lesbian."

Even choosing the right words during translation won't guarantee that nonnative speakers will use an unfamiliar language correctly. For example, Japanese insurance companies warn their policyholders who are visiting North America to avoid their cultural tendency to say "excuse me" or "I'm sorry" if they are involved in a traffic accident.[49] In Japan, apologizing is a traditional way to express goodwill and maintain social harmony, even if the person offering the apology is not at fault. But in North America an apology can be taken as an admission of guilt and result in Japanese tourists being held accountable for accidents in which they may not be responsible.

Difficult as it may be, translation is only a small part of the differences in communication between members of different cultures.

Differences in the way language is used and the very worldview that a language creates make communicating across cultures a challenging task. We see this in our own country. Due to its history and isolation from major centres, there has developed in Newfoundland what is referred to as Newfoundland English. Although not spoken by everyone, Newfoundland English consists of a variety of words and

The History of Black English

It is simple to date the beginning of Black English—the first Blacks arrived in Virginia in 1619, and the history of Black slavery in what is now Canada goes back to those early years as well. Ten years after the arrival of Blacks in Virginia, Oliver Le Jeune, one of the first slaves for whom there is a name, was sold into slavery in New France. Many Loyalists were slave-holders and brought slaves with them into British North America. But in addition to slaves, a large number of Blacks who earned their freedom through loyalty to the Crown immigrated into Nova Scotia and New Brunswick after the American Revolution. In 1833, Parliament in London abolished slavery in Britain's North American colonies, although in actual fact the practice had been under severe restrictions in many parts of the country before that date. Upper Canada restricted slavery in 1793, with the intention of abolishing it. Because of such laws, escaping slaves sought refuge in Canada before and during the American Civil War, though many of them returned to their homes in the United States afterward.

With changes in discriminatory immigration laws, the last half of the twentieth century has brought increased emigration from the Caribbean and Africa. These New Canadians do not speak Black English but rather the English dialect of their former homes; or they have learned Canadian English after settling in their new country. While Black English in the United States has been subjected to intense study in the past few decades, investigation of the English of Black Canadians has been slight. In part this is due to the smaller size of the Black community (approximately 2 percent of the population), in part to the perception that Black citizens have completely assimilated themselves into the general language community and speak the English of their white neighbours. Like many facets of Canadian English, this is, however, an area that remains largely unexplored by all but a few recent students.

Nonetheless, there are communities, settled by Loyalist Blacks and those fleeing from slavery, that have been largely segregated from the surrounding white neighbourhoods and that may reflect earlier forms of Black English. Linguists have begun to explore the nature of the English spoken in these areas in an effort to determine exactly how these dialects relate to the Black English of the United States[52] and to better understand the dialects of Canadian English.

The history and structure of Black English, then, are almost entirely based on a dialect that has been studied in the United States, where at least two views of the origin of that dialect are evident. One view suggests that Black English in North America originated when the African slaves learned English from their colonial masters as a second language. Although the basic grammar was learned, many surface differences persisted, which were reflected in the grammars constructed by the children of slaves, who heard English primarily from their parents. Had the children been exposed to the English spoken by the whites, their grammars would have been more similar if not identical to the general southern dialect. The dialect differences persisted and grew because Blacks in America were isolated by social and racial barriers. The proponents of this view point to the fact that the grammars of Black English and standard American English are basically identical except for a few syntactic and phonological rules, which produce surface differences.

Another view that is receiving increasing support is that many of the unique features of Black English are traceable to influences of the African languages spoken by the slaves. During the seventeenth and eighteenth centuries, Africans who spoke different languages were purposely grouped together to discourage communication and to prevent slave revolts. In order to communicate, the slaves were forced to use the one common language all had access to, namely, English. They invented a simplified form that incorporated many features from West African languages. According to this view, the differences between Black English and other dialects are due more to basic syntactic differences than to surface distinctions.

It is apparent that Black English of the United States is closer to the southern dialect of American English than to other dialects. The theory that suggests that the Negro slaves learned the English of white southerners as a second language explains these similarities. They might also be explained by the fact that for many decades a large number of southern white children were raised by Black women and played with Black children. It is not unlikely that many of the distinguishing features of southern dialects were acquired from Black English in this way. A publication of the American Dialect Society in 1908–1909 makes this point clearly:

> For my part, after a somewhat careful study of east Alabama dialect, I am convinced that the speech of the white people, the dialect I have spoken all my life and the one I tried to record here, is more largely colored by the language of the negroes [sic] than by any other single influence.[53]

The two-way interchange still goes on. Standard Canadian English and American English are enriched by words, phrases, and usage originating in Black English; and Black English, whatever its origins, is influenced by the changes that go on in the many other dialects of English.

Victoria Fromkin, Robert Rodman, Neil Hultin, and Harry Logan

lexical items unique to Newfoundland, or to specific areas of the island. For instance, *drite* refers to dryness in the air; *dwall* to a short, light sleep; *joog* to a drop of liquid; or *quoit* to skipping flat stones over the water. If you're offered a *bung-your-eye* and accept, you'll get a strong alcoholic beverage. The mercantile class in St. John's is referred to as the *fishocracy*. You may also hear individuals use certain past-time constructions such as, "How many times am I after telling you?" as opposed to, "How many times have I told you?" These and other phonological features might be very confusing to an outsider who is unfamiliar with the culture and the language.[50]

Of course, the issue of language and culture is particularly salient here in Canada with its two national languages. To encourage communication between speakers of both languages, education programs have been developed to assist this effort. Since the 1970s and early 1980s, for instance, Canadian children have the option of learning French through immersion programs, and we're seeing a definite increase in bilingualism. In 1981, 17.7 percent of Canada's teens were bilingual, but by 1996 that percentage had increased to 24.4 percent, almost a quarter of all teens, with the highest proportion of bilingual teens in New Brunswick (49.3 percent).[51] According to the *Commissioner of Official Languages Annual Report 1998,* this increase can be attributed to the work of Canadian Parents for French, a dynamic organization that worked to implement French immersion programs across Canada.

Verbal Communication Styles

Using language is more than just choosing a particular group of words to convey an idea. Each language has its own unique style that distinguishes it from others. Matters like the amount of formality or informality, precision or vagueness, and brevity or detail are major ingredients in speaking competently. And when a communicator tries to use the verbal style from one culture in a different one, problems are likely to arise.[54]

One way in which verbal styles vary is in their *directness.* Anthropologist Edward Hall identified two distinct cultural ways of using language.[55] **Low-context cultures** use language primarily to express thoughts, feelings, and ideas as clearly and logically as possible. Low-context communicators look for the meaning of a statement in the words spoken. By contrast, **high-context cultures** value language as a way to maintain social harmony. Rather than upset others by speaking clearly, communicators in these societies learn to discover meaning from the context in which a message is delivered: the nonverbal behaviours of the speaker, the history of the relationship, and the general social rules that govern interaction between people. Table 5–5 summarizes some key differences between the way low- and high-context cultures use language.

North American culture falls toward the low-context end of the scale. Residents of Canada value straight talk and grow impatient

TABLE 5-5	LOW- AND HIGH-CONTEXT COMMUNICATION STYLES

LOW CONTEXT	HIGH CONTEXT
Majority of information carried in explicit verbal messages, with less focus on the situational context.	Important information carried in contextual cues (time, place, relationship, situation). Less reliance on explicit verbal messages.
Self-expression valued. Communicators state opinions and desires directly and strive to persuade others to accept their own viewpoint.	Relational harmony valued and maintained by indirect expression of opinions. Communicators abstain from saying "no" directly.
Clear, eloquent speech considered praiseworthy. Verbal fluency admired.	Communicators talk "around" the point, allowing the other to fill in the missing pieces. Ambiguity and use of silence admired.

with "beating around the bush." By contrast, most Asian and Middle Eastern cultures fit the high-context pattern. In many Asian cultures, for example, maintaining harmony is important, and so communicators will avoid speaking clearly if that would threaten another person's face. For this reason, Japanese or Koreans are less likely than Canadians or Americans to offer a clear "no" to an undesirable request. Instead they would probably use roundabout expressions like "I agree with you in principle, but . . ." or "I sympathize with you. . . ." For example, our Chinese colleague, Dr. Dejun Liu, notes that his communication style is different in Chinese (which he speaks at home) and in English (which he speaks with us). When queried about the differences, he shared that at home he focusses on the listener and doesn't say things in a very clear fashion. He does this on purpose, explaining that one doesn't always want to be clear but that understanding would emerge from the context. However, when Dejun speaks English at the university, he organizes his message so that he is specific, succinct, and assertive. But cultural differences don't fade when we speak another language. Dejun told the story of his friend, another Asian professor, who noted that all her colleagues were being promoted and she wasn't. The friend was well published and felt she, too, was deserving of advancement. She, in the Chinese tradition, was waiting for the leader, her dean, to tell her when it was time to apply. Of course, in Canadian culture this is not the custom. The experience helped her to adapt more to the Canadian way and to speak up for herself.

The same sort of clash between directness and indirectness can aggravate problems between straight-talking, low-context Israelis, who value speaking clearly, and Arabs, whose high-context culture stresses smooth interaction. It's easy to imagine how the clash of cultural styles could lead to misunderstandings and conflicts between Israelis and their Palestinian neighbours. Israelis could view their

Their language is their point of honour, as well as their lever of power. So long as they keep it, they are unconquered. When it ceases to be spoken by their children, a greater loss than Montcalm's will be felt.

Thomas D'Arcy McGee, Father of Confederation, on the speech of the French Canadians, quoted by Graham Fraser in *P.Q.: René Lévesque and the Parti Québécois in Power*

Arab counterparts as evasive, while the Palestinians could perceive the Israelis as insensitive and blunt.

Another way in which language styles can vary across cultures is whether they are *elaborate* or *succinct*. Speakers of Arabic, for instance, commonly use language that is much more rich and expressive than most communicators who use English. Strong assertions and exaggerations that would sound ridiculous in English are a common feature of Arabic. This contrast in linguistic styles can lead to misunderstandings between people from different backgrounds. As one observer put it,

> First, an Arab feels compelled to overassert in almost all types of communication because others expect him [or her] to. If an Arab says exactly what he [or she] means without the expected assertion, other Arabs may still think that he [or she] means the opposite. For example, a simple "no" by a guest to the host's requests to eat more or drink more will not suffice. To convey the meaning that he [or she] is actually full, the guest must keep repeating "no" several times, coupling it with an oath such as "By God" or "I swear to God." Second, an Arab often fails to realize that others, particularly foreigners, may mean exactly what they say even though their language is simple. To the Arabs, a simple "no" may mean indirectly expressed consent and encouragement of a coquettish woman. On the other hand, a simple consent may mean the rejection of a hypocritical politician.[56]

Succinctness is most extreme in cultures where silence is valued. In many Native cultures, for example, the favoured way to handle ambiguous social situations is to remain quiet.[57] When you contrast this silent style to the talkativeness that is common in mainstream North American cultures when people first meet, it's easy to imagine how the first encounter between an Inuktituk speaker and an English speaker might feel uncomfortable to both people.

Along with such differences as directness and indirectness and elaborate and succinct styles, a third way languages differ from one culture to another involves *formality* and *informality*. When one of the authors was learning conversational French, she had to gain a sense of when *vous*, the formal form of the word *you*, was appropriate and when *tu*, the more familiar usage, was not only acceptable but also was the expected format. The informal approach that characterizes relationships in countries like Canada, the United States, Australia, and the Scandinavian countries is quite different from the great concern for using proper speech in many parts of Asia and Africa. Formality isn't so much a matter of using correct grammar as of defining social position. In Korea, for example, the language reflects the Confucian system of relational hierarchies.[58] It has special vocabularies for different sexes, for different levels of social status, for different degrees of intimacy, and for different types of social occasions. For example, there are different degrees of formality for speaking with old friends, nonacquaintances whose background one knows, and complete strangers. One sign of being a learned person in Korea is the ability to use language that recognizes these relational distinctions.

Language and Worldview

Different linguistic styles are important, but there may be even more fundamental differences that separate speakers of various languages. For almost 150 years, some theorists have put forth the notion of **linguistic determinism:** that the worldview of a culture is unavoidably shaped and reflected by the language its members speak. The best-known example of linguistic determinism is the notion that the Inuit have a large number of words (estimated at between 17 and 100) for what we simply call "snow." Different terms are used to describe conditions like a driving blizzard, crusty ice, and light powder. This example suggests how linguistic determinism operates. The need to survive in an Arctic environment led the Inuit to make distinctions that would be unimportant to residents of warmer environments, and once the language makes these distinctions, speakers are more likely to see the world in ways that match the broader vocabulary.

Even though there is some doubt that the Inuit really have so many words for snow,[59] other examples do seem to support the principle of linguistic determinism.[60] For instance, bilingual speakers seem to think differently when they change languages. In one study, French speakers were asked to interpret a series of pictures. When they spoke in French, their descriptions were far more romantic and emotional than when they used English to describe the same kinds of images. Likewise, when students in Hong Kong were asked to complete a values test, they expressed more-traditional Chinese values when they answered in Cantonese than when they spoke English. In Israel, both Arab and Jewish students saw bigger distinctions between their group and "outsiders" when using their native language than when they spoke in English, a

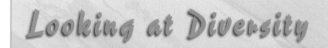

Looking at Diversity

French Immersion

Amy Katz

We studied anatomy in French. We studied geography, physics, and fractals in French. We put on French versions of English plays: *Peter Pan, Fiddler on the Roof* ("Si j'étais un homme riche"). We read *Le Petit Prince* (at least ten times) and later, long before we were ready, *Nausée, Un Amour de Swann,* and *Agaguk*. We were not allowed to speak English to each other in class. Often, we didn't understand what was going on at all. But our teachers optimistically prattled on, lending us their standardized, board-mandated, bowmouthed accents, so that later we would sound like strangers on our exchange trips to Chicoutimi and Quebec City.

We were the third ever French-immersion class to go through Owen Public School in Toronto. (The program continues to be taught there today.) We didn't know it at the time, but our parents were pitting themselves against everyone from neighbours to local principals to lunchroom volunteers. In Ontario, immersion's opponents made death threats and vandalized schools, setting fires and smashing windows, all in defence of the English language. I asked my mother why she bothered to navigate the controversy, and she answered, "I felt they were saying to us, 'Here's a wonderful opportunity for your child, and it's free.' Who's going to say no to that?" In our neighbourhood, everyone except us.

We ate lunch in a separate room from the other kids, because both parents and teachers were afraid we'd ruin their kids' English. The kids wouldn't have talked to us anyway. We were, in playground vernacular, big losers, and this remained our social ranking until well after graduation. Recently I ran into a girl (woman, I guess) from high school in a coffee shop downtown. I smiled, said hello, asked her about her sister. She looked at me blankly. I told her we'd gone to the same high school. She stared. I told her I was in French immersion. Oh, she said, understanding completely.

In the classroom, we learned about Louis Riel and the Plains of Abraham, but not about the Quiet Revolution, or Quebec separatism, or even, really, Quebec. We were taught French but never *why* we were learning French—the strange Canadian alchemy that had projected us into life in this other language.

But we did learn the language. Indelibly. It wasn't until later, after many years of self-imposed unilingualism, that I trotted out the rusty syllables one night in a bar in Montreal, motivated by the need to make a point. The guy I was talking to, who until that moment had been a romantic possibility, told me I sounded like an American tourist. But I felt, however mistakenly, in my element. I found that my vocabulary, acquired in childhood, had retained a visceral hold on my imagination; that a language once used to pose the queries of a seven-year-old resonates differently from one learned as a adult. I dropped the conversation but realized, then and there, that if I could reconfigure my accent, update my seventies terminology, and stop addressing everyone as "vous," I could speak French for real. It reminded me of how I'd silently rejoiced after the first few days of kindergarten, thinking, I get to do this, I really get to learn like this every day. Now, twenty-odd years later, the words are still there—bilingualism's confused, bureaucratic, and most precious gift.

From Amy Katz, "French Immersion," *Saturday Night*

neutral tongue. Examples like these show the power of language to shape cultural identity . . . sometimes for better, and sometimes for worse.

Linguistic influences start early in life. English-speaking parents often label the mischievous pranks of their children as "bad," implying that there is something immoral about acting wild. "Be good!" they are inclined to say. On the other hand, French adults are more likely to say *"Sois sage!"*–"Be wise." The linguistic implication is that misbehaving is an act of foolishness. Swedes would correct the same action with the words *"Var snall!"*–"Be friendly," "Be kind." By contrast, German adults use the command *"Sei artig!"*–literally "Be of your own kind"–in other words, get back in step, conform to your role as a child.[61]

The best-known declaration of linguistic determinism is the **Sapir–Whorf hypothesis,** formulated by Edward Sapir and Benjamin Whorf.[62] Following Sapir's theory, Whorf observed that the language spoken by Hopi Native Americans represents a view of reality that is dramatically different from that of more-familiar tongues. For example, the Hopi language makes no distinction between nouns and verbs. Therefore the people who speak it describe the entire world as being constantly in process. Whereas we use nouns to characterize people or objects as being fixed or constant, Hopi view them more as verbs, constantly changing. In this sense our language represents much of the world rather like a snapshot camera, whereas Hopi reflects a worldview more like a motion picture.

Although there is little support for the extreme linguistically deterministic viewpoint that it is *impossible* for speakers of different languages to view the world identically, the more moderate notion of **linguistic relativism**–that language exerts a strong influence on perceptions–does seem valid. As one scholar put it, "The differences between languages are not so much in what *can* be said, but in what it is *relatively easy* to say."[63] Some languages contain terms that have no English equivalents.[64] For example, consider a few words in other languages that have no English equivalents:

Nemawashi (Japanese): The process of informally feeling out all the people involved with an issue before making a decision

Lagniappe (French/Creole): An extra gift given in a transaction that wasn't expected by the terms of a contract

Lao (Mandarin): A respectful term used for older people, showing their importance in the family and in society

Dharma (Sanskrit): Each person's unique, ideal path in life, and knowledge of how to find it

Koyaanisquatsi (Hopi): Nature out of balance; a way of life so crazy it calls for a new way of living

Once words like these exist and become a part of everyday life, the ideas that they represent are easier to recognize. But even without such terms, each of the preceding concepts is still possible to imagine. Thus, speakers of a language that includes the notion of *lao* would probably treat its older members respectfully, and those who are familiar with *lagniappe* might be more generous. Despite these differences, the words aren't essential to follow these principles. Although language may shape thoughts and behaviour, it doesn't dominate them absolutely.

There used to be a theory that if a language has no term for something, a speaker of that language lacks the concept. The idea has been largely discredited. Languages use circumlocutions; translations, and if necessary explanations, are always possible. But it remains true that richness of vocabulary is a pointer to the importance a culture places upon certain regions of the real rather than upon others.

Margaret Visser,
The Way We Are

The Sapir-Whorf Hypothesis

http://www.aber.ac.uk/~dgc/ whorf.html

The importance of language as a reflection of worldview isn't just a matter of interest for anthropologists and linguists. The labels we use in everyday conversation both reflect and shape the way we view ourselves and others. This explains why businesses often give employees impressive titles, and why a woman's choice of the label "Ms." or "Mrs." can be a statement about her identity.

Relational titles aren't the only linguistic elements that may shape attitudes about men and women. The reading on page 201 suggests that language reforms like avoiding "he" as a gender-neutral pronoun can lead to less-discriminatory thinking. A recent study examined precisely this question.[65] Students were corrected every time they used "he" as a generic pronoun in their writing. At the end of a semester, results showed that the corrections did reduce the use of gender-biased language. However, students did not change their mental images or their attitudes toward language reforms.

SUMMARY

Language is both a marvellous communication tool and the source of many interpersonal problems. Every language is a collection of symbols, governed by a variety of rules. Because of its symbolic nature, language is not a precise vehicle: Meanings rest in people, not in words themselves.

Besides conveying meanings about the content of a specific message, language both reflects and shapes the perceptions of its users. Terms used to name people influence the way they are regarded. The terms used to label speakers and the language they use reflect the level of affiliation, attraction, and interest of a speaker toward a subject. Language patterns also reflect and shape a speaker's perceived power.

When used carelessly, language can lead to a variety of interpersonal problems. The level of precision or vagueness of messages can affect a receiver's understanding of them. Both precise messages and vague, evasive ones have their uses in interpersonal relationships, and a competent communicator has the ability to choose the optimal level of precision for the situation at hand. Language also acknowledges or avoids the speaker's acceptance of responsibility for his or her positions, and competent communicators know how to use "I" and "we" statements to accept the optimal level of responsibility and relational harmony. Some language habits—confusing facts with opinions or inferences, and using emotive terms—can lead to unnecessary disharmony in interpersonal relationships.

The relationship between gender and language is complicated. There are many differences in the ways men and women speak: The content of their conversations varies, as do their reasons for communicating and their conversational style. However, not all differences in language use can be accounted for by the speaker's gender. Occupation, social philosophy, and orientation toward problem solving also influence the use of language, and psychological sex role can be more of an influence than biological sex.

Different languages often shape and reflect the views of a culture. Low-context cultures like Canada use language primarily to express feelings and ideas as clearly and unambiguously as possible. High-context cultures such as Japan and Saudi Arabia, however, avoid specificity in order to promote social harmony. Some cultures value brevity and the succinct use of language, while others have high regard for elaborate forms of speech. In some societies formality is important, while others value informality. Beyond these differences, there is evidence to support linguistic relativism—the notion that language exerts a strong influence on the worldview of the people who speak it.

KEY TERMS

abstraction ladder
"but" statement
convergence
divergence
emotive language
equivocal language
euphemisms
high-context cultures
"I" language

"it" statements
linguistic determinism
linguistic relativism
low-context cultures
phonological rules
powerless speech mannerisms
pragmatic rules
relative words
Sapir–Whorf hypothesis

semantic rules
sex roles
static evaluation
syntactic rules
"we" statements
"you" language

Chapter 6

Nonverbal Communication: Messages Without Words

Observing What You See

When I was a speech communication graduate student, I used to visit the small student union cafeteria each Tuesday and Thursday between classes. There I had my morning tea and bagel and entertained myself by watching all the goings-on. As most people-watchers do, I positioned myself to get a good view of everything, including the cash register where most of the "action" occurred. From my carefully selected seat I was able to watch and make inferences about the various individuals I observed.

I began to notice a good-looking, dark-haired, male student, who appeared to be either in his junior or senior year. He was rather attractive, with strong, white teeth contrasting his tanned complexion, and he sported a trendy haircut. He was about six feet tall and wore hiking boots and blue jeans. Under what looked like a ski jacket (I believe I saw a lift tag), he wore a light-coloured turtleneck and a good wool sweater. He had a strong but not overpowering body, and it was clear that he exercised regularly. In fact, he looked like he had just walked out of an L.L. Bean or Eddie Bauer catalogue.

One day at the cash register he greeted a tall, expensively dressed woman in her fifties with a polite hug. They looked surprised but not unhappy to see one another and began to chat. Their relationship seemed to fall somewhere between professional and informal—it looked as though the two had known each other at one time but had since been separated in some way. After three or four minutes, both smiled, said goodbye to each other, and looked for seats in different parts of the cafeteria.

I observed the male student's behaviour for about a week and a half, when our eyes met. Since I was a married woman at least seven years his senior, I quickly looked away, not wanting to communicate interest. Soon after this encounter, we met at a party. When introduced, we both acknowledged having seen each other in the cafeteria. He noted that he had smiled at me, but that I hadn't returned the smile, and that he had concluded I wasn't a very friendly person as a result. This surprised me; I had no idea my nonverbal response relayed such aloofness.

However, the subject of our conversation gave me an opportunity to express my interpretation of him, as well. Based on my recent observations in the cafeteria, I told him that I guessed that he was from an upper-middle-class background—his parents might be doctors or lawyers. He conceded that his father was a doctor, his mother a lawyer, and was quite amazed that I should have guessed this. It *was* a guess, but based on his appearance—expensive clothing, expensive teeth, and a refined manner. Clearly, he came from a family with money. Then I told him I thought he was probably in the sciences (he was an engineering student), that he skied (he did), and that he lived in a fraternity house (right again). I was correct on all three counts. Again, my predictions were educated guesses, although the lift tag helped a lot. I probably should have guessed he was an engineering student from the start, since the university we attended had a big engineering school. Regarding the fraternity, most of the guys on campus who looked like him lived in frat houses.

By this point he was getting nervous. The final straw came when I mentioned his recent interaction with the older woman. I told him that, based on his friendly but polite and somewhat distant interaction style, the woman was probably not a professor but rather the mother of a friend. It looked like she had asked how he was, how his courses were going, and he had responded in kind. I took another guess and suggested that perhaps she was the mother of a former girlfriend. This was too much for him. He said, "Are you a witch?" I assured him that all I had done was observe and make inferences and that I got lucky with my guesses. He didn't believe me. I had made him very uncomfortable, and he asked me not to say any more (I wondered what secrets he kept!). I joked that I was just getting to the good parts, but he wouldn't have any of it. When I last saw him at the party, he was making a cross sign with his fingers, saying, "Get her away from me," as he quickly left the room. I no longer saw him on those Tuesday and Thursday mornings in the cafeteria.

Am I a witch? Not at all. Anyone who would have taken the time to observe his nonverbal communication within the campus context could have guessed the same things about this student.

However, with the exception of his present reaction, nonverbal behaviour would have told me little about his personal life and philosophies . . . although I could have had some fun guessing.

Judith A. Rolls

Saying "I love you" is not the
words I want to hear from you
It's not that I want you not to
say, but if you only knew
How easy it would be to show me
how you feel.
More than words is all you have
to do to make it real.
Then you wouldn't have to say
that you love me
'Cause I'd already know.

What would you do if my heart
was torn in two?
More than words, to show you
feel that your love for me is
real.
What would you say if I took
those words away?
Then you couldn't make things
new
Just by saying I love you.

Nuno Bettencourt/Gary Cherone,
"More Than Words"

Basic Principles of Nonverbal
Communication

---

http://web.uvic.ca/~susanvan/
hinf315/topic.htm

Have you ever had an experience where someone has told you something, and you sensed that something was not quite right? It wasn't anything that was said or done; you just sensed something. In a situation like this, you were probably responding to your interactional partner's nonverbal clues. Sherlock Holmes might say you were not only watching your partner, but also you were observing him or her.

Observing yourself and others is what this chapter is about. In the following pages you'll become acquainted with the field of nonverbal communication–the way we express ourselves, not by what we say but by what we *do*. Some social scientists have argued that 93 percent of the emotional impact of a message comes from nonverbal sources. Others have reasoned more convincingly that the figure is closer to 65 percent.[1] Whatever the precise figure, the point remains: Nonverbal communication contributes a great deal to conveying meanings. It stands to reason, then, that the ability to understand nonverbal messages is an important part of communicative competence.

We need to begin our study of nonverbal communication by defining that term. At first this might seem like a simple task: If *non* means "not" and *verbal* means "words," then *nonverbal communication* means "communicating without words." In fact, this literal definition isn't completely accurate. For instance, most communication scholars don't define American Sign Language (used by many people with hearing impairments) as nonverbal even though the messages are unspoken. On the other hand, you'll soon read that certain aspects of the voice aren't really verbal. (Can you think of any? Table 6–1 will help you.)

This isn't the place to explore the rather complex debate about exactly what is and what isn't nonverbal. Interesting as that subject may be, we can move along in this introduction by defining **nonverbal communication** as "those messages expressed by other than linguistic means." This rules out not only sign languages but written

TABLE 6–1	TYPES OF COMMUNICATION	
	VOCAL COMMUNICATION	**NONVOCAL COMMUNICATION**
Verbal Communication	Spoken words	Written words
Nonverbal Communication	Tone of voice, sighs, screams, voice qualities (loudness, pitch, and so on)	Gestures, movement, appearance, facial expression, and so on

Adapted from John Stewart and Gary D'Angelo, *Together: Communicating Interpersonally*, 2nd ed. (Reading, MA: Addison-Wesley, 1980), p. 22.

words as well, though it includes messages transmitted by vocal means that don't involve language—the sighs, laughs, and other assorted noises we alluded to a moment ago. In addition, our definition allows us to explore the nonlinguistic dimensions of the spoken word—volume, rate, pitch, and so on.

Our brief definition only hints at the richness of nonverbal messages. You can begin to understand their prevalence by trying a simple experiment.

INVITATION TO INSIGHT

VERBAL AND NONVERBAL COMMUNICATION

Here's an experiment you can try either at home or in class. It will help you begin learning how nonverbal communication works.

1. Pick a partner, and find a place where you have some space to yourselves.

2. Now sit back-to-back with your partner, making sure that no parts of your bodies are touching. You should be seated so that you can talk easily without seeing each other.

3. Once you're seated, take 2 minutes to carry on a conversation about whatever subject you like. The only requirement is that you not look at or touch each other. Communicate by using words only.

4. Next, turn around so that you are facing your partner, seated at a comfortable distance. Now that you can both see and hear each other, carry on your conversation for another 2 minutes.

5. Continue to face each other, but for the next 2 minutes don't speak. Instead, join hands with your partner and communicate whatever messages you want to through sight and touch. Try to be aware of how you feel as you go through this step. There isn't any right or wrong way to behave here—there's nothing wrong with feeling embarrassed, silly, or any other way. The only requirement is to *remain silent.*

After you've finished the experiment, take some time to talk it over with your partner. Start by sharing how you felt in each part of the experience. Were you comfortable, nervous, playful, affectionate? Did your feelings change from one step to another? Could your partner tell these feelings without your expressing them? If so, how? Did your partner communicate his or her feelings, too?

CHARACTERISTICS OF NONVERBAL COMMUNICATION

If this experiment seemed strange to you, we hope you still went through with it because it points out several things about nonverbal communication.

Nonverbal Communication

---

http://www.coe.uh.edu/~shortam/lesson8.html

*Sometimes he'd like to slip
his blackness on a white man
and say,*
walk around a while like this,
see how it really feels . . .

Raymond Souster, "Jazzman"

Nonverbal Communication Exists

Even when you were in the nontalking stage, you probably could pick up some of your partner's feelings by touching hands and noting posture and expressions—maybe more than you could during your conversation. We hope that this exercise showed you that there are other languages besides words that carry messages about your relationships.

The point isn't so much *how* you or your partner behaved during the exercises—whether you were tense or relaxed, friendly or distant. We wanted to show you that even without any formal experience you can recognize and to some degree interpret messages that other people send nonverbally. In this chapter we want to sharpen the skills you already have, to give you a better grasp of the vocabulary of nonverbal language, and to show you how this knowledge can help you understand yourself and others better.

All Nonverbal Behaviour Has Communicative Value

The fact that communication without words took place between you and your partner brings us to this second important feature of nonverbal communication. To understand what we mean here, think about the exercise you just finished. Suppose we'd asked you not to communicate any messages at all while with your partner. What would you have done? Closed your eyes? Withdrawn into a ball? Left the room? You can probably see that even these behaviours communicate messages—that you're avoiding contact. One study (DePaulo 1992) took just this approach.[2] When communicators were told not to express nonverbal clues, others viewed them as dull, withdrawn, uneasy, aloof, and deceptive.

Take a minute now to try *not* communicating. Join a partner, and spend some time trying not to reveal any messages to one another. What happens?

This impossibility of not communicating is extremely important to understand because it means that each of us is a kind of transmitter that cannot be shut off. No matter what we do, we give off information about ourselves.[3]

Stop for a moment, and examine yourself as you read this. If someone were observing you now, what nonverbal clues would that person get about how you're feeling? Are you sitting forward or reclining back? Is your posture tense or relaxed? Are your eyes wide open, or do they keep closing? What does your facial expression communicate? Can you make your face expressionless? Don't people with expressionless faces communicate something to you?

Of course, we don't always intend to send nonverbal messages. Unintentional nonverbal behaviours differ from deliberate ones.[4] For example, we often stammer, blush, frown, and sweat without meaning to do so. Whether or not our nonverbal behaviour is intentional, oth-

"I tell you, Mr. Arthur, this survey has no way of registering a nonverbal response."

ers recognize it and make interpretations about us based on their observations. Some theorists argue that unintentional behaviour may provide information but it shouldn't count as communication. We draw the boundaries of nonverbal communication more broadly, suggesting that even unconscious and unintentional behaviour conveys messages and thus is worth studying as communication.

The fact that you and everyone around you is constantly sending nonverbal clues *is* important because it means that you have a constant source of information available about yourself and others. If you can tune in to these signals, you'll be more aware of how those around you are feeling and thinking, and you'll be better able to respond to their behaviour.

Nonverbal Communication Is Culture-Bound

Cultures have different nonverbal languages as well as verbal ones. Fiorello LaGuardia, legendary mayor of New York from 1933 to 1945, was fluent in English, Italian, and Yiddish. Researchers who watched films of his campaign speeches found that they could tell with the sound turned off which language he was speaking by noticing the changes in his nonverbal behaviour.[5] A somewhat similar study was conducted in Canada, where anglophones and francophones rated the gestures of bilingual speakers, each speaking one language and then the other. The results support the stereotype that the French speak with their hands. Francophones, regardless of which language

Theories of Nonverbal Communication

http://uts.cc.utexas.edu/ ~adgrad/index.html

The men walked hand-in-hand, laughing sleepily together under blinding vertical glare. Sometimes they put their arms round each other's necks; they seemed to like to touch each other, as if it made them feel good to know the other man was there. It wasn't love; it didn't mean anything we could understand.

Graham Greene,
Journey Without Maps

they spoke, gestured more than anglophones.[6] Some anglophones actually gesture more when they are speaking French. One English speaker related that when she spoke French, her whole body spoke.

Some nonverbal behaviours have different meanings from culture to culture. In keeping with the French/English discussion, Pierre Trudeau was noted for using a simple Gallic "shrug" when speaking French, although such a gesture would be considered inappropriate for an English speaker.[7] The "OK" gesture made by joining thumb and forefinger to form a circle is a cheery affirmation to most North Americans, but it has less-positive meanings in other parts of the world.[8] In France and Belgium it means "You're worth zero." In Greece and Turkey it is a vulgar sexual invitation, usually meant as an insult. Given this sort of cross-cultural ambiguity, it's easy to imagine how an exchange student, for example, might wind up in serious trouble.

Less-obvious cross-cultural differences can damage relationships without the parties ever recognizing exactly what has gone wrong. Edward Hall points out that, whereas North Americans are comfortable conducting business at a distance of roughly 1.2 metres, people from the Middle East stand much closer.[9] It is easy to visualize the awkward advance and retreat pattern that might occur when two diplomats or businesspeople from these cultures meet. One of the authors had this very experience when she lived in an international student residence. While in conversation with a Middle Eastern student during a party, she noticed that he moved closer and closer to her. Feeling her personal space being invaded, and interpreting the movement as an undesired sexual advance, she continually moved back a few steps. This persisted until she was in a corner, just where she thought he might want her. However, his interpretation of the same event was quite different: He couldn't understand why she was backing off and being so rude.

DILBERT® reprinted by permission of United Features Syndicate, Inc.

Communicators become more tolerant of others once they understand that unusual nonverbal behaviours are the result of cultural differences. In one study, North American adults were presented with videotapes of speakers from the United States, France, and Germany.[10] When the sound was eliminated, viewers judged foreigners more negatively than their fellow citizens. But when the speakers' voices were added (allowing viewers to recognize that they were from a different country), the critical ratings dropped.

Like distance, patterns of eye contact vary around the world.[11] A direct gaze is considered appropriate for speakers in Latin America, the Arab world, and southern Europe. On the other hand, Asians, Indians, Pakistanis, and northern Europeans gaze at a listener peripherally or not at all. In either case, deviations from the norm are likely to make a listener uncomfortable.

Differing cultural norms for nonverbal behaviour make the potential for cross-cultural misunderstandings great. For example, many Anglo schoolteachers use quasi-questions that hint at the information they are seeking: "Does the name 'Hamilton' ring a bell?" An elementary-school instructor might encourage the class to speak up by making an incorrect statement that demands refutation: "So twelve divided by four is six, right?" Most Anglo students would recognize this behaviour as a way of testing their understanding. But this style of questioning is unfamiliar to many students raised in traditional Black cultures, who aren't likely to respond until they are directly questioned by the instructor.[12] Given this difference, it is easy to imagine how some teachers might view minority children as unresponsive or disinterested, when in fact they are simply playing by a different set of rules.

Despite differences like these, many nonverbal behaviours are universal. Certain expressions have the same meanings around the world. Smiles and laughter are universal signals of positive emotions, for example, while sour expressions convey displeasure in every culture.[13] Charles Darwin believed that expressions like these are the result of evolution, functioning as survival mechanisms that allowed early humans to convey emotional states before the development of language. The innateness of some facial expressions becomes even more clear when we examine the behaviour of children born deaf and blind.[14] Despite a lack of social learning, these children display a broad range of expression. They smile, laugh, and cry in ways virtually identical to seeing and hearing children.

Although nonverbal expressions like these may be universal, the way they are used varies widely around the world. Some cultures discourage the overt demonstration of feelings like happiness or anger. In other cultures the same feelings are perfectly appropriate. Thus, a Japanese might appear much more controlled and placid than an Arab, when in fact their feelings might be identical.

The same principle operates closer to home among subcultures. For example, observations have shown that Black women in all-Black groups are nonverbally more expressive and interrupt each

Resources from the Center for Nonverbal Studies (Nonverbal Dictionary)

http://members.aol.com/ nonverbal2/index.htm

Innumerable travellers' tales involve the visiting hero being offered some horrendous "delicacy" which he has either to eat, or risks offending his host. But we can be put out just because a foreigner raises his eyebrows to mean yes, or asks how much money we make, or stalks off in a rage because we folded our arms or failed to take our hands out of our pockets.

Margaret Visser,
The Rituals of Dinner

Nonverbal Communication in Japan

http://www.shinnova.com/part/99-japa/abj17-e.htm

other more than white women in all-white groups. This doesn't mean that Black women always feel more intensely than their white counterparts. A more likely explanation is that the two groups follow different cultural rules. The researchers found that in racially mixed groups both Black and white women moved closer to each other's style.[15] This nonverbal convergence shows that skilled communicators can adapt their behaviour when interacting with members of other cultures or subcultures in order to make the exchange more smooth and effective.

Nonverbal Communication Is Primarily Relational

Some nonverbal messages serve utilitarian functions. For example, a police officer directs the flow of traffic, and a team of street surveyors uses hand motions to co-ordinate their work. But nonverbal communication more commonly conveys the kinds of relational messages (affinity, control, and respect) that you read about in Chapter 1 and the kinds of identity messages introduced in Chapter 2.

Consider, for example, the role of nonverbal communication in identity management. Chapter 2 discussed how we strive to create an image of ourselves as we want others to view us. Nonverbal communication plays an important role in this process—in many cases more important than verbal messages. Consider, for example, what happens when you attend a party where you are likely to meet strangers you would like to get to know better. Instead of projecting your image verbally ("Hi! I'm attractive, friendly, and easygoing"), you behave in ways that will present this identity. You might smile a lot, and perhaps try to strike a relaxed pose. It's also likely that you dress carefully—even if the image involves looking as though you hadn't given a lot of attention to your appearance.

Along with identity management, nonverbal communication allows us to *define the kinds of relationships we want to have with others.* Think about the wide range of ways you could behave when greeting another person. You could wave, shake hands, nod, smile, clap the other person on the back, give a hug, or avoid all contact. Each one of these decisions would send a message about the nature of your relationship with the other person.

Nonverbal behaviour can be more powerful than words in defining the kind of relationship you are seeking. Recall all the times and ways you have learned that someone you know is upset with you. Most often the first clues don't come from direct statements but from nonverbal clues. Perhaps the message is conveyed through a lack of eye contact, different facial expressions, an increase in distance, or decreased touch. In any case, the change in behaviour clearly proves the power of nonverbal communication to define the status of a relationship.

Nonverbal messages perform a third valuable social function: *conveying emotions* that we may be unwilling or unable to express . . . or ones we may not even be aware of. In fact, nonverbal communication is much better suited to expressing attitudes and feelings than ideas. You can prove this for yourself by imagining how you could express each item on the following list nonverbally:

You're tired.

You're in favour of capital punishment.

You're attracted to another person in the group.

You think prayer in the schools should be allowed.

You're angry at someone in the room.

This list shows that, short of charades, nonverbal messages are much better at expressing attitudes than are other sorts of messages. Among other limitations, nonverbal communication can't convey

simple matters of fact ("The book was written in 2000.")

the past or future tenses ("I was happy yesterday"; "I'll be out of town next week.")

an imaginary idea ("What would it be like if . . .")

conditional statements ("If I don't get a job, I'll have to move out.")

Nonverbal Communication Serves Many Functions

Just because this chapter deals with nonverbal communication, don't get the idea that our words and our actions are unrelated. Quite the opposite is true: Verbal and nonverbal communication are interconnected elements in every act of communication. Nonverbal behaviours can operate in several relationships with verbal messages.

1. **Repeating** If someone asked you for directions to the nearest drugstore, you could say, "Just down this street about two blocks," **repeating** your instructions nonverbally by pointing in that direction. Pointing is an example of what social scientists call **emblems**—deliberate nonverbal behaviours that have a very precise meaning, known to virtually everyone within a cultural group. For example, we all know that a head nod means "yes," a head shake means "no," a wave means "hello" or "goodbye," and a hand to the ear means "I can't hear you."

2. **Substituting** Emblems also can replace a verbal message. When a friend asks, "What's up?" you might shrug your shoulders instead of answering in words. Not all substituting consists of emblems, however. Sometimes **substituting** responses are more ambiguous and less intentional. Many facial expressions operate primarily like verbal interjections, such as "gosh," "really?," "oh,

please!" and so on.[16] In other cases, nonverbal substituting can be useful when communicators are reluctant to express their feelings in words. Faced with a message you find disagreeable, you might sigh, roll your eyes, or yawn when speaking out would not be appropriate.

Courtship is another situation in which nonverbal gestures can signal "I'm interested" when the same message would be awkward to express verbally. Psychologist Monica Moore and a team of graduate students spent hundreds of hours observing women and men courting one another, recording every nonverbal step of the process.[17] Moore discovered that the woman most commonly makes the initial decision about whether to encourage contact by nonverbally signalling her interest to a man. Table 6–2 lists the variety of behaviours used to send this sort of signal. While most of the terms are self-explanatory, a "solitary dance" consists of moving one's body in time to the music.

TABLE 6–2	FLIRTING BEHAVIOURS (Listed in decreasing order of occurrence)	
FACIAL/HEAD PATTERNS	**POSTURE PATTERNS**	**GESTURES**
Smile	Solitary dance	Gesticulation
Room-encompassing glance	Lean	Caress (object)
	Point	Primp
Laugh	Dance (acceptance)	Caress (leg)
Short, darting glance	Parade	Caress (arm)
Fixed gaze	Aid solicitation	Hand hold
Hair flip	Play	Palm
Head toss	Brush	Thigh touch
Head nod	Knee touch	Placement
Giggle	Shoulder hug	Approach
Whisper		Foot to foot
Neck presentation		Request dance
Lip lick		Hug
Pout		Frontal body contact
Coy smile		Breast touch
Face to face		Hang
Kiss		Lateral body contact
Eyebrow flash		Caress (back)
Lipstick application		Arm flexion
		Caress (torso)
		Buttock pat
		Tap
		Caress (face/hair)
		Hike skirt

M. Moore, "Nonverbal Courtship Patterns in Women: Context and Consequences," *Ethnology and Sociobiology* 6 (1985): 237–247.

3. Complementing If you saw a student talking to a teacher, and the student's head was bowed slightly, his voice was low and hesitating, and he shuffled slowly from foot to foot, you might conclude that he felt inferior to the teacher, possibly embarrassed about something he did. The nonverbal behaviours you observed provided the context for the verbal behaviours—they conveyed the relationship between the teacher and student. **Complementing** nonverbal behaviours signal the attitudes the interactants have for one another.

Much complementing behaviour consists of **illustrators**—nonverbal gestures that accompany and support spoken words. Scratching your head when searching for an idea and snapping your fingers when it occurs are examples of illustrators that complement verbal messages. Research shows that North Americans use illustrators more often when they are emotionally aroused—trying to explain ideas that are difficult to put into words when they are furious, horrified, very agitated, distressed, or excited.[18]

4. Accenting Just as we use italics to highlight an idea in print, we use nonverbal devices to emphasize oral messages. Pointing an accusing finger adds emphasis to criticism (as well as probably creating defensiveness in the receiver). **Accenting** certain words with the voice ("It was *your* idea!") is another way to add nonverbal emphasis.

5. Regulating Nonverbal behaviours can serve a **regulating** function by influencing the flow of verbal communication. For example, parties in a conversation often unconsciously send and receive turn-taking cues.[19] When you are ready to yield the floor, the unstated rule is this: Create a rising vocal intonation pattern, then use a falling intonation pattern or draw out the final syllable of the clause at the end of your statement. Finally, stop speaking. If you want to maintain your turn when another speaker seems ready to cut you off, you can suppress the attempt by taking an audible breath, using a sustained intonation pattern (because rising and falling patterns suggest the end of a statement), and avoid any pauses in your speech. There are other nonverbal cues for gaining the floor and for signalling that you do not want to speak.

6. Contradicting People often simultaneously express different and even **contradicting** messages in their verbal and nonverbal behaviours. A common example of this sort of "double message" is the experience we've all had of hearing someone with a red face and bulging veins yelling, "Angry? No, *I'm not angry!*"

Usually, however, the contradiction between words and nonverbal clues isn't this obvious. At times we all try to seem different from what we are. There are many reasons for this contradictory behaviour: to cover nervousness when giving a speech or in a job interview, to keep someone from worrying about us, or to appear more attractive than we believe we really are.

Even though some of the ways in which people contradict themselves are subtle, **double messages** have a strong impact.

I suppose it was something you
said
That caused me to tighten and
pull away.
And when you asked,
"What is it?"
I, of course, said,
"Nothing."

Whenever I say, "Nothing,"
You may be very certain
there is something.
The something is a cold,
hard lump of
Nothing.

Lois Wyse

Beware of the man whose belly does not move when he laughs.

Chinese proverb

As we grow older we become better at interpreting these contradictory messages. Children between the ages of 6 and 12 use a speaker's words to make sense of a message. But as adults, we rely more on nonverbal cues to form impressions. For example, audiences put more emphasis on nonverbal cues than on words to decide whether speakers are honest.[20] They also use nonverbal behaviours to judge the character of speakers as well as their competence and composure; and differences in nonverbal behaviour influence how much listeners are persuaded by a speaker.[21]

Deception is perhaps the most interesting type of double message. Signals of deception—often called **leakage**—can occur in every type of nonverbal behaviour. Some nonverbal channels are more revealing than others, however. Facial expressions are less revealing than body clues, probably because deceivers pay more attention to controlling their faces. Even more useful is the voice, which offers a rich variety of leakage clues.[22] In one experiment, subjects who were encouraged to be deceitful made more speech errors, spoke for shorter periods of time, and had a lower rate of speech than others who were encouraged to express themselves honestly. Another study revealed that the vocal frequency of a liar's voice tends to be higher than that of a truth teller. Research also shows that deceivers delivering a prepared lie responded more quickly than truth tellers, mainly because there was less thinking involved. When unprepared, however, deceivers generally took longer than both prepared deceivers and truth tellers.

As this research shows, deceivers don't always broadcast cues that reveal their lies. Nonverbal evidence of lying is most likely to occur when deceivers haven't had a chance to rehearse, when they feel strongly about the information being hidden, or when they feel anxious or guilty about their lies. Even when **deception cues** are abundant, they aren't necessarily direct signals of lying itself; rather, they may reflect the anxiety that some liars feel. Table 6–3 outlines some conditions under which liars are likely to betray themselves through nonverbal leakage.

Despite the abundance of nonverbal deception cues, it isn't always easy to detect deception. The range of effectiveness in uncovering deceptive messages is broad, ranging from 45 percent to 70 percent.[23] Sometimes the very suspicion that someone is lying can improve the deceiver's attempts to hide the truth. Research shows that communicators who probe the messages of deceptive communicators are no better at detecting lies than those who don't investigate the truth of a message.[24] One explanation for this surprising finding is that deceivers who are questioned become more vigilant about revealing the truth and that their greater caution results in a better cover-up of deception cues.

Some people are better than others at uncovering deception. For example, younger people are better than older ones at uncovering lies.[25] Women are consistently more accurate than men at detecting lying and what the underlying truth really is.[26] The same research

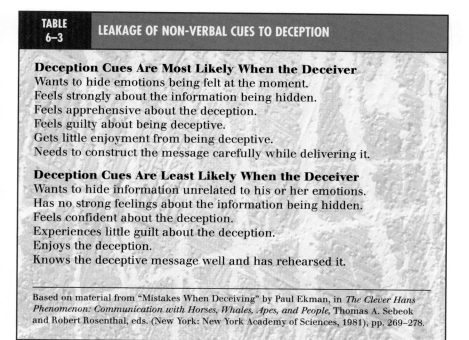

TABLE 6–3	LEAKAGE OF NON-VERBAL CUES TO DECEPTION

Deception Cues Are Most Likely When the Deceiver
Wants to hide emotions being felt at the moment.
Feels strongly about the information being hidden.
Feels apprehensive about the deception.
Feels guilty about being deceptive.
Gets little enjoyment from being deceptive.
Needs to construct the message carefully while delivering it.

Deception Cues Are Least Likely When the Deceiver
Wants to hide information unrelated to his or her emotions.
Has no strong feelings about the information being hidden.
Feels confident about the deception.
Experiences little guilt about the deception.
Enjoys the deception.
Knows the deceptive message well and has rehearsed it.

Based on material from "Mistakes When Deceiving" by Paul Ekman, in *The Clever Hans Phenomenon: Communication with Horses, Whales, Apes, and People,* Thomas A. Sebeok and Robert Rosenthal, eds. (New York: New York Academy of Sciences, 1981), pp. 269–278.

shows that, as people become more intimate, their accuracy in detecting lies declines. This is a surprising fact: Intuition suggests that we ought to be better at judging honesty as we become more familiar with others. Despite their overall accuracy at detecting lies, women are more inclined to fall for the deception of intimate partners than are men. No matter how skillful or inept we may be at interpreting nonverbal behaviour, training can make us better.[27]

Before we finish considering how nonverbal behaviours can deceive, it is important to realize that not all deceptive communication is aimed at taking advantage of the recipient. Some are a polite way to express an idea that would be difficult to handle if expressed in words. For example, recall a time when you became bored with a conversation while your companion kept rambling on. At such a time the most straightforward statement would be, "I'm tired of talking to you and want to get away." It's obvious that the less-direct nonverbal signal–glancing at your watch, for example–is a kinder way to express yourself. In this sense, the ability to deliberately send nonverbal messages that contradict your words can be a kind of communication competence.

Nonverbal Communication Is Ambiguous

You learned in Chapter 5 that verbal messages are easily misunderstood; but nonverbal messages are even more ambiguous. Imagine

Wavelength

I can finish your sentences
You can start my laugh

I can read your dreams
You can touch my mood

Wordless communication
    incarnate by
intangible sensibilities

Without touching
I hold you

With bonding
You free me

You are the gift
I give
    to myself

Jill Meriel Fox

two possible meanings of silence from your companion after a fun-filled evening. Or suppose that a much-admired person with whom you've worked suddenly begins paying more attention to you than ever before. What could some possible meanings of this behaviour be? Although nonverbal behaviour can be very revealing, it can have so many possible meanings that it's impossible to be certain which interpretation is correct.

Not all nonverbal behaviour is equally ambiguous. In laboratory settings, subjects are better at identifying positive facial expressions, such as happiness, love, surprise, and interest, than negative ones like fear, sadness, anger, and disgust.[28] In real life, however, spontaneous nonverbal expressions are so ambiguous that observers are unable to identify the emotions they convey with accuracy any better than blind guessing.[29]

Despite the ambiguity of nonverbal messages, some people are more skillful decoders than others.[30] Those who are better senders of nonverbal messages are also better receivers. Decoding ability also increases with age and training, though there are still differences in

"That was unkind, darling. When their mouths turn up at the corners they want to be friends."

ability because of personality and occupation. For instance, extroverts are relatively accurate judges of nonverbal behaviour, whereas dogmatists are not. Women seem to be better than men at decoding nonverbal messages. Over 95 percent of the studies examined in one analysis showed that women are more accurate at interpreting nonverbal signals.[31] Despite these differences, even the best nonverbal decoders do not approach 100 percent accuracy. To test this principle for yourself, try the experiment below.

This exercise should show you the difference between merely observing somebody's behaviour and actually interpreting it. Noticing

INVITATION TO INSIGHT

READING "BODY LANGUAGE"

In your journey through the supermarket checkout or while waiting for a plane, you've probably noticed books that promise to teach you how to read "body language." These books claim that you can become a kind of mind reader, learning the deepest secrets of everyone around you. But it's not quite as simple as it sounds. Here's an exercise that will both increase your skill in observing nonverbal behaviour and show you the dangers of being too sure that you're a perfect reader of body language. You can try the exercise either in or out of class, and the period of time over which you do it is flexible, from a single class period to several days. In any case, begin by choosing a partner, and then follow these directions:

1. For the first period of time (however long you decide to make it), observe the way your partner behaves. Notice movements, mannerisms, postures, style of dress, and so on. To remember your observations, jot them down. If you're doing this exercise out of class over an extended period of time, there's no need to let your observations interfere with whatever you'd normally be doing: Your only job here is to compile a list of your partner's behaviours. In this step you should be careful *not to interpret* your partner's actions; just record what you see.

2. At the end of the time period, share what you've seen with your partner, who should do the same with you.

3. For the next period of time your job is not only to observe your partner's behaviour but also to *interpret* it. This time in your conference you should tell your partner what you thought his or her actions revealed. For example, does careless dressing suggest oversleeping, loss of interest in appearance, or the desire to feel more comfortable? If you noticed frequent yawning, did you think this meant boredom, fatigue after a late night, or sleepiness after a big meal? Don't feel bad if your guesses weren't all correct. Remember, nonverbal clues tend to be ambiguous. You may be surprised how checking out the nonverbal clues you observe can help build a relationship with another person.

someone's shaky hands or smile is one thing, but deciding what such behaviours mean is quite another. If you're like most people, you probably found that a lot of your guesses were incorrect. Now, if that was true here, it may also be true in your daily life. Being a sharp nonverbal observer can give you some good hunches about how people are feeling, but the only way you can find out if these hunches are correct is to *check them out* verbally, using the skill of perception checking you learned in Chapter 3.

The medium is the message.

Marshall McLuhan,
Understanding Media

DIFFERENCES BETWEEN VERBAL AND NONVERBAL COMMUNICATION

Nonverbal and verbal messages are both indispensable: It's hard to imagine how we could function without either one. Much of the value of these two ways of communicating comes from their differences.

Single vs. Multiple Channels

Most verbal messages—words, sentences, and paragraphs—reach us one at a time, rather like pearls on a string. In fact, it's physically impossible for a person to speak more than one word at a time. Unlike the spoken word, however, nonverbal messages don't arrive in such an orderly, sequential manner. Instead, they bombard us simultaneously from a multitude of channels. Consider the everyday act of meeting a stranger for the first time. On a verbal level there's relatively little information exchanged in the clichés that occupy the first few minutes of most conversations ("How's it going . . ." "Great weather we've been having . . ." "What's your major?"). But at the same moment the number of nonverbal messages available to you is overwhelming: the other people's facial expressions, postures, gestures, the clothing they wear, the distance they stand from you, and so on. In one way this multichannel onslaught of nonverbal messages is a boon, since it provides so many ways of learning about others. In another sense, however, the number of simultaneous messages is a problem, for it's difficult to recognize the overwhelming amount of nonverbal information we receive from others every moment.

Discrete vs. Continuous

Verbal messages—words, sentences, and paragraphs—form messages with clear beginnings and endings. In this sense we can judge whether others are communicating verbally by observing whether they are speaking or writing. Unlike the written and spoken word, however, nonverbal communication is continuous and never ending. As we've already said, nonverbal communication is a constant, unstoppable process. The postures, gestures, and other types of

Nonverbal Stereotyping

Brent Staples

My first victim was a woman—white, well dressed, probably in her early 20s. I came upon her late one evening on a deserted street in a relatively affluent neighbourhood in an otherwise mean, impoverished section of a large city. As I swung onto the avenue behind her, there seemed to be a discreet, uninflammatory distance between us. Not so. She cast back a worried glance. To her, the youngish black man—a broad 6 feet 2 inches with a beard and billowing hair, both hands shoved into the pockets of a bulky military jacket—seemed menacingly close. After a few more quick glimpses, she picked up her pace and was soon running in earnest. Within seconds she disappeared into a cross street. As a softy who is scarcely able to take a knife to a raw chicken—let alone hold on to a person's throat—I was surprised, embarrassed, and dismayed all at once.

That first encounter, and those that followed, signified that a vast, unnerving gulf lay between night-time pedestrians—particularly women—and me.

After dark, on the warrenlike streets where I live, I often see women who fear the worst from me. They seem to have set their faces on neutral, and with their purse straps strung across their chests bandolier-style, they forge ahead as though bracing themselves against being tackled. I understand, of course, that the danger they perceive is not a hallucination. Women are particularly vulnerable to street violence, and young black males are drastically overrepresented among the perpetrators of that violence. Yet these truths are no solace against the kind of alienation that comes of being ever the suspect, a fearsome entity with whom pedestrians avoid making eye contact.

Over the years, I learned to smother the rage I felt at so often being taken for a criminal. Not to do so would surely have led to madness. I now take precautions to make myself less threatening. I move about with care, particularly late in the evening. I give a wide berth to nervous people on subway platforms during the wee hours, particularly when I have exchanged business clothes for

jeans. If I happen to be entering a building behind some people who appear skittish, I may walk by, letting them clear the lobby before I return, so as not to seem to be following them. I have been calm and extremely congenial on those rare occasions when I've been pulled over by the police.

And on late-evening constitutionals I employ what has proved to be an excellent tension-reducing measure: I whistle melodies from Beethoven and Vivaldi and the more popular classical composers. Even steely urbanites hunching toward nighttime destinations seem to relax, and occasionally they even join in the tune. Virtually everybody seems to sense that a mugger wouldn't be warbling bright, sunny selections from Vivaldi's *Four Seasons*. It is my equivalent of the cowbell that hikers wear when they know they are in bear country.

Brent Staples, "Black Men and Public Space"

messages described in the following pages provide a constant flow of messages. Even the absence of a message (an unanswered letter or an unreturned phone call) is a message. As one communication expert said when referring to nonverbal communication, "Nothing never happens."

The first area of nonverbal communication we'll discuss is the broad field of **kinesics,** or body position and motion. In this section we'll explore the role that posture, gestures, body orientation, facial expressions, and eye movements play in our relationships with each other.

Body Orientation

We'll start with **body orientation**—the degree to which we face toward or away from someone with our body, feet, and head. To understand how this kind of physical positioning communicates nonverbal messages, you might try an experiment. You'll need two friends to help you. Imagine that two of you are in the middle of a personal conversation when a third person approaches and wants to join you. You're not especially glad to see this person, but you don't want to sound rude by asking him to leave. Your task is to signal to the intruder that you'd rather be alone, using only the position of your bodies. You can talk to the third person if you wish, but you can't verbally tell him that you want privacy.

When you've tried this experiment or if you've ever been in a real situation similar to it, you know that by turning your body slightly away from an intruder you can make your feelings very clear. An intruder finds himself in the difficult position of trying to talk over your shoulder, and it isn't long before he gets the message and goes away. The nonverbal message here is "We're interested in each other right now and don't want to include you in our conversation." The general rule this situation describes is that facing someone directly signals your interest, and facing away signals a desire to avoid involvement. This explains how we can pack ourselves into intimate distance with total strangers in places like a crowded

There Is Only One of Everything

Not a tree but the tree
we saw, it will never exist, split by the wind and bending down
like that again. What will push out of the earth

later, making it summer, will not be
grass, leaves, repetition, there will
have to be other words. When my

eyes close language vanishes. The cat
with the divided face, half black half orange
nests in my scruffy fur coat, I drink tea,

fingers curved around the cup, impossible
to duplicate these flavours. The table
and freak plates glow softly, consuming themselves,

I look out at you and you occur
in this winter kitchen, random as trees or sentences,
entering me, fading like them, in time you will disappear

but the way you dance by yourself
on the tile floor to a worn song, flat and mournful,
so delighted, spoon waved in one hand, wisps of roughened hair

sticking up from your head, it's your surprised
body, pleasure I like. I can even say it,
though only once and it won't

last: I want this. I want
this.

Margaret Atwood

elevator without offending others. Because there's a very indirect orientation here (everyone is usually standing shoulder to shoulder, facing in the same direction), we understand that despite the close quarters everyone wants to avoid personal contact.

By observing the way people position themselves you can learn a good deal about how they feel. Next time you're in a crowded place where people can choose whom to face directly, try observing who seems to be included in the action and who is being subtly shut out. And in the same way, pay attention to your own body orientation. You may be surprised to discover that you're avoiding a certain person without being conscious of it or that at times you're "turning your back" on people altogether. If this is the case, it may be helpful to figure out why. Are you avoiding an unpleasant situation that needs clearing up, communicating your annoyance or dislike for the other, or sending some other message?

Posture

Another way we communicate nonverbally is through our **posture.** To see if this is true, stop reading for a moment, and notice how you're sitting. What does your position say nonverbally about how you feel? Are there any other people near you now? What messages do you get from their present posture? By paying attention to the postures of those around you, as well as your own, you'll find another channel of nonverbal communication that can furnish information about how people feel about themselves and each other.

An indication of how much posture communicates is shown by our language. It's full of expressions that link emotional states with body postures:

I won't take this lying down!

Take a load off your back.

He can stand on his own two feet.

She has to carry a heavy burden.

Phrases like these show that an awareness of posture exists for us even if it's often unconscious. The main reason we miss most posture messages is that they aren't very obvious. It's seldom that a person who feels weighted down by a problem hunches over so much that she stands out in a crowd, and when we're bored, we usually don't lean back and slump enough to embarrass the other person. In the reading of posture, then, the key is to look for small changes that might be shadows of the way people feel.

For example, a teacher who has a reputation for interesting classes told us how he uses his understanding of postures to do a better job. "Because of my large classes I have to lecture a lot," he said. "And that's an easy way to turn students off. I work hard to make my talks entertaining, but you know that nobody's perfect, and I do have my off days. I can tell when I'm not doing a good job of

The Look of a Victim

Little Red Riding Hood set herself up to be mugged. Her first mistake was skipping through the forest to Grandma's house. Her second mistake was stopping to pick flowers. At this point, as you might remember in the story, the mean, heavy wolf comes along and begins to check her out. He observes, quite perceptively, that she is happy, outgoing, and basically unaware of any dangers in her surrounding environment. The big bad wolf catches these nonverbal clues and splits to Grandma's house. He knows that Red is an easy mark. From this point we all know what happens.

Body movements and gestures reveal a lot of information about a person. Like Little Red Riding Hood, pedestrians may signal to criminals that they are easy targets for mugging by the way they walk. When was the last time you assessed your "muggability rating"? In a recent study two psychologists set out to identify those body movements that characterized easy victims. They assembled "muggability ratings" of 60 big-city pedestrians from the people who may have been the most qualified to judge—prison inmates who had been convicted of assault.

The researchers unobtrusively videotaped pedestrians on weekdays between 10:00 A.M. and 12:00 P.M. Each pedestrian was taped for 6 to 8 seconds, the approximate time it takes for a mugger to size up an approaching person. The judges (prison inmates) rated the "assault potential" of the 60 pedestrians on a 10-point scale. A rating of one indicated someone was "a very easy rip-off," of two, "an easy dude to corner."

Toward the other end of the scale, nine meant a person "would be heavy; would give you a hard time," and ten indicated that the mugger "would avoid it, too big a situation, too heavy." The results revealed several body movements that characterized easy victims: "Their strides were either very long or very short; they moved awkwardly, raising their left legs with their left arms (instead of alternating them); on each step they tended to lift their whole foot up and then place it down (less muggable sorts took steps in which their feet rocked from heel to toe). Overall, the people rated most muggable walked as if they were in conflict with themselves; they seemed to make each move in the most difficult way possible."

Loretta Malandro and Larry Barker

communicating by picking out three or four students before I start my talk and watching how they sit throughout the class period. As long as they're leaning forward in their seats, I know I'm doing OK, but if I look up and see them starting to slump back, I know I'd better change my approach."

Psychologist Albert Mehrabian has found that other postural keys to feelings are tension and relaxation. He says that we take relaxed postures in nonthreatening situations and tighten up when threatened.[34] Based on this observation, he says we can tell a good deal about how others feel simply by watching how tense or loose they seem to be. For example, he suggests that watching tenseness is a way of detecting status differences: The lower-status person is generally the more rigid, tense-appearing one, whereas the one with higher status is more relaxed. This is the kind of situation that often happens when an employee sits ramrod straight while the boss leans back in her chair. The same principle applies to social situations, where it's often possible to tell who's uncomfortable by looking at pictures. Often you'll see someone laughing and talking as if he were perfectly at home, but his posture almost shouts nervousness. Some people never relax, and their posture shows it.

Sometimes posture communicates vulnerability in situations far more serious than mere social or business ones. One study revealed that rapists sometimes use postural clues to select victims they believe are easy to intimidate.[35] Easy targets are more likely to walk slowly and tentatively, stare at the ground, and move their arms and legs in short, jerky motions.

Gestures

We have already discussed how emblems and illustrators convey messages. Sometimes **gestures** like these are intentional—a cheery wave or thumbs-up, for example. In other cases, however, our gestures are unconscious. Occasionally an unconscious gesture will consist of an unambiguous emblem, such as a shrug that clearly means "I don't know." Another revealing set of gestures is what psychiatrist Albert Scheflen calls *preening behaviours*—stroking or combing one's hair, glancing in a mirror, and rearranging one's clothing. Scheflen suggests that these behaviours signal some sort of interest in the other party: perhaps an unconscious sexual come-on or perhaps a sign of less-intimate interest.[36] More often, however, gestures are ambiguous. In addition to illustrators, another group of ambiguous gestures consists of what we usually call *fidgeting*—movements in which one part of the body grooms, massages, rubs, holds, fidgets, pinches, picks, or otherwise manipulates another part. Social scientists call these behaviours **manipulators.**[37] Social rules may discourage us from performing most manipulators in public, but people still do so without noticing.

Research reveals what common sense suggests—that increased use of manipulators is often a sign of discomfort.[38] But not *all* fidgeting

Fie, fie upon her! There's language in her eyes, her cheek, her lip. Nay, her foot speaks; her wanton spirits look out at every joint and motive in her body.

William Shakespeare,
Troilus and Cressida

Showing that the right hand was holding no weapon was probably one origin of our habit of waving; another is said to have been the polite raising of the right arm to make room when passing others in narrow lanes. Pushing back visors and hoods to facilitate recognition of one's face may have led to hat-tipping as well as waving and saluting, and the ancient praying gesture, fist to forehead, looks like another forerunner of the salute.

Margaret Visser,
The Way We Are

signals uneasiness. People also are likely to use manipulators when relaxed. When they let their guard down (either alone or with friends), they will be more likely to fiddle with an earlobe, twirl a strand of hair, or clean their fingernails. Whether or not the fidgeter is hiding something, observers are likely to interpret manipulators as a signal of dishonesty. Since not all fidgeters are liars, it's important not to jump to conclusions about the meaning of manipulations.

Actually, *too few* gestures may be as significant an indicator of double messages as *too many*.[39] Lack of gesturing may signal a lack of interest, sadness, boredom, or low enthusiasm. Illustrators also decrease whenever someone is cautious about speaking. For these reasons, a careful observer will look for either an increase or a decrease in the usual level of gestures.

Face and Eyes

The face and eyes are probably the most noticed parts of the body, but this doesn't mean that their nonverbal messages are the easiest to read. The face is a tremendously complicated channel of expression for several reasons.

First, it's hard even to describe the number and kind of expressions we commonly produce with our face and eyes. For example, researchers have found that there are at least eight distinguishable positions of the eyebrows and forehead, eight more of the eyes and lids, and ten for the lower face.[40] When you multiply this complexity by the number of emotions we feel, you can see why it would be almost impossible to compile a dictionary of facial expressions and their corresponding emotions.

INVITATION TO INSIGHT

THE EYES HAVE IT

Prove for yourself the role eye contact plays in social influence by trying a simple experiment.

1. Choose a situation in which you can make simple requests from a series of strangers. You might, for example, ask to cut in line to use a photocopying machine, or you could ask passersby for a small amount of change to make an important phone call.

2. Make similar requests to at least 20 different people. Use the same words for each request, but alternate your nonverbal behaviour. Half of the time make direct eye contact, and the other half of the time avoid looking directly at the other person when you make your request.

3. Record your results, and see if your eye behaviour played any role in generating compliance with your request.

4. If eye contact does make a difference, describe how you could apply your findings to real-life situations.

Another reason for the difficulty in understanding facial expressions is the speed with which they can change. For example, slow-motion films show expressions fleeting across a subject's face in as short a time as it takes to blink an eye.[41] Also, it seems that different emotions show most clearly in different parts of the face: happiness and surprise in the eyes and lower face; anger in the lower face, brows, and forehead; fear and sadness in the eyes; and disgust in the lower face.

Ekman and Friesen have identified six basic emotions that facial expressions reflect–surprise, fear, anger, disgust, happiness, and sadness. Expressions reflecting these feelings seem to be recognizable in and between members of all cultures. Of course, *affect blends*–the combination of two or more expressions in different parts of the face–are possible. For instance, it's easy to imagine how someone would look who is fearful and surprised or disgusted and angry.

People are quite accurate at judging facial expressions for these emotions. Accuracy increases when judges know the target or the context in which the expression occurs, or when they have seen several samples of the target's expressions.

In spite of the complex way in which the face shows emotions, you can still pick up messages by watching it. One of the easiest ways is to look for expressions that seem to be overdone. Often when someone is trying to fool himself or another, he'll emphasize his mask to a point where it seems too exaggerated to be true. Another way to detect a person's feelings is by watching her expression at moments when she isn't likely to be thinking about her appearance. We've all had the experience of glancing into another car while stopped in a traffic jam, or of looking around at a sporting event and seeing expressions that the wearer would probably never show in more guarded moments. At other times, it's possible to watch a **microexpression** as it flashes across a person's face. For just a moment we see a flash of emotion quite different from the one a speaker is trying to convey. Finally, you may be able to spot contradictory expressions on different parts of someone's face: The eyes say one thing, but the expression of the mouth or eyebrows might be sending quite a different message.

The eyes themselves can send several kinds of messages. Meeting someone's glance with your eyes is usually a sign of involvement, whereas looking away often signals a desire to avoid contact. As we mentioned earlier, this is why solicitors on the street–panhandlers, salespeople, petitioners–try to catch our eye. Once they've managed to establish contact with a glance, it becomes harder for the approached person to draw away.

Another kind of message the eyes communicate is a positive or negative attitude. When someone glances toward us with the proper facial expression, we get a clear message that the looker is interested in us–hence the expression "making eyes." At the same time, when

It was terribly dangerous to let your thoughts wander when you were in any public place or within range of a telescreen. The smallest thing could give you away. A nervous tic, an unconscious look of anxiety, a habit of muttering to yourself–anything that carried with it the suggestion of abnormality, of having something to hide. In any case, to wear an improper expression on your face (to look incredulous when a victory was announced, for example) was itself a punishable offense. There was even a word for it in Newspeak: facecrime, it was called.

George Orwell,
1984

our long glances toward someone else are avoided, we can be pretty sure that the other person isn't as interested in us as we are in him or her. (Of course, there are all sorts of courtship games in which the receiver of a glance pretends not to notice any message by glancing away, yet signals interest with some other part of the body.)

The eyes communicate both dominance and submission. We've all played the game of trying to stare down somebody, and in real life there are also times when downcast eyes are a sign of giving in. In some religious orders, for example, subordinate members are expected to keep their eyes downcast when addressing a superior. And, as noted in Chapter 1, many Native individuals avoid eye contact out of respect.

Even the pupils of our eyes communicate. Researchers measured the amount of pupil dilation while showing men and women various types of pictures.[42] The results of the experiment were interesting: A person's eyes grow larger in proportion to the degree of interest in an object. For example, men's pupils grew about 18 percent larger when looking at pictures of a naked woman, and the degree of dilation for women looking at a naked man's picture was 20 percent. Interestingly enough, the greatest increase in pupil size occurred when women looked at a picture of a mother and an infant. A good salesperson can increase profits by being aware of pupil dilation, as Edward Hall describes. He was once in a Middle Eastern bazaar, where an Arab merchant insisted that a customer looking at his jewellery buy a certain piece that the shopper had been ignoring. But the vendor had been watching the pupils of the buyer's eyes and had known what the buyer really wanted.[43]

In the rest of the chapter, we'll discuss other nonverbal variables such as voice, touch, physical attractiveness, time, and so on.

Voice

The voice itself is another channel of nonverbal communication. Social scientists use the term **paralanguage** to describe nonverbal, vocal messages. The way a message is spoken can give the same word or words many meanings. For example, note how many meanings come from a single sentence just by shifting the emphasis from one word to another:

This is a fantastic communication book.
    (Not just any book, but *this* one in particular.)

This is a *fantastic* communication book.
    (This book is superior, exciting.)

This is a fantastic *communication* book.
    (The book is good as far as communication goes; it may
    not be so great as literature or drama.)

This is a fantastic communication *book*.
    (It's not a play or record; it's a book.)

Throat Duo: The Young Women of Tudjaat Carry on Throat Singing Tradition

Throat singing, traditionally, was a way for Inuit women to escape boredom, a means of entertainment while their husbands were hunting. In order to maintain the rhythm and to keep focussed, throat singers stand face to face, grasping their partner's arms. One woman leads, and her partner, one second behind, imitates the sound she heard. The partner has to listen closely. To repeat the sounds, observes Madeleine Allakarialak, one has to be in a rhythmic movement. A harbinger of happiness, the singers struggle to suppress the smiles which precede laughter while concentrating on each other's rhythms and sounds.

But, inevitably, they are overwhelmed and the songs end in laughter. "After throat singing you tend to laugh," cousin Phoebe Atagotaaluk points out. "You really have to concentrate on the sound. If you aren't in tune you just start to laugh."

Laughing, however, is the purpose of throat singing. "You have to laugh, to be happy," says Dora Pudluk, the girl's aunt, and a veteran throat singer. "When you are mad it doesn't work," she says, "it makes you happy." She points out the sounds do not have a meaning, rather they are just a little play people enjoy doing. "Many women practise when they are packing a baby in their *amounti,* soothing the child."

But to modern, non-Inuit audiences who do not understand the sounds or the Inuit language, the songs are assumed to have meaning. "My aunt told me originally women throat sang to get away from boredom, to entertain themselves," says Allakarialak. "But over time people started putting more meaning into the songs because more and more people asked, 'Why do you throat sing?' and 'What's it for?'"

So, to satisfy their audience, to help them understand their songs, Tudjaat now explains that the sounds represent nature, the birds, and the animals. Atagotaaluk said an elder, Meeko Nastapooka, told her throat singing was used at gatherings, as part of their celebration. Some sounds are about celebrations, others follow the sounds of animals. High tunes represent birds and small animals, low tunes are from larger animals, such as wolves and dogs.

Learning to throat sing involves listening, imitating sounds, and endless hours of practice. Atagotaaluk found the singing made her throat itchy at first but says learning was not too difficult. "Just by following her (Nastapooka) it didn't take long for my throat to get used to it," she says. The more Atagotaaluk practised, the more she wanted to learn. In learning to manipulate her throat muscles to produce music, a young girl reaps the knowledge of generations of throat singers. Being an oral skill, there are no words to explain how to throat sing. Beginners are taught a basic song learned by all throat singers, which is also used to warm up the throat muscles before attempting more complex sounds.

When throat singing, there are no rules, no formulas, no stipulations, except perhaps to have fun. "We can make up any sound we want," says Atagotaaluk. The sounds are numerous and changing, some being forgotten, others being invented. "Everything changes as time goes by," says Allakarialak. But as her cousin philosophizes, "throat singing is throat singing, you have the same sounds, just different tunes."

Regardless of the extent of a throat singer's repertoire, once you've mastered the skill, a person can throat sing with anybody. For instance, when Allakarialak was asked to sing with an elder from Cape Dorset, a community on Baffin Island, she was amazed to discover she could follow her singing. "Some songs are universal, known across the Arctic," she said.

"Since I started young," says Allakarialak, "I had the basic sounds I needed to practise on; it made it easier to pick up other sounds." Her grandmother, Minnie Allakarialak, says throat singers need to have good breathing control and a clean throat. "Lots of talking, yelling, and singing are helpful in exercising the throat," she recommends.

The songs, which are a string of sounds, can be very complicated, and for each sound, breathing has to be worked on, says Atagotaaluk. "You just have to keep practising until you get it," she says. "Once your breathing is on the right track, then the sound is easy. With the right tune, the right movement, and the right concentration with your partner, it sounds good," she says. "There are good sounds somewhere in your throat."

But those sounds do not come without practice.

Suzanne Ngui

An artificially high-pitched tone universally suggests a disarming tentativeness in the speaker. Canadians are noticeably inclined to turn a statement into a question by means of a rising intonation: This expresses hope that there are no objections and simultaneously requests a sign from the listener that the statement has been understood. Corresponding politely hesitant questions might be "OK?" "You know?"

Margaret Visser,
The Way We Are

There are many other ways our voice communicates—through its tone, speed, pitch, volume, number and length of pauses, and **disfluencies** (such as stammering, use of "uh," "um," "er," and so on). All these factors can do a great deal to reinforce or contradict the message our words convey.

Researchers have identified the power of paralanguage through the use of content-free speech—ordinary speech that has been electronically manipulated so that the words are unintelligible, but the paralanguage remains unaffected. (Hearing a foreign language that you don't understand has the same effect.) Subjects who hear content-free speech can consistently recognize the emotion being expressed, as well as identify its strength.[44]

The impact of paralinguistic cues is strong. In fact, when asked to determine a speaker's attitudes, listeners pay more attention to paralanguage than to the content of the words. Furthermore, when vocal factors contradict a verbal message (as when a speaker shouts, "I am *not* angry!"), listeners judge the speaker's intention from the paralanguage, not the words themselves.[45]

Paralanguage can affect behaviour in many ways, some of which are rather surprising. Researchers have discovered that communica-

---

SKILL BUILDER

BUILDING VOCAL FLUENCY

You can become more adept at both conveying and interpreting vocal messages by following these directions.

1. Join a partner and designate one person *A* and the other *B*.

2. Partner A should choose 25 to 50 names from the telephone directory, using his or her voice to convey one of the following attitudes:
   a. egotism
   b. friendliness
   c. insecurity
   d. irritation
   e. confidence

3. Partner B should try to detect the emotion being conveyed.

4. Switch roles and repeat the process. Continue alternating roles until each of you has both conveyed and tried to interpret at least four emotions.

5. After completing the preceding steps, discuss the following questions:
   a. What vocal cues did you use to make your guesses?
   b. Were some emotions easier to guess than others?
   c. Given the accuracy of your guesses, how would you assess your ability to interpret vocal cues?
   d. How can you use your increased sensitivity to vocal cues to improve your everyday communication competence?

tors are most likely to comply with requests delivered by speakers whose rate is similar to their own: People who spoke rapidly responded most favourably to fast talkers, while slow speakers preferred others whose rate was also slow.[46] Besides complying with same-rate speakers, listeners also feel more positively about people who seem to talk at their own rate.

Vocal changes that contradict spoken words are not easy to conceal. If the speaker is trying to hide fear or anger, the voice will probably sound higher and louder, and the rate of talk may be faster than normal. Sadness produces the opposite vocal pattern: quieter, lower-pitched speech delivered at a slower rate.[47]

Sarcasm is one instance in which we use both emphasis and tone of voice to change a statement's meaning to the opposite of its verbal message. Experience this reversal yourself with the following three statements. First say them literally, and then say them sarcastically.

"Thanks a lot!"

"I really had a wonderful time on my blind date."

"There's nothing I like better than lima beans."

As with other nonverbal messages, people often ignore or misinterpret the vocal nuances of sarcasm. Members of certain groups—children, people with weak intellectual skills, and poor listeners—are more likely to misunderstand sarcastic messages than are others.[48]

Communication through paralanguage isn't always intentional. Often our voices give us away when we're trying to create an impression different from our actual feelings. For example, you've probably had experiences of trying to sound calm and serene when you were really seething with inner nervousness. Maybe your deception went along perfectly for a while—just the right smile, no telltale fidgeting of the hands, posture appearing relaxed—and then, without being

A pause in the wrong place, an intonation misunderstood, and a whole conversation went awry.

E.M. Forster,
A Passage to India

cathy®   by Cathy Guisewite

able to do a thing about it, right in the middle of your relaxed comments, your voice squeaked! The charade was over.

Besides reinforcing or contradicting messages, some vocal factors influence the way a speaker is perceived by others. For example, communicators who speak loudly and without hesitations are viewed as more confident than those who pause and speak quietly.[49] People with more attractive voices are rated more highly than those whose speech sounds less attractive.[50] Finally, vocal features can be used for fun. For instance, Inuit throat songs are essentially vocal games with the low-pitched sounds representing birds and animals. Typically created by two females standing face to face, the goal of this exercise is for one person to set a pattern and for the other to quickly imitate the sounds and rhythms. This creates a wonderfully odd sound, produced by inhaling in the throat and varying the pitch while exhaling. Alida Minchella writes, "The first singer tries to throw off the other, either by changing the pattern or forcing her out of breath. The game always finishes with laughter to indicate the end."[51]

Touch

Touch can communicate many messages and signal a variety of relationships:[52]

functional/professional (dental exam, haircut)

social/polite (handshake)

friendship/warmth (clap on back, Spanish *abrazo*)

sexual arousal (some kisses, strokes)

aggression (shoves, slaps)

You might object to the examples following each of these categories, saying that some nonverbal behaviours occur in several types of relationships. A kiss, for example, can mean anything from a polite but superficial greeting to the most intense arousal. What makes a given touch more or less intense? Researchers have suggested a number of factors:

What part of the body does the touching

What part of the body is touched

How long the touch lasts

How much pressure is used

Whether there is movement after contact is made

Whether anyone else is present

The situation in which the touch occurs

The relationship between the persons involved[53]

From this list you can see that there is, indeed, a complex language of touch. Since nonverbal messages are inherently ambiguous,

it's no surprise that this language can often be misunderstood. Is a hug playful or suggestive of stronger feelings? Is a touch on the shoulder a friendly gesture or an attempt at domination? The ambiguity of nonverbal behaviour often leads to serious problems.

Touch plays a powerful role in shaping how we respond to others. For instance, in a laboratory task, subjects evaluated partners more positively when they were touched (appropriately, of course) by them.[54] Besides increasing liking, touch also boosts compliance. In one study, subjects were approached by a female confederate who requested that they return a dime left in the phone booth from which they had just emerged. When the request was accompanied by a light touch on the subject's arm, the probability that the subject would return the dime increased significantly.[55] In a similar experiment, subjects were asked by a male or female confederate to sign a petition or complete a rating scale. Again, subjects were more likely to co-operate when they were touched lightly on the arm. In the rating-scale variation of the study, the results were especially dramatic: Seventy percent of those who were touched complied, whereas only 40 percent of the untouched subjects were willing to co-operate (indicating a predisposition not to comply).[56] An additional power of touch is its on-the-job utility. One study showed that a restaurant waiter's fleeting touches on the hand and shoulder resulted in larger tips.[57]

Besides being the earliest means we have of making contact with others, touching is essential to our healthy development. During the nineteenth and early twentieth centuries, a large percentage of children born every year died. In some orphanages the mortality rate

The unconscious parental feelings communicated through touch or lack of touch can lead to feelings of confusion and conflict in a child. Sometimes a "modern" parent will say all the right things but not want to touch his child very much. The child's confusion comes from the inconsistency of levels: If they really approve of me so much like they say they do, why won't they touch me?

William Schutz

was nearly 100 percent, but even children in the most "progressive" homes, hospitals, and other institutions died regularly. When researchers finally tracked down the causes of this disease, they found that the infants suffered from lack of physical contact with parents or nurses, rather than lack of nutrition, medical care, or other factors. They hadn't been touched enough, and as a result they died. From this knowledge came the practice of "mothering" children in institutions—picking the baby up, carrying it around, and handling it several times each day. At one hospital that began this practice, the death rate for infants fell from between 30 and 35 percent to below 10 percent.[58]

Contemporary research confirms the relationship between touch and health. Studies have shown that premature babies grow faster and gain more weight when massaged.[59] The same researchers demonstrated that massage can help premature children gain weight, aid colicky children to sleep better, improve the mood of depressed adolescents, and boost the immune function of cancer and HIV patients. Research shows that touch between therapists and clients has the potential to encourage a variety of beneficial changes: more self-disclosure, client self-acceptance, and more positive client–therapist relationships.[60]

In traditional North American culture touching is generally more appropriate for women than for men.[61] Males touch their male friends less than they touch their female friends, and also less than females touch their female friends. Fear of homosexuality seems to be a strong reason why men are reluctant to touch one another. Although females are more comfortable about touching than men, gender isn't the only factor that shapes contact. In general, the degree of touch comfort goes along with openness to expressing intimate feelings, an active interpersonal style, and satisfactory relationships.[62]

INVITATION TO INSIGHT

THE RULES OF TOUCH

Like most types of nonverbal behaviour, touching is governed by cultural and social rules. Imagine you are writing a guidebook for visitors from another culture. Describe the rules that govern touching in the following relationships. In each case, describe how the gender of the participants affects the rules.
   a. An adult and a 5-year-old child
   b. An adult and a 12-year-old
   c. Two good friends
   d. Boss and employee

Physical Attractiveness

The importance of beauty has been emphasized in the arts for centuries. More recently, social scientists have begun to measure the degree to which physical attractiveness affects interaction between people.[63] For example, women who are perceived as attractive have more dates, receive higher grades in university or college, persuade males with greater ease, and receive lighter court sentences. Both men and women whom others view as attractive are rated as being more sensitive, kind, strong, sociable, and interesting than their less-fortunate brothers and sisters. Who is most likely to succeed in business? Place your bet on the attractive job applicant. For example, shorter men have more difficulty finding jobs in the first place, and men over 182 cm receive starting salaries that average 12.4 percent higher than comparable applicants under 177 cm.

The influence of attractiveness begins early in life. Preschoolers were shown photographs of children their own age and asked to choose potential friends and enemies. The researchers found that children as young as 3 agreed as to who was attractive ("cute") and unattractive ("homely"). Furthermore, the children valued their attractive counterparts—both of the same and the opposite sex—more highly. Also, preschool children rated by their peers as pretty were most liked, and those identified as least pretty were least liked. Children who were interviewed rated good-looking children as having positive social characteristics ("He's friendly to other children") and unattractive children negatively ("He hits other children without reason").

Teachers also are affected by students' attractiveness. Physically attractive students are usually judged more favourably—more intelligent, friendly, popular than their less-attractive counterparts.[64] Fortunately, attractiveness is something we can control without having to call a plastic surgeon. We view others as beautiful or ugly, not just on the basis of the "original equipment" they come with, but also on how they use that equipment. Posture, gestures, facial expressions, and other behaviours can increase the attractiveness of an otherwise unremarkable person. Exercise can improve the way each of us looks. Finally, the way we dress can make a significant difference in the way others perceive us, as you'll now see.

Clothing

Besides protecting us from the elements, clothing is a means of nonverbal communication. One writer has suggested that clothing conveys at least ten types of messages to others:[65]

1. Economic level
2. Educational level
3. Trustworthiness
4. Social position
5. Sophistication level
6. Economic background
7. Social background
8. Educational background
9. Level of success
10. Moral character

First Impressions

http://www.green-river.com/disc1PRS99_frm.htm

One of the most distinctively modern ideals in clothing is that we ought to avoid bright colours. "Smart" people respond by doggedly and deliberately dressing in grey, beige, black, and brown—perhaps to go with our concrete, tarred, and steel cityscapes. Or, so much colour now being so easily available, we enjoy fastidiously turning it all down for "classy" discretion. Blue is a compromise: a colour, but quiet. Never has it been as popular as it is now: A recent survey established that half of us choose blue as our favourite colour; and TV cameras endorse our preference by reproducing blue extraordinarily well.

Even synthetic indigo fades—and we should hate it not to. As moderns, we are cool, moderate, and far more obedient than the myths about us pretend; we do not often seek to "put ourselves forward."

Margaret Visser,
The Way We Are

Research shows that we do make assumptions about people based on their attire. Communicators who wear special clothing often gain persuasiveness. For example, experimenters dressed in uniforms resembling police officers were more successful than those dressed in civilian clothing in requesting pedestrians to pick up litter and in persuading them to lend a quarter to an overparked motorist.[66] Likewise, solicitors wearing law enforcement officer's and nurse's uniforms increased the level of contributions to law enforcement and health-care campaigns.[67] Uniforms aren't the only kind of clothing that carries influence. In one study, a male and female were stationed in a hallway so that anyone who wished to go by had to avoid them or pass between them. In one condition the conversationalists wore "formal daytime dress"; in the other, they wore "casual attire." Passersby behaved differently toward the couple, depending on the style of clothing: They responded positively with the well-dressed couple and negatively when the same people were casually dressed.[68] Similar results in other situations show the influence of clothing. We are more likely to obey people dressed in a high-status manner. Pedestrians were more likely to return lost coins to well-dressed people than to those dressed in low-status clothing.[69] We are also more likely to follow the lead of high-status dressers, even when it comes to violating social rules. Eighty-three percent of the pedestrians in one study followed a well-dressed jaywalker who violated a "wait" crossing signal, whereas only 48 percent followed a confederate dressed in lower-status clothing.[70] Women who are wearing a jacket are rated as being more powerful than those wearing only a dress or skirt and blouse.[71]

Despite the frequency with which we make them, our clothing-based assumptions aren't always accurate. The stranger wearing wrinkled, ill-fitting old clothes might be a manager on vacation, a normally stylish person on the way to clean a fireplace, or even an eccentric millionaire. As we get to know others better, the importance of clothing shrinks.[72] This fact suggests that clothing is especially important in the early stages of a relationship, when making a positive first impression is necessary to encourage others to know us better. This advice is equally important in personal situations and in employment interviews. In both cases, our style of dress (and personal grooming) can make all the difference between the chance to progress further and outright rejection.

Proxemics

Proxemics is the study of the way people and animals use space. As you'll see by the end of this chapter, you can sometimes tell how people feel toward each other simply by noting the distance between them. To begin to understand how this is so, try the exercise on page 264.

During this experiment your feelings probably changed at least three times. During the first phase, when you were across the room from your partner, you probably felt unnaturally far away. Then as you neared a point about one metre from him or her, you probably felt like stopping; this is the distance at which two people in our culture normally stand while conversing socially. If your partner wasn't someone you're emotionally close to, you probably began to feel quite uncomfortable as you moved through this normal range and

HERMAN®

"I always wear my lucky hat for job interviews."

Proxemics and Chronemics: The Use of Space and Time to Communicate

http://web.uvic.ca/~tbeaumon/ hinf315/topic.htm

INVITATION TO INSIGHT

DISTANCE MAKES A DIFFERENCE

1. Choose a partner, and go to opposite sides of the room and face each other.

2. Very slowly begin walking toward each other while carrying on a conversation. You might simply talk about how you feel as you follow the activity. As you move closer, try to be aware of any change in your feelings. Continue moving slowly toward each other until you are only a few centimetres apart. Remember how you feel at this point.

3. Now, while still facing each other, back up until you're at a comfortable distance for carrying on your conversation.

4. Share your feelings with each other and/or the whole group.

Some thirty inches from my nose
The frontier of my Person goes,
And all the untilled air between
Is private *pagus* or demesne.
Stranger, unless with bedroom eyes
I beckon you to fraternize,
Beware of rudely crossing it:
I have no gun, but I can spit.

W.H. Auden

Copr. © 1943 James Thurber. Copr. © 1971 Helen Thurber and Rosemary A. Thurber. From *Men, Women and Dogs*, published by Harcourt Brace Jovanovich.

came closer; it's possible that you had to force yourself not to move back. Some people find this phase so uncomfortable that they can't get closer than 50 centimetres or so to their partner.

What was happening here? Each of us carries around a sort of invisible bubble of personal space wherever we go. We think of the area inside this bubble as our private territory–almost as much a part of us as our own bodies. As you moved closer to your partner, the distance between your bubbles narrowed and at a certain point disappeared altogether: Your space had been invaded, and this is the point at which you probably felt uncomfortable. As you moved away

I Long to Hold Some Lady

I long to hold some lady
For my love is far away,
And will not come tomorrow
And was not here today.

There is no flesh so perfect
As on my lady's bone,
And yet it seems so distant
When I am all alone:

As though she were a masterpiece
In some castled town,
That pilgrims come to visit
And priests to copy down.

Alas, I cannot travel
To a love I have so deep
Or sleep too close beside
A love I want to keep.

But I long to hold some lady,
For flesh is warm and sweet.
Cold skeletons go marching
Each night beside my feet.

Leonard Cohen

---

again, your partner retreated out of your bubble, and you felt more relaxed.

Of course, if you were to try this experiment with someone very close to you—your mate, for example—you might not feel any discomfort at all, even while touching. This occurs because our willingness to get close to others—physically as well as emotionally—varies according to the person we're with and the situation we're in. And it's precisely the distance that we voluntarily put between ourselves and others that gives a nonverbal clue about our feelings and the nature of the relationship.

Anthropologist Edward T. Hall has defined four distances that we use in our everyday lives.[73] He says that we choose a particular one depending on how we feel toward the other person at a given time, the context of the conversation, and our interpersonal goals.

INTIMATE DISTANCE   The first of Hall's zones begins with skin contact and ranges out to about 45 centimetres. We usually use **intimate distance** with people who are emotionally very close to us, and then mostly in private situations–making love, caressing, comforting, protecting. By allowing someone to move into our intimate distance we're letting that person enter our territory. When we do this voluntarily, it's usually a sign of trust: We've willingly lowered our defences. On the other hand, when someone invades this most personal area without our consent, we usually feel threatened. This explains the discomfort we sometimes feel when forced into crowded places like buses or elevators with strangers. At times like these the standard behaviour in our society is to draw away or tense our muscles and avoid eye contact. This is a nonverbal way of signalling, "I'm sorry for invading your territory, but the situation forced it." Invasions of intimate distance can be perceived as a form of sexual harassment, even if the invader has no malicious intentions. For this reason, it's important to honour the cultural rules of spatial integrity.

PERSONAL DISTANCE   The second spatial zone, **personal distance,** ranges from 45 centimetres at its closest point to 1.2 metres at its farthest. Its closer phase is the distance at which most couples stand in public. But if someone of the opposite sex stands this close to one partner at a party, the other partner is likely to feel uncomfortable. This "moving in" often is taken to mean that something more than casual conversation is taking place. The far range of personal distance runs from about 75 centimetres to 1.2 metres. It's the zone just beyond the other person's reach. As Hall puts it, at this distance we can keep someone "at arm's length." This choice of words suggests the type of communication that goes on at this range: The contacts are still reasonably close, but they're much less personal than the ones that occur a foot or so closer.

SOCIAL DISTANCE   **Social distance** ranges from 1.2 metres to about 3.6 metres. Within it are the kinds of communication that usually occur in business. Its closer phase, from 1.2 to 2.1 metres, is the distance at which conversations usually occur between salespeople and customers and between people who work together. Most people feel uncomfortable when a salesclerk comes as close as 90 centimetres, whereas 1.2 or 1.5 metres nonverbally signals "I'm here to help you, but I don't mean to be too personal or pushy."

We use the far range of social distance—2.1 to 3.6 metres—for more formal and impersonal situations. This is the distance at which we sit from our boss (or other authority figure) as she stares across her desk at us. Sitting at this distance signals a far different and less-relaxed type of conversation than if we were to pull a chair around to the boss's side of the desk and sit only 90 centimetres or so away.

Choosing the optimal distance can have a powerful effect on how we regard others and how we respond to them. For example, students are more satisfied with teachers who reduce the distance between themselves and their classes. They also are more satisfied with the course itself, and they are more likely to follow the teacher's instructions.[74] Likewise, medical patients are more satisfied with physicians who are not standoffish.[75]

PUBLIC DISTANCE   **Public distance** is Hall's term for the farthest zone, running outward from 3.6 metres. The closer range of public distance is the one that most teachers use in the classroom. In the farther reaches of public space—7.5 metres and beyond—two-way communication is almost impossible. In some cases, it's necessary for speakers to use public distance because of the size of their audience, but we can assume that anyone who voluntarily chooses to use it when he or she could be closer is not interested in having a dialogue.

Territoriality

Whereas personal space is the invisible bubble we carry around as an extension of our physical being, **territory** remains stationary. Any geographical area, such as a room, house, neighbourhood, or country, to which we assume some kind of "rights" is our territory. What's interesting about territoriality is that there is no real basis for the assumption of proprietary rights of "owning" some area, but the feeling of "owning" exists nonetheless. Your room in the house is *your* room whether you're there or not (unlike personal space, which is carried around with you), and it's your room because you say it is. Although you could probably make a case for your room's *really* being your room (and not the family's or that of the mortgage holder on the house), what about the desk you sit at in each class? You feel the same way about the desk, that it's yours even though it's certain that the desk is owned by the school and is in no way really yours.

The way people use space can communicate a good deal about power and status. Generally we grant people with higher status more personal territory and greater privacy. We knock before entering our boss's office, whereas she can usually walk into our work area without hesitating. In traditional schools, professors have offices, dining rooms, and even toilets that are private, whereas the students, who are presumably less important, have no such sanctuaries. Among the

Walk down the street. Go into an office building, a mall, or your own home. Art, painting, design, and decoration surround us, reflecting current styles and messages through a universal visual language of texture, colour, and pattern. The need to creatively claim one's environment by marking it with personal art is well documented throughout history.

Sheila McGraw,
Painting and Decorating Furniture

military, greater space and privacy usually come with rank: Privates sleep 40 to a barrack, sergeants have their own private rooms, and generals have government-provided houses.

Physical Environment

In this section, we want to emphasize the ways in which physical settings, architecture, and interior design affect our communication. Begin by recalling for a moment the different homes you've visited lately. Were some of these homes more comfortable to be in than others? Certainly a lot of these kinds of feelings are shaped by the people you were with, but there are some houses where it seems impossible to relax, no matter how friendly the hosts are. We've spent what seemed like endless evenings in what Mark Knapp calls "unliving rooms," where the spotless ashtrays, furniture coverings, and plastic lamp covers seem to send nonverbal messages telling us not to touch anything, not to put our feet up, and not to be comfortable. People who live in houses like this probably wonder why nobody ever seems to relax and enjoy themselves at their parties. One thing is quite certain: They don't understand that this environment they have created can communicate discomfort to their guests.

The impressions that home designs communicate can be remarkably accurate. Researchers showed 99 students slides of the insides or outsides of 12 upper-middle-class homes and then asked them to infer the personality of the owners from their impressions.[76] The students were especially accurate after glancing at interior photos. The decorating schemes communicated accurate information about the homeowners' intellectualism, politeness, maturity, optimism, tenseness, willingness to take adventures, family orientations, and reservedness. The home exteriors also gave viewers accurate perceptions of the owners' artistic interests, graciousness, privacy, and quietness.

Besides communicating information about the designer, an environment can shape the kind of interaction that takes place in it. In one experiment, subjects working in a "beautiful" room were more positive and energetic than those working in "average" or "ugly" spaces.[77] In another study, students saw professors who occupied well-decorated offices as being more credible than those occupying less-attractive work areas.[78] Physicians have shaped environments to improve the quality of interaction with their patients. Simply removing a doctor's desk makes patients feel almost five times more at ease during office visits.[79] Redesigning a convalescent ward of a hospital greatly increased the interaction between patients. In the old design, seats were placed shoulder to shoulder around the edges of the ward. By grouping the chairs around small tables so that patients faced each other at a comfortable distance, the number of conversations doubled.

Time

Social scientists use the term **chronemics** to describe the study of how humans use and structure time. The way we handle time can express both intentional and unintentional messages.[80] For instance, in a culture like ours that values time highly, waiting can be an indicator of status. "Important" people (whose time is supposedly more valuable than that of others) may be seen by appointment only, while it is acceptable to intrude without notice on lesser beings. To see how this rule operates, consider how natural it is for a boss to drop into a subordinate's office unannounced, while the employee would never intrude into the boss's office without an appointment. A related rule is that low-status people must never make more-important people wait. It would be a serious mistake to show up late for a job interview, although the interviewer might keep you cooling your heels in the lobby. Important people are often whisked to the head of a restaurant or airport line, while the presumably less-exalted masses are forced to wait their turn.

At the beginning of the long dash . . .

Dominion Observatory, phrase introducing national time signal since 1941

The use of time depends greatly on culture. In some cultures, punctuality is critically important, while in others it is barely considered. One professor discovered the difference between North and South American attitudes when teaching at a university in Brazil.[81] He found that some students arrived halfway through a 2-hour class, and that most of them stayed put and kept asking questions when the class was scheduled to end. A half-hour after the official end of the period, the professor finally closed off discussion, since there was no indication that the students intended to leave. This flexibility of time is quite different from what is common in most Canadian colleges and universities!

Even within a culture, rules of time vary. Sometimes the differences are geographic. In Toronto, the party invitation may say 9:00, but nobody would think of showing up before 9:30. In Saskatoon, guests are expected to show up on time, or perhaps even a bit early. Even within the same geographic area, different groups establish their own rules about the use of time. Consider your own experience. In school, some instructors begin and end class punctually, while others are more casual. With some people you feel comfortable talking for hours in person or on the phone, while with others time seems to be precious and not "wasted."

SUMMARY

Nonverbal communication consists of messages expressed by nonlinguistic means, such as distance, touch, body posture and orientation, expressions of the face and eyes, movement, vocal characteristics, clothing, physical environment, and time.

Nonverbal communication is pervasive; in fact, it is impossible to not send nonverbal messages. Most nonverbal communication reveals attitudes and feelings, in contrast to verbal messages, which are better suited to expressing ideas. Although many nonverbal behaviours are universal, their use and significance vary from one culture to another. Nonverbal communication serves many functions. It can repeat, substitute for, complement, accent, regulate, and contradict verbal messages.

Nonverbal messages differ from verbal ones in several ways. They involve multiple channels, are continuous instead of discrete, are usually more ambiguous, and are more likely to be unconscious. When presented with conflicting verbal and nonverbal messages, communicators are more likely to rely on the nonverbal ones.

KEY TERMS

accenting
body orientation
chronemics
complementing
contradicting
deception cues
disfluencies
double messages
emblems

gestures
illustrators
intimate distance
kinesics
leakage
manipulators
microexpression
nonverbal communication
paralanguage

personal distance
posture
proxemics
public distance
regulating
repeating
social distance
substituting
territory

Chapter 7

Listening: More Than Meets the Ear

Elements in the Listening Process

Hearing
Attending
Understanding
Responding
Remembering

Types of Ineffective Listening

Pseudolistening
Stage-Hogging
Selective Listening
Insulated Listening
Defensive Listening
Ambushing
Insensitive Listening

Why We Don't Listen

Message Overload
Preoccupation
Rapid Thought
Effort
External Noise
Hearing Problems
Faulty Assumptions
Lack of Apparent Advantages
Lack of Training
Media Influences

Informational Listening

Talk Less
Get Rid of Distractions
Don't Judge Prematurely
Look for Key Ideas
Ask Questions
Paraphrase

Listening to Help

Advising
Judging
Analyzing
Questioning
Supporting
Prompting
Paraphrasing
When and How to Help?

Summary

Key Terms

i have just
wandered back
into our conversation
and find
that you
are still
rattling on
about something
or other
i think i must
have been gone
at least
twenty minutes
and you
never missed me
now this might say
something
about my acting ability
or it might say
something about
your sensitivity
one thing
troubles me tho

when it
is my turn
to rattle on
for twenty minutes
which i
have been known to do
have you
been missing too

Ric Masten

s Ric Masten's poem on the opposite page shows, there's more to listening than gazing politely at a speaker and nodding your head every so often. As you will soon learn, listening is a demanding and complex activity–and just as important as speaking in the communication process.

If frequency is a measure of importance, then listening easily qualifies as the most prominent kind of communication. We spend more time listening to others than in any other type of communication. One study (summarized in Figure 7–1) revealed that postsecondary students spent an average of 14 percent of their communicating time writing, 16 percent speaking, 17 percent reading, and a whopping 53 percent listening. Listening was broken down further into listening to mass communication media, such as radio and television, and listening to face-to-face messages. The former category accounted for 21 percent of the students' communication time, and the latter accounted for 32 percent–more than any other type of communication.[1] On the job, listening is just as important. Studies show that most employees of major corporations in North America spend about 60 percent of each workday listening to others.[2]

Besides being the most frequent form of communication, listening is arguably just as important as speaking in terms of making relationships work. In one survey, marital counsellors identified "failing to take the other's perspective when listening" as one of the most frequent communication problems in the couples with whom they

Do not speak, my son, unless you can improve on silence.

Irving Layton, "Advice for David"

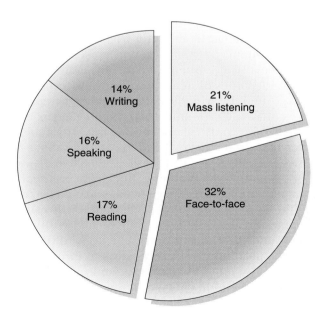

FIGURE 7–1

Types of Listening Activities

All speech . . . is a dead language until it finds a willing and prepared hearer.

Robert Louis Stevenson

work.[3] When a group of adults was asked what communication skills were most important in family and social settings, listening was ranked first.[4] When the same group was asked to identify the most important on-the-job communication skills, listening again ranked at the top of the list. A study examining the link between listening and career success revealed that better listeners rose to higher levels in their organizations.[5] The ability to listen well is closely linked to persuasive skills.[6]

This chapter will explore the nature of listening. After looking at all the elements that make up the process of listening, we will take a look at a variety of poor listening habits and their causes. After reviewing this gloomy picture, you will learn some ways to improve your listening skills, so that your chances of understanding others are better. Finally we'll explore listening and responding skills that can help others solve their problems.

ELEMENTS IN THE LISTENING PROCESS

Before we go any further, it is important to offer a clear definition of listening. There's more to this activity than passively absorbing a speaker's words. In truth, **listening** is a process that consists of five elements: hearing, attending, understanding, responding, and remembering.

Hearing

Hearing is the physiological dimension of listening. It occurs when sound waves strike the ear at a certain frequency and loudness. Hearing is also influenced by background noise. If there are other loud noises, especially at the same frequency as the message we are trying to hear, it becomes difficult to sort out the important signals from the background. Hearing is also influenced by continuous exposure to the same tone or loudness. Marshall Chasin, an audiologist at the University of Toronto who also runs the Musicians Clinic in Toronto, notes that prolonged exposure to sounds above 85 decibels (dB) can cause permanent hearing loss. Eighty-five dB would be the equivalent of the sound of a dial tone. Rock concerts register about 110 dB, and many of us have experienced hearing loss after attending one. Such losses are referred to as temporary threshold shifts (TTS), and, generally, hearing returns to normal within 16–18 hours. Chasin recommends that rock groups take precautions like wearing custom earplugs, positioning speakers so as to minimize hearing loss, and spending time in quiet environments.[7] To preserve our hearing, we listeners should consider taking similar precautions and even reduce the volume of our stereos and Walkmans.

Attending

Attending is the process of filtering out some messages and fo-cussing on others. As you read in Chapter 3, we attend to messages that stand out from background noise in some way: by being more intense, repetitious, different, and so on. Not surprisingly, research shows that we also attend most carefully to messages when we per-ceive that there is a payoff for doing so. Even if you've been day-dreaming, you're likely to attend to a message like, "This will be on the test."

Understanding

Understanding occurs when we make sense of a message. It is pos-sible to hear and attend to a message without understanding it at all. And, of course, it's possible to *misunderstand* a message. This chap-ter describes the many reasons why we misunderstand others—and why they misunderstand us. It also outlines skills that will help you improve your own understanding of others.

Responding

Responding to a message consists of giving observable feedback to the speaker. Listeners don't always respond visibly to a speaker . . . but research suggests that they should. One study of 195 critical incidents in banking and medical settings showed that a major difference between effective and ineffective listening was the kind of feedback offered.[8] Good listeners showed that they were attentive by such nonverbal behaviours as keeping eye contact and reacting with appropriate facial expressions. Their verbal behaviour–answering questions and exchanging ideas, for example–also demonstrated their attention. It's easy to imagine how other responses would signal less-effective listening. A slumped posture, bored expression, and yawning send a clear message that you are not tuned in to the speaker.

Adding responsiveness to our listening model demonstrates the fact we discussed in Chapter 1 that communication is *transactional* in nature. Listening isn't just a passive activity. As listeners we are active participants in a communication transaction. At the same time that we receive messages we also send them.

Remembering

One of the most striking things about the human species is the fluidity of our memory and our capacity to forget.

Wade David, anthropologist
(Quoted in *Saturday Night*)

Remembering is the ability to recall information. Research suggests that people remember only about half of what they hear *immediately* after hearing it. They forget half even if they work hard at listening. This situation would probably not be too bad if the half remembered right after were retained, but it isn't. Within 2 months, half of the half is forgotten, bringing what we remember down to about 25 percent of the original message. This loss, however, doesn't take 2 months: People start forgetting immediately (within 8 hours the 50 percent remembered drops to about 35 percent). Given the

---

INVITATION TO INSIGHT

LISTENING BREAKDOWNS

You can overcome believing in some common myths about listening by recalling specific instances when

    a. you heard another person's message but did not attend to it.

    b. you attended to a message but forgot it almost immediately.

    c. you attended to and remembered a message but did not understand it accurately.

    d. you understood a message but did not respond sufficiently to convey your understanding to the sender.

    e. you failed to remember some or all of an important message.

Not comprehending, they hear like the deaf.

Heraclitus

amount of information we process every day—from teachers, friends, the radio, TV, and other sources—the *residual message* (what we remember) is a small fraction of what we hear.

This high rate of forgetfulness isn't as depressing as it might seem. Although most people recall very few details of their conversations, they do retain an overall impression about the speaker, especially in important relationships.[9]

By now you can see that listening isn't as simple as it might seem. The challenges of attending to, understanding, responding to, and remembering all the messages we hear are tremendous. You can begin to get a sense of how tough it is to listen effectively by trying the exercise on p. 278.

TYPES OF INEFFECTIVE LISTENING

The preceding exercise demonstrated some of the most common types of poor listening. As you read on, you'll begin to recognize them as behaviours that you and those around you probably use quite often. Although you'll soon learn that a certain amount of ineffective listening is inevitable, and sometimes even understandable, it's important to be aware of these types so that you can avoid them when understanding others is important to you.

Looking at Diversity

Listening with the Mind's Eye

Patty Neumeyer became legally blind shortly after high school as the result of a progressive loss of vision. Her disability has not slowed the pace of her life: She is a college graduate, an actress, and a professional singer along with her husband, Bob Burnham, who is also blind. In this profile, Patty dismisses many stereotyped notions about the differences between life with and without vision.

It's not hard for someone who can see to imagine how being blind affects my listening: All of my communication (except the kinds that include touching!) operate like a telephone conversation. The words are still there, and so are vocal cues like tone of voice, pauses, sighs, and so on. I may not be able to see the other person, but there's still plenty of information. Being blind does have its logistical inconveniences, but it doesn't affect my communication as much as you might think.

I won't deny that missing out on visual messages is sometimes a disadvantage, especially with people who don't talk much and who are very nonverbally expressive. With people like this, it can help to have an "interpreter" who tells me what I'm missing. It's also hard to rely on voice alone when I don't know another person. Some people have personalities that affect their voice all the time: They always sound like they're grouchy or in a hurry, for example. Without any knowledge of people with this sort of personality, I sometimes assume that I'm doing

something to affect their attitude, when they treat everyone the same way.

You might think that, despite these problems, blind people are better listeners—especially sensitive to every nuance of voice, or even able to pick up "vibrations" from other people. After all, we *have* to rely on voice. It is certainly true that some blind people are extremely sensitive. Take my husband, Bob. He's so good at understanding others that he can predict their reactions before they speak and adjust what he says to avoid problems. But I think that has to do with his empathic personality, and not his blindness. After all, I'm blind, too, and it's a real challenge for me to put myself in another person's shoes.

I believe that the most important factor in being a good listener is whether you spend mental time focussed on your own thoughts or on the other person. If you're egocentric (either by personality or just for the moment), you won't care much about the other person's ideas. So you are likely to miss some important things he or she is saying, and maybe misin-

terpret other things. But if you really care about the other person's ideas you will do whatever it takes to understand them. That's true whether you're blind or not.

Maybe not all blind people are created equal, and that's why it's harder for some to listen than others. I'm what you could call an auditory person: I use my hearing a lot to make sense of the world. For instance, when I need to learn the lyrics of a new song that Bob and I will perform, I can hear them once and I've basically got them. But Bob is more "visual" even though he's blind: He'll need to study the lyrics in Braille before he can remember them. If this difference between being auditory and visual has any real validity, then it can explain why some people—blind and otherwise—find it easier than others to listen.

What I'm suggesting is that vision may play a big part in how people listen, but it's only one of many variables. It's my opinion that the personality that each person develops, by nature and nurture, is the biggest influence.

Pseudolistening

Pseudolistening is an imitation of the real thing. Pseudolisteners give the appearance of being attentive: They look you in the eye, nod and smile at the right times, and may even answer you occasionally. Behind that appearance of interest, however, something entirely different is going on, for pseudolisteners use a polite façade to mask thoughts that have nothing to do with what the speaker is saying. Often pseudolisteners ignore you because of something on their minds that's more important to them than your remarks. Other times they may simply be bored or think that they've heard what you have to say before and so tune out your remarks. Whatever the reasons, the significant fact is that pseudolistening is really counterfeit communication.

Stage-Hogging

Stage-hogs (sometimes called "conversational narcissists") try to turn the topic of conversations to themselves instead of showing interest in the speaker.[10] One stage-hogging strategy is a "shift-response"–changing the focus of the conversation from the speaker to the narcissist:

A: "I had a great time mountain-biking last weekend!"
B: "Mountain-biking's OK, but I'd rather go running."

A: "My math class is really tough."
B: "You think math is tough? You ought to try my physics class!"

Interruptions are another hallmark of stage-hogging. Besides preventing the listener from learning potentially valuable information, they can damage the relationship between the interrupter and the speaker. For example, applicants who interrupt the questions of employment interviewers are likely to be rated less favourably than job seekers who wait until the interviewer has finished speaking before they respond.[11]

When confronted with stage-hogs, people respond in one of two ways. Sometimes the reaction is passive: talking less, tuning out the speaker, showing disinterest nonverbally, and leaving the conversation. Other strategies are more active: trying to recapture the floor, hinting about the stage-hog's dominance, or confronting the speaker about his or her narcissism. Reactions like these give stage-hogs a taste of their own medicine, turning the conversation into a verbal tug-of-war.

Not all interruptions are attempts at stage-hogging. One study revealed a difference between male and female interrupters.[12] Men typically interrupted conversations far more often than women. Their goals were usually to control the discussion. Women interrupted for very different reasons: to communicate agreement, to elaborate on the speaker's idea, or to participate in the topic of conversation.

Bright-eyed college students in lecture halls aren't necessarily listening to the professor.

If a buzzer went off at sporadic intervals and students were asked to encode their thoughts and moods at that moment, you would discover that:

- *About 20 percent of the students, men and women, are pursuing erotic thoughts.*
- *Another 20 percent are reminiscing about something.*
- *Only 20 percent are actually paying attention to the lecture; 12 percent actively listen.*
- *The others are worrying, daydreaming, thinking about lunch or–surprise–religion (8 percent).*

Paul Cameron,
Wayne State University

EgoSpeak: Why No One Listens to You

http://www.extension.ualberta.ca/ govstudies/adbh/articles/ egospeak.htm

These sorts of responses are more likely to be welcomed as a contribution to the discussion, and not as attempts to grab the stage.

Selective Listening

Selective listeners respond only to the parts of your remarks that interest them, rejecting everything else. All of us are selective listeners from time to time, as, for instance, when we screen out radio commercials and keep an ear cocked for our favourite song. In other cases, selective listening occurs in conversations with people who expect a thorough hearing but pay attention to their partner only when the subject turns to their favourite topic—perhaps money, sex, or some particular person. Unless and until you bring up one of these pet subjects, you might as well talk to the door.

Insulated Listening

Insulated listeners are almost the opposite of their selective cousins just mentioned. Instead of looking for something, these people avoid it. Whenever a topic arises that they'd rather not deal with, insulated listeners simply fail to hear or acknowledge it. You remind them about a problem, perhaps an unfinished job, poor grades, or the like, and they'll nod or answer you and then promptly forget what you've just said.

Defensive Listening

Defensive listeners take others' remarks as personal attacks. The teenager who perceives her parents' questions about her friends and activities as distrustful snooping is a defensive listener, as is the insecure breadwinner who explodes any time his mate mentions money, or the touchy parent who views any questioning by her children as a threat to her authority and parental wisdom. As your reading in Chapter 9 will suggest, it's fair to assume that many defensive listeners are suffering from shaky presenting images and avoid admitting it by projecting their own insecurities onto others.

Ambushing

Ambushers listen carefully to you, but only because they're collecting information they'll use to attack what you say. The cross-examining prosecution lawyer is a good example of an ambusher. Needless to say, using this kind of strategy will justifiably initiate defensiveness in the other person.

Insensitive Listening

Insensitive listeners offer the final example of people who don't receive another person's messages clearly. As we've said before, people

HERMAN®   by Jim Unger

"Ear, Nose and Throat"

often don't express their thoughts or feelings openly but instead communicate them through a subtle and unconscious choice of words or nonverbal clues or both. Insensitive listeners aren't able to look beyond the words and behaviour to understand their hidden meanings. Instead, they take a speaker's remarks at face value.

Fellows who have no tongues are often all eyes and ears.

Thomas C. Haliburton,
Sam Slick's Wise Saws

WHY WE DON'T LISTEN

After thinking about the styles of ineffective listening described in the previous pages, most people begin to see that they listen carefully only a small percentage of the time. It's pretty discouraging to realize that much of the time you aren't hearing others and they aren't getting your messages, but this is a fact of life. Sad as it may be, it's impossible to listen *all* the time, for several reasons.

Message Overload

The amount of speech most of us encounter every day makes careful listening to everything we hear impossible. As you have already read, many of us spend almost half the time we're awake listening to verbal messages–from instructors, co-workers, friends, family,

Most conversations are simply monologues delivered in the presence of a witness.

Margaret Millar,
The Weak-Eyed Bat

salespeople, and total strangers, not to mention radio and television. This means that we often spend 5 hours or more a day listening to people talk. It's impossible to keep our attention totally focussed for this amount of time. Therefore, at times we have to let our attention wander. Given the onslaught of messages, it's understandable—perhaps even justifiable—to use pseudolistening and other less-than-admirable responses.

Preoccupation

Another reason we don't always listen carefully is that we're often wrapped up in personal concerns that are of more immediate importance to us than the messages others are sending. It's hard to pay attention to someone else when you're anticipating an upcoming test or thinking about the wonderful time you had last night with good friends. Yet we still feel we have to "listen" politely to others, and so we continue with our charade.

Rapid Thought

Listening carefully is also difficult for a physiological reason. Although we're capable of understanding speech at rates up to 600 words per minute, the average person speaks between 100 and 150 words per minute.[13] Thus, we have a lot of "spare time" to spend with our minds while someone is talking. And the temptation is to use this time in ways that don't relate to the speaker's ideas, such as thinking about personal interests, daydreaming, planning a rebuttal, and so on. Rather than let your attention wander, the trick is to use this spare time to understand the speaker's ideas.

Effort

Listening effectively is hard work. The physical changes that occur during careful listening show the effort it takes: The heart rate quickens, respiration increases, and body temperature rises.[14] Notice that these changes are similar to the body's reaction to physical effort. This is no coincidence, for listening carefully to a speaker can be just as taxing as more-obvious efforts.

External Noise

The physical world in which we live often presents distractions that make it hard to pay attention to others. The sound of traffic, music, others' speech, and so on interferes with our ability to hear well. Consider, for example, how the efficiency of your listening decreases when you are seated in a crowded, hot, stuffy room that is surrounded by traffic and other noises. In such circumstances even the best intentions aren't enough to ensure clear understanding.

Hearing Problems

Sometimes a person's listening ability suffers from a physiological hearing problem. Once a hearing problem has been diagnosed, it's often possible to treat it. The real tragedy occurs when a hearing loss goes undetected. This is what occurred during the 1990s, with the greatest hearing hazards being continued exposure to music and recreational noise. The Canadian Hearing Society reports that there are more young people with permanent hearing losses as a result of such exposure. While the youth of today are not going deaf, they are definitely becoming hard of hearing.[15] To test your own hearing, try the following. Before attending some noisy event, turn your car radio to a news station and reduce the volume so that it is barely audible. After the event, see if you can hear the voices. You probably won't be able to, which suggests that you have been overexposd to noise or music.[16] If you cannot hear the voices within 24 hours, you should see a physician or audiologist.

*I talk too much
but the manner
of your listening
calls the words
out of me.
You say almost
nothing. Yet
there would be
only silence
if you were not here.*

Alden Nowlan,
"Apology"

Faulty Assumptions

We often make incorrect assumptions that lead us to believe we're listening attentively when quite the opposite is true. For instance, we are less likely to listen when the subject is a familiar one, when we assume the speaker's thoughts are too simple or too complex, or when we think the topic is unimportant. In such circumstances, we should try to pay close attention to compensate for our assumptions.

Lack of Apparent Advantages

It often appears that we have more to gain by speaking than by listening. One big advantage of speaking is that it gives you a chance to control others' thoughts and actions. Whatever your goal—to be hired by a prospective boss, to convince others to vote for the candidate of your choice, or to describe the way you want your hair cut—the key to success seems to be the ability to speak well.

Another apparent advantage of speaking is the chance it provides to gain the admiration, respect, or liking of others. Tell jokes, and everyone will think you're a real wit. Offer advice, and they'll be grateful for your help. Tell them all you know, and they'll be impressed by your wisdom. But keep quiet . . . and you think you'll look like a worthless nobody.

Finally, talking gives you the chance to release energy in a way that listening can't. When you're frustrated, the chance to talk about your problems can often help you feel better. In the same way, you can often lessen your anger by letting it out verbally. It is also helpful to share your excitement with others by talking about it, for keeping it inside often makes you feel as if you might burst.

Although it's true that talking does have many advantages, it's important to realize that listening can pay dividends, too. As you'll soon read, being a good listener is one good way to help others with their problems—and what better way is there to have others appreciate you? As for controlling others, it may be true that it's hard to be persuasive while you're listening, but your willingness to hear others out will often encourage them to think about your ideas in return. Like defensiveness, listening is often reciprocal: You get what you give.

Lack of Training

Even if we want to listen well, we're often hampered by a lack of skill. A common but mistaken belief is that listening is like breathing—an activity that people do well naturally. "After all," the common belief goes, "I've been listening since I was a child. I don't need to study the subject in school."

The truth is that listening is a skill much like speaking: Virtually everybody does it, though few people do it well. One study illustrates this point. In the study, 144 managers were asked to rate their listening skills. Astonishingly, not one of the managers described himself or herself as a "poor" or "very poor" listener, while 94 percent rated themselves as "good" or "very good." [17] The favourable self-ratings contrasted sharply with the perceptions of the managers' subordinates, many of whom said their boss's listening skills were weak. As we have already discussed, some poor listening is inevitable. The good news is that listening can be improved through instruction and training.[18] Despite this fact, the amount of time spent teaching listening is far less than that devoted to other types of communication. Table 7–1 reflects this upside-down arrangement.

Listen or your tongue will keep you deaf.

Native proverb

TABLE 7–1	COMPARISON OF COMMUNICATION ACTIVITIES			
	LISTENING	**SPEAKING**	**READING**	**WRITING**
Learned	First	Second	Third	Fourth
Used	Most	Next to most	Next to least	Least
Taught	Least	Next to least	Next to most	Most

Media Influences

A final challenge to serious listening is the influence of contemporary mass media, especially television and radio. A growing amount of programming consists of short segments: news items, commercials, music videos, and so on. (Think of *Sesame Street* and MuchMusic.) In the same vein, news stories (for example, *The Globe and Mail* and the television news) consist of brief stories with a declining portion of text and a growing amount of graphical information. These trends discourage the kind of focussed attention that is necessary for careful listening, especially to complicated ideas and feelings.

INFORMATIONAL LISTENING

After reading the preceding few pages, you might decide that listening well is impossible. Fortunately, with the right combination of attitude and skill, you can do a reasonably good job. The first step is to realize that different types of listening are suited for different purposes. With informational listening the goal is to make sure you are accurately receiving the same thoughts the other person is trying to convey—not always an easy feat when you consider the forces that interfere with understanding.

The situations that call for informational listening are endless and varied: following the directions of an instructor or boss, listening to a friend's account of a vacation, learning about your family history from a relative's tales, swapping ideas in a discussion about religion

Characteristics of Effective Listeners

http://www.sasked.gov.sk.ca/docs/ mla/speak007/html

I don't mind that you are talking so long as you don't mind that I'm not listening.

Morning Smile,
Cape Breton Post

or politics . . . the list goes on and on. You can become a more effective informational listener by following several guidelines.

Talk Less

Zeno of Citium put it most succinctly: "We have been given two ears and but a single mouth, in order that we may hear more and talk less." If your true goal is to understand the speaker, avoid the tendency to hog the stage and shift the conversation to your ideas. Talking less doesn't mean you should remain completely silent. As you'll soon read, feedback that clarifies your understanding and seeks new information is an important way to understand a speaker. Nonetheless, most of us talk too much when we're claiming to understand others. You can appreciate this point by trying the following exercise.

INVITATION TO INSIGHT

SPEAKING AND LISTENING WITH A "TALKING STICK"

Explore the benefits of talking less and listening more by using a "talking stick." This exercise is based on the Native tradition of "council." Gather a group of people in a circle and designate a particular item as the talking stick. (Almost any manageable object will do.) Participants then pass the object around the circle. Each person may speak

   a. when holding the stick;

   b. for as long as he or she holds the stick; and

   c. without interruption from anyone else in the circle.

When a member is through speaking, the stick passes to the left, and the speaker surrendering the stick must wait until it has made its way around the circle before speaking again.

After each member of the group has had the chance to speak, discuss how this experience differed from more-common approaches to listening. Decide how the desirable parts of this method could be introduced into everyday conversations.

Listening
ear pressed against stone
it isn't quiet but silent
so that the sounds I hear
are not from outside me any
  longer
but gyrating dancing thoughts
or the small noise my body
  makes
in its act of living.

Al Purdy,
"Listening"

Get Rid of Distractions

Some distractions are external: ringing telephones, radio or television programs, friends dropping in, and so on. Other diversions are internal: preoccupation with your own problems, an empty stomach, and so on. If the information you're seeking is really important, do everything possible to eliminate the internal and external noise that interferes with careful listening.

Don't Judge Prematurely

Most people would agree with the principle that it's essential to understand a speaker's ideas before judging them. Despite this

FIGURE 7–2

commonsense fact, all of us are guilty of forming snap judgements, evaluating others before hearing them out. This tendency is greatest when the speaker's ideas conflict with our own. Conversations that ought to be exchanges of ideas turn into verbal battles, with the "opponents" trying to ambush one another in order to win a victory. Disagreements aren't the only kind of conversation in which the tendency to judge others is strong: It's also tempting to counterattack when others criticize you, even when those criticisms may contain valuable truths and when understanding them may lead to a change for the better. Even if there is no criticism or disagreement, we tend to evaluate others based on sketchy first impressions, forming snap judgements that aren't at all valid. Not all premature judgements are negative. It's also possible to jump to overly favourable conclusions about the quality of a speaker's remarks when we like that person or agree with the ideas being expressed. The lesson contained in these negative examples is clear: Listen first. Make sure you understand. *Then* evaluate.

Look for Key Ideas

It's easy to lose patience with long-winded speakers who never seem to get to the point—or *have* a point, for that matter. Nonetheless, most people do have a central idea. By using your ability to think more quickly than the speaker can talk, you may be able to extract the central idea from the surrounding mass of words you're hearing. If you can't figure out what the speaker is driving at, you can always ask in a tactful way by using the skills of questioning and paraphrasing, which we'll examine now.

Ask Questions

The listening methods discussed so far are basically passive in nature; that is, they can be carried out silently. It's also possible to verify or increase your understanding in a more active way by asking questions to be sure you are receiving the speaker's thoughts and feelings accurately.

Despite their apparent benefits, not all questions are equally helpful. Whereas **sincere questions** are aimed at understanding others, **counterfeit questions** are really disguised attempts to send a message, not receive one. Counterfeit questions come in several varieties:

- *Questions that trap the speaker.* When your friend says, "You didn't like that movie, did you?," you're being backed into a corner. It's clear that your friend disapproves, so the question leaves you with two choices: You can disagree and defend your position, or you can devalue your reaction by lying or equivocating—"I guess it wasn't perfect." Consider how much easier it would be to respond to the sincere question, "What did you think of the movie?"

  A tag question like "did you?" or "isn't that right?" at the end of a question can be a tip-off that the asker is looking for agreement,

Listening to Others

http://www.ncpg.com/self17.html

not information. Although some tag questions are genuine requests for confirmation, counterfeit ones are used to coerce agreement: "You said you'd call at five o'clock, but you forgot, didn't you?" Similarly, leading questions that begin with "Don't you" (such as, "Don't you think he would make a good boss?") direct others toward a desired response. As a simple solution, changing "Don't you?" to "Do you?" makes the question less leading.

- *Questions that make statements.* "Are you finally off the phone?" is more of a statement than a question—a fact unlikely to be lost on the targeted person. Emphasizing certain words can also turn a question into a statement: "You lent money to *Tony?*" We also use questions to offer advice. The person who responds with "Are you going to stand up to him and give him what he deserves?" clearly has stated an opinion about what should be done.

- *Questions that carry hidden agendas.* "Are you busy Friday night?" is a dangerous question to answer. If you say "No," thinking the person has something fun in mind, you won't like hearing, "Good,

The Chinese characters that make up the verb "to listen" tell us something significant about this skill.

EAR

EYES

UNDIVIDED
ATTENTION

HEART

FIGURE 7–3

Calligraphy by Angie Au.

"You haven't been listening. I keep telling you that I don't want a product fit for a king."

because I need some help moving my piano." Obviously, such questions are not designed to enhance understanding: They are setups for the proposal that follows. Other examples include, "Will you do me a favour?" and "If I tell you what happened, will you promise not to get mad?" Wise communicators answer questions that mask hidden agendas cautiously, with responses like "It depends" or "Let me hear what you have in mind before I answer."

- *Questions that seek "correct" answers.* Most of us have been victims of questioners who want to hear only a particular response. "Which shoes do you think I should wear?" can be a sincere question—unless the asker has a predetermined preference. When this happens, the asker isn't interested in listening to contrary opinions, and "incorrect" responses get shot down. Some of these questions may venture into delicate territory. "Honey, do you think I look ugly?" can be a request for a "correct" answer.

- *Questions based on unchecked assumptions.* "Why aren't you listening to me?" assumes the other person isn't paying attention. "What's the matter?" assumes that something is wrong. As Chapter 3 explains, perception checking is a much better way of checking out assumptions. As you recall, a perception check offers a description and interpretations, followed by a sincere request for clarification: "When you kept looking over at the TV I thought you weren't listening to me, but maybe I was wrong. *Were* you paying attention?"

Unlike the counterfeit questions we've just examined, sincere questions are genuine requests for new information that clarifies a speaker's thoughts or feelings. Although the value of sincere questioning might seem obvious, there are two reasons why people often don't use this information-seeking approach. First, communicators are often reluctant to show their ignorance by asking for explanation of what seems to be an obvious point. At times like this it's a good idea to recall a quote attributed to Confucius: "He who asks a question is a fool for five minutes. He who does not ask is a fool for life."

A second reason people are often disinclined to ask questions is that they think they already understand a speaker; but do we in fact understand others as often or as well as we think? You can best answer by thinking about how often people misunderstand *you* while feeling certain that they know what you've meant. If you are aware that others should ask questions of you more often, then it's logical to assume that the same principle holds true in reverse.

Paraphrase

Questioning is often a valuable tool for increasing understanding. Sometimes, however, it won't help you understand a speaker's ideas any more clearly, and it can even lead to greater confusion. Consider the common example of asking directions to a friend's home. Sup-

Learn to listen. Opportunity could be knocking at your door very softly.

Frank Tyger

INVITATION TO INSIGHT

COUNTERFEIT QUESTIONS

Check your understanding of counterfeit questions by looking at Jill and Mark's conversation on page 310. Create examples of poor responses that Mark could have given Jill by showing how and where he could have:

a. Asked a question that was really a statement.

b. Asked a question with a hidden agenda.

c. Asked a question that begged for a "correct" answer.

d. Asked a question based on an unchecked assumption.

e. Denied Jill the right to her feelings.

f. Minimized the significance of the situation.

g. Focussed on "then and there" rather than "here and now."

h. Cast judgement on Jill.

In each case, speculate how Jill might have reacted to Mark's poor response.

---

pose you've received these instructions: "Drive about a kilometre and then turn left at the traffic signal." Now imagine that a few common problems exist in this simple message. First, suppose that your friend's idea of a kilometre differs from yours: Your mental picture of the distance is actually closer to two kilometres, whereas your friend's is closer to 300 metres. Next, consider that "traffic signal" really means "stop sign"; after all, it's common for us to think one thing and say another. Keeping these problems in mind, suppose you tried to verify your understanding of the directions by asking, "After I turn at the light, how far should I go?," to which your friend replied that the house is the third from the corner. Clearly, if you parted after this exchange, you would encounter a lot of frustration before finding the elusive residence.

What was the problem here? It's easy to see that questioning might not have helped you, for your original ideas of how far to drive and where to turn were mistaken. Such mistakes exemplify the biggest problem with questioning: Your inquiries don't tell you whether you have accurately received information that has *already* been sent.

The need to understand others is even more important in a variety of everyday situations: making sure you know just what the boss wants, clarifying a school assignment before leaving class, knowing exactly what's behind critical comments others might direct at you, and understanding what others mean when they offer advice.

Since questioning doesn't always provide the information you need, consider another kind of feedback—one that would tell you

Effective Listening & Responding

---

http://www.comunityinc.com/
05articles/0502_listen.html

whether you understood what had already been said before you asked additional questions. This type of feedback involves restating in your own words the message you thought the speaker had just sent, without adding anything new. Statements that reword the listener's interpretation of a message are commonly termed **paraphrasing** or **active listening.** Sometimes a paraphrase will reflect the *ideas* you think a speaker has expressed:

> *(To a direction-giver)* "You're telling me to drive down to the traffic light by the high school and turn toward the mountains, is that it?"

> *(To the boss)* "So you need me both this Saturday *and* next Saturday–right?"

> *(To a professor)* "When you said, 'Don't worry about the low grade on the quiz,' did you mean it won't count against my grade?"

In other cases, a paraphrase will reflect your understanding of the speaker's *feelings:*

"You said you understand, but you look confused. Are you?"

"You seem to be in a hurry. I get the idea you don't want to talk now. Is that right?"

"You said, 'Forget it,' but it sounds like you're mad. Are you?"

SKILL BUILDER

PARAPHRASING PRACTICE

This exercise will help you see that it is possible to understand someone who disagrees with you, without arguing or sacrificing your point of view.

1. Find a partner, then move to a place where you can talk comfortably. Designate one person as *A* and the other *B.*

2. Find a subject on which you and your partner apparently disagree— a current-events topic, a philosophical or moral issue, or perhaps simply a matter of personal taste.

3. Person A begins by making a statement on the subject. Person B's job is then to paraphrase the idea back, beginning by saying something like "What I hear you saying is. . . . " It is very important that in this step B feed back only what she heard A say without adding any judgement or interpretation. B's job is simply to understand her, and doing so in no way should signify agreement or disagreement with A's remarks.

4. Person A then responds by telling B whether her response was accurate. If there was some misunderstanding, A should make the correction, and B should feed back her new understanding of the statement. Continue this process until you're both sure that B understands A's statement.

5. Now it's B's turn to respond to A's statement and for B to help the process of understanding by correcting A.

6. Continue this process until each partner is satisfied that she has explained herself fully and has been understood by the other person.

7. Now discuss the following questions:

   a. When you were a listener, how accurate was your first understanding of the speaker's statements?

   b. How did your understanding of the speaker's position change after you used active listening?

   c. Did you find that the gap between your position and that of your partner narrowed as a result of active listening?

   d. How did you feel at the end of your conversation? How does this feeling compare with your usual emotional state after discussing controversial issues?

   e. How might your life change if you used active listening at home? At work? With friends?

TYPES OF PARAPHRASING STATEMENTS   Whether your paraphrasing reflects a speaker's thoughts or feelings, and whether it focusses on a specific comment or a general theme, the key to success is to restate the other person's comments in your own words as a way of cross-checking the information. If you simply repeat the speaker's comments verbatim, you will sound foolish . . . and you still might well be misunderstanding what has been said. Notice the difference between simply parroting a statement and true paraphrasing:

Speaker: "I'd like to go, but I can't afford it."

Parroting: "You'd like to go, but you can't afford it."

Paraphrasing: "So if we could find a way to pay for you, you'd be willing to come. Is that right?"

Speaker: "Gawd, do you look awful!"

Parroting: "You think I look terrible."

Paraphrasing: "You think I've put on too much weight?"

As these examples suggest, effective paraphrasing is a skill that takes time to develop. You can make your paraphrasing sound more natural by taking any of three approaches, depending on the situation:

1. Change the speaker's wording.
    Speaker: "Social assistance is just another way for Canadians to freeload off the government."
    Paraphrase: "Let me see if I got this right. You're upset because you think social assistance recipients should have to work to receive money."
2. Offer an example of what you think the speaker is talking about.
       When the speaker makes an abstract statement, you may suggest a specific example or two to see if your understanding is accurate.
    Speaker: "Lee is such a jerk. I can't believe the way he acted last night."
    Paraphrase: "You think those jokes were pretty offensive, huh?"
3. Reflect the underlying theme of the speaker's remarks.
       When you want to summarize the *theme* that seems to have run through another person's conversation, a complete or partial perception check is appropriate:
    Paraphrase: "You keep reminding me to be careful. Sounds like you're worried that something might happen to me. Am I right?"

Paraphrasing won't always be accurate. But even if your restatement is off-base, your response gives the other person a chance to make a correction. Besides increasing the chance of understanding others, paraphrasing is an excellent way to keep the tone of a confrontation positive. When you are sincerely trying to understand the other person, you are less likely to engage in the kind of hostile behaviour that can lead to a destructive battle. For this reason, some communication experts suggest that the ratio of active listening to other responses should be at least 5:1, if not more.[19]

TEACHING DOCTORS TO LISTEN

As she looks up at the young faces in the auditorium, Cathy Chovaz's voice wavers slightly. "I could be you," she tells the audience. "You could be me. I went through university like every other student, and when I graduated, the whole world was there waiting for me. Then, bang—that whole reality changed drastically for me and my family."

Chovaz, 35, is telling her story to first-year medical students at the University of Western Ontario (UWO) in London. Her hands never stop gesturing as she speaks, a habit cultivated since she lost her hearing 9 years ago. In and out of hospital about 35 times since then, at times near death, Chovaz was eventually diagnosed with RED-M syndrome, a rare condition associated with constrictions of the small arteries in the brain, eyes, and ears that can result in small strokes and may cause deafness, blindness, and brain dysfunction.

"It wasn't just me lying there in the hospital," Chovaz tells the medical students. "With a patient come her dreams, hopes, and ambitions. When you admit a patient, you admit all of that."

Chovaz's moving words are part of a unique lesson plan at UWO in which patients become teachers, and medical students learn about the human side of medicine.

The brainchild of Dr. John Howard, associate professor of medicine at UWO and co-ordinator of the clinical methods course, it was designed to make medical education more responsive to society. It's all part of a shift toward patient-centred medicine, fostered by Educating Future Physicians for Ontario (EFPO). "Sometimes, doctors need to be encouraged to listen to what the patient wants, rather than simply dispensing treatment," says Dr. Howard.

The aim of EFPO is to create doctors who are good advocates, gatekeepers, collaborators, and, most importantly, communicators, according to Dr. Wayne Weston, site co-ordinator of EFPO at UWO. Patients' number one beef about doctors is poor listening skills, says Weston. "It's one of the most common complaints to the College of Physicians and Surgeons of Ontario and a leading cause of lawsuits." It's also one of the chief reasons why women switch doctors, according to a recent survey of 1,000 Canadian women conducted by Women's College Hospital in Toronto.

Communicating with patients goes beyond making them happy. Studies have shown that patients actually get better more quickly if they perceive their doctor listened and fully discussed the problem with them, says epidemiologist Moira Stewart, a professor at UWO's Centre for Studies in Family Medicine, which teaches and researches patient-centred care. For example, a 1986 London, Ontario, study of 272 patients who sought help for headaches found recovery was statistically related to whether the patients felt their doctor had fully discussed the problem with them at the first visit. A 1989 U.S. study of high blood pressure and diabetes found that blood pressure and blood sugar levels improved in patients who asked their doctor questions and received satisfactory answers, while levels stayed the same in patients who didn't fully participate in their visits.

On the first day of UWO's clinical methods course, which teaches medical students how to talk to patients and conduct medical interviews and physicals, the students listen to the stories of several patients. They are then asked to come up with a mission statement for their class describing the qualities that make good physicians. That mission becomes a focal point of the class's undergraduate medical education for students and instructors alike. "Previously, you went to medical school, you went to a bunch of classes; you didn't really talk about the sort of doctor you wanted to be," says Dr. Howard, who doesn't know of any other Canadian school incorporating a mission statement into its curriculum. "The mission statement encourages the medical students to focus on the people they will serve."

The students say they find the day invaluable, he adds. "First-year students are at their best in terms of wanting to help people. They're at the stage where they hang on every word from the patients."

For Chovaz, whose experience with doctors ranged from those who truly acknowledged the power of her spirit to those who treated her merely as a fascinating collection of symptoms, a more balanced doctor–patient relationship is long overdue. Her advice to students: "Approach your patients as whole people. People who come to you need to be in partnership with you. Keep your minds and hearts open."

Dahlia Reich

Listening Exercises

*http://catsis.weber.edu/comm/
EXlisten.htm*

Because it's an unfamiliar way of responding, paraphrasing may feel awkward at first, but if you start by paraphrasing occasionally and then gradually increase the frequency of such responses, you can begin to learn the benefits of this method.

LISTENING TO HELP

We listen for information out of self-interest. Another reason for listening, however, is to help others with their problems. Sometimes the dilemma is a major one: "I don't know whether we should stay together or split up" or "I keep getting turned down for jobs I want." At other times the problem is less profound. A friend might be trying to decide what birthday gift to buy or how to spend the weekend.

There's no question about the value of receiving help with personal problems. One survey showed that "comforting ability" was among the most important communication skills a friend could have.[20] The value of personal support is clear when big problems arise, but research shows that the smaller, everyday distresses and upsets can actually take a bigger toll on mental health and physical well-being.[21]

Whether the problem is large or small, knowing how to help is a valuable skill. To understand your present style of helping, try the following exercise before reading on.

Most of the responses you made probably fell into one of several categories. None of these ways of responding is good or bad in itself, but there's a proper time and place for each kind of response. The problem usually occurs, however, when we use them in the wrong situations or depend on one or two styles of responses for all situations.

As you read the following descriptions of these ways of responding, see which ones you used most frequently in the previous exercise, and think about the results that probably would have occurred from your response.

Advising

When approached with another's problem, the most common tendency is an **advising response**: to help by offering a solution.[22] Although such a response is sometimes valuable, often it isn't as helpful as you might think.[23]

Often your suggestion may not offer the best course to follow, in which case it can even be harmful. There's often a temptation to tell others how we would behave in their place, but it's important to realize that what's right for one person may not be right for another. A related consequence of advising is that it often allows others to avoid responsibility for their decisions. A partner who follows a suggestion of yours that doesn't work out can always pin the blame on you. Finally, often people simply don't want advice: They may not be ready

INVITATION TO INSIGHT

WHAT WOULD YOU DO?

1. In a moment you'll read a list of situations in which someone tells you of a problem. In each case, write out the words you'd use in responding to this person.

2. Here are the statements:

    a. My parents are driving me crazy. Everything I like seems to go against their values, and they just won't accept my feelings as being right for me. It's not that they don't love me—they do. But they don't accept me.

    b. I've been pretty discouraged lately. I just can't get a good relationship going with anyone. . . . I mean a romantic relationship . . . you know. I have plenty of guys whom I'm friends with, but that's always as far as it goes. I'm tired of being just a pal. . . . I want to be more than that.

    c. (Child to parents) I hate you guys! You always go out and leave me with some stupid sitter. Why don't you like me?

    d. I'm really bummed out. I don't know what I want to do with my life. I'm pretty tired of school, but there aren't any good jobs around, and I sure don't want to join the army. I could just drop out for a while, but that doesn't really sound very good either.

    e. My marriage is a mess. It's not that we fight too much or anything, but there's no excitement any more. It's like we're in a rut, and it keeps getting worse. . . .

    f. I keep getting the feeling that my boss is angry at me. It seems as if lately he hasn't been joking around very much, and he hasn't said anything at all about my work for about 3 weeks now. I wonder what I should do.

3. Once you've written your response to each of these messages, imagine the probable outcome of the conversation that would have followed. If you've tried this exercise in class, you might have two group members role-play each statement. Based on your idea of how the conversation might have gone, decide which responses were helpful and which were unproductive.

to accept it, needing instead simply to talk out their thoughts and feelings.

Before offering advice, then, you need to be sure that three conditions are present:

1. **Be confident that the advice is accurate.** You may be certain about some matters of fact, such as the proper way to solve a school problem or the cost of a piece of merchandise, but resist the temptation to act like an authority on matters you know little about. Furthermore, it is both unfair and risky to make suggestions when you aren't positive that they are the best choices.

Try to feel, in your heart's core, the reality of others. This is the most painful thing in the world, probably, and the most necessary. In times of personal adversity, know that you are not alone. Know that although in the eternal scheme of things you are small, you are also unique and irreplaceable, as are all your fellow humans everywhere in the world. Know that your commitment is above all to life itself.

Margaret Laurence,
Trent University address

Realize that just because a course of action worked for you doesn't guarantee that it will be correct for everybody.

2. Ask yourself whether the person seeking your advice seems willing to accept it. In this way you can avoid the frustration of making good suggestions, only to find that the person with the problem had another solution in mind all the time.

3. Be confident that the receiver won't blame you if the advice doesn't work out. You may be offering the suggestions, but the choice and responsibility for accepting them are up to the recipient of your advice.

Judging

A **judging response** evaluates the sender's thoughts or behaviours in some way. The judgement may be favourable–"That's a good idea" or "You're on the right track now"–or unfavourable–"An attitude like that won't get you anywhere." But in either case it implies that the person doing the judging is in some way qualified to pass judgement on the speaker's thoughts or actions.

Sometimes negative judgements are purely critical. How many times have you heard such responses as "Well, you asked for it!" or "I *told* you so!" or "You're just feeling sorry for yourself"? Although comments like these can sometimes serve as a verbal slap that brings problem-holders to their senses, they usually make matters worse.

In other cases negative judgements are less critical. These involve what we usually call *constructive criticism*, which is intended to help the problem-holder improve in the future. This is the sort of response given by friends about everything from the choice of clothing to jobs to friends. Another common setting for constructive criticism occurs in school, where instructors evaluate students' work to help them master concepts and skills. But whether it's justified or not, even constructive criticism runs the risk of arousing defensiveness because it may threaten the self-concept of the person at whom it is directed.

Judgements have the best chance of being received when two conditions exist:

1. The person with the problem should have requested an evaluation by you. Occasionally an unsolicited judgement may bring someone to his or her senses, but more often this sort of uninvited evaluation will trigger a defensive response.

2. The intent of your judgement should be genuinely constructive and not designed as a put-down. If you are tempted to use judgements as a weapon, don't fool yourself into thinking that you are being helpful. Often the statement "I'm telling you this for your own good . . ." simply isn't true.

If you can remember to follow these two guidelines, your judgements will probably be less frequent and better received.

even more confused by accepting it. Second, even if your analysis is accurate, telling it to the problem-holder might not be useful. There's a chance that it will arouse defensiveness (since analysis implies superiority and evaluativeness), and even if it doesn't, the person may not be able to understand your view of the problem without working it out personally.

How can you know when it's helpful to offer an analysis? There are several guidelines to follow:

1. Offer your interpretation in a tentative way rather than as absolute fact. There's a big difference between saying, "Maybe the reason is . . ." or "The way it looks to me . . ." and insisting, "This is the truth."
2. Your analysis ought to have a reasonable chance of being correct. An inaccurate interpretation—especially one that sounds plausible—can leave a person more confused than before.
3. You ought to be sure that the other person will be receptive to your analysis. Even if you're completely accurate, your thoughts won't help if the problem-holder isn't ready to consider them.
4. Be sure that your motive for offering an analysis is truly to help the other person. It can be tempting to offer an analysis to show how brilliant you are or even to make the other person feel bad for not having thought of the right answer in the first place. Needless to say, an analysis offered under such conditions isn't helpful.

Questioning

A few pages ago we talked about questioning as one way for you to understand others better. A **questioning response** can also be a way to help others think about their problems and understand them more clearly. For example, questioning can help a problem-holder define vague ideas more precisely. You might respond to a friend with a line of questioning: "You said Greg has been acting 'differently' toward you lately. What has he been doing?" Another example of a question that helps clarify is: "You told your roommates that you wanted them to be more helpful in keeping the place clean. What would you like them to do?"

Questions can also encourage a problem-holder to examine a situation in more detail by talking either about what happened or about personal feelings—for example, "How did you feel when they turned you down? What did you do then?" This type of questioning is particularly helpful when you are dealing with someone who is quiet or is unwilling under the circumstances to talk about the problem very much.

Although questions have the potential to be helpful, they also run the risk of confusing or distracting the person with the problem. The best questioning follows these principles:

1. Don't ask questions just to satisfy your own curiosity. You might become so interested in the other person's story that you will

Ideally, when you listen better, you ask better questions. A good objective in a meeting is to hear your client say things such as "That's a good question." That's because it means you have provided some insight to the client that he or she didn't possess.

Neil Grammer, Rogen Canada
(Quoted in *The Globe and Mail*)

Teach me the art of communication
Because, I want to tell you about me
The Indian of today
The lonely stranger to her own land.
But always willing to meet halfway.
Don't disregard my hand if it is offered in freindship.
I was only a child yesterday
But I am expected to be mature and brave
On the battlefield of assimilation.
Please help me.

Rita Joe, "The Art of Communication"

want to hear more. "What did he say then?" you might be tempted to ask. "What happened next?" Responding to questions like these might confuse the person with the problem, or even leave him or her more agitated than before.

2. Be sure your questions won't confuse or distract the person you're trying to help. For instance, asking someone, "When did the problem begin?" might provide some clue about how to solve it—but it could also lead to a long digression that would only confuse matters. As with advice, it's important to be sure you're on the right track before asking questions.

3. Don't use questions to disguise your suggestions or criticism. We've all been questioned by parents, teachers, or other figures who seemed to be trying to trap us or indirectly to guide us. In this way, questioning becomes a strategy that can imply that the questioner already has some idea of what direction the discussion should take, but isn't willing to tell you directly.

Supporting

There are times when other people want to hear more than a reflection of how *they* feel: They would like to know how you feel about them. **Supporting responses** reveal a listener's solidarity with the speaker's situation.

There are several types of support:

Agreement	"You're right—the landlord is being unfair." "Yeah, that class was tough for me, too."
Offers to help	"I'm here if you need me."

	"Let me try to straighten him out. Maybe he'll listen to me."
Praise	"I don't care what the boss said: I think you did a great job!"
	"You're a terrific person, and if she doesn't recognize it, that's her problem!"
Reassurance	"The worst part is over. It will get easier from here."
	"I know you'll do a great job."
Diversion	"Let's catch a movie and get your mind off this."
	"That reminds me of the time we . . ."

Despite their apparent value, supporting responses may not be helpful. In fact, they can even make things worse. Telling a person who is obviously upset that everything is fine or joking about what seems like a serious problem can leave others thinking that you don't regard their problems as very significant. They might interpret your comments as put-downs, leaving them feeling worse than before.

It's easy to identify what effective support *doesn't* sound like. Certain phrases usually indicate a lack of empathy on the part of a listener. You're probably not being supportive if you:

- *Deny others the right to their feelings.* Many non-empathic responses imply that certain emotions are wrong or should be stifled. Consider the stock phrase "Don't worry about it." Although the remark may be intended as a reassuring comment, the underlying message is that the speaker wants the person to feel differently. The irony is that the direction probably won't work—after all, it's unlikely that people can or will stop worrying just because you tell them to do so. Other examples of denying feelings include "It's nothing to get so upset about" and "That's a silly way to feel." Research about such responses is clear: "Messages that explicitly acknowledge, elaborate, and legitimize the feelings and perspective of a distressed person are perceived as more helpful messages than those which only implicitly recognize or deny the feelings and perspective of the other." [24]

- *Minimize the significance of the situation.* Consider the times you've been told, "Hey, it's only _____ ." You can probably fill in the blank in a variety of ways: "a job," "her opinion," "a test," "puppy love," "a party." How did you react when you were told this? You probably thought the person who said it "just didn't understand." To someone who has been the victim of verbal abuse, the hurtful message isn't "just words"; to a child who didn't get an invitation, it isn't "just a party"; to a worker who has been chewed out by the boss, it isn't "just a job." When you minimize the significance of someone else's experience, you aren't responding empathically. Instead, you are interpreting the event from your perspective and rendering judgement—rarely a helpful response.

THE DRUNKARD'S CHILD

A little child stood moaning
   At the hour of midnight lone,
And no human ear was list'ning
   To the feebly wailing tone;
The cold, keen blast of winter
   With funeral wail swept by,
And the blinding snow fell darkly
   Through the murky, wintry sky.

Ah! desolate and wretched
   Was the drunkard's outcast child,
Driven forth amidst the horrors
   Of that night of tempests wild.
The babe so fondly cherished
   Once 'neath a parent's eye,
Now laid her down in anguish
   Midst the drifting snows to die!

"Papa!-papa!"—she murmured,
   "The night is cold and drear,
And I'm freezing!—Oh, I'm freezing!
   In the storm and darkness here;—
My naked feet are stiff'ning,
   And my little hands are numb,—
Papa, can I not come to thee,
   And warm myself at home?"

"Mamma! mamma!"—more wildly,
   The little suff'erer cried—
Forgetting, in her anguish,
   How her stricken mother died—
"Oh, take me to your bosom,
   And warm me on your breast,
Then lay me down and kiss me,
   In my little bed to rest!"

Poor child!—the sleep that gathers
   Thy stiffened eyelid o'er
Will know no weary waking
   To a life of anguish more.
Sleep on!—the snows may gather
   O'er thy cold and pulseless form—
Thou art resting, calmly resting,
   In the wild, dark, midnight storm!

Pamelia Vining Yule

- *Focus on "then and there" rather than "here and now."* Although it is sometimes true that "you'll feel better tomorrow," it sometimes isn't. You can probably remember times when you felt *worse* the next day. More important, focussing on the future avoids empathizing in the present. Even if the prediction that "ten years from now you won't remember her name" proves correct, it provides little comfort to someone experiencing heartbreak today. "Everything is going to turn out fine" and "There are more fish in the sea–you'll land one soon" are variations on the same theme. They are platitudes, because everything may not "turn out fine" and the person might not "land one soon." There are times when "the bigger picture" offers reassurance (see *Analyzing*), but most "then and there" clichés suggest that the listener is uncomfortable dealing with the present.

- *Cast judgement.* It usually isn't encouraging to hear "You know, it's your own fault–you really shouldn't have done that" after you've confessed to making a poor decision. This response suggests the listener is playing judge rather than walking in your shoes. As we'll discuss in Chapter 9, evaluative and

I won't leave you lonely tonight
I want you to hold me all night
It's gonna be alright
I won't leave you lonely tonight

Shania Twain

condescending statements are more likely to engender defensiveness than to help people change for the better.

- *Defend yourself.* When your response to others' concerns is to defend yourself ("Don't blame me; I've done my part"), it's clear you are more concerned with yourself than with the other person. Chapter 9 offers detailed advice for responding nondefensively to criticism. Until then, realize that justifying yourself isn't compatible with understanding or helping others.

- *Rain on the speaker's parade.* Most of the preceding examples deal with difficult situations or messages about pain. Empathizing, however, involves identifying with others' joys as well as their sorrows. Many of us can recall coming home with exciting news, only to be told: "A 5 percent raise? That isn't so great"; "An A-minus? Why didn't you get an A?"; or "Big deal—I got one of those years ago." Taking the wind out of someone's sails is the opposite of empathizing.

Despite the potential drawbacks, supporting responses *can* be helpful. Guidelines for effective supporting include:

1. Recognize that you can support another person's struggles without approving of her or his decisions. Suppose, for instance, that a friend has decided to quit a job that you think she should keep. You could still be supportive by saying, "I know you've given this a lot of thought and that you're doing what you think is best." Responses like this can provide support without compromising your principles.
2. Monitor the other person's reaction to your support. If it doesn't seem to help, consider other types of responses that let him or her explore the issue.

Even if your advice, judgements, and analysis are correct and your questions are sincere, and even if your support comes from the best motives, these responses often fail to help. One survey demonstrated how poorly such traditional responses work.[25] Mourners who had recently suffered from the death of a loved one reported that 80 percent of the statements made to them were unhelpful. Nearly half of the "helpful" statements were advice: "You've got to get out more."

"Don't question God's will." Despite their frequency, these suggestions were helpful only 3 percent of the time. The next most frequent response was reassurance, such as "She's out of pain now." Like advice, this kind of support was helpful only 3 percent of the time. Far more helpful were expressions that acknowledged the mourner's feelings. The remainder of this chapter will explore two kinds of responses that make just this sort of acknowledgement possible: prompting and paraphrasing.

Prompting

Advising, judging, analyzing, questioning, and supporting are all active styles of helping that call for a great deal of input from the respondent. Another approach to problem solving is more passive. **Prompting** involves using silences and brief statements of encouragement to draw others out, and in so doing to help them solve their own problems. Consider this example:

Sajive: Julie's dad is selling a complete computer system for only $500, but if I want it I have to buy it now. He's got another interested buyer. It's a great deal. But buying it would wipe out my savings. At the rate I spend money, it would take me a year to save up this much again.

Katie: Uh huh.

Sajive: I wouldn't be able to take that ski trip over March break . . . but I sure could save time with my schoolwork . . . and do a better job, too.

Katie: That's for sure.

Sajive: Do you think I should buy it?

Katie: I don't know. What do *you* think?

Sajive: I just can't decide.

Katie: (silence)

Sajive: I'm going to do it. I'll never get a deal like this again.

Prompting works especially well when you can't help others make a decision. At times like this your presence can act like a catalyst to help others find their own answers. Prompting will work best when it's done sincerely. Your nonverbal behaviours—eye contact, posture, facial expression, tone of voice—have to show that you are concerned with the other person's problem. Mechanical prompting is likely to irritate instead of help.

Paraphrasing

A few pages ago you read about the value of paraphrasing to understand others. The same skill can be used as a helping tool. When you use this approach, be sure to reflect both the *thoughts* and the *feelings* you hear being expressed. The conversation between two friends in the Communication Transcript on the next page shows how reflecting can offer support and help a person find the answer to her own problem.

But when the child asks me
Because Why
or
Why Because
I can only say
Go outside and play.

Red Lane, "Margins IV"

Communication Transcript

Paraphrasing on the Job

The following conversation between two co-workers shows how paraphrasing can help listeners find solutions to their problems. Notice how Jill comes to a conclusion about her problem without advice from Mark. Notice also how the paraphrasing sounds natural when combined with occasional sincere questions and other helping styles.

Jill I've had the strangest feeling about John [their boss] lately.

Mark What's that? *(A simple question invites Jill to go on.)*

Jill I'm starting to think maybe he has this thing about women—or maybe it's just about me.

Mark You mean he's coming on to you? *(Mark paraphrases what he thinks Jill has said.)*

Jill Oh no, not at all! But it seems like he doesn't take women—or at least me—seriously. *(Jill corrects Mark's misunderstanding and explains herself.)*

Mark What do you mean? *(Mark asks another simple question to get more information.)*

Jill Well, whenever we're in a meeting or just talking around the office and he asks for ideas, he always seems to pick men. He gives orders to women—men, too—but he never asks the women to say what they think.

Mark So you think maybe he doesn't take women seriously, is that it? *(Mark paraphrases Jill's last statement.)*

Jill Yeah. Well, he sure doesn't seem interested in their ideas. But that doesn't mean he's a total woman-hater or a male chauvinist pig. I know he counts on some women in the office. Ling has been here forever, and he's always saying he couldn't live without her. And when Tracey got the new computer system up and running last month, I know he appreciated that. He gave her a day off and told everybody how she saved our lives.

Mark Now you sound confused. *(Reflects her apparent feeling.)*

Jill I am confused. I don't think it's just my imagination. I mean I'm a good producer, but he has never—not once— asked me for my ideas about how to improve sales or anything. And I can't remember a time when he's asked any other women. But maybe I'm overreacting.

Mark You're not positive whether you're right, but I can tell that this has you concerned. *(Mark paraphrases both Jill's central theme and her feeling.)*

Jill Yes. But I don't know what to do about it.

Mark Maybe you should . . . *(Starts to offer advice, but catches himself and decides to ask a sincere question instead.)* So what are your choices?

Jill Well, I could just ask him if he's aware that he never asks women's opinions. But that might sound too aggressive and angry.

Mark And you're not angry? *(Tries to clarify how Jill is feeling.)*

Jill Not really. I don't know whether I should be angry because he's not taking ideas seriously, or whether he just doesn't take my ideas seri-ously, or whether it's nothing at all.

Mark So you're mostly confused. *(Reflects Jill's apparent feeling again.)*

Jill Yes! I don't know where I stand with John, and not being sure is starting to get to me. I wish I knew what he thinks of me. Maybe I could just tell him I'm confused about what is going on here and ask him to clear it up. But what if it's nothing? Then I'll look insecure.

Mark *(Mark thinks Jill should confront the boss, but he isn't positive that this is the best approach, so he paraphrases what Jill seems to be saying.)* And that would make you look bad.

Jill I'm afraid maybe it would. I wonder if I could talk it over with anybody else in the office and get their ideas . . .

Mark . . . see what they think . . .

Jill Yeah. Maybe I could ask Tracey. She's easy to talk to, and I do respect her judgement. Maybe she could give me some ideas about how to handle this.

Mark Sounds like you're comfortable with talking to Tracey first. *(Paraphrases)*

Jill *(Warming to the idea)* Yes! Then if it's nothing, I can calm down. But if I do need to talk to John, I'll know I'm doing the right thing.

Mark Great. Let me know how it goes.

The Communication Transcript suggests several reasons why paraphrasing can be so helpful.[26] First, listeners who reflect the speaker's thoughts and feelings (instead of judging or analyzing, for example) show their involvement and concern. The nonevaluative nature of reflecting encourages the problem-holder to discuss the matter further. Reflecting feelings as well as thoughts allows the problem-holder to unload more of the concerns he or she has been carrying around, often leading to the relief that comes from catharsis. Finally, paraphrasing helps the problem-holder to sort out the problem. The clarity that comes from this sort of perspective can make it possible to find solutions that weren't apparent before.

Although the immediate goal of reflective listening is to help the other person, an additional payoff is that the relationship between speaker and listener improves. For example, couples who communicate in ways that show they understand one another's feelings and ideas are more satisfied with their marriages than couples who express less understanding.[27] The opposite is also true: In marriages where husbands do not give emotional responses to their wives, the stress level grows.

Because empathy is the ingredient that makes paraphrasing thoughts and feelings helpful, it's a mistake to think of reflective listening as a technique that you can use mechanically.[28] It's essential to realize that empathy is a relational matter and not something that can be created just by paraphrasing, or by any other kind of behaviour. Carl Rogers, the psychologist generally considered the foremost advocate of active listening, made the case against mechanical paraphrasing strongly: "I am *not* trying to 'reflect feelings.' I am trying to determine whether my understanding of the client's inner world is correct—whether I am seeing it as he or she is experiencing it at this moment."[29] In other words, reflecting is not an end in itself; rather, it is one way to help others by understanding them better.

There are several factors to consider before you decide to paraphrase:

1. *Is the problem complex enough?* Sometimes people are simply looking for information and not trying to work out their feelings. At times like this, paraphrasing would be out of place. If someone asks you for the time, it would be ridiculous to respond by saying, "You want to know what time it is." If you're fixing dinner and someone wants to know when it will be ready, it would be exasperating to reply "You're interested in knowing when we'll be eating."
2. *Do you have the necessary time and concern?* The kind of paraphrasing we've been discussing here takes a good deal of time. Therefore, if you're in a hurry to do something besides listen, it's wise to avoid starting a conversation you won't be able to finish. Even more important than time is concern. It's not necessarily wrong to be too preoccupied to help or even to be unwilling to exert the considerable effort that active listening requires: You can't help everyone with every problem. It's far better to state honestly that you're unable or unwilling to help than to pretend to care when you really don't.

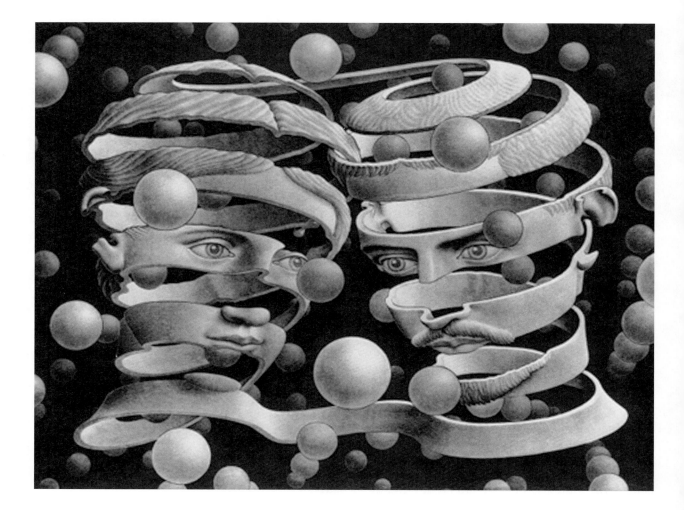

The reality of the other person is not in what he reveals to you, but in what he cannot reveal to you. Therefore, if you could understand him, listen not to what he says but rather to what he does not say.

Kahlil Gibran

5. *Are you genuinely interested in helping the other person?* Sometimes as you listen to others, it's easy to relate their thoughts to your own life or to seek more information just to satisfy your own curiosity. Remember that paraphrasing is a form of helping someone else. The general obligation to reciprocate the other person's self-disclosure with information of your own isn't necessary when the goal is to solve a problem. Research shows that speakers who reveal highly intimate personal information don't expect, or even appreciate, the same kind of disclosure from a conversational partner.[30] Rather, the most competent and socially attractive response is one that sticks to the same topic but is lower in intimacy. In other words, when we are opening up to others, we don't appreciate their pulling a conversational take-away such as "You're worried? So am I! Let me tell you about how I feel. . . ."

4. *Can you withhold judgement?* You've already seen that paraphrasing allows other people to find their own answers. You should use this style only if you can comfortably paraphrase without inject-ing your own judgements. It's sometimes tempting to rephrase others' comments in a way that leads them toward the solution you think is best without ever clearly stating your intentions. As you will read in Chapter 9, this kind of strategy is likely to back-fire by causing defensiveness if it's discovered. If you think the sit-uation meets the criteria for advice described earlier in this chapter, you should offer your suggestions openly.

5. *Is your paraphrasing in proportion to other responses?* Although active listening can be a very helpful way of responding to others' problems, it can become artificial and annoying when it's over-used. This is especially true if you suddenly begin to use it as a major response. Even if such responses are potentially helpful, this sudden switch in your behaviour will be so out of character that others might find it distracting. A far better way to use para-phrasing is gradually to introduce it into your repertoire of help-fulness, so that you can become comfortable with it without appearing too awkward. Another way to become more comfort-able with this style is to start using it on real but relatively minor problems, so that you'll be more adept at knowing how and when to use it when a major crisis does occur.

By now it's clear that there are many ways to help others—proba-bly more than you use. You can also see that each helping style has its advantages and drawbacks. This leads us to the important ques-tion of which style or styles are most helpful. There isn't a simple answer to this question.

When and How to Help?

Before committing yourself to helping another person—even some-one in obvious distress—make sure your help is welcome. There are many occasions in which others prefer to keep their concerns to themselves. In these cases your efforts to get involved may not be useful and can even be harmful. In one survey, some people re-ported occasions when social support wasn't necessary, because they felt capable of handling the problem by themselves.[31] Many regarded uninvited help as an intrusion, and some said it left them feeling more nervous than before. The majority of respondents ex-pressed a preference for being in control of whether their distress-ing situation should be discussed with even the most helpful friend.

When help is welcome, there is no single best way to provide it. Research shows that *all* styles can help others accept their situation, feel better, and have a sense of control over their problems.[32] But there is enormous variability in which approach will work with a given person.[33] This fact explains why communicators who are able to use a wide variety of helping styles are usually more effective than those who rely on just one or two approaches.[34]

Ethical Challenge

Unconditional Positive Regard

Carl Rogers is the best-known advocate of paraphrasing as a helping tool. As a psychotherapist, Rogers focussed on how professionals could help others, but he and his followers were convinced that the same approach could work in all interpersonal relationships.

Rogers used several terms to describe his approach: Sometimes he labelled it "non-directive," sometimes "client-centred," and at other times "person-centred." All these terms reflect his belief that the best way to help others is to offer a supportive climate in which the person seeking help can find his or her own answers. Rogers believed that advising, judging, analyzing, and questioning were not the best ways to help others solve their problems. Instead, Rogers and his followers were convinced people are basically good and that they can improve without receiving any guidance from others, once they accept and respect themselves.

An essential ingredient for person-centred helping is what Rogers called "unconditional positive regard." This attitude requires the helper to treat the speaker's ideas respectfully and nonjudgementally. Unconditional positive regard means accepting others for who they are, even when you don't approve of the help-seeker's posture toward life. Treating a help-seeker with unconditional positive regard doesn't oblige you to agree with everything a speaker thinks, feels, or does; but it does require you to suspend judgement about the rightness or wrongness of the help-seeker's thoughts and actions.

A person-centred approach to helping places heavy demands on the listener. At the skill level, it requires an ability to reflect the speaker's thoughts and feelings perceptively and accurately. Even more difficult, though, is the challenge of listening and responding without passing judgement on the speaker's ideas or behaviour.

Unconditional positive regard is especially hard when we are faced with the challenge of listening and responding to someone whose beliefs, attitudes, and values differ profoundly from our own. This approach requires the helper to follow the scriptural injunction of loving the sinner while hating the sin. One of the best models of this attitude is illustrated in the movie *Dead Man Walking*. This film re-creates the true story of Sister Helen Prejean, a Catholic nun who took on the role of counselling a convicted murderer named Matthew Poncelet. Sister Helen confronts the awful truth of Poncelet's crime while managing to maintain her genuine concern for him as a human being. Few communicators can manage to achieve the level of unconditional positive regard Sister Helen demonstrates, but her story is a model for those who accept a person-centred approach to helping . . . and the values it embodies.

For a better understanding of unconditional positive regard, see the following work by Carl Rogers: *On Becoming a Person* (Boston: Houghton Mifflin, 1961); *Carl Rogers on Personal Power* (New York: Delacorte Press, 1977); and "A Theory of Therapy, Personality and Interpersonal Relationships, as Developed in the Client-Centered Framework," in *Psychology: A Study of Science*, S. Koch, ed. (New York: McGraw-Hill, 1959).

You can boost the odds of choosing the best helping style in each situation by considering three factors. First, think about the *situation* and match your response to the nature of the problem. Sometimes people need your advice. In other cases your encouragement and support will be most helpful, and in still other instances your analysis or judgement may be truly useful. And, as you have seen, there are times when your probes and paraphrasing can help others find their own answer.

Besides considering the situation, you should also think about the *other person* when deciding which approach to use. Some people are able to consider advice thoughtfully, while others use suggestions to avoid making their own decisions. Many communicators are extremely defensive and aren't capable of receiving analysis or judgements without lashing out. Still others aren't equipped to think through problems clearly enough to profit from paraphrasing and probing. Sophisticated helpers choose a style that fits the person.

Finally, think about *yourself* when deciding how to respond. Most of us reflexively use one or two helping styles. You may be best at listening quietly, offering a prompt from time to time. Or perhaps you are especially insightful and can offer a truly useful analysis of the problem. Of course, it's also possible to rely on a response style that is *unhelpful.* You may be overly judgemental or too eager to advise, even when your suggestions aren't invited or productive. As you think about how to respond to another's problems, consider both your strengths and weaknesses.

SUMMARY

Listening is the most common—and perhaps the most overlooked—form of communication. Listening consists of five elements: hearing, attending, understanding, responding, and remembering.

A number of responding styles masquerade as listening, but are only poor imitations of the real thing. We listen poorly for a variety of reasons. Some have to do with the tremendous number of messages that bombard us daily, and with the personal preoccupations and rapid thoughts that distract us from focussing on the information we are exposed to. Another set of reasons includes the considerable effort involved in listening carefully and the mistaken belief that listening is a natural ability that doesn't require skill or work and that lacks the rewards that come from speaking. A few listeners fail to receive messages due to physical hearing defects. One important type of listening involves seeking information from others. Some keys to success in this area are to talk less, reduce distractions, avoid making premature judgements, and seek the speaker's key ideas. Asking questions and paraphrasing are two important ways of seeking information.

A second type of listening focusses on helping others solve their problems. Some common helping styles are advising, judging, analyzing, questioning, and supporting. Prompting and paraphrasing are less-common but effective response styles. The most helpful communicators use a variety of these styles, choosing the one most appropriate for themselves, the situation at hand, and the person with the problem.

KEY TERMS

active listening
advising response
ambushing
analyzing statement
attending
counterfeit questions
defensive listening
hearing

insensitive listening
insulated listening
judging response
listening
paraphrasing
prompting
pseudolistening
questioning response

remembering
responding
selective listening
sincere questions
stage-hogging
supporting response
understanding

Looking at Relationships

Communication and Relational Dynamics

I believe that for friendship there should be similarity; but for love there must be dissimilarity.

L.M. Montgomery,
My Dear Mr. M.: Letters to G.B. Macmillan

"**W**e have a terrific relationship."

"I'm looking for a better relationship."

"Our relationship has changed a lot."

We hear a lot about relationships. You might describe a relationship as anything from your daily interaction with a co-worker, to the way you communicate with your dentist, to how to talk to a newfound lover.

Interpersonal relationships involve the way people deal with one another *socially*. But what is it about social interaction that defines a relationship? This chapter will offer some insights. It will offer explanations for why we form relationships with some people and not with others. It will look at how communication operates as people form, manage, and sometimes end their relationships. You will see that relationships aren't static, like a painting or photograph. Rather, they change over time, like an ongoing dance or drama. Even the most stable and satisfying relationships wax and wane in a variety of ways as communication patterns change. Finally, this chapter will examine the subject of self-disclosure and its alternatives. By the time you finish reading the following pages you will have a better sense of how communication both defines and reflects our interpersonal world.

WHY WE FORM RELATIONSHIPS

What makes us seek relationships with some people and not with others? This is a question social scientists have studied extensively. Though it would take an entire book to describe their findings, we can summarize a number of explanations. As you read them, consider which ones fit you.

Attraction

Sometimes we establish personal relationships because we find others attractive in one way or another. Physical attraction is an obvious plus in some types of relationships, but there are other bases of attraction as well.

SIMILARITY AND COMPLEMENTARITY   A large body of research confirms the fact that we like people who are similar to us, at least in most cases.[1] One of the first steps in getting acquainted with a stranger is the search for common ground—interests, experiences, or other factors you share. When we find similarities, we usually feel some kind of attraction toward the person who is like us.

This doesn't mean that the key to popularity is to agree with everyone about everything. Attraction is greatest when we are similar to others in a high percentage of important areas. For example, a couple who support each other's career goals, like the same friends, and have similar beliefs about human rights can tolerate trivial disagreements about the merits of sushi or jazz. With enough similarity in key areas, they can survive even disputes about more important subjects, such as how much time to spend with their families or whether separate vacations are acceptable. But if the number and content of disagreements become too great, the relationship may be threatened.

Similarity can turn from attraction to repulsion when we encounter people who are like us in many ways but who behave in a strange or socially offensive manner. For instance, you have probably disliked people others have said were "just like you" but who talked too much, were complainers, or had some other unappealing characteristic. In fact, there is a tendency to have stronger dislike for similar but offensive people than for those who are offensive but different. One likely reason is that such people threaten our self-esteem, causing us to fear that we may be as unappealing as they are. In such circumstances, the reaction is often to put as much distance as possible between ourselves and this threat to our ideal self-image.

The familiar saying "opposites attract" seems to contradict the principle of similarity we just described. In truth, though, both are valid. Differences strengthen a relationship when they are *complementary*–that is, when each partner's characteristics satisfy the other's needs. Individuals, for instance, are likely to be attracted to each other when one partner is dominant and the other passive. Relationships also work well when the partners agree that one will exercise control in certain areas ("You make the final decisions about money") and the other will take the lead in different ones ("I'll decide how we ought to decorate the place"). Strains occur when control issues are disputed.

Studies that have examined successful and unsuccessful couples over a 20-year period show the interaction between similarities and differences. The research demonstrates that partners in successful marriages were similar enough to satisfy each other physically and mentally but were different enough to meet each other's

HERMAN®

8-16   © 1986 Jim Unger

"Two round-the-world cruises in opposite directions."

needs and keep the relationship interesting. The successful couples found ways to keep a balance between their similarities and differences, adjusting to the changes that occurred over the years.

RECIPROCAL ATTRACTION We like people who like us—usually. The power of reciprocal attraction is especially strong in the early stages of a relationship. At that time we are attracted to people who we believe are attracted to us. Conversely, we will probably not care for people who either attack or seem indifferent toward us. After we get to know others, their liking becomes less of a factor. By then we form our preferences more from the other reasons listed in this section.

It's no mystery why reciprocal liking builds attractiveness. People who approve of us bolster our feelings of self-esteem. This approval is rewarding in its own right, and it can also confirm a presenting self-concept that says, "I'm a likable person."

However, you can probably think of cases where you haven't liked people who seemed to like you. These experiences usually fall into two categories. Sometimes we think the other person's supposed liking is counterfeit—an insincere device to get something from us. The acquaintance who becomes friendly whenever he needs to borrow your car and the employee who says what the boss wants to hear in order to get a promotion are examples. This sort of behaviour really isn't "liking" at all. The second category occurs when the other person's approval doesn't fit with our own self-concept. As you read in

Chapter 2, we cling to an existing self-concept even when it is unre-alistically unfavourable. When someone says you're good-looking, intelligent, and kind, but you believe you are ugly, stupid, and mean, you may choose to disregard the flattering information and remain in your familiar state of unhappiness. Groucho Marx summarized this attitude when he said he would never join any club that would consider having him as a member.

COMPETENCE   We like to be around talented people, probably because we hope their skills and abilities will rub off on us. On the other hand, we are uncomfortable around those who are *too* competent– probably because we look bad by comparison. Given these contrast-ing attitudes, it's no surprise that people are generally attracted to those who are talented but who have visible flaws that show they are human, just like us. There are some qualifications to this principle. People with especially high or low self-esteem find "perfect" people more attractive than those who are competent but flawed, and some studies suggest that women tend to be more impressed by uniformly superior people of both sexes. Men, on the other hand, are especially impressed by attractive individuals who also display their "human" side. On the whole, though, the principle stands: The best way to gain the liking of others is to be good at what you do but to admit your mistakes.

The fact that a certain degree of imperfection is attractive drives another nail into the coffin of the perfectionistic myth described in Chapter 4. We mistakenly believe that we need to appear flawless in order to gain the respect and affection of others when, in fact, acting "perfect" may drive away the people we want to draw closer.

DISCLOSURE   Revealing important information about yourself can help build liking. Sometimes the basis of this attraction comes from learn-ing about how we are similar, either in experiences ("I broke off an engagement myself") or in attitudes ("I feel nervous with strangers, too"). Self-disclosure also increases liking because it is a sign of re-gard. When people share private information with you, it suggests they respect and trust you–a kind of liking that we've already seen increases attractiveness.

Not all disclosure leads to liking. People whose sharing is poorly timed often meet with bad results. It's probably unwise, for example, to talk about your sexual insecurities with a new acquaintance or to express your pet peeves to a friend at her birthday party. In addition to bad timing, opening up too much too soon can be a mistake. Re-search shows that people are judged as attractive when they match the amount and content of what they share with that of the other person in a relationship. See pages 360–364 for more guidelines about when and how to self-disclose.

PROXIMITY   As common sense suggests, we are likely to develop relationships with people we interact with frequently. In many cases, proximity leads to liking. We're more likely to develop friendships with close neighbours than with distant ones, for instance; and several studies show that the chances are good that we'll choose a mate with whom we often cross paths. Facts like these are understandable when we consider that proximity allows us to get more information about other people and benefit from a relationship with them.

Familiarity, on the other hand, can also breed contempt. Evidence to support this fact comes from police blotters as well as university laboratories. Thieves frequently prey on nearby victims, even though the risk of being recognized is greater. Spouse and child abuse is distressingly common. Most aggravated assaults occur within the family or among close neighbours. Within the law, the same principle holds: You are likely to develop strong personal feelings of either like or dislike regarding others you encounter frequently.

INVITATION TO INSIGHT

ANALYZING INTERPERSONAL ATTRACTION

1. List the names of five people with whom you have strong positive personal relationships. Use the list that follows to identify the basis of your attraction.

   a. Are their interests, attitudes, values, beliefs, or backgrounds similar to yours?
   b. Do they fill a complementary need for you?
   c. Are they attracted to you?
   d. Are they competent but human?
   e. Have they shared personal information with you?
   f. Do you encounter them frequently?

2. Now consider five people with whom you would like to build a stronger relationship. Use the same list to decide whether you are the kind of person they would be attracted to.

A Resource for Improving Communication in Your Relationships

---

http://cyber-source.com/ index.html

Intimacy

Research on attraction helps explain why we seek out relationships with some people more than others. But the question of what we *want* in those relationships can be answered in part by looking at the need for **intimacy.**

In his book *Intimacy,* psychotherapist C. Edward Crowther offers a reminder of just how important close relationships can be.[2] As part of a study of people who were dying in hospices and hospitals, he asked each person individually what mattered most in life. Fully 90 percent of these terminally ill patients put intimate relationships at the top of the list. As a 50-year-old mother of three children who was dying of cancer put it, "You need not wait

until you are in my condition to know nothing in life is as important as loving relationships."

DIMENSIONS OF INTIMACY   What is intimacy? Is it spending time together? Sharing feelings? Having sex? Going through thick and thin? Are intimacy and love the same thing? Answers to these questions can be found by examining the dimensions of intimacy. Intimacy has several dimensions. The first form is *physical*. Even before birth, the developing fetus experiences an incredible physical closeness with its mother that will never happen again, "floating in a warm fluid, curling inside a total embrace, swaying to the undulations of the moving

Men and women suffer equally. The tragedy is not that they suffer, but that they suffer alone.

Margaret Laurence,
quoted by Sinclair Ross in *The Lamp at Noon*

body and hearing the beat of the pulsing heart."[3] As they grow up, fortunate children are continually nourished by physical intimacy: being rocked, fed, hugged, and held. As we grow older, the opportunities for physical intimacy are less regular, but still possible and important. Some, but by no means all, physical intimacy is sexual. In one survey, only one-quarter of the respondents (who were college and university students) stated that intimacy necessarily contained a romantic or sexual dimension.[4] Other forms of physical intimacy include affectionate hugs, kisses, and even struggles. Companions who have endured physical challenges together—in athletics or emergencies, for example—form a bond that can last a lifetime.

In other cases, intimacy comes from *intellectual* sharing. Not every exchange of ideas counts as intimacy, of course. Talking about next week's midterm with your professor or classmates isn't likely to forge strong relational bonds. But when you engage another person in an exchange of important ideas, a kind of closeness develops that can be powerful and exciting.

A third type of intimacy is *emotional:* exchanging important feelings. Surprisingly, this sort of personal communication needn't happen in face-to-face encounters. One study revealed that almost two-thirds of a randomly selected group of e-mail users said they had formed a personal relationship with someone they had met for the first time through an Internet newsgroup.[5] The electronic friends characterized their relationships in ways that sound remarkably similar to traditional friendships: interdependence (e.g., "We would go out of our way to help each other"), breadth ("Our communication ranges over a wide variety of topics"), depth ("I feel I could confide in this person about almost anything"), and commitment ("I am very committed to maintaining this relationship").

If we define intimacy as being close to another person, then *shared activities* can provide another way to achieve this state. Shared activities can include everything from working side by side at a job to meeting regularly for exercise workouts. When partners spend time together, they can develop unique ways of relating that transform the relationship from an impersonal one to one with interpersonal qualities. For example, both friendships and romantic relationships are often characterized by several forms of play. Partners invent private codes, fool around by acting like other people, tease one another, and play games—everything from having punning contests to arm wrestling.[6] Not all shared activities create and express intimacy, of course, but the bonds that come from experiencing significant events with another person are too frequent and significant to ignore.

Some intimate relationships exhibit all four qualities: physical intimacy, intellectual exchanges, emotional disclosure, and shared activities. Other intimate relationships exhibit only one or two. Some relationships, of course, aren't intimate in any way. Acquaintances, roommates, and co-workers may never become intimate. In some cases even family members develop smooth but relatively impersonal relationships.

Not even the closest relationships always operate at the highest
level of intimacy. At times you might share all your thoughts or feelings with a friend, family member, or lover; at other times you might
withdraw. You might freely share your feelings about one topic and
stay more aloof about another one. The same principle holds for
physical intimacy, which waxes and wanes in most relationships.

MASCULINE AND FEMININE INTIMACY STYLES   Until recently most social
scientists believed that women were better than men at developing and maintaining intimate relationships.[7] This view grew from
the assumption that the disclosure of personal information is the
most important ingredient of intimacy. Most research *does* show

that women (taken as a group, of course) are more willing than men to share their thoughts and feelings.[8] In terms of the amount and depth of information exchanged, female–female relationships are at the top of the disclosure list. Male–female relationships come in second, while relationships between men involve less disclosure than any other type. At every age, women disclose more than men, and the information they reveal is more personal and more likely to involve disclosure of feelings. Although both sexes are equally likely to reveal negative information, men are less likely to share positive feelings.[9]

Through the mid-1980s many communication scholars interpreted the relative lack of male self-disclosure as a sign that men were unwilling or even unable to develop close relationships. Some argued that the female trait of disclosing personal information and feelings made women more "emotionally mature" and "interpersonally competent" than men. Personal-growth programs and self-help books urged men to achieve closeness by learning to open up and share their feelings.

But scholarship conducted in the past decade has shown that emotional expression isn't the *only* way to develop close relationships. Unlike women who value personal talk, men grow close to one another by doing things. In one study, more than 75 percent of the men surveyed said that their most meaningful experiences with friends came from activities other than talking.[10] They reported that, through shared activities, they "grew on one another," developed feelings of interdependence, showed appreciation for one another, and demonstrated mutual liking. Likewise, men regarded practical help as a measure of caring. Research like this shows that, for many men, closeness grows from activities that don't depend heavily on disclosure: A friend is a person who does things *for* you and *with* you.

Reprinted with special permission of King Features Syndicate

The difference between male and female measures of intimacy helps explain some of the stresses and misunderstandings that can arise between the sexes. For example, a woman who looks for emotional disclosure as a measure of affection may overlook an "inexpressive" man's efforts to show he cares by doing favours or spending time together. Fixing a leaky faucet or taking a hike may look like ways to avoid getting close, but to the guy who proposes them, they may be measures of affection and bids for intimacy. Likewise, differing ideas about the timing and meaning of sex can lead to misunderstandings. Whereas many women think of sex as a way to express intimacy that has already developed, men are more likely to see it as a way to *create* that intimacy.[11] In this sense, the man who encourages sex early in a relationship or after a fight may not be just a testosterone-crazed lecher: He may view the shared activity as a way to build closeness. By contrast, the woman who views personal talk as the pathway to intimacy may resist the idea of physical closeness before the emotional side of the relationship has been discussed.

CULTURAL INFLUENCES ON INTIMACY   Historically, the notions of public and private behaviour have changed dramatically.[12] What would be considered intimate behaviour in modern terms was quite public at times in the past. For example, in sixteenth-century Germany, the new husband and wife were expected to consummate their marriage upon a bed carried among witnesses who would validate the marriage![13] Conversely, at the same time in England as well as in colonial America, the customary level of communication between spouses was rather formal: not much different from the way acquaintances or neighbours spoke to one another.

Even today, the notion of intimacy varies from one culture to another. In one study, researchers asked residents of Britain, Japan, Hong Kong, and Italy to describe their use of 33 rules that governed interaction in social relationships.[14] The rules governed a wide range of communication behaviours: everything from the use of humour to shaking hands to the management of money. The results showed that the greatest differences between Asian and European cultures focussed on the rules for dealing with intimacy: showing emotions, expressing affection in public, engaging in sexual activity, respecting privacy, and so on.

Disclosure is especially high in North American society. In fact, people from the United States are more disclosing than members of any culture studied.[15] They are likely to disclose more about themselves to acquaintances, and even strangers. By contrast, Germans and Japanese tend to disclose little about themselves except in personal relationships with a select few. Within North American culture, intimacy varies from one group to another. For example, working-class Black men are much more disclosing than their white counterparts.[16] By contrast, upwardly mobile Black men communicate more like white men with the same social agenda, disclosing less with their male friends.

In some collectivist cultures such as Taiwan and Japan there is an especially great difference in the way people communicate with members of their "ingroups" (such as family and close friends) and with those they view as outsiders.[17] They generally do not reach out to strangers, often waiting until they are properly introduced before entering into a conversation. Once introduced, they address outsiders with a degree of formality. They go to extremes to hide unfavourable information about ingroup members from outsiders, on the principle that one doesn't wash dirty laundry in public. By contrast, members of more individualistic cultures like Canada, the United States, and Australia make less distinction between personal relationships and casual ones. They act more familiar with strangers and disclose more personal information, making them excellent "cocktail party conversationalists." Social psychologist Kurt Lewin captured the difference nicely when he noted that Americans were easy to meet but difficult to get to know, while Germans were difficult to meet, but then easy to know well.[18]

Differences like these mean that the level of self-disclosure appropriate in one culture may seem completely inappropriate in another one. If you were raised in Canada or the United States you might view people from other cultures as undisclosing, or even standoffish. But the amount of information that the nonnatives share might actually be quite personal and revealing according to the standards of their culture. The converse is also true: To members of other cultures, North Americans probably appear like exhibitionists who spew personal information to anyone within earshot.

Even in cultures that value high amounts of personal communication, intimacy is not a priority, or even desired in every relationship. Many fellow workers, neighbours, and community members often interact in satisfying ways without ever achieving any real degree of intimacy. Family members also get along well by deliberately keeping their physical and emotional distance from one another. Relationships of this sort might achieve a modest degree of integration, but never go further.

THE LIMITS OF INTIMACY   It's impossible to have a close relationship with everyone: There simply isn't enough time and energy. Even if we could seek intimacy with everyone we encountered, few of us would want that much closeness. Consider the range of everyday contacts that don't require any sort of intimacy. Some are based on economic exchange (for example, the people at work or at the video shop you visit several times a week); some are based on group membership (for example, an AA or school group); some on physical proximity (for example, neighbours, carpooling); and some grow out of third-party connections (for example, mutual friends, child care). Simply engaging in conversational give-and-take can be a kind of enjoyable recreation, not too different from impromptu jam sessions where musicians gather solely to create music, not to exchange personal information.[19]

INVITATION TO INSIGHT

YOUR IQ (INTIMACY QUOTIENT)

What is the level of intimacy in your important relationships? Find out by following these directions.

1. Identify the point on each scale below that best describes one of your important relationships.

   a. Your level of physical intimacy

1	2	3	4	5
low				high

   b. Your amount of emotional intimacy

1	2	3	4	5
low				high

   c. The extent of your intellectual intimacy

1	2	3	4	5
low				high

   d. The degree of shared activities in your relationship

1	2	3	4	5
low				high

2. Now answer the following questions:

   a. What responses to each dimension of intimacy seem most significant to you?

   b. Are you satisfied with the intimacy profile outlined by your responses?

   c. If you are not satisfied, what steps can you take to change your degree of intimacy?

Some scholars have pointed out that an obsession with intimacy can lead to *less*-satisfying relationships.[20] People who consider intimate communication as the only kind worth pursuing place little value on relationships that don't meet this standard. This can lead them to regard interaction with strangers and casual acquaintances as superficial, or at best as the groundwork for deeper relationships. When you consider the pleasure that can come from polite but distant communication, the limitations of this view become clear. Intimacy is definitely rewarding, but it isn't the only way of relating to others.

This doesn't mean that intimacy is unimportant—just that it isn't the *only* measure of relational satisfaction. Even within highly personal relationships, total intimacy isn't desirable. Even the most personal relationships have their impersonal moments. And, as you will read later in this chapter, people need privacy and independence as well as intimacy and connection.

Rewards

Intimacy can be satisfying, but it isn't the only payoff that drives us to seek out and stay in relationships. Some social scientists have argued that all relationships—both impersonal and personal—are based on a semi-economic model called **social exchange theory.**[21] This approach suggests that we often seek out people who can give us rewards—either tangible or emotional—that are greater than or equal to the costs we encounter in dealing with them. Social exchange theorists define rewards as any outcomes we desire. Rewards may be tangible (a nice place to live, a high-paying job) or intangible (prestige, emotional support, companionship). Costs are undesirable outcomes: unpleasant work, emotional pain, and so on. A simple formula captures the social exchange explanation for why we form and maintain relationships:

Rewards − Costs = Outcome

According to social exchange theorists, we use this formula (often unconsciously) to decide whether dealing with another person is a "good deal" or "not worth the effort," based on whether the outcome is positive or negative.

At its most blatant level, an exchange approach seems cold and calculating; but in some types of relationships it seems quite appropriate. A healthy business relationship is based on how well the parties help one another, and some friendships are based on an informal kind of barter: "I don't mind listening to the ups and down of your love life because you rescue me when the house needs repairs." Even close relationships have an element of exchange. Friends and lovers often tolerate each other's quirks because the comfort and enjoyment they get make the less-than-pleasant times worth accepting.

At first glance, the social exchange model seems to present a view of relationships very different from one based on the need to seek intimacy. In fact, the two approaches aren't incompatible. Seeking intimacy of any type—whether emotional, physical, or even intellectual— has its costs; and our decision about whether to "pay" those costs is, in great measure, made by considering the likely payoffs. If the costs of seeking and maintaining an intimate relationship are too great or the payoffs not worth the effort, we may decide to back off.

Costs and rewards don't exist in isolation: We define them by comparing a certain situation with alternatives. For example, consider a hypothetical woman we will call Kim, who is struggling to decide whether to remain in a relationship with Ray, her longtime boyfriend. Ray does love Kim, but he's not perfect: He has a bad temper, and he has become verbally abusive from time to time. Also, Kim knows that Ray was unfaithful to her at least once. In deciding whether to stay with Ray, Kim will use two standards. The first is her **comparison level (CL)**—her standard of what behaviour is acceptable. If Kim believes that relational partners have an obligation to be faithful and treat one another respectfully at all times, then Ray's behaviour will fall below her comparison level. On the other hand, if Kim adopts a "nobody's perfect" standard, she is more likely to view Ray's behaviour as meeting or exceeding her comparison level.

Kim will also rate Ray according to her **comparison level of alternatives (CL_{alt}).** This standard refers to a comparison between the rewards she is receiving in her present situation and those she could expect to receive in others. If, for example, Kim views her choices as staying with Ray or being alone, her CL_{alt} would be lower than her present situation; but if she is confident that she could find a kinder partner, her CL_{alt} would be higher than the status quo.

Table 8–1 outlines all the possible combinations of the outcomes (the present situation), comparison levels, and comparison levels of alternatives. Social exchange theorists suggest that communicators unconsciously use this calculus to decide whether to form and stay in relationships. At first this information seems to offer little comfort to communicators who are in unsatisfying relationships, such as those where $CL >$ $CL_{alt} >$ outcome. But there are alternatives to being stuck in situations where the costs outweigh the rewards. First, you might make sure that you are judging your present relationship against a realistic comparison level. Expecting a situation to be perfect can be a recipe for unhappiness. (Recall the discussion of the "fallacy of

TABLE 8–1	CALCULATING RELATIONAL COSTS AND REWARDS
RELATIVE VALUE OF OUTCOME, CL, CL$_{ALT}$	**STATE OF THE RELATIONSHIP**

Outcome > CL > CL$_{alt}$	Satisfying
	    Stable
	        Dependent

Outcome > CL$_{alt}$ > CL	Satisfying
	    Stable
	        Nondependent

CL$_{alt}$ > CL > Outcome	Not satisfying
	    Break off relationship
	        Happy elsewhere

CL$_{alt}$ > Outcome > CL	Satisfying
	    Unstable
	        Happier elsewhere

CL > CL$_{alt}$ > Outcome	Not satisfying
	    Break off relationship
	        Continue unhappy

CL > Outcome > CL$_{alt}$	Highly unsatisfying
	    Can't break away
	        Dependent and unhappy

Adapted from M.E. Roloff, *Interpersonal Communication: The Social Exchange Approach* (Beverly Hills, CA: Sage, 1981); and E.M. Griffin, *A First Look at Communication Theory,* 2nd ed. (New York: McGraw-Hill, 1994).

INVITATION TO INSIGHT

CALCULATING YOUR RELATIONAL COSTS AND REWARDS

Use Table 8–1 to calculate the costs and rewards in one of your important personal relationships. Does the information in this table accurately reflect your situation? If you are unsatisfied with the situation you identify using Table 8–1, consider what alternatives you might use to improve your present situation:

• Re-evaluating your comparison level

• Searching for new alternatives

• Changing your communication in ways that could improve your present situation

shoulds" in Chapter 4.) If you decide that your present situation is truly inferior to your comparison level, you might explore whether there are other alternatives you haven't considered. And finally, the skills introduced throughout *Looking Out/Looking In* may help you negotiate a better relationship with the other person.

MODELS OF RELATIONAL DEVELOPMENT AND MAINTENANCE

So far we have looked at some factors that influence why we form relationships. But your own experience demonstrates that beginnings are a unique time. How does communication change as we spend time with others and get to know them? Communication scholars have different ways of answering this question. To learn two major perspectives, read on.

Developmental Models

One of the best-known models of relational stages was developed by Mark Knapp, who broke down the rise and fall of relationships into 10 stages, contained in the two broad phases of "coming together" and "coming apart."[22] Other researchers have suggested that any model of relational communication ought to contain a third area of **relational maintenance**–communication aimed at keeping relationships operating smoothly and satisfactorily.[23] Figure 8–1 shows how Knapp's 10 stages fit into this three-part view of relational communication.

The following stages are especially descriptive of intimate, romantic relationships and close friendships. The pattern for other intimate relationships, such as families, would follow different paths. Some valuable associations don't require a high level of intimacy. They are based on other, equally important foundations: career activities, shared political interests, and religion, to mention just a few.[24]

Some Western cultures have rituals to mark the progress of a friendship and to give it public legitimacy and form. In Germany, for example, there's a small ceremony called Duzen, *the name itself signifying the transformation in the relationship. The ritual calls for the two friends, each holding a glass of wine or beer, to entwine arms, thus bringing each other physically close, and to drink up after making a promise of eternal brotherhood with the word* Bruderschaft. *When it's over, the friends will have passed from a relationship that requires the formal* Sie *mode of address to the familiar* Du.

Lillian B. Rubin,
Just Friends: The Role of Friendship in Our Lives

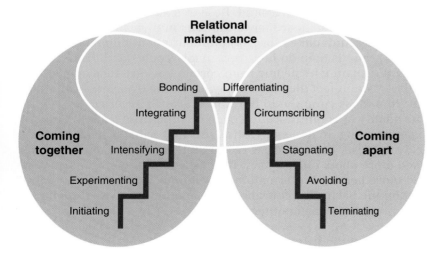

FIGURE 8–1

Stages of Relational Development

Passion is a bonfire that soon burns out but affection can last a lifetime.

Marion Hilliard, physician, quoted in *Chatelaine*

INITIATING The goals in the first stage are to show that you are interested in making contact and to show that you are the kind of person worth talking to. Communication during this **initiating** stage is usually brief, and it generally follows conventional formulas: handshakes, remarks about innocuous subjects like the weather, and friendly expressions. These kinds of behaviours may seem superficial and meaningless, but they are a way of signalling that we're interested in building some kind of relationship with the other person. They allow us to say without saying, "I'm a friendly person, and I'd like to get to know you."

EXPERIMENTING Once we have made contact with a new person, the next step is to decide whether we are interested in pursuing the relationship further. This task involves **uncertainty reduction**—the process of getting to know others by gaining more information about them.[25] The need to reduce uncertainty is especially important when we first meet others. A usual part of uncertainty reduction is the search for common ground, and it involves such conversational basics as "Where are you from?" "What's your major?" From there we look for other similarities: "You're a runner, too? How many kilometres do you do a week?"

The hallmark of the **experimenting** stage is small talk. As Mark Knapp says, this small talk is like Listerine: "We hate it, but we take large quantities every day."[26] We tolerate the ordeal of small talk because it serves several functions. First, it is a useful way to find out what interests we share with the other person. It also provides a way to "audition" the other person—to help us decide whether a relationship is worth pursuing. In addition, small talk is a safe way to ease into a relationship. You haven't risked much as you decide whether to proceed further. Finally, small talk *does* provide some kind of link to others. It's often better than being alone.

The willingness to pursue relationships with strangers is partly a matter of personal style. Some people are outgoing and others more shy, but culture also shapes behaviour toward newcomers, especially ones from a different background. Research suggests that members of high-context cultures are more cautious in their first encounters with strangers and make more assumptions about them based on their backgrounds than do members of low-context cultures.[27] This fact might explain why people from certain backgrounds appear unfriendly, when in fact they are simply operating by a set of rules different from those common in low-context North America.

The quality of communication changes after even a small amount of experimenting. In one study, strangers met with each other for 2, 4, or 6 minutes.[28] In every case, researchers found that, as the parties learned more about one another, they asked fewer questions and disclosed more personal information. In addition, as the amount of information the partners knew about one another increased, so did their attraction for one another.

INTENSIFYING In the **intensifying** stage the kind of truly interpersonal relationship defined in Chapter 1 begins to develop. Several

THE FAR SIDE By GARY LARSON

changes in communication patterns occur during intensifying. The expression of feelings toward the other becomes more common. Dating couples use a wide range of communication strategies to describe their feelings of attraction.[29] About a quarter of the time they express their feelings directly, using metacommunication to discuss the state of the relationship. More often they use less-direct methods of communication: spending an increasing amount of time together, asking for support from one another, doing favours for the partner, giving tokens of affection, hinting and flirting, expressing feelings nonverbally, getting to know the partner's friends and family, and trying to look more physically attractive.

Other changes mark the intensifying stage. Forms of address become more familiar. The parties begin to see themselves as "we" instead of separate individuals. It is during the intensifying stage that we begin to express directly feelings of commitment to one another: "I'm sure glad we met." "You're the best thing that's happened to me in a long time."

Although commitment grows as a relationship intensifies, communication between partners shows that doubts can still remain. Romantic couples use a variety of strategies to test the commitment of one another.[30] These approaches include asking direct questions, "testing" the partner by presenting challenges that require proof of commitment, hinting in order to gain expressions of commitment, asking third parties for information, and attempting to make the partner jealous. Although these behaviours are frequent in the early stages of a relationship, they decline as the partners spend more time together.

INTEGRATING   As the relationship strengthens, the parties begin to take on an identity as a social unit. Invitations begin to come addressed to the couple. Social circles merge. The partners begin to take on each other's commitments: "Sure, we'll spend Thanksgiving with your family." Common property may begin to be designated–our apartment, our car, our song.[31] Partners develop unique, ritualistic ways of behaving.[32] They may even begin to speak alike, using personal idioms and sentence patterns.[33] In this sense, the **integrating** stage is a time when we give up some characteristics of our old selves and become different people.

As we become more integrated with others, our sense of obligation to them grows.[34] We feel obliged to provide a variety of resources, such as class notes and money, whether or not the other person asks for them. Surprisingly, while integration is characterized by more relational solidarity, partners make fewer straightforward requests than they did in earlier relational stages. In dating relationships, for example, there is a curvilinear relationship (shown in Figure 8–2) between the relational stage and the number of explicit requests.[35] This pattern isn't as surprising as it might first seem: As partners become better acquainted, their knowledge of one another makes overt requests less necessary. But later, as the relationship inevitably begins to change, the need for more-explicit statements of wants and needs will increase again.

BONDING   During the **bonding** stage, the parties make symbolic public gestures to show the world that their relationship exists. The most common form of bonding in romantic relationships is a wedding ceremony and the legal ties that come with it. Bonding generates social support for the relationship. Custom and law both impose certain obligations on partners who have officially bonded.

Bonding marks a turning point in a relationship. Up to now the relationship may have developed at a steady pace: Experimenting gradually moved into intensifying and then into integrating. Now, however, there is a spurt of commitment. The public display and declaration of exclusivity make this a critical period in the relationship.

DIFFERENTIATING   Now that the two people have formed this commonality, they need to re-establish individual identities. This **differentiating** stage is the point where the "hold me tight" orientation that has existed shifts, and "put me down" messages begin to occur. Partners use a variety of strategies to gain privacy from one another.[36] Sometimes they confront the other party directly, explaining that

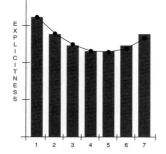

STAGE OF RELATIONAL DEVELOPMENT

FIGURE 8–2

Explicitness of requests varies across relational stages.

Adapted from D.H. Solomon, "A Developmental Model of Intimacy and Date Request Explicitness," *Communication Monographs* 64 (1997): 99–118.

they don't want to continue a discussion. In other cases they are less direct, offering nonverbal cues, changing the topic, or leaving the room.

Differentiation is likely to occur when a relationship begins to experience the first, inevitable stress. This need for autonomy needn't be a negative experience, however. People need to be individuals as well as parts of a relationship, and differentiation is a necessary step toward autonomy. The key to successful differentiation is maintaining a commitment to the relationship, while creating the space for being an individual as well.

CIRCUMSCRIBING   So far we have been looking at the growth of relationships. Although some reach a plateau of development, going on successfully for as long as a lifetime, others pass through several stages of decline and dissolution. In the **circumscribing** stage, communication between members decreases in quantity and quality. Restrictions and restraints characterize this stage, and dynamic communication becomes static. Rather than discuss a disagreement (which requires some degree of energy on both parts), members opt for withdrawal: either mental (silence or daydreaming and fantasizing) or physical (where people spend less time together). Circumscribing doesn't involve total avoidance, which may come later. Rather, it entails a certain shrinking of interest and commitment.

STAGNATING   If circumscribing continues, the relationship enters the **stagnating** stage. Members behave toward each other in old, familiar ways without much feeling. No growth occurs. The relationship is a hollow shell of its former self. We see stagnation in many workers who have lost enthusiasm for their job yet continue to go through the motions for years. The same sad event occurs for some couples who unenthusiastically have the same conversations, see the same people, and follow the same routines without any sense of joy or novelty.

AVOIDING   When stagnation becomes too unpleasant, parties in a relationship begin to create distance between each other. This is the **avoiding** stage. Sometimes they do it under the guise of excuses ("I've been sick lately and can't see you") and sometimes directly ("Please don't call me; I don't want to see you now"). In either case, by this point the handwriting is on the wall about the relationship's future.

The deterioration of a relationship from bonding through circumscribing, stagnating, and avoiding isn't inevitable. One of the key differences between marriages that end in separation and those that are restored to their former intimacy is the communication that occurs when the partners are unsatisfied.[37] Unsuccessful couples deal with their problems by avoidance, indirectness, and less involvement with one another. By contrast, couples who "repair" their relationship communicate much more directly. They confront one another with their concerns and spend time and effort negotiating solutions to their problems.

I cannot describe or even conjure up in my mind the physical appearance of those who are closest to me. They have dropped so securely into my heart that I can't see them.

Betty Jane Wylie,
No Two Alike

Love is the terrible secret people are suspected of unless they're married, then one always suspects they don't.

Jane Rule,
quoted in *The Canadian*

TERMINATING Characteristics of this final **terminating** stage include summary dialogues of where the relationship has gone and the desire to dissociate. The relationship may end with a cordial dinner, a note left on the kitchen table, a phone call, or a legal document stating the dissolution. Depending on each person's feelings, this stage can be quite short, or it may be drawn out over time, with bitter jabs at each other. In either case, termination doesn't have to be totally negative. Understanding each other's investments in the relationship and needs for personal growth may dilute the hard feelings.

In romantic relationships, the best predictor of whether the parties will become friends is whether they were friends before their emotional involvement.[38] The way the couple splits up also makes a difference. It's no surprise to find that friendships are most possible when communication during the breakup was positive: expressions that there were no regrets for time spent together and other attempts to minimize hard feelings. When communication during termination was negative (manipulative, complaining to third parties), friendships were less likely.

According to Knapp, a relationship can exist in only one stage at a time. At any moment it will exhibit the most predominant traits of just one of the 10 levels described on pages 336–340. Despite this fact, elements of other levels are usually present. For example, two lovers deep in the throes of integrating may still do their share of experimenting and have differentiating disagreements. Likewise, family members who spend most of their energy avoiding one another may have an occasional good spell in which their former closeness briefly intensifies. Even though there may be overtones of several stages, one will predominate.

Knapp also argues that movement between stages is generally sequential, so that relationships typically move from one stage to another in a step-by-step manner as they develop and deteriorate. This doesn't mean that every relationship will move through all 10 stages. Some reach a certain point and then go no further. When this occurs, movement is usually across the staircase to the corresponding point of deterioration. There are exceptions to the rule of sequential development. Occasionally partners may skip a stage: Sudden elopements and desertions are an example. Nonetheless, most of the time sequential, one-step-at-a-time progression allows the relationship to unfold at a pace that is manageable for the partners.

At first glance, Knapp's 10 steps of relational communication seem to suggest that all relationships follow the same trajectory, from initiation through termination. Your own experience almost certainly shows that this isn't necessarily the case. Some never make it past the early stages of initiating and experimenting. Others (with fellow workers or neighbours, for example) develop as far as integrating or even intensifying without ever reaching the stage of bonding. The 10-step model illustrates the range of possibilities, but it doesn't describe a guaranteed pathway for every relationship.

INVITATION TO INSIGHT

YOUR RELATIONAL STAGE

You can gain a clearer appreciation of the accuracy and value of relational stages by answering the following questions.

1. Describe the present stage of your relationship and the behaviours that characterize your communication in this stage. Give specific examples to support your assessment.

2. Discuss the trend of the communication in terms of the stages described on pages 341–347. Are you likely to remain in the present stage, or do you anticipate movement to another stage? Which one? Explain your answer.

3. Describe your level of satisfaction with the answer to question 2. If you are satisfied, describe what you can do to increase the likelihood that the relationship will operate at the stage you described. If you are not satisfied, discuss what you can do to move the relationship toward a more satisfying stage.

4. Because both parties define a relationship, define your partner's perspective. Would she or he say that the relationship is at the same stage as you describe it? If not, explain how your partner would characterize it. What does your partner do to determine the stage at which your relationship operates? (Give specific examples.) How would you like your partner to behave in order to move the relationship to, or maintain it at, the stage you desire? What can you do to encourage your partner to behave in the way you desire?

Dialectical Perspectives

Stage-related views like the one described in the preceding pages suggest that communication differs in important ways at various points in the life of a relationship. According to stage-related views, the kinds of interaction that happen during initiating, experimenting, or intensifying are different from the interaction that occurs during differentiating, circumscribing, or avoiding.

Not all theorists agree that a stage-related view is the best way to explain interaction in relationships. Some suggest that communicators grapple with the same kinds of challenges whether a relationship is brand new or has lasted decades. They argue that communicators seek important but inherently incompatible goals throughout virtually all their relationships. The struggle to achieve these goals creates **dialectical tensions:** conflicts that arise when two opposing or incompatible forces exist simultaneously. In recent years, communication scholars have identified the dialectical forces that make successful communication challenging.[39] They suggest that the struggle to manage these dialectical tensions creates the most powerful dynamics in relational communication. In the following pages we will discuss three powerful dialectical tensions.

Events happen every day and in quick succession. We stop talking to our partner about our day-to-day experiences, telling ourselves we do not want to burden them or that it would take too much time to get them up to the point where the information would make sense or be compelling. But the truth is that we have gotten out of the habit—or maybe never really developed the skill—of sharing our lives in the first place.

The process of allowing for separate lives starts innocently enough, but ultimately our lack of communication so radically reduces interest in each other that respect, the bedrock of any relationship, suffers.

Pepper Schwartz,
Peer Marriage

CONNECTION VS. AUTONOMY   No one is an island. Recognizing this fact, we seek out involvement with others. But, at the same time, we are unwilling to sacrifice our entire identity to even the most satisfying relationship. The conflicting desires for connection and independence are embodied in the **connection–autonomy dialectic.** Research on relational breakups demonstrates the consequences for relational partners who can't find a way to manage these very different personal needs.[40] Some of the most common reasons for relational breakups involve failure of partners to satisfy one another's needs for connection: "We barely spent any time together"; "S/he wasn't committed to the relationship"; "We had different needs." But other relational complaints involve excessive demands for connection: "I felt trapped"; "I needed freedom."

The levels of connection and autonomy that we seek can change over time. In his book *Intimate Behavior*, Desmond Morris suggests that each of us repeatedly goes through three stages: "Hold me tight," "Put me down," and "Leave me alone."[41] This cycle becomes apparent in the first years of life when children move from the "hold me tight" phase that characterizes infancy into a new "put me down" stage of exploring the world by crawling, walking, touching, and tasting. This move for independence isn't all in one direction: The same 3-year-old who insists "I can do it myself" in August may cling to parents on the first day of preschool in September. As children grow into adolescents, the "leave me alone" orientation becomes apparent. Teenagers who used to happily spend time with their parents now may groan at the thought of a family vacation, or even the notion of sitting down at the dinner table each evening. More time is spent either with friends or alone. Although this time can be painful for parents, most developmental experts recognize it as a necessary phase in moving from childhood to adulthood.

As the need for independence from family grows, adolescents take care of their "hold me tight" needs by associating with their peers. Friendships during the teenage years are vital, and the level of closeness with contemporaries can be a barometer of happiness. This is the time when physical intimacy becomes an option, and sexual exploration may provide a new way of achieving closeness.

In adult relationships, the same cycle of intimacy and distance repeats itself. In marriages, for example, the "hold me tight" bonds of the first year are often followed by a desire for independence. This need for autonomy can manifest itself in a number of ways, such as the desire to make friends or engage in activities that don't include the spouse, or the need to make a career move that might disrupt the relationship. As the discussion of relational stages earlier in this chapter explained, this movement from closeness to autonomy may lead to the breakup of a relationship; but it can also be part of a cycle that redefines the relationship in a new form that can recapture or even surpass the intimacy that existed in the past.

PREDICTABILITY VS. NOVELTY   Stability is an important need in relationships, but too much of it can lead to feelings of staleness. The

David Hockney, "My Parents" 1977. Oil on Canvas. 72 × 72 © David Hockney/Tate Gallery, London/Art Resource, NY

predictability–novelty dialectic reflects this tension. Humorist Dave Barry exaggerates only slightly when he talks about the boredom that can come when husbands and wives know each other too well:

> After a decade or so of marriage, you know *everything* about your spouse, every habit and opinion and twitch and tic and minor skin growth. You could write a seventeen-pound book solely about the way your spouse

eats. This kind of intimate knowledge can be very handy in certain situations—such as when you're on a TV quiz show where the object is to identify your spouse from the sound of his or her chewing—but it tends to lower the passion level of a relationship.[42]

Although too much familiarity can lead to the risk of boredom and stagnation, nobody wants a completely unpredictable relational partner. Too many surprises can threaten the foundations upon which the relationship is based ("You're not the person I married!").

The challenge for communicators is to juggle the desire for predictability with the need for novelty that keeps the relationship fresh and interesting. People differ in their need and desire for stability and surprises, so there is no optimal mixture of the two. As you will read shortly, there are a number of strategies people can use to manage these contradictory drives.

OPENNESS VS. PRIVACY   As Chapter 1 explained, disclosure is one characteristic of interpersonal relationships. Yet, along with the drive for intimacy, we have an equally important need to maintain some space between ourselves and others. These sometimes conflicting drives create the **openness–privacy dialectic.**

Even the strongest interpersonal relationships require some distance. On a short-term basis, the desire for closeness waxes and wanes. Lovers may go through periods of much sharing and times of relative withdrawal. Likewise, they experience periods of passion and then times of little physical contact. Friends have times of high disclosure where they share almost every feeling and idea, and then disengage for days, months, or even longer. Figure 8–3 illustrates some patterns of variation in openness uncovered in a study of college students' communication patterns.[43] The students reported the degree of openness in one of their important relationships—a friendship, romantic relationship, or marriage—over a range of 30 conversations. The graphs show a definite pattern of fluctuation between disclosure and privacy in every stage of the relationships.

STRATEGIES FOR MANAGING DIALECTICAL TENSIONS   Managing the dialectical tensions outlined in these pages presents communication challenges. There are a number of ways these challenges can be managed.[44] One of the least functional is *denial* that tensions exist. People in denial insist that "everything is fine": that the inevitable tugs of dialectical tensions really aren't a problem. For example, co-workers who claim that they're *always* happy to be members of the team and *never* see conflicts between their personal goals and those of the organization are probably operating in a state of denial.

Disorientation is another response to dialectical tensions. In this mode, communicators feel so overwhelmed and helpless that they are unable to confront their problems. In the face of dialectical tensions they might fight, freeze, or even leave the relationship. A couple who discovers soon after the honeymoon that living a "happily

"Love passes" . . . men say (and women sigh), but it isn't true. Infatuation passes, but not a love that has become one's life!

Henriette Dessaulles,
Hopes and Dreams: The Diary of Henriette Dessaulles, 1874–1881

ever after," conflict-free life is impossible might become so terrified that they would come to view their marriage as a mistake.

In the strategy of *selection,* communicators respond to one end of the dialectical spectrum and ignore the other. For example, a couple caught between the conflicting desires for stability and novelty might find their struggle for change too difficult to manage and choose to stick with predictable, if unexciting, patterns of relating to one another.

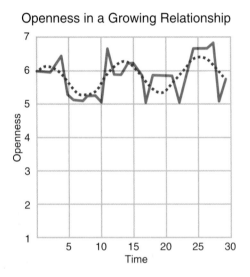

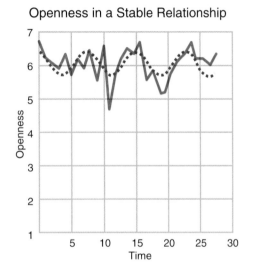

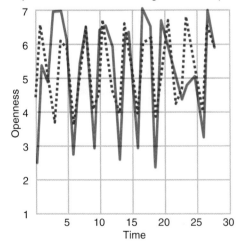

FIGURE 8–3

Cyclical Phases of Openness and Withdrawal in Relationships

From C.A. VanLear, "Testing a Cyclical Model of Communicative Openness in Relationship Development: Two Longitudinal Studies," *Communication Monographs* 58 (1991): 337–361. Copyright held by the Speech Communication Association. Reproduced by permission of the publisher.

Communicators choose the strategy of *alternation* to switch between one end of the dialectical spectrum at some times, and the other end at other times. Friends, for example, might manage the connection–autonomy dialectic by alternating between periods when they spend a large amount of time together and other periods when they live independent lives.

A fifth strategy is *segmentation,* a tactic in which partners compartmentalize different areas of their relationship. For example, a couple might manage the openness–privacy dialectic by sharing almost all their feelings about mutual friends with one another, but keep certain parts of their past romantic histories private.

Moderation is a sixth strategy. This approach is characterized by compromises, in which communicators choose to back off from expressing either end of the dialectical spectrum. Adult children, for example, might manage the openness–privacy dialectic with their inquisitive parents by answering some (though not all) unwelcome parental questions.

Communicators can also respond to dialectical challenges by *reframing* them in terms that redefine the situation so that the apparent contradiction disappears. Consider a couple who wince when their friends characterize them as a "perfect couple." On one hand, they want to escape from the "perfect couple" label that feels confining, but on the other, they enjoy the admiration that comes with this identity. By pointing out to their friends that "ideal couples" aren't always blissfully happy, they can both be themselves and keep the admiration of their friends.

A final approach to dialectical tensions is *reaffirmation*–acknowledging that dialectical tensions will never disappear, accepting or even embracing the challenges they present. The metaphorical view of relational life as a kind of roller coaster reflects this orientation, and communicators who use reaffirmation view dialectical tensions as part of the ride.

INVITATION TO INSIGHT

YOUR DIALECTICAL TENSIONS

Describe how each of the dialectical tensions described in these pages operates in one of your important relationships. Which incompatible goals do you and your relational partner(s) seek? Which of the strategies described on pages 344–346 do you use to manage these tensions? Are you satisfied with this approach, or can you suggest better strategies?

Characteristics of Relational Development and Maintenance

Whether you analyze a relationship in terms of stages or dialectical dynamics, two characteristics are true of every interpersonal relationship. As you read about each, consider how it applies to your own experience.

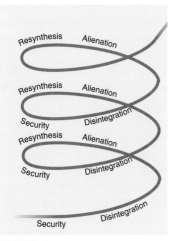

FIGURE 8–4
A Helical Model of Relational Cycles

RELATIONSHIPS ARE CONSTANTLY CHANGING   Relationships are certainly not doomed to deteriorate. But even the strongest ones are rarely stable for long periods of time. In fairy tales a couple may live "happily ever after," but in real life this sort of equilibrium is less common. Consider a husband and wife who have been married for some time. Although they have formally bonded, their relationship will probably shift from one dimension of a relational dialectic to another, and forward or backward along the spectrum of stages. Sometimes the partners will feel the need to differentiate from one another, and at other times they will seek intimacy. Sometimes they will feel secure in the predictable patterns they have established, and at other times one or both will be hungry for novelty. The relationship may become more circumscribed, or even stagnant. From this point the marriage may fail, but this fate isn't certain. With effort, the partners may move from the stage of stagnating to experimenting, or from circumscribing to intensifying.

Communication theorist Richard Conville describes the constantly changing, evolving nature of relationships as a cycle in which partners move through a series of stages, returning to ones they previously encountered . . . although at a new level[45] (see Figure 8–4). In this cycle, partners move from security (integration, in Knapp's terminology) to disintegration (differentiating) to alienation (circumscribing) to resynthesis (intensifying, integrating) to a new level of security. This process repeats itself again and again.

MOVEMENT IS ALWAYS TO A NEW PLACE   Even though a relationship may move back to a stage it has experienced before, it will never be the same. For example, most healthy long-term relationships will go through several phases of experimenting, when the partners try out new ways of behaving with one another. Though each phase is characterized by the same general features, the specifics will feel different each time. As you learned in Chapter 1, communication is irreversible. Partners can never go back to "the way things were." Sometimes this fact may lead to regrets: It's impossible to take back a cruel comment or forget a crisis. On the other hand, the irreversibility of communication can make relationships exciting, since it lessens the chance for boredom.

SELF-DISCLOSURE IN RELATIONSHIPS

One way we judge the strength of relationships is by the amount of information we share with others. "We don't have any secrets," some people proudly claim. Opening up certainly is important. As Chapter 1 explained, one ingredient in qualitatively interpersonal relationships is disclosure. Chapter 7 showed that we find others more attractive when they share certain private information with us. Given the obvious importance of self-disclosure, we need to take a closer look at the subject. Just what is it? When is it desirable? How can it best be done?

The best place to begin is with a definition. **Self-disclosure** is the process of deliberately revealing information about oneself that is significant and that would not normally be known by others. Let's take a closer look at some parts of this definition. Self-disclosure must be *deliberate*. If you accidentally mention to a friend that you're thinking about quitting a job or proposing marriage, that information doesn't qualify as self-disclosure. Besides being intentional, the information must also be *significant*. Volunteering trivial facts, opinions, or feelings—that you like fudge, for example—hardly counts as disclosure. The third requirement is that the information being disclosed is *not known by others*. There's nothing noteworthy about telling others that you are depressed or elated if they already know that.

Degrees of Self-Disclosure

Although our definition of self-disclosure is helpful, it doesn't reveal the important fact that not all self-disclosure is equally revealing—that some disclosing messages tell more about us than others.

Social psychologists Irwin Altman and Dalmas Taylor describe two ways in which communication can be more or less disclosing.[46] Their model of **social penetration** is pictured in Figure 8–5. The first dimension of self-disclosure in this model involves the **breadth** of information volunteered—the range of subjects being discussed. For example, the breadth of disclosure in your relationship with a fellow worker will expand as you begin revealing information about your life away from the job as well as on-the-job details. The second dimension of disclosure is the **depth** of the information being volunteered, the shift from relatively nonrevealing messages to more-personal ones.

Depending on the breadth and depth of information shared, a relationship can be defined as casual or intimate. In a casual relationship the breadth may be great, but not the depth. A more intimate relationship is likely to have high depth in at least one area. The most intimate relationships are those in which disclosure is great in both breadth and depth. Altman and Taylor see the development of a

Social Penetration Theory

http://oak.cats.ohiou.edu/ ~bz372497/socpenbz.htm

Social Penetration Theory and Memory

http://oak.cats.ohiou.edu/ ~sk260695/sksp.html

4 A.M.
I walked around my good intentions
And found that there were none
I blame my father for the wasted years
We hardly talked
I never thought I would forget this hate
the phone call made me realize
I'm wrong

If I don't make it known that	I walked around my room
I've loved you all along	Not thinking
Just like sunny days that	Just sinking in this box
We ignore because	I blame myself for being
We're all dumb and jaded	too much
And I hope God I figure out	Like somebody else
What's wrong	I never thought I would just
	Bend this way

Our Lady Peace

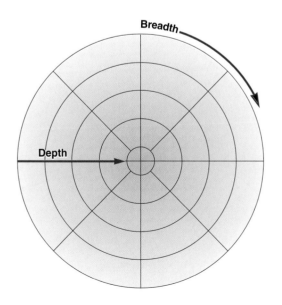

Breadth

Depth

FIGURE 8–5
Social Penetration Model

relationship as a progression from the periphery of their model to its centre, a process that typically occurs over time. Each of your personal relationships probably has a different combination of breadth of subjects and depth of disclosure. Figure 8–6 pictures a student's self-disclosure in one relationship.

What makes the disclosure in some messages deeper than others? One way to measure depth is by how far it goes on two of the dimensions that define self-disclosure. Some revelations are certainly more *significant* than others. Consider the difference between saying, "I love my family" and "I love you." Other statements qualify as deep disclosure because they are *private*. Sharing a secret that you've told only a few close friends is certainly an act of self-disclosure, but it's even more revealing to divulge information that you've never told anyone.

Another way to classify the depth of disclosure is to look at the types of information we share. These include clichés, facts, opinions, and feelings.

CLICHÉS **Clichés** are ritualized, stock responses to social situations—virtually the opposite of self-disclosure: "What's up?" "Not much." "Let's get together for lunch." Remarks such as these usually aren't meant to be taken literally; in fact, the other person would be surprised if you responded to a casual "How's it goin'?" with a lengthy speech on your health, state of mind, love life, or finances. Yet it's a mistake to consider clichés meaningless, for they serve several useful functions. For instance, they can give two speakers time to size each other up and decide whether it's desirable to carry their conversation any further. Our first impressions are generally based more on the

FIGURE 8–6
Sample Model of Social Penetration

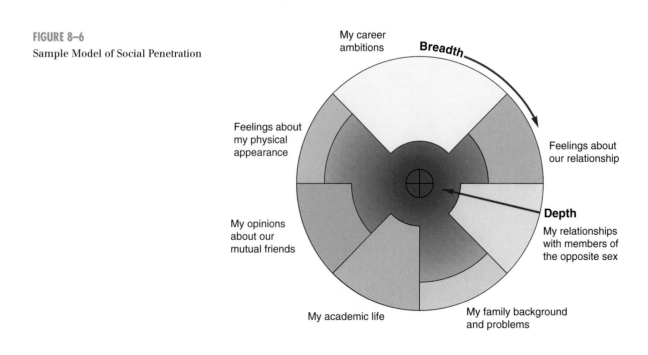

nonverbal characteristics of the other person than on the words we hear spoken. Factors such as eye contact, vocal tone, facial expression, posture, and so on can often tell us more about another person than can the initial sentences in a conversation. Given the value of these nonverbal cues and the awkwardness of actually saying, "I want to take a few minutes to look you over before I commit myself to getting acquainted," the exchange of a few stock phrases can be just the thing to get you through this initial period comfortably.

Clichés can also serve as codes for other messages we don't usually express directly, such as "I want to acknowledge your presence" (for instance, when two acquaintances walk past each other). Additional unstated messages often contained in clichés are "I'm interested in talking if you feel like it" or "Let's keep the conversation light and impersonal; I don't feel like disclosing much about myself right now." Accompanied by a different set of nonverbal cues, a cliché can say, "I don't want to be impolite, but you'd better stay away from me for now." In all these cases clichés serve as a valuable kind of shorthand that makes it easy to keep the social wheels greased and indicates the potential for further, possibly more-profound conversation.

FACTS Not all factual statements qualify as self-disclosure: They must fit the criteria of being intentional, significant, and not otherwise known:

> "This isn't my first try at college. I dropped out a year ago with terrible grades."

> "I'm practically engaged." (On meeting a stranger while away from home)

> "That idea that everyone thought was so clever wasn't really mine. I read it in a book last year."

Facts like these can be meaningful in themselves, but they also have a greater significance in a relationship. Disclosing important information suggests a level of trust and commitment to the other person that signals a desire to move the relationship to a new level.

OPINIONS Still more revealing is the level of opinions:

> "I used to think abortion was totally wrong, but lately I've changed my mind."

> "I really like Karen."

> "I don't think you're telling me what's on your mind."

Opinions like these usually reveal more about a person than facts alone. If you know where the speaker stands on a subject, you can get a clearer picture of how your relationship might develop. Likewise, every time you offer a personal opinion, you are giving others valuable information about yourself.

Self-Disclosure, Emotional Openness, and Effective Communication

http://mentalhelp.net/psyhelp/ chap13/chap13i.htm

FEELINGS The fourth level of self-disclosure—and usually the most revealing one—is the realm of feelings. At first glance, feelings might appear to be the same as opinions, but there is a big difference. As we saw, "I don't think you're telling me what's on your mind" is an opinion. Now notice how much more we learn about the speaker by looking at the different feelings that might accompany this statement:

> "I don't think you're telling me what's on your mind, and *I'm suspicious.*"

> "I don't think you're telling me what's on your mind, *and I'm angry.*"

> "I don't think you're telling me what's on your mind, and *I'm hurt.*"

The difference between these four levels of communication suggests why relationships can be frustrating. One reason has to do with the depth of disclosure, which may not lead to the kind of relationship one or both parties are seeking. Sometimes the communicators might remain exclusively on the level of facts. This might be suitable for a business relationship but wouldn't be very likely in most other circumstances. Even worse, other communicators never get off the level of clichés. And just as a diet of rich foods can become unappealing if carried to excess, the overuse of feelings and opinions can also become disagreeable. In most cases the successful conversation

is one in which the participants move from one level to another, depending on the circumstances.

Another common problem occurs when two communicators want to relate to each other on different levels. If one is willing to deal only with facts and perhaps an occasional opinion and the other insists on revealing personal feelings, the results are likely to be uncomfortable for both. Consider the following meeting between Jack and Brayden at a party.

J: Hi. My name's Jack. I don't think we've met before. *(cliché)*

B: I'm Brayden. Nice to meet you. *(cliché)*

J: Do you know anybody here? I've just moved in next door and don't know a soul except for the host. What's his name . . . Sean? *(fact)*

B: Sean's right. Well, I'm here with my wife–that's her over there–and we know a few other people. *(fact; both speakers are comfortable so far)*

J: Well, I used to have a wife, but she split. She really did me in. *(fact and opinion)*

B: Oh? *(cliché; he doesn't know how to reply to this comment)*

J: Yeah. Everything was going along great–I thought. Then one day she told me she was in love with her gynecologist and that she wanted a divorce. Man, I still haven't gotten over it. *(feeling and fact)*

B: Well, uh, that's too bad. *(cliché; Brayden is now very uncomfortable)*

J: I don't think I'll ever trust another woman. I'm still in love with my wife, and it's killing me. She really broke my heart. *(feeling and fact)*

B: I'm sorry. Listen, I've got to go. *(cliché)*

Clearly, Jack moved to the level of disclosing feelings long before Brayden was prepared to accept this kind of communication. Though this type of discussion might have helped a friendship if it had come at a later time, Jack succeeded only in driving Brayden away by coming on too fast. Remember the hazards of moving too quickly to a level your partner is likely to find uncomfortable.

A Model of Self-Disclosure

One way to look at the important part self-disclosure plays in interpersonal communication is by means of a device called the **Johari Window.**[47] (The window takes its name from the first names of its creators, Joseph Luft and Harry Ingham.) Imagine a frame like Figure 8–7 that contains everything there is to know about you: your likes and dislikes, your goals, your secrets, your needs–everything.

Of course, you aren't aware of everything about yourself. Like most people, you're probably discovering new things about yourself all the time. To represent this, we can divide the frame containing

INVITATION TO INSIGHT

EXAMINING YOUR SELF-DISCLOSURE

Here's a chance to explore the levels of self-disclosure you use with some important people in your life.

1. Choose a "significant other" as the subject of this exercise.

2. Over a 3-day period, record the number of statements you make in each category: clichés, facts, opinions, and feelings.

3. Try to be aware of the topics that you discuss on each level, along with the number of statements in each category.

4. Based on your findings, answer these questions:
   a. Which categories of self-disclosure do you engage in most frequently? Least often?
   b. What type of disclosure (fact, opinion, or feeling) do you use in each topic area?
   c. Explain the reason for omitting topical categories (for example, conflicts, the future) or levels of disclosure or both (for example, feelings).
   d. Explain the consequences of any omissions described in part c.

everything about you into two parts: the part you know about and the part you're not aware of, as in Figure 8–8.

We can also divide this frame containing everything about you in another way. In this division one part represents the things about you that others know, and the second part contains the things about you that you keep to yourself. Figure 8–9 represents this view.

When we impose these two divided frames one atop the other, we have a Johari Window. By looking at Figure 8–10 you can see the *everything about you* divided into four parts.

Part 1 represents the information of which both you and the other person are aware. This part is your *open area.* Part 2 represents the *blind area:* information of which you are unaware but the other person knows. You learn about information in the blind area primarily through feedback. Part 3 represents your *hidden area:* information that you know but aren't willing to reveal to others. Items in this hidden area become public primarily through self-disclosure. Part 4 represents information that is *unknown* to both you and others. At first the unknown area seems impossible to verify. After all, if neither you nor others know what it contains, how can you be sure it exists? We can deduce its existence because we are constantly discovering new things about ourselves. It is not unusual to discover, for example, that you have an unrecognized talent, strength, or weakness. Items move from the unknown area either directly into the open area when you disclose your insight or through one of the other areas first.

Everything about you

FIGURE 8–7

The relative size of each area in our personal Johari Windows changes from time to time, according to our moods, the subject we are discussing, and our relationship with the other person. Despite these changes, most people's overall style of disclosure could be represented by a single Johari Window. Figure 8–11 pictures windows representing four extreme interaction styles.

Diagram I depicts a person who is neither receptive to feedback nor willing to self-disclose. This person takes few risks and may appear aloof and uncommunicative. The largest quadrant is the unknown area: Such people have a lot to learn about themselves, as do others. Diagram II depicts a person who is open to feedback from others but does not voluntarily self-disclose. This person may fear exposure, possibly because of not trusting others. People who fit this pattern may appear highly supportive at first. They want to hear *your* story and appear willing to deny themselves by remaining quiet. Then this first impression fades, and eventually you see them as distrustful and detached. A Johari Window describing such people has a large hidden area.

Diagram III in Figure 8–11 describes people who discourage feedback from others but disclose freely. Like the people pictured in diagram II, they may distrust others' opinions. They certainly seem self-centred. Their largest quadrant is the blind area: They do not encourage feedback, and so fail to learn much about how others view them.

Diagram IV depicts people who are both willing to disclose information about themselves and open to others' ideas. They are trusting enough to seek the opinions of others and disclose their own. In extreme, this communication style can be intimidating and overwhelming because it violates the usual expectations of how non-intimates ought to behave. In moderation, however, this open style provides the best chance for developing highly interpersonal relationships.

Interpersonal communication of any depth is virtually impossible if the individuals involved have little open area. Going a step further, you can see that a relationship is limited by the individual who is less open–that is, who possesses the smaller open area. Figure 8–12 illustrates this situation with Johari Windows. Person A's window is set up in reverse so that A's and B's open areas are adjacent. Notice that the amount of communication (represented by the arrows connecting the two open areas) is dictated by the size of the smaller open area of A. The arrows originating from person B's open area and being turned aside by A's hidden and blind areas represent unsuccessful attempts to communicate.

You have probably found yourself in situations that resemble Figure 8–12. Perhaps you have felt the frustration of not being able to get to know someone who was too reserved. Perhaps you have blocked another person's attempts to build a relationship with you in the same way. Whether you picture yourself more like person A or person B, the fact is that self-disclosure on both sides is necessary

FIGURE 8–8

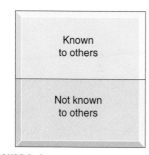

FIGURE 8–9

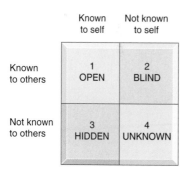

FIGURE 8–10

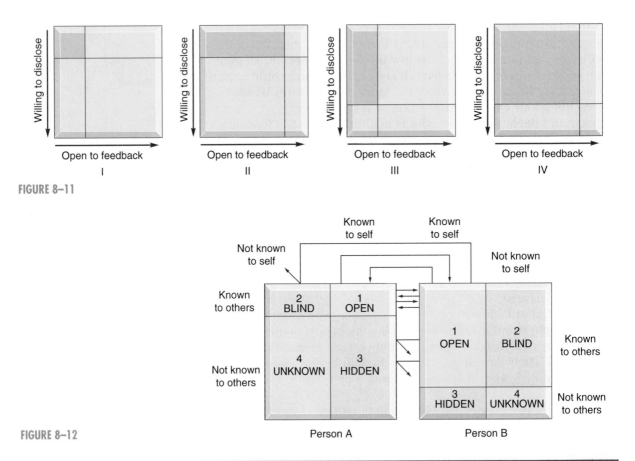

FIGURE 8–11

FIGURE 8–12

INVITATION TO INSIGHT

BUILDING A JOHARI WINDOW

You can use the Johari Window model to examine the level of self-disclosure in your own relationships.

1. Use the format described in the preceding section to draw two Johari Windows representing the relationship between you and one other person. Remember to reverse one of the windows so that your open areas and those of the other person face each other.

2. Describe which parts of yourself you keep in the hidden area. Explain your reasons for doing so. Describe the costs or benefits or both of not disclosing these parts of yourself.

3. Look at the blind area of your model. Is this area large or small because of the amount of feedback (much or little) that you get from your partner or because of your willingness to receive the feedback that is offered?

4. Explain whether you are satisfied with the results illustrated by your answers. If you are not satisfied, explain what you can do to remedy the problem.

for the development of any interpersonal relationship. Just how much and what type of disclosure is optimal are described in the next section.

Characteristics of Self-Disclosure

By now it's clear that self-disclosure isn't a common type of communication, even in close relationships. The following characteristics show the place of self-disclosure in interpersonal affairs.

SELF-DISCLOSURE USUALLY OCCURS IN DYADS   Although it is possible for people to disclose a great deal about themselves in groups, self-disclosure typically occurs in one-to-one settings. Because revealing significant information about yourself involves a certain amount of risk, limiting the disclosure to one person at a time minimizes the chance that your revelations will lead to unhappy consequences.

SELF-DISCLOSURE OCCURS INCREMENTALLY   Although occasions do occur in which partners start their relationship by telling everything about themselves to each other, such instances are rare. In most cases the amount of disclosure increases over time. We begin relationships by

revealing relatively little about ourselves; then if our first bits of self-disclosure are well received and bring on similar responses from the other person, we're willing to reveal more. This principle is important to remember. It would usually be a mistake to assume that the way to build a strong relationship would be to reveal the most private details about yourself when first making contact with another person. Unless the circumstances are unique, such baring of your soul would be likely to scare potential partners away rather than bring them closer.

RELATIVELY FEW TRANSACTIONS INVOLVE HIGH LEVELS OF SELF-DISCLOSURE   Just as it's unwise to seek great self-disclosure too soon, it's also unproductive to reveal yourself too often. Except for unique settings—such as in therapy—there's usually no need to disclose frequently or steadily. When used properly, self-disclosure may strengthen relationships, but like most medicines, large amounts of disclosure are not necessary to produce good results.

SELF-DISCLOSURE IS RELATIVELY SCARCE   What is the optimal amount of self-disclosure? You might suspect that the correct answer is "the more, the better," at least in personal relationships. Research has shown that the matter isn't this simple, however.[48] For example, there seems to be a curvilinear relationship between openness and satisfaction in marriage, so that a moderate amount of openness produces better results than either extreme disclosure or withholding. Most conversations—even among friends—focus on everyday, mundane topics and disclose little or no personal information.[49] Even partners in intimate relationships rarely talk about personal information.[50] One good measure of happiness is how well the level of disclosure matches the expectations of communicators: If we get what we believe is a reasonable amount of candour from others, we are happy. If they tell us too little—or too much—we become less satisfied.

SELF-DISCLOSURE USUALLY OCCURS IN THE CONTEXT OF POSITIVE RELATIONSHIPS
This principle makes sense. We're generally more willing to reveal information about ourselves when we feel accepted by the other person. This doesn't mean that you should avoid making disclosing statements that contain negative messages (for example, "I feel uncomfortable about what happened last night"). Such explanations are likely to be successful if they're designed to be constructive, to help your relationship grow. On the other hand, disclosure that has the effect of attacking the other person ("You sure aren't very bright") is almost guaranteed to be destructive. For this reason, it's especially important to phrase negative messages in the supportive, assertive ways described in Chapters 9 and 10.

Reasons for Self-Disclosure

Self-disclosure has the potential to improve and expand interpersonal relationships, but it serves other functions as well.[51] As you read each of the following reasons why people reveal themselves, see which apply to you.

CATHARSIS   Sometimes you might disclose information in an effort to "get it off your chest." In a moment of candour you might, for instance, reveal your regrets about having behaved badly in the past.

SELF-CLARIFICATION   Sometimes you can clarify your beliefs, opinions, thoughts, attitudes, and feelings by talking about them with another person. This sort of "talking the problem out" occurs with psychotherapists, but it also goes on with others, all the way from good friends to bartenders or hairstylists.

SELF-VALIDATION   If you disclose information ("I think I did the right thing . . .") with the hope of obtaining the listener's agreement, you are seeking validation of your behaviour–confirmation of a belief you hold about yourself. On a deeper level, this sort of self-validating disclosure seeks confirmation of important parts of your self-concept.

RECIPROCITY   A well-documented conclusion from research is that one act of self-disclosure begets another.[52] Thus, in some situations you may choose to disclose information about yourself to encourage another person to do so also.

IDENTITY MANAGEMENT   Sometimes we reveal personal information to make ourselves more attractive. Some observers have made this point bluntly, asserting that self-disclosure has become another way of "marketing" ourselves.[53] Consider a couple on their first date. It's not hard to imagine how one or both partners might share personal information to appear more sincere, interesting, sensitive, or interested in the other person. The same principle applies in other situations. A salesperson might say, "I'll be honest with you . . ." primarily to show that she is on your side, and a new acquaintance might talk about the details of his past to seem more friendly and likable.

RELATIONSHIP MAINTENANCE AND ENHANCEMENT   A large body of research supports the role of self-disclosure in relational success.[54] For example, there is a strong relationship between the quality of self-disclosure and marital satisfaction.[55] The same principle applies in other personal relationships. The bond between grandparents and grandchildren, for example, grows stronger when the honesty and depth of sharing between them are high.[56]

SOCIAL CONTROL   Revealing personal information may increase your control over the other person, and sometimes over the situation in which you and the other person find yourselves. For example, an employee who tells the boss that another firm has made overtures probably will have an increased chance of getting raises and improvements in working conditions.

"Bob, as a token of my appreciation for this wonderful lunch I would like to disclose to you my income-tax returns for the past four years."

DRAWING BY ZIEGLER; © 1984 *The New Yorker* Magazine, Inc.

MANIPULATION Although most of the preceding reasons might strike you as being manipulative, they often aren't premeditated strategies. There are cases, however, when an act of self-disclosure is calculated in advance to achieve a desired result. Of course, if a disclosure's hidden motive ever becomes clear to the receiver, the results will most likely be quite unlike those intended.

The reasons for disclosing vary from one situation to another, depending on several factors. The strongest influence on why people disclose seems to be how well they know the other person.[57] When the target of disclosure is a friend, the most frequent reason people give for volunteering personal information is relationship maintenance and enhancement. In other words, we disclose to friends in order to strengthen the relationship. The second important reason is self-clarification—to sort out confusion to understand ourselves better.

With strangers, reciprocity becomes the most common reason for disclosing. We offer information about ourselves to strangers to learn more about them, so we can decide whether and how to continue the relationship. The second most important reason is impression formation. In other words, we often reveal information about ourselves to strangers to make us look good. This information, of course, is usually positive—at least in the early stages of a friendship.

An Exercise to Help Build Supportive Relationships

http://www.virtualpsych.com/ stress/openupexer.htm

Guidelines for Self-Disclosure

By now it should be clear that deciding when and how much personal information to disclose is not a simple matter. The following guidelines can help you choose the level of self-disclosure that is appropriate in a given situation.

IS THE OTHER PERSON IMPORTANT TO YOU?   There are several ways in which someone might be important. Perhaps you have an ongoing relationship deep enough so that sharing significant parts of yourself justifies keeping your present level of togetherness intact. Or perhaps the person to whom you're considering disclosing is someone with whom you've previously related on a less personal level. But now you see a chance to grow closer, and disclosure may be the path toward developing that personal relationship.

IS THE RISK OF DISCLOSING REASONABLE?   Take a realistic look at the potential risks of self-disclosure. Even if the probable benefits are great, opening yourself up to almost certain rejection may be asking for trouble. For instance, it might be foolhardy to share your important feelings with someone you know is likely to betray your confidences or ridicule them. On the other hand, knowing that your partner is trustworthy and supportive makes the prospect of speaking out more reasonable.

Revealing personal thoughts and feelings can be especially risky on the job.[58] The politics of the workplace sometimes requires communicators to keep feelings to themselves in order to accomplish both personal and organizational goals. You might, for example, find the opinions of a boss or customer personally offensive but decide to bite your tongue rather than risk your job or lose goodwill for the company.

In anticipating risks, be sure that you are realistic. It's sometimes easy to indulge in catastrophic expectations and imagine all sorts of disastrous consequences when in fact such horrors are quite unlikely to occur.

IS THE DISCLOSURE RELEVANT TO THE SITUATION AT HAND?   The kind of disclosure that is often a characteristic of highly personal relationships usually isn't appropriate in less personal settings. For instance, a study of classroom communication revealed that sharing all feelings—both positive and negative—and being completely honest resulted in less cohesiveness than a "relatively" honest climate in which pleasant but superficial relationships were the norm.[59]

Even in personal relationships—with close friends, family members, and so on—constant disclosure isn't a useful goal. The level of sharing in successful relationships rises and falls in cycles. You may go through a period of great disclosure and then spend another interval of relative nondisclosure. Even during a phase of high disclosure sharing *everything* about yourself isn't necessarily constructive. Usually the subject of appropriate self-disclosure involves the relationship rather than personal information. Furthermore, it is usually most constructive to focus your disclosure about the relationship on the "here and now" as opposed to "there and then." "How am I feeling now?" "How are we doing now?" These are appropriate topics for sharing personal thoughts and feelings. At times it's relevant to bring up the past, but only as it relates to what's going on in the present.

ARE THE AMOUNT AND TYPE OF DISCLOSURE APPROPRIATE?   It is usually a mistake to share too much information too soon. Research shows that in most relationships the process of disclosure is gradual.[60] At first most of the information that is exchanged is relatively non-intimate. As the parties move into the intensifying, integrating, and bonding stages of the relationship, the rate of disclosure begins to grow.

As we've already seen, even in relationships in which disclosure is an important feature, the amount of personal information is relatively small when compared with non-intimate information. Most long-term relationships aren't characterized by a constant exchange of intimate details. Rather, they are a mixture of much everyday, non-intimate information and less frequent but more personal messages.

Besides being moderate in amount, self-disclosure should consist of positive information as well as negative details. Hearing nothing but a string of dismal confessions or complaints can be discouraging. In fact, people who disclose an excess of negative information are often considered "negatively adjusted."[61]

Finally, when considering the appropriateness of disclosure in any relationship, timing is also important. If the other person is tired, preoccupied, or in a bad mood, it may be best to postpone an important conversation.

WILL THE EFFECT BE CONSTRUCTIVE?   Self-disclosure can be a vicious tool if it's not used carefully. Psychologists suggest that every person has a psychological "beltline." Below that beltline are areas about which

"I'm a very sensual person. How about you, Mr. Gellerman?"

Drawing by Stan Hunt; © 1982 *The New Yorker Magazine,* Inc.

Communication Transcript

Appropriate and Inappropriate Self-Disclosure

Marcel has been working in an entry-level sales job for almost a year after graduating from university. He likes the company, but he is growing more and more frustrated at his lack of advancement. After much thought, he decides to share his concerns with his boss, Julie. As you read the following transcript, notice that self-disclosure has the potential to enhance or jeopardize personal goals and relationships, depending on whether it follows the guidelines on pages 360–364.

Marcel Do you have a few minutes to talk?

Julie Sure, no problem. Come on in.

Marcel Do you mind if we close the door?

Julie *(looking a bit surprised)* Sure.

Marcel I'd like to talk to you about the future.

Julie The future?

Marcel Well, it's been over a year since I started to work here. One of the things you told me in the interview back then was that people move up fast here . . .

Julie Well, . . .

Marcel . . . and I'm confused because I've been doing pretty much the same work since I was hired.

Julie Well, we *do* think a lot of your work.

Marcel I'm glad to hear that. But I'm starting to wonder how much of a chance I'll have to grow with this company. *(Marcel is disclosing his concerns about career advancement—a very appropriate topic to raise with his boss. There is some risk in this sort of disclosure, but given Marcel's apparently good standing with his boss, it seems*

reasonable. Note that Marcel is deliberately vague about "his future." At this stage, the high level of abstraction is probably a good idea.)

Julie I can understand that you're anxious about taking on more responsibility. I can tell you that you've got a good shot at advancing, if you can just hang in there for a little while.

Marcel *(impatiently)* That sounds good, but I've been waiting—a lot longer than I expected to. I'm starting to wonder if some of the things I've heard around here are true.

Julie *(suspiciously)* What kinds of things are you talking about, Marcel?

Marcel Well, Bill and Latisha were telling me about some people who left here because they didn't get the promotions they were promised. *(Marcel discloses information that was told to him in confidence, jeopardizing the standing of two coworkers with Julie.)*

Julie *(firmly)* Marcel, I'm sure you understand that I can't talk about personnel decisions involving former employees. I can tell you that we try to give people all the challenges and rewards they deserve, though it can take a while.

Marcel *(with some sarcasm)* A year seems like more than "a while." I'm starting to think this company is more interested in having somebody with a French name on the payroll than giving me a real shot at promotion. *(Marcel's concern may be legitimate, but the sarcastic tone of his disclosure isn't constructive.)*

Julie Look: I probably shouldn't be saying this, but I'm as frustrated as you are that it's taking so long to get a promotion arranged for you. I can tell you that there will be some personnel changes soon that will give you a good chance to make the kinds of changes you want. I think you can expect to see some changes in the next 6 weeks. *(Julie offers two items of self-disclosure that encourage Marcel to reciprocate.)*

Marcel That's really good to hear! I have to tell you that I've started to think about other career options. Not because I *want* to leave here, but because I just can't afford to stand still. I really need to start bringing home more money. I don't want to be one of those losers who still can't afford to buy his own house by the time he's 40. *(Marcel makes a big mistake disclosing his opinion about home ownership—a topic that*

Communication Transcript *continued*

has no relevance to the discussion at hand.)

Julie Gee, I'm still renting...

Marcel Oh. I didn't mean that the way it sounded... *(But the damage from the inappropriate disclosure is already done.)*

Julie Anyway, I'm glad you let me know about your concerns.

I hope you can hang in there for just a little while longer.

Marcel Sure. Six weeks, huh? I'll keep an eye on the calendar!

After the conversation, Julie still thinks Marcel is a candidate for promotion, but some of his inappropriate disclosures have left her with doubts about his

maturity and good judgement which she didn't have before they spoke. Julie makes a mental note to keep an eye on Marcel, and to reconsider the amount of responsibility she gives him until he has demonstrated the ability to share his personal feelings and concerns more constructively.

the person is extremely sensitive. Jabbing at a "below-the-belt" area is a surefire way to disable another person, though usually at great cost to the relationship. It's important to consider the effects of your candour before opening up to others. Comments such as "I've always thought you were pretty unintelligent" or "Last year I made love to your best friend" *may* sometimes resolve old business and thus be constructive, but more than likely they will be devastating–to the listener, to the relationship, and to the self-esteem.

IS THE SELF-DISCLOSURE CLEAR AND UNDERSTANDABLE? When you are expressing yourself to others, it's important that you reveal yourself in a way that's intelligible. This means using the guidelines for clear language outlined in Chapter 5. For instance, it's far better to describe another's behaviour by saying, "When you don't answer my phone calls or drop by to visit anymore..." than to complain vaguely, "When you avoid me...."

IS THE DISCLOSURE RECIPROCATED? The amount of personal information you share will usually depend on how much the other person reveals. As a rule, disclosure is a two-way street. For example, couples are happiest when their levels of openness are roughly equal.[62]

There are a few times when one-way disclosure is acceptable. Most of them involve formal, therapeutic relationships in which a client approaches a trained professional with the goal of resolving a problem. For instance, you wouldn't necessarily expect to hear about a physician's personal ailments during a visit to a medical office. Nonetheless, it's interesting to note that one frequently noted characteristic of effective psychotherapists, counsellors, and teachers is a willingness to reveal their feelings about a relationship to their clients.

SKILL BUILDER

APPROPRIATE SELF-DISCLOSURE

Use the guidelines on pages 360–364 to develop one scenario where you might reveal a self-disclosing message. Create a message of this type, and use the information in this chapter to discuss the risks and benefits of sharing this message.

ALTERNATIVES TO SELF-DISCLOSURE

Although self-disclosure plays an important role in interpersonal relationships, it isn't the only type of communication available. To understand why complete honesty isn't always an easy or ideal choice, consider some familiar dilemmas:

A new acquaintance is much more interested in becoming friends than you are. She invites you to a party this weekend. You aren't busy, but you don't want to go. What would you say?

Your boss asks you what you think of the strategic plan process. You think it's a waste of time. Would you tell him?

You're attracted to your best friend's mate, who has confessed that he feels the same way about you. You both agree that you won't act on your feelings and that even bringing up the subject would make your friend feel terribly insecure. Now your friend has asked whether you're attracted at all to the mate. Would you tell the truth?

You've just been given a large, extremely ugly painting as a gift by a relative who visits your home often. How would you respond to the question "Where will you hang it?"

Situations like these highlight some of the issues that surround deceptive communication. On one hand, our moral education and common sense lead us to abhor anything less than the truth. Ethicists point out that the very existence of a society seems based on a foundation of truthfulness.[63] Although isolated cultures do exist where deceit is a norm, they are dysfunctional and on the verge of breakdown.

On the other hand, although honesty is desirable in principle, it often has risky, potentially unpleasant consequences. It's tempting to avoid situations where self-disclosure would be difficult, but examples like the ones you just read show that evasion isn't always possible. Research and personal experience show that communicators—even those with the best intentions—aren't always completely honest when they find themselves in situations in which honesty would be

Words, like Nature, half reveal and half conceal the Soul within.

Alfred, Lord Tennyson

Relationship Quizzes

http://www.positive-way.com/ relationship%20quiz.htm

*We are hard on each other
and call it honesty,
choosing our jagged truths
with care and aiming them
 across
the neutral table.*

*The things we say are
true; it is our crooked
aims, our choices
turn them criminal.*

Margaret Atwood,
Power Politics

uncomfortable.[64] Three common alternatives to self-disclosure are lying, equivocating, and hinting. We will take a closer look at each one.

Lying

To most of us, lying appears as a breach of ethics. At first glance it appears that the very possibility of a society depends on the acceptance of truthfulness as a social norm. Although lying to gain unfair advantage over an unknowing victim seems clearly wrong, another kind of mistruth—the **"white lie"**—isn't so easy to dismiss as completely unethical. A "white lie" is defined (at least by the teller) as unmalicious, or even helpful to the person to whom it is told. Whether or not they are innocent, white lies are certainly common. In one study, 130 subjects were asked to keep track of the truthfulness of their everyday conversational statements.[65] Only 38.5 percent of these statements—slightly more than a third—proved to be totally honest.

REASONS FOR LYING   What reasons do people give for being so deceitful? When subjects in the study were asked to give a lie-by-lie account of their motives for concealing or distorting the truth, five major reasons emerged.

1. *To save face.* Over half the lies were justified as a way to prevent embarrassment. Such lying is often given the approving label "tact" and is used "when it would be unkind to be honest, but dishonest to be kind."[66] Sometimes a face-saving lie saves face for the recipient, as when you pretend to remember someone at a party in order to save that person from the embarrassment of being forgotten. In other cases a lie protects the teller from humiliation. You might, for instance, cover up your mistakes by blaming them on outside forces: "You didn't receive the research paper? I put it in the campus mail."

2. *To avoid tension or conflict.* Sometimes it seems worthwhile to tell a small lie to prevent a large conflict. You might, for example, say you're not upset at a friend's teasing in order to prevent the big deal that would result if you expressed your annoyance. It's often easier to explain your behaviour in dishonest terms than to make matters worse. You might explain your apparent irritation by saying, "I'm not mad at you; it's just been a tough day."

3. *To guide social interaction.* Sometimes we lie to make everyday relationships run smoothly. You might, for instance, pretend to be glad to see someone you actually dislike, or fake interest in a dinner companion's boring stories to make a social event pass quickly. Children who aren't skilled or interested in these social lies are often a source of embarrassment

HAS. LOOMIS DECIDED TO TELL HER HUSBAND HOW
SHE REALLY FELT.

for their parents: "But Mommy said you were a boring old cow."

4. *To expand or reduce relationships.* Some lies are designed to make the relationship grow: "You're going downtown? I'm headed that way. Can I give you a ride?" "I like science fiction, too. What have you read lately?" Lies that make the teller look good also fit into this category. You might try to impress a potential employer by calling yourself a management student when you've taken only a course or two in business. Sometimes we tell untruths to reduce interaction with others. Lies in this category often allow the teller to escape unpleasant situations: "I really have to go. I should be studying for a test tomorrow." In other cases people lie to end a relationship entirely: "You're really great, but I'm just not ready to settle down yet."

5. *To gain power.* Sometimes we tell lies to show we're in control of a situation. Turning down a last-minute request for a date by claiming you're busy can be one way to put yourself in a one-up position, saying in effect, "Don't expect me to sit around waiting for you to call." Lying to get confidential information–even for a good cause–also falls into the category of achieving power.

This five-part scheme isn't the only way to categorize lies. The taxonomy outlined in Table 8–2 is more complicated than the preceding five-part one and covers some types of lies that don't fit into the simpler scheme. Exaggerations, for example, are lies told to boost the effect of a story. In exaggerated tales the fish grow larger, hikes grow longer and more strenuous, and so on. The stories may be less truthful, but they become more interesting–at least to the teller.

Most people think white lies are told for the benefit of the recipient. In the study cited earlier, the majority of subjects claimed such lying was "the right thing to do." Other research paints a less flattering picture of who benefits most from lying. One study found that two out of every three lies are told for "selfish reasons."[67] A look at Table 8–2 seems to make this figure too conservative. Of the 322 lies recorded, 75.8 percent were for the benefit of the liar. Less than 22 percent were for the benefit of the person hearing the lie, while a mere 2.5 percent were intended to aid a third party.

Before we become totally cynical, however, the researchers urge a charitable interpretation. After all, most intentional communication behaviour–truthful or not–is designed to help the speaker achieve a goal. Therefore, it's unfair to judge white lies more harshly than other types of messages. If we define selfishness as the extent to which some desired resource or interaction is denied to the person hearing the lie or to a third party, then only 111 lies (34.5 percent) can be considered truly selfish. This figure may be no worse than the degree of selfishness in honest messages.

EFFECTS OF LIES What are the consequences of learning that you've been lied to? In an interpersonal relationship, the discovery can be traumatic. As we grow closer to others, our expectations about their

I want the man in my life to love me enough to lie to me a little–or at least to be selective about the truth he tells me. As Emerson said, "God offers to every mind its choice between truth and repose." When it comes to love, I'll take repose.

Joan Sutton,
Lovers and Others

TABLE 8–2	TYPES OF WHITE LIES AND THEIR FREQUENCY		
	BENEFIT SELF	**BENEFIT OTHER**	**BENEFIT THIRD PARTY**
Basic Needs	**68**	1	1
A. Acquire resources	29	0	0
B. Protect resources	39	1	1
Affiliation	**128**	1	6
A. Positive	65	0	0
1. Initiate interaction	8	0	0
2. Continue interaction	6	0	0
3. Avoid conflict	48	0	0
4. Obligatory acceptance	3	0	0
B. Negative	43	1	3
1. Avoid interaction	34	1	3
2. Leave-taking	9	0	0
C. Conversational control	20	0	3
1. Redirect conversation	3	0	0
2. Avoid self-disclosure	17	0	3
Self-Esteem	**35**	63	1
A. Competence	8	26	0
B. Taste	0	18	1
C. Social desirability	27	19	0
Other	**13**	5	0
A. Dissonance reduction	3	5	0
B. Practical joke	2	0	0
C. Exaggeration	8	0	0

From C. Camden, M.T. Motley, and W. Wilson, "White Lies in Interpersonal Communication: A Taxonomy and Preliminary Investigation of Social Motivations," *Western Journal of Speech Communication* 48 (1984): 315.

honesty grow stronger. After all, discovering that you've been deceived requires you to redefine not only the lie you just uncovered, but also many of the messages you previously took for granted. Was last week's compliment really sincere? Was your joke really funny, or was the other person's laughter a put-on? Does the other person care about you as much as he or she claimed?

Research has shown that deception does, in fact, threaten relationships.[68] Not all lies are equally devastating, however. Feelings like dismay and betrayal are greatest when the relationship is most intense, the importance of the subject is high, and when there was previous suspicion that the other person wasn't being completely honest. Of these three factors, the importance of the information lied about proved to be the key factor in provoking a relational crisis.

An occasional white lie in an otherwise honest relationship doesn't pose much threat. Major deception, though—especially when it is part of a pattern of deceit—is likely to provoke a relational crisis. In fact, the discovery of major deception can lead to the end of the relationship.

The lesson here is clear: Lying about major parts of your relationship can have the most grave consequences. If preserving a relationship is important, honesty—at least about important matters—really does appear to be the best policy.

Equivocating

Lying isn't the only alternative to self-disclosure. When faced with the choice between lying and telling an unpleasant truth, communicators can—and often do—equivocate. As Chapter 5 explained, **equivocal language** has two or more equally plausible meanings. Sometimes people send equivocal messages without meaning to, resulting in confusion. "I'll meet you at the apartment" could refer to more than one place. But other times we are deliberately vague. For instance, when a friend asks what you think of an awful outfit, you could say, "It's really unusual—one of a kind!" Likewise, if you are too angry to accept a friend's apology but don't want to appear petty, you might say, "Don't mention it."

The value of equivocation becomes clear when you consider the alternatives. Consider the dilemma of what to say when you've been given an unwanted present—that ugly painting we mentioned earlier, for example—and the giver asks what you think of it. How can you respond? On one hand, you need to choose between telling the truth and lying. On the other, you have a choice of whether to make your response clear or vague. Figure 8–13 displays these choices. After considering the alternatives, it's clear that the first option—an equivocal, true response—is far preferable to the other choices in several respects. First, it spares the receiver from embarrassment. For example, rather than flatly saying, "No" to an unappealing invitation, it may be kinder to say, "I have other plans"—even if those plans are to stay home and watch TV.

Besides saving face for the recipient, honest equivocation can be less stressful for the sender than either telling the truth bluntly or lying. Because equivocation is often easier to take than the cold, hard truth, it spares the teller from feeling guilty. It's less taxing on the conscience to say, "I've never tasted anything like this" than to say, "This meal tastes terrible," even though the latter comment is more precise. Few people *want* to lie, and equivocation provides an alternative to deceit.

A study by communication researcher Sandra Metts and her colleagues shows how equivocation can save face in difficult situations.[69] Several hundred college students were asked how they would turn down unwanted sexual overtures from a person whose feelings were important to them: either a close friend, a prospective date, or a

I am in that state of mind where even a lie is a comfort, providing it is a cheerful lie.

Lucy Maud Montgomery,
Rilla of Ingleside

IS MISLEADING YOUR SPOUSE FRAUD OR TACT?

When their marriage of more than a decade ended in divorce, Ronald Askew sued his ex-wife for fraud because she admittedly concealed the fact that she had never felt sexually attracted to him. A jury agreed and ordered Bonnette Askew to pay her ex-husband $242,000 in damages.

"I'm astonished by this verdict, and I've looked at divorce in 62 societies," said Helen Fisher, an American Museum of Natural History anthropologist who authored the recent book *Anatomy of Love: The Natural History of Monogamy, Adultery and Divorce.*

Bonnette Askew, 45, acknowledged in court that she had never been sexually attracted to her husband. But she said she always loved him and noted that their marriage was not sexless and that they had two children together.

She first admitted her lack of sexual desire for him during a joint therapy session in 1991. "I guess he confused sex with love," Bonnette Askew said, adding that she concealed her lack of desire because she "didn't want to hurt his male ego."

But Ronald Askew, 50, said his lawsuit had more to do with honesty and integrity than sex. He felt deceived, especially because he said he repeatedly asked her before their marriage to be honest with him and reveal any important secrets.

If Ronald Askew believes total honesty is the foundation of good marriages, Fisher has a message for him: "Grow up."

"Since when is anyone truly honest with anyone?" Fisher said. "Did this man really want her to say: 'You're short, fat and you're terrible in bed'? Much of the world is amazed at what they see as bru-tal honesty. She was operating on an entirely different set of social values, which much of the world operates on—delicacy as opposed to brutal honesty."

Maria Cone

Equivocal

OPTION I: (Equivocal, True Message) "What an unusual painting! I've never seen anything like it!"	**OPTION II:** (Equivocal, False Message) "Thanks for the painting. I'll hang it as soon as I can find just the right place."
OPTION III: (Clear, True Message) "It's just not my kind of painting. I don't like the colours, the style, or the subject."	**OPTION IV:** (Clear, False Message) "What a beautiful painting! I love it."

True   False

Clear

FIGURE 8–13

Dimensions of Truthfulness and Equivocation

Adapted from J.B. Bavelas, A. Black, N. Chovil, and J. Mullet, *Equivocal Communication* (Newbury Park, CA: Sage, 1990), p. 178.

dating partner. The majority of students chose a diplomatic reaction ("I just don't think I'm ready for this right now") as being more face-saving and comfortable than a direct statement like "I just don't feel sexually attracted to you." The diplomatic reaction seemed sufficiently clear to get the message across, but not so blunt as to embarrass or even humiliate the other person. (Interestingly, men said they would be better able to handle a direct rejection more comfortably than women. The researchers suggest that one reason for the difference is that men stereotypically initiate sexual behaviours and thus are more likely to expect rejection.)

Besides preventing embarrassment, equivocal language can save the speaker from being caught lying. If a potential employer asks

about your grades during an interview, you would be safe saying, "I had a B average last semester," even though your overall grade average is closer to C. The statement isn't a complete answer, but it is honest as far as it goes. As one team of researchers put it, "Equivocation is neither a false message nor a clear truth, but rather an alternative used precisely when both of these are to be avoided."[70]

Given these advantages, it's not surprising that most people will usually choose to equivocate rather than tell a lie. In a series of experiments, subjects chose among telling a face-saving lie, telling the truth, and equivocating. Only 6 percent chose the lie, and between 3 and 4 percent chose the hurtful truth. By contrast, over 90 percent chose the equivocal response.[71]

Hinting

Hints are more direct than equivocal statements. Whereas an equivocal message isn't necessarily aimed at changing another's behaviour, a hint seeks to get a desired response from the other person. Some hints are designed to save the receiver from embarrassment:[72]

Direct statement

You're too overweight to be ordering dessert.

I'm too busy to continue with this conversation. I wish you would let me go.

Face-saving hint

These desserts are terribly overpriced.

I know you're busy; I'd better let you go.

Other hints are less concerned with protecting the receiver than with saving the sender from embarrassment:

Direct statement

Please don't smoke here because it is bothering me.

I'd like to invite you out for lunch, but I don't want to risk a "no" answer to my invitation.

Hint

I'm pretty sure that smoking isn't permitted here.

Gee, it's almost lunchtime. Have you ever eaten at that new Italian restaurant around the corner?

The face-saving value of hints explains why communicators are more likely to be indirect than fully disclosing when they deliver a potentially embarrassing message.[73] The success of a hint depends on the other person's ability to pick up the unexpressed message. Your subtle remarks might go right over the head of an insensitive receiver . . . or one who chooses not to respond. If this happens, you may decide to be more direct. On the other hand, if the costs of a straightforward message seem too high, you can withdraw without risk.

Ethical Challenge

Must We Always Tell the Truth?

"Is there really a Santa Claus?"

"Am I talking too much? . . ."

"Isn't this the cutest baby you've ever seen?"

"Was it good for you?"

Questions like these often seem to invite answers that are less than totally honest. The research summarized on pages 366–369 reveals that, at one time or another, virtually everyone avoids telling the complete truth. Sometimes we remain silent, sometimes we tell "white lies," and sometimes we equivocate. We seem to be caught between the time-honoured commandment "Thou shall not lie" and the fact that everybody *does* seem to bend the truth, if only for altruistic reasons. What, then, are the ethics of honesty?

Philosopher Immanuel Kant had a clear answer: We may be able to evade unpleasant situations by keeping quiet, but we must always tell the complete truth when there is no way to avoid speaking up. He said, "Truthfulness in statements which cannot be avoided is the formal duty of an individual . . . however great may be the disadvantage accruing to himself or another." Kant's unbending position didn't make any exception for lies or equivocations told in the best interests of the receiver. In his moral code, lying is wrong—period.

Kant's unbending moral stance grows from his *categorical imperative*: the dictum that the morality of an action is determined by whether it could be practised universally. At one level, the categorical imperative demands that we ask, "What if everybody lied?" Since it would be intolerable—even impossible—to function in a world in which everyone lied, we have an ethical obligation to refrain from being untruthful, even once.

Not all ethicists have shared Kant's rigid standards of truthtelling. Utilitarian philosophers claim that the way to determine the morality of a behaviour is by exploring whether it leads to the greatest happiness for the greatest number of people. Philosopher Sissela Bok adopts this stance when she argues that the morality (or immorality) of an untruth can be calcu-

lated only by comparing its effect to that of telling the unvarnished truth. She offers some circumstances in which deception may be justified: doing good, avoiding harm, and protecting a larger truth.

Despite her tolerance for some lies, Bok doesn't consider benign falsehoods to be just as acceptable as the truth. Her *principle of veracity* asserts that "truthful statements are preferable to lying in the absence of special considerations." In other words, she encourages truthtelling whenever possible. Of course, the phrase "whenever possible" is open to interpretation, and Bok is realistic enough to recognize that liars are prone to self-deceptive justifications. For this reason, she tempers her utilitarian position with a *test of publicity*. She suggests we ask how others would respond if they knew that we were being untruthful. If most disinterested observers with all the facts supported untruthful speech as the best course, then it passes the test of publicity.

Submit your case for avoiding the truth to a "court of self-disclosure":

1. *Recall recent situations in which you have used each of the following evasive approaches: lying, equivocating, and hinting.*
2. *Write an anonymous written description of each situation, including a justification for your behaviour, on a separate sheet of paper. Submit the cases to a panel of "judges" (most likely fellow students), who will evaluate the morality of these decisions.*

Read Kant's own words on truthtelling in the following works: "On a Supposed Right to Lie from Altruistic Motives," in *Critique of Practical Reason* and *Other Writings in Moral Philosophy*, Lewis White Beck, trans. and ed. (Chicago: University of Chicago Press, 1964); and *Groundwork of the Metaphysic of Morals*, H.J. Paton, trans. (New York: Harper Torchbooks, 1964). Bok's arguments are detailed in her book *Lying: Moral Choice in Public and Private Life* (New York: Vintage, 1979). See also Charles Fried's essay "The Evil of Lying" in *Right and Wrong* (Cambridge, MA: Harvard University Press, 1978).

The Ethics of Evasion

It's easy to see why people choose hints, equivocations, and white lies instead of complete self-disclosure. These strategies provide a way to manage difficult situations that is easier than the alternatives for both the speaker and the receiver of the message. In this sense, successful liars, equivocators, and hinters can be said to possess a certain kind of communicative competence. On the other hand, there are certainly times when honesty is the right approach, even if it's painful. At times like these, evaders could be viewed as lacking the competence or the integrity to handle a situation most effectively.

Are hints, benign lies, and equivocations ethical alternatives to self-disclosure? Some of the examples in these pages suggest the answer is a qualified "yes." Many social scientists and philosophers agree. As the Ethical Challenge on page 373 shows, some argue that the morality of a speaker's *motives* for lying ought to be judged, not the deceptive act itself, and others ask whether the *effects* of a lie will be worth the deception. Perhaps the right questions to ask, then, are whether an indirect message is truly in the interests of the receiver and whether this sort of evasion is the only effective way to behave.

SUMMARY

People form interpersonal relationships for a variety of reasons. Some involve the degree of interpersonal attraction communicators feel for one another. Attraction can come from perceived similarity, complementary personality features, reciprocal interest, perceived competence, disclosure of personal information, and proximity. People also form relationships to satisfy their need for intimacy, which they can achieve through physical means, intellectual and emotional exchanges, and shared activities. Intimacy is not essential to all relationships, and even in relationships where it is important, it is not important all the time. Gender and culture exert a strong influence on both the amount of intimacy in a relationship and how that intimacy is communicated. People also form relationships to achieve various types of rewards. Social exchange theory presents a method for explaining when people will choose to form and remain in relationships by showing how they compare their present situation with other alternatives.

Two models offer somewhat different perspectives on how communication operates in the development and maintenance of interpersonal relationships. A stage-related model characterizes communication as exhibiting different characteristics as people come together and draw apart. Dialectical models characterize communicators in every stage as being driven by the need to manage a variety of mutually incompatible needs. Both models share a variety of characteristics, which were described in this chapter.

An important question in interpersonal relationships is the appropriate type and degree of self-disclosure: honest, revealing messages about the self that are intentionally directed toward others. Disclosing communication contains information that is generally unavailable from other sources. Revealing personal information does not guarantee that this communication will be perceived by others as disclosing. A number of factors govern whether a communicator will be judged as being a high- or low-level discloser. The social penetration model describes two dimensions of self-disclosure: breadth and depth. Disclosure of feelings is usually more revealing than disclosure of opinions, and disclosure of opinions is usually more revealing than disclosure of facts. Clichés are the least revealing.

The Johari Window model is a useful way to illustrate self-disclosure. A window representing a single person can illustrate the amount of information that individual reveals to others, hides from others, is blind to, and is unaware of. Windows representing two communicators reveal how differing levels of disclosure can affect the level of intimacy in a relationship.

Communicators disclose personal information for a variety of reasons: catharsis, self-clarification, self-validation, reciprocal obligations, impression formation, relationship maintenance and enhancement, social control, and manipulation.

The percentage of messages that are self-disclosing is relatively low. Three alternatives to revealing personal facts, feelings, and opinions are lying, equivocating, and hinting. Unmalicious "white lies" serve a variety of functions: saving face for the sender or receiver, avoiding tension or conflict, guiding social interaction, managing relationships, and gaining power. When discovered by the recipient, lies have the potential to provoke a relational crisis, especially if the content of the information lied about is significant. Equivocal messages are an attractive alternative to lying and direct honesty. They allow a communicator to be honest without being blunt and causing undesirable reaction. Hints, more direct than equivocal statements, are used primarily to avoid embarrassment. Hints are risky in that they depend on the other person's ability to pick up unexpressed messages. Lies, equivocations, and hints may be ethical alternatives to self-disclosure; however, whether they are ethical depends on the speaker's motives and the effects of the deception.

KEY TERMS

avoiding
bonding
breadth
circumscribing
clichés
comparison level
comparison level of
  alternatives
connection–autonomy
  dialectic
depth

dialectical tension
differentiating
equivocal language
experimenting
initiating
integrating
intensifying
intimacy
Johari Window
openness–privacy dialectic
predictability–novelty dialectic

relational maintenance
self-disclosure
social exchange theory
social penetration
stagnating
terminating
uncertainty reduction
"white lie"

Chapter 9

Improving Communication Climates

Personal relationships are a lot like the weather. Some are fair and warm, while others are stormy and cold; some are polluted, and others healthy. Some relationships have stable climates, while others change dramatically–calm one moment and turbulent the next. You can't measure the interpersonal climate by looking at a thermometer or glancing at the sky, but it's there nonetheless. Every relationship has a feeling, a pervasive mood that colours the interactions of the participants.

Although we can't change the external weather, we *can* act in ways that improve an interpersonal climate. This chapter will explain the forces that make some relationships happy and comfortable and others unpleasant. You will learn what kinds of behaviour contribute to defensiveness and hostility and what kinds lead to more-positive feelings. After reading these pages you will have a better idea of the climate in each of your important relationships . . . and even more significant, how to improve it.

COMMUNICATION CLIMATE: THE KEY TO POSITIVE RELATIONSHIPS

The term **communication climate** refers to the emotional tone of a relationship. A climate doesn't involve specific activities as much as the way people feel about each other as they carry out those activities. Consider two interpersonal communication classes, for example. Both meet for the same length of time and follow the same syllabus. It's easy to imagine how one of these classes might be a friendly, comfortable place to learn, whereas the other could be cold and tense–even hostile. The same principle holds in other contexts. The role of climate in families and friendships is obvious. So is the impact of climate in the workplace. Have you ever held a job where backbiting, criticism, and suspicion were the norm? Or have you been lucky enough to work where the atmosphere was positive, encouraging, and supportive? If you've experienced both, you know what a difference climate makes. Research has demonstrated that employees have a higher level of commitment at jobs in which they experience a positive communication climate.[1] Studies also show that performance and job satisfaction increase when the communication climate is positive.[2] Whether it's the workplace, the classroom, or the home, people look for and stay in communication climates that affirm and support them.

Like their meteorological counterparts, communication climates are shared by everyone involved. It's rare to find one person describing a relationship as open and positive while another characterizes it as cold and hostile. Also, just like the weather, communication climates can change over time. A relationship can be overcast at one

First we'd climb a tree
and maybe then we'd talk
or sit silently
and listen to our thoughts
with illusions of someday
casting a golden light
no dress rehearsal,
this is our life

The Tragically Hip

time and sunny at another. Carrying the analogy to its conclusion, we need to acknowledge that communication climate forecasting is not a perfect science. Unlike the weather, however, people can influence the communication climates in their relationships. In this chapter we will explore ways to make your communication climates as satisfying as possible. We will begin by describing how communication climates develop. Next, we will explain how and why communicators respond defensively in certain climates. Finally—and most important—we will discuss what can be done to create positive climates and transform negative ones.

Confirming and Disconfirming Communication

What makes a communication climate positive or negative? In large part, the answer is surprisingly simple. The tone of a relationship is shaped by the degree to which the people believe themselves to be valued by one another. Social scientists use the term **confirming communication** to describe messages that convey valuing, and **disconfirming communication** to define those that show a lack of regard. It's obvious that confirming messages are more desirable than disconfirming ones. But what characteristics distinguish them? Actually, it's an oversimplification to talk about one type of confirming message. In truth, confirming communication occurs on three increasingly positive levels.[3]

- *Recognition* The most fundamental act of confirmation is to recognize the other person. Recognition seems easy and obvious, and yet many times we do not respond to others on this basic level. Failure to write or visit a friend is a common example. So is failure to return a phone message. Avoiding eye contact and not approaching someone you know on campus, at a party, or on the street send a negative message. Of course, this lack of recognition may simply be an oversight. You might not notice your friend, or the pressures of work and school might prevent you from staying in touch. Nonetheless, if the other person *perceives* you as avoiding contact, the message has the effect of being disconfirming.

- *Acknowledgement* Acknowledging the ideas and feelings of others is a stronger form of confirmation. Listening is probably the most common form of acknowledgement. Of course, counterfeit listening–ambushing, stage-hogging, pseudolistening, and so on–have the opposite effect of acknowledgement. More-active acknowledgement includes asking questions, paraphrasing, and reflecting. Not surprisingly, employees rate highly managers who solicit their opinions–even when the managers don't accept every suggestion.[4] As you read in Chapter 7, reflecting the speaker's thoughts and feelings can be a powerful way to offer support when others have problems.

- *Endorsement* Whereas acknowledging means you are interested in another's ideas, endorsement means that you agree with them. It's easy to see why endorsement is the strongest type of confirming message, since it communicates the highest form of valuing. The most obvious form of endorsement is agreeing. Fortunately, it isn't necessary to agree completely with another person in order to endorse her or his message. You can probably find something in the message that you endorse. "I can see why you were so angry," you might reply to a friend, even if you don't approve of his outburst. Of course, outright praise is a strong form of endorsement, and one you can use surprisingly often once you look for opportunities to compliment others. Nonverbal endorsement can also enhance the quality of a relational climate. For example, women rate men who agree with them as more physically attractive than those who fail to do so.[5]

In contrast to confirming messages, disconfirming communication shows a lack of regard for the other person, either by disputing or ignoring some important part of that person's message.[6] Disagreement can be one way to disconfirm others, but not all disagreements are disconfirming–especially when compared with a total lack of acknowledgement. Most experts agree that it is psychologically healthier to have someone disagree with you than ignore you.[7] At its worst, a brutal disagreeing message can so devastate another person that the benefits of recognition and acknowledgement are lost. But in more-constructive forms, disagreement includes two confirming components: recognition and acknowledgement. Communication researchers have demonstrated that constructive disagreements can lead to such benefits as enhanced self-concept,[8] communicative competence,[9] and positive climate in the workplace.[10] The key to maintaining a positive climate while arguing is the way you present your ideas. It is crucial to attack issues, not people. In addition, a sound argument is better received when it's delivered in a supportive, affirming manner.[11] The types of supportive messages outlined on page 380 in this chapter show how it is possible to argue in a respectful, constructive way.

Being ignored can be more disconfirming than being dismissed or attacked. The list of disconfirming responses on pages 382–383 shows how impervious, interrupting, irrelevant, tangential, impersonal, ambiguous, and incongruous responses can show lack of respect for a communicator's importance.

It's important to note that disconfirming messages, like virtually every other kind of communication, are a matter of perception. Communicators are likely to downplay the significance of a potentially hurtful message that they consider to be unintentional.[12] On the other hand, even messages that aren't intended to devalue the other person can be interpreted as disconfirming. Your failure to return a phone call or respond to the letter of an out-of-town friend might simply be the result of a busy schedule; but if the other person views the lack of contact as a sign that you don't value the relationship, the effect can be powerful.

How Communication Climates Develop

As soon as two people start to communicate, a relational climate begins to develop. If the messages are confirming, the climate is likely to be a positive one. If they disconfirm one another, the relationship is likely to be hostile, cold, or defensive.

Communication Transcript

Disconfirming Messages

Disconfirming messages convey a lack of respect or appreciation. Like their confirming counterparts, these messages can shape the climate of an entire relationship.

Verbal Abuse The most obvious type of disconfirming response is **verbal abuse:** communication that appears to be meant to cause psychological pain to another person. Where verbal abuse exists in a relationship, it is seldom an isolated event. Some abuse is overt, but at other times it can be disguised in malicious humour or sarcasm:

"Come here, fatty."

"You're such a bitch!"

Complaining Simple **complaining** may be less intense than verbal abuse, but it can still send a powerful disconfirming message. Complaints may be about specific behav-

iour. More-abstract complaints can be especially disconfirming, because they suggest that the flaw extends beyond one incident:

"I wish you would be more friendly."

"Why can't you clean up after yourself?"

"You need to have a more positive attitude."

Impervious Responses Ignoring the other person's attempt to communicate characterizes an **impervious response.** Refusing to answer another person in a face-to-face conversation is the most obvious kind of impervious response, though not the most common.

Failing to return a phone call or write back in answer to a letter are more common impervious responses. So is not responding to a smile or a wave.

Interrupting Beginning to speak before the other person has finished can show a lack of concern about what the other person has to say. The occasional **interrupting response** is not likely to be taken as a disconfirmation, but repeatedly cutting in on a speaker can be both discouraging and irritating.

Irrelevant Responses A comment unrelated to what the other person has just said is an **irrelevant response.**

A   What a day! I thought it would never end. First the car

Verbal messages certainly contribute to the tone of a relationship, but many climate-shaping messages are nonverbal. The very act of approaching others is confirming, whereas avoiding them can be disconfirming. Smiles or frowns, the presence or absence of eye contact, tone of voice, the use of personal space . . . all these and other cues send messages about how the parties feel toward one another.

Once a climate is formed, it can take on a life of its own and grow in a self-perpetuating **spiral:** a reciprocating communication pattern in which each person's message reinforces the other's.[13] In positive spirals, one partner's confirming message leads to a similar response from the other person. This positive reaction leads the first person to be even more reinforcing. Negative spirals are just as powerful, though they leave the partners feeling worse about themselves and each other. Research shows how spirals operate in relationships to reinforce the principle that "what goes around comes around." In one study of married couples, each spouse's response in conflict situations

Communication Transcript *continued*

overheated and I had to call a tow truck, and then the computer broke down at work.

B Listen, we have to talk about a present for Ann's birthday. The party is on Saturday, and I only have tomorrow to shop for it.

A I'm really beat. Could we talk about it in a few minutes? I've never seen a day like this one.

B I just can't figure out what would suit Ann. She's got everything . . .

Tangential Responses

Conversational "take-aways" are called **tangential responses.** Instead of ignoring the speaker's remarks completely, the other party uses them as a starting point for a shift to a different topic.

A I'd like to know for sure whether you want to go skiing during vacation. If we don't decide whether to go soon, it'll be impossible to get reservations anywhere.

B Yeah. And if I don't pass my botany class, I won't be in the mood to go anywhere. Could you give me some help with this homework? . . .

Impersonal Responses

Impersonal responses are loaded with clichés and other statements that never truly respond to the speaker.

A I've been having some personal problems lately, and I'd like to take off work early a couple of afternoons to clear them up.

B Ah, yes. We all have personal problems. It seems to be a sign of the times.

Ambiguous Responses

Ambiguous responses contain messages with more than one meaning, leaving the other party unsure of the responder's position.

A I'd like to get together with you soon. How about Tuesday?

B Uh, maybe so.

A Well, how about it? Can we talk Tuesday?

B Oh, probably. See you later.

Incongruous Responses

An **incongruous response** contains two messages that seem to deny or contradict each other. Often at least one of these messages is nonverbal.

A Darling, I love you.

B I love you, too. *(giggles)*

was similar to the other's statement.[14] Conciliatory statements (for example, offering support, accepting responsibilities, agreeing) were likely to be followed by conciliatory responses. Confrontive acts (such as criticism, hostile questions, and faultfinding) were likely to trigger an aggressive response. The same pattern held for other kinds of messages: Avoidance begat avoidance, analysis evoked analysis, and so on. Table 9–1 illustrates some reciprocal communication patterns that have the potential to create positive and negative spirals.

Escalatory conflict spirals are the most visible way that disconfirming messages reinforce one another.[15] One attack leads to another until a skirmish escalates into a full-fledged battle:

A: *(mildly irritated)* Where were you? I thought we agreed to meet here a half-hour ago.

B: *(defensively)* I'm sorry. I got hung up at the library. I don't have as much free time as you do, you know.

TABLE 9–1	POSITIVE AND NEGATIVE RECIPROCAL COMMUNICATION PATTERNS

NEGATIVE RECIPROCAL PATTERNS

PATTERN	EXAMPLE
Complaint-countercomplaint	A: I wish you weren't so self-centred. B: Well, I wish you weren't so critical.
Disagreement-disagreement	A: Why are you so hard on Marta? She's a great boss. B: Are you kidding? She's the biggest phony I've ever seen. A: You wouldn't know a good boss if you saw one. B: Neither would you.
Mutual indifference	A: I don't care if you want to stay: I'm exhausted, and I'm getting out of here. B: Go ahead if you want, but find your own way home.
Arguments involving metacommunication	A: How can I talk when you won't listen? B: How can I listen when you won't talk?

POSITIVE RECIPROCAL PATTERNS

PATTERN	EXAMPLE
Validation of other's perspective	A: This assignment is really confusing. Nobody can figure out what we're supposed to do. B: I can understand why you would be confused. Let me explain . . .
Recognizing similarities	A: I can't believe you want to take an expensive vacation! We should be saving money, not spending more! B: I agree we should be saving. But I think we can take this trip and still save some money. Let me show you what I've figured out . . .
Supportiveness	A: I'm going crazy with this job. It was supposed to be temporary. I have to do something different, and soon. B: I can see how much you hate it. Let's figure out how we can get the project finished soon, so you can get back to your regular work.

Adapted from W.R. Cupach and D.J. Canary, *Competence in Interpersonal Conflict* (New York: McGraw-Hill, 1997), pp. 51–52.

A: I wasn't *blaming* you, so don't get so touchy. I do resent what you just said, though. I'm plenty busy. And I've got lots of better things to do than wait around for you!

B: Who's getting touchy? I just made a simple comment. You've sure been defensive lately. What's the matter with you?

Although they are less obvious, **de-escalatory conflict spirals** can also be destructive.[16] Rather than fighting, the parties slowly lessen their dependence on one another, withdraw, and become less invested in the relationship.

Spirals–whether positive or negative–rarely go on indefinitely. Most relationships pass through cycles of progression and regression. If the spiral is negative, partners may find the exchange growing so unpleasant that they switch from negative to positive messages without discussing the matter. In other cases they may engage in metacommunication. "Hold on," one might say. "This is getting us nowhere." In some cases, however, partners pass the "point of no return," leading to the breakup of a relationship. Positive spirals also have their limit: Even the best relationships go through periods of conflict and withdrawal, although a combination of time and communication skills can eventually bring the partners back into greater harmony.

The worst sin towards our fellow creatures is not to hate them, but to be indifferent to them; that's the essence of inhumanity.

George Bernard Shaw

INVITATION TO INSIGHT

EVALUATING COMMUNICATION CLIMATES

You can probably recognize the communication climate in each of your relationships without much analysis. But responding to the following statements will help explain why these climates exist. Following these steps may also suggest how to improve negative climates.

1. Identify the communication climate of an important interpersonal relationship. Using weather metaphors (sunny, gloomy, calm) may help.

2. List the confirming or disconfirming communication that created and now maintains this climate. Be sure to identify both verbal and nonverbal messages.

3. Describe what you can do either to maintain the existing climate (if positive) or to change it (if negative). Again, list both verbal and nonverbal behaviours.

DEFENSIVENESS: CAUSES AND REMEDIES

Probably no type of communication pollutes an interpersonal climate more often than defensive spirals. One verbal attack leads to another, and soon the dispute mushrooms out of control, leaving an aftermath of hurt and bitterness that is difficult–sometimes even impossible–to repair.

The word **defensiveness** suggests protecting oneself from attack, but what kind of attack? Surely, few if any of the times you become

Long ago I learned this proverb: If you do something important, there will always be critics. If you don't like critics, don't do anything important.

Marjorie Montgomery Bowker, *On Guard for Thee: An Independent Analysis, Based on the Actual Text of the Canada–U.S. Free Trade Agreement*

defensive involve a physical threat. If you're not threatened by bodily injury, what *are* you guarding against? To answer this question we need to talk more about the notions of the presenting self and face introduced in Chapter 2.

Recall that a person's face consists of the physical traits, personality characteristics, attitudes, aptitudes, and all the other parts of the image he or she wants to present to the world. Actually, it is a mistake to talk about a single face: We try to project different selves to different people. You might, for instance, try to impress a potential employer with your seriousness but want your friends to see you as a joker. Of course, not all parts of your presenting self are equally significant. Letting others know that you are right-handed or a Gemini is probably less important to you than convincing them you are good-looking or loyal.

When others are willing to accept and acknowledge important parts of our presenting image, there is no need to feel defensive. On the other hand, when others confront us with **face-threatening acts**—messages that seem to challenge the image we want to project—we are likely to resist their messages. Defensiveness, then, is the process of protecting our presenting self, our face.

You can understand how defensiveness operates by imagining what might happen if an important part of your presenting self were attacked. Suppose, for instance, that your boss criticized you for making a stupid mistake. Or consider how you would feel if a friend called you self-centred or your boss labelled you as lazy. You would probably feel threatened if these attacks were untrue. But notice that you might very well react defensively even if you knew deep inside that the criticism was justified. For instance, you have probably responded defensively at times when you *did* make a mistake, act selfishly, or cut corners on your work. In fact, we often feel most defensive when criticism is right on target.[17]

One reason for such defensiveness has to do with our need for approval. In response to the question "Why am I afraid to tell you who I am?" author John Powell quotes one actual response: "Because if I tell you who I am, you may not like who I am, and that is all I have."[18] So one reason we wear defensive masks is to appear to be the kind of person who will gain the approval of others.

Responding defensively to unpleasant but accurate criticism involves fooling not only others but also ourselves. We want to believe the act we're putting on, because it's uncomfortable to admit that we are not the person we would like to be. When faced with a situation where the truth might hurt, we are tempted to convince ourselves that we do fit the idealized picture we have constructed.

A Theory of Cognitive Dissonance

http://www.caic.org.au/general/ cogdiss2.htm

Types of Defensive Reactions

When a part of your presenting self is attacked by others and you aren't willing to accept their judgement, you are faced with what psychologists call **cognitive dissonance**—an inconsistency between two conflicting pieces of information, attitudes, or behaviour.[19] Dissonance is an uncomfortable condition, and communicators strive to resolve it by seeking consistency. One way to eliminate the dissonance, of course, is to accept the critic's judgement and revise your presenting self accordingly. You could agree that you were stupid or

mistaken, for example. Sometimes, however, you aren't willing to accept attacks. The accusations of your critic may be false. And even if they are true, you may be unwilling to admit their accuracy. It isn't pleasant to admit that you were lazy, unfair, or foolish. There are three broad ways to resolve dissonance without agreeing with a critic. Each of them is characterized by **defence mechanisms:** psychological devices that resolve dissonance by maintaining a positive presenting image.

ATTACKING THE CRITIC   Counterattacking follows the old maxim that the best defence is a good offence. Attacking defensive manoeuvres can take several forms.

- *Verbal aggression* Sometimes the recipient uses **verbal aggression** to assault the critic directly. "Where do you get off calling me sloppy?" you might storm to a roommate. "You're the one who leaves globs of toothpaste in the sink and dirty clothes all over the bedroom!" This sort of response shifts the blame onto the critic, without acknowledging that the original judgement might be true. Other attacks on the critic are completely off the subject: "You're in no position to complain about my sloppiness. At least I pay my share of the rent on time." Again, this response resolves the dissonance without ever addressing the validity of the criticism.

- *Sarcasm* Disguising the attack in the barbed, humorous message in **sarcasm** is a less direct form of aggression. "You think I ought to study more? Thanks for taking a break from watching soap operas and eating junk food to run my life." Sarcastic responses might score high on wit and quick thinking, but their hostile, disconfirming nature usually leads to a counterattack and a mutually destructive defensive spiral.

Explaining Defensive Reactions

http://fox.klte.hu/~keresofi/
psychotherapy/a-to-z-entries/
defensive_reactions_d.html

DISTORTING CRITICAL INFORMATION   A second way of defending a perceived self under attack is to somehow distort the information in a manner that leaves the presenting self intact—at least in the eyes of the defender. There are a number of ways to distort dissonant information.

- *Rationalization* **Rationalization** is the invention of logical but untrue explanations of behaviour that is unacceptable to the self. "I would help you out, but I really have to study," you might say as a convenient way to avoid an unpleasant chore. "I'm not overeating," you might protest to another critic who you secretly admit is on target. "I have a busy day ahead, and I need to keep my strength up." (See Table 9–2 for other examples.)

- *Compensation* Those using **compensation** emphasize a strength in one area to cover up a weakness in another. A guilty parent might keep up the façade of being conscientious by protesting, "I may not be around much, but I give those kids the best things

TABLE 9–2	RATIONALIZATION READER FOR STUDENTS	
SITUATION	**WHAT IS SAID**	
When the course is offered in lecture format:	We never get a chance to say anything.	
When the course is offered in discussion format:	The professor just sits there. We're not paid to teach the course.	
When all aspects of the course are covered in class:	All she does is follow the text.	
When you're responsible for covering part of the course outside class:	She never covers half the things we're tested on.	
When you're given objective tests:	They don't allow for any individuality.	
When you're given essay tests:	They're too vague. We never know what's expected.	
When the instructor gives no tests:	It isn't fair! She can't tell how much we really know.	

money can buy!" Likewise, you might try to convince yourself and others that you are a good friend by compensating: "Sorry I forgot your birthday. Let me give you a hand with that job." There's nothing wrong with most acts of compensation in themselves. The harm comes when they are used not sincerely but to maintain a fictitious presenting image.

- *Regression* Another way to avoid facing attack is to play helpless, claiming you *can't* do something when in truth you *don't want* to do it. "I'd like to have a relationship with you, but I just can't: I'm not ready." "I wish I could do the job better, but I just can't: I just don't understand it." The test for **regression** is to substitute the word *won't* for *can't.* In many cases it becomes clear that "It's not my fault" is a fiction.

AVOIDING DISSONANT INFORMATION   A third way to protect a threatened presenting image is to avoid information altogether. Avoidance can take several forms.

- *Physical avoidance* Steering clear of people who attack a presenting self is an obvious way to avoid dissonance. Sometimes **physical avoidance** may be wise. There's little profit in being battered by hostile or abusive criticism. In other cases, however, the

ANGEL

spend all your time waiting for that second
   chance,
for a break that would make it okay,
there's always one reason to not feel good
   enough and it's hard at the end of the
   day,
I need some distraction, oh beautiful
   release, memory seeps through my veins,
let me be empty and weightless and maybe
   I'll find some peace tonight,

in the arms of an angel, fly away from
   here, from this dark cold hotel room
   and the endlessness
that you fear,
you are pulled from the wreckage of your
   silent reverie you're in the arms of the
   angel,
may you find some comfort there.

so tired of the straight line and
   everywhere you turn,
there's vultures and thieves at your back
   and the storm keeps on twisting,
you keep on building the lie, that you
   make up for all that you lack,
it don't make no difference, escaping
   one last time,
it's easier to believe in this sweet
   madness,
oh this glorious sadness that brings me
   to my knees,

in the arms of an angel, fly away from
   here, from this dark cold hotel room
   and the endlessness
that you fear,
you are pulled from the wreckage of
   your silent reverie you're in the arms
   of the angel,
may you find some comfort there,
you're in the arms of an angel, may you
   find some comfort there

Sarah McLachlan

relationship may be important enough and the criticism valid enough that avoiding the situation makes matters only worse.

- *Repression* Sometimes we mentally block out dissonant information. You might, for instance, know that you ought to discuss a problem with a friend, boss, or instructor, yet you put the idea out of your mind whenever it arises. It's possible even to repress a problem in the face of a critic. Changing the subject, acting as if you don't understand, and even pretending you don't hear the criticism all fall into the category of **repression.**

- *Apathy* Another avoidance response, **apathy,** is to acknowledge unpleasant information but pretend you don't care about it. You might for instance, sit calmly through a friend's criticism and act as if it didn't bother you. Similarly, you might respond to the loss of a job by acting indifferent: "Who cares? It was a dumb job anyhow."

- *Displacement* **Displacement** occurs when we vent aggressive or hostile feelings against people or objects that are seen as less threatening than the person or persons who threatened us originally. You may be mad at your boss, but rather than risk getting fired, you could displace your aggression by yelling at the people you live with. Despite its obvious costs, displacement almost always lets us preserve (at least to ourselves) the image that we're *potent*–that we're in control and can't be pushed around by forces beyond our control. The very act of displacing proves this a lie, of course–but one the displacer fails to recognize.

INVITATION TO INSIGHT

DEFENCE MECHANISM INVENTORY

List the three defence mechanisms you use most often, and describe three recent examples of each. You can arrive at your list both by thinking about your own behaviour and by asking others to share their impressions of you.

Conclude your inventory by describing

1. the people with whom you become defensive most often.
2. the parts of your presenting self you frequently defend.
3. the usual consequences of using defence mechanisms.
4. any more satisfying ways you could act in the future.

Preventing Defensiveness in Others

By now you understand how easily communicators become defensive when their presenting image is threatened. You probably recognize that the best chances for creating a favourable response come with messages that honour the other person's face by supporting his or her presenting self.[20] These facts might leave you caught in an apparent bind, asking yourself how to send a face-honouring message when you have a genuine gripe with someone.

The solution to this dilemma lies in the two-dimensional nature of communication. On a content level you can express dissatisfaction with the other person, but on a relational level you can be saying—explicitly or nonverbally—that you value him or her. The possibility of handling potentially delicate issues in ways that improve your relationships may seem overwhelming, but the influential work of researcher Jack Gibb offers some useful tools for controlling defensiveness.[21] After observing groups for several years, Gibb was able to isolate six types of defence-arousing communication and six contrasting behaviours that seemed to reduce the level of threat and defensiveness by conveying face-honouring relational messages of respect. The **Gibb categories** are listed in Table 9–3 and summarized in the following pages.

Six Categories of Defensive Communication

http://www.comunityinc.com/ 05articles/0501_defensive.html

EVALUATION VS. DESCRIPTION The first type of defence-arousing behaviour Gibb noted was **evaluative communication.** Most people become irritated at judgemental statements, which they are likely to interpret as indicating a lack of regard. One form of evaluation is "you" language, described in Chapter 5.

Unlike evaluative "you" language, **descriptive communication** focusses on the *speaker's* thoughts and feelings instead of judging the other person. Descriptive messages often are expressed in "I" language, which tends to provoke less defensiveness than "you" statements.[22] Contrast the following evaluative "you" claims with their descriptive "I" counterparts:

TABLE 9–3	THE GIBB CATEGORIES OF DEFENSIVE AND SUPPORTIVE BEHAVIOURS	
DEFENSIVE BEHAVIOURS		**SUPPORTIVE BEHAVIOURS**
1. Evaluation		1. Description
2. Control		2. Problem Orientation
3. Strategy		3. Spontaneity
4. Neutrality		4. Empathy
5. Superiority		5. Equality
6. Certainty		6. Provisionalism

Evaluation: "You don't know what you're talking about!"

Description: "I don't understand how you came up with that idea."

Evaluation: "This place is a *#%+ mess!"

Description: "When you don't clean up, I have to either do it or live with your mess. That's why I'm mad!"

Evaluation: "Those jokes are sick and depraved!"

Description: "When you tell those off-colour jokes, I get really embarrassed."

Note how each of the descriptive statements focusses on the speaker's thoughts and feelings without judging the other person. Despite its value, descriptive language isn't the only element necessary for success. Its effectiveness depends in part on when, where, and how the statement is delivered. You can imagine how each of the preceding descriptive statements would go over if said in front of a room full of bystanders or in a whining tone of voice. Even the best timing and delivery of a descriptive message won't guarantee success. Some people will react defensively to anything you say or do. Nonetheless, it's easy to see that describing how the other person's behaviour affects you is likely to produce better results than judgementally attacking the individual.

CONTROL VS. PROBLEM ORIENTATION   A second defence-provoking message involves some attempt to control another. **Controlling communication** occurs when a sender seems to be imposing a solution on the receiver with little regard for the receiver's needs or interests. The object of control can involve almost anything: where to eat dinner, what TV program to watch, whether to remain in a relationship, or how to spend a large sum of money. Whatever the situation, people who act in controlling ways create a defensive climate. Researchers have found that the communication of abusive couples was characterized by opposition to one another's viewpoints.[23] None of us likes to feel that our ideas are worthless and that nothing we say will change other people's determination to have their way—yet this is precisely the attitude a controller communicates. Whether done with words, gestures, tone of voice, or through some other channel, whether control is accomplished through status, insistence on obscure or irrelevant rules, or physical power, the controller generates hostility wherever she or he goes. The unspoken message such behaviour communicates is "I know what's best for you, and if you do as I say, we'll get along."

In contrast, in **problem orientation** communicators focus on finding a solution that satisfies both their needs and those of the others involved. The goal here isn't to "win" at the expense of your partner but to work out some arrangement in which everybody feels like a winner. Chapter 10 has a great deal to say about "win–win" problem solving as a way to find problem-oriented solutions.

STRATEGY VS. SPONTANEITY Gibb uses the word **strategy** to character-ize defence-arousing messages in which speakers hide their ulterior motives. The terms *dishonesty* and *manipulation* capture the essence of strategy. Even if the intentions that motivate strategic communica-tion are honourable, the victim of deception who discovers an at-tempt to deceive is likely to feel offended at being played for a naive sucker.

Spontaneity is the behaviour that contrasts with strategy. Spon-taneity simply means expressing yourself honestly. Despite the mis-leading label Gibb chose for this kind of behaviour, spontaneous communication needn't be blurted out as soon as an idea comes to you. You might want to plan the wording of your message carefully so that you can express yourself clearly. The important thing is to be honest. Often spontaneity won't get what you want, but in the long run it's usually better to be candid and perhaps miss out on some small goal than to say all the right things and be a fraud. More than once we've heard people say, "I didn't like what he said, but at least I know he was being honest."

Although it sounds paradoxical at first, spontaneity can be a strat-egy, too. Sometimes you'll see peo-ple using honesty in a calculating way, being just frank enough to win someone's trust or sympathy. This "levelling" is probably the most defence-arousing strategy of all because once we've learned someone is using frankness as a manipulation, there's almost no chance we'll ever trust that person again.

You may be getting the idea that using supportive behaviours such as description, problem orienta-tion, empathy, and so on is a good way to manipulate others. Before going any further, we want to say loudly and clearly that if you ever act supportively without being sin-cere in what you're saying, you've misunderstood the idea behind this chapter, and you're running a risk of causing even more defen-siveness than before. None of the ideas we present in this book can go into a "bag of tricks" that can be used to control others: If you ever find yourself using them in this way, beware!

NEUTRALITY VS. EMPATHY   Gibb used the term **neutrality** to describe a fourth behaviour that arouses defensiveness. Probably a better descriptive word would be *indifference*. A neutral attitude is disconfirming because it communicates a lack of concern for the welfare of another and implies that the other person isn't very important to you. This perceived indifference is likely to promote defensiveness because people do not like to think of themselves as worthless, and they'll protect a self-concept that pictures themselves as worthwhile.

The poor effects of neutrality become apparent when you consider the hostility that most people have for the large, impersonal organizations with which they have to deal: "They think of me as a number instead of a person"; "I never get to speak to a person any more, only a computer." These two common statements reflect reactions to being handled in an indifferent way. Gibb has found that **empathy** helps rid communication of the quality of indifference. When people show that they care for the feelings of another, there's little chance that the person's self-concept will be threatened. Empathy means accepting another's feelings, putting yourself in another's place. This doesn't mean you need to agree with that person. By simply letting someone know about your care and respect, you'll be acting in a supportive way. Gibb noted the importance of nonverbal messages in communicating empathy. He found that facial and bodily expressions of concern are often more important to the receiver than the words used.

SUPERIORITY VS. EQUALITY   A fifth behaviour creating a defensive climate involves **superiority.** As Jake Harwood, Howard Giles, and their associates point out, any message that suggests "I'm better than you" is likely to arouse feelings of defensiveness in the recipients. A body of research confirms that patronizing messages irritate receivers ranging from young students to senior citizens, at least in Western cultures.[24] As humorist Dave Barry suggests in the reading on page 396, some superiority comes from the content of messages. In other cases, the *way* we deliver a message suggests a one-up approach. Consider, for example, how using simplified grammar and vocabulary, talking loudly and slowly, not listening, and varying speaking pitch convey a patronizing attitude.

Superior communication can trigger a variety of defensive responses, including "turning off" the speaker, arguing, or even walking away. Another response is a counterattack, which attempts to belittle the sender of the superior message. We'll go to great lengths "to cut them down to size." All these defensive reactions to projected superiority are destructive to an interpersonal climate.

There are plenty of occasions when we communicate with others who possess talents or knowledge greater than ours, but in these cases the other people needn't communicate an attitude of superiority. Gibb has found ample evidence that many who have superior skills and talents are capable of projecting feelings of **equality** rather than superiority. Such people convey that, although they may

How to Argue Effectively

I argue very well. Ask any of my remaining friends. I can win an argument on any topic, against any opponent. People know this and steer clear of me at parties. Often, as a sign of their great respect, they don't even invite me. You, too, can win arguments. Simply follow these rules:

Drink liquor.

Suppose you are at a party, and some hotshot intellectual is expounding on the economy of Peru, a subject you know nothing about. If you're drinking some health-fanatic drink like grapefruit juice, you'll hang back, afraid to display your ignorance, while the hotshot enthralls your date. But if you drink several large martinis, you'll discover you have *strong views* about the Peruvian economy. You'll be a *wealth* of information. You'll argue forcefully, offering searing insights and possibly upsetting furniture. People will be impressed. Some may leave the room.

Make things up.

Suppose, in the Peruvian economy argument, you are trying to prove that Peruvians are underpaid, a position you base solely on the fact that *you* are underpaid, and you'll be damned if you're going to let a bunch of Peruvians be better off. *Don't* say: "I think Peruvians are underpaid." Say instead: "The average Peruvian's salary in 1981 dollars adjusted for the revised tax base is $1,452.81 per annum, which is $836.07 below the mean gross poverty level."

NOTE: Always make up exact figures. If an opponent asks you where you got your information, make *that* up, too. Say: "This information comes from Dr. Hovel T. Moon's study for the Buford Com-

mission published on May 9, 1982. Didn't you read it?" Say this in the same tone of voice you would use to say, "You left your soiled underwear in my bathroom."

Use meaningless but weighty-sounding words and phrases.

Memorize this list:

Let me put it this way

In terms of

Vis-à-vis

Per se

As it were

Qua

So to speak

You should also memorize some Latin abbreviations such as "Q.E.D.," "e.g.," and "i.e." These are all short for "I speak Latin, and you don't." Here's how to use these words and phrases. Suppose you want to say, "Peruvians would like to order appetizers more often, but they don't have enough money." You never win arguments talking like that. But you *will* win if you say, "Let me put it this way. In terms of appetizers vis-à-vis Peruvians qua Peruvians, they would like to order them more often, so to speak, but they do not have enough money per se, as it were. Q.E.D." Only a fool would challenge that statement.

Use snappy and irrelevant comebacks.

You need an arsenal of all-purpose irrelevant phrases to fire back at your opponents when they make valid points. The best are:

You're begging the question.

You're being defensive.

"What do you mean 'Your guess is as good as mine'? My guess is a hell of a lot better than your guess!"

DRAWING BY ROSS. © 1983 *THE NEW YORKER MAGAZINE*, INC.

Don't compare apples to oranges.

What are your parameters?

This last one is especially valuable. Nobody has the vaguest idea what "parameters" means. Here's how to use your comebacks:

You say "As Abraham Lincoln said in 1873 . . ." Your opponent says: "Lincoln died in 1865. " You say: "You're begging the question."

You say "Liberians, like most Asians . . ." Your opponent says: "Liberia is in Africa." You say: "You're being defensive."

Compare your opponent to Adolf Hitler.

This is your heavy artillery, for when your opponent is obviously right and you are spectacularly wrong. Bring Hitler up subtly. Say, "That sounds suspiciously like something Adolf Hitler might say," or "You certainly do remind me of Adolf Hitler."

So that's it. You now know how to out-argue anybody. Do not try to pull any of this on people who generally carry weapons.

Dave Barry

have greater talent in certain areas, they see others as having just as much worth as human beings.

Equality is put to the test when a person *doesn't* have superior skills, yet is in a position of authority.[25] This condition often exists on the job, where supervisors may have less expertise in certain areas than their subordinates but believe it would be beneath them to admit it. You've probably been in situations where you knew more about the subject than the person in charge—a boss, teacher, parent, or salesperson—yet this person acted as if he or she knew more. Did you feel defensive? No doubt. Did that person feel defensive? No doubt as well. You both were challenging each other's presenting self, so the climate probably became hostile. A truly secure person can treat others with equality even when there are obvious differences in knowledge, talent, and status. Doing so creates a positive climate in which ideas are evaluated not on the basis of who contributed them, but rather on the merit of the ideas themselves.

CERTAINTY VS. PROVISIONALISM   Have you ever run into people who are positive they're right, who know that theirs is the only or proper way of doing something, who insist that they have all the facts and need no additional information? If you have, you've met individuals who project the defence-arousing behaviour Gibb calls **certainty.** Communicators who regard their own opinions with certainty while disregarding the ideas of others demonstrate a lack of regard for the thoughts others hold to be important. It's likely the receiver will take the certainty as a personal affront and react defensively.

In contrast to dogmatic communication is **provisionalism,** in which people may have strong opinions but are willing to acknowledge that they don't have a corner on the truth and will change their stand if another position seems more reasonable.

There is no guarantee that using Gibb's supportive, confirming approach to communication will build a positive climate. The other person may simply not be receptive. But the chances for a constructive relationship will be greatest when communication consists of the kind of constructive approach described here. Besides boosting the odds of getting a positive response from others, supportive communication can leave you feeling better in a variety of ways: more in control of your relationships, more comfortable, and more positive toward others.

Responding Nondefensively to Criticism

The world would be a happier place if everyone communicated supportively. But how can you respond nondefensively when others use evaluation, control, superiority, and all the other attacking behaviours Gibb identified? Despite your best intentions, it's difficult to be reasonable when you're faced with a torrent of criticism. Being attacked is hard enough when the critic is clearly being unfair, but it's often even more threatening when the judgements are correct.

The need to be right—the sign of a vulgar mind.

Albert Camus

True feeling is critical as well as honest thought.

John MacNaughton,
Essays

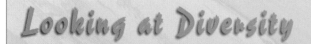

Looking at Diversity

Letters Home

Below is one of a series of letters written to Peter Gzowski by Canadian Jamie Zeppa about life in Bhutan with her Bhutanese husband, Tshewang. The following provides clues about the couple's communication climate.

Being married to Tshewang has been an interesting study in conflicting superstitions and beliefs. I won't walk under ladders, he won't cut his hair or fingernails after dark. I cross my fingers to avert bad luck, he won't travel on a Thursday or take chilies directly out of my hand. He claims, quite correctly, that at least his superstitions have explanations: Thursdays are unlucky for him, and handing chilies or any other "hot" food directly to another person will cause a fight. I've had to learn a whole new set of rules of etiquette: Do not sit with your legs crossed in front of a high official, do not point at religious objects, walk around all holy monuments and temples clockwise, always refuse whatever is offered once or twice, even if you really want to accept,

and always accept things with both hands. A few things I still haven't mastered, like the art of drinking from a communal bottle, Bhutanese style. To prevent the spread of germs, the Bhutanese tip their heads back, hold the bottle a few centimetres from their mouth, and pour the contents in without ever letting their lips touch the bottle. It's actually a very hygienic practice, and it doesn't look so very difficult. Unfortunately, my first attempt at this resulted in a soaked shirt and prolonged choking, and now I bring my own water bottle, or just go thirsty.

When we moved into this bungalow a few months ago, we arranged to borrow a truck, which was only available on Saturday. After we had moved all our furniture in, Tshewang announced that we

had to go back to the old house to sleep.

"Sleep on what?" I asked, incredulous. "The bed is here. The blankets are here. Everything is here."

"It doesn't matter," he explained. "It's extremely unlucky to move on a Saturday."

"But we've already moved," I said.

"Yes, but as long as we don't sleep here, we haven't technically moved," he replied.

"Is there anything else we can't do here today?" I asked grumpily.

It turned out that there was almost nothing we could do in the new house: We couldn't light a fire, take a bath, cook, or eat. We sat around shivering all day and then went to sleep at a neighbour's house.

Despite the accuracy of your critic, the tendency is either to counterattack aggressively with a barrage of verbal aggression or to withdraw nonassertively.

Because neither of these responses is likely to resolve a dispute, we need alternative ways of behaving. There are two such methods. Despite their apparent simplicity, they have proved to be among the most valuable skills many communicators have learned.[26] These are: seeking more information and agreeing with the critic.

SEEK MORE INFORMATION The response of seeking more information makes good sense when you realize that it's foolish to respond to a critical attack until you understand what the other person has said. Even comments that on first consideration appear to be totally unjustified or foolish often prove to contain at least a grain of truth and sometimes much more.

Our son was more than two years old when he had his first haircut. His very fine, curly hair had become knotted into dreadlocks, and I was anxious to cut it. No, no, my husband said, a lama must cut his hair for the first time.

"Does it *absolutely* have to be a lama?" I asked.

"A lama or a maternal uncle," he insisted. "Absolutely."

It would have to be a lama, then: Pema's maternal uncle was on the other side of the planet.

It had to be the right kind of lama, though, and an auspicious time, and a good place, and I soon lost track of the requirements and gave up. Meanwhile, Pema's hair grew longer and wilder, and to keep it out of his face, I tied it back in a ponytail. I thought he looked like a very cool two-year-old, but then someone told him that only girls wore ponytails and Pema refused to let me tie his hair back any more.

One Saturday morning, I told Tshewang that I was taking Pema to a temple—any temple—and asking a lama there—any lama—to cut Pema's hair. "But today might not be an auspicious day," Tshewang protested, and we began a huge argument, which was interrupted by a knock at the door. We opened the door, and there was a lama. Like many lamas, he had left his monastery to beg for alms, part of the spiritual discipline that cuts attachment to worldly comforts. Tshewang and I looked at each other. His unexpected arrival seemed pretty auspicious to us—it did cut short a whopping argument, after all—so we called Pema, who was playing outside.

The lama asked us to bring a bowl of clean water, a bowl of milk, and a pair of scissors. We sat a very nervous-looking Pema on a chair, and the lama then bent his head and prayed, a lovely, half-sung, half-chanted prayer, but a bit too long for Pema, who slid off the chair and tried to escape to his toys in the yard. We reseated him, and then the lama asked for a small leafy branch. I fetched one from a willow tree, and the lama dipped it into the bowls and splashed Pema first with water and then with milk, still praying. Pema giggled. The lama took the scissors, clipped a tiny lock from Pema's hair, and instructed us to burn it outside. We then gave the lama some tea and some money, he said his thanks and told us to take good care of Pema, and that was that.

After he had gone, I expressed surprise that the lama had only cut a tiny piece of hair. "They're lamas," Tshewang muttered, "not *barbers.*" And we took the scissors and trimmed the rest of Pema's hair ourselves.

From Jamie Zeppa, "Letters Home," in *The Morningside Years* by Peter Gzowski (Toronto: McClelland & Stewart, 1997), pp. 83–85.

Many readers object to the idea of asking for details when they are criticized. Their resistance grows from confusing the act *of listening open-mindedly* to a speaker's comments with *accepting* them. Once you realize that you can listen to, understand, and even acknowledge the most hostile comments without necessarily accepting them, it becomes much easier to hear another person out. If you disagree with a speaker's objections, you will be in a much better position to explain yourself once you understand the criticism. On the other hand, after carefully listening to the other's remarks, you might just see that they are valid, in which case you have learned some valuable information about yourself. In either case, you have everything to gain and nothing to lose by paying attention to the critic.

Of course, after one has spent years of instinctively resisting criticism, learning to listen to the other person will take some practice.

INVITATION TO INSIGHT

DEFENSIVENESS FEEDBACK

1. Approach an important person in your life, and request some help in learning more about yourself. Inform the other person that your discussion will probably take at least an hour, so make sure both of you are prepared to invest the necessary amount of time.

2. Begin by explaining all 12 of the Gibb behaviours to your partner. Be sure to give enough examples so that each category is clearly understood.

3. When your explanation is complete and you've answered all your partner's questions, ask him or her to tell you which of the Gibb categories you use. Seek specific examples so that you are certain to understand the feedback fully. (Since you are requesting an evaluation, be prepared for a little defensiveness on your own part at this point.) Inform your partner that you are interested in discovering both the defence-arousing and the supportive behaviours you use and that you are sincerely interested in receiving a candid answer. (Note: If you don't want to hear the truth from your partner, don't try this exercise.)

4. As your partner speaks, record the categories he or she lists in sufficient detail for both of you to be sure that you have understood the comments.

5. When you have finished your list, show it to your partner. Listen to that person's reactions, and make any corrections that are necessary to reflect an accurate understanding of the comments. When your list is accurate, have your partner sign it to indicate that you have understood it clearly.

6. In a concluding statement note
    a. how you felt as your partner was describing you.
    b. whether you agree with the evaluation.
    c. what effect your use of the various Gibb categories has on your relationship with your partner.

To make matters clearer, here are several ways in which you can seek additional information from your critics.

Ask for Specifics   Often the vague attack of a critic is virtually useless even if you sincerely want to change. Abstract accusations such as "You're being unfair" or "You never help out" can be difficult to understand. In such cases it is a good idea to request more-specific information from the sender. "What do I *do* that's unfair?" is an important question to ask before you can judge whether the accusation is correct. "When haven't I helped out?" you might ask before agreeing with or disputing the accusation.

If you already solicit specifics by using questions and are still accused of reacting defensively, the problem may be in the *way* you ask. Your tone of voice and facial expression, posture, or other non-

Assertive Communication

http://is.dal.ca/~hrd/Job_Skills/
Manager/Topics/Relationships/
Assertive_Communication/
assertive_communication.html

verbal clues can give the same words radically different connotations. For example, think of how you could use the words "Exactly what are you talking about?" to communicate either a genuine desire to know or your belief that the speaker is crazy. It's important to request specific information only when you genuinely want to learn more from the speaker, for asking under any other circumstances will make matters only worse.

Guess About Specifics   On some occasions even your sincere and well-phrased requests for specific details won't meet with success. Sometimes your critics won't be able to define precisely the behaviour they find offensive. In these instances, you'll hear such comments as "I can't tell you exactly what's wrong with your sense of humour–all I can say is that I don't like it." In other cases, your critics may know the exact behaviours they don't like, but for some reason they seem to get a perverse satisfaction out of making you struggle to figure it out. At times like this, you hear such comments as "Well, if you don't know what you did to hurt my feelings, I'm certainly not going to tell you!"

Needless to say, failing to learn the details of another's criticism when you genuinely want to know can be frustrating. In instances like these, you can often learn more clearly what is bothering your critic by *guessing* at the specifics of a complaint. In a sense you become both detective and suspect, the goal being to figure out exactly what "crime" you have committed. Like the technique of asking for specifics, guessing must be done with goodwill if it's to produce satisfying results. You need to convey to the critic that for both your sakes you're truly interested in finding out what is the matter. Once you have communicated this intention, the emotional climate generally becomes more comfortable because, in effect, both you and the critic are seeking the same goal.

Here are some typical questions you might hear from someone guessing about the details of another's criticism:

> "So you object to the language I used in writing the paper. Was my language too formal?"

> "OK, I understand that you think the outfit looks funny. What is it that's so bad? Is it the colour? Does it have something to do with the fit? The fabric?"

> "When you say that I'm not doing my share around the house, do you mean that I haven't been helping enough with the cleaning?"

Criticism becomes more sensible when it realizes that it has nothing to do with rejection, only with recognition.

Northrop Frye,
Anatomy of Criticism

Ethical Challenge

Nonviolence: A Legacy of Principled Effectiveness

Among the most familiar and challenging Biblical injunctions is Christ's mandate "If someone strikes you on one cheek, turn to him the other . . ."

The notion of meeting aggression with nonviolence is an ancient one. The Taoist doctrine of *wu-wei*, promulgated over 2,400 years ago in China, advocates nonaction in the face of an attack. In ancient India, the principle of *ahimsa*—nonharming—was shared by Buddhists, Jains, and many Hindus. In the West, some Greek stoics advocated nonaction in the face of threats.

Pacifism has a moral foundation, but by the nineteenth century it was used as a potent strategy for achieving political goals. In the United States, abolitionist William Lloyd Garrison advocated the use of nonviolence to protest slavery. On both sides of the Atlantic, the suffragette movement used nonviolent resistance as a tool to secure rights for women. In czarist Russia, Count Leo Tolstoi led a pacifist movement rejecting war and advocating civil disobedience as a tool for inhibiting violence.

In the twentieth century, nonviolence proved to be a powerful tool for political change. Mahatma Gandhi was demonstrably the most successful practitioner of this approach, first in South Africa and later in India, where his approach of *satyagraha* (truth-force) played a decisive role in the 1947 withdrawal of imperial Britain from India. In the 1950s and 1960s, Martin Luther King Jr. and his followers used nonviolence to demonstrate the evils of racial segregation, contributing to the passage of groundbreaking civil rights laws.

The effectiveness of nonviolence in achieving social change suggests that the strategies of seeking more information from and agreeing with one's critic can be effective in interpersonal situations. These nonconfrontational approaches provide communicators with a communication tool that is both principled and pragmatic.

For more information on nonviolent strategies see Peter Ackerman and Christopher Kruegler, *Strategic Nonviolent Conflict: The Dynamics of People Power in the Twentieth Century* (Westport, CT: Praeger, 1994); and Robert L. Holmes, ed., *Nonviolence in Theory and Practice* (Belmont, CA: Wadsworth, 1990).

Paraphrase the Speaker's Ideas   Another strategy is to draw out confused or reluctant speakers by paraphrasing their thoughts and feelings and using the active listening skills described in Chapter 7. Paraphrasing is especially good in helping others solve their problems; and since people generally criticize you because your behaviour creates some problem for them, the method is especially appropriate at such times.

One advantage of paraphrasing is that you don't have to guess about the specifics of your behaviour that might be offensive. By clarifying or amplifying what you understand critics to be saying, you'll learn more about their objections. A brief dialogue between a disgruntled customer and an especially talented store manager using paraphrasing might sound like this:

Customer: The way you people run this store is disgusting! I just want to tell you that I'll never shop here again.

Manager:	*(reflecting the customer's feeling)* It seems that you're quite upset. Can you tell me your problem?
Customer:	It isn't *my* problem; it's the problem your salespeople have. They seem to think it's a great inconvenience to help a customer find anything around here.
Manager:	So you didn't get enough help locating the items you were looking for, is that it?
Customer:	Help? I spent 20 minutes looking around in here before I even talked to a clerk. All I can say is that it's a hell of a way to run a store.
Manager:	So what you're saying is that the clerks seemed to be ignoring the customers?
Customer:	No. They were all busy with other people. It just seems to me that you ought to have enough help around to handle the crowds that come in at this hour.
Manager:	I understand now. What frustrated you the most was the fact that we didn't have enough staff to serve you promptly.
Customer:	That's right. I have no complaint with the service I get once I'm waited on, and I've always thought you had a good selection here. It's just that I'm too busy to wait so long for help.
Manager:	Well, I'm glad you brought this to my attention. We certainly don't want loyal customers going away mad. I'll try to see that it doesn't happen again.

This conversation illustrates two advantages of paraphrasing. First, the critic often reduces the intensity of the attack once he or she realizes that the complaint is being heard. Often criticism grows from the frustration of unmet needs—which in this case was partly a lack of attention. As soon as the manager genuinely demonstrated interest in the customer's plight, the customer began to feel better and was able to leave the store relatively calm. Of course, this sort of active listening won't always mollify your critic, but even when it doesn't, there's still another benefit that makes the technique worthwhile. In the sample conversation, for instance, the manager learned some valuable information by taking time to understand the customer. The manager discovered that there were certain times when the number of employees was insufficient to help the crowd of shoppers and also that the delays at these times seriously annoyed at least some shoppers, thus threatening a loss in business. This knowledge is certainly important, and by reacting defensively to the customer's complaint, the manager would not have learned from it. As you read earlier, even apparently outlandish criticism often contains at least a grain of truth, and thus a person who is genuinely interested in improving would be wise to hear it out.

Ask What the Critic Wants   Sometimes your critic's demand will be obvious.

"Turn down that music!"

"I wish you'd remember to tell me about phone messages."

"Would you clean up your dirty dishes *now!*"

In other cases, however, you'll need to do some investigating to find out what the critic wants from you:

Anna: I can't believe you invited all those people over without asking me first!

Dejun: Are you saying you want me to cancel the party?

Anna: No, I just wish you'd ask me before you make plans.

Erica: You're so critical! It sounds like you don't like *anything* about this paper.

Maria: But you asked for my opinion. What do you expect me to do when you ask?

Erica: I want to know what's wrong, but I don't *just* want to hear criticisms. If you think there's anything good about my work, I wish you'd tell me that, too.

This last example illustrates the importance of accompanying your questions with the right nonverbal behaviour. It's easy to imagine two ways Maria could have expressed "What do you expect me to do when you ask?" One would show a genuine desire to clarify what Erica wanted, while the other would have been clearly hostile and defensive. As with all the styles in this section, your responses to criticism have to be sincere to work.

Ask about the consequences of your behaviour As a rule, people complain about your actions only when some need of theirs is not being met. One way to respond to this kind of criticism is to find out exactly what troublesome consequences your behaviour has for them. You'll often find that actions that seem perfectly legitimate to you cause some difficulty for your critic; once you have understood this, comments that previously sounded foolish take on a new meaning.

Neighbour A: You say that I ought to have my cat neutered. Why is that important to you?

Neighbour B: Because at night he picks fights with my cat, and I'm tired of paying the vet's bills.

Worker A: Why do you care whether I'm late for work?

Worker B: Because when the boss asks, I feel obligated to make up some story so you won't get in trouble, and I don't like to lie.

Husband: Why does it bother you when I lose money at poker? You know I never gamble more than I can afford.

Wife: It's not the cash itself. It's that when you lose, you're in a grumpy mood for two or three days, and that's no fun for me.

Ask What Else Is Wrong It might seem crazy to invite more criticism, but sometimes asking about other complaints can uncover the real problem:

Raul: Are you mad at me?

Tina: No, why are you asking?

Raul: Because the whole time we were at the picnic you hardly spent any time talking to me. In fact, it seemed like whenever I came over to where you were, you went off somewhere else.

Tina: Is anything else wrong?

Raul: Well, I've been wondering lately if you're tired of me.

This example shows that asking if anything else bothers your critic isn't just an exercise in masochism. If you can keep your defensiveness in check, probing further can lead the conversation to issues that are the source of the critic's real dissatisfaction.

Sometimes soliciting more information from a critic isn't enough. What do you do, for instance, when you fully understand the other person's objections and still feel a defensive response on the tip of your tongue? You know that if you try to protect yourself, you'll wind up in an argument; on the other hand, you simply can't accept what

Nothing is weaker than water;
Yet, for attacking what is hard
  and tough,
Nothing surpasses it, nothing
  equals it.
The principle, that what is weak
  overcomes what is strong,
And what is yielding conquers
  what is resistant, is known to
  everyone.
Yet few utilize it profitably in
  practice . . .

Lao Tzu
Tao Te Ching

The Journal of Cooperative
Communication Skills

http://www.coopcomm.org/
ccejournal.htm

Rebuilding a Relationship After Communication Breakdown

A marriage counsellor booked them for twelve sessions. Each session lasted two hours, twenty-four hours in all. During those twenty-four hours they released into the mild air of the marriage counsellor's office millions of words. Their longest conversation. The polished floor, the walls, the perforated ceiling tile drank in the unstoppable flow. Barbara Cormin wept and shouted. Peter Cormin moaned, retreated, put his head on his arms. The histories they separately recounted were as detailed as the thick, soft novels people carry with them to the beach in the summer. Every story elicited a counterstory, until the accumulated weight of blame and blemish had squeezed them dry. "What are we doing?" Peter Cormin said, moving the back of his hand across and across his mouth. Barbara thought back to the day she had stood by the sunlit tulip bed and said, "Something's wrong," and wondered now what had possessed her. A hunger for words, was that all? She asked the marriage counsellor for a glass of cold water. She feared what lay ahead. A long fall into silence. An expensive drowning.

But they were surprisingly happy for quite some time after, speaking to each other kindly, with a highly specific strategy, little pieces moved on a chess board. What had been tricky territory before was strewn with shame. Barbara was prepared now to admit that marriage was, at best, a flawed and gappy narrative. Occasionally some confidence would wobble forward, and one of them, Barbara or Peter, might look up cunningly, ready to measure the moment and retreat or advance. They worked around the reserves of each other's inattention the way a pen-and-ink artist learns to use the reserve of white space.

Carol Shields, "Milk Bread Beer Ice"

the other person is saying about you. The solution to such a dilemma is outrageously simple and is discussed in the following section.

AGREE WITH THE CRITIC   But, you protest, how can you honestly agree with comments you don't believe are true? The following pages will answer this question by showing that there's virtually no situation in which you can't honestly accept the other person's point of view and still maintain your position. To see how this can be so, you need to realize that there are two different types of agreement, one of which you can use in almost any situation.

Agree with the Facts   This is the easiest type of agreement to understand, though not always to practise. Research suggests that it is also highly effective in restoring a damaged reputation with a critic.[27] You agree with your critic when the accusation is factually correct:

"You're right, I am angry."

"I suppose I *was* being defensive."

"Now that you mention it, I did get pretty sarcastic."

Agreeing with the facts seems quite sensible when you realize that certain matters are indisputable. If you agree to be somewhere at 4:00 and don't show up until 5:00, you *are* late, no matter how good your explanation for tardiness. If you've broken a borrowed object, run out of gas, or failed to finish a job you started, there's no point in denying it. In the same way, if you're honest, you will have to agree with many interpretations of your behaviour even when they're not flattering. You do get angry, act foolishly, fail to listen, and behave inconsiderately. Once you rid yourself of the myth of perfection, it's much easier to acknowledge these truths.

If many criticisms aimed at you are accurate, why is it so difficult to accept them without being defensive? The answer to this question lies in a confusion between agreeing with the *facts* and accepting the *judgement* that so often accompanies them. Most critics don't merely describe the action that offends them; they also evaluate it, and it's this evaluation that we resist:

"It's silly to be angry."

"You have no reason for being defensive."

"You were wrong to be so sarcastic."

It's judgements like these that we resent. By realizing that you can agree with—and even learn from—the descriptive part of many criticisms and still not accept the accompanying evaluations, you'll often have a response that is both honest and nondefensive.

Of course, in order to reduce defensiveness, your agreements with the facts must be honest ones admitted without malice. It's humiliating to accept descriptions that aren't accurate, and maliciously pretending to agree with these only leads to trouble. You can imagine how unproductive the conversation given earlier would have been if the manager

Communication Transcript

Responding Nondefensively to Criticism

Defending yourself—even when you're right—isn't always the best approach. The following dialogue shows the importance of self-control and thinking before responding when you are being criticized. The employee realizes that arguing won't change his boss's mind, and so he decides to reply as honestly as he can without becoming defensive.

Boss How'd things go while I was out?

Employee Pretty well, except for one thing. Mr. Macintosh—he said you knew him–came in and wanted to buy about $200 worth of stuff. He wanted me to charge him wholesale, and I asked him for his tax number, just like you told me. He said he didn't have it, and so I told him he'd have to pay retail. He got pretty mad.

Boss He's a good customer. I hope you gave him the discount.

Employee *(beginning to sound defensive)* Well, I didn't. You told me last week that the law said we had to charge full price unless the customer had a tax number.

Boss Oh my gosh! Didn't Macintosh tell you he had a number?

Employee *(becoming more defensive)* He did, but he didn't have it with him. I didn't want to get you mad at me for breaking the law.

Boss *(barely concealing his exasperation)* Well, customers don't always have their tax numbers memorized. Macintosh has been coming here for years, and we just fill in his number on the records later.

Employee *(deciding to respond nondefensively instead of getting into an argument he knows he can't win)* I can see why it looks like I gave Mr. Macintosh a hard time. You don't ask him for the number, and I

insisted on having it. *(agrees with the boss's perception)*

Boss Yes! There's a lot of competition in this business, and we have to keep our customers happy–especially the good ones– or we'll lose them. Macintosh drives across town to do business with us. There are places right near him. If we jerk him around he'll go there, and we'll lose a good customer.

Employee That's true. *(agrees with the fact that it is important to keep customers happy)* And I want to know how to treat customers right. But I'm confused about how to handle people who want a discount and don't have tax numbers. What should I do? *(asks what the boss wants)*

had spoken the same words in a sarcastic tone. Only agree with the facts when you can do so sincerely. Though this won't always be possible, you'll be surprised at how often you can use this simple response.

Agree with the Critic's Perception Agreeing with your critic may be fine when you acknowledge that the gripes are accurate, but how can you confess when they seem to be completely unjustified? You've listened carefully and asked questions to make sure you understand the objections, but the more you listen, the more positive you are that the critic is totally out of line. Even in these cases there is a way of agreeing–this time not with the critic's conclusions but with that person's right to see things her or his way.

Jacques: I don't believe you've been all the places you were just describing. You're probably just making all this up to impress us.

Boss Well, you need to be a little flexible with good customers.

Employee How should I do that? *(asks for specifics)*

Boss Well, it's OK to trust people who are regulars.

Employee So I don't need to ask regular customers for their tax numbers. I should look them up later? *(paraphrases to clarify boss's ambiguous directions to "trust" regular customers)*

Boss That's right. You've got to use your head in business!

Employee *(ignores the indirect accusation about not "using his head," recognizing that there's no point in defending himself)* OK, so when regular customers come in, I won't even ask them for their tax numbers . . . right? *(paraphrases again, to be sure he has the message correct; the employee has no desire to get criticized again about this matter)*

Boss No, go ahead and ask for the number. If they have it, we won't have to look it up later. But if they don't have the number, just say OK and give them the discount.

Employee Got it. I only have one question: How can I know who the regular customers are? Should I take their word for it? *(asks for specifics)*

Boss Well, you'll get to know most of them after you've been here a while. But it's OK to trust them until then. If they say they're regulars, just take their word for it. You've got to trust people sometimes, you know!

Employee *(ignores the fact that the boss originally told him not to trust people, but to insist on getting their number; decides instead to agree with the boss)* I can see how important it is to trust good customers.

Boss Right.

Employee Thanks for clearing up how to handle the tax num-

bers. Is there anything else I ought to know so things will run smoothly when you're not in the store? *(asks if anything else is wrong)*

Boss I don't think so. *(patronizingly)* Don't get discouraged; you'll catch on. It took me 20 years to build this business. Stick with it and someday you could be running a place like this.

Employee *(trying to agree with his boss without sounding sarcastic)* I guess I could.

The employee's refusal to act defensively turned what might have been a scolding into a discussion about how to handle a business challenge in the future. The employee might not like the boss's patronizing attitude and contradictory directions, but his communication skill kept the communication climate positive–probably the best possible outcome for this situation.

Danielle: Well, I can see how you might think that. I've known people who lie to get approval.

Steve: I want to let you know right from the start that I was against hiring you for the job. I think you got it because you're a woman.

Rachael: I can understand why you'd believe that with all the antidiscrimination laws on the books. I hope that after I've been here for a while, you'll change your mind.

Shannon: I don't think you're being totally honest about your reason for wanting to stay home. You say that it's because you have a headache, but I think you're avoiding Krista and Mike.

Pat: I can see why that would make sense to you because Krista and I got into an argument the last time we were together. All I can say is that I do have a headache.

One key to feeling comfortable acknowledging accurate criticism is to understand that *agreeing* with a critic doesn't necessarily oblige you to *apologize*. Sometimes you aren't responsible for the behaviour that your critic finds objectionable, in which case an explanation might be more appropriate than an apology:

> "I know I'm late. There was an accident downtown, and the streets are jammed." (Spoken in an explanatory, nondefensive tone.)

In other cases, your behaviour might be understandable, if not perfect. When this happens, you can acknowledge the validity of the criticism without apologizing:

> "You're right. I *did* lose my temper. I've had to remind you three or four times, and I guess I finally used up all my patience." (Again, delivered as an explanation, not a defence or counterattack.)

In still other instances, you can acknowledge your critic's right to see things differently than you, without backing off from your position.

> "I can understand why you think I'm overreacting. I know this doesn't seem as important to you as it does to me. I hope you can understand why I think this is such a big deal."

Apologizing is fine if you can do so sincerely; but you will be able to agree with critics more often if you understand that doing so doesn't require you to grovel.

Some critics don't seem to deserve the kinds of respectful responses outlined here. They seem more interested in attacking you than explaining themselves. Before you counterattack these hostile critics, ask yourself whether a defensive response will be worth the consequences.

SUMMARY

Every relationship has a communication climate. Positive climates are characterized by confirming messages, which make it clear that the parties value one another. Communication in negative climates is usually disconfirming. In one way or another, messages in disconfirming relationships convey indifference or hostility. Communication climates develop early in a relationship, both from verbal and nonverbal messages. Once created, reciprocal messages create either positive or negative spirals in which either the frequency and intensity of positive or negative messages is likely to grow.

Farcus

by David Waisglass
Gordon Coulthart

© 1996 Farcus Cartoons   WAISGLASS/COULTHART

"We need to improve morale ... any of you boneheads have a good idea?"

SKILL BUILDER

COPING WITH CRITICISM

Take turns practising nondefensive responses with a partner:

1. Choose one of the following criticisms, and brief your partner on how it might be directed at you:
   a. You're so selfish sometimes. You only think of yourself.
   b. Don't be so touchy!
   c. You say you understand me, but you don't really.
   d. I wish you'd do your share around here.
   e. You're so critical!

2. As your partner criticizes you, answer with the appropriate response from the preceding pages. As you do so, try to adopt an attitude of genuinely wanting to understand the criticism and finding parts you can sincerely agree with.

3. Ask your partner to evaluate your response. Does it follow the forms described in the previous pages? Does it sound sincere?

4. Replay the same scene, trying to improve your response.

Defensive spirals are among the most destructive types of communication. Most defensiveness occurs when people try to protect key parts of a presenting self-image that they believe is under attack. Defensive communicators respond by attacking their critic, distorting critical information, or avoiding critical messages. Using the supportive behaviours defined by Jack Gibb when expressing potentially threatening messages can reduce the likelihood of triggering defensive reactions in others.

When faced with criticism by others, it is possible to respond nondefensively by attempting to understand the criticism and by agreeing either with the facts or with the critic's perception.

KEY TERMS

ambiguous response
apathy
certainty
cognitive dissonance
communication climate
compensation
complaining
confirming communication
controlling communication
de-escalatory conflict spiral
defence mechanism
defensiveness
descriptive communication
disconfirming communication

displacement
empathy
equality
escalatory conflict spiral
evaluative communication
face-threatening act
Gibb categories
impersonal response
impervious response
incongruous response
interrupting response
irrelevant response
neutrality
physical avoidance

problem orientation
provisionalism
rationalization
regression
repression
sarcasm
spiral
spontaneity
strategy
superiority
tangential response
verbal abuse
verbal aggression

Chapter 10

Managing Interpersonal Conflicts

For most people, conflict has about the same appeal as a trip to the dentist. A quick look at the thesaurus offers a clue about the distasteful nature of conflict. Synonyms for the term include *battle, brawl, clash, competition, discord, disharmony, duel, fight, strife, struggle, trouble,* and *violence.* Even the metaphors we use to describe our conflicts show that we view conflict as something to be avoided.[1] We often talk about conflict as a kind of war: "He shot down my arguments." "OK, fire away." "Don't try to defend yourself!" Another metaphor suggests conflict is explosive: "Don't blow your stack!" "I needed to let off steam." "You've got a short fuse." Sometimes conflict seems like a kind of trial, in which one party accuses another: "Come on, admit you're guilty." "Stop accusing me!" "Just listen to my case." Language that suggests conflict is a mess is also common: "Let's not open this can of worms." "That's a sticky situation." "Don't make such a stink!" Even the metaphor of a game implies that one side has to defeat the other: "That was out of bounds." "You're not playing fair." "I give up; you win!"

Despite images like these, the truth is that conflicts *can* actually be constructive. With the right set of communication skills, conflict can be less like a struggle and more like a kind of dance in which partners work together to create something that would be impossible without their co-operation. You may have to persuade the other person to become your partner, and you may be clumsy at first; but with enough practice and goodwill, you can work together instead of at cross-purposes.

The attitude you bring to your conflicts can make a tremendous difference between success and failure. One study revealed that college students in close romantic relationships who believed that conflicts are destructive were most likely to neglect or quit the relationship and less likely to seek a solution than couples who had less negative attitudes.[2] Of course, attitudes alone won't always guarantee satisfying solutions to conflicts. The kinds of skills you will learn in this chapter can help well-intentioned partners handle their disagreements constructively. But without the right attitude, all the skills in the world will be little help.

There are no magic tricks to resolve all the conflicts in your life. On the other hand, there are ways to manage these conflicts constructively. If you follow these methods you may find that your relationships are actually stronger and more satisfying than before.

THE NATURE OF CONFLICT

Before focussing on how to solve interpersonal problems constructively, we need to take a brief look at the nature of conflict. What is it? Why is it an inevitable part of life? How can it be beneficial?

Conflict Defined

Before reading further, make a list of the interpersonal conflicts in your life. They probably involve many different people, revolve around very different subjects, and take many different forms. Some become loud, angry arguments. Others may be expressed in calm, rational discussions. Still others might simmer along most of the time with brief but bitter flare-ups.

Whatever form they may take, all interpersonal conflicts share certain characteristics. Joyce Hocker and William Wilmot provide a thorough definition when they define **conflict** as *an expressed struggle between at least two interdependent parties who perceive incompatible goals, scarce rewards, and interference from the other party in achieving their goals.*[3] A closer look at the key parts of this definition will help you recognize how conflict operates in your life.

EXPRESSED STRUGGLE   A conflict can exist only when both parties are aware of a disagreement. For instance, you may be upset for months because a neighbour's loud stereo keeps you awake at night, but no conflict exists between the two of you until the neighbour learns about the problem. Of course, the expressed struggle doesn't have to be verbal. You can show your displeasure with somebody without saying a word. A dirty look, the silent treatment, or avoiding the other person are all ways of expressing yourself. One way or another, both parties must know that a problem exists before they're in conflict.

PERCEIVED INCOMPATIBLE GOALS   All conflicts look as if one party's gain would be another's loss. For instance, consider the neighbour whose

Husband and Wife

Desire is spent,

but the sharing

remains: it is beautiful to hear
them

bickering, knowing the hurt will
not last,

all will be forgiven, all has been
accepted,

yet the sparks fly

when, as he puts it,

they rub one another

the wrong way–

it is beautiful to watch them,

knowing their forty years

in the same house

have not solved the mystery,

have not extinguished

the last spark of passion.

It is beautiful to think

how, after we are gone

and cannot see or hear them,

they will make their peace

like two proud old warriors.

Alden Nowlan

stereo keeps you awake at night. Doesn't somebody have to lose? If the neighbour turns down the noise, she loses the enjoyment of hearing the music at full volume; but if she keeps the volume up, you're still awake and unhappy.

The goals in this situation really aren't completely incompatible–there are solutions that allow both parties to get what they want. For instance, you could achieve peace and quiet by closing your windows or getting the neighbour to close hers. You might use a pair of earplugs, or perhaps she could get a set of earphones, allowing the music to be played at full volume without bothering anyone. If any of these solutions prove workable, the conflict disappears.

Unfortunately, people often fail to see mutually satisfying answers to their problems. As long as they *perceive* their goals to be mutually exclusive, a conflict exists.

PERCEIVED SCARCE REWARDS   Conflicts also exist when people believe there isn't enough of something to go around. The most obvious example of a scarce resource is money–a cause of many conflicts. If a worker asks for a raise in pay and the boss would rather keep the money or use it to expand the business, the two parties are in conflict.

Time is another scarce commodity. As authors and family members, we constantly face struggles about how to use the limited time we have at home. Should we work on this book? Hang out with our spouses? Talk with our children? Enjoy the luxury of being alone? With only 24 hours in a day, we're bound to wind up in conflicts with our families, editors, students, and friends–all of whom want more of our time than we have to give.

INTERDEPENDENCE   However antagonistic they might feel, the parties in conflict are usually dependent on each other. The welfare and satisfaction of one depend on the actions of another. If not, then even in the face of scarce resources and incompatible goals there would be no need for conflict. Interdependence exists between conflicting nations, social groups, organizations, friends, and lovers. In each case, if the two parties didn't need each other to solve the problem, they would go their separate ways. In fact, many conflicts go unresolved because the parties fail to understand their interdependence. One of the first steps toward resolving a conflict is to take the attitude that "we're all in this together."

INTERFERENCE FROM THE OTHER PARTY   No matter how much one person's position may differ from another's, a full-fledged conflict won't occur until the participants act in ways that prevent one another from reaching their goals. For example, you might let some friends know that you object to their driving after drinking too much alcohol, but the conflict will escalate if you act in ways that prevent them from getting behind the wheel. Likewise, a parent–child dispute about what clothing and music are appropriate will blossom into a conflict when the parents try to impose their position on the youngster.

Conflict Is Natural

Every relationship of any depth at all has conflict.[4] No matter how close, how understanding, how compatible you are, there will be times when your ideas or actions or needs or goals won't match those of others around you. You like rock and country music, but your companion prefers jazz or classical; you want to see other people, but your partner wants to keep the relationship exclusive; you think a paper you've done is fine, but your instructor wants it changed; you like to sleep late on Sunday mornings, but your housemate likes to play the stereo–loudly! There's no end to the number and kinds of disagreements possible. College students who have kept journals of their relationships report that they take part in about seven arguments per week. Most have argued with the other person before, often about the same topic.[5] One survey of couples revealed six broad areas of disagreement:

1. Power (e.g., decision making, conversational control)
2. Social issues (e.g., politics, religion)
3. Personal flaws (e.g., drinking, smoking, appearance)
4. Distrust (e.g., dishonesty, jealousy)
5. Intimacy (e.g., sex, lack of affection)
6. Personal distance (e.g., lack of time together, work or school commitments)[6]

Just as conflict is a fact of life, so are the feelings that go along with it–hurt, anger, frustration, resentment, disappointment. Because these feelings are usually unpleasant, there is a temptation to avoid them or pretend they don't exist. But as sure as conflicts are bound to arise, so are the emotions that go with them.

At first this might seem depressing. If problems are inevitable in even the best relationships, does this mean that you're doomed to relive the same arguments, the same hurt feelings, over and over? Fortunately, the answer to this question is a definite "no." Even though conflict is a part of a meaningful relationship,[7] you can change the way you deal with it.

Conflict Can Be Beneficial

Since it is impossible to *avoid* conflicts, the challenge is to handle them well when they do arise. Effective communication during conflicts can actually keep good relationships strong. People who use the constructive skills described in this chapter are more satisfied with their relationships and with the outcomes of their conflicts.[8]

Perhaps the best evidence of how constructive conflict skills can benefit a relationship focusses on communication between husbands and wives. Over 20 years of research shows that both happy and unhappy marriages have conflicts, but that they manage conflict in very different ways.[9] One 9-year study revealed that unhappy couples argued in ways that we have catalogued in this book as destructive.[10]

We're so much alike that we can't discuss. We can only fight.

Stephen Leacock, "Rebuilding the Cities," Royal Architectural Institute of Canada, *Journal*

They were more concerned with defending themselves than with being problem oriented; they failed to listen carefully to one another, had little or no empathy for their partners, used evaluative "you" language, and ignored one another's nonverbal relational messages.

Many satisfied couples think and communicate differently when they disagree. They view disagreements as healthy and recognize that conflicts need to be faced.[11] Although they may argue vigorously, they use skills like perception checking to find out what the other person is thinking, and they let one another know that they understand the other side of the dispute.[12] They are willing to admit their mistakes, both contributing to a harmonious relationship and helping to solve the problem at hand.

In the following pages, we will review communication skills that can make conflicts constructive, and we will introduce still more methods you can use to resolve the inevitable conflicts you face. Before doing so, however, we need to examine how individuals behave when faced with a dispute.

My Conflict Style

http://p2001.health.org/st01/
5hbox6a.htm#Myconflict

PERSONAL CONFLICT STYLES

There are several ways in which people can act when their needs aren't met (see Table 10–1). Each approach has very different characteristics, as we can show by describing a common problem. At one time or another almost everyone has been bothered by a neighbour's barking dog. You know the story: Every passing car, distant siren, pedestrian, and falling leaf seem to set off a fit of barking that makes you unable to sleep, socialize, or study. In a description of the possible ways of handling this kind of situation, the differences between nonassertive, directly aggressive, passive-aggressive, indirect, and assertive behaviour should become clear.

Nonassertive Behaviour

Nonassertion is the inability or unwillingness to express thoughts or feelings in a conflict. Sometimes nonassertion comes from a lack of confidence. In other cases, people lack the awareness or skill to use a more direct means of expression. Sometimes people know how to communicate in a straightforward way but choose to behave nonassertively.

Nonassertion is a surprisingly common way of dealing with conflicts. One study revealed that dating partners do not express roughly 40 percent of their relational grievances to one another.[13] Another survey examined the conflict level of husbands and wives in "non-distressed" marriages. Over a 5-day period, spouses reported that their partner engaged in an average of 13 behaviours that were "displeasurable" to them, but that they had only *one* confrontation during the same period.[14]

TABLE 10–1	INDIVIDUAL STYLES OF CONFLICT				
	NONASSERTIVE	DIRECTLY AGGRESSIVE	PASSIVE-AGGRESSIVE	INDIRECT	ASSERTIVE
Approach to Others	I'm not OK, you're OK.	I'm OK, you're not OK.	I'm OK, you're not OK. (But I'll let you think you are.)	I'm OK, you're not OK or I'm not OK, you're OK.	I'm OK, you're OK.
Decision Making	Lets other choose	Chooses for others. They know it.	Chooses for others. They don't know it.	Chooses for others. They don't know it.	Chooses for self
Self-Sufficiency	Low	High or low	Looks high, but usually low	High or low	Usually high
Behaviour in Problem Situations	Flees; gives in	Outright attack	Concealed attack	Strategic, oblique	Direct confrontation
Response of Others	Disrespect, guilt, anger, frustration	Hurt, defensiveness, humiliation	Confusion, frustration, feelings of manipulation	Unknowing compliance or resistance	Mutual respect
Success Pattern	Succeeds by luck or charity of others	Feels compelled to beat out others	Wins by manipulation	Gains unwitting compliance of others	Attempts "win–win" solutions

Adapted with permission from Stanlee Phelps and Nancy Austin, *The Assertive Woman*. (San Luis Obispo, CA: Impact, 1975), p. 11; and Gerald Piaget, American Orthopsychiatric Association, 1975. Further reproduction prohibited.

Nonassertion can take a variety of forms. One is **avoidance—** either physical (steering clear of a friend after having an argument), or conversational (changing the topic, joking, or denying that a problem exists). People who avoid conflicts usually believe it's easier to put up with the status quo than to face the problem head-on and try to solve it. **Accommodation** is another type of nonassertive response. Accommodators deal with conflict by giving in, putting the other's needs ahead of their own.

Faced with the annoyance of a barking dog next door, a nonassertive person might try to ignore the noise by closing the windows and turning up the radio. Other nonassertive responses

would be to deny that the problem even exists, or to hope that it would go away. None of these alternatives sounds very appealing. They probably would lead the nonassertive communicator to grow more and more angry at the neighbours, making a friendly relationship difficult. Nonassertion also can lead to a loss of self-respect: It's hard to respect yourself when you can't cope with even an everyday irritation.[15]

Nonassertion isn't always a bad idea. You might choose to keep quiet or give in if the risk of speaking up is too great: getting fired from a job you can't afford to lose, being humiliated in public, or even risking physical harm. You might also avoid a conflict if the relationship it involves isn't worth the effort. Even in close relationships, though, nonassertion has its logic. If the issue is temporary or minor, you might let it pass. It might even make sense to keep your thoughts to yourself and give in if the issue is more important to the other person than it is to you. These reasons help explain why the communication of many happily married couples is characterized by "selectively ignoring" the other person's minor flaws.[16] This doesn't mean that a key to successful relationships is avoiding *all* conflicts. Instead, it suggests that it's smart to save energy for the truly important ones.

Like avoidance, accommodation can also be appropriate, especially in cases in which the other person's needs may be more important than yours. For instance, if a friend wants to have a serious talk and you feel playful, you'd most likely honour her request, particularly if that person is facing some kind of crisis and wants your help. In most cases, however, nonassertive accommodators fail to assert themselves either because they don't value themselves sufficiently, or because they don't know how to ask for what they want.

Direct Aggression

In contrast to nonassertion, **direct aggression** occurs when a communicator expresses a criticism or demand that threatens the face of the person at whom it is directed. Communication researcher

Dominic Infante identified several types of direct aggression: character attacks, competence attacks, physical appearance attacks, maledictions (wishing the other ill fortune), teasing, ridicule, threats, swearing, and nonverbal emblems.[17]

Direct aggression can have a severe impact on the target. Recipients can feel embarrassed, inadequate, humiliated, hopeless, desperate, or depressed. These results can lead to decreased effectiveness in personal relationships and on the job.[18] There is a significant connection between verbal aggression and physical aggression,[19] but even if the attacks never lead to blows, the psychological effects can be devastating. Aggressive behaviour can punish the attacker as well as the victim. Men who view conversations as contests and partners as opponents are 60 percent more apt to die earlier than those who are less aggressive.[20] Newly married couples whose disagreements were marked by sarcasm, interruptions, and criticism suffered a drop in the effectiveness of their immune systems.[21]

Verbal aggression can affect the relationship as well as the individuals involved. One aggressive remark can lead to an equally combative reaction, starting a destructive spiral that can expand beyond the original dispute and damage the entire relationship. This fact explains why verbally abusive couples report significantly less relational satisfaction than do partners who communicate about their conflicts in other ways.[22] Even among well-adjusted couples, negative communication is more likely to be reciprocated than positive—and once hostility is expressed, it usually escalates.[23]

You could handle the barking dog problem with direct aggression by abusively confronting your neighbours, calling them names and threatening to call the dogcatcher the next time you see their hound running loose. If the town in which you live has a leash law, you would be within your legal rights to do so, and thus you would gain your goal of bringing peace and quiet to the neighbourhood. Unfortunately, your direct aggression would have other, less productive consequences. Your neighbours and you would probably cease to be on speaking terms, and you could expect a complaint from them the first time you violated even the most inconsequential of city ordinances. If you live in the neighbourhood for any time at all, this state of hostilities isn't very appealing. This example shows why research confirms what common sense suggests: Unlike other conflict styles, direct aggression is judged incompetent by virtually everyone who encounters it.[24]

Passive Aggression

Passive aggression occurs when a communicator expresses hostility in an obscure way. As the Ethical Challenge on page 423 explains, this behaviour has been termed **"crazymaking."** It occurs when people have feelings of resentment, anger, or rage that they are unable or unwilling to express directly. Instead of keeping these feelings to themselves, the crazymakers send these aggressive messages in subtle, indirect ways, thus maintaining the front of

Sir, it is not you who is not speaking to me! It is I who is not speaking to you!

John V. Clyne,
quoted in the *Vancouver Sun*

Silence needs no messenger.
Stillness runs in all directions
Building thoughts and feelings, each a realm,
To well up and drown the senses,
And overwhelm.

Your silence needs no messenger.
Yet, it makes prisoner my mind.
Wonder becomes worry, then dread
About that which wasn't soundly said.

Neil Towne

---

kindness. This amiable façade eventually crumbles, however, leaving the crazymaker's victim confused and angry at having been fooled. The targets of the crazymaker can either react with aggressive behaviour of their own or retreat to nurse their hurt feelings. In either case, passive aggression seldom has anything but harmful effects on a relationship.

You could respond to your neighbours and their dog in several crazymaking, passive-aggressive ways. One strategy would be to complain anonymously to the city pound and then, after the dog has been hauled away, express your sympathy. Or you could complain to everyone else in the neighbourhood, hoping that their hostility would force the offending neighbours to quiet the dog or face being social outcasts.

There are a number of shortcomings to this sort of approach, each of which illustrates the risks of passive aggression. First, there is the chance that the crazymaking won't work: The neighbours might simply miss the point of your veiled attacks and continue to ignore the barking. On the other hand, they might get your message clearly, but either because of your lack of sincerity or out of sheer stubbornness, they might simply refuse to do anything about it. In either case, it's likely that in this and other instances passive aggression won't satisfy your unmet need.

Even when passive aggression proves successful in the short run, a second shortcoming lies in its consequences over the longer run. You might manage to intimidate your neighbours into shutting up their mutt, for instance, but in winning the battle you could lose what would become a war. As a means of revenge, they could wage their own campaign of crazymaking by such tactics as bad-mouthing you to other neighbours or phoning in false complaints about your loud parties. It's obvious that feuds such as this one are counterproductive and outweigh the apparent advantages of passive aggression.

Isn't it queer that only sensible people agree with you?

Robert C. (Bob) Edwards,
Calgary Eye Opener

Ethical Challenge

Dirty Fighting with Crazymakers

Psychologist George Bach uses the term "crazymakers" to describe passive-aggressive behaviour. His label reflects the insidious nature of indirect aggression, which can confuse and anger a victim who may not even be aware of being victimized. While a case can be made for using all the other approaches to conflict described in this chapter, it is difficult to find a justification for passive-aggressive crazymaking.

The following categories represent a nonexhaustive list of crazymaking. They are presented here as a warning for potential victims, who might choose to use perception checking, "I" language, assertion, or other communication strategies to explore whether the user has a complaint that can be addressed in a more constructive manner.

The Avoider

Avoiders refuse to fight. When a conflict arises, they leave, fall asleep, pretend to be busy at work, or keep from facing the problem in some other way. Because avoiders won't fight back, this strategy can frustrate the person who wants to address an issue.

The Pseudoaccommodator

Pseudoaccommodators pretend to give in and then continue to act in the same way.

The Guiltmaker

Instead of expressing dissatisfaction directly, guiltmakers try to make others feel responsible for causing pain. A guiltmaker's favourite line is "It's OK; don't worry about me . . . " accompanied by a big sigh.

The Mind Reader

Instead of allowing their partners to express feelings honestly, mind readers go into character analysis, explaining what the other person really means or what's wrong with the other person. By behaving this way mind readers refuse to handle their own feelings and leave no room for their partners to express themselves.

The Trapper

Trappers play an especially dirty trick by setting up a desired behaviour for their partners and then when it's met, attacking the very thing they requested. An example of this technique is for the trapper to say, "Let's be totally honest with each other," and then attack the partner's self-disclosure.

The Crisis Tickler

Crisis ticklers almost bring what's bothering them to the surface, but never quite come out and express themselves. Instead of admitting concern about the finances, they innocently ask, "Gee, how much did that cost?" dropping a rather obvious hint but never really dealing with the crisis.

The Gunnysacker

These people don't share complaints as they arise. Instead, they put their resentments into a psychological gunnysack, which after a while begins to bulge with both large and small gripes. Then, when the sack is about to burst, the gunnysacker pours out all the pent-up aggressions on the overwhelmed and unsuspecting victim.

The Trivial Tyrannizer

Instead of honestly sharing their resentments, trivial tyrannizers do things they know will get their partners' goat—leaving dirty dishes in the sink, clipping fingernails in bed, belching out loud, turning up the television too loud, and so on.

The Beltliner

Everyone has a psychological "beltline," and below it are subjects too sensitive to be approached without damaging the relationship. Beltlines may have to do with physical characteristics, intelligence, past behaviour, or deeply ingrained personality traits a person is trying to overcome. In an attempt to "get even" or hurt their partners, beltliners will use intimate knowledge to hit below the belt, where they know it will hurt.

The Joker

Because they are afraid to face conflicts squarely, the jokers kid around when their partners want to be serious, thus blocking the expression of important feelings.

The Withholder

Instead of expressing their anger honestly and directly, the withholders punish their partners by keeping back something—courtesy, affection, good cooking, humour, sex. As you can imagine, this is likely to build up even greater resentments in the relationship.

The Benedict Arnold

These characters get back at their partners by sabotage, by failing to defend them from attackers, and even by encouraging ridicule or disregard from outside the relationship.

For more information about crazymaking, see George Bach and Peter Wyden, *The Intimate Enemy* (New York: Avon, 1968), and George Bach, *Aggression Lab: The Fair Fight Manual* (Dubuque, IA: Kendall-Hunt, 1971).

Indirect Communication

The clearest communication is not necessarily the best approach. **Indirect communication** conveys a message in a roundabout manner, in order to save face for the recipient. Although indirect communication lacks the clarity of an aggressive or assertive message, it involves more initiative than nonassertion. It also has none of the hostility of passive-aggressive crazymaking. The goal is to get what you want without arousing the hostility of the other person. Consider the case of the annoying dog. One indirect approach would be to strike up a friendly conversation with the owners and ask if anything you are doing is too noisy for them, hoping they would get the hint.

Because it saves face for the other party, indirect communication is often kinder than blunt honesty. If your guests are staying too long, it's probably kinder to yawn and hint about your big day tomorrow than to bluntly ask them to leave. Likewise, if you're not interested in going out with someone who has asked you for a date, it may be more compassionate to claim that you're busy than to say "I'm not interested in seeing you."

At other times we communicate indirectly in order to protect ourselves. You might, for example, test the waters by hinting instead of directly asking the boss for a raise, or by letting your partner know indirectly that you could use some affection instead of asking outright. At times like these, an oblique approach may get the message across while softening the blow of a negative response.

The advantages of self-protection and saving face for others help explain why indirect communication is the most common way people make requests.[25] The risk of an indirect message, of course, is that the other party will misunderstand you or fail to get the message at all. There are also times when the importance of an idea is so great that hinting lacks the necessary punch. When clarity and directness are your goals, an assertive approach is in order.

Assertion

Assertion occurs when a message expresses the speaker's needs, thoughts, and feelings clearly and directly without judging or dictating to others. Most assertive messages follow the format described later in this chapter on pages 427–435.

An assertive course of action in the case of the barking dog would be to wait a few days to make sure the noise is not just a fluke. If the barking continues, you could introduce yourself to your neighbours and explain your problem. You could tell them that although they might not notice it, the dog often plays in the street and keeps barking at passing cars. You could tell them why this behaviour bothers you. It keeps you awake at night and makes it hard for you to do your work. You could point out that you don't want to be a jerk and call the pound. Rather than behaving in these ways, you could tell them that

You ask me what it's all about
I say I don't know
Should you stay and work it out
I say I don't think so
Life is short and grief can tear a heart apart

Life is short
Life is sweet
This much I know
Should you stay and work it out
I say I don't think so

From "I Don't Know," Kate and Anna McGarrigle

you've come to see what kind of solution you can find that will satisfy both of you. This approach may not work, and you might then have to decide whether it is more important to avoid bad feelings or to have peace and quiet. But the chances for a happy ending are best with this assertive approach. And no matter what happens, you can keep your self-respect by behaving directly and honestly.

INVITATION TO INSIGHT

YOUR CONFLICT STYLE

1. Think back over your recent history and recall five conflicts you've had. The more current they are, the better, and they should be ones that occurred with people who are important to you, people with whom your relationship matters.

2. Turn an $8\frac{1}{2}$-by-11 sheet of paper horizontally and copy the following chart. To give yourself plenty of room you might extend your chart onto a second page.

I **The Conflict** (Describe whom it was with, what it was about.)	II **How I Managed It** (What did you say? How did you act?)	III **The Results** (How did you feel? How did the others involved feel? Are you happy with the results?)

3. For each of the conflicts, fill in the appropriate spaces on your chart.

4. Based on what you've written here, answer the following questions:
   a. Are you happy with the way you've handled your conflicts? Do you come away from them feeling better or worse than before?
   b. Have your conflicts made your relationships stronger or weaker?
   c. Do you recognize any patterns in your conflict style? For example, do you hold your angry feelings inside? Are you sarcastic? Do you lose your temper easily?
   d. If you could, would you like to change the way you deal with your conflicts?

International Online Training Program on Intractable Conflict

http://www.colorado.edu/conflict/ peace/

Which Style Is Best?

After reading this far, you might think that assertive communication is clearly superior to other styles. It allows you to express yourself honestly and seems to have the greatest chance of success. Actually, it's an oversimplification to say that any communication style is always best. A competent, successful communicator will choose the most effective style for a given situation. How can you decide which style will be most effective? There are several factors to consider.

1. *The Situation* When someone else clearly has more power than you, nonassertion may be the best approach. If the boss tells you to fill that order *"now!"* it may be smart to do it without comment. The more assertive response ("When you use that tone of voice, I feel defensive . . .") might be more clear, but it also could cost you your job. Likewise, there are some situations when an aggressive message is most appropriate. Even the most mild-mannered parents will testify that sooner or later yelling seems to be the only way to get a child to respond: "I've told you three times not to bother the cat. Now *stop it,* or you'll be sorry!"

2. *The Receiver* Although assertiveness has the best chance of success with most people, some receivers respond better to other approaches. One businessman illustrated this point when he described how his normally even-tempered boss used shouting in a phone conversation with a particularly difficult person:

   > I've never heard him so angry. He was enraged. His face was red, and the veins were bulging on his neck. I tried to get his attention to calm him down, but he waved me away impatiently. As soon as the call was over, he turned to me and smiled. "There," he said. "That ought to do it." If I were the guy he'd been shouting at, let me tell you, that would have done it, too. But it was all a put-on.[26]

3. *Your Goals* When you want to solve a problem, assertiveness may seem like the best approach, but there are other reasons for communicating in a conflict. The other person might not like you as much when you assert your rights as when you keep quiet, so if the goal is to maintain harmony, nonassertion may be the best course.[27] The problem might not be worth the potential conflict. In other cases, your overriding concern may be to calm down an enraged or upset person. Tolerating an outburst from your crotchety and sick neighbour, for example, is probably better than standing up for yourself and triggering a stroke. Likewise, you might choose to sit quietly through the nagging of a family member rather than ruin a special dinner. In still other cases, your moral principles might compel an aggressive statement even though it might not get you what you originally sought: "I've had enough of your racist jokes. I've tried to explain why they're so offensive, but you obviously haven't listened. I'm leaving!"

ASSERTION WITHOUT AGGRESSION: THE CLEAR MESSAGE FORMAT

Knowing *when* to behave assertively isn't the same as knowing *how* to assert yourself. The next few pages will describe a method for communicating assertively. It works for a variety of messages: your hopes, problems, complaints, and appreciations.[28] Besides giving you a way to express yourself directly, this clear message format also makes it easy for others to understand you. Finally, because assertive messages are phrased in the kind of descriptive "I" language you learned in Chapter 5, they are less likely than aggressive attacks to cause a defensive reaction that will start a needless fight or shut down discussion altogether.

A complete assertive message has five parts. We'll examine each of these parts one by one and then discuss how to combine them in your everyday communication.

Behaviour

As you read in Chapter 5, a **behavioural description** describes the raw material to which you react. A behavioural description should be *objective*, describing an event without interpreting it.

Two examples of behavioural descriptions might look like this.

Example 1
"One week ago John promised me that he would ask my permission before smoking in the same room with me. Just a moment ago he lit up a cigarette without asking for my OK."

Example 2
"Chris has acted differently over the last week. I can't remember her laughing once since the holiday weekend. She hasn't dropped by my place like she usually does, hasn't suggested we play tennis, and hasn't returned my phone calls."

Notice that in both cases the descriptive statements record only data that are available through the senses. The observer has not attached any meaning. The value of describing the problem

without using emotive language was demonstrated by a study examining conflicts between couples. The study revealed that satisfied partners tend to offer behavioural complaints ("You always throw your socks on the floor"), while unsatisfied couples make more complaints aimed at personal characteristics ("You're a slob").[29] Other research confirmed the fact that personal complaints are more likely to result in an escalated conflict episode.[30] The reason should be obvious–complaints about personal characteristics attack a more fundamental part of the presenting self. Talking about socks deals with a habit that can be changed; calling someone a slob or a pig is a character assault that is unlikely to be forgotten when the conflict is over.

Interpretation

Interpretation is the process of attaching meaning to behaviour. The important thing to realize about interpretations is that they are *subjective.* That is, there is more than one interpretation that we can attach to any behaviour. For example, look at these two different interpretations of each of the preceding descriptions:

Example 1
Interpretation A "John must have forgotten about our agreement that he wouldn't smoke without asking me first. I'm sure he's too considerate to go back on his word on something he knows I feel strongly about."

Interpretation B "John is a rude, inconsiderate person. After promising not to smoke around me without asking, he's just deliberately done so. This shows that he cares only about himself. In fact, I bet he's deliberately doing this to drive me crazy!"

Example 2
Interpretation A "Something must be bothering Chris. It's probably her family. She'll probably just feel worse if I keep pestering her."

Interpretation B "Chris is probably mad at me. It's probably because I kidded her about losing so often at tennis. I'd better leave her alone until she cools off."

These examples show that interpretations are based on more than simple sense data. They grow out of many factors, including

- *Your past experience* "John has always (never) kept his promises in the past" or "When I'm preoccupied with personal problems I draw away from my friends."

- *Your assumptions* "An unkept promise is a sign of uncaring (forgetfulness)" or "Lack of communication with friends is a sign that something is wrong."

- *Your expectations* "John probably wants (doesn't want) to fight" or "I thought the family visit (or kidding about tennis) would upset her."

"I" Statements, not "You" Statements

http://www.colorado.edu/conflict/
peace/treatment/istate.htm

- *Your knowledge* "Long-time, habitual cigarette smokers aren't even aware of lighting up" or "I know Chris's dad has been sick lately."

- *Your current mood* "I feel good about John and about life in general" or "I've been awfully sarcastic lately. I went too far when I kidded Chris about her tennis game."

Once you become aware of the difference between observable behaviour and interpretation, some of the reasons for communication breakdowns become clear. Many problems occur when a sender fails to describe the behaviour on which an interpretation is based. For instance, imagine the difference between hearing a friend say

"You are a tightwad!" *(no behavioural description)*

and explaining

"When you never offer to pay me back for the coffee and snacks I often buy you, I think you're a tightwad." *(behaviour plus interpretation)*

The first speaker's failure to specify behaviour would probably confuse the receiver, who has no way of knowing what prompted the sender's remarks. This failure to describe behaviour also reduces any chance that the receiver will change the offensive behaviour, which, after all, is unknown to that person.

Just as important as specifying behaviour is the need to clarify an interpretation of such behaviour instead of presenting the interpretation as a matter of fact. Consider the difference between saying

"It's obvious that if you cared for me you'd write more often." *(interpretation presented as fact)*

and saying

"When I didn't get a letter or even a postcard from you, I thought that you didn't care for me." *(interpretation made clear)*

As you learned in Chapter 5, your comments are much less likely to arouse defensiveness in others when you present them using "I" language.

A third important rule is to avoid making statements that appear to describe behaviour but that are in fact interpretations. For instance, don't mistake these kinds of statements as objective descriptions:

"I see you're tired." (*Tired* is an interpretation. Your behavioural description might have been "I see your eyes closing and your head nodding.")

"I see you're in a hurry." (*Hurry* is an interpretation. The behavioural description could have been "I see you gathering up your books and looking at the clock.")

"I can tell that you're hungry. (*Hungry* is an interpretation. The behaviour you heard was the sound of your friend's stomach growling.)

"You look anxious to get started." (*Anxious* is an interpretation. What could the behaviour be in this case? The short time it took your friend to answer the door? The coat and hat that the person was already wearing?)

There's nothing wrong with making these interpretations. In fact, this is a necessary step because only by interpreting behaviour do we arrive at a meaning. However, we often make inaccurate interpretations, and when we don't separate behaviour from our interpretations, we fool ourselves into believing that our interpretations are reality—that is, what we *think* is what exists.

SKILL BUILDER

BEHAVIOURS AND INTERPRETATIONS

1. Tell two other group members several interpretations you have recently made about other people in your life. For each interpretation, describe the behaviour on which you based your remarks.

2. With your partners' help, consider some alternate interpretations of the behaviour that might be as plausible as your original ones.

3. After considering the alternate interpretations, decide

   a. which one was most reasonable.
   b. how you might share that interpretation (along with the behaviour) with the other person involved in a tentative, nondogmatic way.

Feeling

Reporting behaviour and sharing your interpretations are important, but *feeling statements* add a new dimension to a message. For example, consider the difference between saying

"When you kiss me and nibble on my ear while we're watching television *[behaviour]*, I think you probably want to make love *[interpretation]*, and *I feel excited.*"

and

"When you kiss me and nibble on my ear while we're watching television, I think you probably want to make love, and *I feel disgusted.*"

Notice how the expression of different feelings can change the meaning of another message.

"When you laugh at me *[behaviour]*, I think you find my comments foolish *[interpretation]*, and *I feel embarrassed.*"

and

"When you laugh at me, I think you find my comments foolish, and *I feel angry.*"

No doubt you can supply other examples in which different feelings can radically affect a speaker's meaning. Recognizing this, we find it logical to say that we should identify our feelings in our conversations with others. Yet if we pay attention to the everyday acts of communication, we see that no such disclosure occurs.

It's important to recognize that some statements *seem* as if they're expressing feelings but are really interpretations or statements of intention. For instance, it's not accurate to say "I feel like leaving" (really an intention) or "I feel you're wrong" (an interpretation). Statements like these obscure the true expression of feelings.

What prevents people from sharing their feelings? Certainly one cause is that making such statements can bring on a great deal of anxiety. It's often frightening to come right out and say, "I'm angry," "I feel embarrassed," or "I love you," and often we aren't willing to take the risks that come with such clear-cut assertions.

A second reason why people fail to express their feelings clearly is simply because they don't recognize them. We aren't always aware that we're angry, confused, impatient, or sad. Asking yourself, "How do I feel?" can often uncover important information that needs to be communicated to your partner.

Consequence

A **consequence statement** explains what happens as a result of the behaviour you have described, your interpretation, the ensuing feeling, or all three. There are three types of consequences:

SKILL BUILDER

NAME THE FEELING

Add a feeling you would be likely to have to each of the following messages:

1. I felt _____ when I found out you didn't invite me on the camping trip. You said you thought I wouldn't want to go, but I have a hard time accepting that.
2. I felt _____ when you offered to help me move. I know how busy you are.
3. When you tell me you still want to be a friend but you want to "lighten up a little," I get the idea you're tired of me and I feel _____.
4. You told me you wanted my honest opinion about your paintings, and then when I tell you what I think, you say I don't understand them. I'm _____.

How would the impact of each message be different if it didn't include a feeling statement?

- *What happens to you, the speaker*
  "When I didn't get the phone message yesterday *[behaviour]*, I didn't know that my doctor's appointment was delayed and I would end up sitting in the office for an hour when I could have been studying or working *[consequences]*. It seems to me that you don't care enough about how busy I am to even write a simple note *[interpretation]*, and that's why I'm so mad *[feeling]*."

  "I appreciate *[feeling]* the help you've given me on my term paper *[behaviour]*. It tells me you think I'm on the right track *[interpretation]*, and this gives me a boost to keep working on the idea *[consequences]*."

- *What happens to the person you're addressing*
  "When you have four or five drinks at a party after I've warned you to slow down *[behaviour]*, you start to act weird: You make crude jokes that offend everybody, and you drive like a maniac *[consequences]*. For instance, last night you almost hit a telephone pole while you were backing out of the driveway *[more behaviour]*. I don't think you realize how differently you act *[interpretation]*, and I'm worried *[feeling]* about what will happen if you keep drinking at this rate."

- *What happens to others*
  "You probably don't know because you couldn't hear her cry *[interpretation]*, but when you rehearse your lines for the play without closing the doors *[behaviour]*, the baby can't sleep *[consequence]*. I'm especially concerned *[feeling]* about her because she's had a cold lately."

  "I thought you'd want to know *[interpretation]* that when you kid Bob about his height *[behaviour]*, he gets embarrassed *[feeling]* and usually quiets down or leaves *[consequences]*."

Consequence statements are valuable for two reasons. First, they help you understand more clearly why you are bothered or pleased by another's behaviour. Just as important, telling others about the consequences of their actions can clarify for them the results of their behaviour. As with interpretations, we often think others *should* be aware of consequences without being told; but the fact is that they often aren't. By explicitly stating consequences, you can be sure that you or your message leaves nothing to the listener's imagination.

When you are stating consequences, it's important simply to describe what happens without moralizing. For instance, it's one thing to say, "When you didn't call to say you'd be late, I stayed up worrying," and another to rant on "How can I ever trust you? You're going to drive me crazy!" Remember, it's perfectly legitimate to express your thoughts and feelings, but it's important to label them as such. And when you want to request change from someone, you can use intention statements, which we'll describe in the next section.

It's easy to confuse some interpretation, feeling, or intention statements with consequences. For example, you might say, "As a consequence of your turning down my invitation *[behaviour]*, I got the idea *[interpretation]* you're mad at me. I'm worried *[feeling]*, and I want to know what you're thinking *[intention]*." To say that these are not consequences as we're using the term is more than semantic hairsplitting. Confusing interpretations, feelings, and intentions with consequences might prevent you from mentioning the true consequence–what has happened as a result of this event. In our example, a real consequence statement might be " . . . and that's why I've been so quiet lately." As you'll read on page 436, sometimes a consequence is combined with another message element. The important point to remember is that you somehow need to explain the consequences of an incident if the other person is to understand your concern completely.

Intention

Intention statements are the final element of the assertive format. They can communicate three kinds of messages:

- *Where you stand on an issue*
  "When you call us 'girls' after I've told you we want to be called 'women' *[behaviour]*, I get the idea you don't appreciate how important the difference is to us *[interpretation]* and how demeaning it feels *[feeling]*. Now I'm in an awkward spot: Either I have to keep bringing the subject up, or else drop it and feel bad *[consequence]*. I want you to know how much this bothers me *[intention]*."

  "I'm really grateful *[feeling]* to you for speaking up for me in front of the boss yesterday *[behaviour]*. That must have taken a lot of courage *[interpretation]*. Knowing that you're behind me gives me a lot of confidence *[consequence]*, and I want you to know how much I appreciate your support *[intention]*."

- *Requests of others*
  "When I didn't hear from you last night *[behaviour]*, I thought you were mad at me *[interpretation]*. I've been thinking about it ever since *[consequence]*, and I'm still worried *[feeling]*. I'd like to know whether you are angry *[intention]*."

  "I really enjoyed *[feeling]* your visit *[behaviour]*, and I'm glad you had a good time, too *[interpretation]*. I hope you'll come again *[intention]*."

- *Descriptions of how you plan to act in the future*
  "I've asked you to repay the $25 I lent you three times now *[behaviour]*. I'm getting the idea that you've been avoiding me *[interpretation]*, and I'm pretty angry about it *[feeling]*. I want you to know that unless we clear this up now, you shouldn't expect me ever to lend you anything again *[intention]*."

"I'm glad *[feeling]* you liked *[interpretation]* the paper I wrote. I'm thinking about taking your advanced writing class next term *[intention]*."

Why is it so important to make your intentions clear? Because failing to do so often makes it hard for others to know what you want from them or how to act. Consider how confusing the following statements are because they lack a clear statement of intention:

"Wow! A frozen Snickers. I haven't had one of those in years." (Does the speaker want a bite, or is she just making an innocent remark?)

"Thanks for the invitation, but I really should study Saturday night." (Does the speaker want to be asked out again, or is she indirectly suggesting that she doesn't ever want to go out with you?)

"To tell you the truth, I was asleep when you came by, but I should have been up anyway." (Is the speaker saying that it's OK to come by in the future, or is he hinting that he doesn't appreciate unannounced visitors?)

You can see from these examples that it's often hard to make a clear interpretation of another person's ideas without a direct statement of intention. Notice how much more direct statements become when the speakers make their position clear:

"Wow! A frozen Snickers. I haven't had one of those in years. *If I hadn't already eaten, I'd be asking for a bite.*"

"Thanks for the invitation, but I really should study Saturday night. *I hope you'll ask me again soon.*"

"To tell you the truth, I was asleep when you came by, but I should have been up anyway. *Maybe the next time you should phone before dropping in so I'll be sure to be awake.*"

As in the preceding cases, we are often motivated by one single intention. Sometimes, however, we act from a combination of intentions, which may even be in conflict with each other. When this happens, our conflicting wants often make it difficult for us to reach decisions.

"I want to be truthful with you, but I don't want to violate my friend's privacy."

"I want to continue to enjoy your friendship and company, but I don't want to get too attached right now."

"I want to have time to study and get good grades, but I also want to have a job with some money coming in."

Although revealing your conflicting intentions is guaranteed to clear up confusion, sometimes an outright statement, such as the preceding, can help you come to a decision. Even when you remain mixed up, expressing your contrary wants has the benefit of letting others know where you stand.

Using the Clear Message Format

Before you try to deliver messages by using the behaviour-interpretation-feeling-consequences-intention format, there are a few points to remember.

1. *The elements may be delivered in mixed order.* As the examples on the preceding pages show, it's sometimes best to begin by stating your feelings. In other cases, you can start by sharing your intentions or interpretations or by describing consequences.

2. *Word the message to suit your personal style.* Instead of saying "I interpret your behaviour to mean . . ." you might choose to say "I think . . ." or "It seems to me . . ." or perhaps "I get the idea. . . ." In the same way, you can express your intentions by saying "I hope you'll understand (or do) . . ." or perhaps "I wish you would. . . ." The words you choose should sound authentic in order to reinforce the genuineness of your statement.

3. *When appropriate, combine two elements in a single phrase.* The statement " . . . and ever since then I've been wanting to talk to you" expresses both a consequence and an intention. In the same way, saying " . . . and after you said that, I felt confused" expresses a consequence and a feeling. Whether you combine elements or state them separately, the important point is to be sure that each one is present in your statement.

4. *Take your time delivering the message.* It isn't always possible to deliver messages such as the ones here all at one time, wrapped up in neat paragraphs. It will often be necessary to repeat or re-state one part many times before your receiver truly understands what you're saying. As you've already read, there are many types of psychological and physical noise that make it difficult for us to understand each other. In communication, as in many other activities, patience and persistence are essential.

Now try your hand at combining all these elements in this exercise.

SKILL BUILDER

PUTTING YOUR MESSAGE TOGETHER

1. Join with two other class members. Each person in turn should share a message he or she might want to send to another person, being sure to include behaviour, interpretation, feeling, consequence, and intention statements in the remarks.

2. The others in the group should help the speaker by offering feedback about how the remarks could be made clearer if there is any question about the meaning.

3. Once the speaker has composed a satisfactory message he or she should practise actually delivering it by having another group member play the role of the intended receiver. Continue this practice until the speaker is confident that he or she can deliver the message effectively.

4. Repeat this process until each group member has had a chance to practise delivering a message.

CONFLICT IN RELATIONAL SYSTEMS

So far we have focussed on individual conflict styles. Even though the style you choose in a conflict is important, your approach isn't the only factor that will determine how a conflict unfolds. In reality, conflict is *relational:* Its character usually is determined by the way the parties interact with one another.[31] You might, for example, be determined to handle a conflict with your neighbour assertively, only to be driven to aggression by his uncooperative nature . . . or even to nonassertion by his physical threats. Likewise, you might plan to hint to a professor that you are bothered by her apparent indifference, but wind up discussing the matter in an open, assertive way in reaction to her constructive response. Examples like these suggest that conflict isn't just a matter of individual choice. Rather, it depends on how the partners interact.

When two or more people are in a long-term relationship, they develop their own **relational conflict style**—a pattern of managing disagreements that repeats itself over time. The mutual influence that parties have on one another is so powerful that it can overcome our disposition to handle conflicts in the manner that comes most easily to one or the other.[32] As we will soon see, some relational conflict styles are constructive, while others can make life miserable and threaten relationships.

Complementary, Symmetrical, and Parallel Styles

Partners in interpersonal relationships—and impersonal ones, too—can use one of three styles introduced in Chapter 1 to manage their conflicts. In relationships with a **complementary conflict style,** the partners use different but mutually reinforcing behaviours. In a **symmetrical conflict style,** both parties use the same tactics. Some relationships are characterized by a **parallel conflict style,** which shifts between complementary and symmetrical patterns from one issue to another. Table 10–2 illustrates how the same conflict can unfold in very different ways, depending on whether the partners' communication is symmetrical or complementary. A parallel style would alternate between these two forms, depending on the situation.

Research shows that a complementary "fight–flight" style is common in many unhappy marriages. One partner—most commonly the wife—addresses the conflict directly, while the other—usually the husband—withdraws.[33] It's easy to see how this pattern can lead to a cycle of increasing hostility and isolation, since each partner punctuates the conflict differently, blaming the other for making matters worse. "I withdraw because she's so critical," a husband might say. The wife wouldn't organize the sequence in the same way, however. "I criticize because he withdraws" would be her perception.

Complementary styles aren't the only ones that can lead to problems. Some distressed marriages suffer from destructively symmetrical communication. If both partners treat each other with matching hostility, one threat or insult leads to another in an escalatory spiral. If the partners both withdraw from each other instead of facing their

TABLE 10–2	COMPLEMENTARY AND SYMMETRICAL CONFLICT STYLES	
SITUATION	**COMPLEMENTARY STYLES**	**SYMMETRICAL STYLES**
Example 1: Wife upset because husband is spending little time at home.	Wife complains; husband withdraws, spending even less time at home.	Wife complains. Husband responds angrily and defensively.
Example 2: Female employee offended when boss calls her "sweetie."	Employee objects to boss, explaining her reasons for being offended. Boss apologizes for his unintentional insult.	Employee turns the tables by calling boss "cutie." Boss gets the hint and stops using the term.
Example 3: Parents uncomfortable about teenager's new friends.	Parents express concerns. Child dismisses them, saying, "There's nothing to worry about."	Teen expresses concern that parents are being too protective.

problems, a de-escalatory spiral results, in which the satisfaction and vitality ebb from the relationship, leaving it a shell of its former self.

As Table 10–2 shows, both complementary and symmetrical behaviour can produce "good" results as well as "bad" ones. If the complementary behaviours are positive, then a positive spiral results and the conflict stands a good chance of being resolved. This is the case in example 2 in Table 10–2, in which the boss is open to hearing the employee's concerns, listening willingly as the employee talks. Here, a complementary talk–listen pattern works well.

Symmetrical styles can also be beneficial, as another look at the boss–employee example shows. Many women have found that giving insensitive men a taste of their own sexist medicine is an effective way to end harassment without provoking an argument. The clearest example of constructive symmetry occurs when both parties communicate assertively, listening to one another's concerns and working together to resolve them. The potential for this sort of solution occurs in example 3, in the parent–teenager conflict. With enough mutual respect and careful listening, both the parents and their teenager can understand one another's concerns, and very possibly find a way to give both parties what they want.

Intimate and Aggressive Styles

Another way to look at conflict styles is to examine the interaction between intimacy and aggression. The following scheme was originally used to describe communication between couples, but it also works well for other types of relationships.

* *Nonintimate–Aggressive* These partners fight, but are unsuccessful at satisfying important content and relational goals. In some relationships aggression is expressed directly: "Forget it. I'm not

going to another stupid party with your friends. All they do is gossip and eat." In other relationships, indirect aggression is the norm: *(Sarcastically)* "Sure, I'd *love* to go to another party with your friends." Neither of these approaches is satisfying, since there are few rewards to justify the costs of the unpleasantness.

- *Nonintimate–Nonaggressive* The individuals avoid conflicts–and one another–instead of facing issues head-on: "You won't be coming home for the holidays? Oh well, I guess that's OK. . . ." Relationships of this sort can be quite stable, but because this pattern of communication doesn't confront and resolve problems, the vitality and satisfaction can decline over time.

- *Intimate–Aggressive* This pattern combines aggression and intimacy in a manner that might seem upsetting to outsiders, but that can work well in some relationships. Lovers may argue like cats and dogs, but then make up just as intensely. Co-workers might argue heatedly about how to get the job done, but still cherish their association.

- *Intimate–Nonaggressive* This sort of relationship has a low amount of attacking or blaming. Partners may confront each other directly or indirectly, but one way or another they manage to prevent issues from interfering with their relationship.

INVITATION TO INSIGHT

UNDERSTANDING CONFLICT STYLES

You can gain a clearer idea of how conflict styles differ by completing the following exercise.

1. Join a partner and choose one of the following conflicts to work on for this exercise. If you prefer, you may substitute a different conflict of your own.

   Roommates disagree about the noise level in their apartment.

   Parents want their son or daughter, who is in second year in college, to stay home for the winter vacation. The son or daughter wants to travel with friends.

   One person in a couple wants to spend free time socializing with friends. The other wants to stay at home together.

2. Role-play the conflict four times, reflecting each of the following styles:

   Nonintimate–aggressive   Intimate–aggressive

   Nonintimate–nonaggressive   Intimate–nonaggressive

3. After experiencing each of these styles, determine which of them characterizes the way conflict is managed in one of your interpersonal relationships. Are you satisfied with this approach? If not, describe what style would be more appropriate.

The pattern that partners choose may reveal a great deal about the kind of relationship they have chosen. Communication researcher Mary Ann Fitzpatrick identified three types of couples: separates, independents, and traditionals.[34] Further research revealed that partners in each type of relationship approached conflict in a different manner.[35] Separates and independents tended to avoid conflict. Traditionals, by contrast, spent the most time focussing on their interaction. They also felt most secure about their relationships. They expressed negative emotions frequently, but also sought and revealed a large amount of personal information. Satisfied traditional couples fit the intimate–nonaggressive pattern, communicating more positive and less negative information than independents.

Information like this suggests that there's no single "best" relational conflict style. Some families or couples may fight intensely but love one another just as strongly. Others might handle issues more rationally and calmly. Even a nonintimate–nonaggressive style can work well when there's no desire to have an interpersonal relationship. You might, for example, be willing to accommodate the demands of an eccentric professor for a semester, since rolling with the punches gets you the education you are seeking without provoking a confrontation that could be upsetting and costly.

Conflict Rituals

When people have been in a relationship for some time, their communication often develops into **conflict rituals**—unacknowledged but very real repeating patterns of interlocking behaviour.[36] Consider a few common rituals:

- A young child interrupts her parents, demanding to be included in their conversation. At first the parents tell the child to wait, but she whines and cries until the parents find it easier to listen than to ignore the fussing.

- A couple fights. One partner leaves. The other accepts the blame for the problem and begs forgiveness. The first partner returns, and a happy reunion takes place. Soon they fight again.

- A boss flies into a rage when the pressure builds at work. Recognizing this, the employees avoid him as much as possible. When the crisis is over, the boss compensates for his outbursts by being especially receptive to employee requests.

There's nothing inherently wrong with the interaction in many rituals, especially when everybody involved accepts them as ways of managing conflict.[37] Consider the preceding examples. In the first, the little girl's whining may be the only way she can get the parents' attention. In the second, both partners might use the fighting as a way to blow off steam, and both might find that the joy of a reunion is worth the grief of the separation. The third ritual might work well for the boss (as a way of releasing pressure) and for employees (in getting their requests met).

Rituals can cause problems, though, when they become the *only* way relational partners handle their conflicts. As you learned in Chapter 1, competent communicators have a large repertoire of behaviours, and they are able to choose the most effective response for a given situation. Relying on one ritual pattern to handle all conflicts is no more effective than using a screwdriver to handle every home repair or putting the same seasoning on every dish you cook: What works in one situation isn't likely to succeed in many others. Conflict rituals may be familiar and comfortable, but they aren't the best way to resolve the variety of conflicts that are part of any relationship.

INVITATION TO INSIGHT

YOUR CONFLICT RITUALS

Describe two conflict rituals in one of your important relationships. One of your examples should consist of a positive ritual and the other of one that generates unsatisfying results. For each example, explain

1. a subject that is likely to trigger the conflict (e.g., money, leisure time, affection).
2. the behaviour of one partner that initiates the ritual.
3. the series of responses by both partners that follow the initiating event.
4. how the ritual ends.

Based on your description, explain an alternative to the unsatisfying ritual and describe how you might be able to change the way you manage the conflict in a more satisfying way.

VARIABLES IN CONFLICT STYLES

By now you can see that every relational system is unique. The communication patterns in one family, business, or classroom are likely to be very different from any other. But along with the differences that arise in individual relationships, there are two powerful variables that affect the way people manage conflict: gender and culture. We will now take a brief look at each of these factors and see how they affect conflict management.

Men and women are supposed to argue, and one of the reasons why they get married is so they won't have to argue with strangers.

H. Gordon Green, *Professor Go Home*

Gender

Men and women often approach conflicts differently. Even in childhood, males are more likely to be aggressive, demanding, and competitive, while females are more co-operative. Studies of children from preschool to early adolescence have shown that boys try to get their way by ordering one another around: "Lie down." "Get off my steps." "Gimme your arm." By contrast, girls are more likely to make proposals for action, beginning with the word "Let's": "Let's go find some." "Let's ask her, 'Do you have any bottles?'" "Let's move *these* out *first*."[38] Whereas boys tell each other what role to take in pretend play ("Come on, be a doctor"), girls more commonly ask each other what role they want ("Will you be the patient for a few minutes?") or make a joint proposal ("We can both be doctors"). Furthermore, boys often make demands without offering an explanation ("Look, man. I want the wire cutters right now"). By contrast, girls often give reasons for their suggestions ("We gotta *clean* 'em first . . . 'cause they got germs").

Differences like these often persist into adulthood. One survey of college students revealed that men and women viewed conflicts in contrasting ways.[39] Regardless of their cultural background, female students described men as being concerned with power and more interested in content than relational issues. Phrases used to describe male conflict styles included: "The most important thing to males in conflict is their egos." "Men don't worry about feelings." "Men are more direct." By contrast, women were described as being more concerned with maintaining the relationship during a conflict. Phrases used to describe female conflict styles included: "Women are better listeners." "Women try to solve problems without controlling the other person." "Females are more concerned with others' feelings." When the actual conflict behaviours of both sexes are observed, women turn out to be more assertive than men about expressing their ideas and feelings, and men are more likely to withdraw from discussing issues.[40]

These sorts of differences don't mean that men are incapable of forming good relationships. Instead, their notions of what makes a good relationship are different. For some men, friendship and aggression aren't mutually exclusive. In fact, many strong male relationships are built around competition—at work or in athletics, for example. Women can be competitive, too, but they also are more likely to use logical reasoning and bargaining than aggression.[41] When men communicate with women, they become less aggressive and more co-operative than they are in all-male groups.

Most theorists suggest that the primary reason for differences in conflict style is socialization.[42] Some social scientists have proposed that a "threshold of assertiveness" may exist for people, especially women, allowing them to behave in an assertive way up to a point, but no further. Because women typically have been perceived as more compliant and co-operative, they may have seen themselves as reaching this threshold sooner than men, at which time they back off. Being less assertive may not feel right to women who justifiably think that they shouldn't be held to a different standard than men. Nonetheless, this is one case where gender equity doesn't produce the best results: Both women and men appear less tolerant of assertive behaviour when it comes from a woman than from a man.[43]

Happiness is driving a taxi in Toronto.

George Gabori, quoted by Ethan Heberman in *The Toronto Star*

In contrast with the "men are from Mars, women are from Venus" view of conflict, a look at the entire body of research on gender and conflict suggests that the differences in how the two sexes handle conflict are rather small, and not at all representative of the stereotypical picture of aggressive men and passive women. However, the influence of gender on these differences is quite small. Although women and men may have characteristically different conflict styles, the situation at hand has a greater influence on shaping the way a person handles conflict. Who is seeking change and how the other person responds determine the way conflict is managed much more than gender.[44]

Culture

The way in which people manage conflict varies tremendously depending on their cultural background. The straight-talking, assertive approach that characterizes many North Americans is not the universal norm.[45]

Perhaps the most important cultural factor in shaping attitudes toward conflict is an orientation toward individualism or collectivism.[46] In individualistic cultures, the goals, rights, and needs of each person are considered important, and most people would agree that it is an individual's right to stand up for himself or herself. By contrast, collectivist cultures (more common in Latin America and Asia)

consider the concerns of the group to be more important than those of any individual. In these cultures, the kind of assertive behaviour that might seem perfectly appropriate to a North American would seem rude and insensitive.

Another factor that distinguishes the assertiveness that is so valued by North Americans and northern Europeans from the behaviour styles of other cultures is the difference between high- and low-context cultural styles.[47] Recall from our discussion in Chapter 6 that low-context cultures like Canada and the United States place a premium on being direct and literal. By contrast, high-context cultures like Japan value self-restraint and avoid confrontation. Communicators in these cultures derive meaning from a variety of unspoken rules, such as the context, social conventions, and hints. Preserving and honouring the face of the other person are a prime goal, and communicators go to great lengths to avoid any communication that might risk embarrassing a conversational partner. For this reason, what seems like "beating around the bush" to a Canadian would be polite to an Asian. In Japan, for example, even a simple request like "close the door" would be too straightforward.[48] A more indirect statement such as "It is somewhat cold today" would be more appropriate. To take a more important example, Japanese are reluctant to say "no" to a request. A more likely answer would be "Let me think about it for a while," which anyone familiar with Japanese culture would recognize as a refusal. When indirect communication is a cultural norm, it is unreasonable to expect more-straightforward approaches to succeed. When people from different cultures face a conflict, their habitual communication patterns may not mesh smoothly. The challenge faced by a Canadian husband and his Taiwanese wife illustrates this sort of problem:

> The husband would typically try to confront his wife verbally and directly, . . . leading her to either become violently defensive or withdraw completely from the discussion. She, on the other hand, would attempt to indicate her displeasure by changes in mood and eye contact (typical of Chinese culture) that were either not noticed (or uninterpretable) by her husband. Thus, neither "his way" nor "her way" was working and they could not see any realistic way to "compromise."[49]

It isn't necessary to look at Asia to encounter cultural differences in conflict. Canadians visiting Greece, for example, often think they are witnessing an argument when they are overhearing a friendly conversation.[50] A comparative study of North American and Italian nursery-school children showed that one of the Italian children's favourite pastimes was a kind of heated debating that Italians call *discussione*, but that we would regard as arguing. Likewise, research has shown that the conversations of working-class Jewish speakers of eastern European origin used arguments as a means of being sociable.

Within Canada, the ethnic background of communicators also plays a role in their ideas about conflict. For instance, in a class discussion on this topic, Dolores Francis, a Mi'kmaq student, noted that it is very difficult for her to learn communication patterns offered in this textbook because conflict is rarely seen in her culture. She explained that even when children say or do inappropriate things, adults do not interfere because to do so shames the children. Instead, parents later talk with their children, who would respect them and not engage in the disorderly behaviour again. Further, when in conflict with non-Native peoples, Dolores added, although she describes a problem in just one word, non-Natives use several; in other words, they tend to go on and on. To adapt to the white approach, she feels she must exaggerate, and this runs contrary to her cultural norms. With differences like these, it's easy to imagine how two friends, lovers, or fellow workers from different cultural backgrounds might have trouble finding a conflict style that is comfortable for them both.

METHODS OF CONFLICT RESOLUTION

No matter what the relational style, gender, or culture of the participants, every conflict is a struggle to have one's goals met. Sometimes that struggle succeeds, and in other cases it fails. In the remainder of this chapter we'll look at various approaches to resolving conflicts and see which ones are most promising.

Win–Lose

In **win–lose problem solving,** one party gets what he or she wants, whereas the other comes up short. People resort to this method of resolving disputes when they perceive a situation as being an "either–or" one: Either I get what I want or you get your way. The most clear-cut examples of win–lose situations are games in which the rules require a winner and a loser. Some interpersonal issues seem to fit into this win–lose framework: two co-workers seeking a promotion to the same job, or a couple disagreeing on how to spend their limited money.

Power is the distinguishing characteristic in win–lose problem solving, for it is necessary to defeat an opponent to get what one wants. The most obvious kind of power is physical. Some parents threaten their children with warnings, such as "Stop that or I'll send you to your room." Adults who use physical power to deal with each other usually aren't so blunt, but the legal system is the implied threat: "Follow the rules or we'll lock you up."

Real or implied force isn't the only kind of power used in conflicts. People who rely on authority of many types engage in win–lose methods without ever threatening physical coercion. In most jobs, supervisors have the authority to assign working hours, promotions, and desirable or undesirable tasks, and, of course, to fire an unsatisfactory employee. Teachers can use the power of grades to coerce students to act in desired ways.

There are two kinds of problems. Those that get better and almost solve themselves and those that get worse. You can afford to let the first type ride, but you better get the second fast.

John Turner,
quoted in *Maclean's*

Intellectual or mental power can also be a tool for conquering an opponent. Everyone is familiar with stories of how a seemingly weak hero defeats a stronger enemy through cleverness, showing that brains are more important than brawn. In a less admirable way, passive–aggressive crazymakers can defeat their partners by inducing guilt, avoiding issues, withholding desired behaviours, pseudoaccommodating, and so on.

Even the usually admired democratic principle of majority rule is a win–lose method of resolving conflicts. However fair it may be, with this system one group gets its way and another is unsatisfied.

There are some circumstances in which the win–lose method may be necessary, as when there are truly scarce resources and only one party can achieve satisfaction. For instance, if two men want to marry the same woman, or vice versa, only one can succeed. And to return to an earlier example, it's often true that only one applicant can be hired for a job. But don't be too willing to assume that your conflicts are necessarily win–lose: As you'll soon read, many situations that seem to require a loser can be resolved to everyone's satisfaction. There is a second kind of situation when win–lose is the best method. Even when co-operation is possible, if the other person insists on trying to defeat you, the most logical response might be to defend yourself by fighting back.

A final and much less frequent justification for trying to defeat another person occurs when the other party is clearly behaving in a wrong manner and when defeating that person is the only way to stop the wrongful behaviour. Few people would deny the importance of restraining a person who is deliberately harming others, even if the aggressor's freedom is sacrificed in the process. The danger of forcing wrongdoers to behave themselves is the wide difference in opinion between people about who is wrong and who is right. Given this difference, it would seem only justifiable in the most extreme circumstances to coerce others into behaving as we think they should.

Lose–Lose

In **lose–lose problem solving,** neither side is satisfied with the outcome. Although the name of this approach is so discouraging that it's hard to imagine how anyone could willingly use it, the reality is that lose–lose is a fairly common way to handle conflicts. In many instances the parties will both strive to be winners, but as a result of the struggle, both wind up losers. We see this in interpersonal relations between best friends, siblings, or parents and children where, as a result of some conflict, they refuse to communicate ever again. For example, we know of two siblings who were very close as children, and remained so into adulthood. However, after a strong disagreement about where their elderly, fragile mother should live, the two never spoke again. Not only was the conflict a lose–lose one for the two parties involved, their spouses, children, and other family members were also deprived of the warm family relationships they

THE FAR SIDE   By GARY LARSON

"OK, crybaby!" You want the last soda?
Well, let me GET IT READY FOR YOU!"

had once enjoyed. Perhaps you have seen such battles of pride where both parties strike out and suffer.

Compromise

Unlike lose–lose outcomes, a **compromise** gives both parties at least some of what they wanted, though both sacrifice part of their goals. People usually settle for compromises when it seems that partial satisfaction is the best they can hope for. Although a compromise may be better than losing everything, this approach hardly seems to deserve the positive image it has with some people. In his valuable book on conflict resolution, Albert Filley makes an interesting observation about our attitudes toward this method.[51] Why is it, he asks, that if someone says, "I will compromise my values," we view the action unfavourably, yet we talk admiringly about parties in a conflict who compromise to reach a solution? Although compromises may be the best obtainable result in some conflicts, it's important to realize that both people in a dispute can often work together to find much better solutions. In such cases "compromise" is a negative word.

Most of us are surrounded by the results of bad compromises. Consider a common example—the conflict between one person's desire to smoke cigarettes and another's need for clean air. The win-lose outcomes on this issue are obvious: Either the smoker abstains or the nonsmoker gets polluted lungs—neither very satisfying. But a compromise in which the smoker gets to enjoy only a rare cigarette or must retreat outdoors and in which the nonsmoker still must inhale some fumes or feel like an ogre is hardly better. Both sides have lost a considerable amount of both comfort and goodwill. Of course, the costs involved in other compromises are even greater. For example, if a divorced couple compromise on child care by haggling over custody and then grudgingly agree to split the time with their children, it's hard to say that anybody has won.

However, some compromises do leave both parties satisfied. You and the seller might settle on a price for a used car that is between what the seller was asking and what you wanted to pay. Although neither of you got everything you wanted, the outcome would still leave both of you

Co-operation is not a one-way street.

Maurice Duplessis, favourite phrase used in speeches as premier of Quebec, 1936–39, 1944–59

To really work out a problem, you need an uninterrupted period of time together. Making a nasty comment as you both leave the house in the morning doesn't get at the issue and it leaves both of you in a bad mood. Make an appointment to talk about it. "I'd like some time with you tonight to talk about a problem I'm having" is a good way to approach it. It doesn't help to start off on the attack: "I want to talk to you about the lousy job you're doing: . . ." This is just another form of the hit and run. And, to be honest, it is your problem. It may be that your partner isn't doing the dishes as promised, but it is really a problem because you are unhappy about it.

If the time you suggest for talking isn't acceptable to your partner, ask when would be. Pin down a specific time. If you just leave it for "sometime on the weekend" there will always be something else one of you would rather be doing.

Lois Richardson,
Working Couples: How to Successfully Combine Family and Work

satisfied. Likewise, you and your companion might agree to see a film that is the second choice for both of you in order to spend an evening together. As long as everyone is satisfied with an outcome, compromise can be an effective way to resolve conflicts.

Win–Win

In **win–win problem solving,** the goal is to find a solution that satisfies the needs of everyone involved. Not only do the parties avoid trying to win at the other's expense, but also they believe that by working together it is possible to find a solution that goes beyond a mere compromise and allows all parties to reach their goals. Consider a few examples:

Scott was an antique collector; his wife, Angela, loved to raise and show championship Dalmatians. Their income didn't leave enough money for both to practise their hobbies, and splitting the cash they did have wouldn't have left enough for either. *Solution:* Put all the first year's money into the puppies, and then, after they were grown, use the income from their litters and show prizes to pay for Scott's collection.

Celine, a store manager, hated rescheduling employee work shifts to accommodate their social and family needs. She and her staff developed an arrangement in which employees arranged schedule swaps on their own and notified her in writing once they were made.

Jenna and Amanda were roommates who had different studying habits. Jenna liked to do her work in the evenings, which left her days free for other things, but Amanda felt that nighttime was party time. *Solution:* Monday through Wednesday evenings Jenna studied at her boyfriend's place while Amanda did anything she wanted. Amanda agreed to keep things quiet around the house on Thursday and Sunday nights.

The point here isn't that these solutions are the correct ones for everybody with similar problems: The win–win approach doesn't work that way. Different people might have found other solutions that suited them better. The win–win method gives you an *approach*–a way of creatively finding just the right answer for your unique problem. By using it you can tailor-make a way of resolving your conflicts that everyone can live with comfortably.

You should understand that the win–win approach doesn't call for compromises in which the participants give up something they really want or need. Sometimes a compromise is the only alternative, but in the method we're talking about you find a solution that satisfies everyone—one in which nobody had to lose.

Although a win–win approach sounds ideal, it is not always possible, or even appropriate. Table 10–3 lists some factors to consider

TABLE 10–3	CHOOSING THE MOST APPROPRIATE METHOD OF CONFLICT

CONSIDER DEFERRING TO THE OTHER PERSON:

When you discover you are wrong
When the issue is more important to the other person than it is to you
To let others learn by making their own mistakes
When the long-term cost of winning may not be worth short-term gains

CONSIDER COMPROMISING:

When there is not enough time to seek a win–win outcome
When the issue is not important enough to negotiate at length
When the other person is not willing to seek a win–win outcome

CONSIDER COMPETING:

When the issue is important and the other person will take advantage of your noncompetitive approach

CONSIDER CO-OPERATING:

When the issue is too important for a compromise
When a long-term relationship between you and the other person is important
When the other person is willing to co-operate

when deciding which approach to take when facing a conflict. There will certainly be times when compromising is the most sensible approach. You will even encounter instances when pushing for your own solution is reasonable. Even more surprisingly, you will probably discover that there are times when it makes sense to willingly accept the loser's role.

WIN–WIN COMMUNICATION SKILLS

Win–win problem solving is clearly superior to the win–lose and lose–lose approaches. Why, then, is it so rarely used? There are three reasons. The first is lack of awareness. Some people are so used to competition that they mistakenly think winning requires them to defeat their "opponent."

Even when they know better, another reason prevents many people from seeking win–win solutions. Conflicts are often emotional affairs, in which people react combatively without stopping to think of better alternatives. Because this kind of emotional reflex prevents constructive solutions, it's often necessary to stop yourself from speaking out

As a country, we are in the incredibly fortunate position of having no problems which cannot be substantially resolved by an act of our own national will. Therefore, let us will once again to live together in peace and equality, respecting each other's rights and freedoms, sharing fairly the rich opportunities of this great land.

Pierre Elliott Trudeau,
New Year's message, published in
The Toronto Star

aggressively in a conflict and starting an escalating spiral of defensiveness. The time-honoured advice of "counting to ten" applies here. Once you've thought about the matter, you'll be able to *act* constructively instead of *reacting* in a way that's likely to produce a lose–lose outcome.

A third reason win–win solutions are rare is that they require the other person's co-operation. It's difficult to negotiate constructively with someone who insists on trying to defeat you. In this case, use your best persuasive skills to explain that by working together you can find a solution that satisfies both of you.

In spite of these challenges, it is definitely possible to become better at resolving conflicts. In the following pages we will outline a method to increase your chances of being able to handle your conflicts in a

Cross

He has leaned for hours
    against the veranda railing
Gazing the darkened garden
    out of mind
While she with battened
    hatches rides out the wind
That will blow for a year or a
    day, there is no telling.

As to why they are cross she
    barely remembers now.
That they are cross, she is
    certain. They hardly speak.
Feel cold and hurt and stony.
    For a week
Have without understanding
    behaved so.

And will continue so to behave
    for neither
Can come to that undemanded
    act of love

Kiss the sleeping princess or
    sleep with the frog
And break the spell which
    holds them each from the
    other.

Or if one ventures towards it,
    the other, shy,
Dissembles, regrets too late the
    dissimulation
And sits, hands slack, heart
    tiny, the hard solution
Having again passed by.

Silly the pair of them. Yet they
    make me weep.
Two on a desert island, back to
    back
Who, while the alien world
    howls round them black
Go their own ways, fall emptily
    off to sleep.

P.K. Page

win–win manner. As you read the following steps, try to imagine yourself applying them to a problem that's bothering you now.

Step 1–Identify Your Problem and Unmet Needs

Before you speak out, it's important to realize that the problem that is causing conflict is yours. Whether you want to return an unsatisfactory piece of merchandise, complain to noisy neighbours because your sleep is being disturbed, or request a change in working conditions from your employer, the problem is yours. Why? Because in each case *you* are the person who "owns" the problem–the one who is dissatisfied. You are the one who has paid for the defective article; the merchant who sold it to you has the use of your good money. You are the one who is losing sleep as a result of your neighbours' activities; they are content to go on as before. You, not your boss,* are the one who is unhappy with your working conditions.

Realizing that the problem is yours will make a big difference when the time comes to approach your partner. Instead of feeling and acting in an evaluative way, you'll be more likely to state your problem in a descriptive way, which not only will be more accurate but also reduce the chance of a defensive reaction.

Once you realize that the problem is yours, the next step is to identify the unmet needs that make you dissatisfied. For instance, in the barking dog incident, your need may be to get some sleep or to study without interruptions. In the case of a friend who teases you in public, your need would probably be to avoid embarrassment.

Sometimes the task of identifying your needs isn't as simple as it first seems. Behind the apparent content of an issue is often a relational need. Consider these examples:

A friend hasn't returned some money you lent long ago. Your apparent need in this situation might be to get the cash back. But a little thought will probably show that this isn't the only, or even the main, thing you want. Even if you were rolling in money, you'd probably want the loan repaid because of your most important need: *to avoid feeling victimized by your friend's taking advantage of you.*

Someone you care about who lives in a distant city has failed to respond to several letters. Your apparent need may be to get answers to the questions you've written about, but it's likely that there's another, more fundamental need: *the reassurance that you're still important enough to deserve a response.*

---

*Of course, others involved in the conflict may have problems of their own. For instance, the shopkeeper, the noisy neighbours, and your boss may all be bothered by your requests. But the fact remains that the reason you are speaking up about these matters is because you are dissatisfied. Thus, the problem is at least initially yours.

> No one said it would be easy,
> but no one said it would be this hard.
> No one said it would be easy,
> but no one thought we'd come this far.
>
> Sheryl Crow

As you'll soon see, the ability to identify your real needs plays a key role in solving interpersonal problems. For now, the point to remember is that before you voice your problem to your partner, you ought to be clear about which of your needs aren't being met.

Step 2—Make a Date

Destructive fights often start because the initiator confronts a partner who isn't ready. There are many times when a person isn't in the right frame of mind to face a conflict, perhaps owing to being fatigued, being in too much of a hurry to take the necessary time, being upset over another problem, or not feeling well. At times like these it's unfair to "jump" a person without notice and expect to get full attention for your problem. If you do persist, you'll probably have an ugly fight on your hands.

After you have a clear idea of the problem, approach your partner with a request to try to solve it. For example, "Something's been bothering me. Can we talk about it?" If the answer is "yes," you're ready to go further. If it isn't the right time to confront your partner, find a time that's agreeable to both of you.

Step 3—Describe Your Problem and Needs

Your partner can't possibly meet your needs without knowing why you're upset and what you want. Therefore, it's up to you to describe your problem as specifically as possible. The best way to deliver a complete, accurate message is to use the assertive behaviour-interpretation-feeling-consequence-intention format. Notice how well this approach works in the following examples:

> *Example 1*
> "I have a problem. It's about your leaving dirty clothes around the house after I've told you how much it bothers me *[behaviour]*. It's a problem because I have to run around like crazy and pick things up whenever guests come, which is no fun at all *[consequence]*. I'm starting to think that either you're not paying attention to my requests or you're trying to drive me crazy *[thoughts]*, and either way I'm getting more and more resentful *[feeling]*. I'd like to find some way to have a neat place without my having to be a maid or a nag."

Example 2

"I have a problem. When you drop by without calling ahead and I'm studying *[behaviour]*, I don't know whether to visit or ask you to leave *[thought]*. Either way, I get uncomfortable *[feeling]*, and it seems like whatever I do, I lose: Either I have to put you off or get behind in my work *[consequences]*. I'd like to find a way to get my studying done and still socialize with you *[intention]*."

Example 3

"Something is bothering me. When you tell me you love me and yet spend almost all your free time with your other friends *[behaviour]*, I wonder whether you mean it *[thought]*. I get insecure *[feeling]*, and then I start acting moody *[consequence]*. I need some way of finding out for sure how you feel about me *[intention]*."

Step 4—Consider Your Partner's Point of View

After stating your problem and describing what you need, it's important to make sure your partner has understood what you've said. As you can remember from the discussion of listening in Chapter 7,

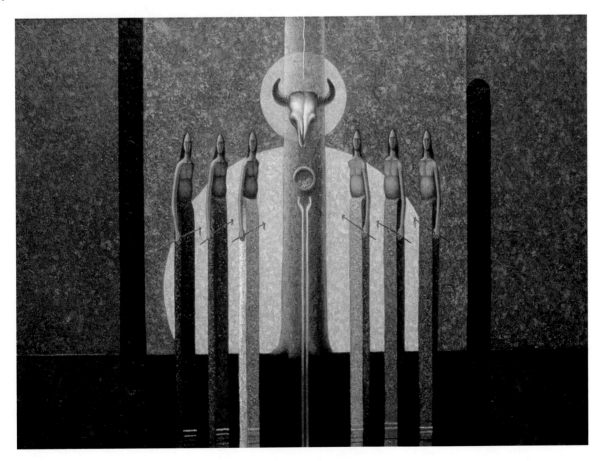

there's a good chance—especially in a stressful conflict—that your words will be misinterpreted.

It's usually unrealistic to insist that your partner paraphrase your statement, and fortunately there are more tactful and subtle ways to make sure you've been understood. For instance, you might try saying, "I'm not sure I expressed myself very well just now—maybe you should tell what you heard me say so I can be sure I got it right." In any case, be absolutely sure that your partner understands your whole message before going any further. Legitimate agreements are tough enough, but there's no point in getting upset about a conflict that doesn't even exist.

Once you have made your position clear, it's time to find out what your partner needs to feel satisfied about this issue. There are two reasons why it's important to discover your partner's needs. First, it's fair. The other person has just as much right as you to feel satisfied, and if you expect help in meeting your needs, it's reasonable that you behave in the same way. But in addition to decency, there's another, practical reason for concerning yourself with what the other person wants. Just as an unhappy partner will make it hard for you to become satisfied, a happy one will be more likely to co-operate in letting you reach your goals. Thus, it's in your own self-interest to discover and meet your partner's needs.

You can learn about your partner's needs simply by asking about them: "Now I've told you what I want and why. Tell me what you need to feel OK about this." Once your partner begins to talk, your job is to use the listening skills discussed earlier in this book to make sure you understand.

Step 5—Negotiate a Solution

Now that you and your partner understand each other's needs, the goal becomes finding a way to meet them. This is done by developing as many potential solutions as possible and then evaluating them to decide which one best meets everyone's needs. Probably the best description of the win–win approach has been written by Thomas Gordon in his book *Parent Effectiveness Training.*[52] The following steps are a modification of this approach:

1. *Identify and define the conflict.* We've discussed identifying and defining the conflict in the preceding pages. It consists of discovering each person's problem and needs, setting the stage for meeting all of them.
2. *Generate a number of possible solutions.* In this step, the partners work together to think of as many means as possible to reach their stated ends. The key word here is *quantity:* It's important to generate as many ideas as you can think of without worrying about which ones are good or bad. Write down every thought that comes up, no matter how unworkable: Sometimes a far-fetched idea will lead to a more workable one.

3. *Evaluate the alternative solutions.* This is the time to talk about which solutions will work and which ones won't. It's important for all parties to be honest about their willingness to accept an idea. If a solution is going to work, everyone involved has to support it.
4. *Decide on the best solution.* Now that you've looked at all the alternatives, pick the one that looks best to everyone. It's important to be sure everybody understands the solution and is willing to try it out. Remember that your decision doesn't have to be final, but it should look potentially successful.

Step 6—Follow Up the Solution

You can't be sure the solution will work until you try it. After you've tested it for a while, it's a good idea to set aside some time to talk over its progress. You may find that you need to make some changes or even rethink the whole problem. The idea is to keep on top of the problem, to keep using creativity to solve it.

As you think about applying this method, it is important to keep two points in mind. First, realize the importance of following every step. Each one is essential to the success of your encounter, and skipping one or more can lead to misunderstandings that might cause the conversation to degenerate into a negative spiral. After you have practised the method a number of times and are familiar with it, this type of problem solving will become almost second nature. You will then be able to approach your conflicts without following this step-by-step approach. But for the time being try to be patient and trust the value of the pattern.

A second point to realize is that in real life this method is not likely to flow smoothly from one step to another. You can expect and prepare for a certain amount of resistance from the other person. As Figure 10–1 shows, when a step doesn't meet with success, simply move back and repeat the preceding ones as necessary.

SKILL BUILDER

WIN–WIN SOLUTIONS AND YOU

1. Make a list of the situations in your life in which a conflict of needs is creating tension between you and someone else.

2. Analyze what you're doing at present to resolve such conflicts, and describe whether your behaviour is meeting with any success.

3. Pick at least one of the problems you just listed, and, with the other people involved, try to develop a win–win solution by following the steps listed in the preceding pages.

4. After working through steps 1 to 5, disclose the results of your conference to the class. After you've had time to test your solution, report the progress you've made and discuss the follow-up conference described in step 6.

FIGURE 10–1

Flow Chart of the Win–Win Negotiation Process

Adapted from Rory Remer and Paul de Mesquita, "Teaching and Learning Skills of Interpersonal Confrontation," in *Intimates in Conflict: A Communication Perspective*, D.D. Cahn, ed. (Hillsdale, NJ: Lawrence Erlbaum, 1990), p. 227.

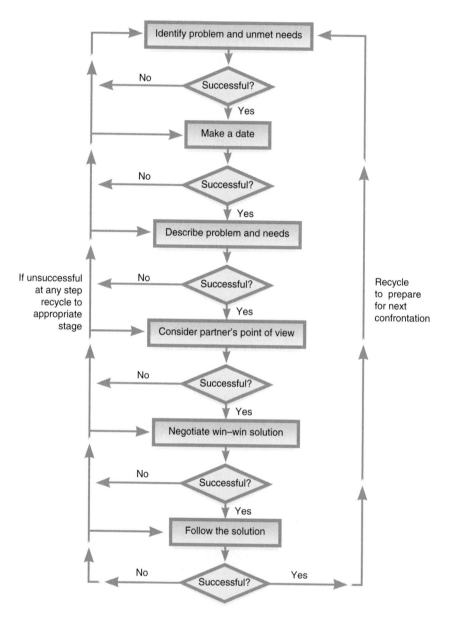

Your climate is the mood
Of living, the hinge of now,
In time the present tense.

Al Purdy, "Where the Moment Is"

Win–win solutions aren't always possible. There will be times when even the best-intentioned people simply won't be able to find a way of meeting all their needs. In cases like this, the process of negotiation has to include some compromises. But even then the preceding steps haven't been wasted. The genuine desire to learn what the other person wants and to try to satisfy those desires will build a climate of goodwill that can help you find the best solution to the present problem and also improve your relationship in the future.

Communication Transcript

Win—Win Problem Solving

It is 7:15 A.M. on a typical school day. Chris enters the kitchen and finds the sink full of dirty dishes. It was her roommate Terry's turn to do them. She sighs in disgust and begins to clean up, slamming pots and pans.

Terry Can't you be a little more quiet? I don't have a class till 10:00, and I want to catch up on sleep.

Chris *[Expressing her aggression indirectly in a sarcastic tone of voice]* Sorry to bother you. I was cleaning up last night's dinner dishes.

Terry *[Misses the message]* Well, I wish you'd do it a little more quietly. I was up late studying last night, and I'm beat.

Chris *[Decides to communicate her irritation more directly, if aggressively]* Well, if you'd done the dishes last night, I wouldn't have had to wash them now.

Terry *[Finally realizes that Chris is angry at her, responds defensively]* I was going to do them when I got up. I've got two midterms this week, and I was studying until midnight last night. What's more important, grades or a spotless kitchen?

Chris *[Perpetuating the growing defensive spiral]* I've got classes, too, you know. But that doesn't mean we have to live like pigs!

Terry *[Angrily]* Forget it. If it's such a big deal, I'll never leave another dirty dish!

Chris and Terry avoid one another as they get ready for school. During the day Chris realizes that attacking Terry will only make matters worse. She decides on a more constructive approach that evening.

Chris That wasn't much fun this morning. Want to talk about it?

Terry I suppose so. But I'm going out to study with Kim and Alisa in a few minutes.

Chris *[Realizing that it's important to talk at a good time]* If you have to leave soon, let's not get into it now. How about talking when you get back?

Terry OK, if I'm not too tired.

Chris Or we could talk tomorrow before class.

Terry OK.

Later that evening Terry and Chris continue their conversation.

Chris *[Defines the issue as her problem by using the assertive clear message format]* I hated to start the day with a fight, but I also hate having to do the dishes when it's not my turn *[behaviour]*. It doesn't seem fair for me to do my job and yours *[interpretation]*, and that's why I got so angry *[feeling]* and nagged at you *[consequence]*.

Terry But I was studying! You know how much I have to do. It's not like I was partying.

Chris *[Avoids attacking Terry by sincerely agreeing with the facts and explaining further why she was upset]* I know. It wasn't just doing the dishes that got me upset. It seems like there have been a lot of times when I've done your jobs and mine too.

Terry *[Defensively]* Like when?

Chris *[Gives specific descriptions of Terry's behaviour]* Well, this was the third time this week that I've done the dishes when it's your turn, and I can think of a couple of times lately when I've had to clean up your stuff before people came over.

Terry I don't see why it's such a big deal. If you just leave the stuff there, I'll clean it up.

Chris *[Still trying to explain herself, she continues to use "I" language.]* I know you would. I guess it's harder for me to put up with a messy place than it is for you.

Terry Yeah. If you'd just relax, living together would be a lot easier!

Chris *[Resenting Terry's judgemental accusation that the problem is all hers]* Hey, wait a second! Don't blame the whole thing on me. It's just that we have different standards. It looks to you like I'm too hung up on keeping the place clean . . .

Terry Right.

continued

Communication Transcript *continued*

Chris   . . . and if we do it your way, then I'd be giving up. I'd have to either live with the place messier than I like it or clean everything up myself. Then I'd get mad at you and things would be pretty tense around here. *[Describes the unpleasant consequences of not solving the problem in a mutually satisfactory way]*

Terry   I suppose so.

Chris   We need to figure out how to take care of the apartment in a way that we can both live with. *[Describes the broad outline of a win–win solution]*

Terry   Yeah.

Chris   So what could we do?

Terry   *[Sounding resigned]* Look, from now on I'll just do the dishes right away. It isn't worth arguing about.

Chris   Sure it is. If you're sore, the apartment may be clean but it won't be worth it.

Terry   *[Skeptically]* OK; what do you suggest?

Chris   Well, I'm not sure. You don't want the pressure of having to clean up right away, and I don't want to have to do my jobs and yours, too. Right?

Terry   Yeah. *[Still sounding skeptical]* So what are we going to do–hire a housekeeper to clean up?

Chris   *[Refusing to let Terry sidetrack the discussion]* That would be great if we could afford it. How about using paper plates? That would make cleaning up from meals easier.

Terry   Yeah, but there would still be pots and pans.

Chris   Well, it's not a perfect fix, but it might help a little. *[Goes on to suggest other ideas]* How about cooking meals that don't take a lot of work to clean up—maybe more salads and less fried stuff that sticks to pans. That would be a better diet, too.

Terry   Yeah. I do hate to scrub crusty frying pans. But that doesn't do anything about your wanting the living room neat and tidy all the time, and I bet I still wouldn't keep the kitchen as clean as you like it. Keeping the place super clean just isn't as big a deal to me as it is for you.

Chris   That's true, and I don't want to have to nag you! *[Clarifies the end she's seeking]* You know, it's not really cleaning up that bothers me. It's doing more than my share of work. I wonder if there's a way I could be responsible for keeping the kitchen clean and picking up if you could do something else to keep the workload even.

Terry   Are you serious? I'd love to get out of doing the dishes! You mean you'd do them . . . and keep the place looking good . . . if I did something else?

Chris   As long as the work was equal and you really did your jobs without me having to remind you.

Terry   What kind of work would you want me to do?

Chris   How about cleaning up the bathroom?

Terry   Forget it. That's worse than doing the dishes.

Chris   OK. How about cooking?

Terry   That might work, but then we'd have to eat together all the time. It's nice to do our own cooking when we want to. It's more flexible that way.

Chris   OK. But what about shopping? I hate the time it takes, and you don't mind it that much, do you?

Terry   You mean shop for groceries? You'd trade that for cleaning the kitchen?

Chris   Sure. And straightening up the living room. It takes an hour each time we shop and we make two trips a week. Doing the dishes would be much quicker.

Terry   Cool! It's a deal.

The plan didn't work perfectly: At first Terry put off shopping until all the food was gone, and Chris took advantage by asking Terry to run other errands during her shopping trips. But their arrangement proved much more successful than the old situation. The apartment was cleaner and the workload more even, which satisfied Chris. Terry was less the object of Chris's nagging and she had no kitchen chores, which made her happier. Just as important, the relationship between Chris and Terry was more comfortable–thanks to win–win problem solving.

CONSTRUCTIVE CONFLICT: QUESTIONS AND ANSWERS

After learning about win–win negotiating, people often express doubts about how well it can work. "It sounds like a good idea," they say, "but. . . ." Three questions arise more than any others, and they deserve an answer.

Isn't the Win–Win Approach Too Good to Be True?

Research shows that seeking mutual benefit is not only desirable–it also works. In fact, the win–win approach produces better results than a win–lose negotiating style.

In a series of experiments, Robert Axelrod presented subjects with a bargaining situation called "prisoner's dilemma," in which they could choose either to co-operate or betray a confederate.[53] There are three types of outcome in prisoner's dilemma: One partner can win big by betraying a confederate, both can win by co-operating, or both can lose by betraying each other.

Although cynics might assume that the most effective strategy is to betray a partner (a win–lose approach), Axelrod demonstrated that co-operation is actually the best hard-nosed choice. He staged a tournament in which participants played against a computer that was programmed to represent several negotiating strategies. The winning strategy was one called "Tit-for-Tat." It starts out by co-operating and continues to co-operate until the other party betrays it. After that, the program always does what the other player did on the previous move. It never punishes an opponent more than once for a betrayal, and it will always co-operate if the other player does.

A win–win Tit-for-Tat strategy succeeds for several reasons.[54] First, it isn't a patsy. It responds quickly to betrayal, discouraging others from taking unfair advantage. At the same time, it is quick to forgive. It doesn't hold a grudge: As soon as the other party co-operates, it does, too. Finally, it isn't too sneaky. By making its behaviour obvious and predictable, Tit-for-Tat creates an atmosphere of trust.

There are certainly some conflicts that can't be resolved with win–win outcomes. Only one suitor can marry the prince or princess, and only one person can be hired for the advertised job. Furthermore, it's impossible to reach a win–win solution when your partner refuses to co-operate. Most of the time, however, good intentions and creative thinking can lead to outcomes that satisfy everyone's needs.

Isn't the Win–Win Approach Too Elaborate?

The win–win approach described in the preceding pages is detailed and highly structured. In everyday life you may rarely use every step:

The Prisoner's Dilemma

http://www.spectacle.org/995/ pd.html

The Complexity of Cooperation

http://pscs.physics.lsa.umich.edu/ Software/ComplexCoop.html

(Reprinted by permission of Jules Feiffer.)

Sometimes the problem at hand won't justify the effort, and other times you and your partner might not need to be so deliberate to take care of the issue. Nonetheless, while learning to use the method, try to follow all the steps carefully. Once you have become familiar and skillful at using them all, you will be able to use whichever ones prove necessary in a given situation. For important issues, you are likely to find that every step of the win–win approach is important. If this process seems time-consuming, just consider the time and energy that will likely be required if you *don't* resolve the issue at hand.

Isn't Win–Win Negotiating *Too* Rational?

Frustrated readers often complain that the win–win approach is so sensible that only a saint could use it successfully. "Sometimes I'm so angry that I don't care about being supportive or empathetic or anything else," they say. "I just want to blow my top!"

When you feel like this, it's almost impossible to be rational. At times like these probably the most therapeutic thing to do is get your feelings off your chest in what George Bach calls a "Vesuvius"—an uncontrolled, spontaneous explosion. A Vesuvius can be a terrific way of blowing off steam, and, after you do so, it's often much easier to figure out a rational solution to your problem.

So we encourage you to have a Vesuvius, with the following qualifications: Be sure your partner understands what you're doing and realizes that whatever you say doesn't call for a response. Your partner should let you rant and rave for as long as you want without getting defensive. Then when your eruption subsides, you can take steps to work through whatever still troubles you.

Is It Possible to Change Others?

Readers often agree that win–win problem solving would be terrific—if everyone had read *Looking Out/Looking In* and understood the method. "How can I get the other person to co-operate?" the question goes.

Though you won't always be able to gain your partner's co-operation, a good attempt can do the trick most of the time. The key lies in showing that it's in the other person's self-interest to work together: "Look, if we can't settle this, we'll both feel miserable. But if we can find an answer, think how much better off we'll be." Notice that this sort of explanation projects both the favourable consequences of co-operating and the costs of competing.

You can also boost the odds of getting your partner's co-operation by modelling the communication skills described in this book. You've read that defence-arousing behaviour is reciprocal, but so is supportive communication. If you can listen sincerely, avoid evaluative attacks, and empathize with your partner's concerns, for example, there's a good chance you'll get the same kind of behaviour in return. And even if your co-operative attitude doesn't succeed, you'll gain self-respect from knowing that at least you behaved honourably and constructively.

SUMMARY

Conflict is a fact of life in every interpersonal relationship. The way in which conflicts are handled plays a major role in the quality of a relationship. When managed constructively, they can lead to stronger and more-satisfying interaction; but when they are handled poorly, relationships will suffer.

There are four ways a person can behave when faced with a conflict. A nonassertive approach avoids the conflict altogether. A directly aggressive approach attacks the other party, while a passive-aggressive approach expresses hostility obliquely. An indirect style hints about the nature of a problem, while an assertive approach confronts the issue directly, but without attacking the other party. A complete assertive message describes the behaviour in question, at least one interpretation, the speaker's feelings, the consequences of the situation, and the speaker's intentions in making the statement.

The way a conflict is handled is not always the choice of a single person, since the parties influence one another as they develop a relational conflict style. This style may be complementary, symmetrical, or parallel; it can involve a combination of intimate and aggressive elements; and it can include constructive or destructive rituals. Besides being shaped by the relationship, a conflict style is also influenced by a person's gender and cultural background.

There are three outcomes to conflicts: win–lose, lose–lose, and win–win. A win–lose approach often disintegrates into a lose–lose outcome in which all the parties suffer. Win–win solutions are often possible, if the parties possess the proper attitude and skills.

KEY TERMS

accommodation
asserion
avoidance
behavioural description
complementary conflict style
compromise
conflict
conflict ritual

consequence statement
crazymaking
direct aggression
indirect communication
intention statement
interpretation
lose-lose problem solving
nonassertion

parallel conflict style
passive aggression
relational conflict style
symmetrical conflict style
win–lose problem solving
win–win problem solving

Endnotes

References for Chapter 1

1. S. Schachter, *The Psychology of Affiliation* (Stanford, CA: Stanford University Press, 1959), pp. 9–10.

2. VPI, *Wisconsin State Journal*, Sept. 7, 1978.

3. J.B. Ross and M.M. McLaughlin, eds., *A Portable Medieval Reader* (New York: Viking, 1949).

4. Three articles in *The Journal of the American Medical Association* 267 (Jan. 22/29, 1992) discuss the link between psychosocial influences and coronary heart disease: R.B. Case, A.J. Moss, N. Case, M. McDermott, and S. Eberly, "Living Alone after Myocardial Infarction" (pp. 515–519); R.B. Williams, J.C. Barefoot, R.M. Califf, T.L. Haney, W.B. Saunders, D.B. Pryon, M.A. Hlatky, I.C. Siegler, and D.B. Mark, "Prognostic Importance of Social and Economic Resources among Medically Treated Patients with Angiographically Documented Coronary Artery Disease" (pp. 520–524); and R. Ruberman, "Psychosocial Influences on Mortality of Patients with Coronary Heart Disease" (pp. 559–560).

5. Sheldon Cohen, *JAMA* (June/July 1997) S. Cohen, "Social Ties and Susceptibility to the Common Cold," *Journal of the American Medical Association* 277 (1997): 1940–1944.

6. R. Narem, "Try a Little TLC," research reported in *Science* 80, no. 1 (1980): 15.

7. J. Lynch, *The Broken Heart: The Medical Consequences of Loneliness* (New York: Basic Books, 1977), pp. 239–242.

8. Ibid.

9. W.D. Rees and S.G. Lutkins, "Mortality of Bereavement," *British Medical Journal* 4 (1967): 13.

10. R. Shattuck, *The Forbidden Experiment: The Story of the Wild Boy of Aveyron* (New York: Farrar, Straus & Giroux, 1980), p. 37.

11. A.M. Nicotera, "Where Have We Been, Where Are We, and Where Do We Go?" in *Interpersonal Communication in Friend and Mate Relationships*, A.M. Nicotera and associates, eds. (Albany: State University of New York Press, 1993).

12. S. Duck, and G. Pittman, "Social and Personal Relationships," in *Handbook of Interpersonal Communication*, 2nd ed., M.L. Knapp and G.R. Phillips, eds. (Newbury Park, CA: Sage, 1994).

13. R.B. Rubin, E.M. Perse, and C.A. Barbato, "Conceptualization and Measurement of Interpersonal Communication Motives," *Human Communication Research* 14 (1988): 602–628.

14. W. Goldschmidt, *The Human Career: The Self in the Symbolic World* (Cambridge, MA: Basil Blackman, 1990).

15. D.B. Curtis, J.L. Winsor, and R.D. Stephens, "National Preferences in Business and Communication Education," *Communication Education* 38 (1989): 6–14. See also M.S. Peterson, "Personnel Interviewers' Perceptions of the Importance and Adequacy of Applicants' Communication Skills," *Communication Education* 46 (1997): 287–291.

16. M.A. McLaughlin, "Employability Skills Profile: What Are Employers Looking For?" *ERIC Clearing House on Counseling and Student Services*, Greensboro, NC; *Canadian Guidance and Counseling Foundation* Eric Document 399484 (1995).

17. A.H. Maslow, *Toward a Psychology of Being* (New York: Van Nostrand Reinhold, 1968).

18. C.E. Shannon and W. Weaver, *The Mathematical Theory of Communication* (Urbana: University of Illinois Press, 1949).

19. See, for example, J.B. Walther, "Computer-Mediated Communication: Impersonal, Interpersonal, and Hyperpersonal Interaction," *Communication Research* 23 (1996): 3–43, and J.B. Walther and J.K. Burgoon, "Relational Communication in Computer-Mediated Interaction," *Human Communication Research* 19 (1992): 50–88.

20. D. Kirkpatrick, "Here Comes the Payoff from PCs," *Fortune* (Mar. 23, 1992): 93–102.

21. D. Tannen, "Gender Gap in Cyberspace," *Newsweek* (May 16, 1994): 52–53.

22. K.R. Colbert, "The Effects of Debate Participation on Argumentativeness and Verbal Aggression," *Communication Education* 42 (1993): 206–214.

23. The issue of intentionality has been a matter of debate by communication theorists. For a sample of the arguments on both sides, see M.T. Motley, "On Whether One Can(not) Communicate: An Examination via Traditional Communication Postulates," *Western Journal of Speech Communication* 54 (1990): 1–20; J.B. Bavelas, "Behaving and Communicating: A Reply to Motley," *Western Journal of Speech Communication* 54 (1990): 593–602; and J. Stewart, "A Postmodern Look at Traditional Communication Postulates," *Western Journal of Speech Communication* 55 (1991): 354–379.

24. E.M. Rogers and D.L. Kincaid, *Communication Networks: Toward a New Paradigm for Research* (New York: Free Press, 1981), pp. 43–48, 63–66.

25. See, for example, R.K. Shelly, "Sequences and Cycles in Social Interaction," *Small Group Research* 28 (1997): 333–356.

26. S. Duck, "Relationships as Unfinished Business: Out of the Frying Pan and into the 1990s," *Journal of Social and Personal Relationships* 7 (1990): 5. See also J.N. Capella, "The Biological Origins of Automated Patterns of Human Interaction," *Communication Theory* 1 (1991): 4–35.

27. B.R. Burleson and W. Samter, "A Social Skills Approach to Relationship Maintenance," in *Communication and Relationship Maintenance,* D. Canary and L. Stafford, eds. (San Diego: Academic Press, 1994), p. 12.

28. M. Dainton and L. Stafford, "The Dark Side of 'Normal' Family Interaction," in *The Dark Side of Interpersonal Communication,* B.H. Spitzberg and W.R. Cupach, eds. (Hillsdale, NJ: Erlbaum, 1993).

29. See T. Clevenger, Jr., "Can One Not Communicate? A Conflict of Models," *Communication Studies* 42 (1991): 340–353. For a detailed rationale of the position argued in this section, see G.H. Stamp and M.L. Knapp, "The Construct of Intent in Interpersonal Communication," *Quarterly Journal of Speech* 76 (1990): 282–299.

30. For a thorough discussion of communication difficulties, see N. Coupland, H. Giles, and J.M. Wiemann, eds., *"Miscommunication" and Problematic Talk* (Newbury Park, CA: Sage, 1991).

31. For a similar list of characteristics, see J.C. McCroskey and V.P. Richmond, *Fundamentals of Human Communication: An Interpersonal Perspective* (Prospect Heights, IL: Waveland, 1996).

32. J.C. McCroskey and L. Wheeless, *Introduction to Human Communication* (Boston: Allyn and Bacon, 1976), p. 5. See also D.H. Cloven and M.E. Roloff, "Sense-Making Activities and Interpersonal Conflict: Communicative Cures for the Mulling Blues," *Western Journal of Speech Communication* 55 (1991): 134–158. See also D. Stiebel, *When Talking Makes Things Worse! Resolving Problems When Communication Fails* (Andrews and McMeel, 1997).

33. M.V. Redmond, "Interpersonal Communication: Definitions and Conceptual Approaches," in *Interpersonal Communication: Readings in Theory and Research,* M.V. Redmond, ed. (Fort Worth, TX: Harcourt Brace, 1995): 4–11.

34. See, for example, G.R. Miller and M. Steinberg, *Between People: A New Analysis of Interpersonal Communication* (Chicago: SRA, 1975), and J. Stewart and C. Logan, *Together: Communicating Interpersonally,* 5th ed. (New York: McGraw-Hill, 1998).

35. For further discussion of the characteristics of impersonal and interpersonal communication, see Arthur P. Bochner, "The Functions of Human Communication in Interpersonal Bonding," in *Handbook of Rhetorical and Communication Theory,* C.C. Arnold and J.W. Bowers, eds. (Boston: Allyn and Bacon, 1984), p. 550; S. Trenholm and A. Jensen, *Interpersonal Communication,* 2nd ed. (Belmont, CA: Wadsworth, 1992), pp. 27–33; J. Stewart and G. D'Angelo, *Together: Communicating Interpersonally,* 5th ed. (New York: McGraw-Hill, 1998), p. 5.

36. K.J. Gergen, *The Saturated Self: Dilemmas of Identity in Contemporary Life* (New York: Basic Books, 1991), p. 158.

37. See P. Wattzlawick, J.H. Beavin, and D.D. Jackson, *Pragmatics of Human Communication* (New York: Norton, 1967), and W.J. Lederer and D.D. Jackson, *The Mirages of Marriage* (New York: Norton, 1968).

38. D. Tannen, *That's Not What I Meant! How Conversational Style Makes or Breaks Your Relations with Others* (New York: Morrow, 1986), p. 190.

39. See, for example, R.A. Bell and J.A. Daly, "The Affinity-Seeking Function of Communication," in *Interpersonal Communication: Readings in Theory and Research,* M.V. Redmond, ed. (Fort Worth, TX: Harcourt Brace, 1995).

40. T.S. Lim and J.W. Bowers, "Facework: Solidarity, Approbation, and Tact," *Human Communication Research* 17 (1991): 415–450.

41. M.T. Palmer, "Controlling Conversations: Turns, Topics, and Interpersonal Control," *Communication Monographs* 56 (1989): 1–18.

42. Watzlawich, Beavin, and Jackson, *Pragmatics of Human Communication.*

43. For a thorough review of this topic, see B.H. Spitzberg and W.R. Cupach, *Handbook of Interpersonal Competence Research* (New York: Springer-Verlag, 1989).

44. See J.M. Wiemann, J. Takai, H. Ota, and M. Wiemann, "A Relational Model of Communication Competence," in *Emerging Theories of Human Communication,* B. Kovacic, ed. (Albany, NY: SUNY Press, 1997).

45. See Y.Y. Kim, "Intercultural Communication Competence: A Systems-Theoretic View," in *Cross-Cultural Interpersonal Communication,* S. Ting-Toomey and F. Korzenny, eds. (Newbury Park, CA: Sage, 1991); and G.M. Chen and W.J. Sarosta, "Intercultural Communication Competence: A Synthesis," in *Communication Yearbook 19,* B.R. Burleson and A.W. Kunkel, eds. (Thousand Oaks, CA: Sage, 1996).

46. B.H. Spitzberg, "An Examination of Trait Measures of Interpersonal Competence," *Communication Reports* 4 (1991): 22–29.

47. L.K. Guerrero, P.A. Andersen, P.F. Jorgensen, B.H. Spitzberg, and S.V. Eloy, "Coping with the Green-Eyed Monster: Conceptualizing and Measuring Communicative Responses to Romantic Jealousy," *Western Journal of Communication* 59 (1995): 270–304.

48. See B.J. O'Kefe, "The Logic of Message Design: Individual Differences in Reasoning about Communication," *Communication Monographs* 55 (1988): 80–103.

49. M. Fitzpatrick, *Between Husbands and Wives: Communication in Marriage* (Newbury Park, CA: Sage, 1989).

50. D.B. Wackman, S. Miller, and E.W. Nunnally, *Student Workbook: Increasing Awareness and Communication Skills* (Minneapolis: Interpersonal Communication Programs, 1976), p. 6.

51. J.M. Wiemann and P.M. Backlund, "Current Theory and Research in Communication Competence," *Review of Educational Research* 50 (1980): 185–199. See also M.V. Redmond, "The Relationship between Perceived Communication Competence and Perceived Empathy," *Communication Monographs* 52 (December 1985): 377–382; and M.V. Redmond, "The Functions of Empathy (Decentering) in Human Relations," *Human Relations* 42 (1989): 593–605.

52. R. Martin, "Relational Cognition Complexity and Relational Communication in Personal Relationships," *Communication Monographs* 59 (1992): 150–163.

53. Burleson and Samter, op. cit, p. 22.

54. B.D. Sypher and T. Zorn, "Communication-Related Abilities and Upward Mobility: A Longitudinal Investigation," *Human Communication Research* 12 (1986): 420–431.

55. Research summarized in D.E. Hamachek, *Encounters with the Self,* 2nd ed. (Fort Worth, TX: Holt, Rinehart and Winston, 1987), p. 8. See also J.A. Daly, A.L. Vangelisti, and S.M. Daughton, "The Nature and Correlates of Conversational Sensitivity," in *Interpersonal Communication: Readings in Theory and Research,* M.V. Redmond, ed. (Fort Worth, TX: Harcourt Brace, 1995).

56. Adapted from the work of R.P. Hart as reported by M.L. Knapp in *Interpersonal Communication and Human Relationships* (Boston: Allyn and Bacon, 1984), pp. 342–344. See also R.P. Hart and D.M. Burks, "Rhetorical Sensitivity and Social Interaction," *Speech Monographs* 39 (1972): 75–91; and R.P. Hart, R.E. Carlson, and W.F. Eadie, "Attitudes toward Communication and the Assessment of Rhetorical Sensitivity," *Communication Monographs* 47 (1980): 1–22.

References for Chapter 2

1. D. Carbaugh, *Situating Selves: The Communication of Social Identities in American Scenes* (Albany, NY: SUNY Press, 1996).

2. For a discussion of how the self-concept develops, see D. Hamachek, *Encounters with the Self,* 3rd ed. (Fort Worth, TX: Holt, Rinehart and Winston, 1992), pp. 5–8.

3. G.H. Mead, *Mind, Self, and Society* (Chicago: University of Chicago Press, 1934). See also P. Killock and J. O'Brien, eds., *The Production of Reality,* 2nd ed. (Thousand Oaks, CA: Pine Forge Press, 1997).

4. C.H. Cooley, *Human Nature and the Social Order* (New York: Scribner's, 1912).

5. J.B. Miller, "Learning from Early Relationship Experience," in *Learning about Relationships,* S. Duck, ed. (Newbury Park, CA: Sage, 1993).

6. T. Adler, "Personality, like Plaster, Is Pretty Stable over Time," *APA Monitor* (Oct. 1992): 18.

7. C. Gilligan, *Making Connections: The Relational Worlds of Adolescent Girls at Emma Willard School* (Cambridge: Harvard University Press, 1990).

8. R.W. Bibby and D.C. Posterski, *The Emerging Generation* (Toronto: Irwin Publishing, 1985).

9. R.W. Bibby and D.C. Posterski, *Teen Trends: A Nation in Motion* (Toronto: Stoddart, 1992).

10. J.D. Brown, N.J. Novick, K.A. Lord, and J.M. Richards, "When Gulliver Travels: Social Context, Psychological Closeness, and Self-Appraisals," *Journal of Personality and Social Psychology* 62 (1992): 717–734.

11. P.N. Myers and F.A. Biocca, "The Elastic Body Image: The Effect of Television Advertising and Programming on Body Image Distortions in Young Women," *Journal of Communication* 42 (1992): 108–134.

12. D. Grodin and T.R. Lindlof, *Constructing the Self in a Mediated World* (Newbury Park, CA: Sage, 1995).

13. J.D. Brown and T.A. Mankowski, "Self-Esteem, Mood, and Self-Evaluation: Changes in Mood and the Way You See You," *Journal of Personality and Social Psychology* 64 (1993): 421–430.

14. M.A. Gara, R.L. Woolfolk, B.D. Cohen, and R.B. Goldston, "Perception of Self and Other in Major Depression," *Journal of Abnormal Psychology* 102 (1993): 93–100.

15. B. Bower, "Truth Aches: People Who View Themselves Poorly May Seek the 'Truth' and Find Despair," *Science News* (Aug. 15, 1992): 110–111; and W.B. Swann, R.M. Wenzlaff, D.S. Krull, and B.W. Pelham, "Allure of Negative Feedback: Self-Verification Strivings among Depressed Persons," *Journal of Abnormal Psychology* 101 (1992): 293–306.

16. L.C. Miller, L.L. Cooke, J. Tsang, and F. Morgan, "Should I Brag? Nature and Impact of Positive and Boastful Disclosures for Women and Men," *Human Communication Research* 18 (1992): 364–399.

17. W.W. Wilmot, *Relational Communication* (New York: McGraw-Hill, 1995), pp. 35–54.

18. H. Giles and P. Johnson, "'Ethnolinguistic Identity Theory': A Social Psychological Approach to Language Maintenance," *International Journal of Sociology of Language* 68 (1987): 69–99.

19. J. Servaes, "Cultural Identity and Modes of Communication," in *Communication Yearbook 12,* J.A. Anderson, ed. (Newbury Park, CA: Sage, 1989), p. 396.

20. A. Bharti, "The Self in Hindu Thought and Action," in *Culture and Self: Asian and Western Perspectives* (New York: Tavistock, 1985).

21. W.B. Gudykunst and S. Ting-Toomey, *Culture and Interpersonal Communication* (Newbury Park, CA: Sage, 1988).

22. L.A. Samovar and R.E. Porter, *Communication between Cultures* (Belmont, CA: Wadsworth, 1991), p. 91.

23. D. Klopf, "Cross-Cultural Apprehension Research: A Summary of Pacific Basin Studies," in *Avoiding Communication: Shyness, Reticence, and Communication Apprehension,* J. Daly and J. McCroskey, eds. (Beverly Hills, CA: Sage, 1984).

24. S. Ting-Toomey, "A Face-Negotiation Theory," in *Theory in Interpersonal Communication,* Y. Kim and W. Gudykunst, eds. (Newbury Park, CA: Sage, 1988).

25. J. Kolligan, Jr., "Perceived Fraudulence as a Dimension of Perceived Incompetence," in *Competence Considered,* R.J. Sternberg and J. Kolligan, Jr., eds. (New Haven, CT: Yale University Press, 1990).

26. B.J. Zimmerman, A. Bandura, and M. Martinez-Pons, "Self-Motivation for Academic Attainment: The Role of Self-Efficacy Beliefs and Personal Goal Setting," *American Educational Research Journal* 29 (1992): 663–676.

27. G. Downey and S.I. Feldman, "Implications of Rejection Sensitivity for Intimate Relationships," *Journal of Personality and Social Psychology* 70 (1996): 1327–1343.

28. P.D. MacIntyre and K.A. Thivierge, "The Effects of Speaker Personality on Anticipated Reactions to Public Speaking," *Communication Research Reports* 12 (1995): 125–133.

29. R. Rosenthal and L. Jacobson, *Pygmalion in the Classroom* (New York: Holt, Rinehart and Winston, 1968).

30. P.D. Blank, ed., *Interpersonal Expectations: Theory, Research, and Applications* (Cambridge, UK: Cambridge University Press, 1993).

31. C.M. Shaw and R. Edwards, "Self-Concepts and Self-Presentations of Males and Females: Similarities and Differences," *Communication Reports* 10 (1997): 55–62.

32. E. Goffman, *The Presentation of Self in Everyday Life* (Garden City, NY: Doubleday, 1959), and *Relations in Public* (New York: Basic Books, 1971).

33. J. Stewart and C. Logan, *Together: Communicating Interpersonally,* 5th ed. (New York: McGraw-Hill, 1998), p. 120.

34. M.R. Leary and R.M. Kowalski, "Impression Management: A Literature Review and Two-Component Model," *Psychological Bulletin* 107 (1990): 34–47.

35. V. Brightman, A. Segal, P. Werther, and J. Steiner, "Ethological Study of Facial Expression in Response to Taste Stimuli," *Journal of Dental Research* 54 (1975): 141.

36. N. Chovil, "Social Determinants of Facial Displays," *Journal of Nonverbal Behavior* 15 (1991): 141–154.

37. M. Snyder, *Public Appearances, Private Realities: The Psychology of Self-Monitoring* (New York: W.H. Freeman, 1987).

38. The following discussion is based on material in Hamachek, *Encounters with the Self,* 3rd ed., pp. 24–26.

39. L.M. Coleman and B.M. DePaulo, "Uncovering the Human Spirit: Moving beyond Disability and 'Missed' Communications," in *"Miscommunication" and Problematic Talk,* N. Coupland, H. Giles, and J.M. Wiemann, eds. (Newbury Park, CA: Sage, 1991), pp. 61–84.

40. J.W. Vander Zanden, *Social Psychology,* 3rd ed. (New York: Random House, 1984), pp. 235–237.

41. J.B. Walther, "Computer-Mediated Communication: Impersonal, Interpersonal, and Hyperpersonal Interaction," *Communication Research* 23 (1996): 3–43.

References for Chapter 3

1. The graphic demonstrations of factors influencing perception in this and the following paragraph are borrowed from Dennis Coon's *Introduction to Psychology,* 7th ed. (St. Paul, MN: West, 1995).

2. G.W. Allport, *The Nature of Prejudice* (New York: Doubleday Anchor, 1958), p. 185.

3. N. Hewstone and R. Brown, "Contact Is Not Enough," in *Contact and Conflict in Intergroup Encounters,* M. Hewstone and R. Brown, eds. (Oxford, UK: Basil Blackwell, 1986), p. 29. See also H. Giles, N. Coupland, J. Coupland, A. Williams, and J. Nussbaum, "Intergenerational Talk and Communication with Older People," *International Journal of Aging and Human Development* 33 (1992): 251–297.

4. P. Watzlawick, J. Beavin, and D.D. Jackson, *Pragmatics of Human Communication* (New York: Norton, 1967), p. 65.

5. See T.N. Bradbury and F.D. Fincham, "Attributions in Marriage: Review and Critique," *Psychological Bulletin* 107 (1990): 3–33; and V. Manusov, "An Application of Attribution Principles to Nonverbal Behavior in Romantic Dyads," *Communication Monographs* 57 (1990): 104–118.

6. V. Manusov, "It Depends on Your Perspective: Effects of Stance and Beliefs about Intent on Person Perception," *Western Journal of Communication* 57 (1993): 27–41.

7. T. Adler, "Enter Romance, Exit Objectivity," *APA Monitor* (June 1992): 18.

8. J.K. Alberts, U. Kellar-Guenther, and S.R. Corman, "That's Not Funny: Understanding Recipients' Responses to Teasing," *Western Journal of Communication* 60 (1996): 337–357.

9. For a detailed description of how the senses affect perception, see N. Ackerman, *A Natural History of the Senses* (New York: Random House, 1990).

10. J. Piaget, *The Origins of Intelligence in Children* (New York: International Universities Press, 1952).

11. C. Cooper and C. McConville, "Interpreting Mood Scores: Clinical Implications of Individual Differences in Mood Variability," *British Journal of Medical Psychology* 63 (1990): 215–225. See also *Biological Rhythms*

and Behavior, J. Mendlewicz and H.M. van Praag, eds. (New York: Karger, 1983).

12. See, for example, J.C. Hoffmann, "Biorhythms in Human Reproduction: The Not-So-Steady States," *Signs* 7 (1982): 829–844.

13. R. Armao, "Worst Blunders; Firms Laugh through Tears," *American Business* (Jan. 1981): 11.

14. R. Harrison, "Nonverbal Behavior: An Approach to Human Communication," in *Approaches to Human Communication,* R. Budd and B. Ruben, eds. (New York: Spartan Books, 1972).

15. E.T. Hall, *The Hidden Dimension* (New York: Doubleday Anchor, 1969), p. 160.

16. H. Giles, N. Coupland, and J.M. Wiemann, "Talk Is Cheap . . . But 'My Word Is My Bond': Beliefs about Talk," in *Sociolinguistics Today: International Perspectives,* K. Bolton and H. Kwok, eds. (London: Routledge & Kegan Paul, 1992).

17. H. Hiller, *Canadian Society: A Macro Analysis* (Scarborough, ON: Prentice-Hall, 1991), p. 36.

18. See S.A. Rathus, *Psychology,* 5th ed. (Fort Worth, TX: Harcourt Brace Jovanovich, 1993), pp. 640–643; and C. Wade and C. Tavris, *Psychology* (New York: Harper & Row, 1987), pp. 488–490.

19. S.L. Bem, "Androgyny and Gender Schema Theory: A Conceptual and Empirical Integration," in *Nebraska Symposium on Motivation: Psychology and Gender,* T.B. Sonderegger, ed. (Lincoln: University of Nebraska Press, 1985).

20. P.G. Zimbardo, C. Haney, and W.C. Banks, "A Pirandellian Prison," *New York Times Magazine,* April 8, 1973.

21. See, for example, P. Baron, "Self-Esteem, Ingratiation, and Evaluation of Unknown Others," *Journal of Personality and Social Psychology* (1974): 104–109.

22. D.E. Hamachek, *Encounters with Others: Interpersonal Relationships and You* (New York: Holt, Rinehart and Winston, 1982), p. 3.

23. For a summary of the narrative paradigm, see E. Griffin, *A First Look at Communication Theory,* 3rd ed. (New York: McGraw-Hill, 1997), pp. 322–332. For a more detailed description, see W.R. Fisher, *Human Communication as Narrative: Toward a Philosophy of Reason, Value, and Action* (Columbia: University of South Carolina Press, 1987).

24. See, for example, E. Stone, "Family Ground Rules," in *Making Connections: Readings in Relational Communication,* K. Galvin and P. Cooper, eds. (Los Angeles: Roxbury, 1996).

25. P.M.M. Sias, "Constructing Perceptions of Differential Treatment: An Analysis of Coworkers Discourse," *Communication Monographs* 63 (1996): 171–187.

26. J.C. Pearson, "Positive Distortion: The Most Beautiful Woman in the World," in *Making Connections: Readings in Interpersonal Communication,* K.M. Galvin and P.

Cooper, eds. (Beverly Hills, CA: Roxbury, 1996), pp. 175–181. See also S.L. Murray, J.G. Holmes, and D.W. Griffin, "The Benefits of Positive Illusions: Idealization and the Construction of Satisfaction in Close Relationships," *Journal of Personality and Social Psychology* 70 (1996): 79–98.

27. Statistics Canada, "Divorces," *The Daily* [Online] (May 18, 1999), p. 1. Available http://www.statcan.ca/Daily/English/990518/d990518b.htm.

28. Statistics Canada, "Divorces," *The Daily* [Online] (May 18, 1999), p. 2. Available http://www.statcan.ca/Daily/English/990518/d990518b.htm.

29. D. Hamachek, *Encounters with the Self,* 3rd ed. (Fort Worth, TX: Harcourt Brace Jovanovich, 1992).

30. For a review of these perceptual biases, see Hamachek, *Encounters with the Self.* See also Bradbury and Fincham, "Attributions in Marriage." For an example of the self-serving bias in action, see R. Buttny, "Reported Speech in Talking Race on Campus," *Human Communication Research* 23 (1997): 477–506.

31. B. Sypher and H.E. Sypher, "Seeing Ourselves as Others See Us," *Communication Research* 11 (Jan. 1984): 97–115.

32. Reported by D. Myers, "The Inflated Self," *Psychology Today* 14 (May 1980): 16.

33. J.B. Stiff, J.P. Dillard, L. Somera, H. Kim, and C. Sleight, "Empathy, Communication, and Prosocial Behavior," *Communication Monographs* 55 (1988): 198–213.

34. This research is described by Goleman in *Emotional Intelligence* (New York: Bantam, 1995), p. 98.

35. M. Davis, "The Heritability of Characteristics Associated with Dispositional Empathy," *Journal of Personality* 62 (1994).

36. B. Burleson, J. Delia, and J. Applegate, "The Socialization of Person-Centered Communication: Parental Contributions to the Social-Cognitive and Communication Skills of Their Children," in *Perspectives in Family Communication,* M.A. Fitzpatrick and A. Vangelistin, eds. (Thousand Oaks, CA: Sage, 1995).

37. R. Lennon and N. Eisenberg, "Gender and Age Differences in Empathy and Sympathy," in *Empathy and Its Development,* N. Eisenberg and J. Strayer, eds. (Cambridge, UK: Cambridge University Press, 1987).

38. T. Adler, "Look at Duration, Depth in Research on Emotion," *APA Monitor* (October 1990): 10.

39. N.D. Feshbach, "Parental Empathy and Child Adjustment/Maladjustment," in *Empathy,* Eisenberg and Strayer, eds.

40. See, for example, "Diversity in the Communication Curriculum: Impact on Student Empathy," *Communication Education* 46 (1977): 234–244.

41. P. Reps, "Pillow Education in Rural Japan," in *Square Sun, Square Moon* (New York: Tuttle, 1967).

References for Chapter 4

1. R.J. Sternberg, *Beyond I.Q.* (New York: Cambridge University Press, 1985).
2. D. Goldman, *Emotional Intelligence: Why It Can Matter More Than I.Q.* (New York: Bantam, 1995).
3. P. Ekman, R.W. Levenson, and W.V. Friesen, "Autonomic Nervous System Activity Distinguishes among Emotions," *Science* 221 (Sept. 16, 1983): 1208–1210.
4. S. Valins, "Cognitive Effects of False Heart-Rate Feedback," *Journal of Personality and Social Psychology,* 4 (1966): 400–408.
5. P. Zimbardo, *Shyness: What It Is, What to Do about It* (Reading, MA: Addison-Wesley, 1977), p. 53.
6. Ibid., p. 54.
7. R. Plutchik, "A Language for the Emotions," *Psychology Today* 14 (Feb. 1980): 68–78. For a more detailed explanation, see R. Plutchik, *Emotion: A Psychoevolutionary Synthesis* (New York: Harper & Row, 1980).
8. C.R. Bush, J.P. Bush, and J. Jennings, "Effects of Jealousy Threats on Relationship Perceptions and Emotions," *Journal of Social and Personal Relationships* 5 (1988): 285–303.
9. M. Mikulincer and J. Segal, "A Multidimensional Analysis of the Experience of Loneliness," *Journal of Social and Personal Relationships* 7 (1990): 209–230.
10. Plutchik, "A Language for the Emotions."
11. W.B. Gudykunst and Y.K. Young, *Communicating with Strangers,* 2nd ed. (New York: McGraw-Hill, 1995), pp. 173–174.
12. J.W. Pennebaker, B. Rime, and V.E. Blankenship, "Stereotypes of Emotional Expressiveness of Northerners and Southerners: A Cross-Cultural Test of Montesquieu's Hypotheses," *Journal of Personality and Social Psychology* 70 (1996): 372–380.
13. Ibid., p. 176. See also C. Gallois, "The Language and Communication of Emotion."
14. H.C. Triandis, *Culture and Social Behavior* (New York: McGraw-Hill, 1994), p. 169. See also F.M. Moghaddam, D.M. Taylor, and S.C. Wright, *Social Psychology in Cross-Cultural Perspective* (New York: Freeman, 1993).
15. D. Matsumoto, "Ethnic Differences in Affect Intensity, Emotion Judgments, Display Rule Attitudes, and Self-Reported Emotional Expression in an American Sample," *Motivation and Emotion* 17 (1993): 107–123.
16. L.R. Brody and J.A. Hall, "Gender and Emotion," in *Handbook of Emotions,* M. Lewis and J.M. Haviland, eds. (New York: Guilford, 1993), pp. 451–452. See also K. Floyd and M.T. Morman, "Affectionate Communication in Nonromantic Relationships: Influences of Communicator, Relational, and Contextual Factors," *Western Journal of Communication* 61 (1997): 278–298.
17. J. Hall, "Gender Effects in Decoding Nonverbal Cues," *Psychological Bulletin* 85 (1978): 845–857.
18. S.E. Snodgrass, "Women's Intuition: The Effect of Subordinate Role on Interpersonal Sensitivity," *Journal of Personality and Social Psychology* 49 (1985): 146–155.
19. S.B. Shimanoff, "Degree of Emotional Expressiveness as a Function of Face-Needs, Gender, and Interpersonal Relationship," *Communication Reports* 1 (1988): 43–53.
20. S.B. Shimanoff, "Rules Governing the Verbal Expression of Emotions between Married Couples," *Western Journal of Speech Communication* 49 (1985): 149–165.
21. S. Duck, "Social Emotions: Showing Our Feelings about Other People," in *Human Relationships* (Newbury Park, CA: Sage, 1992). See also S.B. Shimanoff, "Expressing Emotions in Words: Verbal Patterns of Interaction," *Journal of Communication* 35 (1985): 16–31.
22. E.S. Sullins, "Emotional Contagion Revisited: Effects of Social Comparison and Expressive Style on Mood Convergence," *Personality & Social Psychology Bulletin* 17 (1991): 166–174.
23. Goleman, *Emotional Intelligence,* p. 115.
24. L.B. Rosenfeld, "Self-Disclosure and Avoidance: Why Am I Afraid to Tell You Who I Am?" *Communication Monographs* 46 (1979): 63–74.
25. S.A. McCornack and T.R. Levine, "When Lovers Become Leery: The Relationship between Suspicion and Accuracy in Detecting Deception," *Communication Monographs* 57 (1990): 219–230.
26. D.R. Vocate, "Self-Talk and Inner Speech," in *Interpersonal Communication: Different Voices, Different Minds,* D.R. Vocate, ed. (Hillsdale, NJ: Erlbaum, 1994).
27. M. Booth-Butterfield and M.R. Trotta, "Attributional Patterns for Expressions of Love," *Communication Reports* 7 (1994): 119–129.
28. J.A. Bargh, "Automatic Information Processing: Implications for Communication and Affect," in *Communication, Social Cognition, and Affect,* H.E. Sypher and E.T. Higgins, eds. (Hillsdale, NJ: Erlbaum, 1988).
29. A. Beck, *Cognitive Therapy and the Emotional Disorders* (New York: International Universities Press, 1976).
30. S. Metts and W.R. Cupach, "The Influence of Relationship Beliefs and Problem-Solving Relationships on Satisfaction in Romantic Relationships," *Human Communication Research* 17 (1990): 170–185.
31. A. Meichenbaum, *Cognitive Behavior Modification* (New York: Plenum, 1977).
32. A Chatham-Carpenter and V. DeFrancisco, "Pulling Yourself Up Again: Women's Choices and Strategies for Recovering and Maintaining Self-Esteem," *Western Journal of Communication* 61 (1997): 164–187.

References for Chapter 5

1. O. Sacks, *Seeing Voices: A Journey into the World of the Deaf* (Berkeley: University of California Press, 1989), p. 17.

2. S.I. Hayakawa, *Language in Thought and Action* (New York: Harcourt Brace Jovanovich, 1964), p. 27.

3. M.L. Hecht, M.J. Collier, and S.A. Ribeau, *African American Communication: Ethnic Identity and Cultural Interpretation* (Newbury Park, CA: Sage, 1993), pp. 84–89.

4. R. Allard and R. Landry, "French in New Brunswick," in *Language in Canada*, J. Edwards, ed. (Cambridge, UK: Cambridge University Press, 1998), pp. 202–225.

5. E.K.E. Graham, M. Papa, and G.P. Brooks, "Functions of Humor in Conversation: Conceptualization and Measurement," *Western Journal of Communication* 56 (1992): 161–183.

6. W.B. Pearce and V. Cronen, *Communication, Action, and Meaning* (New York: Praeger, 1980). See also V. Cronen, V. Chen, and W.B. Pearce, "Coordinated Management of Meaning: A Critical Theory," in *Theories in Intercultural Communication*, Y.Y. Kim and W.B. Gudykunst, eds. (Newbury Park, CA: Sage, 1988).

7. M.G. Marcus, "The Power of a Name," *Psychology Today* 9 (Oct. 1976): 75–77, 106.

8. A. Mehrabian, "Interrelationships among Name Desirability, Name Uniqueness, Emotion Characteristics Connoted by Names, and Temperament," *Journal of Applied Social Psychology* 22 (1992): 1797–1808.

9. K.M. Steele and L.E. Smithwick, "First Names and First Impressions: A Fragile Relationship," *Sex Roles* 21 (1989): 517–523.

10. K. Foss and B. Edson, "What's in a Name? Accounts of Married Women's Name Choices," *Western Journal of Speech Communication* 53 (1989): 356–373.

11. K.L. Dion, "What's in a Title? The Ms. Stereotype and Images of Women's Titles of Address," *Psychology of Women Quarterly* 11 (1987): 21–36.

12. See, for example, R.K. Aune and Toshiyuki Kikuchi, "Effects of Language Intensity Similarity of Perceptions of Credibility, Relational Attributions, and Persuasion," *Journal of Language and Social Psychology* 12 (1993): 224–238.

13. H. Giles, J. Coupland, and N. Coupland, eds., *Contexts of Accommodation: Developments in Applied Sociolinguistics* (Cambridge: Cambridge University Press, 1991).

14. M. Weiner and A. Mehrabian, *A Language within Language: Immediacy, a Channel in Verbal Communication* (New York: Appleton-Century-Crofts, 1968).

15. J.J. Bradac, J.M. Wiemann, and K. Schaefer, "The Language of Control in Interpersonal Communication," in *Strategic Interpersonal Communication*, J.A. Daly and J.M. Wiemann, eds. (Hillsdale, NJ: Erlbaum, 1994), pp. 102–104. See also S.H. Ng and J.J. Bradac, *Power in Language: Verbal Communication and Social Influence* (Newbury Park, CA: Sage 1993), p. 27.

16. L.A. Hosman, "The Evaluative Consequences of Hedges, Hesitations, and Intensifiers: Powerful and Powerless Speech Styles," *Human Communication Research* 15 (1989): 383–406.

17. L.A. Samovar and R.E. Porter, *Communication between Cultures,* 3rd ed. (Belmont, CA: Wadsworth ITP, 1998), pp. 58–59.

18. J. Bradac and A. Mulac, "Attributional Consequences of Powerful and Powerless Speech Styles in a Crisis-Intervention Context," *Journal of Language and Social Psychology* 3 (1984): 1–19.

19. J.J. Bradac, "The Language of Lovers, Flovers [sic], and Friends: Communicating in Social and Personal Relationships," *Journal of Language and Social Psychology* 2 (1983): 141–162.

20. D. Geddes, "Sex Roles in Management: The Impact of Varying Power of Speech Style on Union Members' Perception of Satisfaction and Effectiveness," *Journal of Psychology* 126 (1992): 589–607.

21. E.M. Eisenberg, "Ambiguity as Strategy in Organizational Communication," *Communication Monographs* 51 (1984): 227–242; and E.M. Eisenberg and M.G. Witten, "Reconsidering Openness in Organizational Communication," *Academy of Management Review* 12 (1987): 418–426.

22. Reprinted in *Newsweek,* Mar. 7, 1994, 54, and *Time,* Oct. 11, 1993, 24.

23. J.K. Alberts, "An Analysis of Couples' Conversational Complaints," *Communication Monographs* 55 (1988): 184–197.

24. T. Wallsten, "Measuring the Vague Meanings of Probability Terms," *Journal of Experimental Psychology* 115 (1986): 348–365.

25. E.S. Kubany, D.C. Richard, G.B. Bauer, and M.Y. Muraoka, "Impact of Assertive and Accusatory Communication of Distress and Anger: A Verbal Component Analysis," *Aggressive Behavior* 18 (1992): 337–347.

26. T. Gordon, *P.E.T.: Parent Effectiveness Training* (New York: Wyden, 1970), p. 145.

27. R. Raskin and R. Shaw, "Narcissism and the Use of Personal Pronouns," *Journal of Personality* 56 (1988): 393–404; and A.L. Vangelisti, M.L. Knapp, and J.A. Daly, "Conversational Narcissism," *Communication Monographs* 57 (1990): 251–274.

28. A.S. Dreyer, C.A. Dreyer, and J.E. Davis, "Individuality and Mutuality in the Language of Families of Field-Dependent and Field-Independent Children," *Journal of Genetic Psychology* 148 (1987): 105–117.

29. R.F. Proctor and J.R. Wilcox, "An Exploratory Analysis of Responses to Owned Messages in Interpersonal Communication," *ETC: A Review of General Semantics* 50 (1993): 201–220; and Vangelisti et al., "Conversational Narcissism," op. cit.

30. S.L. Kirkland, J. Greenberg, and T. Pysczynski, "Further Evidence of the Deleterious Effects of Overheard Derogatory Ethnic Labels: Derogation beyond the Target," *Personality and Social Psychology Bulletin* 12 (1987): 216–227.

31. See, for example, A. Haas and M.A. Sherman, "Conversational Topic as a Function of Role and Gender," *Psychological Reports* 51 (1982): 453–454; A. Haas and M.A. Sherman, "Reported Topics of Conversation among Same-Sex Adults," *Communication Quarterly* 30 (1982): 332–342.

32. J.T. Wood, *Gendered Lives: Communication, Gender, and Culture* (Belmont, CA: Wadsworth, 1994), p. 141.

33. M.A. Sherman and A. Haas, "Man to Man, Woman to Woman," *Psychology Today* 17 (June 1984): 72–73.

34. J.D. Ragsdale, "Gender, Satisfaction Level, and the Use of Relational Maintenance Strategies in Marriage," *Communication Monographs* 63 (1996): 354–374.

35. Haas and Sherman, "Conversational Topic as a Function of Role and Gender."

36. Research summarized by D. Tannen, *You Just Don't Understand: Women and Men in Conversation* (New York: Morrow, 1990).

37. J. Sachs, "Young Children's Language Use in Pretend Play," in *Language, Gender, and Sex in Comparative Perspective,* S.U. Philips, S. Steele, and C. Tanz, eds. (Cambridge: Cambridge University Press, 1987).

38. For a summary of research on differences between male and female conversational behavior, see H. Giles and R.L. Street, Jr., "Communication Characteristics and Behavior," in *Handbook of Interpersonal Communication,* M.L. Knapp and G.R. Miller, eds. (Beverly Hills, CA: Sage, 1985), pp. 205–261; and A. Kohn, "Girl Talk, Guy Talk," *Psychology Today* 22 (February 1988): 65–66.

39. V. deKlerk, "Expletives: Men Only?" *Communication Monographs* 58 (1991): 156–169.

40. A.J. Mulac, J.M. Wiemann, S.J. Widenmann, and T.W. Gibson, "Male/Female Language Differences and Effects in Same-Sex and Mixed-Sex Dyads: The Gender-Linked Language Effect," *Communication Monographs* 55 (1988): 315–335.

41. L.L. Carli, "Gender, Language, and Influence," *Journal of Personality and Social Psychology* 59 (1990): 941–951.

42. See, for example, D.J. Canary and T.M. Emmers-Sommer, *Sex and Gender Differences in Personal Relationships* (New York: Guilford, 1997); D.J. Canary and K. Hause, "Is There Any Reason to Research Sex Differences in Communication?" *Communication Quarterly* 41 (1993): 482–517; A. Feingold, "Gender Differences in Personality: A Meta-Analysis," *Psychological Bulletin* 116 (1995): 429–456; and B.M. Wilkins and P.A.

Andersen, "Gender Differences and Similarities in Management Communication," *Management Communication Quarterly* 5 (1991): 6–35.

43. C.J. Zahn, "The Bases for Differing Evaluations of Male and Female Speech: Evidence from Ratings of Transcribed Conversation," *Communication Monographs* 56 (1989): 59–74.

44. J.T. Wood, *Gendered Lives: Communication, Gender, and Culture* (Belmont, CA: Wadsworth, 1994).

45. D. Tannen, *Talking from 9 to 5: Women and Men in the Workplace: Language, Sex and Power* (New York: Morrow, 1994).

46. D.G. Ellis and L. McCallister, "Relational Control Sequences in Sex-Typed and Androgynous Groups," *Western Journal of Speech Communication* 44 (1980): 35–49.

47. For a thorough discussion of the challenges involved in translation from one language to another, see L.A. Samovar and R.E. Porter, *Communication between Cultures* (Dubuque, IA: W.C. Brown, 1991), pp. 165–169.

48. The examples of this paragraph are taken from D. Ricks, *Big Business Blunders: Mistakes in International Marketing* (Homewood, IL: Dow Jones-Irwin, 1983), p. 41.

49. N. Sugimoto, "'Excuse Me' and 'I'm Sorry': Apologetic Behaviors of Americans and Japanese." Paper presented at the Conference on Communication in Japan and the United States, California State University, Fullerton, California: March 1991.

50. These examples were taken from W. O'Grady and M. Dobrovolsky, *Contemporary Linguistic Analysis: An Introduction,* 3rd ed. (Toronto: Copp Clark, 1996), pp. 527–528.

51. For more information regarding official language issues, see Commissioner of Official Languages, *Annual Report 1998,* Cat. No. SF1-1998 (Ottawa: Minister of Public Works and Government Services Canada, 1999).

52. S. Poplack and S. Tagliamonte, "African American English in the Diaspora: Evidence from Old-Line Nova Scotians," in *Focus on Canada,* S. Clarke, ed. (Amsterdam and Philadelphia: John Benjamins Publishing Co., 1993).

53. L.W. Payne, "A Word-List from East Alabama," *Dialect Notes* 3 (1909): 279–328, 343–391.

54. A summary of how verbal style varies across cultures can be found in Chapter 5 of W.B. Gudykunst and S. Ting-Toomey, *Culture and Interpersonal Communication* (Newbury Park, CA: Sage, 1988).

55. E. Hall, *Beyond Culture* (New York: Doubleday, 1959).

56. A. Almaney and A. Alwan, *Communicating with the Arabs* (Prospect Heights, IL: Waveland, 1982).

57. K. Basso, "To Give Up on Words: Silence in Western Apache Culture," *Southern Journal of Anthropology* 26 (1970): 213–230.

58. J. Yum, "The Practice of Uye-ri in Interpersonal Relationships in Korea," in *Communication Theory from Eastern and Western Perspectives,* D. Kincaid, ed. (New York: Academic Press, 1987).

59. L. Martin and G. Pullum, *The Great Eskimo Vocabulary Hoax* (Chicago: University of Chicago Press, 1991).

60. H. Giles and A. Franklyn-Stokes, "Communicator Characteristics," in *Handbook of International and Intercultural Communication,* M.K. Asante and W.B. Gudykunst, eds. (Newbury Park, CA: Sage, 1989).

61. L. Sinclair, "A Word in Your Ear," in *Ways of Mankind* (Boston: Beacon Press, 1954).

62. B. Whorf, "The Relation of Habitual Thought and Behavior to Language," in *Language, Thought, and Reality,* J.B. Carrol, ed. (Cambridge, MA.: MIT Press, 1956).

63. H. Hoijer, quoted in T. Seinfatt, "Linguistic Relativity: Toward a Broader View," in *Language, Communication, and Culture: Current Directions,* S. Ting-Toomey and F. Korzenny, eds. (Newbury Park, CA: Sage, 1989).

64. H. Rheingold, *They Have a Word for It* (Los Angeles, CA: Jeremy P. Tarcher, 1988).

65. D.A. Prentice, "Do Language Reforms Change Our Ways of Thinking?" *Journal of Language and Social Psychology* 13 (1994): 3–19.

References for Chapter 6

1. Research summarized by J.K. Burgoon, "Nonverbal Signals," in *Handbook of Interpersonal Communication,* M.L. Knapp and G.R. Miller, eds. (Newbury Park, CA: Sage, 1994), p. 235.

2. B.M. DePaulo, "Spotting Lies: Can Humans Learn to Do Better?" *Current Directions in Psychological Science* 3 (1994): 83–86.

3. Not all communication theorists agree with the claim that all nonverbal behavior has communicative value. For a contrasting opinion, see Burgoon, "Nonverbal Signals," pp. 229–232.

4. F. Manusov, "Perceiving Nonverbal Messages: Effects of Immediacy and Encoded Intent on Receiver Judgments," *Western Journal of Speech Communication* 55 (Summer 1991): 235–253.

5. R. Birdwhistell, *Kinesics and Context* (Philadelphia: University of Pennsylvania Press, 1970), Chapter 9.

6. J.M. Lacroix and Y. Rioux, "La Communication Nonverbal Chez Bilingues," *Canadian Journal of Behavioural Science* 10 (1978): 130–140.

7. For further discussion, see J.E. Alcock, D.W. Carment, and S.W. Sadava, *A Textbook of Social Psychology* (Scarborough, ON: Prentice-Hall, 1996).

8. P. Ekman, W.V. Friesen, and J. Baer, "The International Language of Gestures," *Psychology Today* 18 (May 1984): 64–69.

9. E. Hall, *The Hidden Dimension* (Garden City, NY: Anchor Books, 1969).

10. A.M. Warnecke, R.D. Masters, and G. Kempter, "The Roots of Nationalism: Nonverbal Behavior and Xenophobia." *Ethnology and Sociobiology* 13 (1992): 267–282.

11. Hall, *The Hidden Dimension.*

12. D.L. Rubin, "'Nobody Play by the Rule He Know': Ethnic Interference in Classroom Questioning Events," in *Interethnic Communication: Recent Research,* Y.Y. Kim, ed. (Newbury Park, CA: Sage, 1986).

13. S. Weitz, ed., *Nonverbal Communication: Readings with Commentary* (New York: Oxford University Press, 1974).

14. J. Eibl-Eibesfeldt, "Universals and Cultural Differences in Facial Expressions of Emotions," *Nebraska Symposium on Motivation,* J. Cole, ed. (Lincoln: University of Nebraska Press, 1972).

15. M. Booth-Butterfield and F. Jordan, "'Act Like Us': Communication Adaptation among Racially Homogeneous and Heterogeneous Groups." Paper presented at the Speech Communication Association meeting, New Orleans, 1988.

16. M.T. Motley, "Facial Affect and Verbal Context in Conversation: Facial Expression as Interjection," *Human Communication Research* 20 (1993): 3–40.

17. M. Moore, "Nonverbal Courtship Patterns in Women: Context and Consequences," *Ethnology and Sociobiology* 6 (1985): 237–247.

18. P. Ekman and W.V. Friesen. "The Repertoire of Nonverbal Behavior: Categories, Origins, Usage, and Coding," *Semiotica* 1 (1969): 49–98.

19. See, for example, K. Drummond and R. Hopper, "Acknowledgment Tokens in Series," *Communication Reports* 6 (1993): 47–53; and H.M. Rosenfeld, "Conversational Control Functions of Nonverbal Behavior," in *Nonverbal Behavior and Communication,* 2nd ed., A.W. Siegman and S. Feldstein, eds. (Hillsdale, NJ: Erlbaum, 1987).

20. J. Hale and J.B. Stiff, "Nonverbal Primacy in Veracity Judgments," *Communication Reports* 3 (1990): 75–83; and J.B. Stiff, J.L. Hale, R. Garlick, and R.G. Rogan, "Effect of Cue Incongruence and Social Normative Influences on Individual Judgments of Honesty and Deceit," *Southern Speech Communication Journal* 55 (1990): 206–229.

21. J.K. Burgoon, T. Birk, and M. Pfau, "Nonverbal Behaviors, Persuasion, and Credibility," *Human Communication Research* 17 (1990): 140–169.

22. See, for example, B.M. DePaulo, "Detecting Deception Modality Effects," in *Review of Personality and Social Psychology,* vol. 1, L. Wheeler, ed. (Beverly Hills, CA: 1980); and J. Greene, D. O'Hair, M. Cody, and C. Yen, "Planning and Control of Behavior During Deception," *Human Communication Research* 11 (1985): 335–364.

23. P. Kalbfleisch, "Deceit, Distrust, and Social Milieu: Applications of Deception Research in a Troubled World,"

Journal of Applied Communication Research (1992): 308–334.

24. D.B. Buller, J. Comstock, R.K. Aune, and K.D. Strzyzewski, "The Effect of Probing on Deceivers and Truthtellers," *Journal of Nonverbal Behavior* 13 (1989): 155–170. See also D.B. Buller, K.D. Strzyzewski, and J. Comstock, "Interpersonal Deception: I. Deceivers' Reactions to Receivers' Suspicions and Probing," *Communication Monographs* 58 (1991): 1–24.

25. D.A. Lieberman, T.G. Rigo, and R.F. Campain, "Age-Related Differences in Nonverbal Decoding Ability," *Communication Quarterly* 36 (1988): 290–297.

26. S.A. McCornack and M.R. Parks, "What Women Know That Men Don't: Sex Differences in Determining the Truth behind Deceptive Messages," *Journal of Social and Personal Relationships* 7 (1990): 107–118.

27. M.A. deTurck, "Training Observers to Detect Spontaneous Deception: Effects of Gender," *Communication Reports* 4 (1991): 81–89.

28. D. Druckmann, R. Rozelle, and J. Baxter, *Nonverbal Communication: Survey, Theory, and Research* (Beverly Hills, CA: Sage, 1982), p. 52.

29. M. Motley and C. Camden, "Facial Expression of Emotion: A Comparison of Posed versus Spontaneous Expressions in an Interpersonal Communication Setting," *Western Journal of Speech Communication* 52 (1988): 1–22.

30. M.L. Knapp and J. Hall, *Nonverbal Communication in Human Interaction,* 3rd ed. (Fort Worth, TX: Harcourt Brace Jovanovich, 1992), pp. 466–477.

31. J.A. Hall, "Gender, Gender Roles, and Nonverbal Communication Skills," in *Skill in Nonverbal Communication: Individual Differences,* R. Rosenthal, ed. (Cambridge, MA: Oelgeschlager, Gunn, and Hain, 1979), pp. 32–67.

32. Summarized in Burgoon, "Nonverbal Signals," op. cit.

33. M.T. Palmer and K.B. Simmons, "Communicating Intentions through Nonverbal Behaviors: Conscious and Nonconscious Encoding of Liking," *Human Communication Research* 22 (1995): 128–160.

34. A. Mehrabian, *Silent Messages,* 2nd ed. (Belmont, CA: Wadsworth, 1981), pp. 47–48, 61–62.

35. M.B. Myers, D. Templer, and R. Brown, "Coping Ability of Women Who Become Victims of Rape," *Journal of Consulting and Clinical Psychology* 52 (1984): 73–78. See also C. Rubenstein, "Body Language That Speaks to Muggers," *Psychology Today* 20 (August 1980): 20; and J. Meer, "Profile of a Victim," *Psychology Today* 24 (May 1984): 76.

36. A.E. Scheflen, "Quasi-Courting Behavior in Psychotherapy," *Psychiatry* 228 (1965): 245–257.

37. P. Ekman, *Telling Lies, Clues to Deceit in the Marketplace, Politics, and Marriage* (New York: Norton, 1985), pp. 109–110.

38. P. Ekman and W.V. Friesen, "Nonverbal Behavior and Psychopathology," in *The Psychology of Depression: Contemporary Theory and Research,* R.J. Friedman and M.N. Katz, eds. (Washington, DC: J. Winston, 1974).

39. Ekman, *Telling Lies,* p. 107.

40. P. Ekman and W.V. Friesen, *Unmasking the Face: A Guide to Recognizing Emotions from Facial Clues* (Englewood Cliffs, NJ: Prentice-Hall, 1975).

41. Ibid., p. 150.

42. E.H. Hess and J.M. Polt, "Pupil Size as Related to Interest Value of Visual Stimuli," *Science* 132 (1960): 349–350.

43. E.T. Hall, *The Silent Language* (New York: Fawcett, 1959).

44. For a summary, see Knapp and Hall, *Nonverbal Communication,* pp. 344–346.

45. A. Mehrabian and M. Wiener, "Decoding of Inconsistent Communications," *Journal of Personality and Social Psychology* 6 (1967): 109–114; also, A. Mehrabian and S. Ferris, "Interference of Attitudes from Nonverbal Communication in Two Channels," *Journal of Consulting Psychology* 31 (1967): 248–252.

46. D. Buller and K. Aune, "The Effects of Speech Rate Similarity on Compliance: Application of Communication Accommodation Theory," *Western Journal of Communication* 56 (1992): 37–53. See also D. Buller, B.A. LePoire, K. Aune, and S.V. Eloy, "Social Perceptions as Mediators of the Effect of Speech Rate Similarity on Compliance," *Human Communication Research* 19 (1992): 286–311; "The Effects of Vocalics and Nonverbal Sensitivity in Compliance: A Speech Accommodation Theory Explanation," *Human Communication Research* 14 (1988): 301–332.

47. Ekman, *Telling Lies,* p. 93.

48. P.A. Andersen, "Nonverbal Communication in the Small Group," in *Small Group Communication: A Reader,* 4th ed., R.S. Cathcart and L.A. Samovar, eds. (Dubuque, IA: W.C. Brown, 1984).

49. C.E. Kimble and S.D. Seidel, "Vocal Signs of Confidence," *Journal of Nonverbal Behavior* 15 (1991): 99–105.

50. M. Zuckerman and R.E. Driver, "What Sounds Beautiful Is Good: The Vocal Attractiveness Stereotype," *Journal of Nonverbal Behavior* 13 (1989): 67–82.

51. A Minchella, "Inspired by Throat Singing," University of Toronto, *The Bulletin* [Online] (July 22, 1996). Available http://www.library.utoronto.ca/bulletin/july22_96/art11.htm (Dec. 1, 1999).

52. R. Heslin and T. Alper, "Touch: A Bonding Gesture," in *Nonverbal Interaction,* J.M. Wiemann and R.P. Harrison, eds. (Beverly Hills, CA: Sage, 1983), pp. 47–75.

53. Ibid.

54. J. Burgoon, J. Walther, and E. Baesler, "Interpretations, Evaluations and Consequences of Interpersonal Touch," *Human Communication Research* 19 (1992): 237–263.

55. C.R. Kleinke, "Compliance to Requests Made by Gazing and Touching Experiments in Field Settings," *Journal of Experimental Social Psychology* 13 (1977): 218–223.

56. F.N. Willis and H.K. Hamm, "The Use of Interpersonal Touch in Securing Compliance," *Journal of Nonverbal Behavior* 5 (1980): 49–55.

57. A.H. Crusco and C.G. Wetzel, "The Midas Touch: Effects of Interpersonal Touch on Restaurant Tipping," *Personality and Social Psychology Bulletin* 10 (1984): 512–517.

58. H. Bakwin, "Emotional Deprivation in Infants," *Journal of Pediatrics* 35 (1949): 512–521.

59. T. Adler, "Congressional Staffers Witness Miracle of Touch," *APA Monitor* (Feb. 1993): 12–13.

60. M.S. Driscoll, D.L. Newman, and J.M. Seal, "The Effect of Touch on the Perception of Counselors," *Counselor Education and Supervision* 27 (1988): 344–354; and J.M. Wilson, "The Value of Touch in Psychotherapy," *American Journal of Orthopsychiatry* 52 (1982): 65–72.

61. V.J. Derlega, R.J. Lewis, S. Harrison, B.A. Winstead, and R. Costanza, "Gender Differences in the Initiation and Attribution of Tactile Intimacy," *Journal of Nonverbal Behavior* 13 (1989): 83–96.

62. D.K. Fromme, W.E. Jaynes, D.K. Taylor, E.G. Hanold, J. Daniell, J.R. Rountree, and M. Fromme, "Nonverbal Behavior and Attitudes toward Touch," *Journal of Nonverbal Behavior* 13 (1989): 3–14.

63. For a summary, see Knapp and Hall, *Nonverbal Communication in Human Interaction,* pp. 93–132.

64. V. Ritts, M.L. Patterson, and M.E. Tubbs, "Expectations, Impressions, and Judgments of Physically Attractive Students: A Review," *Review of Educational Research* 62 (1992): 413–426.

65. W. Thourlby, *You Are What You Wear* (New York: New American Library, 1978), p. 1.

66. L. Bickman, "The Social Power of a Uniform," *Journal of Applied Social Psychology* 4 (1974): 47–61.

67. S.G. Lawrence and M. Watson, "Getting Others to Help: The Effectiveness of Professional Uniforms in Charitable Fund Raising," *Journal of Applied Communication Research* 19 (1991): 170–185.

68. H. Fortenberry, J. Maclean, P. Morris, and M. O'Connell, "Mode of Dress as a Perceptual Cue to Deference," *The Journal of Social Psychology* 104 (1978).

69. L. Bickman, "Social Roles and Uniforms: Clothes Make the Person," *Psychology Today* 7 (April 1974): 48–51.

70. M. Lefkowitz, R.R. Blake, and J.S. Mouton, "Status of Actors in Pedestrian Violation of Traffic Signals," *Journal of Abnormal and Social Psychology* 51 (1955): 704–706.

71. L.E. Temple and K.R. Loewen, "Perceptions of Power: First Impressions of a Woman Wearing a Jacket," *Perceptual and Motor Skills* 76 (1993): 339–348.

72. T.F. Hoult, "Experimental Measurement of Clothing as a Factor in Some Social Ratings of Selected American Men," *American Sociological Review* 19 (1954): 326–327.

73. Hall, *The Hidden Dimension.*

74. M. Hackman and K. Walker, "Instructional Communication in the Televised Classroom: The Effects of System Design and Teacher Immediacy," *Communication Education* 39 (1990): 196–206. See also J.C. McCroskey and V.P. Richmond, "Increasing Teacher Influence through Immediacy," in *Power in the Classroom: Communication, Control, and Concern,* V.P. Richmond and J.C. McCroskey, eds. (Hillsdale, NJ: Erlbaum, 1992).

75. C. Conlee, J. Olvera, and N. Vagim, "The Relationships among Physician Nonverbal Immediacy and Measures of Patient Satisfaction with Physician Care," *Communication Reports* 6 (1993): 25–33.

76. E. Sadalla, "Identity and Symbolism in Housing," *Environment and Behavior* 19 (1987): 569–587.

77. A. Maslow and N. Mintz, "Effects of Aesthetic Surroundings: Initial Effects of Those Aesthetic Surroundings upon Perceiving 'Energy' and 'Well-Being' in Faces," *Journal of Psychology* 41 (1956): 247–254.

78. J.J. Teven and M.E. Comadena, "The Effects of Office Aesthetic Quality on Students' Perceptions of Teacher Credibility and Communicator Style," *Communication Research Reports* 13 (1996): 101–108.

79. R. Sommer, *Personal Space: The Behavioral Basis of Design* (Englewood Cliffs, NJ: Prentice-Hall, 1969).

80. R. Levine, "The Pace of Life across Cultures," in *The Social Psychology of Time,* J.E. McGrath, ed. (Newbury Park, CA: Sage, 1988).

81. R. Levine and E. Wolff, "Social Time: The Heartbeat of Culture," *Psychology Today* 19 (March 1985): 28–35.

References for Chapter 7

1. L. Barker, R. Edwards, C. Gaines, K. Gladney, and R. Holley, "An Investigation of Proportional Time Spent in Various Communication Activities by College Students," *Journal of Applied Communication Research* 8 (1981): 101–109.

2. Research summarized in A.D. Wolvin and C.G. Coakley, "A Survey of the Status of Listening Training in Some *Fortune* 500 Corporations," *Communication Education* 40 (1991): 152–164.

3. A.L. Vangelisti, "Communication Problems: The Counselor's Perspective," *Journal of Applied Communication Research* 22 (1994): 106–126.

4. A.D. Wolvin, "Meeting the Communication Needs of the Adult Learners," *Communication Education* 33 (1984): 267–271.

5. B.D. Sypher, R.N. Bostrom, and J.H. Seibert, "Listening Communication Abilities and Success at Work," *Journal of Business Communication* 26 (1989): 293–303. See also E.R. Alexander, L.E. Penley, and I.E. Jernigan, "The

Relationship of Basic Decoding Skills to Managerial Effectiveness," *Management Communication Quarterly* 6 (1992): 58–73.

6. See, for example, D.E. Ifert and M.E. Roloff, "Overcoming Expressed Obstacles to Compliance: The Role of Sensitivity to the Expressions of Others and Ability to Modify Self-Presentation," *Communication Quarterly* 45 (1997): 55–67.

7. M. Chasin, "Fast Facts on Noise, Loud Music & Hearing Loss," *Vibes* [Online] (July 1997). Available http://www.chs.ca/resources/vibes/1997/july/noise.htm; M. Chasin, "Musicians and Hearing Loss," *Vibes* [Online] (Oct. 1995). Available http://www.chs.ca/resources/vibes/1995/october/musician.htm.

8. M.H. Lewis and N.L. Reinsch, Jr., "Listening in Organizational Environments," *Journal of Business Communication* 23 (1988): 49–67.

9. B.A. Pisher, *Interpersonal Communication: The Pragmatics of Human Relationships* (New York: Random House, 1987), p. 390.

10. A.L. Vangelisti, M.L. Knapp, and J.A. Daly, "Conversational Narcissism," *Communication Monographs* 57 (1990): 251–274.

11. K.B. McComb and F.M. Jablin, "Verbal Correlates of Interviewer Empathic Listening and Employment Interview Outcomes," *Communication Monographs* 51 (1984): 367.

12. A. Mulac, J.M. Wiemann, S.J. Widenmann, and T.W. Gibson, "Male/Female Language Differences and Effects in Same-Sex and Mixed-Sex Dyads: The Gender-Linked Language Effect," *Communication Monographs* 55 (1988): 315–335.

13. A. Wolvin and C.G. Coakley, *Listening,* 3rd ed. (Dubuque, IA: W.C. Brown, 1988), p. 208.

14. R. Nichols, "Listening Is a Ten-Part Skill," *Nation's Business* 75 (September 1987): 40.

15. M. Chasin, "Musicians and Hearing Loss," *Vibes* [Online] (Oct. 1995). Available http://www.chs.ca/resources/vibes/1995/october/musician.htm.

16. M. Chasin, "Fast Facts on Noise, Loud Music & Hearing Loss," *Vibes* [Online] (July 1997). Available http://www.chs.ca/resources/vibes/1997/july/noise.htm.

17. J. Brownell, "Perceptions of Effective Listeners: A Management Study," *Journal of Business Communication* 27 (1990): 401–415.

18. N. Spinks and B. Wells, "Improving Listening Power: The Payoff," *Bulletin of the Association for Business Communication* 54 (1991): 75–77.

19. R. Remer and P. DeMesquita, "Teaching and Learning Skills of Interpersonal Confrontation," in *Intimates in Conflict: A Communication Perspective*, D. Cahn, ed. (Norwood, NJ: Erlbaum, 1991), p. 242.

20. B. Burleson and W. Samter, "Cognitive Complexity, Communication Skills, and Friendship." Paper presented at the Seventh International Congress on Personal Construct Psychology, Memphis, TN, August 1987.

21. See, for example, J. Ekenrode, "Impact of Chronic and Acute Stressors on Daily Reports of Mood," *Journal of Personality and Social Psychology* 46 (1984): 907–918; A.D. Kanner, J.C. Coyne, C. Schaefer, and R.S. Lazarus, "Comparison of Two Modes of Stress Management: Daily Hassles and Uplifts versus Major Life Events," *Journal of Behavioral Medicine* 4 (1981): 1–39; and A. DeLongis, J.C. Coyne, G. Dakof, S. Polkman, and R.S. Lazarus, "Relation of Daily Hassles, Uplifts, and Major Life Events to Health Status," *Health Psychology* 1 (1982): 119–136.

22. C.J. Notarius and L.R. Herrick, "Listener Response Strategies to a Distressed Other," *Journal of Social and Personal Relationships* 5 (1988): 97–108.

23. D.J. Goldsmith and K. Fitch, "The Normative Context of Advice as Social Support," *Human Communication Research* 23 (1997): 454–476.

24. W. Samter, B.R. Burleson, and L.B. Murphy, "Comforting Conversations: The Effects of Strategy Type of Evaluations of Messages and Message Producers," *Southern Speech Communication Journal* 52 (1987): 263–284.

25. M. Davidowitz and R.D. Myrick, "Responding to the Bereaved: An Analysis of 'Helping' Statements," *Death Education* 8 (1984): 1–10.

26. Adapted from B.R. Burleson, "Comforting Messages: Features, Functions, and Outcomes," in *Strategic Interpersonal Communication*, J.A. Daly and J.M. Wiemann, eds. (Hillsdale, NJ: Erlbaum, 1994), p. 140.

27. Research summarized in J. Pearson, *Communication in the Family* (New York: Harper & Row, 1989), pp. 272–275.

28. See J. Bruneau, "Empathy and Listening: A Conceptual Review and Theoretical Directions," *Journal of the International Listening Association* 3 (1989): 1–20; and K.N. Cissna and R. Anderson, "The Contributions of Carl R. Rogers to a Philosophical Praxis of Dialogue," *Western Journal of Speech Communication* 54 (1990): 137–147.

29. C.R. Rogers, "Reflection of Feelings," *Personal-Centered Review* 1 (1986): 375–377.

30. L.A. Hosman, "The Evaluational Consequences of Topic Reciprocity and Self-Disclosure Reciprocity," *Communication Monographs* 54 (1987): 420–435.

31. R.A. Clark and J.G. Delia, "Individuals' Preferences for Friends' Approaches to Providing Support in Distressing Situations," *Communication Reports* 10 (1997): 115–121.

32. See, for example, R. Silver and C. Wortman, "Coping with Undesirable Life Events," in *Human Helplessness: Theory and Applications,* J. Garber and M. Seligman, eds. (New York: Academic Press, 1981), pp. 279–340; and C.R. Young, D.E. Giles, and M.C. Plantz, "Natural Networks: Help-Giving and Help-Seeking in Two Rural Communities," *American Journal of Community Psychology* 10 (1982): 457–469.

33. Clark and Delia, "Individuals' Preferences."

34. See research cited in B. Burleson, "Comforting Communication: Does It Really Matter?" Paper presented at the annual convention of the Western Speech Communication Association, San Diego, 1988; and in B. Burleson, "Comforting Messages: Their Significance and Effects," in *Communicating Strategically: Strategies in Interpersonal Communication,* J.A. Daly and J.M. Wiemann, eds. (Hillsdale, NJ: Erlbaum, 1990).

References for Chapter 8

1. See, for example, B.R. Burleson and W.H. Denton, "A New Look at Similarity and Attraction in Marriage: Similarities in Social-Cognitive and Communication Skills as Predictors of Attraction and Satisfaction," *Communication Monographs* 59 (1992): 268–287; and B.R. Burleson and W. Samter, "Similarity in the Communication Skills of Young Adults: Foundations of Attraction, Friendship, and Relationship Satisfaction," *Communication Reports* 9 (1996): 127–139.

2. C.E. Crowther and G. Stone, *Intimacy: Strategies for Successful Relationships* (Santa Barbara, CA: Capra Press, 1986), p. 13.

3. D. Morris, *Intimate Behavior* (New York: Bantam, 1973), p. 7.

4. K. Floyd, "Meanings for Closeness and Intimacy in Friendship," *Journal of Social and Personal Relationships* 13 (1996): 85–107.

5. M.R. Parks and K. Floyd, "Making Friends in Cyberspace," *Journal of Communication* 46 (1996): 80–97.

6. L.A. Baxter, "A Dialogic Approach to Relationship Maintenance," in *Communication and Relational Maintenance,* D. Canary and L. Stafford, eds. (San Diego: Academic Press, 1994).

7. J.T. Wood and C.C. Inman, "In a Different Mode: Masculine Styles of Communicating Closeness," *Applied Communication Research* 21 (1993): 279–295; and K. Floyd, "Gender and Closeness among Friends and Siblings," *Journal of Psychology* 129 (1995): 193–202.

8. See, for example, K. Dindia and M. Allen, "Sex Differences in Self-Disclosure: A Meta-Analysis," *Psychological Bulletin* 112 (1992): 106–124; D. Ivy and P. Backlund, *Exploring GenderSpeak* (New York: McGraw-Hill, 1994), p. 219; and K. Floyd, "Communicating Closeness among Siblings: An Application of the Gendered Closeness Perspective," *Communication Research Reports* 13 (1996): 27–34.

9. See, for example, Floyd, "Gender and Closeness among Friends and Siblings."

10. S. Swain, "Covert Intimacy in Men's Friendships: Closeness in Men's Friendships," in *Gender in Intimate Relationships: A Microstructural Approach,* B.J. Risman and P. Schwartz, eds. (Belmont, CA: Wadsworth, 1989).

11. C.K. Reissman, *Divorce Talk: Women and Men Make Sense of Personal Relationships* (New Brunswick: Rutgers University Press, 1990).

12. J. Adamopoulos, "The Emergence of Interpersonal Behavior: Diachronic and Cross-Cultural Processes in the Evolution of Intimacy," in *Cross-Cultural Interpersonal Communication,* S. Ting-Toomey and F. Orzenny, eds. (Newbury Park, CA: Sage, 1991). See also G. Fontaine, "Cultural Diversity in Intimate Intercultural Relationships," in *Intimates in Conflict: A Communication Perspective,* D.D. Cahn, ed. (Hillsdale, NJ: Erlbaum, 1990).

13. J. Adamopoulos and R.N. Bontempo, "Diachronic Universals in Interpersonal Structures," *Journal of Cross-Cultural Psychology* 17 (1986): 169–189.

14. M. Argyle and M. Henderson, "The Rules of Relationships," in *Understanding Personal Relationships,* S. Duck and D. Perlman, eds. (Beverly Hills, CA: Sage, 1985).

15. W.B. Gudykunst and S. Ting-Toomey, *Culture and Interpersonal Communication* (Newbury Park, CA: Sage, 1988), pp. 197–198.

16. C.W. Franklin, "'Hey Home—Yo Bro': Friendship among Black Men," in *Men's Friendships,* P.M. Nardi, ed. (Newbury Park, CA: Sage, 1992).

17. H.C. Triandis, *Culture and Social Behavior* (New York: McGraw-Hill, 1994), p. 230.

18. K. Lewin, *Principles of Topological Psychology* (New York: McGraw-Hill, 1936).

19. E.M. Eisenberg, "Jamming: Transcendence through Organizing," *Communication Research* 17 (1990): 139–164.

20. See, for example, R. Bellah, W.M. Madsen, A. Sullivan, and S.M. Tipton, *Habits of the Heart: Individualism and Commitment in American Life* (Berkeley: University of California Press, 1985); R. Sennett, *The Fall of Public Man: On the Social Psychology of Capitalism* (New York: Random House, 1974); and S. Trenholm and A. Jensen, "The Guarded Self: Toward a Social History of Interpersonal Styles." Paper presented at the Speech Communication Association meeting, San Juan, Puerto Rico, 1990.

21. See, for example, M.E. Roloff, *Interpersonal Communication: The Social Exchange Approach* (Beverly Hills, CA: Sage, 1981).

22. M.L. Knapp and A.L. Vangelisti, *Interpersonal Communication and Human Relationships,* 2nd ed. (Boston: Allyn and Bacon, 1992), pp. 32–56.

23. D.J. Canary and L. Stafford, eds., *Communication and Relational Maintenance* (San Diego: Academic Press, 1994).

24. For a discussion of relational development in nonintimate relationships, see A. Jensen and S. Trenholm, "Beyond Intimacy: An Alternative Trajectories Model of Relationship Development." Paper presented at the Speech Communication Association annual meeting, New Orleans, 1988.

25. C.R. Berger, "Communicating under Uncertainty," in *Interpersonal Processes: New Directions in Communication Research,* M.E. Roloff and G.R. Miller, eds. (Newbury Park, CA: Sage, 1987). See also C.R. Berger and R.J. Calabrese, "Some Explorations in Initial Interaction and Beyond: Toward a Developmental Theory of Interpersonal Communication," *Human Communication Research* 1 (1975): 99–112.

26. Knapp and Vangelisti, *Interpersonal Communication and Human Relationships,* p. 37.

27. Gudykunst and Ting-Toomey, *Culture and Interpersonal Communication,* p. 193.

28. W. Douglas, "Uncertainty, Information-Seeking, and Liking during Initial Interaction," *Western Journal of Speech Communication* 54 (1990): 66–81.

29. J.H. Tolhuizen, "Communication Strategies for Intensifying Dating Relationships: Identification, Use and Structure," *Journal of Social and Personal Relationships* 6 (1989): 413–434.

30. R.A. Bell and N.L. Buerkel-Rothfuss, "(S)he Loves Me, S(he) Loves Me Not: Predictors of Relational Information-Seeking in Courtship and Beyond," *Communication Quarterly* 38 (1990): 64–82.

31. L.A. Baxter, "Symbols of Relationship Identity in Relationship Culture," *Journal of Social and Personal Relationships* 4 (1987): 261–280.

32. C.J.S. Buress and J.C. Pearson, "Interpersonal Rituals in Marriage and Adult Friendship," *Communication Monographs* 64 (1997): 25–46.

33. R.A. Bell and J.G. Healey, "Idiomatic Communication and Interpersonal Solidarity in Friends' Relational Cultures," *Human Communication Research* 18 (1992): 307–335.

34. M. Roloff, C.A. Janiszewski, M.A. McGrath, C.S. Burns, and L.A. Manrai, "Acquiring Resources from Intimates: When Obligation Substitutes for Persuasion," *Human Communication Research* 14 (1988): 364–396.

35. D.H. Solomon, "A Developmental Model of Intimacy and Date Request Explicitness," *Communication Monographs* 64 (1997): 99–118.

36. J.K. Burgoon, R. Parrott, B.A. LePoire, D.L. Kelley, J.B. Walther, and D. Perry, "Maintaining and Restoring Privacy through Different Types of Relationships," *Journal of Social and Personal Relationships* 6 (1989): 131–158.

37. J.A. Courtright, F.E. Miller, L.E. Rogers, and D. Bagarozzi, "Interaction Dynamics of Relational Negotiation: Reconciliation versus Termination of Distressed Relationships," *Western Journal of Speech Communication* 54 (1990): 429–453.

38. S. Metts, W.R. Cupach, and R.A. Bejllovec, "'I Love You Too Much to Ever Start Liking You': Redefining Romantic Relationships," *Journal of Social and Personal Relationships* 6 (1989): 259–274.

39. See, for example, L.A. Baxter and B.M. Montgomery, *Relating: Dialogues and Dialectics* (New York: Guilford, 1996); W.K. Rawlins, *Friendship Matters: Communication, Dialectics, and the Life Course* (New York: Aldine de Gruyter, 1992); and B.H. Spitzberg, "The Dark Side of (In)Competence," in *The Dark Side of Interpersonal Communication,* W.R. Cupach and B.H. Spitzberg, eds. (Hillsdale, NJ: Lawrence Erlbaum, 1993).

40. Summarized by L.A. Baxter, "A Dialogic Approach to Relationship Maintenance," in *Communication and Relational Maintenance,* D.J. Canary and L. Stafford, eds. (San Diego: Academic Press, 1994).

41. Morris, *Intimate Behavior,* pp. 21–29.

42. D. Barry, *Dave Barry Turns 40* (New York: Fawcett, 1990), p. 47.

43. C.A. VanLear, "Testing a Cyclical Model of Communicative Openness in Relationship Development," *Communication Monographs* 58 (1991): 337–361.

44. Adapted from Baxter and Montgomery, *Relating: Dialogues and Dialectics,* pp. 185–206.

45. R.L. Conville, *Relational Transitions: The Evolution of Personal Relationships* (New York: Praeger, 1991), p. 80.

46. I. Altman and D.A. Taylor, *Social Penetration: The Development of Interpersonal Relationships* (New York: Holt, Rinehart and Winston, 1973). See also D.A. Taylor and I. Altman, "Communication in Interpersonal Relationships: Social Penetration Processes," in *Interpersonal Processes: New Directions in Communication Research,* M.E. Roloff and G.R. Miller, eds. (Newbury Park, CA: Sage, 1987).

47. J. Luft, *Of Human Interaction* (Palo Alto, CA: Natural Press, 1969).

48. J.C. Pearson, *Communication in the Family,* 2nd ed. (New York: HarperCollins, 1993), pp. 292–296.

49. K. Dindia, M.A. Fitzpatrick, and D.A. Kenny, "Self-Disclosure in Spouse and Stranger Interaction: A Social Relations Analysis." Paper presented at the annual meeting of the International Communication Association, New Orleans, 1988; and S.W. Duck and D.E. Miell, "Charting the Development of Personal Relationships,"

in *Studying Interpersonal Interaction,* R. Gilmour and S.W. Duck, eds. (NJ, 1991), pp. 133–144.

50. S. Duck, "Some Evident Truths about Conversations in Everyday Relationships: All Communications Are Not Created Equal," *Human Communication Research* 18 (1991): 228–267.

51. Adapted from V.J. Derlega and J. Grezlak, "Appropriateness of Self-Disclosure," in *Self-Disclosure,* G.J. Chelune, ed. (San Francisco: Jossey-Bass, 1979).

52. See V.J. Derlega and A.L. Chaikin, *Sharing Intimacy: What We Reveal to Others and Why* (Englewood Cliffs, NJ: Prentice-Hall, 1975).

53. H.L. Wintrob, "Self-Disclosure as a Marketable Commodity," *Journal of Social Behavior and Personality* 2 (1987): 77–88.

54. E. Aronson, *The Social Animal,* 4th ed. (New York: W.H. Freeman, 1984), p. 316.

55. F.D. Fincham and T.N. Bradbury, "The Impact of Attributions in Marriage: An Individual Difference Analysis," *Journal of Social and Personal Relationships* 6 (1989): 69–85.

56. V.G. Downs, "Grandparents and Grandchildren: The Relationship between Self-Disclosure and Solidarity in an Intergenerational Relationship," *Communication Research Reports* 5 (1988): 173–179.

57. L.B. Rosenfeld and W.L. Kendrick, "Choosing to Be Open: Subjective Reasons for Self-Disclosing," *Western Journal of Speech Communication* 48 (Fall 1984): 326–343.

58. E.M. Eisenberg and M.G. Witten, "Reconsidering Openness in Organizational Communication," *Academy of Management Review* 12 (1987): 418–428.

59. L.B. Rosenfeld and J.R. Gilbert, "The Measurement of Cohesion and Its Relationship to Dimensions of Self-Disclosure in Classroom Settings," *Small Group Behavior* 20 (1989): 291–301.

60. T.E. Runge and R.L. Archer, "Reactions to the Disclosure of Public and Private Self-Information," *Social Psychology Quarterly* 44 (Dec. 1981): 357–362.

61. C.L. Kleinke, "Effects of Personal Evaluations," in Chelune, *Self-Disclosure.*

62. L.B. Rosenfeld and G.I. Bowen, "Marital Disclosure and Marital Satisfaction: Direct-Effect versus Interaction-Effect Models," *Western Journal of Speech Communication* 55 (1991): 69–84.

63. J.A. Jaksa and M. Pritchard, *Communication Ethics: Methods of Analysis,* 2nd ed. (Belmont, CA: Wadsworth, 1993), pp. 65–66.

64. D. O'Hair and M.J. Cody, "Interpersonal Deception: The Dark Side of Interpersonal Communication?" in *The Dark Side of Interpersonal Communication,* B.H. Spitzberg and W.R. Cupach, eds. (Hillsdale, NJ: Erlbaum, 1993).

65. R.E. Turner, C. Edgely, and G. Olmstead, "Information Control in Conversation: Honesty Is Not Always the Best Policy," *Kansas Journal of Sociology* 11 (1975): 69–89.

66. J. Bavelas, "Situations That Lead to Disqualification," *Human Communication Research* 9 (1983): 130–145.

67. D. Hample, "Purposes and Effects of Lying," *Southern Speech Communication Journal* 46 (1980): 33–47.

68. S.A. McCornack and T.R. Levine, "When Lies Are Uncovered: Emotional and Relational Outcomes of Discovered Deception," *Communication Monographs* 57 (1990): 119–138.

69. S. Metts, W.R. Cupach, and T.T. Imahori, "Perceptions of Sexual Compliance-Resisting Messages in Three Types of Cross-Sex Relationships," *Western Journal of Communication* 56 (1992): 1–17.

70. J.B. Bavelas, A. Black, N. Chovil, and J. Mullett, *Equivocal Communication* (Newbury Park, CA: Sage, 1990), p. 171.

71. Ibid.

72. M.T. Motley, "Mindfulness in Solving Communicators' Dilemmas," *Communication Monographs* 59 (1992): 306–314.

73. S.B. Shimanoff, "Degree of Emotional Expressiveness as a Function of Face-Needs, Gender, and Interpersonal Relationship," *Communication Reports* 1 (1988): 43–53.

References for Chapter 9

1. R. Guzley, "Organizational Climate and Communication Climate: Predictors of Commitment to the Organization," *Management Communication Quarterly* 5 (1992): 379–402.

2. D. Pincus, "Communication Satisfaction, Job Satisfaction, and Job Performance," *Human Communication Research* 12 (1986): 395–419.

3. K. Cissna and E. Seiberg, "Patterns of Interactional Confirmation and Disconfirmation," in *Interpersonal Communication: Readings in Theory and Research,* M.V. Redmond, ed. (Fort Worth, TX: Harcourt Brace, 1995).

4. M.W. Allen, "Communication Concepts Related to Perceived Organizational Support," *Western Journal of Communication* 59 (1995): 326–546.

5. B. Bower, "Nice Guys Look Better in Women's Eyes," *Science News* (March 18, 1995): 165.

6. E. Seiberg, "Confirming and Disconfirming Communication in an Organizational Setting," in *Communication in Organizations,* J. Owen, P. Page, and G. Zimmerman, eds. (St. Paul, MN: West, 1976), pp. 129–149.

7. See, for example, A. Holte and L. Wichstrom, "Disconfirmatory Feedback in Families of Schizophrenics," *Scandinavian Journal of Psychology* 31 (1990): 198–211.

8. A.S. Rancer, R.L. Kosberg, and R.A. Baukus, "Beliefs about Arguing as Predictors of Trait Argumentativeness: Implications for Training in Argument and Conflict

Management," *Communication Education* 41 (1992): 375–387.

9. E.O. Onyekwere, R.B. Rubin, and D.A. Infante, "Interpersonal Perception and Communication Satisfaction as a Function of Argumentativeness and Ego-Involvement," *Communication Quarterly* 39 (1991): 35–47.

10. D.A. Infante, B.L. Riddle, C.L. Horvath, and S.A. Tumlin, "Verbal Aggressiveness: Messages and Reasons," *Communication Quarterly* 40 (1992): 116–126.

11. D.A. Infante and W.I. Gorden, "Argumentativeness and Affirming Communicator Style as Predictors of Satisfaction/Dissatisfaction with Subordinates," *Communication Quarterly* 37 (1989): 81–90.

12. A.L. Vangelisti, "Messages That Hurt," in *The Dark Side of Interpersonal Communication,* W.R. Cupach and B.H. Spitzberg, eds. (Hillsdale, NJ: Erlbaum, 1994).

13. W.W. Wilmot, *Dyadic Communication* (New York: Random House, 1987), pp. 149–158.

14. C. Burggraf and A.L. Sillars, "A Critical Examination of Sex Differences in Marital Communication," *Communication Monographs* 54 (1987): 276–294. See also D.A. Newton and J.K. Burgoon, "The Use and Consequences of Verbal Strategies during Interpersonal Disagreements," *Human Communication Research* 16 (1990): 477–518.

15. J.L. Hocker and W.W. Wilmot, *Interpersonal Conflict,* 4th ed. (Dubuque, IA: Brown & Benchmark, 1995), p. 34.

16. Ibid., p. 36.

17. G.H. Stamp, A.L. Vangelisti, and J.A. Daly, "The Creation of Defensiveness in Social Interaction," *Communication Quarterly* 40 (1992): 177–190.

18. J. Powell, *Why Am I Afraid to Tell You Who I Am?* (Chicago: Argus Communications, 1969), p. 12.

19. L. Festinger, *A Theory of Cognitive Dissonance* (Stanford, CA: Stanford University Press, 1957).

20. A.M. Nicotera, *Interpersonal Communication in Friend and Mate Relationships* (Albany: State University of New York, 1993).

21. J. Gibb, "Defensive Communication," *Journal of Communication* 11 (September 1961): 141–148. See also W.F. Eadie, "Defensive Communication Revisited: A Critical Examination of Gibb's Theory," *Southern Speech Communication Journal* 47 (1982): 163–177.

22. R.F. Proctor and J.R. Wilcox, "An Exploratory Analysis of Responses to Owned Messages in Interpersonal Communication," *ETC: A Review of General Semantics* 50 (1993): 201–220.

23. T.C. Sabourin and G.H. Stamp, "Communication and the Experience of Dialectical Tensions in Family Life: An Examination of Abusive and Nonabusive Families," *Communication Monographs* 62 (1995): 213–243.

24. Research summarized in J. Harwood, E.B. Ryan, H. Giles, and S. Tysoski, "Evaluations of Patronizing Speech and Three Response Styles in a Non-Service-Providing Context," *Journal of Applied Communication Research* 25 (1997): 170–195.

25. C.E. Beck and E.A. Beck, "The Manager's Open Door and the Communication Climate," in *Making Connections: Readings in Relational Communication,* K.M. Galvin and P. Cooper, eds. (Los Angeles: Roxbury, 1996).

26. Adapted from M. Smith, *When I Say No, I Feel Guilty* (New York: Dial Press, 1975), pp. 93–110.

27. W.L. Benoit and S. Drew. "Appropriateness and Effectiveness of Image Repair Strategies," *Communication Reports* 10 (1997): 153–163. See also Stamp, et al., "The Creation of Defensiveness in Social Interaction."

References for Chapter 10

1. J.L. Hocker and W.W. Wilmot, *Interpersonal Conflict,* 4th ed. (Madison, WI: Brown & Benchmark, 1995), pp. 21–30. See also P.M. Buzzanell and N.A. Burrell, "Family and Workplace Conflict: Examining Metaphorical Conflict Schemas and Expressions across Context and Sex," *Human Communication Research* 24 (1997): 109–146.

2. S. Metts and W. Cupach, "The Influence of Relationship Beliefs and Prolem-Solving Responses on Satisfaction in Romantic Relationships," *Human Communication Research* 17 (1990): 170–185.

3. Hocker and Wilmot, *Interpersonal Conflict,* pp. 20–28.

4. For a summary of research detailing the prevalence of conflict in relationships, see W.R. Cupach and D.J. Canary, *Competence in Interpersonal Conflict* (New York: McGraw-Hill, 1997), pp. 5–6.

5. W.L. Benoit and P.J. Benoit, "Everyday Argument Practices of Native Social Actors," in *Argument and Critical Practices,* J. Wenzel, ed. (Annandale, VA: Speech Communication Association, 1987).

6. L.A. Kurdek, "The Nature and Correlates of Relationship Quality in Gay, Lesbian, and Heterosexual Cohabitating Couples: A Test of the Individual Difference, Interdependence, and Discrepancy Models," in *Psychological Perspectives on Lesbian and Gay Issues,* B. Greene and G.M. Herek, eds. (Thousand Oaks, CA: Sage 1994).

7. J.M. Gottman, "Emotional Responsiveness in Marital Conversations," *Journal of Communication* 32 (1982): 108–120. See also W.R. Cupach, "Communication Satisfaction and Interpersonal Solidarity as Outcomes of Conflict Message Strategy Use." Paper presented at the International Communication Association Conference, Boston, May 1982.

8. P. Koren, K. Carlton, and D. Shaw, "Marital Conflict: Relations among Behaviors, Outcomes, and Distress," *Journal of Consulting and Clinical Psychology* 48 (1980): 460–468.

9. Hocker and Wilmot, *Interpersonal Conflict,* p. 37.

10. J.M. Gottman, *Marital Interaction: Experimental Investigations* (New York: Academic Press, 1979). See also D.A. Infante, S.A. Myers, and R.A. Buerkel, "Argument and Verbal Aggression in Constructive and Destructive Family and Organizational Disagreements," *Western Journal of Communication* 58 (1994): 73–84.

11. S.E. Crohan, "Marital Happiness and Spousal Consensus on Beliefs about Marital Conflict: A Longitudinal Investigation," *Journal of Science and Personal Relationships* 9 (1992): 89–102.

12. D.J. Canary, H. Weger, Jr., and L. Stafford, "Couples' Argument Sequences and Their Associations with Relational Characteristics," *Western Journal of Speech Communication* 55 (1991): 159–179.

13. M.E. Roloff and D.H. Cloven, "The Chilling Effect in Interpersonal Relationships: The Reluctance to Speak One's Mind," in *Intimates in Conflict: A Communication Perspective*, D.D. Cahn, ed. (Hillsdale, NJ: Erlbaum, 1990).

14. G.R. Birchler, R.L. Weiss, and J.P. Vincent, "Multimethod Analysis of Social Reinforcement Exchange between Maritally Distressed and Nondistressed Spouse and Stranger Dyads," *Journal of Personality and Social Psychology* 31 (1975): 349–360.

15. For a detailed discussion of the drawbacks of nonassertion, see Roloff and Cloven, "The Chilling Effect in Interpersonal Relationships."

16. D.D. Cahn, *Conflict in Intimate Relationships* (New York: Guilford, 1992), p. 100.

17. D.A. Infante, "Aggressiveness," in *Personality and Interpersonal Communication*, J.C. McCroskey and J.A. Daly, eds. (Newbury Park, CA: Sage, 1987).

18. D.A. Infante, A.S. Rancer, and F.F. Jordan, "Affirming and Nonaffirming Style, Dyad Sex, and the Perception of Argumentation and Verbal Aggression in an Interpersonal Dispute," *Human Communication Research* 22 (1996): 315–334.

19. D.A. Infante, T.A. Chandler, and J.E. Rudd, "Test of an Argumentative Skill Deficiency Model of Interspousal Violence," *Communication Monographs* 56 (1989): 163–177.

20. B.K. Houston, M.A. Babyak, M.A. Chesney, and G. Black, "Social Dominance and 22-Year All-Cause Mortality in Men," *Psychosomatic Medicine* 59 (1997): 5–12.

21. "Marital Tiffs Spark Immune Swoon," *Science News*, Sept. 4, 1993, p. 153.

22. T.C. Sabourin, D.A. Infante, and J.E. Rudd, "Verbal Aggression in Marriages: A Comparison of Violent, Distressed but Nonviolent, and Nondistressed Couples," *Human Communication Research* 20 (1993): 245–267.

23. Cahn, *Conflict in Intimate Relationships*, pp. 29–30.

24. B.H. Spitzberg, D.J. Canary, and W.R. Cupach, "A Competence-Based Approach to the Study of Interpersonal Conflict," in *Conflict in Personal Relationships*, D.D. Cahn, ed. (Hillsdale, NJ: Erlbaum, 1994), p. 191.

25. J. Jordan and M.E. Roloff, "Acquiring Assistance from Others: The Effect of Indirect Requests and Relational Intimacy on Verbal Compliance," *Human Communication Research* 16 (1990): 519–555.

26. C. Tavris, "Anger Defused," *Psychology Today* 16 (November 1982): 34.

27. Spitzberg, Canary, and Cupach, "A Competence-Based Approach," p. 190.

28. Adapted from S. Miller, E.W. Nunnally, and D.B. Wackman, *Alive and Aware: How to Improve Your Relationships through Better Communication* (Minneapolis, MN: International Communication Programs, 1975). See also R. Remer and P. deMesquita, "Teaching and Learning the Skills of Interpersonal Confrontation," in Cahn, *Intimates in Conflict*.

29. J.K. Alberts, "An Analysis of Couples' Conversational Complaints," *Communication Monographs* 55 (1988): 184–197.

30. J.K. Alberts and G. Driscoll, "Containment versus Escalation: The Trajectory of Couples' Conversational Complaints," *Western Journal of Communication* 56 (1992): 394–412.

31. Hocker and Wilmot, *Interpersonal Conflict*; M.L. Knapp, L.L. Putnam, and L.J. Davis, "Measuring Interpersonal Conflict in Organizations: Where Do We Go from Here?" *Management Communication Quarterly* 1 (1988): 414–429.

32. C.S. Burggraf and A.L. Sillars, "A Critical Examination of Sex Differences in Marital Communication," *Communication Monographs* 53 (1987): 276–294.

33. J.M. Gottman and L.J. Krokoff, "Marital Interaction and Satisfaction: A Longitudinal View," *Journal of Consulting and Clinical Psychology* 67 (1989): 47–52; and G.R. Pike and A.L. Sillars, "Reciprocity of Marital Communication," *Journal of Social and Personal Relationships* 2 (1985): 303–324.

34. M.A. Fitzpatrick, "A Typological Approach to Communication in Relationships," in *Communication Yearbook 1*, B. Rubin, ed. (New Brunswick, NJ: Transaction Books, 1977).

35. M.A. Fitzpatrick, J. Fey, C. Segrin, and J.L. Schiff, "Internal Working Models of Relationships and Marital Communication," *Journal of Language and Social Psychology* 12 (1993): 103–131. See also M.A. Fitzpatrick, S. Fallis, and L. Vance, "Multifunctional Coding of Conflict Resolution Strategies in Marital Dyads," *Family Relations* 21 (1982): 61–70.

36. Hocker and Wilmot, *Interpersonal Conflict*, p. 142.

37. Cupach and Canary, *Competence in Interpersonal Conflict*, p. 109.

38. Research summarized by D. Tannen in *You Just Don't Understand: Women and Men in Conversation* (New York: William Morrow, 1989), pp. 152–157, 162–165.

39. M.J. Collier, "Conflict Competence within African, Mexican, and Anglo-American Friendships," in *Cross-Cultural Interpersonal Communication*, S. Ting-Toomey and F. Korzenny, eds. (Newbury Park, CA: Safe, 1991).

40. D.J. Canary, W.R. Cupach, and S.J. Messman, *Relationship Conflict* (Newbury Park, CA: Sage, 1995).

41. See M.J. Papa and E.J. Natalle, "Gender, Strategy Selection, and Discussion Satisfaction in Interpersonal Conflict," *Western Journal of Speech Communication* 52 (1989): 260–272.

42. See, for example, J.C. Pearson, *Gender and Communication*, 2nd ed. (Dubuque, IA: W.C. Brown, 1991), pp. 183–184.

43. Spitzberg, Canary, and Cupach, "A Competence-Based Approach," p. 190.

44. Research summarized in Cupach and Canary, *Competence in Interpersonal Conflict*, pp. 63–65.

45. For a more detailed discussion of culture, conflict, and context, see W.B. Gudykunst and S. Ting-Toomey, *Culture and Interpersonal Communication* (Newbury Park, CA: Sage, 1988), pp. 153–160.

46. S. Ting-Toomey, "Managing Conflict in Intimate Intercultural Relationships," in *Conflict in Personal Relationships,* D.D. Cahn, ed. (Hillsdale, NJ: Erlbaum, 1994).

47. See, for example, S. Ting-Toomey, "Rhetorical Sensitivity Style in Three Cultures: France, Japan, and the United States," *Central States Speech Journal* 39 (1988): 28–36.

48. K. Okabe, "Indirect Speech Acts of the Japanese," in *Communication Theory: Eastern and Western Perspectives,* L. Kincaid, ed. (San Diego: Academic Press, 1987), pp. 127–136.

49. G. Fontaine, "Cultural Diversity in Intimate Intercultural Relationships," in Cahn, *Intimates in Conflict.*

50. The following research is summarized in Tannen, *You Just Don't Understand,* p. 160.

51. A.C. Filley, *Interpersonal Conflict Resolution* (Glenview, IL: Scott, Foresman, 1975), p. 23.

52. T. Gordon, *Parent Effectiveness Training* (New York: Wyden, 1970), pp. 236–264.

53. R. Axelrod, *The Evolution of Cooperation* (New York: Basic Books, 1984).

54. M. Kinsley, "It Pays to Be Nice," *Science* 222 (1984): 162.

Glossary

Abstraction ladder A range of more to less abstract terms describing an event or object.

Accenting Nonverbal behaviours that emphasize part of a verbal message.

Accommodation A nonassertive response style in which the communicator submits to a situation rather than attempt to have his or her needs met.

Active listening Restating a speaker's thoughts and feelings in the listener's own words.

Advising response A helping response in which the receiver offers suggestions about how the speaker should deal with a problem.

Affinity The degree to which persons like or appreciate one another.

Ambiguous response A disconfirming response with more than one meaning, leaving the other party unsure of the responder's position.

Ambushing A style in which the receiver listens carefully in order to gather information to use in an attack on the speaker.

Analyzing statement A helping style in which the listener offers an interpretation of a speaker's message.

Androgynous Possessing both masculine and feminine traits.

Apathy A defense mechanism in which a person avoids admitting emotional pain by pretending not to care about an event.

Assertion A direct expression of the sender's needs, thoughts, or feelings, delivered in a way that does not attack the receiver's dignity.

Attending The process of filtering out some messages and focussing on others.

Attribution The process of attaching meaning to behaviour.

Avoidance A nonassertive response style in which the communicator is unwilling to confront a situation in which his or her needs are not being met.

Avoiding A stage of relational development immediately prior to terminating in which the parties minimize contact with one another.

Behaviour Observable actions that can be interpreted as communicative messages.

Behavioural description An account that refers only to observable phenomena.

Body orientation Type of nonverbal communication characterized by the degree to which we face toward or away from someone.

Bonding A stage of relational development in which the parties make symbolic public gestures to show that their relationship exists.

Breadth First dimension of self-disclosure involving the range of subjects being discussed.

"But" statements Statements in which the word "but" cancels out the expression that preceded it.

Certainty Attitude behind messages that dogmatically imply that the speaker's position is correct and that the other person's ideas are not worth considering. Likely to generate a defensive response.

Channel The medium through which a message passes from sender to receiver.

Chronemics The study of how humans use and structure time.

Circumscribing A stage of relational development in which partners begin to reduce the scope of their contact and commitment to one another.

Cliché A ritualized, stock statement delivered in response to a social situation.

Cognitive complexity The ability to construct a variety of frameworks for viewing an issue.

Cognitive conservatism The tendency to seek and attend to information that conforms to an existing self-concept.

Cognitive dissonance An inconsistency between two conflicting pieces of information, attitudes, or behaviours. Communicators strive to reduce dissonance, often through defense mechanisms that maintain an idealized presenting image.

Communication A continuous, transactional process involving participants who occupy different but overlapping environments and create relationships through the exchange of messages, many of which are affected by external, physiological, and psychological noise.

Communication climate The emotional tone of a relationship between two or more individuals.

Communication competence The ability to accomplish one's personal goals in a manner that maintains a relationship on terms that are acceptable to all parties.

Comparison level (CL) The present level of rewards accruing to a person in a given situation.

Comparison level of alternatives (CL$_{alt}$) A comparison between the rewards a person is receiving in his/her present situation and those s/he could expect to receive in others.

Compensation   A defense mechanism in which a person stresses a strength in one area to camouflage a shortcoming in some other area.

Complaining   A disconfirming response that implicitly or explicitly attributes responsibility for the speaker's displeasure to another party.

Complementary conflict style   A relational conflict style in which partners use different but mutually reinforcing behaviours.

Complementary relationship   One in which the distribution of power is unequal, with one party occupying a "one-up" and the other a "one-down" position.

Complementing   Nonverbal behaviour that reinforces a verbal message.

Compromise   An approach to conflict resolution in which both parties attain at least part of what they wanted through self-sacrifice.

Confirming communication   A message that expresses caring or respect for another person.

Conflict   An expressed struggle between at least two interdependent parties who perceive incompatible goals, scarce rewards, and interference from the other party in achieving their goals.

Conflict ritual   An unacknowledged repeating pattern of interlocking behaviour used by participants in a conflict.

Connection-autonomy dialectic   The dialectical tension between a desire for connection and a need for independence in a relationship.

Consequence statement   An explanation of the results that follow either from the behaviour of the person to whom the message is addressed or from the speaker's interpretation of the addressee's behaviour. Consequence statements can describe what happens to the speaker, the addressee, or others.

Content message   A message that communicates information about the subject being discussed. *See also* Relational message.

Contradicting   Nonverbal behaviour that is inconsistent with a verbal message.

Controlling communication   Messages in which the sender tries to impose some sort of outcome on the receiver, usually resulting in a defensive reaction.

Convergence   The process of adapting one's speech style to match that of others with whom the communicator wants to identify. *See also* Divergence.

Counterfeit questions   Questions that disguise the speaker's true motives, which do not include a gen-

uine desire to understand the other person. *See* Sincere questions.

Crazymaking   *See* Passive aggression.

Debilitative emotions   Emotions that prevent a person from functioning effectively.

Deception cues   Nonverbal behaviours that signal the untruthfulness of a verbal message.

Decision control   The power to influence which person in a relationship decides what activities will take place.

Decode   The process in which a receiver attaches meaning to a message. Synonymous with *Interpretation.*

De-escalatory conflict spiral   A communication spiral in which the parties slowly lessen their dependence on one another, withdraw, and become less invested in the relationship.

Defense mechanism   A psychological device used to maintain a presenting self-image that an individual believes is threatened.

Defensive listening   A response style in which the receiver perceives a speaker's comments as an attack.

Defensiveness   The attempt to protect a presenting image a person believes is being attacked.

Depth   A dimension of self-disclosure involving a shift from relatively nonrevealing messages to more-personal ones.

Descriptive communication   Messages that describe the speaker's position without evaluating others. Synonymous with "I" language.

Dialectical tensions   Inherent conflicts that arise when two opposing or incompatible forces exist simultaneously.

Differentiating   A stage of relational development in which the parties reestablish their individual identities after having bonded together.

Direct aggression   A criticism or demand that threatens the face of the person at whom it is directed.

Disconfirming communication   A message that expresses a lack of caring or respect for another person.

Disfluency   A nonlinguistic verbalization, for example, "um," "er," "ah."

Displacement   A defense mechanism in which a person vents hostile or aggressive feelings on a target that cannot strike back, instead of on the true target.

Divergence   Speaking mannerisms that emphasize a communicator's differences from others. *See also* Convergence.

Double message   Contradiction between a verbal message and one or more nonverbal cues.

Dyad   Two individuals communicating. The interaction may or may not be interpersonal in nature.

Emblems   Deliberate nonverbal behaviours with precise meanings, known to virtually all members of a cultural group.

Emotional contagion   The process by which emotions are transferred from one person to another.

Emotive language   Language that conveys the sender's attitude rather than simply offers an objective description.

Empathy   The ability to project oneself into another person's point of view, so as to experience the other's thoughts and feelings.

Encode   The process of putting thoughts into symbols, most commonly words.

Environment   The field of experiences that leads a person to make sense of another's behaviour. Environments consist of physical characteristics, personal experiences, relational history, and cultural background.

Equality   A type of supportive communication described by Gibb, suggesting that the sender regards the receiver as worthy of respect.

Equivocal language   Ambiguous language that has two or more equally plausible meanings.

Escalatory conflict spiral   A communication spiral in which one attack leads to another until the initial skirmish escalates into a full-fledged battle.

Euphemisms   Pleasant terms substituted for blunt ones in order to soften the impact of unpleasant information.

Evaluative communication   Messages in which the sender judges the receiver in some way, usually resulting in a defensive response.

Exchange theory   A socioeconomic theory of relational development that suggests people seek relationships in which the rewards they receive from others are greater than or equal to the costs they encounter.

Experimenting   An early stage in relational development, consisting of a search for common ground. If the experimentation is successful, the relationship will progress to intensifying. If not, it may go no further.

Face-threatening act   Behaviour by another that is perceived as attacking an individual's presenting image, or face.

Facilitative emotions   Emotions that contribute to effective functioning.

Fallacy of approval   The irrational belief that it is vital to win the approval of virtually every person a communicator deals with.

Fallacy of catastrophic expectations   The irrational belief that the worst possible outcome will probably occur.

Fallacy of causation   The irrational belief that emotions are caused by others and not by the person who has them.

Fallacy of helplessness   The irrational belief that satisfaction in life is determined by forces beyond one's control.

Fallacy of overgeneralization   Irrational beliefs in which (1) conclusions (usually negative) are based on limited evidence or (2) communicators exaggerate their shortcomings.

Fallacy of perfection   The irrational belief that a worthwhile communicator should be able to handle every situation with complete confidence and skill.

Fallacy of shoulds   The irrational belief that people should behave in the most desirable way.

Feedback   The discernible response of a receiver to a sender's message.

Gestures   Motions of the body, usually hands or arms, that have communicative value.

Gibb categories   Six sets of contrasting styles of verbal and nonverbal behaviour. Each set describes a communication style that is likely to arouse defensiveness and a contrasting style that is likely to prevent or reduce it. Developed by Jack Gibb.

Hearing   The physiological dimension of listening.

High-context cultures   Cultures that avoid direct use of language, relying on the context of a message to convey meaning.

"I" language   A statement that describes the speaker's reaction to another person's behaviour without making judgements about its worth. *See also* "You" language.

Ideal self   The person each wishes to be. *See also* Perceived self and Presenting self.

Identity   *See* Presenting self.

Identity management   The communication strategies people use to influence how others view them.

Illustrators   Nonverbal behaviours that accompany and support verbal messages.

Impersonal communication   Behaviour that treats others as objects rather than individuals. *See* Interpersonal communication.

Impersonal response A disconfirming response that is superficial or trite.

Impervious response A disconfirming response that ignores another person's attempt to communicate.

Impression management *See* Identity management.

Incongruous response A disconfirming response in which two messages, one of which is usually nonverbal, contradict one another.

Indirect communication An oblique way of expressing wants or needs in order to save face for the recipient.

Influence *See* Control.

Initiating The first stage in relational development, in which the parties express interest in one another.

Insensitive listening Failure to recognize the thoughts or feelings that are not directly expressed by a speaker; instead, accepting the speaker's words at face value.

Instrumental goals Goals aimed at getting others to behave in desired ways.

Insulated listening A style in which the receiver ignores undesirable information.

Integrating A stage of relational development in which the parties begin to take on a single identity.

Intensifying A stage of relational development preceding integrating, in which the parties move toward integration by increasing the amount of contact and the breadth and depth of self-disclosure.

Intention statement A description of where the speaker stands on an issue, what he or she wants, or how he or she plans to act in the future.

Interaction constructs Perceptual schema that categorize people according to their social behaviour.

Interpersonal communication In a quantitative sense, communication (usually face-to-face) between two individuals. (*See also* Dyad.) In a qualitative sense, communication in which the parties consider one another as unique individuals rather than objects. It is characterized by minimal use of stereotyped labels; unique, idiosyncratic rules; and a high degree of information exchange.

Interpersonal relationship An association in which the parties meet each other's social needs to a greater or lesser degree.

Interpretation The process of attaching meaning to sense data; synonymous with *Decode*.

Interrupting response A disconfirming response in which the listener begins to speak before the other person has finished.

Intimacy A state of personal sharing arising from physical, intellectual, and/or emotional contact.

Intimate distance One of Hall's four distance zones, ranging from skin contact to 45 cm.

Irrelevant response A disconfirming response in which one communicator's comments bear no relationship to the previous speaker's ideas.

"It" statements Statements that replace the personal pronoun "I" with the less immediate word "it," often reducing the speaker's acceptance of responsibility for the statement.

Johari Window A model that describes the relationship between self-disclosure and self-awareness.

Judging response A reaction in which the receiver evaluates the sender's message either favourably or unfavourably.

Kinesics The study of body position and motion.

Leakage Nonverbal behaviours that reveal information a communicator does not disclose verbally.

Linear communication model A characterization of communication as a one-way event in which a message flows from sender to receiver.

Linguistic determinism The theory that a culture's worldview is unavoidably shaped and reflected by the language its members speak.

Linguistic relativism A more moderate form of linguistic determinism which argues that language exerts a strong influence on the perceptions of the people who speak it.

Listening Process that consists of hearing, attending, understanding, responding, and remembering an aural message.

Lose–lose problem solving An approach to conflict resolution in which neither side achieves its goals. Sometimes lose–lose outcomes result from both parties seeking a win–lose victory over one another. In other cases, the parties settle for a lose–lose outcome (for example, compromise) because they cannot find any better alternative.

Low-context cultures Cultures that use language primarily to express thoughts, feelings, and ideas as clearly and logically as possible.

Manipulators Movements in which one part of the body grooms, massages, rubs, holds, fidgets, pinches, picks, or otherwise manipulates another part.

Membership constructs Perceptual schema that categorize people according to the groups to which they belong.

Message Information sent from a sender to a receiver.

Metacommunication   Messages (usually relational) that refer to other messages: communication about communication.

Microexpressions   Brief facial expressions.

Mixed emotions   Emotions that are combinations of primary emotions. Some mixed emotions can be expressed in single words (that is, *awe, remorse*), whereas others require more than one term (that is, *embarrassed and angry, relieved and grateful*).

Narrative   A perception of the world shared by a collection of people. Narratives can be described in terms of a dramatic theme.

Neutrality   A defense-arousing behaviour described by Gibb in which the sender expresses indifference toward a receiver.

Noise   External, physiological, and psychological distractions that interfere with the accurate transmission and reception of a message.

Nonassertion   The inability to express one's thoughts or feelings when necessary. Nonassertion may be due to a lack of confidence or communication skill or both.

Nonverbal communication   Messages expressed by other than linguistic means.

Openness-privacy dialectic   The dialectical tension between a desire for open communication and the need for privacy in a relationship.

Organization   The stage in the perception process that involves arranging data in a meaningful way.

Paralanguage   Nonlinguistic means of vocal expression: rate, pitch, tone, and so on.

Parallel conflict style   A relational conflict style in which the approach of the partners varies from one situation to another.

Parallel relationship   One in which the balance of power shifts from one party to the other, according to the situation.

Paraphrasing   Restating a speaker's thoughts and/or feelings in the listener's own words.

Passive aggression   An indirect expression of aggression, delivered in a way that allows the sender to maintain a façade of kindness.

Passive listening   *See* One-way communication.

Perceived self   The person we believe ourselves to be in moments of candor. It may be identical with or different from the presenting and ideal selves.

Perception checking   A three-part method for verifying the accuracy of interpretations, including a description of the sense data, two possible interpretations, and a request for confirmation of the interpretations.

Perceptual schema   Cognitive frameworks that allow individuals to organize perceptual data that they have selected from the environment.

Personal distance   One of Hall's four distance zones, ranging from 45 cm to 1.2 m.

Phonological rules   Linguistic rules that govern how sounds are combined to form words.

Physical avoidance   A defense mechanism whereby the person steers clear of people who attack a presenting self to avoid dissonance.

Physical constructs   Perceptual schema that categorize people according to their appearance.

Pillow method   A method for understanding an issue from several perspectives rather than with an egocentric "I'm right and you're wrong" attitude.

Posture   The way in which individuals carry themselves–erect, slumping, and so on.

Powerless speech mechanisms   Ways of speaking that may reduce perceptions of a communicator's power.

Pragmatic rules   Linguistic rules that help communicators understand how messages may be used and interpreted in a given context.

Predictability-novelty dialectic   The dialectical tension between a desire for stability and the need for novelty in a relationship.

Presenting self   The image a person presents to others. It may be identical with or different from the perceived and ideal selves.

Primary emotions   Basic emotions. Some researchers have identified eight primary emotions: joy, acceptance, fear, surprise, sadness, disgust, anger, and anticipation.

Problem orientation   A supportive style of communication described by Gibb in which the communicators focus on working together to solve their problems instead of trying to impose their own solutions on one another.

Prompting   Using silences and brief statements of encouragement to draw out a speaker.

Provisionalism   A supportive style of communication described by Gibb in which the sender expresses a willingness to consider the other person's position.

Proxemics   The study of how people and animals use space.

Pseudolistening   An imitation of true listening in which the receiver's mind is elsewhere.

Psychological constructs   Perceptual schema that categorize people according to their apparent personalities.
Public distance   One of Hall's four distance zones, extending outward from 3.6 m.
Punctuation   The process of determining the causal order of events.

Qualitative interpersonal communication   *See* Interpersonal communication.
Quantitative interpersonal communication   *See* Interpersonal communication.
Questioning response   A style of helping in which the receiver seeks additional information from the sender. Some questioning responses are really disguised advice.

Rationalization   A defense mechanism in which logical but untrue explanations maintain an unrealistic desired or presenting self-image.
Receiver   One who notices and attends to a message.
Reference groups   Groups against which we compare ourselves, thereby influencing our self-concept and self-esteem.
Reflected appraisal   The theory that a person's self-concept matches the way the person believes others regard him or her.
Regression   A defense mechanism in which a person avoids assuming responsibility by pretending that he or she is unable to do something instead of admitting to being simply unwilling.
Regulating   One function of nonverbal communication, in which nonverbal cues control the flow of verbal communication among individuals.
Relational conflict style   A pattern of managing disagreements that repeats itself over time in a relationship.
Relational maintenance   Communication aimed at keeping relationships operating smoothly and satisfactorily.
Relational message   A message that expresses the social relationship between two or more individuals.
Relationship   *See* Interpersonal relationship.
Relative words   Words that gain their meaning by comparison.
Remembering   Ability to recall information.
Repeating   Nonverbal behaviours that duplicate the content of a verbal message.
Repression   A defense mechanism in which a person avoids facing an unpleasant situation or fact by denying its existence.
Respect   The social need to be held in esteem by others.

Responding   Giving observable feedback to the speaker.
Role constructs   Perceptual schema that categorize people according to their social position.

Sapir–Whorf hypothesis   Theory of linguistic determinism in which language is determined by a culture's perceived reality.
Sarcasm   A potential defensive reaction in which an individual redirects a perceived threat to his or her presenting self by attacking the critic with contemptuous, often ironical remarks.
Selection   The first stage in the perception process in which some data are chosen to attend to and others to ignore.
Selective listening   A listening style in which the receiver responds only to messages that interest him or her.
Self-concept   The relatively stable set of perceptions each individual holds of himself or herself.
Self-disclosure   The process of deliberately revealing information about oneself that is significant and that would not normally be known by others.
Self-fulfilling prophecy   A prediction or expectation of an event that makes the outcome more likely to occur than would otherwise have been the case.
Self-monitoring   The process of attending to one's behaviour and using these observations to shape the way one behaves.
Self-serving bias   The tendency to interpret and explain information in a way that casts the perceiver in the most favourable manner.
Self-talk   The nonvocal process of thinking. On some level, self-talk occurs as a person interprets another's behaviour.
Semantic rules   Rules that govern the meaning of language, as opposed to its structure. *See also* Syntactic rules.
Sender   The creator of a message.
Sex role   The social orientation that governs behaviour, rather than the biological gender.
Significant other   A person whose opinion is important enough to affect one's self-concept strongly.
Sincere questions   Questions that are aimed at soliciting information that enable the asker to understand the other person. *See* Counterfeit questions.
Social comparison   Evaluation of oneself in terms of or by comparison to others.
Social distance   One of Hall's distance zones, ranging from 1.2 to 3.6 m.
Social exchange theory   A socioeconomic theory that suggests people seek relationships in which the

rewards they receive from others are greater than or equal to the costs they encounter.

Social penetration   A model that describes relationships in terms of their breadth and depth.

Spiral   A reciprocal communication pattern in which each person's message reinforces the other's. *See also* De-escalatory conflict spiral, Escalatory conflict spiral.

Spontaneity   A supportive communication behaviour described by Gibb in which the sender expresses a message without any attempt to manipulate the receiver.

Stage-hogging   A listening style in which the receiver is more concerned with making his or her own point than with understanding the speaker.

Stagnating   A stage of relational development characterized by declining enthusiasm and standardized forms of behaviour.

Static evaluation   The tendency to view people or relationships as unchanging.

Stereotyping   Categorizing individuals according to a set of characteristics assumed to belong to all members of a group.

Strategy   A defense-arousing style of communication described by Gibb in which the sender tries to manipulate or deceive a receiver.

Substituting   Nonverbal behaviour that takes the place of a verbal message.

Superiority   A defense-arousing style of communication described by Gibb in which the sender states or implies that the receiver is not worthy of respect.

Supportive responses   Responses that demonstrate solidarity with a speaker's situation.

Symmetrical conflict style   A relational conflict style in which both partners use the same tactics.

Symmetrical relationship   A relationship in which the partners seek an equal amount of control.

Sympathy   Compassion for another's situation. *See also* Empathy.

Syntactic rules   Rules that govern the ways symbols can be arranged, as opposed to the meanings of those symbols. *See also* Semantic rules.

Tangential response   A disconfirming response that uses the speaker's remark as a starting point for a shift to a new topic.

Terminating   The concluding stage of relational development, characterized by the acknowledgement of one or both parties that the relationship is over.

Territory   A stationary area claimed by an individual.

Transactional communication model   A characterization of communication as the simultaneous sending and receiving of messages in an ongoing, irreversible process.

Uncertainty reduction   The process of getting to know others by gaining more information about them.

Understanding   Occurs when sense is made of a message.

Verbal abuse   A disconfirming response intended to cause psychological pain to another.

Verbal aggression   A defense mechanism in which a person avoids facing unpleasant information by verbally attacking the confronting source.

"We" statement   Statement that implies that the issue is the concern and responsibility of both the speaker and receiver of a message. *See also* "I" language and "You" language.

White lie   A lie defined by the teller as unmalicious, or even helpful, to the person to whom it is told.

Whorf–Sapir hypothesis   The theory that the structure of a language shapes the worldview of its users.

Win–lose problem solving   An approach to conflict resolution in which one party reaches its goal at the expense of the other.

Win–win problem solving   An approach to conflict resolution in which the parties work together to satisfy all their goals.

"You" language   A statement that expresses or implies a judgement of the other person. *See also* Evaluative communication, "I" language.

Photo Credits

CHAPTER 1 **2** Private Collection/Diana Ong/Superstock. **4** *Mother and Child* by Paul Peel, 1888, Art Gallery of Ontario: Gift of the Estate of Luella McCleary, 1969. Photo by Carlo Catenazzi/AGO. **6** *Thanks, Girlfriend* by Athena Hampton. Copyright © Athena Hampton/EthnoGraphics. **10** Edvard Munch, *The Scream* (1893), oil on cardboard. Erich Lessing/Art Resource, NY. **15** Chaim Soutine, *Portrait of a Boy*, Chester Dale Collection, © 1999 Board of Trustees, National Gallery of Art, Washington, 1928, canvas, .921 × .651 m. (36¼″ × 25⅝″); framed: 1.124 × .857 × .082 m. (44¼″ × 33¾″ × 3¼″). **20** *Play It Again, Sam* by Dale Kennington. Courtesy of Suzanne Brown Galleries. Copyright © Dale Kennington. **24** *They Brought Their Dog, Mid August* by Kathy Ruttenberg, 60″ × 60″, oil on linen. © Copyright Kathy Ruttenberg. **33** Hiyochika, Kobayashi, "In High Spirits; Envy; Crocodile Tears; Man of Wealth" (from *One Hundred Faces: Supplement to Thirty-Two Faces*). Colour woodblock print, 13⅞″ × 9⅜″. Santa Barbara Museum of Art, Gift of Mr. and Mrs. Roland A. Way.

CHAPTER 2 **42** Malvin Gray Johnson, *Self Portrait*. National Museum of American Art, Washington DC/Art Resource, NY. **46** Pablo Picasso, *Self-Portrait* (1907). Oil on canvas, 22″ × 18″. Art Resource, NY. **50** *Woman Curling in on Herself* by Mary Weymark Goss. Copyright © Mary Weymark Goss. Reproduced by permission of the artist. **52** Sheri Adler. **60** *Four Women with Hands On Earth* by Isabelle Hervé/Stock Illustration Source. **71** Eugene Weston III. **79** Edward Hopper, *Soir Bleu* (1914), oil on canvas, 36″ × 72″ (91.4 × 182.9 cm). Collection of Whitney Museum of American Art, Josephine N. Hopper Bequest 70.1208. Photography Copyright © 1999: Whitney Museum of American Art. **80** *Masquerade* by James Mallakai Letaw, ink wash. Copyright © 1997 James Mallakai Letaw. **83** *Unity Rally III, Montreal* by Evangeline Murray, oil on canvas, 24″ × 30″, 1996. Copyright © Evangeline Murray.

CHAPTER 3 **86** *Raphaelesque Head Exploding* by Salvador Dali (1951), oil on canvas, 43 cm × 33.3 cm. Private collection. **89** M.C. Escher's "Relativity" © 1999 Cordon Art B.V., Baarn, Holland. All rights reserved. **100** *William Chin, 1911* by George Agnew Reid, Art Gallery of Ontario. Photo credit Carlo Catenazzi/AGO. **102** *Unforgettable* by Claire Carew, 1995, oil on canvas. Dedicated to Harry Van Helm Braam. Reproduced by permission of the artist. **107** *Adoration* by Paul Peel, 1885, Art Gallery of Ontario: Gift of Mrs. Robert Wood in memory of her husband, 1940. Photo by Larry Ostrom/AGO. **108** Reproduced by permission of the RCMP Centennial Museum, Regina. **118** *Summer Date August Eleven PM* by Kathy Ruttenberg, 14″ × 18″, oil on canvas, Gallery Henoch, NY. **121** *Elephant and Blind Men*, late nineteenth century,

ivory, height 1⅝″. Signed: Kuku Joso to (literally, "Kuku Joso's knife"). Gift of Mrs. Russell Sage, 1910, 10.211.900. Metropolitan Museum of Art.

CHAPTER 4 **128** *Free Spirit*, Spirit of Mississippi Collection by Mary Bertoli, Holy Name Sister, tissue paper collage. **138** Eugene Weston III. **144** Detail of *Hermes*, Collections royales. Louvre. © R.M.N. Paris. 1991 IC.00.5364. **145** *Isaak* by Kent Harfst, oil on canvas, 23¼″ × 19¼″. Reproduced by permission of the artist. **152** Leonetto Cappiello, *Les Parapluies Revel* 1922. © 1999 Artists Rights Society (ARS), NY/ADGP, Paris. **153** *Screaming Faces* by Manasie Akpaliapik, 1991, Art Gallery of Ontario. Photo by Carlo Catenazzi/AGO. **154** Giraudon/Art Resource, NY. **155** *Self-Portrait* by Jenny Munro, oil on canvas. Copyright © Jenny Munro. **158** *Cup and Cover: Hercules Supporting a Globe* by Hans Rudolph Ulrich, boxwood, gilded silver, silver, Art Gallery of Ontario, Toronto. On Loan from the Thomson Collection. Photo by Carlo Catenazzi/AGO.

CHAPTER 5 **168** *The Bridge Between* by Daphne Odjig, 32″ × 30″, acrylic on canvas. Reproduced by permission. Image provided by Gallery Gevik, Toronto. **170** Pieter Brueghel, *Tower of Babel* (1563), oil on oak panel. Kunsthistorisches Museum, Vienna. **171** *Typography for the Word Music* by Nehal Sheth. Reproduced by permission of the artist. **174** *Seated Woman with Bent Knee*, 1917 (gouache, w/c and black crayon on paper) by Egon Schiele (1890-1918). Narodni Galerie, Prague, Czech Republic/Bridgeman Art Library. **181** *Distant Storm* by Luann K. Bond, 12″ × 16″, oil, © Luann K. Bond. Reproduced by permission of the artist. **183** *The Other Side of the Question* by George Agnew Reid, 1890, Art Gallery of Ontario. Photo by Carlo Catenazzi/AGO. **184** *Psyche ranimee par le baiser de l'Amour* by Antonio Canova, detail, 1793. © RMN. **197** *Petroushka* by Paraskeva Clark, 1937, oil on canvas, National Gallery of Canada, Ottawa. Copyright permission by Clive and Ben Clark. **211** Scene 2, Comparison of celebrated beauties and the loyal league, c. 1797 (colour woodblock print) by Kitagawa Utamaro (1753–1806). Fitzwilliam Museum, University of Cambridge, UK/Bridgeman Art Library. **217** Book cover from *Le Petit Prince* by Antoine de Saint-Exupery, copyright 1943 by Harcourt, Inc., and renewed 1971 by Consuelo de Saint-Exupery, reprinted by permission of the publisher.

CHAPTER 6 **222** *Mime* by Misha Lenn/Stock Illustration Source. **229** Wooden mask reproduced by permission of the Milwaukee Public Museum. **232** *Oedipe explique l'enigme du Sphinx*, Jean-Auguste-Dominique Ingres, © RMN. **238** *Dream & Reality* by Angelo Morbelli/Superstock. **243** Eugene Weston III. **245** *Two Waitresses on a Streetcar Crossing the*

Reverse Falls by Miller Gore Brittain, 1939, oil on Masonite: 55.8″ × 45.7″. Art Gallery of Ontario. Photo by Carlo Catenazzi/AGO. **247** *Ballerina* by Edgar Degas. Erich Lessing/Art Resource, NY. **248** *Children at Night* by Philip Henry Surrey, 1939, Art Gallery of Ontario. Photo by Sean Weaver/AGO. **251** Eugene Weston III. **252** George Tooker, *The Subway* 1950, egg tempera on composition board, sight 18⅛″ × 36⅛″ (46 × 91.8 cm), frame 26″ × 44″ (66 × 111.8 cm). Collection of Whitney Museum of American Art. Purchased with funds from the Juliana Force Purchase Award, 50.23. Photograph Copyright © 2000: Whitney Museum of American Art. **259** Michelangelo, detail from *The Creation of Adam*. Scala/Art Resource, NY. **262** Hyacinthe Rigaud, *Louis XIV, Roi de France* © RMN. **269** *Annette with Clocks No. 3* by Matthew Carver, 1998, 10″ × 10″, acrylic on canvas. Reproduced by permission of the artist.

CHAPTER 7 272 *People Whispering Under Window with Bird* by Dave Cutler/Stock Illustration Source. **277** Eugene Weston III. **279** *Pink Couch* by Andrew Benyei, 1993, fiberglass, 24″ × 15″ × 19″. Reproduced by permission of the artist. **282** *Reddy #2* by Diana Ong. Diana Ong/ Superstock. **285** *Circus Performers* by Wendy Boyd, acrylic on canvas. Reproduced by permission of the artist. **294** Dale Kennington, *Undivided Attention*. Courtesy of Suzanne Brown Galleries, Scottsdale, AZ. **301** Scala/Art Resource, NY. **302** *Conversation Piece* sculpture by Hanna Damasio. **304** *Cathie* by Arthur Shilling, 1976, oil on Masonite. Reproduced by permission of the Arthur Shilling Estate and Beckett Fine Art Ltd., Toronto. Photographed by Simon Glass. **306** Bradley Parrish, *Cosette*, 1994, oil on canvas, 30″ × 42″. Reproduced by permission of Parrish Fine Arts. **312** M.C. Escher's *Bond of Union* © 1998 Cordon Art B.V. Baarn, Holland. All rights reserved.

CHAPTER 8 318 William Kurelek, *Christmas at Otter Lake, Quebec*, 1977. Mixed media on Masonite. Art Gallery of Hamilton, Gift of the Polish Alliance of Canada and Wintario, 1978. **322** Copyright © Beryl Cook 1995. Reproduced by permission of the artist c/o Rogers, Coleridge & White Ltd., 20 Powis Mews, London W11 1JN. **325** 1963.10.137. (1801)/PA: Guy Pene du Bois, *Hallway Italian Restaurant*, Chester Dale Collection © 1998 Board of Trustees, National Gallery of Art, Washington, 1922, canvas .638 × .512 m. (25⅛″ × 20⅛″); framed .809 × .682 m. (31⅞″ × 26⅞″). **327** Luini Bernadino (1480/90–1532), *Les sommeil de l'enfant Jesus*. Louvre © Photo RMN–Arnaudet. **329** Barbara Kruger, *Untitled* (You construct intricate rituals which allow you to touch the skin of other men), 37″ × 50″ photograph, 1980. Collection: Museum of Fine Arts, Boston, Massachusetts. Courtesy: Mary Boone Gallery, New York.

333 *Singing Round Dance Songs* by Dr. Allen Sapp, R.C.A., O.C., S.O.M., 1989, 16 × 20″, acrylic on canvas. Reproduced by permission of Allen Sapp Paintings, Inc. **340** *The Tiff* by Florence Carlyle, Art Gallery of Ontario: Gift of the Province of Ontario, 1972. Photo by Carlo Catenazzi/AGO. **343** David Hockney, *My Parents*, 1977, oil on canvas, 182.9 × 182.9 cm. Tate Gallery, London/Art Resource, NY. **349** *Travelling Companions* by Sharon White/Superstock. **352** Francois Jouffroy, *Jeune Fille contiant son premier secret au Venus*, 1.620 × 0.550 m. Photo: J. Emer-Louvre, RMN IC.00.7039. **368** *Clowns* by Janet Mitchell, 1952, oil, 66 × 76 cm. Reproduced by permission. Collection of Mr. & Mrs. W.E. Code. Photograph by John Dean Photographs.

CHAPTER 9 376 *Two Women with the Black Cat on the Table* by Joy Zemel Long, oil on canvas, 26″ × 32″. Reproduced by permission of the artist. **379** *Interesting Story* by Laura Muntz Lyall, 1898, Art Gallery of Ontario: Gift of the Government of the Province of Ontario, 1972. Photo by Carlo Catenazzi/AGO. **381** Edward Hopper, *Office at Night*, 1940. Oil on canvas, 22⅛″ × 25″. Collection Walker Art Center, Minneapolis. Gift of the T.B. Walker Foundation, Gilbert M. Walker Fund, 1948. **387** Santa Barbara Museum of Art, Gift of Emily Hall, Baroness von Romberg, in memory of Maximilian von Romberg. Photo by Scott McClaine. © Artists Rights Society, Inc., New York, NY. **390** *Triptych of the Day* by Gaetana Previati/Superstock. **394** Emiliano Di Cavalcanti, *Five Girls of Guaratingueta*. Museu de Arte de Sao Paolo. **401** *Quito Hats* by Irene Klar. Reproduced by permission of the artist. **404** William Kurelek, *Damned Pollack*, 1977. Mixed media on Masonite. Art Gallery of Hamilton, Gift of the Polish Alliance of Canada and Wintario, 1978.

CHAPTER 10 412 Rudolf Stussi, *Battleship Toronto*, 1995. Oil on linen. 40″ × 60″. Reproduced with permission of the artist. **415** Francisco de Goya, *Fight with Cudgels* 1820–23. Oil on plaster transferred to canvas, 4′ ⅜″ × 8′ 8¾″. Prado, Madrid. Scala/Art Resource, NY. **437** Corbis-Bettmann. **421** *The Shadow Dance* by Jan Winton, serigraph, 1986. Reproduced by permission of the artist. **425** *The Lament* by Sir Edward Burne-Jones, 1866, gouache, William Morris Gallery, Walthamstow. Reproduced by permission of The Bridgeman Art Library, New York. **428** *L'amour, la morte* by Irina Florov. Reproduced with permission of the artist. **444** © Christopher Arnesen/Tony Stone Images. **449** *Rembrandt's Hands, Vermeer's Frame and the Passing of the Moth* by Juan Gonzalez, 1990, oil and acrylic on honeycomb panel. Reproduced by permission. Courtesy of Nancy Hoffman Gallery, New York. **455** *The Tree* by Joe Geshick, oil, 6 × 4. Reproduced by permission of the artist.

Literary Credits

PREFACE **ix** *Peanuts* reprinted by permission of United Features Syndicate, Inc.

CHAPTER 1 **7** Table: "National Preferences in Business and Communication Education" by D.B. Curtis, J.L. Winsor, and R.D. Stephens, *Communication Education* 38 (1989): 6–14. Used by permission of the National Communication Association. **9** Excerpt from © 1995 article, "Online Affair Leads to Divorce," used with permission of The Associated Press. **26** Drawing by Gail Machlis, *Quality Time*. Pub. date: 7/21/1994. *Quality Time* © 1994 Gail Machlis. Reprinted with permission of the artist. All rights reserved. **27** From *The Accidental Tourist* by Anne Tyler. © 1985 Anne Tyler Modaressi. Reprinted by permission of Alfred A. Knopf, a division of Random House, Inc. **28** Drawing by Mike Ewers. Reprinted by permission. **37** *Calvin and Hobbes* © Watterson 1994. Dist. by Universal Press Syndicate. Reprinted with permission. All rights reserved. **38** Reprinted by permission of Maroushka Kanywani.

CHAPTER 2 **48** *Ziggy* by Tom Wilson. © Ziggy and Friends, Inc. Dist. by Universal Press Syndicate. All rights reserved. **49** From *Children Learn What They Live: Parenting to Inspire Values* by Dorothy Law Nolte and Rachel Harris, foreword by Jack Canfield. **52 & 53** "Cipher in the Snow" by Jean Mizer from *Today's Education*, 11-1964. Used by permission from Jean Todhunter Mizer and *Today's Education*. **54** Drawing by Benard Shoenbaum. © 1990 from *The New Yorker* Collection. All rights reserved. **56** Table: Summarized by Don E. Hamachek, *Encounters with the Self*, 2nd ed. (New York: Holt, Rinehart and Winston, 1982), pp. 3–5. **63** *Cathy* © Cathy Guisewite; © 1994. Reprinted by permission of Universal Press Syndicate. All rights reserved. **64** Excerpt from *Crazy Talk, Stupid Talk* by Neil Postman © 1976. Used courtesy of Neil Postman. **67** Drawing by Gahan Wilson; © Gahan Wilson. Reprinted by permission. **68** Drawing reprinted by permission of Ellison Robertson. **72** Drawing by Dana Fradon. © 1983 from *The New Yorker* Collection. All rights reserved. **76** Self-Monitoring Inventory from "The Many Me's of the Self-Monitor" by Mark Snyder. Published in *Psychology Today*, 1983. Reprinted courtesy of Mark Snyder. **78** Drawing by William Haefeli © 1998 from The Cartoon Bank. All rights reserved. **80 & 81** Excerpted from Anthony Wilson-Smith, "In the World of Spin Doctors," *Maclean's*, May 31, 1999, p. 17. **82** Reprinted by permission of Ron Keough. **84** Drawing by Peter Steiner. © 1993 from *The New Yorker* Collection. All rights reserved.

CHAPTER 3 **90** *Cathy* © Cathy Guisewite; © 1986. Reprinted with permission of Universal Press Syndicate. All rights reserved. **94** *Farcus* by Waisglass/Coulthart; © 1993 FARCUS® is reprinted with permission from LaughingStock Licensing, Inc., Ottawa, Canada. All rights reserved. **95** *Sally Forth* by Greg Howard © 1982. Reprinted with special permission of King Features Syndicate. **100** From "Trying on Old Age" by Holly Hall. Reprinted with permission from *Psychology Today Magazine*. © 1988 (Sussex Publishers, Inc.). **101** Drawing reprinted by permission of Ellison Robertson. **104** Drawing by John Jonik. **105** By David Suzuki from *Breaking Through: A Canadian Literary Mosaic*, edited by John Borovilos. © 1990 Prentice-Hall. Used courtesy of David Suzuki. **108 & 109** "Field Experiment: Preparation for the Changing Police Role" by Fred Ferguson. Used courtesy of the author. **113** Drawing by Lorenz. Reprinted with permission from the *Saturday Evening Post*. **120** From *Siblings without Rivalry: How to Help Your Children Live Together So You Can Too* by Adele Faber and Elaine Mazlish. © 1987 by Adele Faber and Elaine Mazlish. Reprinted by permission of W.W. Norton & Company, Inc.

CHAPTER 4 **135** Drawing by Robert Weber. © 1981 from *The New Yorker* Collection. All rights reserved. **139-140** Isabelle Knockwood, *Out of the Depths* (Lockeport, NS: Roseway Publishing, 1992). Reprinted by permission of the author. **142** Drawing by Robert Weber. © 1993 from the *New Yorker* Collection. All rights reserved. **144** From *Yevgeny Yevtushenko: The Collected Poems, 1952–1990*, edited by Albert C. Todd, © 1991 by Henry Holt and Company, Inc. Reprinted by permission of Henry Holt and Company, Inc. **146** Drawing by Leo Cullum © 1998 from the Cartoon Bank. All rights reserved. **155 & 156** Alanis Morissette, *supposed former infatuation junkie* CD, 1998. Lyrics reprinted by permission. All rights reserved. © 1998 Maverick Recording Company. **161** Drawing by Steve Delmonte. © 1998 by Steve Delmonte. Used by permission.

CHAPTER 5 **173** *Calvin and Hobbes* © Watterson 1992. Dist. by Universal Press Syndicate. Reprinted with permission. All rights reserved. **174 & 175** "It's a 'Girl' Thing for Women" by Carla Hall. © 1997. Reprinted by permission of Los Angeles Times Syndicate. All rights reserved. **180 & 181** "Challenging the 'S' Word" by Christina Koenig. Reprinted with the permission of Christina Koenig. **184** Excerpt from *Conversation and Communication* by J.A.M. Meerloo. Reprinted by permission of International Universities Press, Inc. © 1952 by International Universities Press, Inc. **186** *Herman*® is reprinted with permission from LaughingStock Licensing Inc., Ottawa, Canada. All rights reserved. **189** *Cathy* © Cathy Guisewite; © 1983. Reprinted with permission of Universal Press Syndicate. All rights reserved. **203** Drawing by Marian Henley; © 1998 from The Cartoon Bank. All rights reserved. **207** Excerpt from "Man to Man, Woman to Woman" by Mark Sherman and Adelaide Haas. Reprinted with permission from *Psychology Today* magazine. © 1984

Index